Immigration Detention and
Human Rights

Immigration and Asylum Law and Policy in Europe

VOLUME 19

Editors

Elspeth Guild
*Kingsley Napley Solicitors, London,
Centre for Migration Law, Radboud University Nijmegen*

Jan Niessen
Migration Policy Group, Brussels

The series is a venue for books on European immigration and asylum law and policies where academics, policy makers, law practitioners and others look to find detailed analysis of this dynamic field. Works in the series will start from a European perspective. The increased co-operation within the European Union and the Council of Europe on matters related to immigration and asylum requires the publication of theoretical and empirical research. The series will contribute to well-informed policy debates by analyzing and interpreting the evolving European legislation and its effects on national law and policies. The series brings together the various stakeholders in these policy debates: the legal profession, researchers, employers, trade unions, human rights and other civil society organizations.

Immigration Detention and Human Rights

Rethinking Territorial Sovereignty

By
Galina Cornelisse

LEIDEN • BOSTON
2010

This book is printed on acid-free paper.

Library of Congress Cataloging-in-Publication Data

Cornelisse, Galina.
　Immigration detention and human rights : rethinking territorial sovereignty / by Galina Cornelisse.
　　p. cm. -- (Immigration and asylum law and policy in Europe ; v. 19)
　Includes bibliographical references and index.
　ISBN 978-90-04-17370-5 (hardback : alk. paper) 1. Emigration and immigration law--Europe. 2. Asylum, Right of--Europe. 3. Refugees--Civil rights--Europe. 4. Detention of persons--Europe. 5. Freedom of movement--Europe. I. Title. II. Series.

KJC6044.C67 2010
342.408'2--dc22

2009053782

ISSN 1568-2749
ISBN 978 90 04 17370 5

Copyright 2010 by Koninklijke Brill NV, Leiden, The Netherlands.
Koninklijke Brill NV incorporates the imprints Brill, Hotei Publishing, IDC Publishers, Martinus Nijhoff Publishers and VSP.

All rights reserved. No part of this publication may be reproduced, translated, stored in a retrieval system, or transmitted in any form or by any means, electronic, mechanical, photocopying, recording or otherwise, without prior written permission from the publisher.

Authorization to photocopy items for internal or personal use is granted by Koninklijke Brill NV provided that the appropriate fees are paid directly to The Copyright Clearance Center, 222 Rosewood Drive, Suite 910, Danvers, MA 01923, USA.
Fees are subject to change.

PRINTED IN THE NETHERLANDS

Contents

Acknowledgements xi
Abbreviations xiii

Chapter 1 Introduction: Immigration Detention in Contemporary Europe 1

1.1 Immigration Detention and Modern Constitutionalism 1
1.2 Detention as a Tool of Immigration Control in Europe: An Overview 7
    1.2.1 Detention upon Arrival 8
    1.2.2 The Use of Detention within the Asylum System 11
    1.2.3 Detention and Removal 15
1.3 Immigration Detention: Current Research and Outline of this Book 22

Part I Theory

Chapter 2 Sovereignty, People and Territory 33

2.1 Introduction 33
2.2 A Claim to Ultimate Political Power 34
    2.2.1 The Development of the Modern Notion of Sovereignty 35
    2.2.2 The People as the Source of Legitimate Power 41
2.3 A Territorial Solution to the Problem of Universality versus Particularity 44
    2.3.1 Territorialisation: Changing Identities and Allegiances 46
    2.3.2 The Discovery of the Nation: Inconsistent Universalism? 49
    2.3.3 National Identity as the Basis for Territorial Sovereignty 55
2.4 On Sovereignty's Content and Form, and the (Il)Legitimacy of Violence 59

Chapter 3 Limiting Sovereign Power **64**

3.1 Introduction.. 64
3.2 Constitutionalism as the Theory and Practice
 of the Limits on Political Power 66
  3.2.1 Formal Limits on Government and
   Rules of Institutional Design 67
  3.2.2 Individual Rights as Material Limits
   to Political Power.. 69
  3.2.3 A Brief Note on Constitutionalism's Limits 71
3.3 Citizenship, Individual Rights, and Territory........................... 72
  3.3.1 Citizenship: An Apparent Paradox?.............................. 73
  3.3.2 National Citizenship as a Condition for
   Access to Universal Rights 79
  3.3.3 Citizenship's Structuring Role in a Global
   Territorial Structure 82
3.4. International Law and Violence 85
  3.4.1 The Sovereign State as the True and Only
   Subject of International Law 87
  3.4.2 Types of Violence Regulated by Classical
   International Law 89
  3.4.3 International Human Rights Law................................. 97
3.5 Human Rights: Closing the Gap between Us and
 Them/Inside and Outside?... 101
  3.5.1 'Us' and 'Them' within the Contemporary
   State: Post-national Citizenship................................... 103
  3.5.2 Human Rights and Sovereignty's
   Territorial Claims 113
3.6 Conclusions: A Particularistic Universalism?........................ 126

Part II Doctrine and Practice

**Chapter 4 Freedom of Movement I: The Right to Leave as a
Human Right** **135**

4.1 Introduction... 135
4.2 Development of the Right to Emigrate 137
4.3 General Legal Framework of the Right to Leave 147
4.4 The Right to Leave in the Context of
 Immigration Control.. 154

4.5 On the Right to Leave and the Visibility of the
Content of Sovereignty 158

**Chapter 5 Freedom of Movement II: Decisions on Entry as a
Sovereign Prerogative? 161**

5.1 Introduction 161
5.2 Development of a Sovereign Right to Exclude 163
5.3 The Right to Enter and Remain in International Law 175
    5.3.1 General Limitations on the Sovereign
        Right to Exclude 176
    5.3.2 Refugee Law and the Prohibition of *Non-refoulement* 182
    5.3.3 Family Life and Limits on Immigration Control 195
5.4 Immigration into and within the EU: The Obduracy
of the National Border? 202
    5.4.1 Freedom of Movement *within* an Area
        without Internal Borders 203
    5.4.2 The External Border: The Common
        Immigration and Asylum Policy 208
5.5 Free Movement: Territoriality Shapes the
Relation between State Power and Rights 217
    5.5.1 Territoriality and Limitations on the
        State's Exclusionary Powers 218
    5.5.2 Territoriality and the Asymmetry of
        International Movement 224

**Chapter 6 Reaffirming Sovereignty and Reproducing Territoriality:
Deportation and Detention 229**

6.1 Introduction 229
6.2 Deportation as Administrative Practice 232
6.3 Immigration Detention, State Power, and Territoriality 238
6.4 Maintaining the Territorial Order 245

**Chapter 7 International Human Rights Law on Immigration
Detention 247**

7.1 Introduction 247
7.2 The Human Right to Personal Liberty: A Prohibition
on Arbitrary Detention 249

  7.2.1 The Prohibition on Arbitrariness in
     Article 9 ICCPR 251
  7.2.2 Article 9 ICCPR and Procedural Guarantees
     for Immigration Detainees 256
  7.2.3 Conditions of Immigration Detention: An
     Indication of Arbitrariness? 259
7.3 Human Rights and the Detention of Refugees
  and Asylum Seekers 261
7.4 Regional Discourse: The Council of Europe
  and Immigration Detention 265
7.5 Emerging EC Law on the Detention of Immigrants
  and Asylum Seekers 268
7.6 The Right to Personal Liberty vs. Territorial
  Sovereignty 272

Chapter 8 The ECtHR: Detention as a 'Necessary Adjunct' to an 'Undeniable Sovereign Right'? 277

8.1 Introduction 277
8.2 Immigration Detention and the Right to
  Personal Liberty in the ECHR 278
  8.2.1 The Immigration Context: Deprivations
     or Restrictions upon Liberty? 280
  8.2.2 'Lawful' Detention in 'Accordance with
     a Procedure Prescribed by Law' 282
8.3 Procedural Safeguards against Arbitrary
  Detention 285
  8.3.1 The Right to be Informed of the Reasons
     for Detention 286
  8.3.2 *Habeas Corpus* or the Right to Challenge
     the Lawfulness of Detention 287
  8.3.3 Compensation for Unlawful Deprivations
     of Liberty 290
8.4 The Notion of Arbitrariness in the Strasbourg Case
  Law on Immigration Detention 290
  8.4.1 *Chahal* and *Saadi*: Unnecessary and
     Disproportionate, but Lawful Detention 291
  8.4.2 Immigration Detention and the ECtHR:
     Proportionality 'Lite'? 296
8.5 How to Reconcile the Human Right to Liberty with
  the Public Interest? 300

  8.5.1 The Proportionality Principle as a
     General Principle in the ECHR 301
  8.5.2 Detention of Persons who are Mentally Ill,
     Alcoholics and Vagrants 305
8.6 Immigration Detention as the Blind Spot
  of the ECtHR? 308

Part III Conclusions

Chapter 9 Destabilising Territorial Sovereignty through Human Rights Litigation in Immigration Detention Cases 315

9.1 Introduction 315
9.2 Territorial Sovereignty as an Institution: The Shaping
  of Norms and Practices 316
  9.2.1 Nationalism as Social Practice and the
     Reification of Territorial Sovereignty 317
  9.2.2 The Territorial Limitations of Modern
     Constitutionalism 320
  9.2.3 Constitutionalism's Limits Exemplified:
     The Legal Regulation of Human Movement 322
9.3 Territorial Sovereignty as an Institution with Ontological
  Significance and Immigration Detention as the Litmus Test
  for the Modern Territorial Order 326
9.4 Destabilising Territorial Sovereignty through
  Human Rights Law 332
  9.4.1 The Restrained but Radical Potential of Human Rights 332
  9.4.2 Human Rights as Destabilisation Rights:
     Towards Territoriality 'Lite'? 335
9.5 Conclusions 341

Bibliography 345
Table of Cases 369
Index 379

Acknowledgments

This book would not have been written if it had not been for the help of a great many people. Here I would like to express my debts of gratitude to a few of them in particular. I am immensely grateful to Neil Walker for his inspiring encouragement and kind support as my supervisor at the European University Institute in Florence, where I began this project in 2001 as a PhD student. I also wish to thank the members of the examining jury before which I defended the thesis at the EUI in May 2007: Pieter Boeles, Marise Cremona, and Dora Kostakopoulou. Their insightful and helpful comments have proven very valuable when I was developing the thesis for publication. I have also greatly benefited from discussions with my fellow researchers at the EUI, a number of colleagues at Utrecht University, and many other people that I have met over the last eight years. Here I would like to mention Heli Askola, Leonard Besselink, Eva Hilbrink, Victor Igreja and Chris Townley in particular. I wish to express my gratitude to Elspeth Guild for the confidence she has put in my work. I owe a very great debt to Professor H.G. Schermers and Hanneke Steenbergen – persons without whom I would perhaps never have ventured an academic career. I am very sorry that I cannot tell them anymore how much I have learned and benefited from their exemplary teaching and words of encouragement.

I gratefully acknowledge the grants I received from the NUFFIC and the European University Institute so that I could write my thesis at the EUI. It was a privilege to spend a few years there, a privilege the magnitude of which I have come to appreciate fully only after I left Florence. I express my thanks to the European Commission for its financial support with regard to the programme Framework 6 CHALLENGE. I wish to thank my colleagues at the Department of Constitutional and Administrative Law at Utrecht University for facilitating the completion of the manuscript through their flexibility and companionship. I would like to thank Peter Morris for his excellent work in editing the text. During the final stages of the manuscript, Paulien de Morree assisted me in preparing the bibliography and editing the footnotes, for which I am thankful.

I thank all my friends for their kindness and their generosity. I want to mention Caroline, Chris, Eva, Eekta, Johanna, Jeroen and Vonneke here in particular, simply because I could not have finished this book without their help and hospitality during difficult times. Finally, and above all, I want to thank my family for their love and support. It is to them that I dedicate this book.

Abbreviations

CAT	Convention against Torture and Other Cruel, Inhuman or Degrading Punishment
CPT	European Committee for the Prevention of Torture and Inhuman or Degrading Treatment or Punishment
CSCE	Conference on Security and Co-operation in Europe
ECHR	European Convention on Human Rights
ECJ	European Court of Justice
ECommHR	European Commission of Human Rights
ECRE	European Council on Refugees and Exiles
ECtHR	European Court of Human Rights
ExCom	Executive Committee of the United Nations High Commissioner for Refugees
HRC	United Nations Human Rights Committee
IACHR	Inter-American Commission on Human Rights
ICJ	International Court of Justice
IRO	International Refugee Organisation
NATO	North Atlantic Treaty Organization
PCIJ	Permanent Court of International Justice
ICCPR	International Covenant on Civil and Political Rights
JRS	Jesuit Refugee Service
UDHR	Universal Declaration of Human Rights
UNHCR	United Nations High Commissioner for Refugees
UNRRA	United Nations Relief and Rehabilitation Administration

Chapter 1

Introduction: Immigration Detention in Contemporary Europe

> From a sociological point of view, camps or transit zones may present the institutionalisation of temporariness as a form of radical social exclusion and marginalisation in modern society and a conservation of borders as dividing lines.[1]

1.1 *Immigration Detention and Modern Constitutionalism*

All Member States of the European Union have provisions in their immigration legislation on the basis of which they can deprive foreigners of their liberty. The use of detention for reasons of immigration law enforcement by these countries has increased enormously over the past few years.[2] Concerning asylum seekers this increase seems to be related to the extended use of accelerated procedures and the frequent use of detention when it concerns asylum seekers who await a 'Dublin transfer'.[3] Concerning immigration in general, Member States perceive growing problems related to irregular immigration and one of their responses has been an ever increasing exercise of their powers to detain irregular immigrants. These tendencies are reflected in several instruments of EC legislation which have been adopted over the last few years under title IV of the EC Treaty,

---

[1] J. Tóth, *Briefing Paper: A typology of Transit Zones* (European Parliament, Directorate-General Internal Policies, Citizens Rights and Constitutional Affairs, 2006), 3.

[2] M. Kelly, *Immigration-related detention in Ireland. A research report for the Irish Refugee Council, Irish Penal Reform Trust and Immigration Council of Ireland*, (Dublin: Irish Refugee Council, Irish Penal Reform Trust/Immigrant Council of Ireland, 2005). See also A.M. van Kalmthout, F.B.A.M. Hofstee-van der Meulen and F. Dünkel, *Foreigners in European Prisons* (Nijmegen: Wolf Legal Publishers, 2007).

[3] On the basis of Council Regulation (EC) No. 343/2003 of 18 February 2003 establishing the criteria and mechanisms for determining the Member State responsible for examining an asylum application lodged in one of the Member States by a third-country national, OJ L 222/03, 5 September 2003 (Dublin II Regulation).

authorising the use of detention by Member States in asylum procedures and in the context of removal proceedings.[4] As a result of these developments, the institutionalised practice of immigration detention has become an inherent part of a policy package that has as its main aims to deter future migrants and to remove those already on national territory as rapidly and as effectively as possible. If these policies are criticised by NGOs or other social actors, Member States defend their policies with arguments along the lines of the growing numbers of foreigners, the need to maintain the integrity of border controls and security-related issues.

The detention of immigrants is seldom a transparent practice: information concerning detention facilities is often not made public and many of these facilities are located in isolated places, and as such it has been difficult to raise extensive public awareness for the situation of immigration detainees. In addition, journalists are habitually denied access to places where immigrants are held, allegedly in order to respect the privacy of the detainees, but resulting in the absence of public control over the conditions, legality and procedures within immigration detention centres.[5] In 2004, an Italian journalist infiltrated a detention centre in Sicily by acting as a Kurdish refugee and he published an article on humiliating conditions that he had witnessed and experienced during his stay there.[6] Instead of taking legal steps that might have resulted in improving the conditions at the centre, the Italian state commenced a case against the journalist on charges of presenting a false identity.[7] After the Italian section of *Médecins Sans Frontiers* had published a critical report on the circumstances in various closed centres for migrants, this organisation was accused of disloyalty by the Italian government and denied further access to immigration detention centres.[8]

In spite of the obvious difficulties in obtaining detailed information about what is precisely occurring in detention centres, the public media increasingly

---

[4] Council Directive 2003/9/EC of 27 January 2003 laying down minimum standards for the reception of asylum seekers, OJ L 31/18, 6 February 2003; Council Directive 2005/85/EC of 1 December 2005 laying down minimum standards on procedures in Member States for granting and withdrawing refugee status, OJ L 326/13, 13 December 2005; and Directive 2008/115/EC of the European Parliament and the Council of 16 December 2008 on common standards and procedures in Member States for returning illegally staying third-country nationals, OJ L 348/98, 24 December 2008.
[5] Tóth (2006), 8.
[6] F. Gatti, "Io, Clandestino a Lampedusa," *L'Espresso*, 7 October 2005.
[7] International Helsinki Federation for Human Rights, *Report 2006: Human Rights in the OCSE Region: Italy* (Vienna: IHF and IHF Research Foundation, 2006), 215.
[8] Statewatch, "Update: MSF accused of 'disloyalty' over CPT Report," June 2004, available at http://www.statewatch.org/news/2004/jun/23it-msf.htm.

publish evidence of unacceptable conditions in closed centres for immigrants, reflecting a growing concern in civil society about the practice of immigration detention. Moreover, numerous reports by NGOs over the years have described instances of the use of unlawful force by government officials, illegal detention beyond the foreseen time-limits, a lack of judicial remedies, limited access to legal aid and serious overcrowding.[9] These findings have often been confirmed by the European Committee for the Prevention of Torture and Inhuman or Degrading Treatment or Punishment (CPT) during its visits to places where individuals are deprived of their liberty.[10] In some countries, such as the Netherlands, France, and Malta, the treatment of foreigners detained under immigration legislation is worse than that of prisoners who are detained on a criminal basis.[11] Furthermore, detaining children and unaccompanied minors is becoming standard practice in the majority of EU Member States, contrary to international legal norms and sometimes even against national legislation protecting children's rights.[12] In addition, serious logistic and material problems exist with regard to the detention of non-citizens under immigration legislation. Immigrants are being accommodated in police cells or makeshift shelters for extended periods, and the lack of space in the reception centres is often compensated with accommodation in prisons where immigration detainees are held together with persons who have been convicted of criminal offences. Schemes of legal assistance are flawed, adequate medical structures absent, and the incidence

---

[9] I.e. Amnesty International, *The Netherlands: The Detention of Irregular Migrants and Asylum Seekers*, AI Index 35/02/2008 (Amnesty International, June 2008), Jesuit Refugee Service, *Civil Society Report on Administrative Detention of Asylum Seekers and Illegally Staying Third Country Nationals in the 10 New Member States of the European Union* (Malta, October 2007); ANAFE, *Visites dans la zone d'attente de l'aéroport de Paris-Orly: Observations et recommandations* (juillet 2007–janvier 2008), Paris, September 2008.

[10] See amongst many others: CPT, *Report to the authorities of the Kingdom of the Netherlands on the visits carried out to the Kingdom in Europe, Aruba, and the Netherlands Antilles in June 2007*, CPT/Inf (2008) 2 (Strasbourg, 5 February 2008); and CPT, *Report to the Government of Greece on the visit to Greece from 23 to 29 September 2008*, CPT/Inf (2009) 20 (Strasbourg, 30 June 2009).

[11] Kalmthout, Hofstee-van der Meulen and Dünkel (2007), 55.

[12] STEPS Consulting, *The conditions in centres for third-country nationals (detention camps, open centres as well as transit centres and transit zones) with a particular focus on provisions and facilities for persons with special needs in the 25 EU Member States* (European Parliament, Directorate-General Internal Policies, Citizens Rights and Constitutional Affairs, 2006), 16–17; and S. Bolton, *Briefing Paper: The detention of children in Member States' migration control and determination processes* (European Parliament, Directorate-General Internal Policies, Citizens Rights and Constitutional Affairs, 2006).

of auto-mutilation and (attempted) suicides among the population in immigration detention is very high.[13]

Under these circumstances, the detention of thousands of people in Europe, merely because they have allegedly breached the state's territorial sovereignty, may easily be labelled as an anomaly for Western liberal democracies, especially when seen in the context and development of citizenship discourse, constitutionalism and human rights. Nevertheless, portraying immigration detention solely as an incongruity for otherwise liberal regimes would not do justice to a reality that is much more complex. Thus, in this book I shall put forward the more intricate claim that the practice of depriving unwanted foreigners of their liberty and the lack of adequate constitutional control of this practice is a consequence of the territorial foundations of the global political system, and – more specifically – their impact on constitutional discourse. Some forms of state violence have become so inextricably linked to our understanding of the state and the structure of which it forms part that they have become insulated against the usual forms of legal correction and political control. I shall argue that immigration detention in contemporary Europe exemplifies the way in which, in the dominant political imagery, the mere absence of state authorisation for presence on national territory legitimately and self-evidently constitutes a ground for the use of state violence.[14] At the same time it is precisely these very forms of state violence – so deeply bound up with inequality, injustice and human suffering on a global scale – that should be the most pressing concern for any form of present-day constitutionalism that merits being called that at all.

Before providing an outline of the way in which I intend to address these issues in this book, I shall attempt to bring to life the structural features of state practice in the EU Member States in order to contextualise my subsequent discussion of the law and theory pertaining to immigration detention in later chapters. In this book, the term immigration detention is used to designate deprivations of liberty under administrative law for reasons that are directly linked to the administration of immigration policies. Consequently, both irregular migrants and asylum seekers fall under the scope of this work. At certain points, the distinction between the two groups will be made explicit,

---

[13] On the psychological problems brought about by detention see: D. Silove and M. Fazel, "Detention of refugees," *British Medical Journal* 332 (2006), 251–252. See also STEPS Consulting (2006), 121.

[14] In Poland, for example, the fact that immigration detainees are kept in prison-like places is justified by the authorities by recalling that these people have disobeyed Polish law by entering the country without authorisation. See the report by Caritas Poland in: Jesuit Refugee Service (2007), 90.

for example when the relevant legal norms are applicable to only one of the two categories or when the description of state practice requires the distinction to be made. However, it is important to make clear from the outset that the focus of this book is not on the deprivation of liberty of either asylum seekers or irregular migrants as distinct categories, but on the administrative detention of individuals on account of the lack of state authorisation for their presence on national territory.[15]

With regard to this focus on administrative detention, another preliminary remark needs to be made concerning the tendency towards the increasing criminalisation of illegal entry or stay on national territory.[16] A state that has defined these acts as criminal offences can "detain, charge, convict and sentence to further detention under criminal law" irregular migrants and even applicants for asylum.[17] Cyprus, for example, appears to have no closed centres for irregular migrants and asylum seekers in surveys on immigration detention in Europe.[18] However, irregular immigrants in Cyprus are detained in police custody while awaiting verification of their identity. And as illegal entry and stay are penal offences under Cypriot law, punishable by up to two years in prison, detention is in most cases not an administrative measure, but a penal one.[19] In some other Member States, even if they do not regard unauthorised stay and entry as criminal offences, the legal position of the foreign detainee who was initially apprehended on criminal charges is often unclear, due to the interaction between criminal proceedings, on the one hand, and the

---

[15] In addition, the focus in this study is on the detention of *third-country nationals*, as the detention of EU citizens under immigration law may only be very exceptionally resorted to if the citizen concerned constitutes a genuine threat to public policy. ECJ Case C-215/03 *Salah Oulane v. Minister voor Vreemdelingenzaken en Integratie* [2005] ECR I-1215, par. 40–44.

[16] In addition to national legislation relevant EU law exists here as well: Council Framework Decision 2002/946/JHA of 28 November on the strengthening of the penal framework to prevent the facilitation of unauthorised entry, transit and residence, OJ L 328/1, 5 December 2002; and Council Directive 2002/90/EC of 28 November 2002 defining the facilitation of unauthorised entry, transit and residence, OJ L 328/4, 5 December 2002.

[17] E. Guild, *Report for the European Parliament: Directorate General Internal Policies of the Union: A typology of different types of centres in Europe* (DG Internal Policies of the Union, Citizens Rights and Constitutional Affairs, 2006). See on international law in this field: A. Pacurar, "Smuggling, Detention and Expulsion of Irregular Migrants, A Study on International Legal Norms, Standards and Practices," *European Journal of Migration and Law* 5 (2003).

[18] See the report on Cyprus by the NGO Symfiliosi in: Jesuit Refugee Service (2007), 9.

[19] A. Ellinas, "Cyprus," in: Kalmthout, Hofstee-van der Meulen and Dünkel (2007), 167–168. Other countries that define irregular stay or entry under certain conditions as criminal offences that are punishable by prison sentences are Estonia, France, Germany, Greece, Hungary, Ireland, Italy and Lithuania. See the respective country reports in Kalmthout, Hofstee-van der Meulen and Dünkel (2007).

administrative procedure of expulsion on the other.[20] Although the steadily increasing trend towards the criminalisation of irregular migration is a highly significant one, for reasons concerning the length of this book, it shall only deal with detention as an *administrative* measure.

A last preliminary remark concerns the terms 'detention' and 'deprivation of liberty', which shall be used interchangeably in this book. The line between a *deprivation* of liberty, on the one hand, and a *restriction* upon personal liberty, on the other, is not always that easy to draw. The European Court of Human Rights (ECtHR) has observed that in many cases the difference is merely one of degree or intensity; not one of nature or substance, and that some borderline cases are a "matter of pure opinion".[21] The ECtHR regards the cumulative impact of the restrictions, as well as the degree and intensity of each one separately, when deciding whether one can speak of deprivation of liberty, in which case different guarantees apply than in the case of mere restrictions on free movement.[22] Arguably, in the area of migration law, the line between a deprivation of liberty and a restriction upon free movement may be even more blurred than usual. The most common distinction made in this regard is that between closed and open centres for immigrants, the latter often referred to as reception centres where the individuals who are required to reside can leave at will or within reasonable limits.[23] These so-called open centres, generally housing applicants for asylum, shall not be included in my analysis. Neither do I look at the situation of migrants who are subjected to mandatory residence requirements, as these individuals are merely restricted in their personal liberty, just as those who are obliged to report frequently to the authorities. Only the practice of placing individuals in closed centres or in any other narrowly confined location, which they are not able to leave, will be the subject matter of this book.

Especially with regard to the situation of irregular migrants and asylum seekers who are kept in transit zones – such as the international zone at an airport – specific problems may arise with regard to the question whether one can define their situation as a deprivation of liberty. States have repeatedly argued that individuals who are held in these zones are not deprived of their liberty, either because they are free to leave at will, or because they are not yet

---

[20] S. Snacken, "Belgium," in: Kalmthout, Hofstee-van der Meulen and Dünkel (2007), 147.
[21] ECtHR, *Guzzardi v. Italy*, 6 November 1980, A-39, par. 93.
[22] Ibid., par. 95. See also UNHCR, *Revised Guidelines on Applicable Criteria and Standards relating to the Detention of Asylum Seekers*, IOM/22/99/Rev.1-FOM/22/99/Rev.1 (February 1999), Guideline 1.
[23] Guild (2006), 3.

present on the territory of the state in question. These issues will receive detailed attention in later chapters where the impact of international human rights law on the practice of immigration detention is discussed, but in the sections below, transit zones will be explicitly included in my presentation of a general overview of state practice with regard to immigration detention.

1.2 Detention as a Tool of Immigration Control in Europe: An Overview

A first difficulty that one encounters when attempting to present an overview of the use of immigration detention by the Member States is to obtain reliable figures.[24] Many governments do not have coherent systems of recording statistics concerning immigration detention, especially when it comes to the duration of the detention and the reasons for ending it. Even the total numbers of immigration detainees are at times unknown to national governments themselves, as different categories of persons or different places for detention may fall under different regulations and authorities. In France, for example, some of the administrative detention facilities fall under the control of the *Sécurité Public Regional*, some under the border police and again some others under the *Gendarmerie*.[25] In a federal state such as Germany these difficulties are compounded because the federal states each have different regulations.[26]

If states do keep statistics, they are often rather reticent to make them available to the public.[27] Thus, in Greece, the lack of published data by the Ministry of Public Order makes the calculation of the number of persons affected by administrative detention nearly impossible.[28] In the UK, the Home Office only releases snapshot figures that range from 1105 detained asylum seekers on a given day to 1515.[29] The official haziness surrounding immigration detention

---

[24] On grounds of partially available data, the Jesuit Refugee Service estimates that the number of immigration detainees in Europe may be in the hundreds of thousands of persons per year.
[25] P. Décarpes, "France," in: Kalmthout, Hofstee-van der Meulen and Dünkel (2007), 333.
[26] F. Dünkel, A. Gensing and C. Morgenstern, "Germany," in: Kalmthout, Hofstee-van der Meulen and Dünkel (2007), 377.
[27] Guild (2006), 4.
[28] M. Akritidou, A. Antonopoulou and A. Pitsela, "Greece," in: Kalmthout, Hofstee-van der Meulen and F. Dünkel (2007), 416.
[29] N. Hammond, "United Kingdom," in: Kalmthout, Hofstee-van der Meulen and Dünkel (2007), 841. In addition, the figures released by the UK Border Agency do not include detentions which are carried out in prison. See London Detainee Support Group, *Indefinite detention in the UK: Length of detention snapshot statistics for 1 June 2009* (London, June 2009), at: www.ldsg.org.uk.

is exacerbated by the fact that in many countries not only the media but also human rights organisations are frequently denied access to places where migrants are kept in detention.[30]

Partly drawing on Elspeth Guild's classification in her report for the European Parliament on a typology of different types of centres in Europe, I will distinguish between three types of immigration detention in order to present some of the structural features of state practice in this area. These are detention upon arrival; detention of individuals within the asylum system; and detention as a result of a decision to deport or expel the foreigner.[31]

1.2.1 Detention upon Arrival

> From southern Algeria to Malta, from the Island of Lampedusa to the Ukrainian border, and from the Canaries to Slovenia, camps of all types are now strung out like so many nets for migrants, with the common aim of impeding, if not blocking, their way into Europe.[32]

Most EU Member States are familiar with legislation that provides for the detention of foreigners upon arrival in the state. In such cases, detention is used to prevent unauthorised entry, and it serves to clarify whether the conditions for lawful entry have been met, thereby including verification of identity. At times it is also justified by states with an appeal to health hazards or in order to implement readmission agreements.[33] Detention upon entry is often ordered by border guards and it is frequently carried out in a so-called transit

---

[30] With regard to the situation in France: see Council of Europe Commissioner for Human Rights, *Memorandum by Thomas Hammarberg, Commissioner for Human Rights of the Council of Europe further to his visit to the Zones d'Attente (Waiting Areas) at Roissy Airport and the Mesnil-Amelot Administrative Holding Centre*, CommDH (2008) 5 (Strasbourg, 20 November 2008), and Décarpes (2007), 333 and 337.

[31] Guild (2006), 5. It should be noted that these categories are not always separate in practice. Asylum seekers are often detained upon entry. Asylum legislation in the Czech Republic for example states that asylum seekers applying for international protection at the international airport shall be detained at the reception centre in the transit zone. See the report by the Counselling Centre for Refugees in: Jesuit Refugee Service (2007), 23–34. Similarly, detention as a result of the decision to expel or deport in many cases also affects asylum seekers. For example, in the United Kingdom, when the application of an asylum seeker who was detained in a 'fast-track centre' is rejected, he or she remains in detention until removal is carried out. See Hammond (2007), 842.

[32] C. Rodier, "Not in my backyard, keeping refugees in camps outside Europe," *Vacarme* 24 (2003).

[33] P. Škvain, "Czech Republic," in: Kalmthout, Hofstee-van der Meulen and Dünkel (2007), 203; and Szabó et al., "Hungary," in: Kalmthout, Hofstee-van der Meulen and Dünkel (2007), 443.

zone, which can be the international zone of an airport,[34] or any other place located close to border crossings.[35] Thus, in France, detention upon entry takes place in a so-called *zone d'attente*, of which there are more than 100 in the country, most of them small rooms, for instance in police stations, hotel rooms, administration offices, and which are located near the borders, airports, harbours or railway stations.[36] Some countries also use regular prisons or centres specifically designed for immigrants, as for instance the *Grenshospitium* in the Netherlands.[37]

Serious concerns have been expressed by NGOs and other political actors about detention upon arrival, as the legal position of the detainee is often unclear and not enough guarantees are applicable to the deprivation of liberty.[38] Although the majority of Member States provide for the possibility for third-country nationals to challenge their detention before a judicial authority, in many cases the remedies provided by domestic laws are neither speedy, nor effective, for example because the rights of the individual are not clearly defined.[39] Insufficient access to legal aid appears to be structural, either through the lack of financial means,[40] or because detainees are not told of the

---

[34] Such as the transit zone detention cente at the Lanzarote Airport Terminal in Spain. See Asóciation Pro Derechos Humanos de Andalucía, *Centros de Retencíon e Internamiento en Espana* (October 2008).

[35] In Romania, apparently an old hangar is used at Bucarest-Bănesa Aiport. See CPT, *Rapport au Gouvernement de Roumanie relatif à la visite effectuée en Roumanie par le Comité européen pour la prévention de la torture et des peines ou traitements inhumains ou dégradants du 8 au 19 juin 2006*, CPT/Inf (2008) 41, (Strasbourg, 11 December 2008).

[36] Although the great majority of those detained upon arrival in France are found in the waiting zone at Roissy-Charles de Gaulle in Paris. See Décarpes (2007), 337.

[37] A. van Kalmthout and F. Hofstee-van der Meulen, "The Netherlands," in: Kalmthout, Hofstee-van der Meulen and Dünkel (2007), 650.

[38] Formally, people in transit zones have not yet legally entered the national territory. See ECJ Case C-170/96, *Commission of the European Communities v Council of the European Union* [1988] ECR I-2763. The French term for the deprivation of liberty in these zones d'attente is 'retention', in which case lesser safeguards are applicable to the persons concerned than in the case of detention. See Décarpes (2007), 337. In Hungary the Aliens Act of 2007 abolished 'detention for refusal' and the cases that were formerly covered under this type of detention now fall under the rules on expulsion, and as such important additional safeguards have become applicable. See the report of the Hungarian Helsinki Committee in: Jesuit Refugee Service (2007), 44–57.

[39] EU Network of Independent Experts on Fundamental Rights, *Report on the situation of fundamental rights in the EU and its Member States in 2005: conclusions and recommendations* (Ref.: CFR-CDF&backslash;Conclusions 2005, 2005), 74–75.

[40] Many countries do not provide free legal aid to immigration detainees. See for example the report by Caritas Latvia in: Jesuit Refugee Service (2007), 59; Council of Europe Commissioner for Human Rights, *Report by the Commissioner for Human Rights Mr Thomas Hammarberg on*

reasons for their detention at all, and when they are, not always in a language that they understand.[41] As such, the exercise of formal rights is highly restricted in practice, not in the least also because of many practical obstacles, such as the lack of access to a telephone in order to contact a lawyer.[42] These problems are compounded by the fact that many of the detention centres are far removed from anywhere, which makes contacts with lawyers even more difficult.[43] Furthermore, the conditions in these places are regularly below national constitutional and international legal standards.[44]

The length of time that a migrant may spend in pre-admittance detention varies greatly from less than 24 hours to several weeks, even months, and only some states have the duration of this kind of detention limited by law. Even then ways have been devised by national authorities to evade time-limits set by the law. In Ireland, for example, the detention of an individual 'refused to land' may not exceed 8 weeks. However, if the individual brings legal proceedings to challenge the validity of the detention, the 'clock is stopped' concerning this 8-week period.[45]

---

his visit to Austria 21–25 May 2007, CommDH (2007) 26 (Strasbourg, 12 December 2007); and Council of Europe Commissioner for Human Rights, *Report by the Commissioner for Human Rights Mr Thomas Hammarberg on his visit to Germany, 9–11 and 15–20 October 2006*, CommDH (2007) 14 (Strasbourg, 11 July 2007).

[41] See CPT (11 December 2008) and CPT, *Report to the Hungarian Government on the visit to Hungary carried out by the European Committee for the Prevention of Torture and Inhuman or Degrading Treatment or Punishment from 30 March to 8 April 2005*, CPT/Inf (2006) 20 (Strasbourg, 29 June 2006), 24–25. In Malta the right to be informed about the reasons for detention is not even provided for in national legislation. See Jesuit Refugee Service (2007).

[42] Council of Europe Commissioner for Human Rights, CommDH (2008) 5 (20 November 2008), 4.

[43] On the situation in the United Kingdom, see Council of Europe Commissioner for Human Rights, *Report on his Visit to the United Kingdom (4–12 November 2004) for the attention of the Committee of Ministers and the Parliamentary Assembly*, CommDH (2005) 6 (Strasbourg, 8 June 2005), 17.

[44] The INADS centre at Brussels Airport for persons who arrive without documentation and who are refused entry to Belgian territory (INADS) has been criticised on several occasions by the CPT, in particular with regard to factual access to a lawyer and the lack of any activity for people that are kept in waiting zones for weeks, sometimes even months. See CPT, *Rapport au Gouvernement de la Belgique relatif a la visite effectuée en Belgique par le Comité Européen pour la prévention de la torture et des peines ou traitements inhumains ou dégradants du 18 au 27 avril 2005*, CPT/Inf (2006) 15 (Strasbourg, 20 April 2006). Also Germany has received criticism in this respect, especially regarding the situation in the transit zone at Frankfurt am Main Airport. CPT, *Report to the German Government on the visit to Germany carried out by the European Committee for the Prevention of Torture and Inhuman or Degrading Treatment or Punishment from 3 to 15 December 2000*, CPT/Inf (2003) 20 (Strasbourg, 12 March 2003), 60.

[45] Kelly (2005).

The southern borders of the EU deserve special mention with regard to detention upon arrival. Large numbers of migrants who have been apprehended while attempting to reach mainland Europe are held in Malta, Lampedusa and the Canary Islands in what have been described as "internment camps of dubious legality where people are deprived of their freedom yet supposedly are not prisoners."[46] These centres in particular have repeatedly been condemned on account of both the deplorable material conditions in which the detainees are held, and their legality. A delegation from the European Parliament that visited some of the Maltese administrative detention centres described the conditions as appalling, "unacceptable for a civilised country and untenable in Europe which claims to be the home of human rights."[47] Along the same lines, the Spanish Ombudsman has expressed severe criticism as regards the situation in Fuerteventura and Lanzarote, addressing overpopulation, inadequate facilities, a lack of transparency, a lack of interpreters and a lack of regular medical care.[48]

1.2.2 The Use of Detention within the Asylum System

Regarding the detention of asylum seekers, state practice shows a diverse pattern as well. All European governments detain people in the asylum procedure, but the conditions, the maximum duration and the actual time spent in detention by an asylum seeker vary widely in the Member States. It is important to note that with regard to this type of detention, relevant EC law exists. According to the Asylum Procedures Directive, the Member States shall not hold a person in detention for the sole reason that he or she has applied for asylum.[49] Furthermore, the Reception Conditions Directive provides that Member States are authorised to confine an applicant to a particular place in accordance with their national law, but only "when it proves necessary, for example for legal reasons or reasons of public order".[50]

Nevertheless, state practice shows that asylum seekers are often detained merely and precisely *because* they are asylum seekers, sometimes for a short

---

[46] European United Left/Nordic Green Left, *Report by the GUE/NGL Delegation on the visit to the Canary Islands 10–11 April 2006* (GUE/NGL Website and Publications Unit, May 2006), 11.

[47] European Parliament, Committee on Civil Liberties Justice and Home Affairs, Rapporteur G. Catania, *Report by the LIBE delegation on its visit to the administrative detention centres in Malta*, PV 613713EN.doc (Brussels, 30 March 2006), 9.

[48] J.L. de la Cuesta, "Spain," in: Kalmthout, Hofstee-van der Meulen and Dünkel (2007), 776.

[49] Article 18(1) of Council Directive 2005/85/EC on minimum standards on procedures in Member States for granting and withdrawing refugee status.

[50] Article 7 of Council Directive 2003/9/EC laying down minimum standards for the reception of asylum seekers in the Member States.

time in order to determine the admissibility of the application or to identify the individuals and to initiate the asylum procedure.[51] Thus, in Portugal, asylum seekers are detained until the authorities decide that they have legitimate grounds for asking for asylum, which takes an average of three days. Thereafter, those that are considered to have applied for asylum on legitimate grounds are transferred to open reception centres.[52] In Finland, asylum seekers may be detained after they have received a negative decision on their application, and then their detention in fact serves removal.[53] In Latvia, asylum seekers are detained if their identity is not confirmed or if their claims have been rejected and they await expulsion.[54] In Italy, asylum seekers are *de facto* detained in reception centres (*Centro de Accoglienza*) until they are provided with a document certifying their status as asylum seekers, a practice which, however, seems to lack a clear and unequivocal basis in Italian legislation.[55] Also, if asylum seekers are issued with an expulsion or rejection order before they file their asylum application in Italy, they will no longer be hosted in open centres, but they will be deprived of their liberty for a maximum period of 60 days.[56]

Whereas in some countries detention thus occurs during a certain stage in the asylum procedure, in others the deprivation of liberty may form an inherent part of the entire procedure.[57] In Cyprus, for example, domestic legislation restricts the use of detention with regard to asylum seekers by only allowing it in order to ascertain identity and the facts upon which the application is based. Legally, detention may not exceed eight days, after which the detention can be prolonged by a court for a maximum of 32 days. Nevertheless, Cypriot practice is very different: if asylum seekers entered Cyprus illegally before they submitted their application for asylum, they are detained for that

---

[51] In the Czech Republic all applicants for asylum are initially detained – also because they could pose 'health hazards' to the general population. See Škvain (2007), 203.
[52] R. Abrunhosa Gonçalves, "Portugal," in: Kalmthout, Hofstee-van der Meulen and Dünkel (2007), 75–76.
[53] T. Lappi-Seppälä, "Finland," in: Kalmthout, Hofstee-van der Meulen and Dünkel (2007), 312.
[54] L. Zeibote, "Latvia," in: Kalmthout, Hofstee-van der Meulen and Dünkel (2007), 533.
[55] UN Human Rights Council, *Report of the Working Group on Arbitrary Detention, Addendum, Mission to Italy*, Tenth session, Agenda item 3, A/HRC/10/21/Add.5, 16 February 2009, par 70–72.
[56] Council of Europe Commissioner for Human Rights, *Report by Thomas Hammarberg, Commissioner for Human Rights of the Council of Europe following his visit to Italy on 13–15 January 2009*, CommDH (2009) 16 (Strasbourg, 16 April 2009), 15.
[57] As is the case in Malta. See the country report by JRS Malta in: Jesuit Refugee Service (2007); and Council of Europe Commissioner for Human Rights, *Follow-Up Report on Malta (2003–2005): Assessment of the progress made in implementing the recommendations of the Council of Europe Commissioner for Human Rights*, CommDH (2006) 14 (Strasbourg, 29 March 2006).

reason and they remain in detention until a decision is given on their applications, even though the removal order is suspended for the duration of the asylum procedure.[58] Polish practice is similar: there asylum seekers are not detained unless they apply for asylum while staying 'illegally' on national territory; or during border control while they have no right to enter; or when they attempt to cross Polish borders contrary to the law. Taking into account that few persons seeking international protection await a decision on a visa application in their countries of origin before applying for asylum in another country, the majority of asylum seekers in Poland may be detained upon arrival.[59] In Austria, asylum seekers are detained until a procedural notice is issued by the Federal Asylum Authority during the admissibility proceedings stating that the application is likely to be dismissed or rejected. It is not possible to appeal against such a notice.[60] In Greece, not all asylum seekers are detained, but those who file an application whilst in immigration detention (i.e. on the grounds of illegal entry or stay) remain in detention until a decision on their applications is given, or until the time-limit of three months expires.[61] In the United Kingdom, the vast majority of those detained have applied for asylum at one stage or another.[62]

The United Kingdom is also one of several countries that detain asylum seekers in the context of 'fast-track procedures', where detention seems to serve mere administrative expediency.[63] This practice in particular has led to allegations by NGOs that "detention is resorted to on the basis that a bed is available in a detention centre," rather than considering the "necessity, legality and appropriateness" of detaining asylum seekers.[64] Furthermore, Member

---

[58] See the report by Symfiliosi in: Jesuit Refugee Service (2007), 11–12.
[59] B. Stando-Kawecka, "Poland," in: Kalmthout, Hofstee-van der Meulen and Dünkel (2007), 679.
[60] EU Network of independent experts (2005), 75–76.
[61] M. Akritidou, A. Antonopoulou and A. Pitsela (2007), 416.
[62] Hammond (2007), 841; and Council of Europe Commissioner for Human Rights (8 June 2005).
[63] Doubts have been raised about the effectiveness of the detention of asylum seekers in the context of accelerated procedures. See Council of Europe Commissioner for Human Rights, *Report by Thomas Hammarberg on his visit to the Netherlands 21–25 September 2008*, CommDH (2009) 2 (Strasbourg, 11 March 2009), 15.
[64] Amnesty International, EU Office, *The human cost of "Fortress Europe": Detention and expulsion of asylum-seekers and migrants in the EU: Open letter to Incoming UK Presidency on the occasion of World Refugee Day* (Amnesty International, 20 June 2005). With regard to Hungary, for example, it has been argued that the detention of asylum seekers seems to depend largely on "accidental circumstances and arbitrary decisions of the authorities", as the question whether someone is to be detained seems to be entirely dependent on the moment of border control. See Szabó et al. (2007), 444.

States are increasingly resorting to detention in order to prepare or carry out transfers under the Dublin system,[65] in which case the deprivation of liberty may last for a substantial amount of time, during which no substantial assessment is made with regard to the claim by the individual to international protection.[66]

With regard to the detention of asylum seekers, widespread discrimination on the grounds of nationality exists, as some states routinely detain certain nationalities (or ethnic groups),[67] whereas others seldom or never end up in an immigration prison. Although some countries, amongst which are Germany and Estonia, only allow for the detention of asylum seekers if it is ordered by a judicial authority,[68] in many other countries, the decision to detain is taken administratively. In that case, often extensive discretion exists for individual immigration officers to decide on the detention of asylum seekers.[69] An automatic judicial review is frequently absent,[70] or it can take a long time.[71] In the Czech Republic, asylum seekers who are detained under the Dublin II regulation do not even have the right to challenge their detention at all, and in Malta, asylum seekers cannot effectively challenge the lawfulness of their detention.[72] In other countries, even though they formally recognise the right of the third-country national to challenge the detention, the exercise thereof is restricted

---

[65] ECRE and ELENA, *Report on the Application of the Dublin II Regulation in Europe* (March 2006), at http://www.detention-in-europe.org/images/stories/ecre%20report%20dublii.pdf.

[66] In the Netherlands, the deprivation of liberty which is used against persons detained at the border who are awaiting a Dublin transfer lasts for an average of 86 days. See VluchtelingenWerk, *Gesloten OC Procedure voor Asielzoekers, Onderzoek in Opdracht van UNHCR* (Vluchtelingenwerk Nederland, September 2007).

[67] Such as Roma in the United Kingdom. See L. Weber, "Down that Wrong Road: Discretion on Decisions to Detain Asylum Seekers Arriving at UK Ports," *Howard Journal of Criminal Justice* 42 (2003).

[68] Dünkel, Gensing and Morgenstern (2007), 383; and the report by the Estonian Refugee Council in Jesuit Refugee Service (2007), 35–57.

[69] UNHCR Executive Committee (4 June 1999), 168. See Council of Europe Commissioner for Human Rights, *Memorandum by Thomas Hammerberg following his visits to the United Kingdom on 5–8 February and 31 March–2 April 2008*, CommDH (2008) 23 (Strasbourg, 18 September 2008); Council of Europe Commissioner for Human Rights (8 June 2005); and Weber (2003).

[70] If an automatic judicial review is absent, the detention may be subject to periodical automatic *administrative* review. See Council of Europe Commissioner for Human Rights (18 September 2008).

[71] In the Netherlands, an automatic review by a court of the lawfulness of the detention is provided, but it can take up to 7 weeks until it actually takes place. See P.J.A.M. Baudoin, "De Vreemdelingenwet gewijzigd: rechterlijke toetsing terug naar af," *Migrantenrecht* 6 (2004).

[72] See the report by the Counselling Centre for Refugees, in: Jesuit Refugee Service (2007), 23–34 and the report by JRS Malta, in: Jesuit Refugee Service (2007), 74.

due to the lack of information provided to the detainees or insufficient access to legal aid. In this respect, similar problems are encountered as were discussed above with regard to detention upon arrival.[73]

The detention of refugees in particular may also prejudice their legal position as persons applying for international protection, as they are not always informed about the possibility of applying for asylum while in detention.[74] Even more worrying is that in some instances individuals are even impeded from accessing the asylum procedure as a result of their detention.[75]

1.2.3 *Detention and Removal*

The last category that I shall address is detention as a result of a decision to deport or expel the foreigner in question. If a third-country national has been ordered to leave national territory, the immigration legislation of most EU countries provides for the possibility of administrative detention. In theory, this type of detention is neither a punishment, nor a "means of directly coercing the foreigner to leave the country", but it serves to safeguard removal, such as expulsion or deportation.[76] Thus, the sole fact of irregular residence is usually not a sufficient justification for detention in the EU Member States.[77] Nevertheless, foreigners are frequently kept in detention for significant periods

---

[73] Jesuit Refugee Service (2007); Council of Europe Commissioner for Human Rights, *Memorandum by Thomas Hammarberg following his visit to France from 21 to 23 May 2008*, CommDH (2008) 34 (Strasbourg, 20 November 2008). See also Kelly (2005), 35; and Council of Europe Commissioner for Human Rights (8 June 2005), 18.

[74] See the report by the Hungarian Helsinki Committee in: Jesuit Refugee Service (2007), 52.

[75] Which seems to be the case in some of the *zones d'attente* in France. See Council of Europe Commissioner for Human Rights, CommDH (2008) 5 (20 November 2008), and also European Parliament, Committee on Civil Liberties, Justice and Home Affairs, Rapporteur A. Diaz de Mera Garcia-Consuegra, *Report by the LIBE delegation on its visit to the adminstrative detention centres in Paris*, PV 607993EN.doc (Brussels, 22 March 2006). In Greece, similar problems exist. See Council of Europe Commissioner for Human Rights, *Report by Thomas Hammarberg following his visit to Greece 8–10 December 2008*, CommDH (2009) 6 (Strasbourg, 4 February 2009), 6. See also Amnesty International, *Greece: Out of the spotlight*, AI Index 25/016/20052005 (Amnesty International, 5 October 2005); and CPT, *Report on the visit to Greece carried out by the European Committee for the Prevention of Torture and Inhuman or Degrading Treatment or Punishment from 27 August to 9 September 2005*, CPT/Inf (2006) 41 (Strasbourg, 20 December 2006), 38.

[76] Dünkel, Gensing and Morgenstern (2007), 377. Nonetheless, there are countries that have provisions in their legislation that suggest the coercive nature of detention: in Ireland, the purpose of detention is to ensure that the person will actually co-operate in making arrangements, such as securing travel documents. See M. Moore, "Ireland," in: Kalmthout, Hofstee-van der Meulen and Dünkel (2007), 471.

[77] Guild (2006), 5.

of time before their deportation is practically arranged.[78] Thus, with regard to Hungary, the Commissioner for Human Rights of the Council of Europe has expressed concern that irregular aliens are detained for up to 12 months on the sole ground that they have been found on Hungarian territory without a valid residence.[79] Hungary also has the possibility of enforcing detention even if the deportation order is suspended.[80] In addition, some countries provide for the possibility of detention in *preparation* of deportation procedures, therewith including the verification of the identity of the foreigner and clarification of his residence status.[81] Moreover, although various national laws require that detention is to be necessary (often with a view to public policy or national security interests),[82] in everyday practice the national authorities detain without due regard to the necessity and proportionality of the detention, often as a result of wide discretionary powers conferred upon them by domestic laws.[83]

Even in judicial procedures where the legality of the detention is challenged, the question whether the administration has employed its discretionary powers in accordance with otherwise important constitutional principles is often not addressed.[84] It remains to be seen whether this situation will change as a result of Member States' implementation of the Returns Directive, which binds detention for the purpose of removal to the principle of proportionality, and stipulates that detention may be resorted to in order to prepare the return or carry

---

[78] EU Network of Independent Experts (2005), 73.

[79] Council of Europe Commissioner for Human Rights, *Follow-Up Report on Hungary (2002–2005), Assessment of the progress made in implementing the recommendations of the Council of Europe Commissioner for Human Rights*, CommDH (2006) 11 (Strasbourg, 29 May 2006), 20.

[80] Szabó et al. (2007), 443.

[81] Id. In Germany so-called 'preparatory detention' may not exceed 6 weeks. See Dünkel, Gensing and Morgenstern (2007), 383.

[82] I.e. in Sweden, the law provides for detention if a decision to expel has been taken and the person is likely to abscond or engage in criminal activity. See A.K. Johnson, "Sweden," in: Kalmthout, Hofstee-van der Meulen and Dünkel (2007), 802.

[83] UNHCR, "Detention of Asylum Seekers and Refugees: The Framework, the Problem and Recommended Practice," 15th Meeting of the Executive Committee of the High Commissioner's Programme Standing Committee, Doc. No. EC/49/SC/CRP.13, 4 June 1999, Reprinted in *Refugee Survey Quarterly* 18 (1999), 168; and Amnesty International (June 2008).

[84] Thus, it has been said that the Hungarian courts seem to render their decisions "almost automatically" without due regard to all the circumstances of the case. See the report by the Hungarian Helsinki Committee in: Jesuit Refugee Service (2007), 47. See for a rather restrictive view of the role of the courts in respectively the United Kingdom and the Netherlands: House of Lords, *Regina v. Secretary of State for the Home Department (Respondent) ex parte Khadir (FC) (Appellant)*, 16 June 2005, [2005] UKHL 39, par. 32; and Afdeling Bestuursrechtspraak Raad van State, 6 September 2005, *Jurisprudentie Vreemdelingenrecht* 452 (2005).

out the removal process, but only if *other sufficient but less coercive measures* cannot be applied *effectively in a specific case*.⁸⁵

Most European Member States have the duration of this type of detention limited by law.⁸⁶ Thus, in Belgium, detention for removal is normally imposed for a maximum of two months, but it may be extended to five months. A further extension up to the absolute maximum of eight months is only permitted if it is necessary for the protection of public order or national security.⁸⁷ In the Czech Republic, irregular migrants can only be detained when an administrative decision on expulsion is imposed, and such detention is subject to a time-limit of 180 days.⁸⁸ In Finland, there is no time-limit laid down in legislation, but the courts will order the release of the person in question after three months.⁸⁹ In Greece, if the foreigner is not expelled within three months, he must be released immediately. In Hungary, detention in preparation for expulsion may not last longer than 30 days, but detention in order to deport is subject to a legal limit of twelve months.⁹⁰ According to Latvian aliens' legislation, administrative detention may not exceed twenty months.⁹¹ Whereas in Malta before 2005, there was no legal limit to the duration of the detention – and it was not unusual for persons to be detained for several years – government *policy* now sets a general time-limit of 18 months. However, in practice, release does not always take place automatically after the expiry of this period.⁹² Germany has a maximum length of pre-deportation detention of 18 months.⁹³ According to Polish and Slovenian laws, the total time spent in immigration detention may not exceed one year.⁹⁴ In Spain, if it is foreseeable

---

⁸⁵ Directive 2008/115/EC on common standards and procedures in Member States for returning illegally staying third-country nationals. See also Chapter 7.
⁸⁶ The United Kingdom and the Netherlands are the only Member States where there is no maximum term for detention. See Commissioner for Human Rights (Strasbourg, 11 March 2009), 15. In Estonia detention can be prolonged endlessly by the administrative court upon requests by the Police or the Citizenship and Migration Board. See the report by the Estonian Refugee Council in: Jesuit Refugee Service (2007), 37.
⁸⁷ Snacken (2007), 152.
⁸⁸ Škvain (2007), 203.
⁸⁹ Lappi-Seppälä (2007), 311.
⁹⁰ Which is a significant improvement compared to legislation that was in force before 2001, when the duration of immigration detention was not limited by law. See the report by the Hungarian Helsinki Committee in: Jesuit Refugee Service (2007), 47.
⁹¹ See the report by Caritas Latvia in: Jesuit Refugee Service (2007), 59.
⁹² See the report by JRS Malta, in: Jesuit Refugee Service (2007), 75.
⁹³ Council of Europe Commissioner for Human Rights (11 July 2007), 40.
⁹⁴ Stando-Kawecka (2007), 682; and D. Petrovec, "Slovenia," in: Kalmthout, Hofstee-van der Meulen and Dünkel (2007), 746.

that expulsion is not possible within 40 days, the court has to be notified immediately so that it can release the detainee.[95]

Even though the legislation of the majority of Member States thus provides for release after a period of detention, many of the released detainees are not always able to leave the country (the reason for their prolonged detention being that deportation could not be organised) and are subsequently re-apprehended and again detained. Consequently, in many countries, irregular migrants may spend very long periods in detention with small breaks of freedom that are once again followed by detention.[96] This actual situation is neither apparent from legal provisions that lay down time-limits, nor is it reflected in statistics that record the duration of detention. It is in this context in particular that the Working Group on Arbitrary Detention has called attention to the fact that national laws and executive practice appear to take insufficient account of the fact that in some cases it is clear from the outset that removal is not possible and that detention can therefore not be justified.[97]

Concerning the legal position of the immigration detainee who is to be expelled or deported, similar remarks can be made as were made with regard to the two types of detention discussed above. Countries that provide for a periodical and automatic judicial review of the detention constitute a minority.[98] The exercise of the right to challenge the legality of the detention by detainees is often impeded due to a lack of (understandable) information regarding that right or insufficient access to legal aid.[99] Often the basis for

---

[95] In Spain, if it is foreseeable that expulsion is not possible within the 40-day limit to the detention, the judge has to be notified immediately so that the detainee can be released. See *Organic Law 8/2000 of 22 December, Reforming Organic Law 4/2000, of 11 January, Regarding the Rights and Freedoms of Foreign Nationals Living in Spain and Their Social Integration* [Spain], 22 December 2000.

[96] Akritidou, Antonopoulou and Pitsela (2007), 419.

[97] UN Human Rights Council, *Report of the Working Group on Arbitrary Detention, Addendum, Mission to Italy*, Tenth session, Agenda item 3, A/HRC/10/21/Add.5, 26 January 2009, par. 81.

[98] An automatic judicial review is provided for in Hungarian legislation. See the report by the Hungarian Helsinki Committee in: Jesuit Refugee Service (2007), 47.

[99] See Council of Europe Commissioner for Human Rights (12 December 2007); CPT, *Report to the Austrian Government on the visit to Austria carried out by the European Committee for the Prevention of Torture and Inhuman or Degrading Treatment or Punishment, from 14 to 23 April 2004*, CPT/Inf (2005) 13 (Strasbourg, 21 July 2005), 31–32; HM Chief Inspector of Prisons, A. Owers, *Report on the unannounced inspections of five non-residential short-term holding facilities: Queen's Building and Terminals 1–4, Heathrow Airport 10–13 October 2005* (London: Her Majesty's Inspectorate of Prisons, 2006), 25–26; Kelly (2005), 40–42; and Council of Europe Commissioner for Human Rights, A. Gil-Robles, *Report on his visit to Spain (10–19 March 2005)*, CommDH (2005) 8 (Strasbourg, 9 November 2005), 36. In Poland, the appeal must have been lodged within 7 days from the day upon which the immigrant received the

detention is not adequately explained, and at times even the immigration status of the persons detained remains unclear to them.[100]

I shall conclude this overview of state practice with some brief observations regarding the conditions of detention. The CPT has repeatedly held that "a prison is by definition not a place in which to detain someone who is neither convicted nor suspected of a criminal offence"[101] and it has urged states to put an end to holding immigration detainees in ordinary law enforcement agency detention facilities.[102] Even so, many Member States keep detaining persons who are subject to a removal order in ordinary prisons or police custody facilities, sometimes as a result of a lack of available places in special centres,[103] but often it is also common policy. Thus, in France, although there are many administrative detention centres, foreigners who are subject to removal may be detained with prisoners who are detained under criminal law.[104] And in Austria, detention for the purpose of removal is often practised in normal prisons.[105] In Germany, special institutions for administrative detention under immigration legislation are only to be found in a few federal states. Most cases of administrative detention of foreigners are thus carried out in penitentiary institutions and prisons.[106] Greece has only a few administrative detention centres. Consequently, the detention facilities of police stations all over the country constitute *de facto* institutions for administrative detention, where the

---

detention order, which is not enough for them to contact lawyers and to obtain legal aid. See the report by Caritas Poland in: Jesuit Refugee Service (2007), 91.

[100] Chief Inspector of Prison, A. Owers, *Report on an unannounced inspection of Harmondsworth Immigration Removal Centre 17–21 July 2000* (London: Her Majesty's Inspectorate of Prisons, 2006), 26.

[101] See for example CPT, *Report to the Government of Ireland on the visit to Ireland carried out by the European Committee for the Prevention of Torture and Inhuman or Degrading Treatment or Punishment from 20 to 28 March 2002*, CPT/Inf (2003) 36 (Strasbourg, 18 September 2003), par 69. Cf. UN Commission on Human Rights, *Deliberation No. 5 of the Working Group on Arbitrary Detention*, Fifty-sixth session, Item 11(a) of the provisional agenda, Report of the Working Group on Arbitrary Detention, Annex II, E/CN.4/2000/4, 28 December 1999.

[102] CPT (20 December 2006), 24.

[103] As seems to be the case in Finland where the law states that detention should be carried out in a specialised facility, but as there is only one immigration detention centre in Finland, detention in police cells occurs frequently. See CPT, *Report on the visit to Finland carried out by the European Committee for the Prevention of Torture and Inhuman or Degrading Treatment or Punishment from 20 to 30 April 2008*, CPT/Inf (2009) 5 (Strasbourg, 20 January 2009).

[104] Décarpes (2007), 337.

[105] A. Pilgram and V. Hofinger, "Austria," in: Kalmthout, Hofstee-van der Meulen and Dünkel (2007), 119.

[106] Dünkel, Gensing and Morgenstern (2007), 377.

vast majority of the immigration detainees are held.[107] In Ireland, only ordinary prisons are used.[108] The Netherlands has special places for administrative detention, but detention is also regularly carried out in police custody facilities or prisons.[109] In Portugal, irregular migrants may be placed in prisons with convicted prisoners or in transit zones of international airports.[110] However, the legislation of some states, even though it provides for detention in ordinary prisons or police cells, subjects such detention to strict time-limits (Latvia and Lithuania);[111] or reserves it for special circumstances (Sweden);[112] or alternatively stipulates that immigration detainees are to be kept separate from those that are held under criminal law (Hungary).[113] Persons subject to an expulsion order are at times also kept in transit zones. The latter situation calls for extra scrutiny as some states have argued that in these situations it is not depriving individuals of their liberty at all.[114]

Even when special holding centres exist for immigration detainees, conditions are at times worse than in ordinary prisons, with circumstances reminiscent of high security prisons and regulations that are not appropriate to the legal status of the detainees and the low security risk that they pose.[115] Indeed,

---

[107] Akritidou, Antonopoulou and Pitsela (2007), 416.

[108] Kelly (2005).

[109] P. Baudoin, A. Van de Burght, and B. Hendriksen, *Vrijheidsontneming van vreemdelingen* (The Hague: Boom Juridische Uitgevers, 2002), 211. According to a recent judgment, detention in a *police custody facility* may not last longer than 120 hours, after which period the immigration detainee should be transferred to remand prisons or special facilities. See the judgment by Rechtbank Haarlem, 20 March 2009, *Jurisprudentie Vreemdelingenrecht* 197 (2009).

[110] Abrunhosa Gonçalves (2007), 706.

[111] Zeibote (2007), 533 and S. Malisauskaite-Simanaitiene, "Lithuania," in: Kalmthout, Hofstee-van der Meulen and Dünkel (2007), 565.

[112] Johnson (2007), 803.

[113] Szabó et al. (2007), 447.

[114] Belgium argues that as the foreigners in question have no right of residence in Belgium, they are not being detained by being placed in the transit zone, but simply escorted to Belgium's border, where they are free to leave by boarding a flight to their country of origin or a third country. See Amnesty International, *Europe and Central Asia: Summary of Amnesty International's Concerns in the Region (January-June 2004)*, AI Index EUR/01/005/2004 (Amnesty International, 1 September 2004).

[115] Such as systematically handcuffing immigration detainees when they are taken to and from hospital and the use of military search methods (Malta); the inappropriate use of isolation and violent security measures (Germany and Romania); and allowing communication with family members only through a glass partition (Austria). See for example CPT (12 March 2003), 32; CPT (21 July 2005), 32; and Council of Europe Commissioner of Human Rights (29 March 2006), 12; and Council of Europe Commissioner for Human Rights, A. Gil-Robles, *Report on his visit to Malta from 20-21 October 2003*, CommDH (2004) 4 (Strasbourg, 12 February 2004), 8.

in many countries the rules concerning the detention of illegal immigrants are more restrictive than those applied to persons convicted of criminal offences.[116] In Luxembourg, the Commissioner for Human Rights of the Council of Europe observed that the restrictions on the visits to immigration detainees are more severe than those applicable to normal prisoners.[117] And as regards the situation of immigration detainees in the Netherlands, the CPT has asked that country to clarify the reasons for the decision to classify immigration detention centres as remand prisons.[118] There are also exceptions: in Finland, detainees have access to better and more relaxed living conditions than normal prisoners and the possibilities for receiving visits by friends and family are not limited.[119]

Many immigration detention centres suffer from problems resulting from serious overpopulation, inadequate medical and hygienic care and limited possibilities for contact with the outside world. In 2006, the Commissioner for Human Rights of the Council of Europe called the conditions in the administrative holding centre for men under the *Palais de Justice* in Paris "disastrous and unworthy of France" and urged its closure because he deemed a place of this kind at the heart of the French judicial system to be unacceptable.[120] In the report following its visit to the Czech Republic in 2002, the CPT criticised the conditions of detention and was alarmed by allegations of ill-treatment and verbal abuse in some of the facilities.[121] In Poland, the CPT observed that health care and psychological and psychiatric support for immigration detainees were not adequate. In addition, no regimes of activities appropriate to the detainees' legal status and the length of their stay were available.[122] Conditions of immigration detention in Greece are so bad that some other EU Member States no longer send third-country nationals there under the Dublin Convention. These

---

[116] See Zeibote (2007) and Décarpes (2007).
[117] Council of Europe Commissioner for Human Rights, A. Gil-Robles, *Report on his visit to the Grand Duchy of Luxembourg 2–3 February 2004*, CommDH (2004) 11 (Strasbourg, 8 July 2004), 11.
[118] CPT (5 February 2008), 32.
[119] Lappi-Seppälä, 311; and CPT (20 January 2009).
[120] Council of Europe Commissioner for Human Rights, A. Gil-Robles, *Report on the effective respect for Human Rights in France following his visit from 5 to 21 September 2006*, CommDH (2006) 2 (Strasbourg, 15 February 2006), 62, and for similar criticism see also European Parliament, Committee on Civil Liberties, Justice and Home Affairs (22 March 2006).
[121] CPT, *Report to the Czech Government on the visit to the Czech Republic carried out by the European Committee for the Prevention of Torture and Inhuman or Degrading Treatment or Punishment from 21 to 30 April 2002*, CPT/Inf (2004) 4 (Strasbourg, 12 March 2004).
[122] CPT, *Report to the Polish Government on the visit to Poland carried out by the European Committee for the Prevention of Torture and Inhuman or Degrading Treatment or Punishment from 4 to 15 October 2004*, CPT/Inf (2006) 11 (Strasbourg, 12 March 2006), 22–27.

appalling conditions have not only been repeatedly condemned by the CPT,[123] but they have also led the ECtHR to conclude that immigration detainees in Greece have been subjected to inhuman and degrading treatment, contrary to Article 3 of the Convention.[124]

In view of these problems, it is a welcome development that the Returns Directive lays down requirements regarding the conditions of detention by stipulating that detention shall be carried out in specialised facilities.[125] Moreover, according to the Directive, immigration detainees shall, upon request, be allowed without delay to establish contact with legal representatives, family members and competent consular authorities as well as with relevant international and non-governmental organisations. In addition, Member States have to ensure that international and non-governmental organisations have the possibility to visit places where deprivations of liberty under immigration legislation are carried out. It remains to been seen whether the implementation of the Directive by the Member States will lead to a much needed improvement with regard to the conditions of immigration detention in Europe.

1.3 *Immigration Detention: Current Research and Outline of this Book*

Where, 15 years ago, academic interest in the practice of immigration detention was negligible, the increase in the use of that measure by national states has been accompanied by a steadily growing academic interest. A large part of the emerging research in the legal studies stems from criminological roots, and it has tended to view the growing use of immigration detention as part of a general tendency in contemporary societies towards risk minimisation and societal control, and in which unwanted migrants are seen as a 'dangerous' group that needs to be identified and managed by the use of measures from the criminal justice system, such as "police, penalties and prisons".[126] In order

---

[123] Such as men and women detained in the same cells, not enough food for detainees, the absence of adequate sanitary facilities, flea-inflected blankets and very serious overcrowding. See CPT (30 June 2009) and CPT (20 December 2006), 31-39; and Amnesty International (5 October 2005). See also Council of Europe Commissioner for Human Rights (Strasbourg, 4 February 2009).

[124] *S.D. v. Greece*, 11 June 2009, Appl. No. 53541/07; and *Dougoz v. Greece*, 6 March 2001, Reports 2001-II. See also *K.R.S. v. United Kingdom*, 2 December 2008, Appl. No. 32733/08.

[125] If this is not possible, they should in any case be held separate from ordinary prisoners.

[126] M. Welch, *Detained: Immigration Law and the Expanding I.N.S. Jail Complex* (Philadelphia: Temple University Press, 2002), 23. See also L. Schuster, "A Sledgehammer to Crack a Nut: Deportation, Detention and Dispersal in Europe," *Social Policy and Administration* 39 (2005).

to explain the growth in immigration prisons, several authors have pointed to the emergence of the 'New Penology', a concept embracing both the theory and practice of punishing, and supposedly entailing a novel way of controlling and responding to crime and deviant behaviour.[127] The New Penology differs from traditional penology in that it focuses on "categories of potential and actual offenders rather than on individuals, and on managerial aims rather than rehabilitation or transformation of the offender."[128] As a result, enforcement and coercion is no longer primarily directed at the individual, but focuses unevenly across categories of specific populations, whose potential for risk is assessed by means of actuarial policies and technological tools and contained by increased reliance on imprisonment.[129]

It is inherent in the very paradigm of the New Penology that it encompasses forms of social control which fall outside the traditional sphere of criminal law enforcement, and as such it is not surprising that a link has been made between the New Penology and contemporary tools of immigration law enforcement.[130] Indeed, the increasing criminalisation of 'illegal' stay, the setting up of annual quota to be achieved for deportation, and the steep increase in the use of technological tools in order to 'combat' illegal migration can be seen as reflecting the contemporary rise of 'actuarial justice' in a risk-obsessed society. With regard to immigration detention in particular, it has been argued

---

Mary Bosworth also uses immigration detention in order to identify interesting parallels between the management of foreigners and offenders. See M. Bosworth, "Border Control and the Limits of the Sovereign State," *Social and Legal Studies* 17 (2008); and also M. Lee, "Women's imprisonment as a mechanism of migration control in Hong Kong," *British Journal of Criminology* 47 (2007).

[127] J. Simon, "Refugees in a carceral age: the rebirth of immigration prisons in the United States," *Public Culture* 10 (1998); M. Welch, "The Role of the Immigration and Naturalization Service in the Prison Industrial Complex," *Social Justice* 27 (2000).

[128] S. Easton and C. Piper, *Sentencing and Punishment: The Quest for Justice* (Oxford: Oxford University Press, 2008), 21. See also Welch (2000), 74. On the 'New Penology' in general, see: M. Feeley and J. Simon, "The New Penology: Notes on the Emerging Strategy of Corrections and Its Implications," *Criminology* 30 (1992); and M. Feeley and J. Simon, "Actuarial Justice. The Emerging New Criminal Law," in: *The Futures of Criminology*, ed. D. Nelken (London: Sage, 1994).

[129] On the more widespread reliance upon mass incarceration and the way that relates to new forms of anxiety in contemporary societies, see Z. Bauman, "Social Issues of Law and Order," *British Journal of Criminology* 40 (2000).

[130] Feeley and Simon (1992); T. A. Miller, "Citizenship & Severity: Recent Immigration Reforms and the New Penology," *Georgetown Immigration Law Journal* 17 (2003); and T.A. Miller, "Blurring the Boundaries Between Immigration and Crime Control After September 11th," *Boston College Third World Law Journal* 25(2005). But see A.M. Lucas, "Huddled Masses, Immigrants in detention," *Punishment and Society* 7 (2005).

that this practice reflects a "globalizing culture of control" driven by "perceptions of difference and putative threats".[131] The way in which the detention of 'illegal' migrants resonates with the contemporary political 'management of risk' has also been emphasised by authors who claim that immigration detention has primarily become an instrument to "assuage public fears concerning supposed 'risks' and potential dangers to 'security'".[132]

Undeniably, the everyday practice of immigration detention in the EU Member States fits these observations. While in most countries immigration detention was originally intended as an individual measure of last resort (and was accordingly used relatively sparsely until the early nineties), contemporary practice shows that immigration detention has become a large-scale instrument – almost punitive in character – that explicitly targets categories of persons, leaving ever less scope for the consideration of the individual circumstances of each and every case. This holds true not only for the decision by the executive to resort to detention, but it often also applies to the way in which the judiciary assesses its legitimacy. Thus, according to the highest administrative court in the Netherlands, the fact that someone is detained on grounds which are applicable to nearly every applicant for asylum does not mean that these grounds in themselves are not enough to justify the use of detention in an individual case.[133] The inexorable result of such a line of reasoning is that it is no longer the specific situation of the individual that is decisive for the application of a particularly coercive form of social control. Instead, depriving the individual of his or her liberty is seen as legitimate merely because he or she is designated as belonging to a specific group, a mechanism that is even more explicitly at work in countries that have mandatory detention provisions for certain nationalities.[134] The discourse of 'efficiency, management and control' even seems to have found its way to the European Court of Human Rights. In the case of *Saadi*, the Grand Chamber did not deem the detention of an

---

[131] L. Schuster and M. Welch, "Detention of asylum seekers in the US, UK, France, Germany, and Italy: A critical view of the globalizing culture of control," *Criminal Justice* 5 (2005). See also Z. Bauman, *Globalization: The Human Consequences* (New York: Columbia University Press, 1998).

[132] M.S. Malloch and E. Stanley, "The detention of asylum seekers in the UK: Representing risk, managing the dangerous," *Punishment and Society* 53 (2005).

[133] See the judgement by the Afdeling Bestuursrechtspraak Raad van State 22 January 2008, *Jurisprudentie Vreemdelingenrecht* 115 (2008). See also the judgements by the same administrative court from 11 January 2008, *Jurisprudentie Vreemdelingenrecht* 109 (2008); and 31 October 2007, *Jurisprudentie Vreemdelingenrecht* 543 (2007).

[134] Such as Bulgaria. See V. Ilareva, *Immigration Detention in International Law and Practice: In search of solutions to the challenges faced in Bulgaria* (2008), available at: http://www.statewatch.org/news/2008/jan/valeria-illareva-immigration-detention-bulgaria.pdf.

asylum seeker for reasons of mere 'administrative convenience' to be in violation of the right to personal liberty, even if the decision to detain Mr Saadi, a Kurdish asylum seeker from Northern Iraq, was primarily based on his nationality.[135] Decisive for its judgment were *"the difficult administrative problems"* with which the national state concerned was confronted as a result of *"an escalating flow of huge numbers of asylum seekers"*.[136]

Approaches that draw on the paradigm of the New Penology to explain the institutionalisation of immigration detention in contemporary liberal democracies are valuable because they encourage a critical stance towards this practice in light of important constitutional principles. More specifically, as its proponents argue that deprivation of liberty as a means of immigration law enforcement is increasingly based on an instrumental order that almost exclusively targets categories, they urge us to engage in a thorough investigation of this practice from the perspective of the rights of the *individual*. However, any approach that emphasises the 'new' also runs a risk of losing sight of lines of continuity. Thus, it can be convincingly argued that there are important similarities between the practice of immigration detention in contemporary societies and other coercive forms of social control and the exclusion of groups in the history of the modern state, such as the large-scale incarceration of vagrants in seventeenth century Europe, or the internment of the stateless and the refugees during the 1930s and 1940s.[137]

But perhaps even more importantly, we need to be aware of the fact that immigration detention cannot be reduced to a mere punitive measure – even if contemporary developments may bear witness to an uneasy blurring of the line between criminal law and immigration policies. Moreover, it has been observed that "were immigration detention policy actually to reflect the tenets of the new penology, the treatment of immigration detainees might improve."[138] If this is true, and contemporary practice certainly seems to suggest that immigration detainees are in many respects worse of than those who are kept in prison because they are convicted for a criminal offence, we can only account

---

[135] *Saadi v. United Kingdom*, 29 January 2008, Appl. No. 13229/03, par. 24.
[136] Id., par. 80.
[137] An excellent discussion of such lines of continuity in the Australian context is provided by Alison Bashford and Carolyn Strange, who present quarantine detention and the internment of 'enemy aliens' in wartime as historic precedents for the current detention of asylum seekers. See A. Bashford and C. Strange, "Asylum Seekers and National Histories of Detention," *Australian Journal of Politics and History* 48 (2002). On the development of the law on immigration detention in the UK, France and the United States, see D. Wilsher, *The Liberty of Foreigners: A History, Law and Politics of Immigration Detention* (Nijmegen: Wolf Legal Publishers, 2009).
[138] Lucas (2005), 325.

for the difference in the legal position of the two categories of detainees by fully grasping the distinctiveness of the context in which immigration detention takes place, one that differs profoundly from the purely domestic, national context within which criminal law enforcement is principally carried out. Immigration law enforcement is particular because the legal framework within which it takes place is determined by the relationship between the individual, the nation state and territory in a global system of sovereign, territorial nation states. This book attempts to account fully for this particularity, because only by so doing may it be possible to pose effective challenges to the way in which immigration detention in contemporary societies is increasingly presented as a logical and inevitable part of the fight against unwanted migration.

As such, the aim of this book is threefold. First, it seeks to argue that the particular development of sovereignty, neither a natural nor a self-evident notion but the result of historical contingencies, has led to a situation in which the use of force against outsiders is justified in a way which is fundamentally different from the way in which the use of force against insiders is scrutinised.

The second argument expands and elaborates upon the first one by positing that the contemporary application of human rights has not been able to formulate adequate answers to the use of force in the instances that the national state wishes to verify and enforce its sovereignty against those who have violated its material or symbolic boundaries. I shall argue that this so-called blind spot of human rights protection, which is nowhere more visible than in the contemporary practice of immigration detention, is due to an enduring perception of territoriality as a self-evident and innocent concept for the organisation of the global political system.

At the heart of this second argument is the premise that the concept of territory and the idea of rights are firmly linked and that the international legal discourse regards the 'jurisdictional' content of sovereignty in a way that fundamentally differs from the way in which it considers its territorial form. However, it is important to be aware from the outset that sovereignty's form and content are necessarily intertwined. Both play an equally significant role with regard to the definition of the political community, although their relationship within the context of political organisation has varied over time.

Before the advent of the modern state, political power was based upon personal relations. After the Peace of Westphalia in 1648, this structure began to change slowly into a system where clearly demarcated and independent territorial units formed the basis for political power. The fact that the foundation of political power has over time shifted from the personal to the territorial does not entail that power over people has diminished in importance, nor does it mean that territory was politically insignificant before the emergence of the modern state. It means that, at present, jurisdiction is exercised over individuals because of their presence in a certain territory instead of on account of their specific position in the body politic. In addition, the state uses its spatial powers to protect its territorial borders. The enormous growth of state power during the last few centuries has been accompanied with increasing demands for safeguards against the state abusing its jurisdiction over people, resulting in a multifaceted system for the protection of individual liberties. However, in this book, I shall argue that with regard to the state's spatial powers and sovereignty's territorial frame, a corresponding development is lacking. Precisely because territorial sovereignty is deeply taken for granted, modern constitutionalism is blind to the way in which territorial sovereignty involves the interests of the individual. This blindness is integral to the whole structure of international and domestic constitutionalism. Put differently, territorial sovereignty can be regarded as a structural limitation that stands in the way of the very communicability of individual interests; a claim that is perhaps best substantiated by the existence of the contemporary immigration prison.

The administrative detention of irregular migrants and asylum seekers is one of the ways in which European states seek to protect their territories from unwanted immigration. As authorised presence on national territory increasingly gives rise to an entitlement to rights (so-called post-national citizenship), ever stricter and more coercive tools of immigration law enforcement are resorted to by national states in order to sustain the territorial logic of systems of individual rights protection. However, immigration detention is special amongst the other instruments and policies by which states try to stem the flows of migration.

In the first place, it is special because deprivation of liberty is the sharpest technique by which the state attempts to sustain and reproduce the territorial logic of modern constitutionalism. We shall see that personal liberty and sovereignty are conceptually intertwined: in modern political imagery, the protection of the former is the reason for the existence of the latter. In societies based upon the rule of law there is no more serious interference with an individual's fundamental rights as depriving him or her of his or her liberty. Secondly, immigration detention is not only a way in which states violently guard the territorial logic of modern constitutionalism, but as a practice itself it attempts to make ultimate use of that very logic. Thus, a certain silence/blindness on the part of the rule of law – one that states seem only too eager to protect – has made the detention of thousands of people in contemporary Europe, simply because they have crossed international boundaries without state consent, not only possible, but also commonplace.

The second argument thus presents the administrative detention of foreigners as an inevitable consequence of the way in which we conceive the relationship between individual rights, territory and the state. However, as I have already mentioned above, this book shall not merely portray immigration law enforcement in the form of detention as an illiberal practice by liberal regimes, resulting from a structural feature of contemporary political organisation. In addition, it hopes to introduce a complementary but more hopeful approach by showing how the administrative detention of foreigners, however deplorable as a contemporary political practice, may also provide opportunities to erase the artificial distinction in modern constitutionalism; that is, between the state's exercise of jurisdiction within a given body politic and the territorial frame in which this power is exercised. As such, a stubborn and consistent application of human rights norms to the practice of immigration detention may in time deconstruct the narrow linkage between territoriality and personal rights.

Thus, drawing on Roberto Unger's idea of 'destabilization rights',[139] the third aim of this study is to argue that the capacity of the refugee and the irregular migrant – while interned by European states on European territory – to appeal to the guarantees embodied in modern human rights law, however marginal such guarantees may be in their specific cases, has the potential to destabilise the institution of territorial sovereignty, and therewith it may in time strike at the conceptual innocence and perceived neutrality of territorial borders in constitutional discourse, domestically as well as internationally.

This study sets out with an investigation into the conceptual background of immigration detention from the perspective of the sovereignty paradigm. What is sovereignty (chapter 2), and whether and how can it be limited (chapter 3) are questions which will be dealt with in the first part (theory). The second part (doctrine and practice) will first provide a general contextualisation of immigration detention by exploring the development and nature of the international legal framework regulating the international freedom of movement (chapters 4 and 5), and by investigating the logic of modern immigration law enforcement (chapter 6). Thereafter, I deal specifically with the limits that have been set to the use of immigration detention by human rights law. First, I address the way in which these limits are formally given shape in various general human rights instruments (chapter 6). Secondly, I shall analyse in depth how the European Court of Human Rights (ECtHR) applies fundamental rights to cases of immigration detention (chapter 7). These two

---

[139] R.M. Unger, *False Necessity: Anti-Necessitarian Social Theory in the Service of Radical Democracy* (Cambridge: Cambridge University Press, 1987). See also C.F. Sabel and W. Simon, "Destabilization Rights: How Public Law Litigation Succeeds," *Harvard Law Review* 117 (2004).

chapters intend to determine whether the limits that are set to the use of detention in immigration policy are satisfactory when considered in the light of other contemporary discourses on limiting the potential for violence inherent in sovereign power. Where I find that this is not the case, I maintain that the reason that immigration detainees receive inadequate protection is related to the idea of territoriality. I argue that the problem is not so much territoriality in itself, but has to be sought in the fact that the territorial frame of sovereignty does not have the same history of being subjected to critical scrutiny as its jurisdictional content.

Although territorial sovereignty has so far remained largely immune to forces of domestic and international legal correction, in the last part of the book (chapter 8) I shall contend that the international human rights discourse has the capacity to change the meaning of territorial borders in modern legal discourse. Full constitutional scrutiny of immigration detention by means of human rights may well undermine one of the basic assumptions that underlie the hitherto largely unrestrained exclusionary power of the sovereign state: territorial sovereignty as a neutral and self-evident basis for contemporary political organisation. Paradoxically then, the practice of immigration detention, instead of being only illiberal practice, may hand us the tools to mitigate the exclusive effects of modern sovereignty and transform the international and domestic legal order into one that is more true to some of its underlying universalistic ideals.

Part I
Theory

Chapter 2

Sovereignty, People and Territory

2.1 *Introduction*

In this chapter I shall explore how the notion of sovereignty moulds our understanding of the relationship between people, territory, and authority, a thorough appreciation of which is crucial in order to address the way in which national states respond to international migration and its legal regulation. In the first place, I shall discuss the development of sovereignty in its original, internal manifestation as a particular way to conceptualise and justify ultimate political authority within the state. This substantive aspect of sovereignty – as the exercise of political power over individuals – will be referred to as sovereignty's *content*. Internal sovereignty is bound up with the state's monopoly on the legitimate means of violence, but it is also intricately linked with the claim to determine what constitutes the boundary between the 'inside' and 'outside'.[1] We shall see that the modern concept of sovereignty has brought about a specific understanding of 'inside' and 'outside' through the concept of territoriality: the linkage of political power to clearly demarcated territory. As a result of historical contingencies, ultimate political power came to be framed territorially. It should be noted from the outset that sovereignty's *territorial form* impacts deeply on the particular way in which political power may be exercised over people.

In the second place, throughout the chapter, I shall also focus on the external manifestations of modern sovereignty. Any account of the national territorial state must be integrated in the larger context of the global territorial structure of which it forms part. Indeed, the discursive practice of territorial sovereignty only makes sense when it is embedded in the conception of a system of territorially exclusive, national states exercising sovereign control over fixed populations within clearly demarcated and exclusive territories.

---

[1] N. Walker, "Late sovereignty in the European Union," in *Sovereignty in transition*, ed. N. Walker (Oxford: Hart Publishing; 2003), 22; and W.G. Werner and J.H. de Wilde, "The Endurance of Sovereignty" *European Journal of International Relations* 7(2001), 288.

The structure of this chapter is as follows. Section 2.2 provides a brief overview of the development of theories of sovereignty as a legitimating discourse for ultimate political power within the body politic. Subsequently, in section 2.3 I shall explore the manner in which the modern state has construed its understanding of inside and outside by the use of territory and notions of political identity. We shall see that territorialisation, the process by which political authority came to be linked to clearly demarcated territorial units, determined the way in which the modern state conceives of identity and political community.

Sections 2.2 and 2.3 thus make a division within the concept of sovereignty by dealing with, respectively, the way in which the exercise of power in a given body politic has been legitimised, and the way in which understandings of inside and outside have been constructed. Nonetheless, we shall see that the historical processes that gave rise to both aspects of sovereignty cannot be neatly categorised as relating solely to either the one or the other. On the one hand, the way in which the theory of popular sovereignty has legitimised political authority has strongly influenced the manner in which modern states have drawn their boundaries. On the other hand, the process of territorialisation has facilitated the emergence of the very notion of sovereignty as the legitimation of ultimate power within the body politic. In the conclusions to this chapter in section 2.4, I collect my findings together in order to evaluate the impact of the institution of territorial sovereignty on the question of the (il)legitimacy of violence. The intricate connection between sovereignty's various aspects is briefly reiterated with particular reference to contemporary national responses to international migration.

2.2 *A Claim to Ultimate Political Power*

Amongst other things, modern sovereignty entails a claim to hold a monopoly on the legitimate use of force. And even though modern states, if they are to be regarded as legitimate, should not exercise power mainly through direct or indirect coercion, organised force is generally seen as a legitimate act of last resort in enforcing political decisions.

> Ultimate violence may not be used frequently. There may be innumerable steps in its application, in the way of warnings and reprimands. But if all the warnings are disregarded, even in so slight a matter as paying a traffic ticket, the last thing that will happen is that a couple of cops show up at the door with handcuffs and a Black Maria. […] In Western democracies, with their ideological emphasis on voluntary compliance with popularly legislated rules, this constant presence of

official violence is underemphasized. It is all the more important to be aware of it. Violence is the ultimate foundation of any political order.[2]

The question as to what makes this ultimate threat of violence legitimate is perennial. Its history certainly dates further back than the point at which I shall begin my analysis, which is at the early emergence of sovereignty during the late middle ages. We shall see that the manner in which men have attempted to legitimise the exercise of political power, thereby turning it into authority instead of mere force, has varied from appeals to religion and the natural order to the notion of the people. And although it has been argued that the 'legitimate use of force' is a contradiction in terms – as it seems absurd that "an institution should be able to project its moral injunctions through acts of brute force"[3] – theorists of sovereignty have generally incorporated the capacity to use force explicitly in their conception of legitimate political power. They have done so on the grounds of raison d'État; or because in their theory subjects surrendered their right to self-defence to the sovereign, whose task it then became to protect them, or because sovereignty is logically impossible without complete control and free disposal over the means of violence. My account of the development of the notion of sovereignty as a claim to ultimate political power within the body politic is divided into two parts. In section 2.2.1, I provide an overview of the emergence of a theory of sovereignty against the historical backdrop of the gradual territorialisation of political authority. Section 2.2.2 addresses the distinctively modern theory of popular sovereignty.

2.2.1 The Development of the Modern Notion of Sovereignty

Thinking about sovereignty predated a world in which independent territorial units were the main building blocks for political life.[4] In medieval Europe, political power was not characterised by territoriality, but different territorial entities overlapped each other, and power structures were complex and hierarchical in varying degrees. Political power manifested itself in personal relations rather than with regard to territory, and these relations could be manifold. However, by the end of the fifteenth century, monarchical power had grown

---

[2] P.L. Berger, *An invitation to sociology: a humanistic perspective* (Garden City, NY: Anchor Books, 1963), 69.
[3] J. Hoffman, *State, Power and Democracy* (Brighton: Wheatsheaf Books, 1988), 73.
[4] A.B. Murphy, "The sovereign state system as a political-territorial ideal: historical and contemporary considerations," in *State Sovereignty as a Social Construct*, ed. T.J. Biersteker and C. Weber (Cambridge: Cambridge University Press, 1996), 82; F.H. Hinsley, *Sovereignty* (Cambridge: Cambridge University Press, 1986) 21; and Werner and Wilde (2001), 289.

enormously in almost all of Europe at the expense of medieval institutions, such as feudalism, free city states and the Church, the latter perhaps being the most conspicuous of all medieval institutions. The role of the Reformation in the breakdown of the medieval order should not be underestimated, as before the Reformation Europe was perceived as a single community, even if only in theory: the Res Publica Christiana with its head as the agent of God.[5]

The gradual consolidation of power and territory under a single and supreme ruler, especially in France, but also in Spain and England, changed the modes of political thought and it provided the opportunity for the notion of sovereignty to re-emerge from Roman imperial law and from the theory of divine right.[6] In order to grasp how the notion of sovereignty was able to secure its fundamental place in political thought, it is instructive to take a brief look at the writings of Machiavelli, and not only because it was mainly these writings that created the meaning that is still attached to the term state in political usage.[7]

Machiavelli (1469–1527) lived exactly at the time when the medieval political order, defined by a hierarchy of authorities, started to change slowly into the modern decentralised system of independent political entities defined by territory. The move in Europe from the medieval to the modern was not smooth and peaceful – on the contrary, it was accompanied by civil wars and chaos caused by competing claims to political power. It is no coincidence that theorists of sovereignty have been preoccupied with political stability and the unity of the body politic. Machiavelli, although he did not develop a theory on sovereignty and merely hinted at the notion, was no exception. He was deeply disturbed by the particularly chaotic state which Italy found itself in at the end of the fifteenth century; for although medieval institutions had broken down there was no power which was strong enough to unite the whole of Italy and bring order and stability to the region. According to Machiavelli, the preservation and continuance of the state is the aim of politics. Every prince must seek to maintain his state and "a wise prince is guided above all by the dictates of necessity."[8]

> When the safety of one's country wholly depends on the decision to be taken, no attention should be paid either to justice or injustice, to kindness or cruelty, or to

---

[5] D. Philpott, "Ideas and the evolution of sovereignty," in *State Sovereingty: Change and Persistance in International Relations*, ed. S.H. Hashmi (Pennsylvania: Pennsylvania State University Press, 1997), 28.

[6] See Hinsley (1986) on earlier manifestations of sovereignty.

[7] G.H. Sabine, *History of Political Theory* (London/Calcutta/Sydney: George G. Harrap & Co.,1941), 351; and N. Bobbio, *Democracy and Dictatorship* (Cambridge: Polity Press, 1989), 57.

[8] Q. Skinner, *Machiavelli* (Oxford: Oxford University Press, 1981), 38.

its being praiseworthy or ignominious. On the contrary, every other consideration set aside, that alternative should be wholeheartedly adopted which will save the life and preserve the freedom of one's country.[9]

Thus, it appears that Machiavelli perceived of the polity as an abstract entity, a conception of the state that would eventually give birth to the notion of sovereignty.[10] Linked to his perception of the ruler, placed outside and above the legal and moral framework that applies to the ruled, is Machiavelli's conception of the supreme importance of the legislator in a society, even though he never developed his belief in the omnipotent legislator into a general theory of sovereignty or absolutism. Similarly, he was aware of the idea of the body politic as an instrument in the hands of the ruler in the interest of the political community, and as such he displayed a strong preference for popular rule by the citizens. Nevertheless, and in spite of the republican idealism underpinning the Prince and the Discourses, he did not conceive of a theory in which the ruler and the community were tied together in a body politic which itself would possess sovereign power.[11]

Jean Bodin (1529–1596) was the first to make a systematic statement of the modern idea of sovereignty. He did so in his Six Livres de la République (1576), a work written in and clearly influenced by the disorder of a secularising France in the late sixteenth century. According to Bodin the existence of a sovereign power – 'la puissance perpétuelle et absolue d'une république' – is necessary in the interests of the community. Sovereignty for Bodin is indivisible and inalienable, and it consists of an unlimited power to make law. However, his views on the limitless quality of sovereign power are not altogether clear. For although he stated that sovereignty cannot be limited in function, time, or law, he also maintained that the sovereign is bound by divine and natural law, as well as by the fundamental and customary laws of the political community and the property rights of the citizens.[12]

---

[9] N. Machiavelli, *The Discourses*, ed. B. Crick (Harmondsworth: Penguin Books, 1987), 515.
[10] J. Plamenatz, *Man and Society: Political and social theories from Machiavelli to Marx*, vol I, *From the Middle Ages to Locke* (Longman Publishing Group: New York, 1992), 55.
[11] Hinsley (1986), at 113. See on his liberal republican legacy: Paul A. Rahe (ed.), *Machiavelli's Liberal Republican Legacy* (Cambridge: Cambridge University Press, 2006).
[12] J.W. Allen, *A History of Political Thought in the Sixteenth Century* (London: Dawsons of Pall Mall, 1967), 56. Carl Schmitt relates the way in which Bodin deals with the question as to what extent the sovereign is bound by the laws to what he defines as the very idea of sovereign power: the power to decide on the exception, without which the catch-phrase 'ultimate power in the body politic' would be empty rhetoric. See C. Schmitt, *Political Theology, Four Chapters on the Concept of Sovereignty*, trans. G. Schwab (Chicago: University of Chicago Press, 2005), 8–9. I will come back to Schmitt's definition of sovereign power in the next chapter.

For Bodin, government is not possible without sovereignty: without the existence of a sovereign power, there will just be anarchy. Sovereignty is the essence of the state, for the latter cannot exist without the former. This led him to conclude that the character of the political community made it necessary that this power be legally recognised as sovereignty.[13] Thus, the existence of sovereign power does not need to be justified with an appeal to God, but rather it is explained by the nature of the political community as such.[14] Bodin distinguished between different forms of body politic, depending on where the sovereign power was located, but he himself preferred that form in which the sovereign power resided in one person, a monarchy. The originality of Bodin consisted in his partial conceptual detachment of the notion of sovereignty from God, Pope, Emperor or King, and by presenting it as a legal theory logically necessary in all political associations.[15] Although theories of sovereignty have evolved significantly since Bodin's introduction of the concept, its rudimentary conceptual foundation has remained largely the same. We will see that contemporary sovereignty, just as it was for Bodin and subsequent theorists, is still concerned with the unity of the body politic.

In medieval Europe, political society was conceived as an order instituted by God, in which the ruler and the people were distinct from each other, each with their own position, rights and duties. The implications of this belief remained tangible even in the seventeenth century; there was little awareness of a conception of the ruler as the personification of the body politic, of the people as more than a collection of individuals, let alone of the idea that the body politic could in itself be a sovereign entity in which ruler and people were linked.[16]

The separateness of the ruler and the ruled in the thoughts of most men in this period led them to think that sovereignty had to be vested in one and only one of the two. Thus, on the one hand, there were monarchists who used Bodin's theory of sovereignty to strengthen the theory of Divine Right. On the other hand, a thinker such as Johannes Althusius (1557–1638) insisted that sovereign power belonged exclusively to the people, basing his ideas on popular sovereignty equally upon the legislative foundations of sovereignty

---

[13] Hinsley (1986), 121; Pot, van der, and Donner, *Handboek van het Nederlandse Staatsrecht* (Zwolle: Tjeenk Willink; 1995) 15.

[14] Plamenatz writes that there is not a trace of the doctrine of the Divine Right of Kings in his *Six Livres de la République*. See Plamenatz (1992) 161.

[15] Allen (1967), 59. But see D. Engster, "Jean Bodin, scepticism and absolute sovereignty," *History of Political Thought* 17 (1996).

[16] Hinsley (1986), 130.

laid by Bodin.¹⁷ There were inherent contradictions in both positions, and writers such as Grotius (1583–1645), who in De Jure Belli ac Pacis attempted to reconcile both positions in a single theory, were not successful.¹⁸ The notion of sovereignty did not attain logical coherence until Hobbes (1588–1679), using some elements already present in Bodin's legal theory, based it on radically new premises.

In Leviathan, written in 1651, Hobbes takes as a starting point for his theory of sovereignty a state of nature in which people are only driven by instincts of self-preservation and a will to power which is never satisfied. People have no natural rights and there would accordingly be war between all against all. This image of the state of nature was completely at odds with the portrayal of mankind in medieval Christendom. Moreover, natural law had always been linked with God and normative concepts such as justice, while Hobbes regarded (human) nature as nothing other than a system of causes and effects. Since even the weakest can under certain circumstances be a threat to the life of the strongest, nobody can ever be safe in Hobbes' state of nature.

> Nature hath made men so equall, in the faculties of body, and mind; as that though there bee found one man sometimes manifestly stronger in body, or of quicker mind then another; yet when all is reckoned together, the difference between man, and man, is not so considerable, as that one man can thereupon claim to himselfe any benefit, to which another may not pretend, as well as he. For as to the strength of body, the weakest has strength enough to kill the strongest, either by secret machination, or by confederacy with others, that are in the same danger with himselfe.¹⁹

As everybody is equal in the state of nature – which for Hobbes is clearly not a normative statement – no one will enter into conditions of peace if not upon equal terms. Yet, even if all would agree to respect each other's 'rights', it would not be rational for the individual to keep to such an agreement. Relations of power will always be temporary, a stable order is impossible. To establish such an order, a conscious choice is necessary, made by all, unconditionally and upon equal terms, to surrender completely their freedom to one power, the sovereign.

In the sovereign, the will of all is united; it is a supreme power whose only command is complete obedience, sanctioned with his complete and exclusive control over the means of violence. Only at the moment of surrender does a

---

[17] A. London Fell, *Origins of Legislative Sovereignty and the Legislative State* (Westport: Praeger Publishers; 1999), 13.
[18] Hinsley (1986), 139.
[19] Thomas Hobbes, *Leviathan*, ed. R. Tuck (Cambridge: Cambridge University Press, 1996), Chapter 13, 60.

mere collection of individuals become a people; the multitude constitutes only the people by the will of the sovereign. There cannot be any distinction between state and society, just as the distinction between state and government is an illusion. If there is no state, there can be neither government, nor a society. Sovereignty is indivisible and unlimited. The multitude enters into a covenant with each other in which they agree to surrender to the sovereign, but the latter is not a party to it. For if he could be bound, the absolute power would lie elsewhere, and accordingly he would not be sovereign. Questions of the legitimacy of government do not play a role for Hobbes at all – a government is a government by its capacity to govern and a tyranny is merely a government which is disliked. That being said, sovereign power was also limited for Hobbes in the sense that the sovereign should employ his unlimited and absolute power for the preservation of the lives and property of the governed and as such:

> The Obligation of Subjects to the Soveraign, is understood to last as long, and no longer, than the Power lasteth, by which he is able to protect them."[20]

Whereas for Bodin sovereign power had meant the power to make law, for Hobbes it was to be understood as the exclusive control over coercive force:

> In substance his theory amounted to identifying government with force; at least, the force must always be present in the background whether it has to be applied or not.[21]

After the turmoil and civil wars of the sixteenth and seventeenth centuries, European monarchies were increasingly able to consolidate their powers and the idea of sovereign monarchical power became commonly accepted.[22] The remarkable shift from previous theories of political power was that conceptually the state united the ruler and the ruled, in that the ruler was seen as the personification of the state, and in him was absorbed the personality of the people. Related to this was the conception of an independent territorial state system, for which the Peace of Westphalia provided the first formal step.[23] However, there was no writer in Europe who defended the absolutism of the sovereign power that was for Hobbes a logical consequence of the very idea of

---

[20] *Leviathan*, Chapter 21, 114. Hobbes (1996). Accordingly, the sovereign was thus entitled to enforce on his subjects only those things that he believed necessary for their preservation. However, if he went beyond this limit, subjects would have to accept his judgment. See for the 'rights' of the subjects against the sovereign: *Leviathan*, Chapter 21, 11–113. Ibid.
[21] Hinsley (1986), 468. See also G. Poggi, *The State: its nature, development & prospects* (Cambridge: Polity Press; 1990) 44. See also Sabine (1941), 468.
[22] Pot and Donner (1995), 21.
[23] Murphy (1996), 86.

sovereignty. Defenders of Divine Right concurred that divine and natural law placed constraints on the sovereign ruler. A natural lawyer such as Pufendorf (1632–1694) insisted that even though to be sovereign meant to be absolute and supreme, sovereignty was not equivalent to absolutist power in relation to the society that was subjected to it.[24] The question was now how to reconcile the notion of sovereignty with the idea that the ruler is responsible to the community that he governs.

The notion of popular sovereignty was to provide the answer to this question. The idea that sovereignty rests with the people who have conferred it, by means of a contract, on the ruler was certainly not new. Nonetheless, the clarity that Hobbes had given to the very notion of sovereignty, combined with the wish of most thinkers to refute the absolutist implications of Hobbes' theory, made a new version of social contract theories unavoidable.

2.2.2 The People as the Source of Legitimate Power

In his *Two Treatises of Government*, Locke (1632–1704) attempted to counter Hobbes' arguments for the logical necessity of political absolutism with a theory of constitutional government.[25] In the first Treatise, the theory of Divine Right of Kings was rejected, whereas the second analysed the "True Original, Extent, and End" of political power.[26] Locke's thinking illustrates the approaching enlightenment: instead of a medieval fixation on the spiritual world, he believed that the use of empirical experience and reason would teach and enable man to live a good life. Like Hobbes, he too took the state of nature as a starting point for his theory of government. But unlike Hobbes, Locke believed that in the state of nature, natural law governed, the content of which could be known by reason. If, in the state of nature, someone would transgress this law, entailing that no one ought to harm another, neither in his life, nor in his liberty or possessions, the inflicted party had a right to redress the injury, but only in a manner that was proportionate to the infraction.[27] Only if natural law would be altogether ignored would a situation comparable to Hobbes'

---

[24] Hinsley (1986), 151.
[25] Sabine (1941), 524.
[26] Locke's definition of political power covers legislative and executive power (coercion) and it pays attention to its internal as well as to its external component: "*Political power* then I take to be *a Right* of making Laws with Penalties of Death, and consequently all less penalties, for the Regulating and Preserving of Property, and of employing the force of the Community, in the Execution of such Laws, and in the Defence of the Common-wealth from Foreign Injury, and all this only for the Publick Good." *Second Treatise*, §2. John Locke, *Two Treatises of Government*, ed. P. Laslett (Cambridge University Press: Cambridge, 1967).
[27] *Second Treatise*, § 9. See Locke (1967), 290.

state of nature be brought about, but this would be an exceptional situation, no longer to be called the state of nature but the state of war.[28]

Whereas medieval thinking had emphasised the duties of a mankind that was divided into a natural (divine) order, Locke instead accorded a central place to the unity of mankind and saw natural law as a claim to inalienable rights inherent in each individual.[29] Locke argued that a government is necessary in order to guarantee individual rights and with this presumption, the limits of governmental power are simultaneously established. The state is created by a society of contracting individuals, but sovereignty remains with the people who have the right to revolt against a government, to which they have delegated their supreme power, if it fails to protect their rights. In order to make the idea of individual consent plausible, Locke resorted to a fiction, whereby every member of society gives his "tacit Consent" by making use of its government or, alternatively, by "the very being of any one within the Territories of that Government".[30]

Locke's theory on sovereignty was thus profoundly modern in that it no longer attempted to find answers to the question of what constitutes legitimate power in a divine or natural order. Instead the individual and his rights were accorded a central place in the answer. As such, it was also a theory of constitutional government because its normative assumptions establish clear limitations on the exercise of sovereign power. However, it is important to keep in mind that the question of the legitimisation of the foundation for political power is different from the question of the legality of its exercise. This chapter deals only with the former question; theories of individual rights, the doctrine of government by law, and related concepts will be dealt with in chapter 3.

The theory of popular sovereignty would eventually find a clear expression in the French and American Bills of Rights. However, revolutions were needed before these bills of rights were established, revolutions that would radically change the thinking about the state and power and which would anchor the principle of popular sovereignty firmly in Western political thought and practice. But in the eighteenth century, established government still strongly resisted claims that the community was free to decide how much power to give up to government and how much to retain for itself, and insisted that the Ruler, as the personification of the community, was the sovereign.[31]

---

[28] Ibid. § 17–19.
[29] Pot and Donner (1995), 24; Sabine (1941), 525.
[30] *Second Treatise*, § 120. See Locke (1967), 366. Hobbes adhered to a similar solution " for whosoever entreth into anothers dominion, is subject to all the Laws thereof". *Leviathan*, Chapter XXI, 114. Hobbes (1996).
[31] Hinsley (1986), 152–153.

In *Du Contrat Social*, Rousseau (1712-1778) dismissed this absolutist interpretation and presented a radical new version of the concept of popular sovereignty. Rousseau in fact adopted Hobbes' absolutist implications of the notion of sovereignty,[32] but in his theory absolute power is unconditionally and permanently transferred to the people. In order to arrive at this position, Rousseau started with the state of nature as well, but in contrast to the usual account thereof, he reversed the situation completely by arguing that in the state of nature people were good and innocent.[33] It was, according to him, civilisation with its constant appeal to reason that had spoiled mankind. In a sense, Rousseau broke radically with the Enlightenment ideals; not by progress and the use of reason will men find out how to live the good life, but they need to return to nature, with which he meant the common sentiments with regard to which people hardly differ at all. As such, Rousseau emphasised the importance of community, and he opposed the systematic individualism on which the theories of Hobbes and Locke were built. People do not really exist if not within a community, "for apart from society there would be no scale of values in terms of which to judge well-being."[34] The ideals of the Enlightenment with their emphasis on the individual have created the kind of civilisation in which man cannot find his true self. A return to the liberty and equality of the state of nature is only possible when every man submits himself completely to the community.[35] The state is the community, but as the people possess exclusive and omnipotent sovereignty that is inalienable, government is merely the executor of the general will of the community.

Whereas Locke had accorded the people a right to revolt under certain conditions – that is, when the government had not kept the terms of the contract – for Rousseau such a construction was inconceivable because the government always has to respect the general will and can thus be dissolved at any moment should the community so wish.[36] The volonté générale is not the same as the sum of all individual wills, nor is it the will of the majority, for in both cases Rousseau's theory would equally be based on the individualism that he

---

[32] Rousseau was indeed aware of some similarities between him and Hobbes. R. Tuck, introduction to *Leviathan*, by Thomas Hobbes (Cambridge: Cambridge University Press, 1996), xxxvi.
[33] See also the early version of the Social Contract, also known as the *Geneva Manuscript*, Book II, Chapter 2, 18 where Rousseau contrasted his vision on the state of nature with that of Hobbes. Jean-Jacques Rousseau, *The Social Contract and other later political writings*, ed. V. Gourevitch (Cambridge: Cambridge University Press, 1997), 159.
[34] Sabine (1941), 588.
[35] Through the social compact. See Book 1, Chapter 6 of *Du Contrat Social*, Jean Jacques Rousseau (1997), 50.
[36] Book 1, Chapter 7 of *Du Contrat Social*, Rousseau (1997), 52.

attacked. The general will of a community is a collective good, with its own life and destiny, which is not the same as the private interests of its members together.[37] Man becomes man only as a member of the community and accordingly it is unthinkable that rights can ever be exercised against the community but instead they are something to be enjoyed within it. Since Rousseau's time the doctrine of popular sovereignty has frequently been restated. But it can be found that, while Rousseau's statement thereof can be modified in detail, it cannot in essence be outdone. Since the American and French Revolutions toward the end of the eighteenth century, sooner or later it became the prevalent doctrine, at least in all the more advanced political societies.[38]

However, what Rousseau really wanted was to eradicate the distinction between state and community, by extracting a unitary state personality out of the abstract notion of the general will. The problem was that this left the people without a possibility for governance with actual power over them.[39] As a result, although his account of popular sovereignty has prevailed, the practical need for governance has made its accommodation necessary. Indeed, while the modern notion of sovereignty has created congruence between the ruler and the ruled, it has not been able to resolve the disparity between society and the state. One of ways in which liberal democracies have dealt with the tension that exists between the ideal of the executive state as merely the agent of the people's will, and the reality that it has the potential to turn into Hobbes' absolute sovereign, is by resorting to constitutional government, as will be dealt with in the next chapter.

2.3 A Territorial Solution to the Problem of Universality versus Particularity

> The present approach to the determination of ownership of territory is exclusive, partial and silencing. [...] Territorial boundaries have become barriers. They determine and identify those within and those without the boundary, based on a particular conception of sovereignty.[40]

In the previous sections, I have explored how a theory of sovereignty became a conceptual necessity in order to legitimise the state's exercise of political

---

[37] Sabine (1941), 588.
[38] Hinsley (1986), 154.
[39] Ibid., 155.
[40] R. McCorquodale, "International Law, Boundaries and Imagination" in *Boundaries and Justice: Diverse Ethical Perspectives*, eds. D. Miller and S. Hashmi, 136–163 (Princeton/Oxford: Princeton University Press, 2001), 145 and 152.

authority within the body politic. Different theories on the source and nature of sovereignty were addressed and we have seen how popular sovereignty became the still current, prevalent way in which to legitimise ultimate political power within the body politic.[41] It is important to grasp that the modern notion of sovereignty distinguishes itself from earlier notions of political authority by its very abstraction. Indeed, the modern state is different from those forms of political organisation that preceded it, in that factual relations between the ruler and the ruled no longer provide the basis for political authority. Instead, the abstract notion of the people has assumed that role by forging a symbolic identity between the ruler and the ruled. In the sections below I will elaborate on the way in which that identity has been substantiated in terms of the nation, and the role that the process of territorialisation has played with regard to the nationalisation of political identity. In these sections we shall see that the impact of the particular, territorial solution that modern sovereignty has provided to the problem of particularity versus universality[42] has stretched far beyond the precise location in which territorial boundaries are drawn.

Above, some attention has already been paid to the fact that in the period stretching from the sixteenth until the eighteenth century the idea of territoriality gained ground due to the increasing power of the European monarchs. Apart from touching upon this context of the historical process of the consolidation of exclusive territorial rule, section 2.3.1 will describe how medieval ideas of allegiance, under the influence of changing ideas about the nature and location of sovereignty, transformed and acquired new significance in the concept of nationality. Subsequently, in section 2.3.2 we shall see how the interplay between territoriality and the notion of popular sovereignty led to the formation of exclusive political identities. As theories of popular sovereignty fail to define what is meant by the concept of the people, the notion of territoriality and its accompanying notion of Westphalian sovereignty profoundly influenced the answer to this question. The result was that the universalistic ideals on which theories of popular sovereignty were based translated into a particularistic practice. The tension between the universal and the particular

---

[41] Which is why I do not go into more recent history with regard to the conceptual foundations of modern sovereignty. For whatever the implications and interpretations thereof might have been, as we will see below the basic conceptualisation of modern sovereignty has not really changed since Rousseau. See J. Bartelson, *The Critique of the State* (Cambridge: Cambridge University Press, 2000).

[42] Which is a different way of denoting the distinction between inside and outside, which sovereignty by its very nature must draw. See also A. Giddens, *The nation state and violence* (Cambridge: Polity Press, 1985) 88.

has remained at the heart of the modern state, and its implications for the precise way in which the modern state distinguishes the inside from the outside is discussed in section 2.3.3.

2.3.1 Territorialisation: Changing Identities and Allegiances

In medieval Europe, the feudal system had determined the relationship between people and territory.[43] However, relations of authority, such as command over loyalties, were based more on personal ties than on territorial considerations. Feudal concepts of fealty were not at all comparable to nationality in the modern sense, and social groups had complex and multiple relations with each other, some based on speech, some on religion and some on administrative loyalty. The governance of any such group could depend on many different authorities and the idea of rule was certainly not determined by "a conception of permanent borders within which such rule applied and outside of which it did not apply."[44] The overlap between (political) identities entailed that there was no clear or uniform mechanism by which to distinguish 'us' from 'them', 'inside from outside'. We have seen above that the medieval order characterised by pluralism under the umbrella of universal Christendom changed slowly because of the consolidation of monarchical power and the influence of the Reformation.

The process of state formation in Europe was exclusionist practice: before territorial boundaries hardened, attempts had already been made by states to homogenise populations by expulsing peoples, such as religious minorities whose allegiance a ruler could not be sure of.[45] Indeed, monarchs increasingly tried to reduce regional differences in their territories; fashioned distinctions between insiders and 'aliens'; and encouraged the use of standardised languages in order to create stronger loyalties between the inhabitants of their territories, something that was deemed necessary in order to engage their subjects in the waging of war against other emerging states. The emerging territorial state struck the right balance between the possession of the means of violence and capital accumulation so that this form of political organisation became the dominant one during the sixteenth and seventeenth centuries.[46] Sovereign states survived because their size was ideal for the fighting of wars:

---

[43] A. Dummet and A. Nicol, *Subjects, Citizens, Aliens and Others: Nationality and Immigration Law* (London: Weidenfeld and Nicolson, 1990).

[44] J.A. Caporaso, "Changes in the Westphalian Order: Territory, Public Authority and Sovereignty," *International Studies Review* 2, no. 2 (2000), 22.

[45] Andrew Linklater, *The transformation of political community* (Cambridge: Polity Press, 1998), 28.

[46] Charles Tilly, *Coercion, Capital and European States: AD 990–1992* (Oxford: Basil Blackwell, 1992), 30–31.

they were large enough to withstand attack and small enough to enable administration from a central point.[47] Territory started to play a greater role in political life, but initially the perception that relations of authority were decidedly personal, remained. This was only logical in view of the fact that sovereignty was seen as vested in the King, as we have seen above. As the sovereign was the state, 'nationality' – thus better described as subjecthood – had implied allegiance to the King, not to a certain demarcated territory, and certainly not to a particular social group.

When the feudal order started to transform gradually into absolutism, everybody became, in addition to his status in the hierarchical feudal order, a subject of the King. In time, the doctrine of perpetual allegiance developed, entailing that none of his subjects could unilaterally renounce his obligations towards the King. Subjecthood was generally acquired by birth and could not be subsequently changed. As the will of the King was the source of allegiance, it was also the King who decided who would be conferred with subjecthood. Ideologies such as nationalism, alluding to a deeper relationship between people and territory, or other ideological convictions tying the notions of people and their state to each other in a more profound way were not yet conceivable. Formally, people were subjects by virtue of their being subjected to the sovereign, and not because they had a special relation with each other or with the territory in which they lived. In practice, however, territorialisation led to a situation in which the people over whom the sovereign ruled were defined by virtue of their location within certain borders.[48] This situation became a structural aspect of political organisation after 1648, the year when the Peace of Westphalia, by establishing external sovereignty as a principle of international relations, ascribed to each territorial state the exclusive government of the population within its territory.[49]

During the Enlightenment, earlier attitudes with regard to allegiance and political authority started to change. Due to changing perceptions about the location and nature of sovereignty, the object and foundation of allegiance altered. On the one hand, allegiance became a less stringent condition, for this

---

[47] Linklater (1998) 27. Of course there were many more factors influencing the establishment of the modern system of states. See John G. Ruggie, "Territoriality and Beyond: Problematizing modernity in International Relations," *International Organization* 47 (1993). However, I will not go into these; here it suffices to observe that the modern state system developed as the result of specific historical circumstances. See also Mary Kaldor, *New and Old Wars. Organized Violence in a Global Era* (Cambridge: Polity Press; 1999), 11–20.

[48] Philpott (1997), 19.

[49] Barry Hindess, "Divide and Rule: The International Character of Modern Citizenship" *European Journal of Social Theory* 1, no. 1 (1998), 65.

duty, finding its source in the tie between sovereign and subject established at birth, "an implied, original and virtual allegiance, antecedently to any express promise",[50] was replaced by a notion that, as we saw above, deduced political obligations from consent or voluntary contract:

> "'Tis plain then, …by the Law of right reason, that a Child is born a Subject of no Country, or Government. He is under his Fathers Tuition and Authority, till he come to the Age of Discretion; and then he is a Free-man, at Liberty what Government he will put himself under; what Body Politick he will unite himself to."[51]

However, according to Locke, after an individual had consciously chosen to be a member of society, he could never again possess the liberty he would have had in a state of nature. Thus Locke's lifelong contract still implies perpetual allegiance. Later thinkers, such as Thomas Jefferson (1743–1826), extended the scope of Locke's initial voluntary choice to a choice on an ongoing basis. Unsurprisingly, it was precisely the American Revolution that challenged the principle of perpetual allegiance. This was not only caused by political problems that the Revolution brought about,[52] but it was also the result of the very ideals that inspired the Revolution.[53] As already mentioned, these Enlightenment ideals did not only challenge the foundation of the principle of allegiance, they also changed its object. The idea that allegiance was owed to the kingdom instead of the King gained in importance, explainable by altering perceptions on the location of sovereignty. When sovereignty had passed from the King to the people, allegiance acquired a completely different meaning: it was replaced by the abstract notion of nationality, the bond expressing the fact of a person's belonging to a certain state.

> La notion de nationalité, lien de droit public qui assujettit un individu à un Etat, a succédé à la veille idée féodale d'allégeance, lien personnel unissant le souverain à son sujet.[54]

---

[50] William Blackstone, *Commentaries on the Laws of England*, Vol. I. (London: Murray; 1865), 369.
[51] *Second Treatise*, Chapter 8, § 118. Locke (1967), 365.
[52] The doctrine of perpetual allegiance eventually led to war between Britain and America in 1812 as Britain had been stopping ships on the high seas to impress British-born seamen, despite their claims of American citizenship. See Alan Dowty, *Closed Borders, The Contemporary Assault on Freedom of Movement* (New Haven and London: Yale University Press, 1987), 45.
[53] At the outbreak of the Revolution each inhabitant of America was given the choice whether he wanted to remain a British subject or become an American citizen. Richard Plender, *International Migration Law* (Leiden: Sijthof, 1972), 13.
[54] Raymond Boulbès, *Droit Francais de Nationalité: Les Textes, la Jurisprudence, les Regles Administrative* (Paris: Sirey, 1956), 16.

Even if the concept of nationality can be seen as the successor to the feudal notion of allegiance in the sense that they both unite the sovereign with his subjects, important distinctions between the two concepts make them otherwise disparate. Apart from changing ideas on the location and source of sovereignty, which altered perceptions of allegiance, the process of territorialisation led to a situation in which the individual's relation to the sovereign was factually determined by territory, and no longer by any personal attribute of the subject, as it had done in the feudal order. States were able to establish, to a large degree, exclusive control over their territories and the populations within it. The resulting internal sovereign claim corresponds with the state's external sovereignty in the Westphalian structure through which each territorial state was ascribed the exclusive government of the population within its territory. The concept of sovereignty, linking territory, political community and political power plays a fundamental role in the division of humanity into distinct national populations, with their own territories and states. The precise way in which these concepts have been merged together in the modern state will be addressed below.

2.3.2 The Discovery of the Nation: Inconsistent Universalism?

The secularisation of political theory, combined with other, more practical circumstances, which resulted in the consolidation of exclusive territorial rule, led to perceptions of the state as a unified force, with supreme and exclusive authority over the population within a certain territory.[55] The modern territorial state began to take shape, and with its emergence, identity became a clear matter of inside and outside:

> Legitimations of identity gave way to legitimations of difference, with difference here becoming a matter of absolute exclusions. The principle of identity embodied in Christian universalism was challenged by the principle of difference embodied in the emerging territorial state. This was perhaps not much more than a change in emphasis. But this change in emphasis had enormous repercussions. From then on, the principle of identity, the claim to universalism, was pursued within states.[56]

With the emergence of the territorial state, there came to be clear demarcations by which to differentiate, and those were not only territorial ones. The modern state, apart from claiming exclusive territorial jurisdiction, also asserts a specific national identity. Its borders are "inscribed both on maps and in the

---

[55] Plender (1972), 10.
[56] R.B.J. Walker, *Inside/outside: International Relations as Political Theory* (Cambridge / New York: Cambridge University Press; 1993), 117.

souls of citizens."[57] Yet, it should be noted, the formation of the territorial state and the building of the nation were different, although convergent, processes.[58] How does nationalism – a primarily political principle that holds that the political and national unit should be congruent[59] – relate to the Westphalian state system? Is nationalism, as some argue, solely the product of the struggle for state power: monarchs attempting to homogenise their populations in order to augment and facilitate their rule? Or, instead, is it only logical that pre-political communities – people related to each other by shared culture, ancestry, and lineage – wish to choose their own sovereign?[60] In other words, do the state and nation exist apart, and is it possible to distinguish between the various collective bodies of human beings, which are called nations, on grounds other than common government?[61]

A different, although related, question is how nationalism and the political philosophy that accompanied the emergence of independent territorial states relate to each other. At first sight they seem to contradict each other, for it is difficult to see how one can reconcile the universalistic ideals of eighteenth century enlightenment thinking – expressed in the theory of popular sovereignty – with the formation of exclusive political communities during that same era. We will not find an answer to these difficult questions

---

[57] Nicholas Xenos, "Refugees: The Modern Political Condition" in *Challenging Boundaries. Global Flows, Territorial Identities*, eds. Michael J. Shapiro, and Hayward R. Alker (Minneapolis: University of Minneapolis Press; 1996), 239.

[58] J. Habermas, "The European Nation-state - Its Achievements and Its Limits. On the Past and Future of Sovereignty and Citizenship," in *Mapping the Nation*, ed. G. Balakrishnan (London: Verso, 1996), 283.

[59] Ernest Gellner's definition of nationalism. See Gellner, E, *Nations and Nationalism* (London: Basil Blackwell, 2006).

[60] These questions can be related to the two broad categories into which theories of nationalism can generally be divided: instrumentalism and primordialism. See D. Conversi, "Reassessing Current Theories of Nationalism: Nationalism as Boundary Maintenance and Creation," *Nationalism and Ethnic Politics* 1 (1995) 73. It should be noted that theories that emphasise the instrumental role of nationalism can do so from various perspectives: Ernest Gellner accords industrialisation in modern societies a central role (Gellner, 2006) whereas others criticise his view for its neglect of military processes. D. Conversi, "Homogenisation, nationalism and war: Should we still read Ernest Gellner?" *Nations and Nationalism* 13, no. 3 (2007). See for various theories of nationalism: Benedict Anderson, *Imagined Communities: Reflections on the Origin and Spread of Nationalism* (London: Verso, 1991); A. Dieckhoff and C. Jaffrelot (eds.) *Revisiting Nationalism. Theories and Processes* (London: C. Hurst, 2005); and U. Ozkirimli, *Theories of Nationalism: A Critical Overview* (Basingstoke: Macmillan, 2000).

[61] I. Veit-Brause, "Rethinking the State of the Nation," in *The State in Transition: Reimagining Political Space*, eds. J.A. Camilleri, A.P. Jarvis and A.J. Paolini (Boulder: Lynne Rienner Publishers, 1995), 63.

in early liberal theory itself, for that failed to address the inconsistency between "universal man, which is its point of departure and the citizen or subject of a state, which is its point of arrival."[62] For Hobbes the body politic is not a natural body, but it is created by men from the state of nature. Community does not pre-exist the body politic – indeed, we saw that in his theory it is artificial to make a distinction between society and state: the idea of community is utterly dependent on the notion of the sovereign power. But his theory leaves unanswered the question why particular communities exist and not one, universal community. This could be explained by the fact that Hobbes' writings were occasioned by civil wars and internal chaos, and his Leviathan was a fiction to explain and justify the kind of political power that he deemed logically necessary in a given body politic as well as a practical necessity in his own country.

Also Locke failed to provide a satisfactory answer to the problem caused by territorial particularism in the face of universal humanity. While for Hobbes there is no community at all without the body politic, for Locke there exists a universal community of mankind in the state of nature, in which all men are free and equal: a moral statement flowing from natural law. We saw how Locke explained why men would want to make a contract with each other in order to opt out of this state of nature but he did not clarify why this contract is not made between all members of the natural community of mankind instead of just between members of particular communities. Indeed, most social contract theories failed to explain how, if pre-political humanity was one, anyone could be made sovereign if it were not with the universal consent of all humanity.[63] A notable exception in this respect amongst early liberal theorists is Samuel Pufendorf. He believed that people have a natural right to create separate societies, for they need to associate only with those with whom they share special inclinations; and where possible political boundaries should thus converge with an existing harmony of dispositions.[64]

Nevertheless, although nationalism and the theory of popular sovereignty – in fact, modern ideas concerning equality of mankind in general, seem to contradict each other, the two must somehow be connected. Nationalism is not

---

[62] S. Seth, "Nationalism in/and Modernity," in *The State in Transition: Reimagining Political Space*, eds. J.A. Camilleri, A.P. Jarvis and A.J. Paolini (London: Lynne Rienner Publishers; 1995), 44.

[63] Which was also Sir Robert Filmer's critique of such theories. Sir Robert Filmer was a fervent defender of the theory of Divine Right to patriarchal kingship, and Locke wrote his First Treatise to refute his arguments. See Seth (1995), 48; and Linklater (1998), 105–106.

[64] Linklater (1998), 51.

some "primitive and tribal idea" which survived despite modernity.[65] On the contrary, nationalism is profoundly modern, and wherever theories of popular sovereignty emerged, nationalism appeared. This tension at the heart of modernity cannot be explained by a simple cause but it is instead the result of the conflictive and ambiguous processes that led to the formation of the territorial state based on popular sovereignty. The French Revolution and the radically new notion of citizenship, to which it gave birth, illustrate these ambiguities very well. The Revolution was inspired by the ideal of universal mankind, but the spreading of revolutionary ideals over Europe led to demands for national rights of people, not to claims concerning the universality of mankind.[66] If we look at the Declaration of the Rights of Man and Citizen, we see that it declares that the source of all sovereignty resides in the nation. Thus, all of a sudden, the concept of the people in the theory of popular sovereignty was defined as the nation. The struggle for the control of state power was surely no longer a matter of Divine Right, but neither was it solely an issue of natural rights for the people: instead, it had shifted to the area of national identity.[67] What had caused the concept of the people to be translated into the notion of the nation?

Part of the answer to that question is to be found in the fact that political reformers inspired by Enlightenment ideals were operating in a pre-existing territorial framework. They were rebelling against a monarch whose struggle for power had gradually led to the breakdown of the medieval Christian order and to the establishment of the territorial state. In this struggle, boundaries were gradually drawn[68] and attempts to homogenise populations were made in order to secure loyalties. Extended periods of war, which had consolidated the territorial state during the sixteenth, seventeenth and early eighteenth centuries, had sowed feelings of identity and patriotism.[69] All this had caused the Christian ideal of universal humankind to lose ground during the seventeenth century, and its revival in the eighteenth century did not take place in a vacuum, but in a certain political environment. Thus, the ideals of popular sovereignty were elaborated upon in an emerging system of territoriality where political rule was defined by territory. As a result, they

---

[65] D. Deudney, *Ground Identity: Nature, Place and Space in Nationalism. Lapis, Y and Kratochwil, F. The Return of Culture and Identity in IR Theory* (Boulder: Lynne Rienner Publishers; 1996), 129. See also Seth (1995), 54; and Veit Brause (1995), 61.
[66] J. Kristeva, *Strangers to Ourselves* (New York: Columbia University Press; 1991), 151.
[67] Xenos (1996), 238.
[68] Although it would take a long time before these boundaries actually hardened.
[69] R.L. Hough, *The Nation-States, Concert or Chaos* (Lanham: University Press of America; 2003), 8.

were unavoidably shaped by that very framework. If there had not been absolutist, centralised government on the scale that the territorial state provided, it is doubtful whether political philosophy would have developed as it did. More importantly, territoriality was a fact by the time that ideas of popular sovereignty were brought into practice.

A brief look at France will illustrate the consequences of the fact that the political ideals had to be executed within the framework of the territorial state of which the boundaries had already been drawn previously. Before the Revolution there was no other bond uniting Frenchmen with each other than their common allegiance to the monarch.[70] After the Revolution, governance became impersonal, based on abstract ideas of equality as a replacement for the personal ties that had hitherto provided the basis for political power. Two different processes were necessary in order to realise the ideal of equality. First, privilege and feudalism were abolished. Individual political equality, by the use of the concept of citizenship, was gradually realised, although important exceptions to this ideal never disappeared completely. Second, the different parts of the territorial entity that was France, formerly joined by personal chains of command that had been vertical, had to be integrated into the abstract idea of the body politic based on popular sovereignty. A new idea was needed to imagine this new abstract idea of the body politic, governed by the people, just as a new political identity had to be devised to give expression to political equality. The nation became the all-compassing political entity that was the source of equality, and citizenship indicated membership of this political community. The people became the people by their transformation from the subjects of the King to citizens of a nation. That a universalistic ethic came to be construed in the particularistic language of nation and national citizenship was caused by the fact that it was not within a universal empire but within the territorial state that Enlightenment ideals were politically translated.

The same mechanism can be observed in the concept of citizenship. In most accounts of citizenship, its rights and equality aspect are emphasised. However, it should not be overlooked that citizenship is not only a complex package of rights with which the free and equal individual is endowed, but that he is endowed with them precisely because of his membership in a certain polity. This aspect of citizenship has been called "the gatekeeper between humanity in general and communities of character."[71] The French Revolution merged

---

[70] M.P. Fitzsimmons, "The National Assembly and the Invention of Citizenship," in *The French Revolution and the Meaning of Citizenship*, eds. R. Waldinger, P. Dawson and I. Woloch (Westport, London: Greenwood Press, 1993), 29.

[71] F. Kratochwil, "Citizenship: On the Border of Order," in *The Return of Culture and Identity in IR Theory*, eds. Y. Lapid, and F. Kratochwil (Boulder: Lynne Rienner Publishers; 1996), 182.

the two aspects together, and in the same way as with regard to the concept of the nation, identity is thus constructed by "straddling the claims of the universal and the particular."[72] Also here, territoriality played a major role: the Treaties of Westphalia, long before modern ideas of equality became politically significant, firmly anchored the principle of sovereignty in 'international' relations, by establishing mutually independent territorial political units with supreme and exclusionary authority within their territories. The resulting division of 'humanity'[73] into distinct populations defined by territory was largely a fact at the time that the modern reformers brought their political ideals into practice.

So, it may be, as Julia Kristeva observes, regrettable to find the duality of man/citizen at the heart of the maximum demand for equality that the French Declaration of the Rights of Man and Citizen actually was.[74] However true this is in the light of later developments, as we shall see in more detail in the next chapter, the drafters of the Declaration could not foresee the consequences to which the identification of the citizen with man could give rise. Citizenship was intended to provide equality to all those subject to the power of the state, and the distinction between man and citizen in the eighteenth century did not pose the kind of problems that would arise in later times.[75]

Practical circumstances, of which the organisation of political life on the basis of territoriality constitutes the most important, may explain the birth of a concept such as the nation, but they do not explain the importance that that concept subsequently acquired. Nationalism has proven to be a strong force. The romantic reaction against the Enlightenment played a crucial role with regard to the importance that nationalism as an ideology gained in later times. But it has also been argued that it is liberal theory itself that makes the turn to nationalism possible, although at first sight this does not seem logical. For not only is there tension between the universalistic ethic of early liberal theory and the particularistic attitude that nationalism takes, but in addition it is difficult to see how the self-interested, rational individual on which theories of the modern state are based would want to fight and ultimately die for a

---

[72] A.P. Jarvis, and A.J. Paolini, "Locating the State," in *The State in Transition, Reimagining Political Space*, eds. J.A. Camilleri, A.P. Jarvis, and A.J. Paolini (London: Lynne Rienne Publishers; 1995), 10.

[73] It should be noted that the term humanity is misleading in more than one sense in the context of modernity, considering that the discourse was exclusively European and predominantly male.

[74] Kristeva (1991), 150.

[75] L. Ferrajoli, "Beyond Sovereignty and Citizenship: a Global Constitutionalism" in *Constitutionalism, Democracy and Sovereignty: American and European Perspectives*, ed. R. Bellamy (Aldershot: Avebury; 1996).

political community called the nation. In order to understand the appeal of nationalism we need to grasp the very abstraction of the concept of popular sovereignty. The principle of order and legitimacy in pre-modern political entities, whether they were kingdoms, empires or city states, was based on "inequality, difference and complementarity."[76] As already mentioned, in the medieval world all individuals had their own position, rights and duties, which unified them personally with the sovereign in an order instituted by God. The unity of the modern state is based on an opposite principle: individualism expressed in a contract based on equality. According to Arthur Melzer, this individualism and the concept of equality has led to the identification that is the root of all forms of nationalism.[77]

In addition, the spread of popular sovereignty, by introducing the abstract and intangible concept of the people, changed the understandings of the political community which were not immediately self-evident.[78] In the words of Bernard Yack, it has, on the one hand, led to the nationalisation of the political community, exactly because liberal theory has no justification for the existence of territorial boundaries, boundaries that were a fact when liberal theory came about. As a consequence, it facilitates imaginations of a national community that is pre-political. Yack explains how, on the other hand, theories of popular sovereignty have given rise to the politicisation of national communities. The exclusive nature of territorial control in the concept of sovereignty in general, when applied to popular sovereignty in particular, means that there can be only one 'people' that controls a certain demarcated territory. And although this concept of the people in liberal theory is certainly not a national community, the problem is, once again, that liberal theory does not show us how to define the concept of the people. Accordingly, it invites "assertions of national sovereignty by justifying the right of peoples to de-establish and reconstruct the authority of the state."[79]

2.3.3 National Identity as the Basis for Territorial Sovereignty

We have seen above that the interplay between territorialisation and liberal theory led to the formation of political identities that contain a large potential for political particularism. By the time that the Napoleonic Wars had swept over Europe, the abstract concepts of national citizenship, the nation state,

---

[76] A. Melzer, "Rousseau, Nationalism, and the Politics of Sympathetic Identification" in *Educating the Prince, Essays in Honor of Harvey Mansfield*, eds. M. Blitz and W. Kristol (Lanham: Rowman & Littlefield Publishers, 2000), 126.
[77] Ibid., 125–126.
[78] Bernard Yack, "Popular sovereignty and nationalism" *Political Theory* 29, no. 4 (2001), 518.
[79] Ibid., 528.

and territoriality were established concepts in political thought. Independent sovereign territorial entities had become the building blocks for political life; their borders defined the identity of individuals, and their territorial integrity was seen as essential to prevent destruction and violence. Successive shifts in the Westphalian system during the nineteenth and twentieth century were not so much caused by changes in its underlying premises, but more by alterations in emphasis.[80]

As the nineteenth century advanced, nationalism irrevocably lost its early implications of individual freedom and rights. Nationalism was no longer about encouraging the integration of diverse populations and classes into one nation, based on the idea of an inclusive political community, as it had been for the French Revolutionaries. Instead, it became a tool for states' exclusionist practices. The trend that accorded national identity, as a criterion by which to distinguish between 'us' and 'them', unique importance was initiated by the reaction that took place against the Enlightenment. Romanticism placed emphasis on tradition, emotion and the community. Above, I have already discussed the thought of Rousseau with regard to the location and nature of sovereignty. The volonté générale is not, as we saw, a construct based on rationality and self-interest, but is something that is inherent in the concept of community. The cosmopolitanism of the Enlightenment, according to Rousseau, was an empty promise, and ties that resulted from a common feeling of belonging were infinitely more important than abstract ideas of universal mankind. Hence, he warned of cosmopolites "who, justifying their love of fatherland by their love of mankind, boast of loving everyone so that they might have the right of loving no one."[81] For Rousseau, man becomes human by his membership of a community: "we do not properly begin to become men until after having been Citizens."[82] And although the community in the sense meant by Rousseau is not necessarily the nation, it is not difficult to see how his thoughts could be applied to the newly emerging idea of the nation, which was exactly what subsequent thinkers, such as Georg Hegel (1770–1831), would do.

In Hegel's philosophy there is no distinction between community, state and nation. The significant unit is neither the individual, nor just any group of individuals, but it is the nation. For Rousseau sovereignty is expressed in the general will; for Hegel state sovereignty is the fundamental expression of the national will. If, up until contemporary times, nationality is the primary

---

[80] See Caporaso (2000), 8–11.
[81] See Book 1, Chapter 2 of the *Geneva Manuscript*. Jean-Jacques Rousseau (1997), 158.
[82] Id.

political identity, leaving all other loyalties and ties far behind, that trend was started by Hegel, by whom the state is continually represented as standing for the highest possible ethical value.[83] Increasing nationalism noticeably changed the role of the state: just as in Hegel's philosophy the state became identified with the nation.

In addition, nationalism, as the struggle over the definition of territorial boundaries, reinforced the sovereign territorial ideal.[84] Thus, by the end of the nineteenth century, sovereignty, territory and the identity of the political community had become inextricably linked. In the period between the two world wars, national identity had become the highest political priority; states generally did not recognise any other identity or loyalty. The national state had a monopoly control on violence, it was the highest court of appeal and it had an exclusive right of representation in the international sphere.[85]

The structural importance of clearly demarcated and inviolable territory, ruled by the nation as a discrete social unit, was strengthened by the Treaty of Versailles. People were defined by virtue of to which state they belonged, and the political community became increasingly closed in upon itself, and more and more hostile to outsiders, due to nationalistic forces and new state structures that intensified the totalising project.[86] These outsiders were not only people belonging to other states, but also those belying a different identity within the state. However, it was not only nationalism that changed conceptions of the relationship between people, territory and the state. After the First World War, many regimes proclaimed a collectivist ethic. Instead of the ethnic or cultural homogeneity towards which nationalists strive, collectivism aims at social homogeneity. Collectivism maintains that the will of the individual coincides with the will of the state – the interests of the individual are identical to the interests of the state. In practice, this meant that the aspirations of the individual were completely subordinated to those of the state.

Although the Second World War clearly demonstrated the dangers of unbridled nationalism, nationalism as an acceptable political ideology was not discarded, as was shown by decolonisation and the transformation of the former USSR republics into nation states. The tendency to fuse the meanings of state and nation is still evident today, and the perception of the territorial state as a

---

[83] Sabine (1941), 639.
[84] Murphy (1996), 97. See aso Y. Lapid, "Identities, Borders, Orders: Nudging International Relations Theory in a New Direction," in *Identities, Borders, Orders: Rethinking IR Theory*, eds. M. Albert, D. Jacobson and Y. Lapid (Minneapolis and London: University of Minnesota Press, 2001).
[85] E.H. Carr, *The Twenty Years Crisis: 1919–1939* (London: Macmillan; 1946), 228.
[86] Linklater (1998), 4.

"container of society"[87] is a persistent one. The territorial state is seen as the proper unit for organising political life, and "the categories through which we have attempted to pose questions about the political are precisely those that have been constructed in relation to the state."[88] Thus, the exercise of citizenship has become inseparable from belonging to the nation: a very specific kind of membership in a territorially defined political community.[89] Territorial boundaries are to be guarded jealously and strictly, especially with regard to the movement of persons, because the territorially fixed population has become one of the foundations of the concept of sovereignty: "when the rules for differentiating between the inside and the outside become blurred and ambiguous, the foundations of sovereignty become shaky."[90]

Of course, in some areas there are exceptions to this fundamental place of the territorial nation state in politics, most notably the case of the European Union. Within the Union, Member States are limited in their use of territorial borders to maintain a strict divide between inside and outside. Nevertheless, with regard to the Union's external frontiers, it has been argued extensively that no such movement away from a traditional conception of sovereignty can be discerned. The external frontiers of the EU have the long-established meaning that territorial boundaries have in distinguishing between 'us' and 'them' and they may even have reinforced the importance of such distinctions.[91] The fact that the EU in this sense is not as novel as some like to believe is perhaps best illustrated by the denial of full EU citizenship for long-term residents of the EU. Nationality, territory and the community become increasingly decoupled for insiders, but for outsiders their linkage remains strong. Indeed, something strangely familiar about this very project of the abolition of internal borders, while simultaneously reinforcing external ones, comes to mind when reading Joseph Weiler's criticism of the exclusion of third-country nationals from EU citizenship at the time of its birth:

---

[87] J. Agnew, and S. Corbridge, *Mastering space: Hegemony, territory and international political economy* (London: Routledge, 1995), 82–92. See also Murphy (1996), 103; and J. Tully, *Strange multiplicity: Constitutionalism in an age of diversity* (Cambridge: Cambridge University Press, 1997), 187.

[88] Jarvis and Paolini (1995), 7.

[89] See E. Balibar, "Propositions on Citizenship" *Ethics* 98, no. 4 (1988), 726; and Caporaso (2000), 22.

[90] R. Doty, "Sovereignty and the nation: constructing the boundaries of national identity," in *State Sovereignty as a Social Construct*, eds. T.J. Biersteker and C. Weber (Cambridge: Cambridge University Press; 1996), 122.

[91] See E. Balibar, "World Borders, Political Borders" *Proceedings of the Modern Language Association of America* 117 (2002); and D. Kostakopoulou and R. Thomas, "Unweaving the Threads: Territoriality, National Ownership of Land and Asylum Policy," *European Journal of Migration and Law* 6, no. 1 (2004), 6.

> The successful elimination of internal frontiers will of course accentuate in a symbolic way (and in a very real sense too) the external frontiers of the Community [...] In one way, the more that these external borders are accentuated, the greater the sense of internal solidarity [...] in the very concept of European citizenship a distinction is created between the insider and the outsider that tugs at their common humanity.[92]

In addition, as we shall see when addressing the Europeanisation of immigration policies in chapter 5, the perceived self-evidence of the link between territorial exclusion and the individual who is defined as the 'other'– which may well be the essence of the nationalism that plays such a fundamental role in the self-understanding of the modern state – has found a definite place within 'post-national Europe'.

2.4. *On Sovereignty's Content and Form, and the (Il)Legitimacy of Violence*

In this chapter we have seen how territorialisation, "a historically specific, contradictory, and conflictual process rather than a pre-given, fixed, or natural condition"[93], has led to the current perception of sovereignty as a self-evident and natural abstraction that links state power, people and territory. I have attempted to demonstrate that the question as to what constitutes legitimate political power cannot be seen in isolation from the modern state's claim to determine its boundaries. On the one hand, the process of territorialisation facilitated the emergence of the abstract notion of sovereignty as the legitimation of ultimate power within the body politic. On the other hand, the way in which the theory of popular sovereignty subsequently legitimised ultimate political authority within the body politic has made possible an exclusive ideal of the political community. In addition, the territorial aspect of the modern state's claim to determine its boundaries cannot be understood properly when we fail to take into account the Westphalian structure in which each and every state necessarily operates. However, the intricate historical relation between all sovereignty's aspects is often ignored, resulting in an uncritical acceptance of the status quo of contemporary political organisation on the basis of territory.

---

[92] J. Weiler, "Thou shall not oppress a stranger: On the judicial Protection of the Human Rights of Non-EC Nationals – A Critique" *European Journal of International Law* 3 (1992), 65 and 68. Strangely familiar seeing that nationalism "simultaneously strives at the reinforcement of external borders and the elimination of internal borders". Conversi (1995) 78.

[93] N. Brenner, "Beyond State-Centrism? Space, Territoriality and Geographical Scale in Globalization Studies" *Theory and Society* 28 (1999), 12.

In concluding this chapter I want to draw attention to the way in which sovereignty's claim to distinguish from the inside and the outside has impacted on the question of legitimate political violence. Charles Tilly aptly expresses the link between violence and the state, when he writes that the state made war while war made the state.[94] Tilly refers to factual circumstances of armed conflict that caused the territorial state to become the dominant form of political organisation. However, we have also seen how the religious wars of the seventeenth century gave a strong impulse to the theory of sovereignty as the foundation for ultimate political authority in the body politic. The notion of sovereignty was partly formulated as an answer to the violence that ravaged Europe. An essential feature of the consolidation of the European state system was that the state's monopoly on the use of force was vigorously institutionalised.[95] With the advent of popular sovereignty, one of the tasks of the modern state was to provide security, and one of the reasons why the modern state was successful in establishing its monopoly on the use of violence was its very ability to provide citizens with security. From then on, individuals no longer had the right to use force against each other. We have seen that most theorists on sovereignty were primarily concerned with its internal claims, but in international relations the concept came to bear upon the relations between states as well. Similar to its role internally, the external aspect of exclusive territorial sovereignty, for which the Treaties of Westphalia provided the first step, was also perceived as a necessity in order to prevent the recurrence of the violence that had devastated Europe during the Thirty Years War. The way in which the modern state distinguished, from then onwards, between inside and outside, by the use of territorial boundaries and later by the assumption of a "necessary alignment between territory and identity, state and nation"[96] profoundly influenced the question of legitimate violence.

Indeed, through the process of territorialisation a novel structure by which to distinguish between legitimate and illegitimate violence would materialise. Before the modern territorial state came into existence, it was difficult to distinguish between war and mere crime within the widespread violence that Europe continually suffered. The absence of a clear mechanism to determine 'us' from 'them', due to the overlap between identity-based boundaries, made it impossible to make a distinction between those forms of violence that were legitimate and those that were not, and it was only when the territorial state

---

[94] Tilly (1992).
[95] Hough (2003), 7.
[96] D. Campbell, "Violent Performances: Identity, Sovereignty, Responsibility," in *The Return of Culture and Identity in IR Theory*, eds. Y. Lapid and F. Kratochwil (Boulder: Lynne Rienner Publishers; 1996), 171.

had taken shape that distinctions of this kind could be made.[97] War was legitimate if it was waged by the authority that had the right to wage it: the state, and as such it was distinguished from mere crime by simply defining it as something that only sovereign states engaged in.[98] In nineteenth century conceptions of international law, the right of a state to wage war in order to settle disputes with other states was regarded as a fundamental aspect of that state's sovereignty.[99] The inter-state order that was the result of the establishment of Westphalian sovereignty led to an additional, albeit related, distinction within the concept of violence. On the one hand, there was internal violence, perpetrated against the individual within the territorial boundaries of the sovereign state; the regulation of which was the prerogative of the sovereign state alone, consistent with the idea of sovereignty as the supreme political authority over the population within a certain territory. On the other hand, external violence such as the use of force between states was regulated by the articulation of international norms, which were based on strong territorial assumptions. These issues will receive further attention in the next chapter, but for now it is important to point to the role played by the very process of territorialisation in shaping norms that delimit legitimate from illegitimate violence. Thus, as we shall see later, the territorialisation of political authority has impacted deeply on the specific modes of its exercise.

However, as is convincingly argued by John Agnew and Stuart Corbridge, the lack of attention to the relationship between the exercise of state power through political institutions and the clear spatial demarcation of the territory on which this power is exercised has led to a reification of the principle of territoriality.[100] Notwithstanding the fact that territoriality is a relative latecomer on the global political stage, at present the linkage of political power to clearly demarcated territory is still seen as a natural and neutral way of organising the global political system. As a result, the territorial form that sovereignty has assumed over the course of history is generally perceived as separate

---

[97] R.W. Mansbach, and F. Wilmer, "War, Violence and the Westphalian State System as a Moral Community" in: *Identities, Borders, Orders: Rethinking IR Theory*, eds. M. Albert, D. Jacobson and Y. Lapid (Minneapolis: University of Minnesota Press, 2000), 56.

[98] M. Van Creveld, *Transformation of War* (New York, London, Free Press; 1991), 41; and A.M. Rifaat, *International Agression: A Study of the Legal Concept, its development and definiton in international law* (Stockholm: Almqist and Viksell International; 1979), 12.

[99] R.A. Brand, "Sovereignty: The State, the Individual, and the International Legal System in the Twenty First Century," *Hastings International and Comparative Law Review* 25 (2002), 287.

[100] Agnew and Corbridge (1995), 82. See also Walker (1993); and M. Anderson and D. Bigo, "What are EU frontiers for and what do they mean?" in *In Search of Europe's Borders*, eds. K. Groenendijk, E. Guild and P. Minderhoud (The Hague: Kluwer Law International; 2002), 17.

from its jurisdictional content. Nevertheless, even if the way in which sovereignty's various aspects have traditionally been categorised and discussed – that is, according to its external and internal manifestations; or according to its substantive content as the exercise of power through political institutions and its territorial form – may at times serve the sake of doctrinal clarity; these distinctions and categorisations fail to do justice to the complex historic reality of sovereign state power. The territorial frame in which the modern state operates, and the jurisdictional claims over persons that it makes within this frame, do not make sense if analysed in isolation from each other. Indeed, the territorial basis of the state intends to "fix and enforce boundaries of identity so that the distinction between inside and outside [becomes] defensible."[101] These boundaries of identity have everything to do with the unity of the body politic and the definition of the political community. The state uses both the form and content of sovereignty to protect the political community and maintain a collective identity. The vague and overlapping identities of medieval Europe gave rise to violence, chaos and destruction, but we will see later in this study that the way in which the modern state perceives, construes, and protects the political community gives rise to its own sort of violence.

The intricate and complex way in which sovereignty's various aspects are interrelated is nowhere more visible than in the field of international migration. Indeed, national responses to international migration exemplify that the Westphalian distinction between the state's internal and external sovereign claims is blurred and they illustrate the narrow intertwinement of the territorial frame and the 'jurisdictional' content of sovereign power: The movement of people across borders engages the external sovereign claims of national states in a Westphalian structure that divides humanity in distinct and separate entities. At the same time, international migration engages the internal sovereign claims of the national state in a policy area where its identity-based boundaries and its territorial borders converge. A state which regards immigration as a threat, attempts to guard its territorial boundaries, inter alia with the use of military patrols to intercept illegal migrants at the border and military police to carry out expulsions. Simultaneously, it establishes controls within society, ranging from obligatory language courses for foreigners to checks on 'bogus' marriages, to ensure that its identity remains unthreatened. Immigration is thus perceived as both a "resistant element to a secure identity on the inside" as

---

[101] Mansbach and Wilmer (2001), 56. See also D. Newman, "Boundaries, Borders and Barriers: Changing Geographic Perspectives on Territorial Lines," in *Identities, Borders, Orders. Rethinking IR Theory*, eds. M. Albert, D. Jacobson and Y. Lapid (Minneapolis: University of Minnesota Press; 2001), 139 and 145.

well as a territorial "threat identified and located on the outside of the state through a discourse of danger that contains elements applicable to both."[102]

Later in this study, I will demonstrate that the reification of the institution of territorial sovereignty has led to a structural blindness in the law for the involvement of personal interests whenever the state bases its claims on sovereignty's territorial frame. We shall see that such blindness is exacerbated whenever the very individuals who are affected by the state's spatial powers are rendered invisible, either because they are far away and unknown or alternatively because they are very different from 'us'. If anything, the tension between the universal and the particular that lies at the heart of the modern state is thus made more acute by an uncritical acceptance of the institution of territorial sovereignty and a strict separation between the form and content of modern sovereignty. The distinction between the 'innocent' territorial form of the modern state and its resulting spatial powers, on the one hand, and the exercise of jurisdiction over people within a certain territory, on the other, obscures the fact that constraints on individual behaviour and freedom are always motivated on account of the notion of political community and the unity of the body politic. Consequently, just as its jurisdictional content, the territorial form of sovereignty has enormous repercussions for individual behaviour and freedom, as we will see in the second part of this book. But before turning to the way in which the sovereign claims of the national state influence questions of international migration in later chapters, I shall address a more immediate concern in the next chapter, where I discuss the legal discourses that limit and make accountable the exercise of sovereign state power.

---

[102] Campbell (1996), 169. See also E. Balibar, "The Borders of Europe," in *Cosmopolitics: Thinking and Feeling beyond the Nation*, eds. P. Cheah and B. Robbins (Minneapolis: University of Minnesota Press; 1998), 220.

Chapter 3

Limiting Sovereign Power

3.1 *Introduction*

In the previous chapter, I have explored the way in which the concept of sovereignty legitimised ultimate political power within a body politic defined by clearly demarcated territorial boundaries. Because such power is amongst other things expressed as a legitimate (i.e. considered to be legitimate) claim to a monopoly of violence, physical force is a defining element in the construction of the state and sovereignty.[1] We have seen how, due to the way in which it determined boundaries and later also because it turned into *popular* sovereignty, sovereignty became a legitimate site for violence. However, that is not to say that it is an unproblematic site for violence. As a response to the growing power of the modern state and its particular notion of sovereignty, ways have been devised to circumscribe the power of the state to resort to the "specific *means* peculiar to it […] namely the use of physical force."[2] This has been necessary because, even though the modern notion of sovereignty attempts to attain congruence between ruler and the ruled, it has not been able to resolve the disparity between people and the state – a disparity that stems from the very abstraction of the modern notion of sovereignty. The legal discourses that seek to limit the power of the modern state are the direct result of the divergence between state and society: as it is the sovereign *state* that is in possession of the legitimate means of coercion, safeguards for the people are necessary. These safeguards, first embodied in domestic constitutionalism and the discourse of citizenship, and later also in the international human rights regime, are the subject matter of this chapter.

---

[1] Max Weber famously defined the state as "a human community that (successfully) claims the *monopoly of the legitimate use of physical force* within a given territory". See M. Weber, "Politics as Vocation," in *From Max Weber: Essays in sociology*, trans./eds. H.H. Gerth and C.W. Wright Mills (New York: Oxford University Press, 1946), 78.
[2] Id.

I shall attempt to demonstrate that in the legal discourses that seek to limit state violence, we can discern both universality and particularity. Indeed, the tension between universality and particularity that we encounter in the very concept of the modern state has been reproduced in the instruments that aim at the protection of the individual against the power of that specific form of political organisation. In some of these discourses the balance tends to fall more towards an ideal of universality, whereas in others political particularism is strongly and explicitly emphasised. But while there are thus important differences in emphasis in this respect, I shall argue that the reification of the territorial form of sovereignty in the contemporary world sets limits to the universalistic potential of *all* these discourses, therewith including the most recent expression of modern constitutional ideas: human rights law. In the second part of this book, we shall see that the practice of immigration detention provides an outstanding example of the implications on the life of the individual of such apparent naturalness and inevitability of territorial sovereignty in constitutionalist discourses. Certainly, immigration law and policy is one of the areas in which the tension between the universal and the particular is bound to emerge most distinctly, as it is a field that is defined by the way in which the distinction is drawn between 'us' and 'them'. The regulation of international migration also shows distinctly that the territorial form of sovereignty and the jurisdictional claims of the modern state are deeply intertwined: In order to preserve the unity of the state and to protect collective identity, the state bases the exercise of power on sovereignty as a whole. Thus, the tension between the universal and the particular as well as the conceptual division within sovereignty between its territorial form and its substantive content will be recurrent themes in my exploration of the legal discourses that aim at the protection of the individual against state power.

This chapter is structured as follows. Section 3.2 sets the stage by presenting some general aspects of a theory of constitutionalism. This is followed by a discussion of the notion of citizenship as a particular institutionalisation of constitutionalism's fundamental guarantees in section 3.3. We shall see that the very process of territorialisation caused a political particularistic reality to triumph over citizenship's original universalistic ideals. After that, in section 3.4, I shall explore the way in which the use of force has been governed by international law. Amongst other things, the regulation of inter-state violence will be addressed in order to reveal territoriality's shaping impact on the discourse of classic international law. However, particular emphasis will be placed on modern human rights law, as a distinctive branch of international law that emerged as an explicit attempt to overcome traditional particularistic forces in the field of individual rights protection. Whether it has succeeded in doing so will be considered in section 3.5, which deals with the implications of modern human rights law for sovereignty's claim to distinguish the inside from the outside. In the conclusions to this chapter, I shall elaborate upon the notion of territoriality as an impediment to the realisation of the radical promise of human rights.

3.2 Constitutionalism as the Theory and Practice of the Limits on Political Power

> In framing a government which is to be administered by men over men, the great difficulty lies in this: you must first enable the government to control the governed; and in the next place oblige it to control itself. A dependence on the people is, no doubt, the primary control on government; but experience has taught mankind the necessity of auxiliary protections.[3]

At no point in history has sovereignty entailed absolute rule without accountability, and the arbitrary use of power by the sovereign has never gone unchallenged. Certainly, it would have seemed strange to Bodin that the sovereign could be bound by law – in his theory that would have meant that the sovereign is bound by his own will, something he found inconceivable.[4] Nonetheless, we have seen that also according to Bodin, sovereign power is subject to limits, albeit not embodied by any human law, but incorporated in the law of God and nature. Even Hobbes' sovereign is not absolute once it is appreciated that his power is only absolute if it is effective.

We have seen that in the modern state, the legitimacy of political power is founded on the idea of popular sovereignty, while popular sovereignty itself is based on ideals of individual liberty and equality. Consequently, not only the foundation, but also the exercise of political power will have to be based on the same principles of liberty and equality: If the idea of sovereign power is necessary to secure each individual's natural rights, it follows that, apart from an obligation to protect these rights against violations by other individuals, the sovereign state is obliged to respect these rights in its own actions towards individuals as well. As such, it is necessary to limit and control the powers of the state. In the modern state, this is achieved through constitutionalism's fundamental principles of *limited government* (government only exists to serve specified ends) and the *rule of law* (it should only govern according to specific

---

[3] James Madison, Alexander Hamilton, and John Jay, *The Federalist Papers*, ed. I. Kramnick (London: Penguin Books, 1987), 319–320.
[4] J.W. Allen, *A History of Political Thought in the Sixteenth Century* (London: Dawsons of Pall Mall, 1967), 50.

rules).[5] Constitutionalism thus poses the issue of limits to political power primarily in terms of the relation between power and law.[6]

Already before the modern state came into existence, there were theories about the limits to political power. However, compared with traditional 'constitutional' theories, the constitutionalism of the modern state based on ideas of popular sovereignty and each citizen's equality is more successful in imposing effective and consistent limits to the exercise of political power.[7] Indeed, in the modern constitutional state, individual rights determine the limits, scope, and aim of governmental power while the prohibition on the arbitrary use of power is shaped by the notion of equality. Moreover, through its requirement that the state itself is bound by the law, constitutionalism seeks to prevent the arbitrary use of power by the state on a more formal level as well.

While the principles of limited government and the rule of law find their origins in the Enlightenment, in most states their consolidation in law generally took place during the nineteenth century.[8] As such, modern constitutionalism "finds its fullest expression in the constitution that establishes not just formal but also material limits to political power."[9] Below, I shall first deal with the formal limits that modern constitutionalism places on the power of the modern state, after which I shall investigate more substantive requirements that are brought about by the notion of individual rights.

3.2.1 Formal Limits on Government and Rules of Institutional Design

Formal limits on government as they have developed within the framework of the modern nation state can be found in the principle of legality, the doctrine of separation of powers, and the existence of an independent judiciary. In the first place, the principle of legality prevents the arbitrary use of state power through its requirement that the exercise of power by the state is in accordance with and finds its formal basis in the law. The principle of equality compels these laws to consist of general rules, equally applicable to every citizen, and as such the risk of arbitrariness in the exercise of state power is minimised. Ultimately, the legal basis for the exercise of political power is to

---

[5] G.J. Schochet, "Introduction: constitutionalism, liberalism, and the study of politics," in *Constitutionalism*, eds. J.R. Pennock and J.W. Chapman (New York: New York University Press, 1979), 1.
[6] N. Bobbio, *Democracy and Dictatorship* (Cambridge: Polity Press; 1989), 89.
[7] Schochet (1979), 3–4.
[8] C.M. Zoethout, "Wat is de rechtsstaat?" in *De rechtsstaat als toetsingskader*, eds. F.J. van Ommeren and S.E. Zijlstra (The Hague: Boom Juridische Uitgevers, 2003), 69; and F.J. van Ommeren, "De rechtsstaat als toetsingskader," *De rechtsstaat als toetsingskader*, eds. F.J. van Ommeren and S.E. Zijlstra (The Hague: Boom Juridische Uitgevers, 2003), 11.
[9] Bobbio (1989), 97.

be found in a constitution, which 'constitutes' the various branches of government, their powers and the limits thereto.[10]

In the second place, any arbitrary and unaccountable exercise of state power is prevented through rules of institutional design. John Locke argued in his *Second Treatise* that, as the supreme power of the people had to be delegated, it would be best for political power to be divided amongst several independent spheres of right in order to prevent abuse. This line of thought was developed further by Montesquieu (1689–1755), whose name it is which is first and foremost associated with the doctrine of separation of powers, an idea he alleged to have discovered by a study of the English constitution.[11] Montesquieu was afraid that the despotism of the French monarchy, which in his eyes equalled law with the sovereign's will, had so damaged the traditional constitution of France that freedom had become forever impossible.[12] For him, personal liberty was paramount and would be best secured if the legislative, executive, and judiciary powers of the state were to be divided amongst different branches of government, which would then be able to control each other.

The idea of separation of powers was not a new one, but Montesquieu made it into a coherent legal system of checks and balances between the different parts of the constitution, a legal doctrine that is still a central feature of contemporary constitutional democracies.[13] Each power is accorded its own status and tasks while it is at the same time to a certain extent dependent on the others, which results in a system of checks and balances in which the different branches of government can exercise a degree of control on each other. A variety of systems of checks and balances can be found amongst existing constitutional democracies. However, central to any constitutional practice that is based upon the doctrine of separation of powers is that the basis for restrictions on individual freedom is to be enacted by the legislature; that actions of the executive are bound by the rules which are laid down by the legislature; and that an independent judiciary ensures that the executive acts within the limits that are set by the legislature.

In the third place, the existence of an independent judiciary occupies a central role in any theory of constitutionalism. Its role is central to the extent that

---

[10] Zoethout (2003), 60. As such, as Carl Schmitt observes, the legal order ultimately rests on a decision, not a norm. See C. Schmitt, *Political Theology, Four Chapters on the Concept of Sovereignty*, trans. G. Schwab (Chicago: University of Chicago Press, 2005), 10.

[11] Although at the time that Montesquieu was studying the English constitution the Civil Wars had destroyed the remnants of medieval mixed government and the Revolution in 1688 had settled Parliamentary supremacy. See G.H.A. Sabine, *History of Political Theory* (London, Calcutta, Sydney: George G. Harrap & Co., 1941), 560.

[12] Ibid., 552.

[13] Ibid., 558. See also Bobbio (1989), 96.

it is indispensable to ensure that constitutionalism as a whole can actually work, and as such it is generally seen as an independent feature of constitutional government, instead of forming a mere part of the doctrine of separation of powers.[14] An independent judiciary is in the best position to ensure that any action by the state is based upon and in conformity with the law. Furthermore, in ensuring a fair application of the law as well as overseeing its strict enforcement, an independent judiciary guarantees the principle of equality. But perhaps most importantly of all, the protection of individual rights is simply not possible without the existence of an independent judiciary. In the next section I will address the manner in which they interact in further detail.

3.2.2 Individual Rights as Material Limits to Political Power

As the very principles relating to each man's freedom and equality constitute the basis for the idea of limited government, constitutionalism is certainly not confined to matters of procedure or questions of institutional design. Indeed, individual liberties are intrinsic to it and the way in which the constitution establishes material limits to political power is thus "well represented by the barrier which fundamental rights – once recognised and legally protected – raise against the claims and presumptions of the holder of sovereign power to regulate every action of individuals or groups."[15]

We have seen in the previous chapter that social contract theories were founded on the idea of natural rights. A first impulse towards such an idea of rights can be observed in the Christian tradition, probably most notably in the writings of Thomas Aquinas (1225–1274).[16] However, in medieval feudal Europe individual rights were not perceived as such, but they consisted of privileges split off from feudal authority. Instead of a conceptual foundation that spoke of rights inherent in men because they were men, these privileges were of a contractual character, a famous example of which is constituted by the Magna Carta of 1215.[17] The modern idea of fundamental rights only developed in the seventeenth century. In the Enlightenment tradition, natural law was seen as a claim to inalienable rights inherent in each individual, and

---

[14] S. Gordon, *Controlling the state: Constitutionalism from ancient Athens to today* (Cambridge/Massachusetts: Harvard University Press, 1999), 43.
[15] Bobbio (1989), 97.
[16] See J. Finnis, *Aquinas: Moral, Political, and Legal Theory* (Oxford: Oxford University Press, 1998) 132–186.
[17] G. Shafir, "Citizenship and Human Rights in an Era of Globalisation," in *People out of Place: Globalization, Human Rights and the Citizenship Gap*, eds. A. Brysk and G. Shafir (New York/London: Routledge, 2004), 13; and M.C. Burkens, *Algemene Leerstukken van Grondrechten naar Nederlands Constitutioneel Recht* (Zwolle: W.E.J. Tjeenk Willink, 1989), 3.

fundamental rights are thus accorded to man by virtue of his humanity and not because of his particular position in the body politic. Such a notion of rights as a guarantee for the individual's freedom that exists independently from and prior to any political community finds a clear expression in the Bill of Rights of the American States and the French Declaration of the Rights of Man and the Citizen. The ambiguities to which these documents have subsequently given rise will be addressed shortly; for now, I want to focus on the original conception of the nature of individual rights.

Their very character, which is primarily not one of "legal entitlements", but one of "spheres of *freedom*",[18] is most clearly visible in the classical fundamental rights, or civil rights, the most important of which are the right to life, liberty, physical integrity, and equality, and diverse freedoms such as the freedom of thought, religion, and expression. These rights in particular exist prior to the state and as a result, their content cannot depend on the positive laws that have been enacted by the state.

Later developments with regard to the regulation of governmental power and the tasks of the modern state led to the articulation of additional kinds of fundamental rights: political rights and social or economic rights. Political rights, such as the right to vote and to fulfil a public office, aim to ensure equal participation for every citizen in the body politic. Their purpose is to translate the ideal of popular sovereignty into political practice. The emergence of economic and social rights is directly related to changing conceptions at the beginning of the twentieth century regarding the role that the modern state should play in the life of its citizens. Social demands were reframed in the language of rights when governments became obliged to promote actively the well-being of their citizens. In contemporary legal discourse civil, political, and social rights are all accorded the status of fundamental rights, and in political practice, the exercise by the individual of these rights shows that they are intimately related, as is most clearly illustrated in the concept of citizenship.[19]

In some instances, it may not be possible or desirable that individuals exercise the full scope of their fundamental rights. One example is the case in which the fundamental rights of two individuals clash; another example is the case in which the state's task of providing security for all conflicts with individuals' unrestricted exercise of these rights. However, the very nature of such rights makes that they cannot be 'simply traded away for other social

---

[18] Schmitt, *Constitutional Theory*, trans. J. Seitzer, eds. J. Seitzer and E. Kennedy (North Carolina: Duke University Press, 2008), 202.
[19] Shown by Marshall in his theory of citizenship. See T.H. Marshall, "Citizenship and Social Class" in *Citizenship and Social Class and other essays* (Cambridge: Cambridge University Press, 1950).

gains'.[20] Indeed, the state may only interfere with these rights to an extent that is "clearly definable and then only through a regulated procedure."[21] This means that interferences by the executive with the individual's fundamental rights should be based on restrictions that are endorsed by the legislature. Moreover, when his rights are interfered with, the individual has the right to have the interference reviewed by an independent judiciary. When assessing whether an infringement of a fundamental right has occurred, judges should not merely examine whether the executive has acted in accordance with the rules laid down by the legislature, but they should also assess whether the interference itself is not in breach with the core of the right in question. When called upon to resolve conflicts between human rights and competing public interests, judges will thus have to reconcile the 'special status' of such rights with the legitimate power of the state to set limits to their exercise. Although legal theorists disagree over the question as to whether the very act of balancing human rights with considerations of public utility is adequate for the adjudication of human rights claims,[22] the practice of constitutional adjudication shows that the proportionality principle plays a fundamental role in safeguarding the special status of human rights by ensuring that they are not *simply* traded away for other social gains.[23]

3.2.3 A Brief Note on Constitutionalism's Limits

The idea of constitutionalism thus thwarts assertions of sovereignty as power without restraint. Especially when it concerns the fundamental rights of the individual, political power is clearly circumscribed according to legal rules that simultaneously set formal and material limits to its exercise. Nonetheless, it should not be forgotten that there are situations in which the normal

---

[20] 'The language may be that of Nozickian "side-constraints" or Dworkinian "rights as trumps" or the Rawlsian "lexical priority of basic rights" but the moral instinct of the liberal is typically to give some special status (even if not an absolute priority) to the protection of basic liberties, which means that they cannot simply be traded away for other social gains.' I. Loader and N. Walker, *Civilizing Security* (Cambridge: Cambridge University Press, 2007), 55.

[21] Schmitt (2008), 202.

[22] J. Habermas, *Between Facts and Norms: Contributions to a Discourse Theory of Law and Democracy* (Cambridge: MIT Press, 1996), 256. See also B. Çalı, "Balancing Human Rights? Methodological Problems with Weights, Scales and Proportions," *Human Rights Quarterly* 29 (2007), 251; and R. Alexy, "Balancing, constitutional review and rationality," *Ratio Juris* 16 (2003), 136.

[23] S. Greer, "Balancing" and the European Court of Human Rights: A Contribution to the Habermas-Alexy Debate," *Cambridge Law Journal* 63 (2004); and A. McHarg, "Reconciling Human Rights and the Public Interest: Conceptual Problems and Doctrinal Uncertainty in the Jurisprudence of the European Court of Human Rights," *Modern Law Review* 62 (1999), 672.

constitutional guarantees of the state no longer apply. According to Carl Schmitt, it is precisely (and only) in these exceptional situations that the definition of sovereign power as the highest power makes any sense at all.

> It is precisely the exception that makes relevant the subject of sovereignty, that is, the whole question of sovereignty. The precise details of an emergency cannot be anticipated, nor can one spell out what may take place in such a case, especially when it is truly a matter of extreme emergency and of how it is to be eliminated. [...] The most guidance the constitution can provide is to indicate who can act in such a case. If such action is not subject to controls, if it is not hampered in some ways by checks and balances, as is the case in a liberal constitution, then it is clear who the sovereign is.[24]

As Schmitt writes, an exception in this sense is not the same as anarchy and chaos, and therefore order in the juristic sense may still prevail when sovereign power emerges as 'principally unlimited authority'.[25] The appearance of sovereign power in this sense will be warranted in cases where the unity of the body politic is threatened, and in such cases the sovereign state will suspend the normal order ('the law') by reasons of self-preservation. Schmitt points at the difference between natural law theorists such as Pufendorf and Bodin on the one hand, who were very much concerned with the meaning of the exception in their theories on political power, and later, rationalist theorists on the other hand, who provided the theoretical foundation for the *constitutional* state, such as Locke and Kant. However, that is not to say that the exception has no place in today's liberal democracies that are committed to constitutional government as may well be exemplified by the contemporary security discourse in these democracies.[26]

> All tendencies of modern constitutional development point toward eliminating the sovereign in this sense. [...] But whether the extreme exception can be banished from the world is not a juristic question. Whether one has confidence and hope that it can be eliminated depends on philosophical, especially on philosophical-historical or metaphysical convictions."[27]

3.3 *Citizenship, Individual Rights, and Territory*

Constitutionalism is the product of specific historical processes that, from the seventeenth century onwards, took place within sovereign states defined by territoriality. With regard to rules regulating institutional design, their

---

[24] Schmitt (2005), 7.
[25] Ibid., 12–13.
[26] I shall come back to securitisation in the modern state and its link with migration in Chapter 5.
[27] Schmitt (2005), 7.

embeddedness in the territorial state is logical and does not bring about serious inconsistencies.[28] However, concerning individual rights, the consequences of their "particular historical institutionalisation in sovereign states"[29] may turn out to be in contradiction with their underlying ideals of the equality and dignity of universal humankind. The institutionalisation of individual rights in the state has mainly occurred in the concept of citizenship, a concept that impinges also significantly on life outside constitutional affairs.[30] My account of modern citizenship is divided into three parts. Section 3.3.1 addresses the factual circumstances that gave birth to modern citizenship, and I shall argue there as well that the very tension that we find at the heart of the modern state between an ideal of universal humankind and a particularistic reality also expresses itself in the concept of citizenship. In section 3.3.2 the implications of this tension for the rights of the individual are discussed. We will not only see that universal rights have been actualised mostly within national states, but that *national citizenship* became a necessary condition for access to those rights that one supposedly enjoys by virtue of belonging to universal humankind. Subsequently, in section 3.3.3, I shall focus on citizenship's role in a *global structure of sovereign states* based on clearly demarcated territory in order to argue that 'outsiders' are not only denied access to fundamental rights on account of the internal sovereign claims of the national state, but that discrimination against them is also a structural aspect of the Westphalian state system.

3.3.1 Citizenship: An Apparent Paradox?

The idea of citizenship itself is much older than the existence of the territorial state. Since ancient Athens, theories of citizenship have rested on some idea of political participation.[31] However, citizenship as a status that accords people, at least formally, a uniform collection of rights and duties by virtue of their membership of the polity is a distinctly modern idea, which developed in the

---

[28] Which is not to say that the forms of accountability they create may be found wanting in view of the current trends of globalisation. See for examples of these problems and the possible solutions thereto: J. Cohen and C. Sabel, "Gobal Democracy," *International Law and Politics* 37 (2005); and E. Erman, "Rethinking Accountability in the Context of Human Rights," *Res Publica* 12 (2006).
[29] J. Huysmans, "Discussing Sovereignty and Transnational Politics," in *Sovereignty in transition*, ed. N. Walker (Oxford: Hart Publishing, 2003) on democratic forms of politics.
[30] C. Tilly, "Why worry about Citizenship?" in *Extending Citizenship, Reconfiguring States*, eds. M. Hanagan and C. Tilly (Lanham: Rowman and Littlefield Publishers, 1999), 253.
[31] K. Rubenstein, "Globalization and Citizenship and Nationality," in *Jurisprudence for an interconnected globe*, ed. C. Dauvergne (Aldershot: Ashgate, 2003), 160.

framework of the emerging nation state. In all accounts of citizenship as it emerged after the French Revolution, two notions are emphasised. The first represents membership of the polity, which, as a marker of identity, creates a clear boundary between inside and outside, and the second connotes a legal status, endowing the individual with a set of rights and responsibilities. Most writers on citizenship have depicted these two elements of citizenship as conflicting with each other; the tension that exists between them making their synthesis in a single concept seem a paradox. Partly this tension is explained by the fact that modern citizenship fused two ways of thinking about liberty.[32]

The first, dating much further back than the second, relates to the extent to which the individual can partake in political affairs. Citizenship of ancient Greece was based on such a republican notion of liberty. The idea of political participation in the modern state is determined by the collective right to exercise popular sovereignty.[33] The second way of thinking about liberty is a modern one, and its appearance on the political stage dates from the Enlightenment era. Instead of a political concept, it is a legal notion, which is based on equality and is characterised by the rights of the individual.[34] When these two ways of thinking about liberty are merged in the single concept of citizenship a certain tension will surface. For to lay claim to a right based on the universal equality of mankind one does not need any further qualifying conditions than to be human, but in order to claim a part in collective decision making about the future of the polity, one has to form, by definition, part of that collective. Precisely this tension is what Pietro Costa refers to when he writes that citizenship is a seemingly successful synthesis between two very different traditions, the first being the one based on the unbreakable ties between the individual and the body politic and the second embodied by the natural law paradigm in which the individual is the symbol of sovereignty and the immediate titleholder of rights.[35]

However, there is more to modern citizenship. Ties between the individual and the body politic are not stable and neither are they necessarily unbreakable. Furthermore, they need not be based on criteria that are exclusive. As such, the republican notion of citizenship as participation in the body politic is not the same as citizenship as a marker of identity as the communitarian

---

[32] R. de Lange, "Paradoxes of European Citizenship," in *Nationalism, Racism and the Rule of Law*, ed. P. Fitzpatrick (Aldershot: Dartmouth Publishing Company, 1995).
[33] Ibid., 97.
[34] Ibid., 98.
[35] P. Costa, "The Discourse of Citizenship in Europe, A Tentative Explanation," in *Privileges and rights of citizenship: law and the juridical construction of civil society*, eds. J. Kirshner and L. Mayali (Berkeley: Robbins Collection Publications, 2002), 218-219.

tradition has it. Nonetheless, modern citizenship developed simultaneously with the modern state and accordingly it was influenced by the very ambiguities that are inherent in the concept of the modern state. Indeed, citizenship's innate tension is the same as that which can be discerned in the concept of the modern state and which indeed lies at the heart of modernity: tension between ideals concerning the universality of mankind and particularistic claims of distinct communities, *in casu* distinguished by varying national origins – however these may be understood or defined. In the course of history, nationalism determined which ties between people and state were to be politically relevant. As such, by putting citizenship on a par with *national identity*, nationalism has magnified the potential for conflict between the different ideas that underlie citizenship. More than in contemporary nationalism, which has become a particularistic claim *per se*, the paradox between human universality and political particularism remains deeply ingrained in the discourse on citizenship. Indeed, much of the 'moral capital' that has accumulated in the course of resistance to the growth of state power is embodied in the concept of citizenship.[36] Nevertheless, through its equation with nationality and identity the very concept of citizenship is simultaneously employed to defend a certain distinction between the inside and the outside.[37]

> The citizenship project is about the expansion of equality among citizens. But as equality is based upon membership, citizenship status forms the basis of an exclusive politics and identity.[38]

Chapter 2 made clear how the universalistic ideals inspired by the French Revolution developed into particularistic realities. The question that I will seek to answer here is how this development relates to the notion of citizenship, as we know it today. Before the French Revolution, certain parts of Europe did have urban citizenship, providing those who were fortunate enough to possess it with autonomy, control of guild institutions and even social welfare entitlements at the local level.[39] However, after the Revolution a new kind of citizenship spread over Europe. As the Revolutionaries wished to abolish all titles of distinction that were current during the old regime, the concept of equality of all members of the body politic required a novel notion. Accordingly, the French Declaration of the Rights of Man and Citizen expressed the very ideal

---

[36] A. Linklater, *The transformation of political community* (Cambridge: Polity Press, 1998), 169.
[37] As such, citizenship has turned into an issue of identity in the communitarian tradition, which is not necessarily the result of a republican view of citizenship.
[38] Rubenstein (2003), 163.
[39] M. Hanagan, "Recasting citizenship: Introduction," *Theory and Society* 26 (1997), 398; and Marshall (1950).

of the equality of universal mankind in the concept of *citizenship*. Rights and freedoms based on a notion of universal humankind thus found their place in a political discourse that would retain its relevance in the future as it could be adapted to fit all kinds of struggles for equality on a national scale. Fitzsimmons captures very well how the new idea of equality related to the concept of the *nation*, when he writes that "membership in the nation, rather than privilege mediated through the monarch, became the basis for political rights in the polity."[40] Thus, theories of popular sovereignty were the driving force behind the transformation of subjects of a King to citizens of a nation. It should be noted that for the early Revolutionaries the distinction between man and citizen was not problematic: the title of French Citizen could be accorded to foreigners, living in France or abroad, who "in various areas of the world, [had] caused human reason to ripen and blazed the trail of liberty"[41].

However, citizenship was profoundly affected by the changing character of the concept of the nation. As we have seen in the previous chapter, that concept – originally founded on equality and liberty – acquired completely different connotations in the course of the nineteenth century when its emphasis shifted from 'demos' to 'ethnos'. As a result, citizenship became a tool in states' exclusionist practices, instead of a principle that aimed at the realisation of ideals concerning universal humankind, albeit on a small (territorial!) scale. But before turning to these changing connotations of nation and citizenship, the beginning of which were marked by the Revolutionary Wars, it is necessary to add some additional observations regarding the early emergence and development of citizenship.

Ideals of popular sovereignty have led to citizenship as a theoretical notion. However, it is important to bear in mind that the 'moral capital' that accumulated in the notion of citizenship was not just a result of political ideals and a theoretical discourse based on universalistic conceptions of justice and equality. Certainly, sovereignty in the form of direct rule based on representation required the notion of citizenship in order to solve the legitimation problem posed by the abstract notion of popular sovereignty and to perceive of equality in a logically coherent manner. But in addition to the revolutionary ideals that made citizenship as a concept ideologically conceivable, it was direct rule as was exercised by the modern state which made citizenship practically possible

---

[40] M.P. Fitzsimmons, "The National Assembly and the Invention of Citizenship," in *The French Revolution and the Meaning of Citizenship*, eds. R. Waldinger, P. Dawson and I. Woloch (Westport, London: Greenwood Press, 1993), 32.

[41] J. Kristeva, *Strangers to Ourselves* (New York: Columbia University Press, 1991), 156. See also L. Ferrajoli, "Beyond sovereignty and citizenship: a global constitutionalism," in *Constitutionalism, Democracy and Sovereignty*, ed. R. Bellamy, (Aldershot: Avebury, 1996), 153.

and necessary. Put more prosaically, the content of modern citizenship is the result of war, coercion and violence, and of struggles from below.⁴²

This link between citizenship and state power is emphasised in the writings of Charles Tilly, who describes the role played by warfare, state expansion and direct rule with regard to the emergence of citizenship. When, in the second half of the eighteenth century, states were in need of continually bigger armies, they no longer relied so much on mercenaries, but started to draw troops from their own populations. Taxation of the population was the way in which they financed increasing military activity. Resistance by domestic populations to these practices led to citizenship:

> Both ordinary people and their patrons fought war-impelled taxation, conscription, seizures of goods and restrictions on trade by means ranging from passive resistance to outright rebellion, put down with varying combinations of repression, persuasion and bargaining. The very acts of intervening, repressing, persuading and bargaining formed willy-nilly the institutions of direct rule. Out of struggle emerged citizenship, a continuing series of transactions between persons and agents of a given state in which each has enforceable rights and obligations uniquely by virtue of the persons' membership in an exclusive category, a category of native born or naturalized people.⁴³

Thus Tilly emphasises the role played by warfare and state expansion in the processes that led to the establishment of citizenship – what he calls "the causal chain from military activity to citizenship". In a similar vein, Andrew Linklater regards citizenship as a reaction to the "totalising project", with which he refers to the efforts that were made by central governments to homogenise communities, and their creation of clear mechanisms to distinguish inside from outside in order to meet the challenges of war.⁴⁴ As such, he argues, states' totalising practices led to the elaboration of citizenship rights, because when 'subjects' were confronted with the extension of state power and the increasingly demanding and restrictive character of political communities, they were simply forced to organise political and legal rights.⁴⁵ In addition, he stresses the importance of capitalism and production processes in the process of establishing direct rule and the expansion of citizenship's moral potential.⁴⁶

I have briefly dealt with these more factual roots of citizenship because it is essential to understand that citizenship is not merely a concept which was

---

⁴² C. Tilly, "The Emergence of Citizenship in France and Elsewhere," *International Review of Social History* 40, suppl. 3 (1995).
⁴³ Ibid., 230.
⁴⁴ Linklater (1998), 6.
⁴⁵ Ibid., 146–147.
⁴⁶ See also Marshall (1950).

conjured up in an age dominated by ideals regarding equality and universality of mankind, but that it is very much linked to actual processes of state formation and the operations of sovereign power. For these reasons, a thorough grasp of the notion of citizenship cannot limit itself to a mere investigation into the way in which that concept features in political theory, but it needs to take into account the actualities of political power. Only a combination of both perspectives of citizenship is able to capture its transformative potential by making explicit that it has been adapted to support all kinds of struggles for equality. Indeed, in Marshall's classic account of modern citizenship, depicting the evolution of civil to political to social rights, its powerful potential for equality and universality clearly surfaces.

Nevertheless, as I have mentioned above, there is also a particularistic side to citizenship, one that was emphasised by the role which the nation assumed on Europe's political stage during the nineteenth century and onwards. As we have seen in the previous chapter, by the time that the Napoleonic wars had swept over Europe, territoriality and sovereignty were firmly anchored political concepts. Citizenship became inextricably linked to these concepts. Citizenship was territorial because the population over which the state exercised its rule was territorially defined. But the role that nationalism was to play in the subsequent century with regard to the setting of boundaries to the political community shaped citizenship's political particularism in an even more decisive (and insidious) way. Nationality and citizenship developed into interchangeable terms in a manner that could not have been foreseen by the Revolutionaries who drew up the Declaration of the Rights of Man and the Citizen. We have seen how nationalism in the nineteenth century caused the discourse of sovereignty to become thoroughly particularistic, therewith leaving behind universalistic approaches that were based on the idea of a common humanity. These tendencies reached their zenith in the twentieth century during the period between the two World Wars.[47] Citizenship became an indicator as well as an instrument of exclusion and provided protection only for those who 'belonged'.

The conflicting tendencies of the modern state are thus exemplified by the role and content of citizenship during this period. The contraction of the political community in the twentieth century was synchronous with the extension of citizenship rights internally. These may seem contradictory tendencies, but perhaps it is more accurate, following Linklater, to depict them as trends that reinforced each other.[48] When welfare rights became part of the citizenship

---

[47] Linklater (1998), 161.
[48] Ibid., 150.

package, states acquired more influence in the everyday lives of their citizens. The totalising project thus received new impetus, national feelings were strengthened, and as a result transnational loyalties weakened. On the other hand, it was also nationalism that shaped the conditions for unprecedented levels of social and political mobilisation.[49] Although the interaction between nationalism and citizenship is complex and cannot be regarded as solely leading to a more exclusive notion of citizenship, citizenship's political particularism was undoubtedly enhanced by nationalism. The hostile way in which national governments responded to the issue of displaced people after the First World War and dealt with large migration flows in the latter half of the twentieth century emphasises the new function that citizenship has assumed since its invention in the nineteenth century.

Thus, the universalistic ideals that originally underpinned modern citizenship were gradually overshadowed by the instrumentalist use that the modern state made of the concept in order to distinguish the inside from the outside. In this respect it is important to remember that before the modern *nation state* came into existence, states also defined their social boundaries in terms of who is and who is not included in the community. However, when government was not yet based on popular sovereignty, membership had just meant that one was subjected to the authorities of that state.[50] Popular sovereignty, social contract theories and the idea of natural rights changed the meaning of membership in ways that are not immediately self-evident. Finally, in order to understand territoriality's fundamental role in the particularistic connotations that citizenship has acquired in the course of history, it is important to emphasise once again that the initial question of membership of the political community cannot be settled by social contract theories. Whether one does or does not belong to 'the people' is ultimately only determined by territoriality and jurisdiction, instead of by any (implied) contract.[51] The precise implications of citizenship's particularism for the rights of the individual shall be dealt with below.

3.3.2 National Citizenship as a Condition for Access to Universal Rights

Whereas in the eighteenth century citizenship was meant to provide equality to all because the distinction between man and citizen was not seen as

---

[49] Ibid., 145.
[50] J. Habermas, "The European Nation-state - Its Achievements and Its Limits. On the Past and Future of Sovereignty and Citizenship," in *Mapping the Nation*, ed. G. Balakrishnan, (London: Verso, 1996), 285.
[51] F. Kratochwil, "Citizenship: On the Border of Order," in *The Return of Culture and Identity in IR Theory*, eds. Y. Lapid, and F. Kratochwil (Boulder: Lynne Rienner Publishers, 1996), 183.

problematic, presently we live in an age in which this distinction has become a highly significant one. In this section we will see that universal rights have not only been actualised mostly within national states, but that citizenship became a necessary condition for access to those rights that one supposedly has by virtue of belonging to universal humankind. In order to understand this process properly, we need to take into account the political forces that shaped the nation state and take a closer look at the development of the concept of the Rights of Man and their subsequent implementation in political reality.

When the Rights of Man were reinvented in the Enlightenment era, they were proclaimed as inalienable. They no longer flowed from religion, nor were they privileges granted by the King or any other ruler, but man himself was their source. However, we have seen that at the same time they became linked to the right of the people to self-government. Thus, when for the first time in history man appeared as an individual who carried rights without reference to a larger order, these rights almost immediately came to be identified with the rights of peoples, guaranteed by the concept of the nation.[52] As Julia Kristeva observes, "the man supposedly independent of all government turns out to be the citizen of a nation."[53]

The explanation for the duality of man/citizen at the heart of the French Declaration is the interdependence of sovereignty and rights. And if, on the one hand, the modern state based on popular sovereignty was an effective and powerful vehicle for the protection and implementation of the Rights of Man, that state at the same time set obvious limits to the universalism of those rights.[54] Equal rights and freedoms were secured through membership in the nation that was constituted by the 'people'. Even though the French Revolution, with its emphasis on universal humankind, is hostile to any pre-constitutional concept of the people,[55] we have seen in the previous chapter how theories of popular sovereignty open the door to particularistic nationalist claims due to the fact that liberal theory fails to define what is meant by a concept as intangible and elusive as the people. The resulting potential for nationalist claims is

---

[52] H. Arendt, *The Origins of Totalitarianism* (San Diego/New York/London: Harcourt Brace and Company, 1976), 291; and N. Xenos, "Refugees: The Modern Political Condition," in *Challenging Boundaries. Global Flows, Territorial Identities*, eds. M.J. Shapiro, and H.R. Alker (Minneapolis: University of Minneapolis Press, 1996), 233.
[53] Kristeva (1991), 150.
[54] Shafir (2004), 24.
[55] H. Brunkhorst, "Rights and the Sovereignty of the People in the Crisis of the Nation State," *Ratio Iuris*. 13 (2000), 51.

strengthened in a system where the organisation of political life on the basis of clear territorial demarcations is a fact.

Nationalism played an ambiguous role in the development of citizenship. Without it, the political mobilisation that led to the extension and expansion of citizenship would perhaps not have been possible because for that an appeal was needed that was stronger than the abstract ideas on human rights and popular sovereignty.[56] However, the result was that only national citizenship seemed to be able to secure the actual enjoyment of the rights of man. In *The Origins of Totalitarianism* Hannah Arendt depicted this process unambiguously:

> The whole question of rights [...] was quickly and inextricably blended with the question of national emancipation; only the emancipated sovereignty of the people, of one's own people, seemed to be able to ensure them. As mankind, since the French Revolution, was conceived in the image of a family of nations, it gradually became self-evident that the people, and not the individual was the image of man.[57]

Arendt wrote that the disastrous consequences of this identification of the rights of man with the rights of citizen became clear only in the twentieth century. By then, nationalism had long lost its original function of integrating diverse social strata and peoples in one nation. Instead it had led to an exclusive ideal of the nation state purportedly constituted by a people whose bonds to each other and to its territory were pre-political. The plight of the refugees and the stateless and the sufferings of the victims of totalitarian governments in this era showed that "the Rights of Man, supposedly inalienable, proved to be unenforceable – even in countries whose constitutions were based upon them – whenever people appeared who were no longer citizen of any state."[58]

Without belonging to an organised political community of a particular sort – the territorial nation state – rights had become illusionary: the loss of national rights in practice meant the loss of human rights. The attempts of the stateless and the minorities to fight for their own national states only strengthened the perception of a natural and necessary link between the territorial state, citizenship and individual rights. In a similar manner was such a perception of the inevitability of the link between national sovereignty and rights reinforced by the minority treaties that were concluded after the First World War, which were deemed necessary to protect the rights of minorities that did not have a state of their own.[59]

---

[56] Habermas (1996), 285.
[57] Arendt (1976), 291.
[58] Ibid., 293.
[59] Shafir (2004), 23. See section 3.4.2.

After the Second World War the dangers inherent in a system in which the rights of man had "no reality and no value except as political rights, rights of the citizen"[60] was recognised. The idea of natural rights based on a truly universal humankind received new impetus, and although the nationality-territory link as such still grants unconditional access to many entitlements, formal citizenship status and rights have to a certain extent become decoupled in contemporary political societies. Human rights discourse and/or constitutional norms underlying Western liberal democracies have led to what some scholars describe as post-national citizenship, an approach to rights which is allegedly not linked to territorial or national exclusivity and to which I shall come back to in section 3.5.2, after I have dealt with the emergence of human rights law.

3.3.3 *Citizenship's Structuring Role in a Global Territorial Structure*

However, before we turn to international law, there is another aspect of citizenship that is deserving of our attention. Whereas most accounts of citizenship focus on the relation between the individual and the state, the role of citizenship on a global scale in the Westphalian state system is often ignored. Barry Hindess is a scholar who turns away from this wholly internal perspective on citizenship and examines its global role instead.[61] He argues that discrimination is not merely a result of the internal sovereign claims that contemporary states make on behalf of their own populations, but that it constitutes a requirement of the modern state system.[62]

We have already seen in chapter 2 that, by establishing external sovereignty as a principle of international relations, the Peace of Westphalia ascribed to each territorial state the exclusive government of the population within its territory.[63] States were able to establish to a large degree exclusive control over their territories and the populations within them. The important point made by Hindess is that the modern state system as such does not only regulate the conduct of states amongst each other, but that it simultaneously constitutes

---

[60] E. Balibar, *Masses, Classes and Ideas* (New York: Routledge, 1994), 212. See also J. Edwards, "Asylum Seekers and Human Rights," *Res Publica* 7 (2001).

[61] It can be argued that the concept of nationality, and not citizenship, should be used to describe the external manifestation of membership. However, in this chapter I seek to argue that precisely because of territoriality, the two notions have become inextricably intertwined as exemplified by the term 'national citizenship'.

[62] B. Hindess, "Citizenship in the international management of populations," *American Behavioral Scientist*. 43 (2000); and B. Hindess, "Divide and Rule: The International Character of Modern Citizenship" *European Journal of Social Theory* 1 (1998).

[63] Hindess (1998), 65.

"a dispersed regime of governance covering the overall populations of the states concerned."[64] This regime of governance is dependent on the division of humanity into distinct national populations, with their own territories and states. The notion of national citizenship serves as an instrument for a system of global governance that determines who belongs where. Citizenship's particularism is accordingly not only the result of the internal sovereign claim of the state to determine its own boundaries. Distinctions between nationals and foreigners are also an inevitable outcome of the Westphalian state system that partitions "humanity into citizens of a plurality of states (and a minority who are both displaced and stateless)."[65]

By looking at citizenship's structural role in the territorial state system important insights surface that are lost when we depict citizenship solely as a national project that gradually turned the privileges of the few into the rights of the many. In our contemporary global system, citizenship is an important tool for an ongoing construction of territory as a political concept. It is a fundamental notion in order to maintain a global political system based on territoriality, as it perpetuates "an image of a world divided into 'national' populations and territories, domiciled in terms of state membership."[66] The notion of the nation state as a container of society plays an important role here: the assumption that various sovereign states constitute a world system of separate, closed and homogenous units.[67] The era after the Second World War provides a clear example of the process by which identity and territory are linked and by which the latter is inscribed with strong political meaning: massive population transfers based on ethnicity were tellingly called 'repatriation' and those people without a nationality were termed 'displaced'.

A purely internal account of citizenship ignores the structural role of citizenship in the Westphalian state system. Citizenship can be understood as a project that gradually led to turning the privileges of the few into the rights of the many *only* if the national state is perceived as a closed container, in which the only relevant political processes take place. If, in contrast, we perceive territorial boundaries not as natural and self-evident, but as features of political life that have grown out of particular historical contingencies, then it becomes, to say the least, doubtful whether citizenship has really turned the privileges of the few into the rights of the many. The boundary between the privileged and

---

[64] Id.
[65] Ibid., 66.
[66] W. Walters, "Deportation, Expulsion, and the International Police of Aliens," *Citizenship Studies* 6 (2002), 282.
[67] J. Tully, *Strange multiplicity: Constitutionalism in an age of diversity* (Cambridge: Cambridge University Press, 1997), 187.

those without rights may simply have been relocated or changed in character when the territorial state came into existence.

In addition, by focussing on the citizens of the most prosperous and democratic countries, most theoretical accounts of citizenship ignore the fact that all human beings are supposed to be citizens of some kind of political community.[68] It is exactly with regard to individuals whose national rights do not match the standard account of citizenship that citizenship's particularism becomes truly problematic. People detained in waiting zones at European airports, or those intercepted on the Mediterranean certainly are citizens of one state or another. But instead of being a guarantee for social, political or economic rights in their home countries (the absence of which in many cases constituted the very reason for their departure), the discourse of citizenship denies these people the possibility to pursue these rights elsewhere. Thus, by allocating populations to specific states, the *global institution* of national citizenship implicitly endorses the view that only national self-emancipation is suitable for securing the Rights of Man.

Hence, the two aspects of citizenship that I have discussed in this chapter – citizenship as a condition for access to rights and citizenship as a tool for allocating populations to specific territories – interact to reinforce the ideal of national sovereignty and territoriality. Hannah Arendt explained the lack of attention for the concept of human rights during the nineteenth century by arguing that such rights were supposed to be embodied in the notion of citizenship and that, in theory, all members of humanity could achieve citizenship rights.

> All human beings were supposed to be citizens of some kind of political community; if the laws of their country did not live up to the demands of the rights of Man, they were supposed to change them, by legislation in democratic countries, or through revolutionary action in despotisms.[69]

The idealisation of national sovereignty and the interconnectedness of the concept of rights and territoriality, both inherent in a perception of citizenship as recounted by Arendt, are apparent when we realise that the words with which Hindess condemns the contemporary international discourse of citizenship essentially express the same idea:

> The teleological discourse of citizenship promises the poorest of the world that, if only they would stay at home and learn to behave themselves, they too could be citizens like us.[70]

---

[68] Hindess (2000), 1495.
[69] Arendt (1976), 293.
[70] Hindess (2000), 1496.

As such, for many people citizenship offers far less than protection against sovereign power: it justifies their exclusion and it sustains inequality on a global scale. In section 3.5 I shall investigate whether so-called post-national citizenship has severed the link between nationality, rights and territory so as to offer more inclusive protection against sovereign power. Post-national conceptions of citizenship, which are based upon a notion of rights that is no longer nationally exclusive, partly emerged in response to developments in international law. It is to these developments that I shall turn first.

3.4. *International Law and Violence*

In this section I shall investigate the way in which international law has set limits to the use of violence by the state. However, before I do that, some preliminary remarks about the relationship between sovereignty and international law are necessary. Realists have often portrayed the Westphalian system as providing law and morality solely within states while outside these states anarchy and chaos reign. The international environment is seen as a permanent Hobbesian state of nature. And how else could it be, these realists ask, in the absence of an international Leviathan: a 'supranational' authority that manages the relations between sovereigns? According to thinkers such as Hobbes, Rousseau and Morgenthau the very concept of state sovereignty necessarily entails anarchy in international relations. And certainly, in view of the sheer number of international conflicts, "the history of international relations since the days of the Westphalia treaties provides overwhelming evidence that [theirs] is a reasonably accurate depiction of the dynamics of relations between states."[71] It is true that the concept of sovereignty as elaborated upon in the previous chapter precludes an 'international sovereign' who rules over sovereign nation states. A realist account of international relations is inevitable in Hobbes' theory of sovereignty, where government is identified with force and it is a logical impossibility for the sovereign to be bound.

However, contemporary international reality also demonstrates that restrictions on the liberty of states to manage their affairs are legion.[72] To understand these restrictions it is essential to be aware that sovereignty is not only a monopoly over the legitimate means of coercion, and neither does it constitute merely ultimate authority, but that these aspects of sovereignty are also

---

[71] K.J. Holsti, *International Politics. A framework for analysis* (New Jersey: Prentice Hall, 1995), 6.
[72] I. Brownlie, *Principles of Public International Law* (Oxford: Oxford University Press, 2003), 369; and B.Z. Tamanaha, *On the rule of law* (Cambridge: Cambridge University Press, 2004), 131.

exercised exclusively within a certain territory. Westphalian sovereignty entails the exclusion of external authority from the territory of the state. Thus, although sovereignty was initially thought of as a concept to conceptualise and justify authority within the state, its territorial form inevitably came to bear upon relations among states.

The result was that a system of international law came into existence alongside the emergence of the system of sovereign states. Nevertheless, in spite of the normative and regulating character of international law, it should be clear from the outset that there are limits to what international law in its current form can achieve. Some authors have found the reason for these limits generally in the configurations of state interest and the distribution of state power.[73] In this book, I argue more specifically that the existence of these limits, expressed in the near immunisation of territorial sovereignty against legal forms of correction, are due to the reification of territoriality as an organising principle for the modern state system.

We will see below that in international law, the regulation of violence and territorial boundaries are connected to each other by much the same logic as that which binds people, territory and authority within the nation state. Similarly, the same tension that exists between particularism and universalism in the idea of the nation state and its accompanying concepts, such as citizenship, comes to the fore in international law, albeit in a different fashion. Here the tension between universalistic ideals and a reality that is to a high degree particularistic is expressed in differing conceptions about who are the subjects of international law. The way in which this tension is resolved has profound implications for which kinds of violence have become a matter of concern for international law. Whether one believes that "only states have international legal personality" or assumes that, on the contrary, "individuals are the true and exclusive legal persons"[74] makes an enormous difference, especially in this area of international law.

In section 3.4.1, I shall recount how classical international law has resolved this tension in favour of the national territorial state. Section 3.4.2 addresses the types of violence that classical international law deals with. The consequences of the ideal of the national territorial state dominating the international legal discourse regarding state violence will be illustrated with examples relating to the regulation of interstate violence, diplomatic protection and the treatment of minorities under international law. Lastly, in section 3.4.3, I shall

---

[73] J.L. Goldsmith and E.A. Posner, *The Limits of International Law* (Oxford: Oxford University Press, 2005), 13.

[74] J.E. Nijman, *The concept of international legal personality: An inquiry into the history and theory of international law* (The Hague: T.M.C. Asser Press, 2004), 6.

focus on international human rights law and will seek an answer to the question whether the state-based approach of classical international law, based upon the same obdurate link between sovereignty, territory and identity as is embodied in the notion of citizenship, has been abandoned there.

3.4.1 *The Sovereign State as the True and Only Subject of International Law*

International law emerged at a time when the state was not yet the decisive political entity it was later to become, and in early international law, the individual was fully included. The influence of ideas which had their roots in the *Res Publica Christiana*, such as the notion that the rights of individuals were morally prior to the rights of the body politic to which they belonged, were for a long time palpable in international law. Indeed, early theorists of international law were natural lawyers and they argued that assertions of what is now called Westphalian sovereignty are subject to clear limits. Francisco de Vitoria (1480–1546) and Francisco Suarez (1548–1617) grounded international law in the divine order, in which the individual had its own place. Hugo Grotius (1583–1645) modernised the law of nations, as he maintained that its content could be based on reason. For him, international law was still natural law, but no longer divine. In Grotius' law of nations the individual featured as a subject, inevitably, in view of the foundation for his *ius gentium*: a society of sovereigns and their subjects who were united in the natural bond of mankind.[75]

Chapter 2 described how the emergence of the modern state with its reliance on territory and the concept of the nation caused the universalistic ideals from the Enlightenment era to translate in a political particularistic reality. Similarly, with the emergence of the modern state, the tension in international law, which expresses itself *inter alia* with regard to the question as to who are its subjects, gradually began to be decided in favour of the nation state, and the individual loses much of his relevance as a subject of international law. Paradoxical as it may seem (again), Enlightenment ideals influenced this process in a twofold manner.

First, that influence was indirect, as a result of the process by which the state based on the modern notion of popular sovereignty clearly differentiated between inside and outside. A consequence was that the nation state was gradually perceived as a unified force, with supreme and exclusionary authority within a clearly demarcated territory. The manner in which this conception of the state influenced international law is aptly illustrated by the work of Christian Wolff (1679–1754). While still a natural law theorist, instead of according natural rights to individuals, he ascribes them to states which are to

---

[75] Ibid., 46–47.

him the exclusive subjects of international law. One of the natural rights of states was the right to non-interference by other states.[76]

A second trend that contributed to the demise of the individual in international law was the emergence of empiricist theories during the Enlightenment. Instead of deriving international law from absolute principles, it was reinterpreted in terms of what actually happened between states.[77] The work of Emmerich de Vattel (1714–1767) marks the transition from natural law theories in international law to an approach that identified the law of nations with positive law between sovereign states. To him, as to Wolff, the exclusion of external authority, as a characteristic of sovereignty, was one of the cornerstones of the law of nations. Under the influence of legal positivism in the eighteenth century, the law of nations came to rely fully upon national sovereignty, and legal personality in international law became dependant on absolute sovereignty.[78]

In this way, the role of the state in international law was doubly emphasised. Eighteenth century ideals of individualism and human equality did not lead to a strengthening of the position of the individual in international law. On the contrary, just as they had contributed towards nationalism and hostility towards outsiders within the nation state, they consolidated the importance of the sovereign state in international law as the sole bearer of rights. In the nineteenth century, this tendency in international law was reinforced as idealised concepts such as nation and state were romantically perceived as one. As a result, the idea of the individual as a subject of international law had become unthinkable in the late nineteenth century, with its Hegelian glorification of the state and national sovereignty. In short, a positivist approach which obscured the natural law origins of international law, combined with the mythic dimension the state had acquired, by use of idealised or constructed concepts such as territory and nationality, led to a perception of international law as law solely for and by states.[79]

In those few cases where the individual featured, his position was derived from and dependent on the will of the sovereign state,[80] as we will see below.

---

[76] Ibid., 82.
[77] M.N. Shaw, *International Law* (Cambridge: Cambridge University Press, 1997), 22.
[78] Nijman (2004), 111.
[79] Note that sovereignty did not only function as a shield between the individual and the international legal system. By defining it as something exclusively European, it excluded for a long time non-Western states and indigenous communities from international law. See A. Orford, "The destiny of international law," *Leiden Journal of International Law* 17 (2004), 470.
[80] C. Harding and C.L. Lim, "The significance of Westphalia: an archaeology of the international legal order" in *Renegotiating Westphalia. Essays and commentary on the European and conceptual foundations of modern international law*, eds. C. Harding and C.L. Lim (The Hague: Kluwer Law International, 1999), 5.

This situation would last until 1945, although already before that time voices were heard to make the international legal system more inclusive by deconstructing the "artificial and absolute separation" that existed between the state and its citizens in international law.[81] A perception of the territorial state as the sole subject of international law has had a strong impact on the regulation and legitimisation of violence by international law, as we will see shortly.

3.4.2 Types of Violence Regulated by Classical International Law

Here I shall outline the forms of violence that traditional international law regulates and the ways in which it purports to do that. Far from being an in-depth investigation of this field of international law, this outline serves to further elucidate some aspects of the relationship between sovereign power, territory, and people. As a result, we will see that both the way in which international law offers protection against state violence and the way in which it determines whether the use of force is legitimate or not is to a large degree determined by the concept of national sovereignty. Although the relevance of inter-state violence, humanitarian law, diplomatic protection and the treatment of minorities may not seem directly apparent for the subject under consideration in this book, I shall elaborate on these issues in order to illustrate that the international legal regime dealing with violence is decisively shaped by the way in which territorial boundaries were drawn in the past and by the meanings that were subsequently ascribed to them. Only a thorough understanding of this structural characteristic of international law will make it possible to evaluate the alleged novelty of international human rights law.

Inter-state Violence
We have seen in chapter 2 that the emergence of a territorial state system led to a new structure delimiting legitimate and illegitimate violence. Before political authority came to be framed territorially, the absence of a clear mechanism to determine 'us' from 'them' made it impossible to distinguish between war and mere crime, even though there were religious theories justifying the use of violence in specific instances, such as the doctrine of just war.[82] It was only through the establishment of the Westphalian order that war could be distinguished from mere crime by defining it as something that only sovereign states engaged in.[83] In nineteenth century conceptions of international law, the

---

[81] Nijman (2004), 128.
[82] R.W. Mansbach, and F. Wilmer, "War, Violence and the Westphalian State System as a Moral Community" in *Identities, Borders, Orders: Rethinking IR Theory*, eds. M. Albert, D. Jacobson and Y. Lapid (Minneapolis: University of Minnesota Press, 2000), 56.
[83] M. Van Creveld, *Transformation of War* (New York, London, Free Press, 1991), 41.

right of a state to wage war in order to settle disputes with other states was regarded as a fundamental aspect of that state's sovereignty and the sovereign state's interest was perceived as a legitimate reason for resorting to violence against other states, if only conditioned by the requirement that it should be a last resort.[84]

Thus, territorialisation diminished the importance of non-state actors in this area in a twofold way: as we have seen above, only the sovereign state was in possession of international legal personality, and only violence waged by the sovereign state was regarded as legitimate. The result was that whenever the individual featured in the laws of war, his position was derived from the sovereign state's right to resort to force. The regulation of violence was monopolised by national states in a very literal sense: combatants who did not fight for a national army, such as religious minorities and sub-state rebels, were not accorded rights, just as indigenous peoples were not protected by the laws of war.[85]

After the First World War, the attitude in which the right to wage war was perceived as inherent in sovereignty changed. The Kellogg-Briand Pact of 1928 renounced war as an instrument of foreign policy except when it was resorted to in self-defence. This shift was reinforced by the Tokyo and Nuremberg trials in which Japanese and German individuals were prosecuted for planning aggressive wars: so-called crimes against the peace. Pursuant to Article 2(4) of the Charter of the United Nations, the use of force is forbidden in contemporary international relations, and the territorial integrity of sovereign states is a cornerstone of contemporary international law.[86] Nevertheless, even if the right to wage war is no longer regarded as inherent in sovereignty, the language of war has principally remained the language of the state. This is illustrated by the way in which international law has formulated exceptions to the prohibition on the use of force and the present framework of international humanitarian law (i.e. the law of armed conflict).

To begin with the legal framework dealing with the laws of war, it suffices to note that international humanitarian law remains largely constructed

---

[84] R.A. Brand, "Sovereignty: The State, the Individual, and the International Legal System in the Twenty First Century," *Hastings International and Comparative Law Review* 25 (2002), 287; and H.J. Steiner and P. Alston, *International Human Rights in Context: Law, Politics, Morals* (Oxford: Oxford University Press, 2000), 114.

[85] Mansbach and Wilmer (2001), 61.

[86] UN Charter Article 2(4): "All Members shall refrain in their international relations from the threat or use of force against the territorial integrity or political independence of any state, or in any other manner inconsistent with the purposes of the United Nations." See also International Court of Justice, 27 June 1986, *Case concerning Military and Paramilitary Activities in and Against Nicaragua (Nicaragua v. U.S.A.)*, Merits, 1986 ICJ Reports 4.

against the background of the Westphalian state system. This is exemplified by the fact that norms regarding international responses to civil wars are less developed than those that regulate interstate wars; humanitarian law regulating internal conflict offers less protection than that which pertains to interstate wars; and only states can become parties to the Geneva Conventions.[87]

If we look at the exceptions to the prohibition on the threat or the use of force in inter-state relations that are currently recognised by international law, it becomes clear that these exceptions, of which there are two, are similarly modelled on the ideal of the Westphalian state system. The first one consists of the "inherent right to individual or collective self-defence if an armed attack occurs" on the state's territory.[88] In that case the use of force is entirely consistent with a structure of independent territorial entities with exclusive rule within their territories. Chapter 7 of the Charter of the United Nations furthermore allows the Security Council to take military action in case of "the existence of any threat to the peace, breach of the peace, or act of aggression", terms which have traditionally been understood as denoting war between national states. More recent developments in international law with regard to humanitarian interventions in which purely internal situations are capable of being deemed a threat to the peace, and thus justify the collective use of force under Chapter VII of the Charter, are related to the emergence of an international human rights regime, which shall be dealt with below. For now it is important to note that the law of humanitarian intervention has been criticised as being profoundly related to the way in which boundaries between 'us' and 'them' are drawn.[89] Accordingly, instead of merely emphasising the territorial component of the Westphalian system as such, the relation between humanitarian intervention and that system is more complex, and is reminiscent of the way in which it partitions humanity into distinct groups that can be territorially compartmentalised.

---

[87] J. Fitzpatrick, "Sovereignty, Territoriality and the Rule of Law," *Hastings International and Comparative Law Review* 25 (2002). See also Y. Dinstein, *The International Law of Belligerent Occupation* (Cambridge: Cambridge University Press, 2009) and M. Kaldor, *New and Old Wars: Organized Violence in a Global Era* (Cambridge: Polity Press, 1999), 116.

[88] Article 51 of Chapter VII of the UN Charter.

[89] See A. Orford, *Reading Humanitarian Intervention* (Cambridge: Cambridge University Press, 2003). When commenting on modern humanitarian wars Costas Douzinas writes that "war and just war have been important strategies through which sovereignty has come into existence and has been put to work. War is a central element of the Western symbolic, of the way in which the West has conceived of its existence, territory and importance." C. Douzinas, *Human Rights and Empire: The political philosophy of cosmopolitanism* (Milton Park: Routledge Cavendish, 2007), 87.

> Humanitarian intervention narratives work in this way – to reassure the international community that there is a differentiated other, and to locate this other 'somewhere else, outside'. [...] The notion that the suffering or chaotic other is located elsewhere is reinforced through the act of intervention – we use force to maintain 'safe havens' or to protect (local) civilians at home, while at the same time evacuating foreigners.[90]

Interestingly, Anne Orford goes on to write that it is precisely the refugee who unsettles this separation and that it is thus through the claims of the 'other' who does not stay at home that our sense of security and safety is unsettled.[91] These issues will receive closer attention in the second part of the book.

Diplomatic Protection and the Treatment of Minorities
In Chapter 2 we have seen how the Westphalian structure did not only result in a new structure by which to differentiate between legitimate and illegitimate violence, but that it also resulted in a division between internal and external violence. Violence that was resorted to by the state within its own territory has long remained within the exclusive sphere of domestic jurisdiction, consistent with the idea of sovereignty as the supreme legitimate authority within a territory. However, although international law has largely ignored the question of violence by the state within the state,[92] the treatment of minorities and foreigners constitutes exceptions to this notion of *domain réservé* in classical international law.

We have seen how in the course of history ties of allegiance, nationality and citizenship have provided the basis for the legal community of the state.[93] The protection of the rights of aliens in international law demonstrates the relevance of those very same ties in international law. International law's recognition of their significance has led to the paradox that "the individual in his capacity as an alien [enjoyed] a larger measure of protection by traditional international law than in his character as the citizen of his own state."[94] Generally speaking, classical international law decrees that foreigners may not be unlawfully discriminated against, that they have the right to respect for their life and property, and most importantly, that they are entitled to judicial

---

[90] Orford (2003),124.
[91] Id.
[92] Mansbach and Wilmer (2001), 63; J. Donelly, "Human Rights in a New World Order: Implications for a New Europe," in *Human Rights in the New Europe*, ed. D.P. Forsythe (Lincoln/London: Nebraska University Press, 1994), 8; and L. Henkin, "That 'S' Word: Sovereignty, and Globalization, and Human Rights, et Cetera," *Fordham Law Review* 68 (1999), 4.
[93] Brownlie (2003), 497.
[94] H. Lauterpacht, *International law and human rights* (Hamden: Archon Books, 1968), 121.

protection to vindicate their rights in the host country.[95] Although the significance of the individual in this field of international law is thus obvious, the traditional stance with regard to international legal personality is not abandoned here: only the sovereign state is actually accorded rights, as individuals wronged by a foreign state cannot appeal to international law. Indeed, solely national states can claim compliance with international rules to the benefit of their nationals residing abroad, which is the right to exercise so-called diplomatic protection. Neither can individuals under classical international law claim a right to seek and obtain diplomatic protection from their national state; legal entitlements to such forms of protection are a matter of domestic law alone.[96]

Diplomatic protection with respect to nationals in foreign countries has existed since the Middle Ages, but practice with modern features appeared in the late eighteenth century.[97] During the nineteenth century issues of diplomatic protection increased enormously because more people resided outside their national states than ever before.[98] From that time onwards, the place that diplomatic protection occupies in international law is determined by two features of the modern state: a strong linkage between identity and sovereignty internally, and a powerful assertion of sovereignty externally. Vattel's argument that an injury to an alien is an injury to his state,[99] illustrates the assumption by international law that the interference by one state with another one's national may constitute a breach of the sovereignty of the former state.

> In taking up a case of one of its nationals, by resorting to diplomatic protection or international judicial proceedings on his behalf, a state is in reality asserting its own right, the right to ensure in the persons of its nationals respect for the rules of international law.[100]

In the discourse concerning limitations upon a state's treatment of foreigners we can distinguish two different approaches: one which argues that it is

---

[95] A. Cassese, *International Law* (Oxford: Oxford University Press, 2005), 121. Diplomatic protection can only be invoked when the individual has exhausted the domestic remedies available in the host state.
[96] Ibid., 122.
[97] Brownlie (2003), 500.
[98] "In the century after 1840 some sixty mixed claims commissions were set up to deal with disputes arising from injury to the interests of aliens." Ibid., 500.
[99] M.S. McDougal, H.D. Lasswell and L. Chen, "The protection of aliens from discrimination and world public order: responsibility of states conjoined with human rights," *American Journal of International Law* 70 (1976).
[100] Permanent Court of International Justice, 28 February 1939, *Panavezys-Saldutiskis Railway Case (Estonia v. Lithuania)*, Ser A/B No 76 (1939).

sufficient for foreigners to be treated as nationals; the other maintaining that their treatment should live up to a minimum standard of civilisation, the so-called international minimum standard.[101] In the latter discourse, a purely state-centred discourse is abandoned in favour of an approach based on the dignity of the individual. As the latter approach prevailed it can be contended that, even though international law does not confer individuals directly with rights regarding their treatment by a foreign state, universalistic ideals based on the dignity of the individual came to play an important role in this field of law.[102]

However, the very fact that the modern state is based on ties of allegiance, nationality and citizenship, *and* its linkage of sovereignty and identity provide a rationale for the existence of a right of diplomatic protection in international law. The weight which international law attaches to the meaning of these ties is proven by its insistence that the presence of such ties is not merely a formal question. A clear illustration of the centrality of the link between sovereignty and identity in this field is provided by the International Court of Justice's decision in the *Nottebohm Case*, a case which concerned a claim that Liechtenstein had made against Guatemala regarding the treatment of one of its nationals.[103] Although the Court stated that it is the sovereign right of all states to determine the criteria for becoming a citizen in domestic law, these criteria and their subsequent application by the national state would have to be scrutinised on the international plane in questions of diplomatic protection. It found that Nottebohm's nationality could not be validly invoked by Liechtenstein against Guatemala because it did not correspond to a factual situation. According to the Court, international law can only recognise naturalisation if it constitutes a legal recognition of a person's *factual membership* of a state's population. In the Court's view, such membership is expressed by adherence to the state's traditions, its interests, way of life and by assuming the obligations and rights of its citizens. The concept of diplomatic protection in international law as applied by the Court in *Nottebohm* fits perfectly with the way in which the structural, gobal role of citizenship and the internal sovereign claims of the modern state reinforce each other. Just as legal protection within the state has traditionally been largely contingent on national identity, the principle of 'effective nationality' in the law of diplomatic protection thus makes sure that the same principle operates on the international plane.

---

[101] McDougal, Laswell and Chen (1976), 443.
[102] Although the two approaches often reflect conflicting economic and political interests. See Cassese (2005), 120; and Brownlie (2003), 503.
[103] International Court of Justice, *Nottebohm Case (Liechtenstein v. Guatemala)*, 6 April 1955, 1955 I.C.J. 4.

As such, it reinforces the Westphalian system through its insistence that each state bears responsibility only for those that supposedly have the same 'identity': those that truly 'belong' to the body politic. Perhaps superfluously, I take the opportunity to emphasise once again that such a system of allocation to the sovereign of those that 'belong' finds its basis in territorial demarcations that were made in the past. In this respect, it is imperative to take a closer look at the place that so-called minorities occupy in such a system, which by definition must be a special one. And indeed, their protection has always been a concern for international law. Chapter 2 described how the Treaties of Westphalia anchored the notion of external sovereignty in international relations by establishing mutually independent territorial political units with supreme and exclusionary authority within their domains. It is generally perceived that these treaties accordingly gave the sovereign the right to determine the religion within his territory. Nevertheless, such is not a complete account of the Treaties.[104] These also contained restrictions on the sovereign's right to regulate religious affairs in his territory by giving minority religious groups the right to practice their religion and by prohibiting religious discrimination to a certain extent.[105]

Thus, although the Peace of Westphalia established sovereignty as a principle governing international relations by ascribing a fixed territory to the sole jurisdiction of a sovereign and by categorising populations as belonging to one state or another, at the same time these Treaties impinged significantly on the supreme right of the sovereign by placing him under an obligation to protect and respect certain religious freedoms within his territory. The enforcement mechanism for these rights was largely effective, as it consisted of "a clear and easy-to-implement threat of retaliation: protestant states would conduct reprisals against their own minority population and vice versa."[106] Here it is possible to observe a conspicuous parallel with diplomatic protection: Sovereign states would regard coreligionists living in another state as a matter of their concern, just as they consider the treatment of their nationals by another state as not falling entirely within the domestic jurisdiction of the latter state. The identity of the body politic, itself largely determined by the process of territorialisation may thus in certain, well-defined cases override a purely territorialised conception of sovereign power.

After WWI, the issue of minorities was brought to the forefront of international law and the protection of minorities was placed under the guarantee

---

[104] See S.D. Krasner, "Abiding Sovereignty," *International Political Science Review* 22 (2001).
[105] Goldsmith and Posner (2005), 113.
[106] Ibid., 155.

of the League of Nations. The design of a system of minority protection by the League of Nations was prompted by the fact that many claims of self-determination by national groups in Europe were not satisfied.[107] This system was built on the basis of several documents, which regulated the situation of specific states and certain population groups living in these states.[108] Obligations concerning minority protection did not amount to a closed system of international law, as they were only imposed on certain states, and only concerned some of the minorities living under their jurisdiction.[109] The Permanent Court of International Justice formulated two general principles that form the basis of the minority protection by the Treaties. First, nationals belonging to racial, religious or linguistic minorities were to be "placed in every respect on a footing of perfect equality with the other nationals of the state." Secondly, these minorities had a right to "the preservation of the racial peculiarities, their traditions and their national characteristics."[110]

The cases of minority protection and diplomatic protection constitute an exception to the assumption that the deployment of internal violence is a matter for the sovereign state alone, in which classical international law has no role to play. Nevertheless, international laws that protect minorities and aliens do not depart from a traditional understanding of sovereignty which links authority, territory and people and makes a strict distinction between the 'inside' and the 'outside'. By providing 'outsiders' (i.e. foreigners and minorities) with protection against sovereign power, international law in this area reinforces the ideal of the nation state with its perfect link between identity and territory. Such an ideal led to a perception in which "only nationals could be citizens, only people of the same national origin could enjoy the full protection of legal institutions," and in which "people of a different national origin needed some law of exception."[111]

In addition, it should be emphasised that the Minority Treaties had a clear geopolitical aim as well which consisted of maintaining the territorial ideal: "the system of protection of minorities (…) is also intended (…) to ensure that States with a minority within their boundaries should be protected from the danger of interference by other powers in their internal

---

[107] K. Henrard, *Devising an Adequate System of Minority Protection: Individual Human Rights, Minority Rights and the Right to Self-Determination* (The Hague: Martinus Nijhoff Publishers, 2000), 4.
[108] Ibid., 4–5.
[109] See Arendt (1976), 272.
[110] Permanent Court International Justice, *Minority Schools in Albania*, Advisory Opinion of 6 April 1936.
[111] Arendt (1976), 275.

affairs."[112] Accordingly, just as with regard to the discourse of citizenship and the regulation of interstate violence, the law with regard to diplomatic protection and minorities affirms once more that "the relationship between identity and borders underlies both the process of norm articulation and the kinds of violence identified as problematic".[113]

3.4.3 *International Human Rights Law*

We have seen above that the rise of territorial concentrations of power in the Westphalian era has been checked by developments in two different areas.[114] These developments took place along separate lines and to a certain extent each followed a different logic. Internally, the growth of state power led to the demand for citizenship rights, offering protection to the people against the arbitrary use of power by the state. Externally, the state was to undergo constraints formulated by international law. The separateness of the discourses regulating internal and external restraints on state power led to a gap between national and international law. International law was the law between sovereign states, in which the regulation of violence was determined by strong territorial assumptions and in which the individual as such did not feature. The treatment by a state of its territorially defined population usually did not involve any question of international law, with its acceptance of sovereignty's exclusive link between power, territory and population. Internally, the concept of fundamental rights, based on the dignity of the individual, became linked to national sovereignty, which involved a similar exclusive linkage between territory, nationality, and citizenship. Accordingly, within the nation state, the original universality of citizenship rights gradually turned into a particularistic conception of rights, based on national belonging.

When, during the period between the two world wars, sovereignty's narrow link – internally as well as externally – between power, territory, identity and rights was at its firmest, the existence of the gap between international and domestic law resulted in the absence of any enforceable rights for large groups of individuals. The terrible consequences thereof became clear during the Second World War, exemplified as they were in factual spaces of rightlessness, such as the concentration and extermination camps and, to a lesser degree, the internment camps for displaced people and refugees.

After 1945, the welfare of the individual, irrespective of his nationality, was increasingly considered as a matter of international concern by the

---

[112] League of Nations Official Journal, Volume 9, 1928, 942.
[113] Mansbach and Wilmer (2001), 56.
[114] Linklater (1998), 213.

international community.¹¹⁵ The Nuremberg War Crimes Trials prosecuted individuals on the novel charge of crimes against humanity. Crimes committed against a state's own population became a general matter of concern for international law. Note that the Nuremberg Trials did not break completely with the territorially defined "process of norm articulation and the traditional kinds of violence identified as problematic", seeing that crimes against humanity could only be committed in connection with war crimes or crimes against the peace. Accordingly the treatment of Germany's Jewish population by the Nazis prior to 1939 was not adjudicated. However, the Trials marked an important first step in deconstructing sovereignty's function as a barrier between the individual and the international legal order. Although the criminalisation of aggression in the Trials amounted to erecting "a wall around state sovereignty", the effect of criminalising certain acts carried out against a state's own population was "to pierce the veil of sovereignty."¹¹⁶ Indirectly, the enactment of 'crimes against humanity' constituted the recognition in international law of individual rights that are superior to the law of the sovereign state.¹¹⁷

The emerging human rights regime captured in various legal documents carried this process a step further. In the Charter of the United Nations, human rights were explicitly listed as a matter of concern for the new organisation, and it imposed on its members the obligation to respect such rights, irrespective of nationality.¹¹⁸ The post-war period saw an immense proliferation of international institutions and norms dedicated to protecting human rights. Many of these norms acquired binding legal force as they became embodied in multilateral frameworks for the protection of human rights.¹¹⁹ Apart from

---

[115] S. Oda, "The Individual in International Law," in *Manual of Public International Law*, ed. M. Sørensen, 469–530 (London: MacMillan & Co, 1968), 495.

[116] D. Luban, *Legal Modernism* (Ann Arbor: University of Michigan Press, 1994), 336.

[117] Lauterpacht (1968), 38. As I am concerned with individual rights and protection against violence employed by the state, I will not look into developments that deal with individual criminal responsibility under international law. These developments, however, also give a clear indication of the diminishing importance of sovereignty as shielding the individual from the international legal system.

[118] Donnelly (1994), 8; and Lauterpacht (1968), 347.

[119] The most important of which: *Convention against Torture and Other Cruel, Inhuman or Degrading Treatment or Punishment*, 10 December 1984, G.A. Res. 39/46, U.N. GAOR, 39th Session., Supp. No. 51, at 197, U.N. Doc. A/Res/39/708 (1984); *Convention on the Elimination of all Forms of Discrimination Against Women*, 18 December 1979, G.A. Res. 34/180, U.N. GAOR 34th Sess., Supp. No. 46, at 193, U.N. Doc. 34/46/ (1980); *International Convention on the Elimination of All Forms of Racial Discrimination*, opened for signature on 7 March 1966, 660 U.N.T.S. 195; ICCPR; *International Convention on Economic, Social and Cultural Rights*, 19 December 1966, 993 U.N.T.S. 3; *Convention on the Prevention and Punishment of the Crime of Genocide*, 9 December 1948, 78 U.N.T.S. 277.

treaties that were open for signature to all states, irrespective of their geographic location, human rights were also incorporated into international law on a regional scale.[120]

In addition, certain rights of individuals have become customary international law. Irrespective of the fact whether a state has entered into specific treaty obligations with regard to the rights of the people under its jurisdiction, the prohibition on torture, genocide, slavery, racial discrimination, extra-judicial killings and disappearances have acquired the status of customary international law, or even *ius cogens*.[121] International law no longer permits states to defend violations of these rights as legitimate exercises of national sovereignty. The status of international law in this area is confirmed by the fact that states, even when violating basic human rights norms, generally do not assert a legal entitlement to do so; instead, they deny that such violations have taken place.[122]

Not only the development of individual rights was suddenly taking place beyond the nation state, aspects relating to their enforcement and implementation were in some cases transferred to the international sphere as well. International institutions, such as the United Nations' Commission on Human Rights, acquired monitoring tasks with regard to member states' human rights obligations, and in case of violations, the individual in some cases can appeal directly to an international body.[123] Nonetheless, the real enforcement and implementation of universal human rights, going further than monitoring and pressure procedures, have largely remained national.[124]

This does not mean that the real effect of international law is nugatory in this area. First of all, in the absence of effective international institutions, national judges of liberal states have assumed an important role with regard to the enforcement of international human rights norms, as will be looked into more closely below.[125] Secondly, there is an indirect effect of international

---

[120] ECHR; American Convention on Human Rights, 1969; African Charter on Human and Peoples' Rights, 1981.

[121] R. McCorquodale, "An Inclusive International Legal System," *Leiden Journal of International Law* 17 (2004), 486; and W.J. Aceves, "Relative Normativity: Challenging the Sovereignty Norm Through Human Rights Litigation," *Hastings International and Comparative Law Review* 25 (2002), 261. See also the ICJ in the *Barcelona Traction Case* (*Barcelona Traction Light and Power Co. Case (Belgium v. Spain)*, 5 February 1970 I.C.J. 3.).

[122] G.H. Fox, "New approaches to International Human Rights: The Sovereign State Revisited," in *State sovereignty: change and persistence in international relations*, ed. S.H. Hashmi (Pennsylvania: The Pennsylvania State University Press, 1997), 115–116.

[123] See the first Optional Protocol to the ICCPR.

[124] Donnelly (1994), 9.

[125] See also Aceves (2002).

human rights law in domestic systems, even when that law concerns so-called soft law: national judges may interpret national law in conformity with standards laid down in international instruments, even when those are not binding, or not ratified.[126] Thirdly, the existence and acknowledgement of international norms with regard to the dignity of the human person have important normative consequences: demands can now be framed in the language of law which make those demands more powerful and lends them a legitimacy they might have been lacking otherwise.[127]

The regional record with regard to the implementation and enforcement of human rights shows a diverse picture.[128] Asia and the Middle East lack intergovernmental regional human rights organisations, whereas Africa, Europe and the Americas have established international mechanisms to ensure the protection of fundamental rights. By far the most effective and extensive of these is the protection of human rights in the framework of the Council of Europe.

The ECHR covers mainly civil and political rights, and is ratified by all forty-one Member States of the Council of Europe. Its influence is not only felt in the domestic systems of the Member States, the majority of which have incorporated it into national law, but also the European Union, although not yet a party to the ECHR,[129] has undertaken to respect the fundamental rights as guaranteed by it.[130] The ECHR accords the individual a right of appeal to an international body, the European Court of Human Rights (ECtHR), in the case of an alleged breach of the fundamental rights protected by the Convention. Contracting parties to the ECHR have undertaken to abide by the judgments of the Court, which has, if it finds a violation of one of the rights enumerated in the Convention, the right to oblige a state to pay just satisfaction to a victim, or to take other measures. The Committee of Ministers of the Council of Europe supervises the execution of judgments, and makes recommendations with regard to general measures, in the case that domestic legislation or administrative arrangements make subsequent similar breaches

---

[126] A. Gurowitz, "International law, politics and migrant rights," in *The politics of international law* ed. C. Reus-Smit (Cambridge: Cambridge University Press, 2004), 144.

[127] Ibid., 149; D.A. Martin, "Effects of International Law on Migration Policy and Practice: The Uses of Hypocrisy," *International Migration Review* 23 (1989); and Tamanaha (2004), 131.

[128] Donnelly (1994), 9.

[129] The Reform Treaty establishes in Article 6(2) the legal basis for the EU's accession to the European Convention on Human Rights. *Treaty of Lisbon amending the Treaty on European Union and the Treaty establishing the European Community*, signed at Lisbon, 13 December 2007, OJ C 306/13, 17 December 2007.

[130] Article 6 TEU. See Spielmann, "Human Rights Case Law in the Strasbourg and Luxembourg Courts: Conflicts, Inconsistencies, and Complementarities," in *The EU and Human Rights*, ed. P. Alston (Oxford: Oxford university Press, 1999), 759–760.

of the ECHR foreseeable. Member States of the Council of Europe generally comply with the judgments of the Court, encouraged as they are by a number of pressures and interests.[131]

By its transfer to the international sphere of constitutional principles which had thus far only featured in the domestic sphere, international human rights law intends to close the aforementioned gap between national and international law. Perhaps this is best illustrated by the way in which human rights are protected in the framework of the Council of Europe, with the ECHR as an "instrument of European public order",[132] in which individuals are not only accorded international rights, but are able to secure the protection of these rights on the international plane as well.

In order to understand the way in which international human rights affect the modern state, it is helpful to distinguish between the internal and external effects of international law in this area. Externally, the sovereign state can no longer maintain that the treatment of its population is a matter of domestic jurisdiction. The individual has become a subject of international law, and it has been said that "the development of international law in this century is likely to be framed and judged not so much by the way international law defines relations between states, as by the way it defines relations between persons and states."[133] Internally (i.e. within the nation state) national citizenship can no longer legitimately be the only foundation upon which rights are determined, as international law guarantees fundamental rights irrespective of a person's nationality. The precise implications of such a 'piercing of the veil of sovereignty' in these two directions for the way in which the modern state distinguishes between inside and outside shall be dealt with in the next section.

3.5 Human Rights: Closing the Gap between Us and Them/Inside and Outside?

We have seen above that in traditional international law, Westphalian sovereignty entailed that the state was able to maintain a distinction between inside and outside. Amongst other things, it did so by designing certain areas

---

[131] For an exception, see *Loizidou vs. Turkey*, Judgments of 23 March 1995 (preliminary objections), A-310; 18 December 1996 (merits), Reports 1996-VI; and 28 July 1998 (just satisfaction), Reports 1998-IV. See also C. Ovey and R.C.A. White, *European Convention on Human Rights* (Oxford: Oxford University Press, 2002), 431–435.

[132] The ECtHR in *Loizidou v. Turkey*, (preliminary objections), 23 March 1995, par. 75.

[133] Brand (2002), 280. The development of international criminal law is of course highly significant in this regard as well.

as falling under its domestic jurisdiction, where international law had no role to play. The treatment of individuals within its territory, apart from some exceptions (in which the status of individuals under international law was derived from the sovereign status of the state), constituted one such area of domestic jurisdiction. Presently, international law has changed in this respect: the incorporation of norms concerning human dignity in international law results in an inability on the part of states to argue that national sovereignty entails that the treatment of the individuals under their jurisdiction is not a matter for international law.

As a result of these developments, contemporary international law has brought about congruence between the ideas underlying Westphalian and domestic sovereignty. Internally, sovereignty has always been "authority, not might."[134] Externally, however, it was actual power and not legal authority which constituted the basis for Westphalian sovereignty, where statehood was determined by effective control over a defined territory and a permanent population. With the recognition of human rights (and before that, the prohibition on the use of force) in modern international law, this standard of material effectiveness has been diluted, as the international community can refuse to recognise statehood when effective control within a territory is established in violation of fundamental human rights, the principle of self-determination, or the prohibition on the use of force.[135] Thus, in this respect as well, we see that sovereignty is no longer capable of bringing about a strict divide between the domestic and the international. Formerly, such a divide entailed a territorialisation of the rule of law, containing the legal within the territorially defined state where authority is defined and bound by the rule of law, and defining the international as a space that lacks a constitutional order (at least with respect to the individual).[136]

Consequently, human rights law has instituted a constitutional order over and across national boundaries and, as a result, a blurring between domestic and international law has occurred in the field of individual rights. International

---

[134] C.H. McIlwain, *Constitutionalism & The Changing World: Collected Papers* (Cambridge: Cambridge University Press, 1969), 30.

[135] C. Warbrick, States and Recognition in International Law in *International Law*, ed. M.E. Evans (Oxford: Oxford University Press, 2003), 205; and A. Nollkaemper, *Kern van het internationaal publiekrecht* (The Hague: Boom Juridische Uitgevers, 2004), 116–118. Examples are the resolutions of the U.N. Security Council in which the establishment of the South African homelands (a violation of the prohibition of apartheid), and the establishment of North Cyprus by Turkey (a violation of the prohibition on the use of force) were deemed to be in violation of international law. See S/Res/181 and S/Res/182 (1962) and S/Res/541 (1983).

[136] Huysmans (2003), 215–216. See also Fox (1997), 113–114.

human rights norms add a new dimension to the rule of law within the constitutional state with particular repercussions concerning its practice of judicial review. As such, human rights can simultaneously be seen as a tool to close the gap between national and international law, *and* as an attempt to overcome the tension between particularism and the universality of a global structure of sovereign states that each have jurisdiction within clearly demarcated territories. Whether it truly succeeds in establishing a guarantee for individual freedom that is not trapped within "the image of the sovereign, the territorial state and its traditional [...] institutions"[137] will be investigated in this section.

In addition to the domestic/international divide, we have seen that sovereignty traditionally distinguished the inside from the outside through two related claims: the first concerning territory, the second regarding matters of identity. I shall first explore the effect of the blurring between domestic and international law on matters of identity with specific attention to individual rights in section 3.5.1, which will show that distinctions regarding inside and outside that are based on identity *within* the nation state have lost much of their former importance. Due to international human rights norms, so-called postnational conceptions of citizenship have developed within the modern state. However, with regard to the modern state's *territorially based claims*, which shall be dealt with in section 3.5.2, the picture is more ambiguous, and I shall argue that territoriality as an organising principle has not been weakened by international human rights norms. On the contrary, we will see that the limits to the validity of these norms are often determined precisely by territoriality.

3.5.1 'Us' and 'Them' within the Contemporary State: Post-national Citizenship

Human Rights and Post-national Citizenship
I have described above[138] how citizenship and nationality acquired identical meanings when the meanings of statehood and nationhood coincided.[139] Just like nationality, the institution of national citizenship was centred on exclusive allegiance,[140] and legal personhood became linked to nationality. Individual rights were in reality national rights. The result was that non-citizens fell into

---

[137] Huysmans (2003), 223 with regard to transnational democracy.
[138] See section 3.3.1.
[139] U.K. Preuß, "Two challenges to European citizenship," in *Constitutionalism in Transformation: European and Theoretical Perspectives*, eds. R. Bellamy and D. Castiglione (Oxford: Blackwell, 1996), 128.
[140] S. Sassen, "The Repositioning of Citizenship," in *People out of Place: Globalization, Human Rights and the Citizenship Gap*, eds. A. Brysk and G. Shafir (London/New York: Routledge, 2004), 194.

a gap that existed between national and international law, without any real possibilities for the enforcement of those rights that were originally perceived of as universal and inalienable. However, the linkage between nationality and citizenship does not need to be "indispensable, inevitable or necessary."[141] On the contrary, we have seen that the bundling of the rather diverse elements in the single institution of citizenship came about as a result of historical contingencies. In this section, I shall argue that contemporary developments indicate in some respects a gradual weakening of the linkage between nationality and citizenship, if not with regard to citizenship as a formal status, then at least with regard to citizenship as a normative project. According to Saskia Sassen, the tension between citizenship as a formal status or as an increasingly comprehensive social membership has been fuelled by "globalisation and human rights, therewith furthering the elements of a new discourse on rights."[142]

Thus, not only the increased prominence of the international human rights regime features in Sassen's analysis of how globalisation destabilises the particular bundling of diverse elements in the institution of citizenship, and how it "brings to the fore the fact itself of that bundling and its particularity."[143] In addition to the international human rights discourse, Sassen accords a crucial role to various forms of globalisation, such as economic deregulation and the subsequent prominence of the markets. Important as such developments are, the scope of this book does not allow for a discussion of these issues when I examine the changing legal connotations of social membership. Moreover, I take the opportunity to point out that in this section I will not investigate the way in which international human rights norms involve a right of non-citizens to be present on the territory of the state. Although an important part of any exploration of the way in which international human rights norms limit state sovereignty and their capacity to transform citizenship as a normative project, questions with regard to the right to cross national boundaries will be addressed in the second part of this book.

Under the influence of human rights norms, formal membership of the territorially exclusive nation state ceases to be the only ground for an entitlement to rights. Although, as we will see in later in this study, international law is largely silent with regard to the nation state's discretion to admit or refuse aliens, once these aliens are present within the territory of the national state, international human rights norms impose important obligations upon the state with regard to these non-citizens. As governments are obliged to

---

[141] F. Dell'Olio, *The Europeanization of citizenship: between the ideology of nationality, immigration and European identity* (Aldershot: Ashgate, 2005), 13.
[142] Sassen (2004), 198.
[143] Ibid., 191.

guarantee some fundamental rights, irrespective of nationality, rights based on universal personhood seem to have broken the state's monopoly on granting membership rights.[144]

At this point, it is important to reiterate the blurring which human rights law has caused between national and international law. The *international* human rights regime operates partially *within* the nation state because adherence to the rule of law within the nation state, as I have discussed above,[145] ensures that international human rights norms are grounded in national institutions and practices. As a result, these norms have changed the domestic constitutional order by their implication that an individual is protected by the law as an individual, and no longer because of formal citizenship status. In addition, most of the enforcement of human rights norms takes place within the nation state, with domestic courts playing an especially important role.[146] These courts have become obliged to extend basic legal protection to anyone falling under the state's jurisdiction.[147] Consequently, any tension between sovereignty as absolute power and international human rights should not be perceived as a conflict between a clear-cut inside and outside because this tension may surface purely *within* the national state.[148] In the case of rights protection for non-citizens, the tension between international human rights and sovereignty acquires an additional dimension, as human rights interests in that case do not compete merely with states' jurisdictional independence, but with another central element of sovereignty that I have addressed in the previous chapter: the right to determine who belongs to the community.[149]

Under the influence of human rights norms, a blurring has occurred between the position of nationals and long-term or legal residents within the nation state. I shall not deal with the question whether this gradual increase in rights for aliens is the result of international developments, or whether it is rather due to the "liberalness of liberal states" and the way in which domestic courts in these states have been guaranteeing rights for aliens over the past

---

[144] M. Murphy and S. Harty, "Post-Sovereign Citizenship," *Citizenship Studies* 7 (2003), 181.
[145] In section 3.2.
[146] See Aceves (2002), 277; Martin (1989), p. 564; and S. Sassen, "Beyond Sovereignty: De-Facto Transnationalism in Immigration Policy," *European Journal of Migration and Law* 1 (1999), 181.
[147] See McDougal, Lasswell, and Chen (1976), 461–463.
[148] Sassen (1999), 61.
[149] L. Bosniak, "Human Rights, State Sovereignty and the Protection of Undocumented Migrants," in *Irregular Migration and Human Rights: Theoretical, European and International Perspectives*, eds. B. Bogusz, R. Cholewinski, A. Cygan and E. Szyszczak, (Leiden/Boston: Martinus Nijhoff Publishers, 2004), 329.

years, as has been argued by Christian Joppke.[150] As I have already mentionened, the human rights discourse operates both *within* and *outside* the nation state, which is precisely one of its defining characteristics. The fact that an extension of rights to non-citizens has taken place mostly in Western states under the rule of law through domestic judiciaries does not necessarily diminish the importance of an international dimension to human rights, but instead it could underscore the unique quality of these norms when compared to other forms of (international) law.

Human rights norms have secured civil and a certain amount of political as well as social rights for non-citizens, who as a result become part of the community of the state. Even if these non-citizens do not acquire citizenship as a formal status, their position in the nation state is anchored in an explicit discourse on rights and belonging, which has been called post-national citizenship.[151]

However, with regard to discourses on post-national citizenship, it is important to make a distinction between the various categories of fundamental rights, as not the full range of political and economic rights forms part of the 'post-national citizenship package'. Furthermore, with regard to non-citizens' status in the nation state, lawful residents should be distinguished from persons who do not have the authorisation of the state to be present on its territory. Accordingly, even more so than with regard to national citizenship, the content of post-national citizenship is impossible to define, as it is a scale on which diverse factors determine the extent of rights and the degree of belonging for each individual.

International human rights instruments oblige the state to respect classical individual rights, such as the right to life, liberty, physical integrity, freedom of thought, conscience and religion, etc., to anyone under their jurisdiction, without regard to nationality. Thus, anyone present on the territory of the state – citizens, legal residents and illegal immigrants alike – is entitled to the enjoyment of fundamental civil rights. Especially in the case of undocumented migrants, international norms, such as those laid down in instruments such as the ECHR and the ICCPR, are frequently invoked, as those people have no formalised status within the state to rely on.

However, with regard to their entitlement to rights, important differences exist between documented and undocumented migrants. The way in which

---

[150] C. Joppke, "Why Liberal States accept Unwanted Immigration," *World Politics* 50 (1998), 292–293.

[151] Y. Soysal, *Limits of Citizenship* (Chicago: University of Chicago Press, 1994). On the *decline* of citizenship see: D. Jacobson "The Global Political Culture," in *Identities, Borders, Orders. Rethinking International Relations Theory*, eds. M. Albert, D. Jacobson and Y. Lapid (Minneapolis: University of Minnesota Press, 2001).

human rights norms weakened the link between nationality and social membership is most distinctly illustrated in the case of legal, long-term residents. In addition to civil rights, most European states grant long-term legal residents many social rights on an almost equal footing with their own citizens. The gradual expansion of social rights to this class of non-citizens is emphasised by Sassen, who argues that concerning social services, citizenship status is of minor significance in Europe: "What matters is residence and legal alien status."[152] In contrast, the status of illegal immigrants within the nation state, although not devoid of access to rights, can hardly be described as approaching something like citizenship status.

With regard to political rights, the distance between the post-national citizenship of legal residents and national citizenship remains the greatest. Notwithstanding the fact that in many European countries long-term residents have the right to vote in municipal elections, foreigners, when they do not naturalise, are by far not accorded the full range of political rights within the national state. A clear example of the universality of civil rights versus the enduring particularity of political rights is provided by the ECHR. Most rights which this Convention guarantees are civil rights that are thus to be secured to anyone under the jurisdiction of one of the Contracting Parties, as is required by Article 1 ECHR. However, with regard to Articles 10 and 11 ECHR, respectively securing freedom of expression and freedom of assembly and association – freedoms that consist of the exercise of political rights, Article 16 ECHR expressly stipulates that nothing in these provisions shall be regarded as preventing the Contracting Parties from imposing restrictions on the political activity of aliens. The fact that political rights are only to a very limited extent included in the post-national citizenship package is due to the direct link of such rights with the concept of popular sovereignty, and as such with a resounding particularistic connotation of the concept of the people.

With specific regard to post-national citizenship, it is once again important to stress the importance of the existence of the rule of law domestically, in order for human rights norms to reach their full potential and as such to transform the traditional domestic legal order. I have already remarked several times upon the fundamental role which domestic courts play with regard to the enforcement of such norms. The judiciary in a state based upon the rule of law is able to mediate between the international and the domestic legal order. Sassen contends that, as domestic courts have to accept the existence of

---

[152] S. Sassen, "The de facto Transnationalization of Immigration Policy," in *Challenge to the Nation-State: immigration in Western Europe and the United States*, ed. C. Joppke (Oxford: Oxford University Press, 1998), 71.

undocumented migrants making rights-based claims, a new social contract comes into being between these aliens and society at large.[153]

The same holds true, even much more so, for immigrants who have acquired legal residence status. Such a new form of social contract may partly make up for the lack of political rights for non-nationals. David Jacobson and Galya Ruffer claim that there is a replacement of the traditional democratic route of voting, civic participation and political mobilisation by the concept of judicial agency: "Through this new mode of political engagement, litigants challenge legislative and executive authority as they cross organisational and even national boundaries."[154] In line with Sassen's argument, they contend that judicial agency, a term which designates individual access to a dense web of judicially mediated rights and restraints, changes the connotations of the traditional social contract, for also outsiders can avail themselves of such access, and as such become part of the organised political community. Exclusive measures taken by the executive are challenged at the level of the nation state, where the judiciary assesses their legality in light of the international human rights obligations of the state. Conflicting forces between the judiciary and the executive lead to a "shift of power towards formal commitment to human rights",[155] which thwarts executive but also legislative attempts to exclude non-nationals from the enjoyment of rights which were originally retained for nationals.[156]

European Union Citizenship
Any account of post-national citizenship would be incomplete if it ignores citizenship of the European Union, which is the only formal constitutionalisation of 'post-national' citizenship. The Treaty on the European Union, which was agreed upon and signed by the Member States in Maastricht in 1992, introduced the concept of citizenship of the European Union. Article 17 EC Treaty provides that every person holding the nationality of a Member State shall be a citizen of the Union, which citizenship shall complement and not replace national citizenship. The most important right which European citizenship enshrines is the right to move and reside freely within the territory of all Member

---

[153] Sassen (1996), 96.
[154] D. Jacobson and G.B. Ruffer, "Courts across Borders: The Implications of Judicial Agency for Human Rights and Democracy," *Human Rights Quarterly* 25 (2003), 74. See also Helen Stacy who argues that the human rights regime results in political requests being framed in the language of rights. H. Stacy, "Relational Sovereignty," *Stanford Law Review* 55 (2003), 2050.
[155] Jacobson and Ruffer (2003), 79.
[156] See also S. Bibler Coutin, "Contesting criminality, Illegal immigration and the spatialization of legality," *Theoretical Criminology* 9 (2005).

States (Article 18 EC Treaty), but it should be emphasised that the right to reside in another Member State for a period exceeding three months is granted only to certain classes of Union citizens.[157] Citizens of the Union who reside lawfully in the territory of another Member State have the right to equal treatment within the material scope of Community law, giving them in effect much the same social and economic rights as nationals of that Member State. Freedom of movement and the prohibition of discrimination on the grounds of nationality in Article 12 EC Treaty were codified long before the notion of Union citizenship came into being. Indeed, as these principles constitute cornerstones of EC law, the concept of Union citizenship formalised already existing Community law in the field of socio-economic rights. Nonetheless, it should be noted that the approach which the ECJ has taken to the concept of citizenship has the effect of significantly extending access to fundamental rights for EU citizens, at times arguably even contrary to secondary Community legislation.[158]

Furthermore, citizenship of the Union entails more than the right to move and a prohibition on discrimination on the ground of nationality. In addition, in the territory of a non-Member State in which their Member State is not represented, Union citizens are entitled to protection by the diplomatic authorities of any Member State, according to the same conditions as nationals of that State.[159] Moreover, every citizen of the Union has the right to vote and stand as a candidate for the municipal and European Parliament elections of the Member State in which he or she resides.[160] Although to a limited extent, Union citizenship is thus complemented with political rights.

The impact of Community law in this respect extends outside the Community legal framework into other areas of international law, which more specifically aim at the protection of human rights proper. In *Piermont v. France*, France relied on the aforementioned Article 16 ECHR to restrict the freedom of expression of a German national who was present in French Polynesia.[161] Contending that neither European citizenship, nor the status of

---

[157] Directive 2004/38/EC of the European Parliament and the Council of 29 April 2004 on the right of the citizens of the Union and their family members to move and reside freely within the territory of the Member States grants a right of residence for a period longer than three months to Union citizens who are workers or self-employed, who have sufficient resources not to become a burden on the social assistance system of the host state, students and family members of these citizens.

[158] See Case C-184/99, *Grzelczyk v. Centre public d'aide social d'Ottignies-Louvain-la-Neuve* [2001] ECR I-6193; Case C-209/03, *Bidar v. London Borough of Ealing* [2005] ECR I-2119; and Case C-456/02, *Trojani v. Centre Public D'Aide Sociale de Bruxelles* [2004] ECR I-7573.

[159] Article 20 ECT.

[160] Article 19 ECT.

[161] ECtHR, *Piermont v. France*, 27 April 1995, A-314.

Ms Piermont as a member of the European Parliament was relevant, France argued before the ECtHR that Ms Piermont fell within the scope of Article 16 ECHR, as did anyone who was not a national of the country in which he intended to exercise the freedoms of Article 10 and 11 ECHR. However, according to the Court in Strasbourg, although it did not take into account the concept of European citizenship, as the Community Treaties at the material time did not recognise any such citizenship, EU Member States were precluded from raising Article 16 against anyone in possession of the nationality of one of the Member States.[162]

Nonetheless, Union citizenship is traditional in the sense that it maintains a strong link between the very concept of nationality and access to rights. Only individuals who possess the nationality of one of the Member States are endowed with Union citizenship. Long-term residents who do not possess the nationality of one of the Member States – those who according to Yasemin Soysal benefit from access to rights on the ground of post-national citizenship – do not benefit from the right of free movement and other Union citizenship rights, save the right to petition the Parliament and the Ombudsman. So although discrimination on grounds of nationality becomes increasingly prohibited with regard to persons who posses the nationality of one of the Member States, such discrimination is permitted with regard to the large numbers of non-European citizens present on the same territory.[163] Council Directive 2003/109/EC attempts to improve the status of third-country nationals, but essential differences remain.[164] Most significant in this respect is that Member States retain the final power of deciding on whom to confer long-term resident status through the possibility of requiring integration requirements in accordance with national laws.[165] As a result, instead of a European status that is beyond the national sovereign ideal, long-term resident status is ultimately a status that can be made contingent upon the national state's notion of its 'nationness'. It is worth mentioning that this situation is buttressed by the Reform Treaty, seeing that it explicitly excludes any harmonisation of laws concerning the integration of third-country nationals.[166] The aim of achieving

---

[162] Ibid., par. 64.
[163] S. Boelaert-Suominen, "Non-EU nationals and Council Directive 2003/109/EC on the status of Third Country Nationals who are long-term residents: Five paces forward and possibly three paces back," *Common Market Law Review* 42(2005), 1015.
[164] Council Directive 2003/109/EC of 25 November 2003 concerning the status of third-country nationals who are long-term residents, O.J. L 16 of 23 January 2003, p. 44.
[165] Article 5(2) of Council Directive 2003/109/EC concerning the status of third-country nationals who are long-term residents.
[166] Article 63a paragraph 4.

'near equality' is furthermore substantially weakened by Article 11(2) and (3) of the Directive.[167] Article 11(2) stipulates that Member States may restrict equal treatment in the field of public goods to cases where the registered or usual place of residence of the long-term resident lies *within* the territory of the Member State concerned, and Article 11(3) allows for limiting equal treatment also within the Member State where a third-country national usually resides. In addition, Directive 2003/109 gives host Member States the possibility of restricting the free movement rights of those who are in possession of long-term resident status on the grounds of economic considerations,[168] whereas economic ends are explicitly excluded from the public policy exceptions to the freedom of movement and residence of EU citizens.[169]

Even if voices are heard advocating that Union citizenship should be based on residence status,[170] in light of Member States' reluctance this will probably not happen in the near future. It is arguable that if EU membership were to be truly post-national, the link between nationality and the entitlement to rights would have to be disconnected more radically. From the outside – in the eyes of most individuals who do not possess the nationality of one of the Member States[171] – with the establishment of Union citizenship, the EU as a whole acquired the characteristics of the traditional territorial state. According to some authors Union citizenship has even enhanced national citizenship.[172] Support for such a view can be found in a legal instrument such as Directive 2003/109, which seems to reinforce the predominant perception that the link between nationality, citizenship and territorial exclusion is a natural one, instead of questioning the deeper assumptions that buttress this view. Rainer Bauböck contends that taking Union citizenship seriously entails that such citizenship should be accessible under fair conditions to all long-term residents in the Member States. He argues that the fact that nationality laws of

---

[167] See in detail: L. Halleskov, "The Long-Term Residents Directive: A Fulfilment of the Tampere Objective of Near-Equality?" *European Journal of Migration and Law* 7 (2005).

[168] Article 14(3) of Council Directive 2003/109/EC concerning the status of third-country nationals who are long-term residents.

[169] See Article 27 of Directive 2004/38/EC on the right of citizens of the Union and their family members to move and reside freely within the territory of the Member States.

[170] See for example European Parliament, *Working Document on the Fourth Report of Citizenship of the Union (1 May 2001 –30 April 2004)*, Committee on Civil Liberties, Justice and Home Affairs, 30 June 2005; and also the Parliamentary Assembly of the Council of Europe, *Recommendation 1714 (2005), Abolition des Restrictions au Droit de Vote*, text adopted by the Assembly on 24 June 2005.

[171] Although there are some important exceptions to this, mostly the result of the case law of the ECJ. I will come back to these important exceptions in chapter 6.

[172] See Dell'Olio (2005).

Member States are not harmonised, and in addition are illiberal and exclusionary, is "a matter of concern to the Union as a whole as it is through them that membership in the Union is regulated."[173] We shall see in chapter 5 that the status of third-country nationals in the EU is to a very large extent determined by Member States' national immigration rules, although there are some important exceptions to this, mainly brought about by the case law of the European Court of Justice.

Denationalising the Rule of Law
We have seen above that the internalisation of international human rights norms has led to a shading of the distinction between insiders and outsiders *within* the national state. Such a distinction can no longer be made by simply drawing an unambiguous line between nationals and foreigners, but the question as to whether someone does or does not 'belong' is rather a matter of degree. Wholly inside are those who possess the nationality of the nation state, entitled to the full range of civil, political and social rights. Wholly outside are those that do not find themselves under the jurisdiction of the state concerned. Inside, albeit to a lesser degree than nationals, are foreigners who are in possession of a formal residence status that secures their entitlement to civil rights, a range of social and economic rights, and in some cases a limited amount of political rights. Partially inside and partially outside are foreigners who are illegally present on the nation state's territory: their entitlement to rights concerns mainly civil rights – and not even these rights are guaranteed to the full extent – as we shall see in the second part of this book.

Apart from the erosion of the once 'necessary and inevitable' linkage between nationality, citizenship status and access to rights, it should be noted that under the influence of international law issues related to the concept of nationality itself no longer fall exclusively under the national state's domestic jurisdiction. Although international law still largely allows each state to determine whom it regards as its citizens,[174] it is possible to discern developments at the international plane indicating that the state no longer enjoys an unlimited discretion with regard to all matters relating to nationality. These developments relate mostly to the prevention of statelessness and issues of dual nationality and should not be overstated.[175] Nonetheless, with regard to these issues, international law treats questions of nationality increasingly from a

---

[173] R. Bauböck, *Multilevel citizenship and territorial borders in the EU polity* (Vienna: Österreichische Akademie der Wissenschaften, 2003), 6. See also de Lange (1995), 109–10.
[174] Rubenstein (2003), 168–169.
[175] As can be seen in a recent decision by the HRC. See *Tsarov v. Estonia*, decision of 26 October 2007, Comm. No. 1223/2003, CCPR/C/91/D/1223/2003.

rights-oriented perspective. As such, they may signal a departing from international law's traditional approach to nationality law, which consisted of a "matter of human geography confronted on the same terms as territorial geography", predicated to the maintenance of international order instead of directly accounting for individual interests.[176] Kim Rubenstein argues along the same lines, suggesting a movement away from the centrality of the state in international law towards a rights-based, individualised focus: "as international law becomes more flexible in its use of nationality so too it becomes part of citizenship's progressive project."[177]

This section has argued that international law has increasingly taken account of the individual interests that are involved in the exercise of jurisdiction over people by the state within its territory. International human rights have factually led to a weakening of the tie between formal citizenship status and individual rights within the nation state. In this sense, one can speak of what I will call the 'denationalisation of modern constitutionalism'. In the next section I shall explore how human rights have affected territoriality: what is their impact on the territorial claims of the modern state? Are human rights norms capable of transforming the territorial form of sovereignty in a similar manner as they have affected its content so as to be able to speak of a 'de-territorialisation of modern constitutionalism'?

3.5.2 *Human Rights and Sovereignty's Territorial Claims*

In the previous section, we have seen that human rights norms have led to an extension of citizenship status, if not formally then at least with regard to citizenship as a status indicating membership of and access to rights in the organised political community. Although this has certainly been beneficial for large groups of individuals living in states which are not their own, in this section I shall argue that advancing human rights norms have not led to a truly radical new approach to citizenship, one that is able to negotiate more radically the distinction between universalism and particularism. We shall see that formal citizenship status remains of fundamental importance for a territorial regime of governance and access to fundamental rights for the individual.

> While it may be true that advancing human rights norms increasingly commit countries to granting the same civil and social (though not political) rights to those merely resident in their territories as accorded their full citizens, this

---

[176] P.J. Spiro, "Mandated Membership, Diluted Identity: Citizenship, Globalization and International Law," in *People out of Place: Globalization, Human Rights and the Citizenship Gap*, eds. A. Brysk and G. Shafir (London/New York: Routledge, 2004), 94–95.
[177] Rubenstein (2003), 185–186.

development does not necessarily signal the "decline of citizenship" for most people. These arguments primarily concern the access to rights only of immigrants, not of the main stock of the populations that constitute and replenish the bodies of citizens that constitute states. Such arguments tend to overstate the significance of what are, in fact, relatively marginal phenomena. From this point of view, it seems quite exaggerated to claim that, "in terms of translation into rights and privileges, [national citizenship] is no longer a significant construction".[178]

We have seen that within the nation state, the status of legal residents and undocumented aliens differ in important respects. According to Linda Bosniak, it is the state's claim to territorial sovereignty that accounts for this difference in treatment. She argues that with regard to undocumented immigrants, the state's territorial sovereignty has been breached, which explains why the state accords these persons far less rights than legal residents.[179] Indeed, the way in which the modern state perceives and wishes to maintain its territorial sovereignty may impact deeply on the rights of the individual. As such, the modern state's territorial and jurisdictional claims are intrinsically intertwined. Nevertheless, the image of neutrality and self-evidence that the territorial form of sovereignty has acquired has brought about a perception in which the territorial claims of the modern state and its exercise of jurisdiction over individuals whose presence within national territory is officially authorised are firmly kept apart. And whereas international law has increasingly conceded that the 'jurisdictional' content of sovereignty thus understood implicates the rights of the individual, any acknowledgement of the fact that the territorial form of sovereignty involves individual interests as well is very rare.

Below, I shall argue that territoriality exerts a limiting influence on the universality of human rights law. The role of territoriality in this respect is established by examining the territorial scope of human rights obligations of the national state and the way in which access to rights is factually guaranteed to the individual. Furthermore, by investigating the way in which human rights norms limit the state's spatial powers (i.e. its assertions of territorial sovereignty), I shall contend that human rights norms have made very few inroads whenever the state bases the exercise of power on the notion of *territorial* sovereignty. I will conclude that international law regards the notion of territoriality and sovereignty's territorial frame as being essential to the preservation

---

[178] J. Torpey, *The Invention of the Passport* (Cambridge: Cambridge University Press, 2000), 156.
[179] L. Bosniak, *The Citizen and the Alien, Contemporary Dilemmas of Contemporary Membership* (Princeton/Oxford: Princeton University Press, 2006), 70. See for a detailed discussion also L.S. Bosniak, "Human Rights, State Sovereignty and the Protection of Undocumented Migrants Under the International Migrant Workers Convention," *International Migration Review* 25 (1991), 753–756.

of a particular international order. The result is that the individual interests that are involved in sovereignty's territorial form are still only marginally accounted for, a proposition that will be investigated further in the second part of this book.

Territorial Scope of Human Rights Protection: Duties beyond Borders?

> The concept of universal human rights is antithetical to the [...] geographic distinctions that cause the protection of humanitarian law and the Constitution to be variable and unpredictable.[180]

Most human rights instruments provide that the state is to ensure individual rights protection to anyone under its jurisdiction.[181] Thus, at least in theory, actions by states *within* their national territory may not violate the human rights of individuals. However, with regard to the actions of states outside national territory the situation is more complex. Concerning European states' human rights obligations, the admissibility decision of the ECtHR in *Bankovic*[182] has led to a certain ambiguity with regard to the question as to how the notion of jurisdiction in Article 2 ECHR is to be interpreted in an extraterritorial context. The Court's approach to this issue has been criticised as being fundamentally flawed.[183] Before considering the implications of *Bankovic* and other recent ECtHR case law, I will discuss the approach that the Strasbourg organs have traditionally taken towards the extraterritorial application of the Convention, as well as the way in which other international human rights bodies have dealt with the question of extraterritoriality.

Taking into account the object and purpose of human rights obligations of national states, there is no *a priori* reason why they should not be held responsible for those violations attributable to them that occurred outside national territory.[184] Both the European Commission for Human Rights and the ECtHR have repeatedly held that in certain instances the national state can be held

---

[180] Fitzpatrick (2002), 334.
[181] Article 1 ECHR, Article 1 American Convention on Human Rights, Article 2 ICCPR.
[182] *Bankovic and Others v. Belgium* (Decision), 12 December 2001, Reports 2001-XII.
[183] K. Altiparmak, "*Bankovic*: An Obstacle to the Application of the European Convention on Human Rights in Iraq?" *Journal of Conflict and Security Law* 9 (2004); V. Mantouvalou, "Extending Judicial control in International Law: Human Rights Treaties and Extraterritoriality," *International Journal of Human Rights* 9 (2005); A. Ruth and M. Trilsch, "Bankovic v. Belgium (Admissibility), App. No. 52207/99," The *American Journal of International Law* 97 (2003) and M. Happold, "Bankovic v Belgium and the territorial scope of the European Convention on Human Rights," *Human Rights Law Review* 1 (2003).
[184] Th. Meron, "Extraterritoriality of Human Rights Treaties," *The American Journal of International Law*, 89 (1995), 78.

responsible for the actions of its authorities outside its national territory, as the term jurisdiction is not limited to the national territory of the contracting states.[185] According to the Commission, "it is clear from the language [...] and the object of [Article 1] and the purpose of the Convention as a whole, that High Contracting Parties are bound to secure the said rights and freedoms to all persons under their actual authority and responsibility, whether that authority is exercised within their own territory or abroad."[186]

Apart from the situation in which it has occupied foreign territory,[187] a state can be held responsible for violations of Convention rights and freedoms of persons who were in the territory of another state, but who were "found to be under the former state's authority and control through its agents operating – whether lawfully or unlawfully – in the latter state."[188] Before the *Bankovic* case, the case law of both the Strasbourg Commission and the Court showed that in order to engage a state's liability under the ECHR, the overall exercise of jurisdiction is not always required and even a specific act committed abroad is capable of bringing a person within the jurisdiction of the state to which that act can be attributed.[189]

> Nationals of a State are partly within its jurisdiction wherever they may be, and authorised agents of a State not only remain under its jurisdiction when abroad, but bring any other person "within the jurisdiction" of that State to the extent that they exercise authority over such persons. Insofar as the State's acts or omissions affect such persons, the responsibility of that State is engaged.[190]

---

[185] ECtHR, *Drozd and Janousek v. France and Spain*, 26 June 1992, A-240; and EcommHR, *Hess. v. United Kingdom*, 28 May 1975, D&R 2, p. 72. In particular, actions by a state's consular and diplomatic representatives may involve the liability of a national state under the ECHR. See EcommHR, *X. v. Germany*, 25 September 1965, Yearbook of the European Convention on Human Rights 8, 158; and C. Lush, "The territorial application of the European Convention on Human Rights: Recent case law," *International and Comparative Law Quarterly* 42(1993), 898. In *Drozd and Janousek*, the Court accepted that France had limited its jurisdiction *ratione loci* by a declaration under Article 63, but it concluded that it exercised jurisdiction *ratione personae*. Lush (2003, 898) concludes that the Convention thus seems to be "*hybrid, not without a measure of internal consistency*."

[186] EcommHR, *Cyprus v. Turkey*, 26 May 1975, D&R 2, p. 136; and EcommHR, *X. and Y. v. Switzerland*, 14 July 1977, D&R 9, p. 57.

[187] And exercises effective control of an area outside its national territory. See *Loizidou v. Turkey*, 23 March 1995 (preliminary objections), par. 62; and 18 December 1996 (merits), par 52.

[188] EcommHR, *M v. Denmark*, 14 October 1992, D&R 73, 193; and *Illich Sanchez Ramirez v. France*, 24 June 1994, D&R 86, 155.

[189] EcommHR, *W. v. Ireland*, 28 February 1983, D&R 32, 211, par. 17. Altiparmak (2004), 233–244.

[190] EcommHR, *Stocké v. Germany*, Report of 12 October 1989, A-199, par. 166–167. See also EcommHR, *Chrysostomides and others v. Turkey*, 4 March 2003 Appl. Nos. 15299/89; 15300/89; and 15318/89.

The Inter-American Commission on Human Rights and the UN Human Rights Committee take a similar approach in order to establish extraterritorial responsibility for human rights violations.[191] According to these bodies, the meaning of the term jurisdiction is not to be equated with territorial competence but it should also cover extraterritorial acts by the state or its agents that violate the fundamental rights protected by respectively the IACHR and the ICCPR outside national territory.[192]

This broad interpretation of the term jurisdiction, taking as a starting point the "relationship between the person affected and the state concerned, not [...] the geographical location of the violation"[193] may perhaps not reflect the ordinary meaning of jurisdiction in international law but it is consistent with the object and purpose of international human rights documents. When the term jurisdiction is used in international law to discuss the relationship between states amongst each other, it is clear that its scope is limited by the territorial claims made by other states on behalf of their sovereignty over a certain territory. The concept of jurisdiction in human rights documents deals with the relationship between the state and the individual, and should be understood as having a direct relationship with the rules concerning state responsibility in international law, which determine that responsibility derives from control.[194] This line of reasoning is confirmed by the Commission's observations in *Stocké*:

> An arrest made by the authorities of one State on the territory of another State, without the prior consent of the State concerned, does not [...] only involve State responsibility vis-à-vis the other State, but [it] also affects that person's individual right to security under Article 5(1). The question whether or not the other State claims reparation for violation of its rights under international law is not relevant for the individual right under the Convention.

Thus, although a state's jurisdictional competence is primarily territorial, responsibility for violations of fundamental rights is not restricted to national

---

[191] IACHR, *Coard et al. v. The United States*, Decision of 29 September 1999, Report no. 109/99, Case no. 10.951, par. 37, 39, 41; HRC, *Lopez Burgos v. Uruguay*, 29 July 1981, Comm. No. 52/1979, U.N. Doc. Supp. No. 40 (A/36/40) at 176 (1981), par. 12.3 and HRC, *Celiberti de Casariego v. Uruguay*, 29 July 1981, Comm. No. 56/1979, U.N. Doc. CCPR/C/OP/1 at 92 (1984), par. 10.3.

[192] Lush (1993).

[193] Altiparmak (2004), 239.

[194] R.A. Lawson and H.G. Schermers, *Leading cases of the European Court of Human Rights* (Nijmegen: Ars Aequi Libri, 1999), 603. See also International Law Commission, *Draft articles on Responsibility of States for internationally wrongful acts*, adopted by the ILC at its fifty-third session (2001) (extract from the Report of the International Law Commission on the work of its Fifty-third session, Official Records of the General Assembly, Fifty-sixth session, Supplement No. 10 (A/56/10), chp.IV.E.1) November 2001.

territory. The case law of the Strasbourg organs, the IACHR and the HRC makes it clear that responsibility *ratione personae* for extraterritorial acts, although it may not be as straightforward to establish as responsibility *ratione loci*, is not exceptional.[195] This approach is in fact required by the idea of the modern version of the rule of law that aims at overcoming the particularist, territorially limited universalism of traditional constitutional discourses. In the words of the IACHR, "no person under the authority and control of a state, regardless of his or her circumstances, is devoid of legal protection for his or her fundamental and non-derogable human rights."[196]

However, in *Bankovic*, the ECtHR seemed to depart from some of the principles generally accepted as established jurisprudence by both the Commission and the Court. The application originated in the 1999 NATO bombing of Radio Televizije Srbije in Belgrade and was lodged by an individual who had been injured by the bombing and five surviving relatives of those killed by it. They alleged that by bombing the Serbian Television Station, the respondent States had violated Articles 2, 10 and 13 of the Convention. The Court declared their application inadmissible, as it was not satisfied that the applicants and their deceased relatives were within the jurisdiction of the respondent states on account of the extraterritorial act in question.[197] Although it has been argued that the Court's conclusion can be supported on the ground that NATO did not at any moment assert authority or exercise effective control over the individuals,[198] the decision of the Court was framed in much wider terms that certainly signalled a departure from the stance that the Strasbourg bodies had previously taken towards the question of extraterritorial jurisdiction.

In the first place, the Court referred to the 1969 Vienna Convention in order to ascertain the "ordinary meaning" of the term jurisdiction. It went on to state that, from the standpoint of international law, the jurisdictional competence of a state is primarily territorial. If extraterritorial jurisdiction is exercised, the suggested bases of such jurisdiction are defined and limited by the sovereign territorial rights of other states:

---

[195] In addition to the cases quoted above see also IACHR, *Salas v. The United States*, 14 October 1993, Case 10.573, Report No. 51/96; and *the Haitian Centre for Human Rights* et. Al. *v. United States*, decision of 13 March 1997, Report no. 51/96, Case No. 10.675.

[196] IACHR, *Detainees in Guantanamo Bay, Cuba; Request for Precautionary Measures*, at: http://www1.umn.edu/humanrts/cases/guantanamo-2003.html.

[197] *Bankovic v. Belgium*, par. 82.

[198] See Happold (2003), 90 who calls it the right decision for the wrong reasons. 'Right' as there was no structured relationship between NATO and the victims of the bombing who were merely unfortunate enough to be in a building targeted by NATO forces.

> Article 1 of the Convention must be considered to reflect this ordinary and essential territorial notion of the term jurisdiction, other bases of jurisdiction being exceptional and requiring special justification in the particular circumstances of each case.[199]

In reaching this conclusion, the Court referred to its previous case law, which it interpreted as entailing that

> the recognition of the exercise of extra-territorial jurisdiction is exceptional: [the Court] has done so when the respondent state, through the effective control of the relevant territory and its inhabitants abroad as a consequence of military occupation or through the consent, invitation or acquiescence of the Government of that territory, exercises all or some of the public powers normally ascribed to that government.[200]

It is rather unfortunate that the Court did not refer to decisions of the ECommHR, such as in the above-cited *Stocké case*, where the question as to whether the extraterritorial act occurred with or without the consent of the state on whose territory it took place was deemed irrelevant for the interpretation of Article 1. The Court's adherence to the ordinary meaning in international law of the term jurisdiction in *Bankovic*[201] is problematic for a number of reasons, such as involving a danger "to embroil the Court in disputes as to whether a state has acted lawfully or unlawfully".[202] More fundamentally, it adheres to an understanding of the territorial form of sovereignty that thwarts international human rights law's underlying principles. That it is no longer the sovereignty of the violating state that constitutes a barrier for the individual to lay a claim to rights that are supposed to be inalienable, but instead the sovereignty of the state on whose territory the violation took place does not matter much from the viewpoint of those whose rights are violated.

In the second place, the Court's interpretation of previous cases that were decided or pending is problematic. It stated that in the admissibility decisions in the cases of *Issa*,[203] *Öcalan*,[204] and *Xhavara*[205] that the respondent states did not raise the jurisdiction issue.[206] Apart from the fact that the absence of claims

---

[199] *Bankovic v. Belgium*, par. 61.
[200] Ibid. par. 71.
[201] Its approach was repeated in *Gentilhomme and Others v. France*, Judgment of 14 May 2002, Appl. Nos. 48205/99, 48207/99 and 48209/99, par. 20.
[202] Happold (2003), 83. See also M. Milanovic, "From Compromise to Principle: Clarifying the Concept of State Jurisdiction in Human Rights Treaties," *Human Rights Law Review* 8 (2008).
[203] ECtHR, *Issa and others v. Turkey* (Decision), 30 March 2000, Appl. No. 31821/96.
[204] *Öcalan v. Turkey* (Decision), 14 December 2000, Appl. No. 46221/99.
[205] *Xhavara and others v. Italy and Albania* (Decision), 11 January 2001, Appl. No. 39473/98.
[206] *Bankovic v. Belgium*, par. 81.

by the parties concerning admissibility has not impeded the Court from addressing the issue of admissibility, the circumstance that the respondent states refrained from raising admissibility objections that were related to the jurisdiction issue at least indicates state practice that does not adhere to the 'ordinary meaning' of the term jurisdiction. But it is the Court's referral to its judgment in the *Cyprus v. Turkey Case*[207] that is perhaps most unsettling. Its observation in the latter case that there was a need to avoid "a regrettable vacuum in the system of human rights protection" in Northern Cyprus was to be read in the territorial context of that case:

> [...] the inhabitants of Cyprus would have found themselves excluded from the benefits of the Convention safeguards and system which they had previously enjoyed, by Turkey's effective control of the territory and by the accompanying inability of the Cypriot government, as a contracting state, to fulfil the obligations it had undertaken under the Convention.[208]

It went on to state that the desirability of avoiding a vacuum in human rights protection has so far been relied on by the Court in order to establish jurisdiction solely with regard to territories that would normally be covered by the Convention. Accordingly, the Court excluded the Federal Republic of Yugoslavia from the legal space in which contracting states have to ensure respect for the Convention, even in respect of their own conduct. This analysis has been criticised as turning an argument that was originally intended to expand the court's jurisdiction into one that limits extraterritorial jurisdiction.[209] In fact, the Court's approach in *Bankovic* illustrates that it is at times decisively and unnecessarily influenced by territoriality and the resultant (territorial) division of humanity as falling under the responsibility of one particular state, even though this construction may obstruct the important principle of effective protection of the Convention's Rights and Freedoms, so often invoked by the Strasbourg Court itself.[210] However, when deciding on the merits of the *Issa Case*,[211] the Court once again seemed to mitigate its restrictive interpretation of the term jurisdiction. This time it did refer to some of the cases decided by the HRC and former decisions of the ECommHR, and it declared that a state may be held accountable for any violation of Convention

---

[207] *Cyprus v. Turkey*, Judgment of 10 May 2001, Reports 2001-IV.
[208] *Bankovic v. Belgium*, par. 80.
[209] Ruth and Trilsch (2003), p. 172.
[210] See for example ECtHR in *Loizidou v. Turkey* (preliminary objections), 23 March 1995, par. 72.
[211] *Issa and others v. Turkey*, Judgement of 16 November 2004, Appl. No. 31821/96. It is worth noting that the Turkish Government submitted post-admissibility observations in this case, in which it was contended that in Bankovic the Court had departed from its previous case law on the scope of interpretation of Article 1. See par. 52 of the judgment.

rights of persons "who are in the territory of another state but who are found to be under the authority and control of the former state through its agents operating – whether lawfully or unlawfully – in the latter state."[212] However, the Court concluded that the applicants did not fall within the jurisdiction of Turkey as they could not prove that the Turkish armed forces had conducted operations in the area were the alleged violations took place.[213]

Also in its judgment on the merits in the *Öcalan case*, the Court referred to the ECommHR decision in *Stocké*.[214] According to the Court, the *Öcalan case* was to be distinguished from *Bankovic* as the "applicant was physically forced to return to Turkey by Turkish officials and was subject to their authority and control following his arrest and return to Turkey."[215] When it decided on the merits in the *Ilascu Case*, the Court again stressed the ordinary meaning of the term jurisdiction in public international law and referred to *Banković* to stress the prevalence of the territorial principle in the application of the Convention. However, it added that the concept of 'jurisdiction' is not necessarily restricted to the national territory of the contracting states.[216]

We may conclude that when a state is acting extraterritorially it is theoretically bound by international human rights obligations, even though there may be important limits to their responsibility. Nevertheless, everyday reality may well pose limits to extraterritorial responsibility that are much more difficult to overcome than those formulated in a court of law. This concern is especially urgent in the field of contemporary immigration policy, where states' focus increasingly on extraterritorial control of migration flows. Even if the measures that prevent immigrants from reaching national territory frequently result in breaches of fundamental rights, these measures are seldom

---

[212] Ibid., par. 71.
[213] Ibid., par. 81.
[214] *Öcalan v. Turkey*, Judgment of 12 March 2003, Appl. No 46221/99, par. 88.
[215] Ibid. par. 93. See also ECtHR, *Saddam Hussein v. Albania and others* (Decision), 14 March 2006, Appl. No. 23276/04, in which the Court decided that the arrest of Saddam Hussein in Iraq did not fall within the jurisdiction of the respondent European States as he had not substantiated any evidence of a jurisdictional link between himself and those States.
[216] *Ilascu and others*, Judgment of 8 July 2004, Reports 2004-VII, par. 310–314. See also *Markovich and others v. Italy*, 14 December 2008, Appl. No. 1398/03. In this case the Court did not depart from its interpretation in *Bankovic*, but it established that the respondent state exercised jurisdiction with regard to the complaint made under Article 6 ECHR in the domestic proceedings that applicants had commenced in Italy. Although the mere fact that individuals seek a remedy in domestic courts is not sufficient to bring about a 'jurisdictional link', "if the domestic law recognises a right to bring an action and if the right claimed is one which prima facie possesses the characteristics required by Article 6 of the Convention, the Court sees no reason why such domestic proceedings should not be subjected to the same level of scrutiny as any other proceedings brought at the national level".

challenged judicially, which is not in the least because persons affected by them are not likely to be able to bring their cases to court.

This practical obstacle brings us to an additional issue to be investigated in order to understand territoriality's limiting influence on the universalistic potential of modern human rights law. Indeed, apart from looking at the territorial scope of human rights obligations as provided for in various legal instruments, one needs to investigate the way in which access to those rights is factually guaranteed in order to comprehend the importance of sovereignty's territorial frame for the notion of individual rights. This line of investigation brings us back to John Torpey's scepticism concerning the decline of citizenship in a world where territory is exclusively divided amongst nation states. Indeed, we shall need to investigate citizenship once more, but now its postnational version in terms of a global system of governance in order to grasp the fundamental role which space as a political construct plays in determining access to rights.

Human rights and their realisation depend on the state system, a global structure in which governance is still largely undertaken on a territorial basis.[217] Celebrations of post-national citizenship overlook the territorial aspect of the global political system, and thus fail to appreciate the importance of territory in the practice of fundamental rights protection.[218] As such, just as traditional accounts of citizenship, accounts of post-national citizenship take a predominantly internal perspective. As they focus primarily on the modern, liberal state under the rule of law as the site for investigating the implementation of human rights, citizenship is portrayed as a process that takes place within the nation state as a closed container; a territorially defined entity in which the only politically relevant processes take place.

And indeed, from a wholly internal perspective, it makes sense to claim that nationality no longer determines the status of an individual. In other words, nationality is no longer decisive for the extent of access to rights but only *if* and *for as long as* an individual is present within the territory of the nation state. However, from a global perspective that takes into account the numerous individuals living in states not governed by the rule of law, nationality, citizenship and the issue of human rights protection remain still firmly linked. The Universal Declaration of Human Rights of 1948 (UDHR) states that fundamental rights are to be guaranteed, not only without distinction as to the personal characteristics of an individual, but additionally without distinction

---

[217] Henkin (1999), 7; and Shafir (2004), 23.
[218] See Murphy and Harty (2003) who make the same argument with regard to what they call models of post-sovereign citizenship and the self-determination of sub-state nations.

on the basis of the political, jurisdictional or international status of the country or territory to which a person belongs. However, the concept of territoriality, continuously confirmed and reinforced by international law,[219] bears witness to a completely different reality. We have seen above that the ECtHR has stated unambiguously that Article 1 ECHR sets limits on the reach of the Convention.[220] Even apart from the question of responsibility for extraterritorial acts, these limits in general can only be explained in a system that divides responsibly and population on the basis of territory. Territoriality's limiting influence on the universality of human rights ensures that, in daily practice, rights remain "territorially limited at the level of the nation state."[221]

Accordingly, and in spite of the fact that *within* the territory of the nation state citizenship as a normative project and nationality may well have become increasingly decoupled, outside its territory the two remain doctrinally linked. Although, as Sassen has asserted, the ascendance of human rights may strengthen the tendency to move away from nationality as an absolute category, the territorial borders of the nation state at the same time determine the exact limits of this tendency. Hence, I disagree with her argument that human rights equally contribute to a move away from national territory.[222] Similarly, I contest the claim made by Yasemin Soysal, who argues that, as national belonging per se is no longer the basis for rights, we witness the emergence of a new "model of membership, anchored in deterritorialized notions of person's rights."[223] On the contrary, it may well be that a reassertion of territorial sovereignty is the modern state's answer to the growing significance of individual rights protection – irrespective of nationality – within its territory. In a system where one's presence on the territory of the nation state is decisive for the extent of rights to be enjoyed, states may actually benefit from keeping people out of their territories. Whether there are limits to such assertions of territorial sovereignty will be investigated below.

Limits to the State's Spatial Powers
Dora Kostakopoulou and Robert Thomas argue that the British asylum regime cannot be understood without reference to a specific understanding of territoriality, which is modelled upon the law of private ownership.[224] According to

---

[219] McCorquodale (2004), 480.
[220] *Loizidou v. Turkey*, 23 March 1995, par. 62.
[221] D. Chandler, "New Rights for Old? Cosmopolitan Citizenship and the Critique of State Sovereignty;" *Political Studies* 51 (2003), 332.
[222] Sassen (1999), 185.
[223] Y. Soysal, *Limits of Citizenship* (Chicago: University of Chicago Press, 1994), 3.
[224] D. Kostakopoulou and R. Thomas, "Unweaving the Threads: Territoriality, National Ownership of Land and Asylum Policy" *European Journal of Migration and Law* 6 (2004), 7.

these authors, the idea of territoriality is conducive to the formation of what they call a geo-authoritarian culture, a culture which not only impedes the recognition of duties beyond borders, as we have seen above, but also increases the spatial powers of governments.[225] Asylum and matters relating to freedom of movement more generally will be addressed in the next two chapters, but here I will sketch the context in which the state is able to make use of its spatial powers when dealing with these issues.

First, it has become clear in the sections of this chapter that have dealt with citizenship, be it national or post-national, that territory is the means through which governments compartmentalise and control populations.[226] Furthermore, we have seen in the section on international law that the inviolability of national territory is one of the key principles of international law. In international law, sovereignty stands for the ownership of territory, and international law functions as a distributive mechanism for determining which state can exercise sovereignty over a certain territory.[227] International law organises power and authority into territorially defined sovereign units, and the inviolability of national territory and the maintenance of the territorial status quo are its elemental principles. In this particular context, David Luban discusses what he calls Nuremberg's "equivocal and immoral legacy". He argues that although the veil of sovereignty was pierced by criminalising certain acts which are carried out by the state against its own population, the criminalisation of aggression in the Trials amounted to erecting a wall around state sovereignty, resulting in the old European model of 'unbreachable' nation states.[228]

It follows that international law makes a difference between sovereignty's territorial form and the exercise of its jurisdiction within this 'predestined' territorial framework. Although the state is no longer permitted to employ the latter in whatever way it pleases, the maintenance of the integrity of its territorial boundaries remains its exclusive prerogative. It seems that human rights norms have transformed international law, but only with regard to the sovereign state's jurisdictional claims over persons within a given territory. Regarding territorial sovereignty, international law is still the law for and by sovereign states alone and its main aim is to serve the narrow interests of the stability of international order and those of already existing states.[229]

---

[225] Id.
[226] Newman (2001), 144.
[227] R. McCorquodale "International Law, Boundaries and Imagination", in *Boundaries and Justice: Diverse Ethical Perspectives*, eds. D. Miller and S. Hashmi (Princeton/Oxford: Princeton University Press, 2001), 142.
[228] Luban (1994), 336.
[229] See McCorquodale (2001), 138.

Perhaps the prohibition on the use of force can hardly be used as an example to demonstrate that the state's spatial powers are not limited by international law. However, we have seen in section 3.4.2 how the notions of war and legitimate violence, and the way in which territorial boundaries are drawn, are intertwined. They mutually influence each other in a discourse that attempts to reduce every transnational problem to a territorial solution. And, as Mary Kaldor writes, "the stylised notion of war [...] as a construction of the centralised, 'rationalised', hierarchically ordered, territorialized modern state, [...] dominates, even today, the way policy makers conceive of security."[230] Accordingly, the nearly absolute value of territorial integrity extends far beyond the language of armed force between national states, while it is at the same time decisively shaped by that language. In this respect, international law still sees territorial sovereignty with much the same eyes as the United States Supreme Court did in the *Chinese Exclusion Case*, which was decided in 1889:

> to preserve its independence, and give security against foreign aggression and encroachment, is the highest duty of every nation, and to attain these ends nearly all other considerations are to be subordinated. It matters not in what form such aggression and encroachment come, whether from the foreign nation acting in its national character or from vast hordes of its people crowding in upon us[231]

The second part of this book shall explore in depth the relationship between the regulation of the 'permeability of the national border', international law, and individual interests. There I shall examine in closer detail the allegation that "human rights norms have seen states yielding jurisdiction, but not territory, which remains doctrinally enclosed."[232] In this section, I have investigated the link that exists between territory and rights. I have argued that territoriality impedes the realisation of human rights' universal aspirations. At the same time, it seems that human rights have not made any significant inroads in the state's assertion of its territorial sovereignty, a provisional conclusion that will be examined in detail in the second part of this book. With regard to territorial sovereignty, international law seems to be still largely the law for and by sovereign states alone. In this respect, it seems justified to conclude that human rights have failed to establish a constitutional order over and across physical borders.

---

[230] Kaldor (1999), 15.
[231] Chae Chan Ping v. United States (*Chinese Exclusion Case*), 130 U.S. (1889) 581, at 606.
[232] R.C. Panglangan, "Territorial Sovereignty: Command, Title and the Expanding Claims of the Commons," in *Boundaries and Justice: Diverse Ethical Perspectives*, eds. D. Miller and S. Hashmi (Princeton/Oxford: Princeton University Press, 2001), 165.

In addition, it can be argued that human rights norms even have a reifying effect on territoriality, as the progressive development of these norms has "formally enshrined modern ideals of legitimate statehood in the normative fabric of international society."[233] When we regard human rights from this perspective, it seems that they form an inherent part of the modern discourse of legitimate statehood, a discourse that still seeks to justify territorial particularism on the grounds of ethical universalism.[234]

3.6 Conclusions: A Particularistic Universalism?

In this chapter, I have explored the ways in which, over time, the use of violence by the state has been limited by various discourses. We have seen that in the general concept of the rule of law we can discern material and formal limits on the exercise of political power. The former are constituted by fundamental rights, whereas with regard to the latter, the separation of powers and an independent judiciary deserve special attention.

It is important to bear in mind that there exists a difference between the legitimacy of the exercise of political power (legality), and the legitimacy of its foundations. The latter question is decided by the concept of sovereignty as the construction of a particular legal order; an intrinsically political concept the foundations of which cannot be cannot be assessed with reference to that same legal order.[235] In contrast, the exercise of state power within a constitutional framework can be subjected to the requirements of the rule of law, and can accordingly be judged as to its legality or legitimacy. Consequently, at the moment that the rule of law or the normal constitutional guarantees of the modern state do not fully apply, we can observe sovereignty's undisguised claim to distinguish the inside from the outside, a claim that is, as we have seen in chapter 2, based on both territory and identity. The emergence of the exposed core of state power in this sense is likely in the field of migration, associated as it is with the "essence of the nation"[236] and the unity of the political community

---

[233] C. Reus-Smit, "Human rights and the social construction of sovereignty," *Review of International Studies* 27(2001), 531.

[234] Ibid., 522. See also Costas Douzinas (2007), who argues that "every polity, state or empire promotes a version of morality and of people's entitlement that accords with its priorities and interests. [...] Human rights became an instrument for underpinning the power of states". Douzinas (2007), 178–179.

[235] See Schmitt (2005), 10.

[236] C. Dauvergne, "Sovereignty, Migration and the Rule of Law in Global Times," *The Modern Law Review* 67 (2004), 592.

in contemporary Western states. In the second part of this book, we shall see that extensive executive discretion and the traditional deference of the judiciary indeed go hand in hand when it concerns the regulation of international human mobility. Consequently, in modern constitutionalism the relevance of the distinction between insiders and outsiders is not only that outsiders generally enjoy a lesser degree of access to judicial protection, but the particularity of the rule of law goes further than that: its territorial assumptions are illustrated with the fact that in the field of migration we encounter "power which does not conform to judicial or legislative modes of exercise."[237] The exact way in which migration law and policy may engage the exposed core of state power, where the arbitrary exercise of political power is most likely to manifest itself, will be addressed in detail in the remainder of this book.

We have seen in this chapter that citizenship's potential for universalism was nipped in the bud on account of territorialisation, both by the resulting Westphalian order as a global structure (the structural dimension of citizenship) and by the ensuing internal sovereign claims of the territorial state. This led to a construction by which membership in the territorially defined state became a necessary condition for access to those rights that were supposed to be universal: the loss of national rights in practice entailed the loss of human rights. Citizenship's internal and structural dimensions interact to reinforce the ideal of national territorial sovereignty, and it presents the link between rights and territorial belonging as natural and necessary.

However, it is not only citizenship's linkage between rights and identity which shows how territorial boundaries drawn in the past influence the question of which kinds of state violence are prone to correction through the law. Also international law's regulation of state violence is strongly shaped by the way in which territorial demarcations were brought about. The result is that in the international legal regulation of state violence, matters of identity and territorial boundaries are connected to each other by the same sovereign logic as that which binds together people, territory and authority within the nation state. And just as tension exists between the universal and the particular within the nation state, the same tension is present in all accounts of international law, expressed in differing conceptions of who are the subjects of international law. A stubborn conception of the territorial state as the sole subject of international law has had a strong impact on the regulation and legitimisation of violence. International law, until the advent of international human rights, largely ignored domestic violence, but it has attempted to regulate those kinds of violence that crossed national boundaries. When in the course of the

---

[237] Id.

twentieth century territorial integrity became a cornerstone of international law, sovereignty in international law no longer entailed a right to wage war as an instrument of foreign policy. Nonetheless, the old language of war, a state-based discourse with emphasis on the territorial component of sovereignty that is firmly rooted in the Westphalian state system, still decisively shapes the way in which we conceive of sovereignty, the political community and the state prerogatives with regard to its territorial boundaries.

Even classical international law exceptions to the rule that internal violence is a matter for the sovereign state alone, such as pertaining to minorities and foreigners, affirm a particularistic conception of the modern state and the system that it forms part of. As these rules only confer states with rights, they are consistent with citizenship's structuring role in the global world, in which national sovereignty is supposed to embody a perfect link between territory and identity. In addition, legal norms concerning the treatment of minorities and foreigners prove and reinforce the rule that decrees that territorial belonging is essential in order to enjoy rights that were supposed to be universal and inalienable.

The way in which both citizenship and classical international law afford protection against state violence is thus profoundly shaped by sovereignty's claim to distinguish the inside from the outside. The argument by Richard Mansbach and Franke Wilmer that "the relationship between identity and borders underlies both the process of norm articulation and the kinds of violence identified as problematic"[238] thus proves to be true, not only in the international arena, but equally with regard to the domestic order.

Different discourses traditionally regulated internal and external state violence. The existence of the notion of *domain réservé* in international law exemplified the separateness of the domestic and international orders. Even though not directly apparent, the strict separation between international and domestic law that was brought about by the territorial state and the system of which it forms part made a theoretical division within the concept of sovereignty possible. Sovereignty's claim to distinguish the inside from the outside is based on both power over territory and power over people; nevertheless, in due time sovereignty's territorial frame became conceptually distinct from the exercise of jurisdiction over people within a body politic. The state's jurisdiction within a clearly demarcated territory was regulated by *domestic law* only, whereas matters relating to the territorial frame of sovereignty were dealt with by *international law*, as external violence was perceived as engaging the territorial sovereignty of the modern state in an area where only the interests of states were

---

[238] Mansbach and Wilmer (2001), 56.

legally recognised. The result was that the exercise of power through political institutions and the clear spatial demarcation of the territory on which this power was exercised became distinct aspects in the definition of the state,[239] and the intrinsic bond that existed between them was seldom accounted for.

After the Second World War, the international community recognised the inherent dangers of the old system. Human rights law was intended to close the gap between national and international law. From then onwards, international law has decreed that all individuals present within the territory of the nation state, citizens and non-citizens alike, are entitled to have their fundamental rights protected. Human rights law has thus to a certain degree resulted in a convergence between national and international law. Internally, citizenship can no longer be the only foundation for access to rights, and the domestic judiciary in the constitutional state plays an important role with regard to the implementation of international norms protecting human dignity. Externally, the individual has become a subject of international law, and the treatment by the national state of persons under its jurisdiction is no longer a mere matter of sovereign discretion.

Nevertheless, even though human rights have resulted in convergence between national and international law with regard to the rule of law, they have not succeeded in abolishing the conceptual distinction between the content and form of sovereignty, which in turn results in the immunisation of the territorial component of sovereignty against legal forces of correction. In order to see this clearly, I have investigated the way in which modern human rights law affects sovereignty's claim to distinguish the inside from the outside. We have seen that human rights norms have significantly limited the state's claim to decide matters of inside and outside within its territory by reference to identity. Nevertheless, when sovereignty's claim to distinguish the inside and the outside is based on territory, human rights law has not achieved a similar transformation. In spite of notions of post-national citizenship, the modern version of the rule of law remains territorially limited for two reasons.

In the first place, in most cases, access to fundamental rights is factually determined by one's presence on the territory. National states refuse to be held accountable for actions that have taken place outside their national territories, an attitude that in the European context may be facilitated by ambiguous recent case law of the ECtHR that seems to revert to a territorial version of the legal space in which the ECHR applies. In addition, territorialisation ensures that territory and rights remain linked in a more structural way. Celebrations

---

[239] J. Agnew, and S. Corbridge, *Mastering space: Hegemony, territory and international political economy* (London: Routledge, 1995).

of post-national citizenship suffer essentially from the same shortcomings as any theory that presents citizenship simply as a project that gradually turned the privileges of the few into the rights of the many. The viewpoint from which they investigate citizenship is the territory of the national (liberal) state. When the territorial basis of the global state system is disregarded or taken for granted, it makes sense to claim that nationality and rights have become untangled. However, the internal perspective that such theories take conceal the fact that this is only the case within the territory of the liberal, Western democracy. Outside its territory, questions of identity and rights remain firmly linked. As a result, territoriality causes "the stateless, the refugee and the citizen of dictatorships" to remain largely beyond the fundamental rights protection of the constitutional state.[240] As long as the political community is predominantly based on space, in other words, when the "territorial compartmentalisation of the globe remains based on the existing pattern of sovereign states,"[241] the true universality of human rights remains a mere theory. In this context, Gershon Shafir has argued that human rights can only be really effective if they are transformed into membership of a global community that has its own distributive and enforcing institutions.[242] As I shall argue later in this book, in order to grasp the full potential of such and other instances of citizenship, which are not dependent on territorially demarcated units such as the nation state, we need to create a space in which we are really free to imagine alternative conceptions of the institutional expression of the values that underlie the human rights discourse.

The second reason that contributes to the 'territorial limitation' of human rights law lies in the fact that human rights have hitherto left the state's exercise of its spatial powers largely unhampered. Territorial integrity is a cornerstone of international law, and the protection of its territorial boundaries has remained the exclusive prerogative of the national state. Chapter 5 takes a closer look at these issues, but for now it is important to reiterate that the way in which the notions of sovereignty and territorial boundaries interact is still decisively shaped by a state-centred discourse which adheres to the sanctity of territorial boundaries in order to maintain a stable order of sovereign

---

[240] J.C.A. Isaac, "A new guarantee on earth: Hannah Arendt on human dignity and the politics of human rights," *American Political Science Review* 90 (1996), 162.

[241] D. Newman, "Boundaries, Borders and Barriers: Changing Geographic Perspectives on Territorial Lines" in *Rethinking International Relations Theory: Identities, Borders, Orders*, eds. M. Albert, D. Jacobson and Y. Lapid (Minneapolis: University of Minnesota Press; 2001), 138.

[242] Shafir (2004), 24. See also E.O. Eriksen, "Why a Charter of Fundamental Rights in the EU?" *Ratio Juris* 16 (2003), 369–370.

states, instead of achieving a just community of individuals. In addition, we need to be aware of the possibility that in a situation in which one's presence on national territory automatically leads to an entitlement to fundamental rights, the sovereign state may wish to keep people outside its territory in order not to have to accord them these fundamental rights. Hence, in spite of its increasing 'denationalisation', the modern rule of law remains territorially limited, and it seems that the status of sovereignty's territorial frame in international law has remained largely the same as it was before the advent of modern human rights law.

Nuremberg's "equivocal and immoral legacy" combined with the reification of territoriality has led to a structural blindness concerning the involvement of personal interests whenever the state bases its claims on the notion of territorial sovereignty, a proposition which will be investigated in further detail in the next chapters. There we will see that the territorial blind spot of the modern version of the rule of law affects individual rights most obviously and disadvantageously in the global context of immigration from poor, underprivileged citizens of non-Western countries into the Western, liberal democracies. A version of the rule of law that keeps the content of sovereignty within a territorially defined body politic and its territorial form apart, scrutinising the former aspect while it is largely silent with regard to the latter aspect, obscures the fact that constraints on individual behaviour and freedom are always motivated on account of the notion of the political community and the unity of the body politic, interests that concern both the form and content of sovereignty. The fact that the modern version of the rule of law has not acknowledged the interrelatedness between the nation state's exercise of jurisdiction over people within a given body politic and the territorial framework in which those jurisdictional claims take place is a particularly serious concern when it comes to the national state's perception of and responses to 'new threats' such as immigration, which by its very nature engage sovereignty's territorial frame as well as its jurisdictional content.

Part II
Doctrine and Practice

Chapter 4

Freedom of Movement I: The Right to Leave as a Human Right

4.1 *Introduction*

> Theoretically, in the sphere of international law, it had always been true that sovereignty is nowhere more absolute than in matters of emigration, naturalization, nationality and expulsion; the point, however, is that practical consideration and the silent acknowledgement of common interests restrained national sovereignty until the rise of totalitarian regimes.[1]

The previous chapter dealt with the way in which the sovereign power of the state has been restrained through a range of (legal) discourses. I have argued that the notion of territoriality has obstructed the realisation of the universalistic potential of each of these discourses. Citizenship, which is much more than a mere legal concept, is the most obvious example of the potentially 'explosive tensions' between universalism and particularism, but also the way in which a political particularistic reality has triumphed over a universalistic idealism in classical international law is to a large extent the result of the Westphalian territorial constellation. Until the advent of international human rights, the few instances in which international law concerned itself with the interests of individuals were those in which the 'territory-identity ideal' of the sovereign state was most clearly not reflected in reality, as in the case of minorities and resident aliens.

Another significant 'anomaly' in a structure that perceives of the territory-identity ideal as a critical element for its stability is the phenomenon of international migration. There is nothing that exposes the social constructedness of territoriality and its concomitant imagery of the nation state as a closed container as unequivocally as human beings that cross national borders. In this chapter and the next, I shall explore the development and the nature of

---

[1] H. Arendt, *The Origins of Totalitarianism* (San Diego/New York/London: Harcourt Brace and Company, 1976), 278.

the legal framework regulating the international movement of persons. We shall see that the decisive impact of territoriality upon modern constitutionalism, resulting in the immunisation of territorial sovereignty against most forms of legal correction, is unambiguously expressed in the legal norms dealing with international migration.

Studies that deal with questions directly related to contemporary immigration policies have predominantly ignored the issue of exit and the way in which legal norms regulate leaving the nation state. Nicholas De Genova has argued that whenever immigration law is addressed, a detailed empirical investigation of its actual operations is often not provided, which results in a perception in which existing laws appear to provide merely a neutral framework.[2] While this book is not a socio-legal study, nor the result of detailed empirical research on the way in which immigration law affects the lives of individuals,[3] I intend to explore its actual operations more carefully by including the issue of emigration. In this way, I shall seek to demonstrate that the laws dealing with immigration do anything but provide a neutral framework. Instead, these legal norms reflect changing perceptions on political authority, and as such they are intimately related to the way in which we perceive the nation state. In this context, John Torpey has argued that the nation is not merely an "imagined community" but is in need of detailed and documented rules for its sustenance. Following the rhetoric of Max Weber, Torpey thus adds an extra dimension to our understanding of the state when he writes that the "monopolisation of the right to regulate movement" has been intrinsic to the very construction of the modern territorial state.[4] As such, "regulation of movement contributes to the very state-ness of the state."[5] And while in current scholarship the import of the rules pertaining to immigration for the 'nation's nationness' is increasingly acknowledged, it is often forgotten that until very recently legal norms dealing with emigration were just as central to the nation state. The centrality of emigration for the notion of national sovereignty and the various ways in which one can conceive of

---

[2] N.P. De Genova, "Migrant "Illegality" and Deportability in Everyday Life," *Annual Review of Anthropology* 31 (2002), 423–424.

[3] See for some interesting examples of such work: J. Schapendonk, "Stuck Between the Desert and the Sea: The Immobility of Sub-Saharan African 'Transit Migrants' in Morocco," in *Rethinking Global Migration: Practices, Policies and Discourses in the European Neighbourhood*, eds. H. Rittersberger-Tiliç et al. (Ankara: KORA, METU & Zeplin Iletisim Hizm, 2008); and N. Peutz, "'Criminal Alien' Deportees in Somaliland: An Ethnography of Removal," in *The Deportation Regime: Sovereignty, Space, and the Freedom of Movement*, eds. Nicholas De Genova and Nathalie Peutz (Durham, NC: Duke University Press, forthcoming 2009).

[4] J. Torpey, *The Invention of the Passport* (Cambridge: Cambridge University Press, 2000), 4.

[5] Ibid., 6.

political power is well exemplified by the quotation taken from Hannah Arendt cited above, which mentions emigration first and does not even refer directly to immigration.

By investigating the overall legal framework regulating movement, one of territoriality's most significant implications on the rule of law shall be exposed: the artificial distinction between sovereignty's territorial frame and its content as the exercise of jurisdiction over individuals within a given body politic. This chapter deals with the right to leave, leaving most questions of immigration to chapter 5. Section 4.2 presents an overview of the way in which perceptions on the issue of exit have developed over time. We shall see that at certain points in history, emigration was looked upon in much the same way as immigration is at present: it had to be directed in channels which the state deemed favourable in the national interest.[6] However, after the Second World War the possibility of an individual to leave his or her country became recognised as a human right in international law. Section 4.3 deals with the international legal norms regulating emigration with particular emphasis on the permitted restrictions on the exercise of the right to leave. In spite of its recognition by international law, contemporary developments show that the exercise of the right to leave becomes increasingly problematic once again, but now it is due to immigration policies of Western democracies. The relationship between measures of immigration control and the individual right to leave shall be dealt with in section 4.4. In the conclusions to this chapter I shall seek an answer to the question as to why sovereignty has decreased in importance when it comes to matters merely concerning exit.

4.2 Development of the Right to Emigrate

The right to leave one's country is the ultimate form of self-determination. Not to be able to leave a country amounts to deprivation of liberty: imprisonment within imagined lines on the surface of the earth instead of incarceration behind concrete walls. Centuries ago, the right to leave was already recognised in the Magna Carta of 1215:

> In future it shall be lawful for any man to leave and return to our kingdom unharmed and without fear, by land or water, preserving his allegiance to us, except in time of war, for some short time, for the common benefit of the realm.[7]

---

[6] See D. Christie Tait, "International aspects of Migration," *Journal of the Royal Institute of International Affairs* 6 (1927).
[7] Chapter 42 of the Magna Carta of 1215.

Thus, the Magna Carta simultaneously qualified the right that it accorded to free men: in the first place it was made subject to the condition that allegiance to the Kingdom was guaranteed, and in the second place it provided for restrictions on exit in times of war. The latter limitation is still to be found in present formulations of the right to leave, which I shall address below. For now, it is the qualification 'preserving his allegiance to us' that merits closer attention as it clearly illustrates the changes that the feudal order was undergoing under the influence of the growing powers of European monarchs.

In medieval Europe, the extent of the freedom of movement had been determined by the feudal order and many people were tied to territory because of obligations to their feudal lord. Indeed, the system of serfdom granted no individual freedom of movement to serfs whatsoever as these were not allowed to leave their place of employment.[8] However, for those whose status was free the situation was quite the opposite, as national borders "were insignificant to the individual traveller, though state boundaries were of warlike concern to rulers."[9] In the restriction on the right to leave as formulated in the Magna Carta an early shift from feudalism to absolutism can be observed, entailing that everybody, in addition to their status in the feudal hierarchy, became a subject of the King. These shifts gave birth to the doctrine of perpetual allegiance, as we have seen in chapter 1. Consequently, permanent emigration as we know it now was inconceivable because it was assumed that a subject could always be recalled to his duties to his King.

Even so, the recognition of the qualified right to leave in the Magna Carta of 1215 was only short-lived. Due to the assertion by later kings of an absolute power to control exit, it is not to be found in later versions of that document, a situation which did not differ much from that in other European countries. From the fifteenth century onwards it would be the relationship between the sovereign and his subjects that determined the extent of actual freedom of movement. In the era stretching from the sixteenth to the eighteenth century, the relationship between people, territory and authority was determined by "mercantilism in the service of absolutism"[10] and the right to leave was virtually non-existent. Population was considered a scarce economic and military resource, and rulers prohibited emigration almost entirely in their efforts to

---

[8] It should be noted that serfdom in Europe was an economic relationship between lord and serf which implied that serfs could in theory (and sometimes also in practice) buy their freedom. See A. Dowty, *Closed Borders, The Contemporary Assault on Freedom of Movement* (New Haven and London: Yale University Press, 1987), 25.

[9] A. Dummet, and A. Nicol, *Subjects, Citizens, Aliens and Others: Nationality and Immigration Law* (London: Weidenfeld and Nicolson, 1990), 11.

[10] Dowty (1987), 29.

maximise economic growth and military power. Early state building was thus intimately linked with regulating movement, although it should be noted that the prohibition of emigration in this era was mainly instrumental in securing a concrete state interest. Conceptions of freedom of movement still had nothing to do with ideologies such as nationalism – alluding to a deeper, symbolic relationship between people and territory, or other ideological convictions – tying the notions of people and their state to each other in a more profound way. This was reflected by the fact that immigration was in most cases welcomed: European monarchs even attempted to acquire populations from what was for them the outside world.[11]

We have seen that at the end of the seventeenth century, the absolute power of the sovereign came under attack by the idea of natural rights and changing ideas about the location of sovereignty. While until then emigration had been considered as a matter that was entirely subject to the discretion of the sovereign (i.e. the monarch), theorists of international law increasingly perceived the right to emigrate as a natural right.[12] This was only logical if the idea of political society as a voluntary contract was to be taken seriously. For if every individual must by free choice be able to determine whether he wants to be a member of that society, he should also be free at any time to break his ties and leave.[13]

Nonetheless, the actual practice of the new regimes that were inspired by Enlightenment ideals was not always consistent with those same ideals. In France, restrictions were imposed on freely leaving the country on grounds of national security soon after the Revolution even though the revolutionary regime had abolished the passport, and even in spite of the fact that the right to leave was recognised in the French Constitution of 1791.[14]

Nevertheless, liberal ideals continued to penetrate governments so that at the end of the nineteenth century it had become possible to leave almost any European state.[15] Very few countries required passports or other documents in order to exit their territories. Their liberal attitude in this regard was not

---

[11] A. Zolberg, "International Migrants and Refugees in Historical Perspective," *Refugees* 91 (1992), 37.

[12] S. Jagerskiold, "The Freedom of Movement," in *The International Bill of Rights: The Covenant on Civil and Political Rights*, ed. L. Henkin (New York: Columbia University Press, 1981), 169.

[13] F.G. Whelan, "Citizenship and the right to leave," *American Political Science Review* 75 (1981), 650.

[14] See on the rather complicated issue of freedom of movement during the Revolutionary years: Torpey (2000), 21–56. The American government did not recognise the right of voluntary expatriation until 1907. See Dowty (1987), 49.

[15] Dowty (1987), 46.

only due to Enlightenment ideals that had influenced daily political practice. Indeed, also the fact that under-population was no longer a problem in these states made those states regard emigration without concern. All European and American states, except Russia, in practice regarded the right to leave as a basic right that was inalienable.[16] Thus, when serfdom was finally entirely abolished throughout Europe in the nineteenth century, thousands of people left their homes to sail for the Americas, Australia or Asia. Nonetheless, the freedom of movement was typically not granted to inhabitants of the colonies. It was clearly in the interests of the imperial powers that these citizens should not leave the colonies. As in many other instances, the rulers applied liberalism at home, but in Africa and Asia they held on to medieval ideas.

The First World War signalled the end of the liberal era regarding freedom of movement and caused passports to reappear on the international stage. During the twentieth century, possession of these documents would develop into a requirement for lawful exit.[17] In the twenties and thirties, more and more European countries restricted their citizens' possibilities to leave.[18] Various factors contributed towards this narrowing of the right to leave. To begin with, there were the losses caused by the First World War combined with reduced birth rates, which made population once again a scarce resource. However, due to xenophobia and racism among their populations and their own nationalistic aspirations, states did not resolve the problems caused by such scarcity by allowing more immigration. Therefore it is important to be aware that restrictions on freedom of movement in this period were not at all comparable to those in the mercantilist era.

The difference between them is to be found in altering conceptions of the relationship between people, territory and the state. We have seen how nationalism led to a perception of sovereignty as entailing an unbreakable and self-evident link between territory, population and authority. National identity became an instrument to distinguish between 'us' and 'them', and cultural and ethnic homogeneity in a state was to be aspired. In the previous chapter we have seen how legal discourses – domestically and internationally – reflected the way in which individuals were defined by virtue of where they 'belonged'. It was nationalism that intensely nourished (even if it did not exactly gave birth to) "the intimate relationship between identities and borders".[19] For the

---

[16] Ibid., 54 and 82.
[17] R. Hofmann, *Die Ausreisefreiheit nach Völkerrecht und staatlichem Recht* (Berlin: Springer, 1988), 3; and Torpey (2000), 21.
[18] Christie Tait (1927), 31.
[19] Y. Lapid, "Identities, Borders, Orders: Nudging International Relations Theory in a New Direction," in *Identities, Borders, Orders: Rethinking International Relations Theory*, eds. M. Albert, D. Jacobson and Y. Lapid (Minneapolis and London: University of Minnesota Press, 2001), 10.

nationalistic mind a liberal attitude to emigration is inconceivable: it cannot be possible to choose freely one's allegiance with a state or abandon it at will if such allegiance is conceived as belonging to a community of individuals bound to each other and 'their' land by common identity, history and 'blood'.

Moreover, the collectivist ethic proclaimed by many regimes after the First World War contributed to a restrictive view of the right to leave as well. Rather than ethnic and cultural homogeneity dictated by the ideology of nationalism, collectivism aims at social homogeneity. Likewise the collectivist state cannot regard emigration without suspicion as leaving the society will inevitably be an act of disloyalty, even treason.[20] In addition, it becomes difficult to maintain that the interests of citizens are the same as those of the state when these citizens are leaving the country en masse. Finally, a regime which is purely or predominantly sustained by coercion, or in which there is no room for dissent can presumably only survive by restricting exit.[21]

After the Second World War, the idea of natural rights revived. Human rights as they were now called were codified and amongst them was the right to leave. Over time, the right to leave was laid down in a range of binding human rights treaties, as we shall see below. However, perhaps the most immediate effect of the codification of the right to leave in international law was that the practice of a substantial number of countries was only the more conspicuous. The most obvious violators of the right to leave were the Communist countries: while the collectivist ethic inspired by the extreme right had not survived the Second World War,[22] its counterpart on the other side of the political spectrum had expanded.

None of the countries united by the Warsaw Pact recognised the right to leave as a human or constitutional right.[23] Quite the opposite: it was regarded as a favour, the granting of which fell wholly within the state's discretion.[24]

---

[20] Dowty (1987), 60; and Torpey (2000), 124–125.

[21] Dowty (1987), 60.

[22] Of course there were still authoritarian regimes in Europe such as Spain under Franco and the Estada Novo in Portugal. The motto of the regime in Portugal was *Deus, Pátria e Familia*, which was obviously meant as a counterpart to the motto of the French Revolution. According to Article 31 of the 1933 Constitution of the Estada Novo, the state had "the right and the obligation to coordinate and regulate the economic and social life of the Nation with the objective of populating the national territories, protecting emigrants, and disciplining emigration." See further M.I.B. Baganha, "From Close to Open Doors: Portuguese Emigration under the Corporative Regime," *e-Journal of Portuguese History* 1 (2003).

[23] G. Brunner, *Before Reforms: Human Rights in the Warsaw Pact States 1971–1988* (London: Hurst and Company, 1990), 204.

[24] This did not mean that policies regarding exit permits were the same in all these countries; neither were they equally restrictive Dowty (1987), 111–127; and H. Hannum, *The right to leave and return in international law and practice* (Dordrecht: Martinus Nijhoff Publishers, 1987), 95–105.

The erection of the Berlin Wall in 1961 was the ultimate illustration of the Communist view on freedom of movement. And even while in due course it would become easier for citizens of the East-Bloc countries to visit other countries of the 'socialist world system', permission for this kind of travelling was by no means obtained as a matter of course.[25]

Moreover, although actual travel to the West did somewhat increase over time, the right to leave was certainly not recognised for the purpose of visiting Western countries or for permanent emigration. According to its penal code the German Democratic Republic (DDR) was able to prosecute those seeking official permission to emigrate for the crime of "incitement hostile to the state."[26] Its constitutional legal doctrine justified the lack of a basic right to emigrate by the socialist government's concern for each of its citizens: Allowing a citizen to emigrate to the West "was tantamount to delivering him up to an imperialist, aggressive and anti-social system of exploitation".[27] The East German policy of prohibiting its citizens from visiting Western countries was additionally defended on the grounds that the Federal Republic did not recognise the citizenship of the German Democratic Republic.[28]

In Russia, the right to leave had never been recognised, not even before the Communist era.[29] After serfdom was abolished in Russia in 1861, the former serfs had lived in village communities from which no one could leave without communal permission. Communist ideology strengthened traditional restrictive notions concerning the right to leave to such an extent as to equal it with treason.

For other East-Bloc countries restrictive views on the right to leave similarly arose from Communist ideologies, but they were certainly also influenced by economic considerations. These states had a keen interest in population building in general and in having educated professionals at their service in particular.

---

[25] Brunner (1990), 208.
[26] D.C. Turack, "Freedom of Transnational movement: The Helsinki Accord and Beyond," *Vanderbilt Journal of International Law* 11 (1978), 55.
[27] Brunner (1990), 217.
[28] The Federal Republic maintained that an all-German nationality still existed and accorded West-German identity papers to all East-Germans who applied for such documents. See D.C. Turack, "A Brief Review of the Provisions in Recent Agreements Concerning Freedom of Movement Issues in the Modern World," *Case Western Reserve Journal of International Law* 11 (1979), 110–111.
[29] Alan Dowty argues that Communist countries which applied restrictive exit policies were copying the Soviet Union policies that were not so much Communist as Russian. This would explain the relative absence of such strict policies in countries with related ideologies but less political links to the USSR if compared to those countries heavily under Soviet political influence, such as the countries of the Warsaw Pact. See Dowty (1987), 208.

The fact that these countries were closely linked to Western Europe and had in the past been relatively open would have made it easier for their citizens to cross borders in pursuit of more rewarding opportunities than it was for Soviet nationals.[30] If these countries had permitted free emigration presumably a large part of their population would have left for the West.

Despite the international obligations of countries entailing the obligation to guarantee the right to leave as laid down in the Universal Declaration of Human Rights and binding instruments, the reality of East-Bloc practice was acknowledged in the Helsinki Accord.[31] This document proclaimed that the participating states should act in accordance with the purposes and principles of the UDHR, and that they should fulfil their obligations as set forth in international human rights instruments by which they are bound. It seems to be in direct contradiction with this statement that the Helsinki Accord then, instead of recognising a general right for citizens to leave their countries permanently, requires the signatories solely "to facilitate freer movement on the basis of family ties, family reunification, proposed marriages and personal or professional travel."[32] Furthermore, the document enumerates certain 'obligations' for states to achieve this aim which are not exactly far-reaching, and certainly do not reflect what contracting states committed themselves to under the ICCPR.[33]

The Helsinki Accord could be described as realpolitik in view of the East-West relationship during the Cold War, seeking to improve the practice of the Communist states in the area of human rights in a manner open to political compromise.[34] Nevertheless, in bilateral relations Western countries

---

[30] Dowty (1987), 116. Evidently, this was especially so with regard to emigration from East Germany to West Germany. See also F.W. Reinke, "Treaty and non-Treaty Human Rights Agreements: A Case Study of Freedom of Movement in East Germany," *Columbia Journal of Transnational Law* 24 (1986), 665.

[31] *Final Act of the Conference on Security and Co-operation in Europe of 1975*, Reprinted in *International Legal Materials* 14 (1975), 1292.

[32] Turack (1978), 44.

[33] "In order to promote further development of contacts on the basis of family ties the participating States will favourably consider applications for travel with the purpose of allowing persons to enter or leave their territory temporarily." Obligations might be a misleading term in more than one way as the legal status of the Helsinki Accord was unclear. It was not a treaty and could thus not be registered as such. See H.G. Schermers, "Mensenrechten in de Slotacte van Helsinki," *Nederlands Juristenblad* 31 (1977), 801; and D.A. Martin, "Effects of International Law on Migration Policy and Practice: The Uses of Hypocrisy," *International Migration Review* 23 (1989), 556.

[34] Some authors write that such a strategy of *realpolitik* was more effective in securing increased protection of individual rights in this area. See Reinke (1986), 658; and Martin (1989), 556–557.

continued to express indignation over the denial of the right to leave. The United States did so by according most-favoured-nation treatment only to those non-market countries which did not deny or make impossible for their citizens the right or opportunity to emigrate.[35] Western countries further attempted to undermine the East-German practice of restricting exit by insisting that access to West Berlin should be free on the western side of the border wall, i.e. possible without passport or customs control.[36] Most individuals who did manage to leave Communist countries were consequently accepted as political refugees by the Western democracies – even though many of them were motivated by economic considerations – something which should be understood in the light of the ongoing ideological battle.

Other countries that breached their obligations with regard to the right to leave after the Second World War were developing countries and dictatorships. After decolonisation former colonies embarked on a process of nation building, a process which was perceived as necessary in view of the fact that the territories of many of these countries were determined by boundaries which did not reflect cultural, linguistic or ethnic divisions. The policies of the ruling class to strengthen national unity often consisted of targeting groups that did not fit in with their image of national unity. These policies inevitably caused conflict, internal struggle and civil war, which in turn produced refugees and displaced persons. Nevertheless, many developing countries that produced great numbers of refugees were not always happy to lose parts of their population, especially if these consisted of educated people seeking a better future in the developed world. Thus, in some of these countries, restrictions on exit were justified by invoking the problem of the so-called brain drain. Their policies of restricting exit – while at the same time carrying out forced expulsions[37] – can

---

[35] Turack (1979), 104; and R.B. Lillich, "Civil Rights," in *Human rights in international law: legal and policy issues*, ed. T. Meron (Oxford: Clarendon Press, 1984), 149–150. The consequence for a country which denied its citizens the right or the opportunity to emigrate was not only that it was not eligible for most-favoured-nation treatment, but it could neither receive US credits, credit guarantees, investment guarantees, nor conclude a US commercial agreement. The legislation led to the end of the first period of *détente* between the US and the Soviet Union as the latter regarded it as interference in its internal affairs. See F.A. Gabor, "Reflections on the Freedom of Movement in light of the dismantled 'Iron Curtain,'" *Tulane Law Review* 65 (1991), 853–854. At the same time it resulted in a liberalisation of China's emigration policies. See Dowty (1987), 234.

[36] Turack (1979), 113. This practice was defended by the view of France, Great Britain and the US that Berlin was under the joint command of the Allies and should not be a divided territory. The GDR also insisted that East Germans were not required to have a passport in order to enter West Germany because the frontier between the two states was not an external border. See Torpey (2000), 147.

[37] An infamous example is Idi Amin's expulsion of 40,000 Asians from Uganda in 1972.

be explained by the ruling elite's wish to sustain their illegitimate rule, economic motivations and their ideas of nation building. However, there are many developing countries that, although they have repeatedly expressed concerns over the brain drain, do not resort to prohibiting emigration. Countries that currently deny the right to leave, such as Burma under military rule, and Iran under the Shah and the Ayatollahs appear to have done so more as a result of their ideology and dictatorial practices.[38]

The Cold War also influenced the exercise of the right to leave for citizens of Western States. Since 1918 it had been illegal to leave the United States without a passport, the issuing of which fell under the competence of the State Department. In the 1950s it was usual for the State Department to deny passports on the basis of individual political beliefs. Refusals were frequently not sufficiently motivated and the Internal Security Act of 1950 even prohibited the issuing of passports to members of the Communist Party.[39] The State Department held that its decisions, being an exercise of governmental foreign policy powers, could not be reviewed by the judiciary.[40] Consequently, during this period, the right to leave the United States lost its character as a fundamental right, and factually assumed the character of a favour, the granting of which fell wholly within the discretion of the State Department.

Nevertheless, decisions of the State Department were regularly challenged in court, and the Supreme Court ruled in 1958 that the right of exit is a part of the 'liberty' of which a citizen cannot be deprived without due process of law under the Fifth Amendment.[41] In 1964, that same Court ruled that political belief alone was not a sufficient reason for a denial of the right to leave and it held that the Section of the Internal Security Act which forbade the issuing of passports to members of the Communist Party was unconstitutional.[42] Nevertheless, the decision of the Secretary of State to revoke the passport of a former CIA agent who disclosed information concerning US

---

[38] Hannum (1987), 127. See also Dowty (1989), 184–187. And of course there are the countries that still adhere to a collectivist socialist ethic, and which impose severe restrictions on exit, such as Cuba and China. Chinese citizens need permission from the government to emigrate. See G. Liu, *The Right to Leave and Return and Chinese Migration Law* (The Hague/Boston: Martinus Nijhoff, 2007). In Cuba, one can even end up in prison by merely discussing emigration. See B. Corbett, *This is Cuba: An Outlaw Culture Survives* (Cambridge, MA: Westview Press, 2002), 241. An account of the horrifying manner in which persons who attempt to emigrate have been treated by Cuban border guards is provided by H.E. Fontova, *Fidel: Hollywood's Favorite Tyrant* (Washington, D.C.: Regnery Publishing, 2005), 157–164.

[39] Dowty (1987), 128; and Torpey (2000), 148.

[40] Dowty (1987), 128.

[41] U.S. Supreme Court, *Kent v. Dulles* 357 U.S. (1958) 116, 125–127.

[42] U.S. Supreme Court, *Aptheker v. Secretary of State*, 378 U.S. (1964) 500, 505–514.

intelligence activities was upheld by the Supreme Court, stating that national security and foreign policy considerations were superior to the freedom to travel abroad and that the latter right could therefore be made subject to reasonable government regulation.[43] Furthermore, the restriction of travel to certain areas by invalidating passports for travel to specific countries was not deemed illegitimate by the Supreme Court, if it was justified by considerations of national security or foreign policy.[44]

In 1989 a revolution, peaceful in character but nonetheless a revolution in view of the deep and abrupt transformations it brought about, changed the political landscape of Central and Eastern Europe. One of the first manifestations of these changes was people's exercise of their right to leave.[45] Hungary was the first nation that demolished a part of the Iron Curtain on its Austrian border. When, in September 1989, Hungary allowed East Germans to depart for the West across that border, East Germans had for the first time since 1961 a real possibility to leave their country. Consequently, thousands of them reached West Germany through Hungary and Czechoslovakia, where the Iron Curtain had been dismantled as well. In view of this exodus, Honecker decided to ease travel restrictions in East Germany, hoping that if East Germans were openly given the possibility to emigrate, many might choose to stay.[46] However, East Germans continued to leave by the thousands and after Honecker's resignation, the new leadership in East Germany confirmed the right of free and unrestricted travel. As the Berlin Wall had been "the foremost symbol of the denial of the basic human right of self-determination"[47] its opening up on 9 November 1989 can be seen as symbolic of the reassertion of this right for the people living in the former East-bloc countries.[48]

Similar changes in the Soviet Union did not have to be waited upon for a long time. Already under Gorbatchov's policy of glasnost, traditional Soviet views on emigration were changing. Such altering views were most obviously expressed in the easing of travel restrictions for one group of Soviet citizens who had perhaps suffered most seriously under the denial of the right to leave, the Soviet Jews.[49] After the collapse of communism in the Soviet Union, that

---

[43] U.S. Supreme Court, *Haig v. Agee*, 453 U.S. (1981) 280. See also Dowty (1987), 130; and Hannum (1987), 53.
[44] U.S. Supreme Court, *Zemel v. Rusk*, 381 U.S. (1965) 1.
[45] Gabor (1991), 854.
[46] R.R. Palmer and J.A. Colton, *A History of the Modern World*. 8th ed. (New York: Mc Graw-Hill, 1995), 1021.
[47] Gabor (1991), 855.
[48] On the changes in the practice of these countries see Turack (1993) 292–302.
[49] The Jews in the Soviet Union were not completely denied the possibility to leave at all times since the Second World War, but it was very difficult and at times impossible to obtain

state dissolved into various republics each of which formally recognised the right to leave. The importance of freedom of movement was confirmed in the Charter of Paris for a New Europe by the Conference on Security and Co-operation in Europe, an organisation that originated from the Helsinki process.[50] As we shall see below, also after 1989, this organisation has also paid considerable attention to what had turned into a human right to leave.

4.3 General Legal Framework of the Right to Leave

We have seen above that in the course of history restrictions on exit have been justified by considerations about the nature of political authority, and later more specifically by the interests of the sovereign state. From modernity onwards, views on a right to leave were thus grounded in secular ideologies such as allegiance to the King, nationalism, and collectivism in the name of communism. As the end of the cold war in 1989 has been said to have "brought in its train the end of all secular ideologies except the ideology of human rights"[51] we shall now turn to the way in which international human rights law perceives of and regulates the issue of emigration.

The right to leave any country, including one's own, is laid down in the UDHR, the first international document in which human rights were codified after the Second World War. The right to leave was also codified in human rights instruments of a later date with binding force, such as the ICCPR; the Convention on the Elimination of Racial Discrimination;[52] the ECHR; the African Charter of Human and People's Rights; and the American Convention of Human Rights.[53] In the following paragraphs, the main emphasis will be on

---

permission to emigrate to Israel. This policy seems not to have been only justified by Soviet ideology, but also by the Soviet Union's wish to maintain good relations with the Arab states.

[50] Conference on Security and Co-operation in Europe, 21 November 1990, *Charter of Paris for a New Europe and Supplementary Document to give effect to certain provisions of the Charter*, 21 November 1990, reprinted in *International Legal Materials*, XXX (1991), 199.

[51] R. Gaete, "Postmodernism and Human Rights: Some Insidious Questions," *Law and Critique* 2 (1991), 150.

[52] In this treaty the right to leave is not guaranteed as such, but Article 5 states that the right to leave should be enjoyed without discrimination on grounds of race, colour, or national or ethnic origin.

[53] There are more international binding documents which have a bearing on the right to leave, such as the 1951 Convention on Refugees, the 1961 UN Convention on the Elimination or Reduction of Statelessness. See V.P. Nanda, "The Right to Movement and Travel Abroad: Some Observations on the U.N. Deliberations," *Denver Journal of International Law and Policy* 1 (1971), 112–113. Another example is the European Social Charter: in Article 18 §4 the

the legal framework of the right to leave as established by the ICCPR and the ECHR. Article 12(2) ICCPR and Article 2 of Protocol 4 ECHR guarantee the right to leave in identical terms. They read as follows:

Everybody shall be free to leave any country, including his own.

The right to leave should be protected for nationals and non-nationals alike. Furthermore, the right to leave places obligations on both the state of residence and the state of nationality. The state of nationality is under a positive obligation to provide a passport because that will provide a national with the means to exercise the right to freedom of movement including the right to leave one's state.[54] The state of residence is under the (mainly) negative obligation to permit exit.

Neither the ICCPR nor the ECHR accord the individual an absolute right to leave. Certain circumstances may justify restrictions on the right to leave. However, according to the UN Human Rights Committee (HRC) these are exceptional circumstances, and restrictions may not impair the essence of the right.[55] In a similar vein, the CSCE Declaration of the Copenhagen Meeting of 29 June 1990 states that restrictions on the right to leave must be very rare exceptions, only necessary if they respond to a specific public need, pursue a legitimate aim, are proportionate to that aim and are not abused or applied arbitrarily.[56] The Strasbourg Declaration on the Right to Leave and Return

---

Contracting Parties recognise the right to leave of their nationals who wish to pursue an activity on the territory of the other Parties.

[54] HRC in *El Dernawi v. Libyan Arab Jamahiriy*, 20 July 2007, Comm. No. 1143/2002; CCPR/C/90/D/1143/2002; and *Loubna El Ghar v. Libyan Arab Jamahiriya*, 15 November 2004, Comm. No. 1107/2002, U.N. Doc. CCPR/C/82/D/1107/2002 (2004). See also *Vidal Martins v. Uruguay*, 23 March 1982, Comm. No. 57/1979, U.N. Doc. Supp. No. 40 (A/37/40) at 157 (1982), par. 7; *Pereira Montera v. Uruguay*, 31 March 1981, Comm. No. 106/1981, CCPR/C/18/D/106/1981 (1983), par. 9.4; *Lichtensztejn v. Uruguay*, 31 March 1983, Comm. No. 77/1980, U.N. Doc. Supp. No. 40 (A/38/40) at 166 (1983), par. 8.3; and *Varela Nunez v. Uruguay*, 22 July 1983, Comm. No. 108/1981, U.N. Doc. CCPR/C/OP/2 at 143 (1990), par. 9.3.

[55] HRC, *General Comment 27*, Freedom of movement (Art.12), (Sixty-seventh session, 1999), Compilation of General Comments and General Recommendations Adopted by Human Rights Treaty Bodies, U.N. Doc. HRI/GEN/1/Rev.6 at 174 (2003), 11–13.

[56] Article 9.4 of the *Document of the Copenhagen Meeting of the Conference of the Human Dimension of the CSCE*, reprinted in: Human Rights Law Journal 11 (1990), 232–246. See also Articles 20 and 21 of the *Concluding Document of the Vienna Conference on Security and Co-operation in Europe*, held in 1989, reprinted in: Human Rights Law Journal 10 (1989); the *Draft Declaration on Freedom and Non-Discrimination in Respect of the Right of Everyone to Leave any Country, including his Own and to Return to his Country*, by the Special Rapporteur Mubanga-Chipoya, UN Doc. E/CN.4/Sub.2/1988/35/Add.1 (1988). See also Article 6 of "The Right to Leave and Return, A Declaration adopted by the Uppsala Colloquium on 21 June 1972," reprinted in: *Israel Yearbook on Human Rights* 4 (1974).

similarly emphasises that restrictions on the right to leave must be construed narrowly.[57] Moreover, it declared that such restrictions should be subject to international scrutiny, in which the burden of justification lies with the state. Indeed, Article 13 ECHR and Article 2(3) ICCPR require an effective remedy whenever someone presents an arguable complaint that his or her right to leave has been violated.

When examining the permissible restrictions on the right to leave, it will become apparent that the scope of that right in particular relies heavily on the relationship between people, territory and authority. Whereas human rights in general can be described as claims of the individual concerning his or her relationship to authority, the right to leave has a very direct bearing on that relationship. After a person has left, the state is in most cases neither capable of exercising nor competent to exercise jurisdiction over that person. That specific characteristic of the right to leave, taken together with the fact that freedom of movement in general may have a great impact on social and economic circumstances in a country in many cases constitute the ratio behind possible restrictions.[58] Paragraph 3 of Article 12 ICCPR reads as follows:

> The above mentioned rights shall not be subject to any restrictions except those which are provided by law, are necessary to protect national security, public order (ordre public), public health or morals or the rights and freedoms of others, and are consistent with the other rights recognised in the present Covenant.

In Paragraph 4 of Article 2 of the Fourth Protocol ECHR, the limitation clause with regard to the right to leave is framed in a slightly different manner, similar to the way in which exceptions to fundamental rights are generally formulated by the ECHR:

> No restrictions shall be placed on the exercise of these rights other than such are in accordance with law and are necessary in a democratic society in the interests of national security or public safety, for the maintenance of "ordre public", for the prevention of crime, for the protection of health and morals, or for the protection of the rights and freedoms of others.

In spite of obvious differences in their wording, it can be assumed that both limitation clauses have the same scope and effect.[59] The denial or seizure of a

---

[57] International Institute of Human Rights, "Strasbourg Declaration on the Right to Leave and Return (and the Recommendation of the Meeting of Experts on the Right to Leave and Return to One's Country)," adopted by the Meeting of Experts, Strasbourg, France, 26 November 1986, reprinted in: *Human Rights Law Journal* 8 (1987).

[58] See A. Cassese, "International protection of the right to leave and return," in *Studi in Onore di Manlio Udina*, ed. A. Giuffre (Milan: Multa Pacis AG, 1975), 222.

[59] M. Nowak, *U.N. Covenant on Civil and Political Rights: CCPR Commentary* (Kehl am Rein: N.P. Engel, 1993), 212.

passport or other necessary travel documents constitutes a direct interference with the right to leave and in order to be legitimate such interference needs to satisfy the requirements for the permissible restrictions.[60] Also indirect limitations on the right to leave, such as restrictions on the export of foreign currency or high costs for obtaining the necessary documents need to satisfy the requirements of Article 12 ICCPR or Article 2 Protocol 4 ECHR.[61]

Restrictions on the right to leave need to be in accordance with (ECHR), or provided for by (ICCPR) law: the source of the restriction should be a general rule.[62] This requirement should be understood as referring to substantive law. Instead of embodying a purely formal requirement it also calls for a certain qualitative standard of the laws in question, which should be accessible and foreseeable.[63] As we have seen in the previous chapter, the legality requirement arises from the claims of a society based on the rule of law and serves to prevent arbitrary and discriminatory practices.[64]

The prohibition of discrimination in general plays an important role with regard to the freedom of movement, and there will clearly be a violation of Article 12 ICCPR or Article 4 Protocol 2 ECHR if there is not an objective justification for differences in treatment between persons exercising their right to leave.[65] It is not accidental that the UN Sub-Commission on Prevention of Discrimination and Protection of Minorities has paid considerable attention to the right of freedom of movement.[66] The emphasis on discrimination

---

[60] ECtHR, *Baumann v. France*, Judgment of 22 May 2001, Reports 2001-V, par. 63–67; and ECtHR, *Napijalo v. Croatia*, Judgment of 13 November 2003, Appl. No. 66485/01, par. 73.

[61] But see ECommHR, *S. v. Sweden*, 6 May 1985, D&R 42, 224, in which case the Commission decided that the right to take property out of a country is not embodied in the right to leave.

[62] Jagerskiold (1981), 172.

[63] ECtHR, *Sunday Times v. the United Kingdom*, 26 April 1979, A-30, par. 49.

[64] See also J.D. Inglés, *Study of Discrimination in Respect of the Right of Everyone to Leave any Country, Including His Own, and to Return to His Country*, Report submitted on 23 November 1962 to the Commission on Human Rights, Sub-Commission on Prevention of Discrimination and Protection of Minorities, 15th Session, UN Doc E/CN.4/Sub.2/220/Rev.1 (1963) (hereinafter (1963)), 47.

[65] R. Higgins, "La Liberte de Circulation des Personnes en Droit International," in *Liberte de Circulation des Personnes en Droit International*, eds. M. Flory and R. Higgins (Paris: Economica, 1988), 343 and 353; and C. Mubanga-Chipoya, *Analysis of the current trends and development regarding the right to leave any country, and some other rights or considerations arising therefrom*, UN doc. E/CN.4/Sub.2/1988/35 (1988), 27–28.

[66] The first substantive study that was requested by the Sub-Commission focussed on discrimination with regard to freedom of movement. See Inglés (1963). See also Inglés, *Draft Report of the Special Rapporteur: Study of discrimination in respect of the right of everyone to leave any country, including his own, and to return to his country*, E/CN.4/Sub.2/L.234 (13 December 1961).

in this area is understandable: contemporary history has shown time and again that the sovereign state has linked the extent of the right to leave with matters of identity.

The character of the right to leave as a human right is emphasised by the requirement by the ECHR and the ICCPR that exceptions to the right to leave need to be necessary (in a democratic society).[67] The most important component of the necessity requirement in human rights law is that restrictive measures must abide by the principle of proportionality: They must be appropriate to achieve the legitimate aims enumerated in the provisions; they must be the least intrusive measure available to achieve those aims; and they should not place a disproportionate burden on the individual concerned when compared with the aim to be achieved.[68] The principle of proportionality in the human rights context also means that restrictions can never be applied generally, but their legitimacy must always be assessed on a case by case basis.

Proportionality should not only be guaranteed in the laws dealing with restrictions on the right to leave, but administrative and judicial authorities are also bound to respect this principle, which requires inter alia that proceedings relating to the exercise of the right be expeditious and that subsequent decisions are sufficiently reasoned.[69] Necessity has also been interpreted as implying a pressing public and social need, for example by the UN Special Rapporteur in his Draft Declaration on the Right to Leave.[70] It is not difficult for a state to maintain that restrictions on the right to leave fall under one of the enumerated state interests, but the requirement of proportionality prevents a too extensive use of these state interests in order to justify interferences.[71] In addition, in the ICCPR, the requirement that limitations on the right to leave must be in accordance with the other rights guaranteed in the ICCPR could well be adopted in order to avoid such

---

[67] In contrast to the ECHR, the ICCPR does not use the term "democratic society" but it can be assumed that the word necessary refers to that concept. K.J. Partsch, "The Right to Leave and Return in the Countries of the Council of Europe," *Israel Yearbook on Human Rights* 5 (1975), 261.

[68] ECtHR, *Riener v. Bulgaria*, Judgment of 23 May 2006, Appl. No. 46343/99, par. 118–130; and HRC, *Miguel González del Río v. Peru*, 28 October 1992, Comm. No. 263/1987, U.N. Doc. CCPR/C/46/D/263/1987 (1992), par. 5.3.

[69] HRC, *General Comment 27* (1999), 15.

[70] Article 7(c) of the *The Draft Declaration on Freedom and Non-Discrimination in Respect of the Right of Everyone to Leave any Country* (Mubanga-Chipoya, 1988).

[71] The first draft of Article 12 ICCPR contained an exhaustive list of all grounds of restriction. Nowak (1993), 206; and Jagerskiold (1981), 171.

extensive use of the permissible grounds for restriction that a codification of the right to leave would in effect be rendered meaningless.

Problems of interpretation have played a role especially with regard to the concepts of national security and public order, while to a much lesser extent with regard to the protection of health and morals and the rights of others.[72] It is argued that national security as a general ground for restricting exit should only be invoked in the case of a political or military threat to the entire nation.[73] However, the drafters of the ICCPR seem to have been primarily concerned with control over military personnel.[74] Also other persons with access to "sensitive" information regarding the military or security of the state may be subjected to wider restrictions with regard to freedom of movement than ordinary citizens.[75] However, also in these cases the necessity and proportionality of the restrictions need to be assessed on a case by case basis.[76]

Furthermore, a person may be prevented from leaving the country with the purpose of ensuring security against the international spread of diseases, a restriction based on public health considerations, which must be temporary.[77] It is difficult to think of permissible restrictions on exit based on morality,[78] although public health and morality can be of significance with regard to the internal freedom of movement, an issue that is also regulated by Article 12 ICCPR or Article 4 Protocol 2 ECHR. The rights and freedoms of others can also constitute a ground on which the right to leave can be restricted. Restrictions of this kind will be justifiable if someone is not willing to fulfil contractual obligations or is trying to escape family maintenance obligations by leaving the country.[79]

---

[72] Higgins (1988), 9.
[73] Article 4(d) of the "Strasbourg Declaration on the Right to Leave and Return" (International Institute of Human Rights, 1987); and Article 7(d) of the *Draft Declaration on Freedom and Non-Discrimination in Respect of the Right of Everyone to Leave any Country* (Mubanga-Chipoya, 1988), 51–52; and Nowak (1993), 212.
[74] Jagerskiold (1981), 172 and 178. See also ECommHR, *Peltonen v. Finland*, 20 February 1995, D&R 80-B, 38.
[75] Hofmann (1988), 311; and L.B. Sohn and T. Buergenthal, *The Movement of Persons across Borders* (Washington: American Society of International Law, 1992), 77.
[76] See ECtHR, *Bartik v. Russia*, Judgment of 21 December 2006, Appl. No. 55565/00.
[77] *Analysis of the current trends and development regarding the right to leave any country, and some other rights or considerations arising therefrom* (Mubanga-Chipoya, 1988), 55.
[78] Nowak (1993), 216. It has been argued that the prevention of trafficking in persons for the purpose of prostitution would fall within this category. See Jagerskiold (1981), 179 and Hofmann (1988), 312. However, in this case of trafficking it would make more sense to base such restrictions on more tangible grounds such as the prevention of crime, or the protection of the rights and freedoms of others.
[79] Jagerskiold (1981), 179; and Hofmann (1988), 312.

Public order or 'ordre public' is the most elusive of all the permissible grounds for restriction. It is has been argued that a broad conception of public order applies in Article 12 ICCPR and Article 2 Protocol 4 ECHR, entailing "all those universally accepted fundamental principles, consistent with respect for human rights, on which a democratic society is based."[80] The grounds of public safety and the prevention of crime in the ECHR are included in the concept of public order as understood by the ICCPR. Someone who is suspected of or sentenced for committing a crime may be prevented from leaving the country,[81] just as persons who are detained with a view to bringing them before the competent legal authority.[82] However, if those judicial proceedings are unduly delayed, restrictions on the right to leave cannot be said to serve public order.[83] The lawful detention of persons for other reasons, for example in a labour institution, also constitutes a permissible ground for restricting the right to leave.[84] The legality of restrictions on exit on the grounds of outstanding public debts, such as taxes, is questioned by some authors.[85] It is argued that, since imprisonment for an inability to fulfil contractual obligations is not allowed in international human rights law, it can neither be a reason for prohibiting exit. However, this argument loses sight of the fact that the international legal protection of the right to personal liberty differs from the international legal protection of the right to freedom of movement. Furthermore, as the proportionality of restrictions on exit of this kind can be easily reviewed, these should not necessarily be deemed illegal.[86]

Much more difficult to assess are restrictions based on considerations of a general character about the well-being of the state, such as economic

---

[80] Article 4(e) of the "Strasbourg Declaration on the Right to Leave and Return." (International Institute of Human Rights, 1987); and Article 6(e) of the *Draft Declaration on Freedom and Non-Discrimination in Respect of the Right of Everyone to Leave any Country* (Mubanga-Chipoya, 1988). See also E.I.A. Daes, *Freedom of the Individual under Law: an Analysis of Article 29 of the Universal Declaration of Human Rights* (New York: United Nations, 1990), 121 and 126–127; R. Aybay, "The Right to Leave and the Right to Return: the International Aspect of Freedom of Movement," *Comparative Law Yearbook* 1 (1977); and Inglés (1963), 48.

[81] ECommHR, *X v. Federal Republic of Germany*, 14 December 1970, D&R 37, 69; ECommHR, *C. v Federal Republic of Germany*, 2 December 1985, D&R 45, 198.

[82] ECommHR, *X. v. Federal Republic of Germany*, 16 May 1977, D&R 9, 190.

[83] HRC, *Miguel González del Río v. Peru v. Peru*, 28 October 1992, Comm. No. 263/1987, U.N. Doc. CCPR/C/46/D/263/1987 (1992), par. 5.3.

[84] ECommHR, *X. v. Federal Republic of Germany*, 5 February 1970, Yearbook of the European Convention on Human Rights 13 (1970), 688.

[85] Jagerskiold (1981), 179; and Nowak (1993), 214.

[86] Cf. the *travaux préparatoires* of Article 12 ICCPR; see also *Analysis of the current trends and development regarding the right to leave any country, and some other rights or considerations arising therefrom* (Mubanga-Chipoya, 1988), 53–54.

considerations or grounds connected to migration and population policies.[87] Restrictions on exit to prevent a brain drain is one example of a broad application of the concept of public order. The fact that restrictions must always be justified on the grounds of proportionality and necessity in each individual case makes it difficult to maintain that far-reaching restrictions on such general grounds are permitted. In precisely these cases caution is particularly warranted because measures of this kind are only meaningful if they target a whole group, instead of one individual, which is an approach that is in itself incompatible with the concept of a human right. Regarding the right to leave in particular, we have seen above that interferences with the right to leave must be narrowly interpreted exceptions to a general rule permitting exit and that discriminatory practices are forbidden. In addition, the outflow of professionals from developing countries often has to do with the lack of adequate possibilities for them in these countries, as there is a lack of effective demand for educated professionals in developing nations, although an almost unlimited need exists.[88] Hence, it has been argued that restrictions on exit in such a situation do not seem to provide a solution to the problem of the brain drain, and their necessity has been severely doubted.[89]

4.4 The Right to Leave in the Context of Immigration Control

Already in 1948 the British Delegation in the Human Rights Commission tabled a proposal to permit restrictions on the right to emigrate in order to

---

[87] See Hofmann (1988), 43; and P. van Dijk and G.J.H. van Hoof, *Theory and Practice of the European Convention on Human Rights* (The Hague: Kluwer, 1998), 670. The majority of the Committee of Experts on Human Rights preparing the ECHR Protocol was against the inclusion of a provision permitting restrictions on the ground of economic welfare. See Explanatory Report to the Fourth Protocol, par. 15, 16 and 18. Similarly, grounds such as general welfare and economic and social well-being of the state were proposed by some representatives in the Commission of Human Rights when drafting Article 12, but they were rejected because they were considered to be too far-reaching. See Inglés (1963), Annex IV, Development of Article 12 of the Draft Covenant on Civil and Political Rights, 2.

[88] *Analysis of the current trends and development regarding the right to leave any country, and some other rights or considerations arising therefrom* (Mubanga-Chipoya, 1988), 84. See also the Recommendation of the Meeting of Experts on The Right to Leave and Return to One's Country, Attached to the Strasbourg Declaration on the Right to Leave and to Return (International Institute of Human Rights, 1987), 483-484.

[89] Jagerskiold (1981), 178; and Higgins (1973), 354. According to Special Rapporteur Inglés, restrictions of this kind are only justified in times of war or national emergency, but not in normal times. Inglés (1961), 31.

help neighbouring states fight illegal immigration.[90] Even in the case that one would concede that the concept of public order in the ICCPR and the ECHR may be understood to cover such a general and ambiguous aspect of the public order of another state, it is difficult to see how in practice this approach can be reconciled with the status of the right to leave as a human right. The most pressing question in this regard is how to evaluate such measures in the light of their necessity and proportionality vis-à-vis each individual.[91] In this respect it is important to reiterate that any measure that in reality consists of an automatic, blanket measure of indefinite duration is incompatible with the right to leave and the corresponding obligations of the state, whose authorities should "take appropriate care to ensure that any interference with the right to leave one's country remains justified and proportionate throughout its duration in the individual circumstances of the case".[92] It follows that restrictions on the right to leave that are maintained over lengthy periods should be assessed periodically.[93] These requirements in particular seem irreconcilable with contemporary measures of immigration control that consist of patrolling the coastal waters of West-African countries by vessels of European Member States in order to prevent 'clandestine emigrations'. These policies have the declared aim of being a deterrent for people who want to leave:

> L' objectif est dissuasif. Il faut que les candidats à l'émigration réalisent que les pays Européens sont là, bien présents, et qu'ils ne pourront pas partir.[94]

During 2006 and 2007 thousands of migrants were thus intercepted in the territorial waters of Senegal and Mauritania and were diverted back to the coast of the territories that they attempted to leave.[95] Even if we leave aside the more

---

[90] UN Commission on Human Rights, *Report of the Third Session of the Commission on Human Rights at Lake Success*, 24 May to 18 June 1948, U.N. Doc. E/800 (28 June 1948), 26.
[91] Which is the crucial difference with the case that restrictions on the right to leave based on public order are applied to persons who constitute a serious danger to the country to which they intend to travel.
[92] ECtHR, *A.E. v Poland*, 31 March 2009, Appl. No. 14480/04, par. 49; Bessenyei v. Hungary, 31 October 2008, Appl. No. 37509/06, par. 24. See also ECtHR, *Földes and Földesné Hajlik v. Hungary*, Judgment of 31 October 2006, Appl. No. 41463/02, par. 36.
[93] *Riener v. Bulgaria*, par. 124.
[94] Eduardo Lobo, the Spanish coordinator of a project that commenced in June 2006 in which several Spanish boats patrol Mauritanian territorial waters. Source: Le Monde (12 August 2006).
[95] Amnesty International, *Mauritania: Nobody wants to have anything to do with us, Collective expulsions of migrants denied entry into Europe*, 1 July 2008. See also the Frontex Annual Report 2006 and the documents that it makes available to the press on its website: www.frontex.europa.eu.

substantial concerns relating to the proportionality and necessity of these measures and the way in which they may be subjected to judicial control, there is a conspicuous problem with regard to their legality. The interception of migrants in the territorial waters of a state such as Mauritania is based upon bilateral agreements between that state and Spain, the precise content of which is kept secret. In addition, in the domestic legislation of Mauritania there is no provision that prohibits leaving the country 'irregularly' – that is, without documentation.[96]

Whereas the HRC has conceded that measures of externalisation may adversely affect the right to leave and admonished states to be aware of the impact of measures of immigration control on the exercise of the right to leave,[97] the Court in Strasbourg has adopted a rather deferential position towards a state which aims at protecting its territory from unauthorised entry in such a manner. Such deference transpired from its decision in Xhavara – which is hitherto the only case in which it was argued before the Court that the right to leave was violated as a result of measures which were taken in the context of immigration control.[98] This case was brought before the ECtHR by Albanian citizens who were trying to enter Italy irregularly when their boat sank on 28 March 1997, following a collision with an Italian naval vessel whose crew was attempting to board the vessel. The Italian operation was based upon a number of measures that the Italian and Albanian authorities had jointly decided upon, as a response to increasing irregular migration from Albania to Italy. Thus a naval blockade had been set up and it was agreed between the two countries that the Italian navy was authorised to board and search Albanian vessels. Although the ECtHR held that that the interception activities which extended to international waters and to the territorial waters of Albania fell under Italian jurisdiction, it dismissed the claim that the measures complained of interfered with the applicants' interference of the right to leave, as it considered that these measures were meant to prevent them from entering Italian territory instead:

---

[96] Amnesty International (1 July 2008). See on international legal provisions that may or may not authorise a state to prohibit leaving the state with fraudulent documents C. Harvey and R.P. Barnidge, "Human rights, Free Movement and the Right to Leave in International Law," *International Journal of Refugee Law* 19 (2007).

[97] See *General Comment 27* (1999) in which the HRC requires state parties to "include information in their reports on measures that impose sanctions on international carriers which bring to their territory persons without required documents, where those measures affect the right to leave another country".

[98] *Xhavara and others v. Italy and Albania* (Decision), 11 January 2001, Appl. No. 39473/98.

> La Cour relève que les mesures mises en cause par les requérants ne visaient pas à les priver du droit de quitter l'Albanie, mais à les empêcher d'entrer sur le territoire italien. Le second paragraphe de l'article 2 du Protocole n° 4 ne trouve donc pas à s'appliquer en l'espèce.[99]

However, such a reading of Article 2 of Protocol 4 seems to disregard the status of the right to leave as a human right in a manner which seems somewhat two-faced, as it is precisely sovereign states which have always been the first to argue that the right to leave is not a right that other states need to complete through a 'duty to admit'. The implications of the independent standing of the right to leave in existing international law are well captured by Violeta Moreno Lax who, referring to the 1969 Vienna Convention of the Law of Treaties, insists that

> Richer countries cannot shield themselves behind a 'collectivized' reading of the right to leave to negate its *Wirkung* in their own regard. The opposite would amount to make some other indefinite poorer State in the South, less able to manage at will migration flows, responsible for any given undesired migrant. The truth is that *each and every* Signatory State of an instrument recognizing the right to leave, exercising power beyond its territorial jurisdiction through interception, remains bound to its obligation to guarantee it to everyone subject to its authority and control.[100]

Remarkable is also the decision by the European Commission of Human Rights in a case involving detention with a view to deportation.[101] The Commission decided that a person whose deportation has been ordered and is detained with a view to the enforcement of the order may not avail himself of the right to freely leave the country.[102] Here the Commission seemed to be handling the concept of public order in a rather contradictory manner: if someone is detained because public order requires his removal from the country, it cannot at the same time be argued that on account of his detention, public order does not allow him to leave the country. The paradoxical way in which the Commission thus dealt with the relation between immigration detention and the right to leave suggests that immigration detention possesses a logic of its own, a subject which we shall delve a littler deeper into in chapter 6.

---

[99] *Xhavara and others v. Italy and Albania*, par. 3.
[100] V. Moreno Lax, "Must EU Borders Have Doors for Refugees? On the Compatibility of Schengen Visas with EU Member States' Obligations to Provide International Protection to Refugees," *European Journal of Migration and Law* 10(2008). 353-354. An increasing number of non-Western countries are currently criminalising "illegal emigration".
[101] ECommHR, *X. v. Federal Republic of Germany*, 26 May 1970, Yearbook of the European Convention on Human Rights 13 (1970), 1028.
[102] Ibid., 1034.

4.5 On the Right to Leave and the Visibility of the Content of Sovereignty

Few rights have been so widely proclaimed, and of few rights has their violation been regarded so plainly as a symptom of tyranny as the right to leave one's country. Yet, it should be borne in mind that a right to leave is a relatively recent notion that is immediately linked with ideas on popular sovereignty and the nature of the sovereign territorial state.[103] If in liberal theory the conceptual basis for the body politic is a voluntary contract, then a fundamental right to leave has to be recognised. In this light it is understandable that non-liberal governments, underpinned as they are by very different views on the nature of political authority, have consistently refused to recognise an individual right to leave.

However, not only illiberal states have regarded the issue of exit as a favour, the granting of which was within their sovereign power alone. We have seen that even after the Second World War, when the right to leave was already codified in various international instruments, also liberal democracies have at times regarded the question of exit as a matter falling entirely under the discretionary power of the executive. The stance of the United States' federal government in its fight against communism was particularly contradictory: while insisting on the right to leave for citizens of the communist countries, it maintained at the same time that its own decisions on exit were not for the judiciary to review as they constituted acts of foreign policy. The US Supreme Court, however, considered the right to leave to be a fundamental right, the interference of which should be subject to judicial scrutiny.

Indeed, recognising that the issue of exit is a fundamental right does not entail that its exercise may never be limited. We have seen in the previous chapter that at times the collective interest (which is ultimately to be defined by the sovereign state) may collide with individuals' unrestricted exercise of their fundamental rights. However, the special status of a human right means that it cannot just be traded away for other social gains. Thus, international law only permits restrictions on the right to leave on the grounds of a limited number of state interests. In addition, the basis for the restrictions is to be laid down by law, and these restrictions need to be proportionate and necessary in view of the circumstances of each individual case. Moreover, Article 13 ECHR

---

[103] See Alen Gamlen on the way in which territorial states relate to their diaspora's abroad and how this unsettles notions of the "modern geopolitical imagination": A. Gamlen, "The emigration state and the modern geopolitical imagination," *Political Geography* 27 (2008).

and Article 2(3) ICCPR require an effective remedy if the individual can present an arguable complaint that his right to leave is violated.

The right to leave is held to encompass the right of the individual to choose the state of destination.[104] This also entails that an alien who is expelled from one state is allowed to determine to which state he or she will be expelled, albeit this is dependent on the consent of the state that he or she wishes to enter.[105] In his study on the right to leave in 1988, Chama Mubanga-Chipoya considered that it is the need for this consent in particular that makes international movement problematic in the contemporary world, rather than the question of exit in itself.[106] However, contemporary immigration policies in themselves may profoundly affect the actual exercise of the right to leave for numerous individuals as well. Indeed, it has been said that we seem to be witnessing "the re-emergence of a notion that in the past was reserved for countries inspired by the Soviet model".[107] The term 'illegal emigration' is again becoming commonplace, but now as a tool in the fight against unwanted immigration.[108] The fact that it is a concept that is, at least when it is employed in a general sense (i.e. without due regard to the circumstances of each individual case), in violation of international legal norms appears to make little difference. How else can we possibly explain that the Moroccan Minister of the Interior, Mustafah Sahel, visiting his French counterpart Nicholas Sarkozy, could proudly declare that in 2004 his country had succeeded in curbing by 27% the number of candidates for illegal emigration?[109] And how are we to interpret the statement made by the Conference of the Interior Ministers of the Western Mediterranean (CIMO) of May 2006, "welcoming the efforts made by the countries on the southern shore of the Mediterranean to limit illegal emigration towards Europe"?[110] Furthermore, the notion of illegal emigration turns up increasingly frequently in newspaper articles, reporting for

---

[104] See ECommHR in *Peltonen v. Finland*.

[105] HRC, *General Comment 27* (1999), 8. See also HRC *General Comment 15: The position of aliens under the Covenant* (Twenty-seventh session, 1986), Compilation of General Comments and General Recommendations Adopted by Human Rights Treaty Bodies, U.N. Doc. HRI/GEN/1/Rev.6 at 140 (2003), 9.

[106] See also V. Boutkevitch, *Working paper on the right to freedom of movement and related issues*, prepared in implementation of Decision 1996/109 of the Sub-Commission on Prevention of Discrimination and Protection of Minorities, U.N. Doc. E\CN.4\Sub.2\1997\22 (29 July 1997).

[107] C. Rodier, "'Emigration illégale': une notion á bannir," *Libération*, 13 June 2006.

[108] Id.

[109] Source: Morrocotimes, 6 October 2005. The law of 11 November 2003 makes it possible to severely punish people who illegally leave Moroccan territory.

[110] Quoted by Rodier (2006).

example that Libya succeeded in arresting more than a thousand candidates for illegal emigration during the second half of July 2006.[111] The Moroccan Minister of the Interior announced publicly that the Moroccan authorities had arrested 383 "illegal emigrants" in the same period, the majority of whom were Moroccan citizens.[112]

We shall see in the next chapter that a world completely divided up into territorial states cannot guarantee the right to leave adequately if it holds on to the view that matters relating to the entry and stay of non-nationals fall wholly within the sovereign prerogative of the sovereign state. But even more significantly, we shall see that a sovereign right to decide on the entry and stay of non-nationals is often defended with much the same arguments that were used to submit matters relating to exit to the sovereign discretion of the nation state in the past. Thus, both the extent to which an individual is able to leave and the extent to which he or she is able to enter the state have always been contingent on what has been perceived by the sovereign state as the collective interest. The way in which international law currently differentiates between the human interests that lie respectively in leaving and entering a state is brought about by the fact that with regard to the right to leave, the content of sovereignty as the exercise of jurisdiction over persons in a given body politic has become visible and explicit, while with regard to the issue of entering or staying in a state that is not one's own, sovereignty's content remains largely concealed on account of the way in which the state presents immigration as predominantly engaging sovereignty's territorial frame. The second part of this argument shall be fleshed out in the next chapter.

---

[111] Le Soleil (Senegal), 8 August 2006.
[112] Source: Libération (Casablanca), 28 July 2006.

Chapter 5

Freedom of Movement II: Decisions on Entry as a Sovereign Prerogative?

> The present international legal system is so determined to protect the interests of states and their territorial boundaries that any people who seek to move across those boundaries are seen as intruders. If they can enter at all, they enter at their own risk.[1]

5.1 Introduction

In the previous chapter, I have discussed the right to leave, the international recognition of which constitutes an evident interference with the domestic competence of the state.[2] Indeed, the development of that right in particular shows that the reserved domain of domestic jurisdiction is not an absolute and invariable notion, but one that is relative and which varies with the development of political theory and international law, and the extent of obligations imposed and undertaken.[3] It is not so long ago that national executives attempted to restrain the right to leave with much the same reasoning that, as we shall see below, is currently being used to portray decisions on entry as falling almost wholly within executive discretion. But while *both* aspects of freedom of movement pose direct challenges to the concept of community, we find that concerning emigration, the jurisdictional content of sovereignty is emphasised and its territorial frame remains hidden, whereas with regard to immigration the situation is precisely the other way around. In contemporary

---

[1] R. McCorquodale, "International Law, Boundaries and Imagination," in *Boundaries and Justice: Diverse Ethical Perspectives*, eds. D. Miller and S. Hashmi (Princeton/Oxford: Princeton University Press, 2001) 145, 152.
[2] M.S. Vazquez, "Self-Determination and the Right to Leave," *Israel Yearbook on Human Rights* 12 (1982), 92–93.
[3] G.S. Goodwin Gill, *International law and the movement of persons between states* (Oxford: Oxford University Press, 1978), 55.

geopolitical imagination immigration is predominantly perceived as behaviour of individuals "disturbing the geographical sovereignty of states (as political refugees or otherwise)."[4] Related to this understanding of immigration as threatening the *internal* manifestation of territorial sovereignty, refugees and large flows of unauthorised migration are also seen as jeopardising *international* stability and security because territorial boundaries are crossed without state consent and thus contrary to the rules and expectations of the international legal system.[5] Thus, with regard to the modern state's responses to immigration, focussed attention is drawn to sovereignty's territorial frame, and the fact that jurisdictional aspects are inevitably involved as well whenever a state enforces its immigration policies on the life of the individual is often disregarded. Contemporary immigration policies by Western states thus express the dominant perception according to which contemporary patterns of migration pose a problem to the global system based on territory and the social system of the territorial state, which therefore needs to be prevented and contained by the use of violent dissuasive measures.[6] However, one can also drastically reverse the angle from which migration is considered:

> Anthropologists understand humans as a 'migratory species' (Massey et al., 1998) and interpret migration as normal behaviour (Kubat and Nowotny, Hoerder, 2003). In that view, it is rather the way, the existing social systems are organised, that poses a problem for the principally mobile human species. In order to vision policies, which would be more adequate to the migratory species one could try to put the entire debate upside down. And instead of analysing the reasons for migration, tackling what are perceived as migration crises, and combating illegal migration, one could alternatively analyse why the social systems fail to integrate mobile populations.[7]

To the extent that modern law, as an integral part of our social systems, fails to take full account of the individual interests of 'mobile populations', I believe that its failure to do so is due to the perceived self-evidence and innocence of territory as the foundation for political organisation, and the resultant inoculation of territorial sovereignty against the transformative power of most

---

[4] C. Harding and C.L. Lim, "The significance of Westphalia: an archaeology of the international legal order" in *Renegotiating Westphalia. Essays and commentary on the European and conceptual foundations of modern international law*, eds. C. Harding and C.L. Lim (The Hague: Kluwer Law International, 1999), 18.

[5] McCorquodale (2001), 151.

[6] F. Düvell, *Illegal immigration: What to do about it*, Working Paper Working Group Migration-Mobility-Minorities-Membership (Florence: EUI/RSCAS, 2004), 9; and Médecins Sans Frontieres, *Violence and Immigration. Report on illegal sub-Saharan immigrants (ISSs) in Morocco* (30 September 2005), 4.

[7] Ibid., 9.

modern constitutional discourse. I shall argue in this chapter that the way in which immigration is portrayed and perceived as impinging first and foremost on the 'integrity of national borders' overpowers the consideration of most – albeit not all – individual rights that may be at stake in its regulation. In order to present my argument convincingly, I shall first trace the development over time of the sovereign right to exclude (section 5.2). Thereafter (section 5.3) I shall explore the legal framework regulating the entry and stay of nationals in a state other than their own. The legal regulation of immigration by third-country nationals into and within the European Union is addressed in a separate section (5.4). Instead of a detailed analysis of the various EU policies and legislation, this section is included in order to explore the way in which territoriality features in the allegedly post-national constellation of the EU. In the conclusions (section 5.5) I shall draw together my findings from this and the previous chapters, and I shall argue that the asymmetry in the legal framework regulating international human movement is the inevitable result of the way in which territoriality has shaped modern constitutional discourse.

5.2 *Development of a Sovereign Right to Exclude*

It is a commonly accepted position that matters concerning the entry and sojourn of aliens fall within the reserved domain of domestic jurisdiction of the national state, which possesses an almost absolute right of exclusion largely unfettered by international law.[8]

> It is an accepted maxim of international law, that every sovereign nation has the power, as inherent in the sovereignty, and essential to its self-preservation, to forbid the entrance of foreigners within its dominions, or to admit them only in such cases and upon such conditions as it may seem fit to describe.[9]

---

[8] L.F.L. Oppenheim, *International Law*, ed. H. Lauterpacht (London: Longmans, 1955), 692; R.B. Lillich, *The Human Rights of Aliens in Contemporary International Law* (Manchester: Manchester University Press, 1984), 35; S. Oda, "The Individual in International Law," in *Manual of Public International Law*, ed. M. Sørensen, (London: MacMillan & Co, 1968), 481; P. Jean, "Le Contenu de la Liberte de Circulation," in *Liberte de Circulation des Personnes en Droit International*, eds. M. Flory and R. Higgins, (Paris: Economica, 1988), 33; K. Doehring, "Aliens, Expulsion and Deportation" in *Encyclopeda of International Law*, R. Bernhardt (Amsterdam: Elsevier Science Publishers, 1992), 107-108. For a summary of these views see R. Plender, *International Immigration Law* (Dordrecht: Kluwer Academic Publishers, 1988), 1-4.

[9] United States Supreme Court, *Nishimura Ekiu v. U.S.*, 142 U.S. (1892), 659.

Before investigating the validity of this claim in contemporary international law, I will address the way in which, historically, questions of the entry and sojourn of foreigners have become so explicitly and intimately bound up with sovereignty. We have seen in chapter 2 that the contemporary understanding of sovereignty accords crucial importance to territorial boundaries. These are to be guarded jealously and strictly, especially with regard to the movement of persons, because the territorially fixed population has become one of the foundations of the concept of sovereignty. However, as we have also seen, due to changing perceptions about the nature and source of the ultimate power of the state, the concept of sovereignty decreased in importance when it came to matters concerning exit: a process which found its culmination in the codification of the right to leave in international law in the twentieth century.

We will see that regarding the entrance and, albeit to a somewhat lesser extent, sojourn, of aliens, altering views on the notion of sovereignty have in general led to a reverse development. But it should be emphasised from the outset that the extensive exercise of a sovereign right to regulate immigration is a relatively recent phenomenon, and the allegedly classical perspective that the right to exclude aliens is an essential attribute of modern sovereignty may turn out to be no more than "a late nineteenth century artefact".[10] Early theorists of international law did not recognize an absolute right of the sovereign to exclude. Hugo de Groot, for example, was insistent on a right of foreign refuge for those who had been expelled from their homes, and in his eyes expulsion was only acceptable when it was justified by a due cause.[11] Francisco de Vittoria as well, in his eagerness to establish as a fundamental human right the faculty of trading with residents of other lands, favoured the individual right of freedom of movement above a sovereign's right of exclusion.[12] Similarly, Immanuel Kant conditioned the right of the stranger to hospitality on the possibility of commerce by the original inhabitants of a country. In his essay *Zum Ewigen Frieden*, written in 1795, Kant's discussion of world citizenship distinguishes between a right of temporary sojourn (the right of a visitor) and the right to permanent sojourn (the right of a guest):[13]

---

[10] D.A. Martin, "Effects of International Law on Migration Policy and Practice: The Uses of Hypocrisy," *International Migration Review* 23 (1989), 547.

[11] J.A. Nafziger, "The general admission of aliens under international law," *American Journal of International Law* 77 (1983), 811; and Plender (1988), 63.

[12] D.P. O'Connell, *International Law* (London: Stevens and Sons, 1970), 693.

[13] See on this further: S. Benhabib, *The Rights of Others* (Cambridge University Press, 2004).

> Hospitality means the right of a foreigner not to be treated with hostility by mere reason of his arrival on foreign soil. The natives may turn him away – if this can be done without his perishing – but so long as he behaves peaceably they may not show hostility towards him.[14]

In Kant's view, then, recognition of the right of hospitality shall bring mankind nearer to a cosmopolitan constitution, and as such it is underbuilt by two universalist premises: mankind must endure each other's proximity as the surface of the earth – which is in communal possession – is finite, and "originally no one had more right than another to be in any one particular place."[15] And although it is his name that is most often associated with an absolute right of exclusion, even Emmerich de Vattel (1714–1767) applied significant limitations to external sovereignty when it comes to the entry or sojourn of aliens.[16]

In medieval Europe, when the nation state did not yet exist, it was not so much the possibility to enter territory that gave rise to problems. Instead, as we have seen, for many individuals the right to depart from it was problematic, as a large part of the population was tied to territory due to the institution of serfdom. Nonetheless, for free people there was ample opportunity for freedom of movement and choice of residence, due to the imperatives of economic trade, even though medieval cities often controlled immigration strictly.[17] In any case, *national* borders (in so far as one could already speak of them), possessed little significance for the individual traveller, even as they were of concern to rulers with regard to warfare. Entry could be refused, and removal imposed, but such measures were usually directed against certain individuals and not against foreigners as such.[18] Exile was an individual measure used against members of the polity as a punishment, mainly for political offences, and in those cases that expulsion was a mass measure, it was directed at religious minorities. However, it should be acknowledged that the expulsion of these minorities was indeed bound up with early attempts of monarchs to homogenise populations in order to form strong states, inhabited by a population whose allegiance they could be sure of:

---

[14] Immanuel Kant, *Perpetual Peace, A Philosophical Proposal*, transl. H. O'Brien (London: Sweet and Maxwell, 1927), 23.

[15] Id.

[16] Nafziger, (1983), 814; Goodwin Gill, *International law and the movement of persons between states* (1978), 95; and S. McGrath Dale, "The Flying Dutchman Dichotomy: The International Right to Leave v. The Sovereign Right to Exclude," *Dickinson Journal of International Law* 9 (1991), 365.

[17] Nafziger (1983), 810.

[18] A. Dummet and A. Nicol, *Subjects, Citizens, Aliens and Others: Nationality and Immigration Law* (London: Weidenfeld and Nicolson, 1990), 11.

The fact that questions of religion and political loyalty are intertwined is clear by the sixteenth and seventeenth century. Corporate expulsion can be seen as a tool of state formation, occurring against the backdrop of the break-up of the universal church. Indeed, for some observers its frequency and concentration in the western part of Europe is related to the fact that it goes hand in hand with the emergence of the modern state system there.[19]

Another example in which the 'right to remain' was infringed upon, apart from exile for those who had attempted to undermine the authority of the state and expulsions of religious minorities, was the practice in early modern Europe to restrict poor relief to the local poor. By placing deportation in a historical perspective, William Walters shows that the policing – in the sense of governing – of the foreign poor had become, by the late nineteenth century, a major preoccupation of deportation policy.[20] Yet, in the sixteenth and seventeenth centuries, the foreigner was not yet defined in national terms, but it was the distinction between *local* versus foreigner which was deemed relevant for the application of poor laws.[21]

The Westphalian system of territorial states, dividing populations and allocating these to specific territories, conflicts with the ideal of individual freedom of movement. We have seen that in the era of mercantilism, this friction again came mainly to the surface with regard to the right to leave. The possibility to enter remained largely unaffected as states were generally happy to welcome immigrants, perceiving immigration as a way to increase the population. At the time that the absolute power of the sovereign ruler was being attacked, free movement across state boundaries became the norm. Not only the right to emigrate was perceived as a natural right, also the freedom to enter was scarcely subject to restrictions. The French Constitution of 1791 guaranteed "*liberté de aller, de rester, de partir*" and initially the Revolution with its cosmopolitan spirit was very welcoming towards foreigners. Thus, refugees and exiles were received with encouragement, in the hope that cosmopolitan ideals and principles of human rights would "contaminate neighbouring people and incite uprisings against tyrants."[22]

Nevertheless, during the Revolutionary Wars, the situation changed dramatically. Foreigners, especially those from countries with which France was at war, suddenly became suspicious individuals, who could be banished from

---

[19] W. Walters, "Deportation, Expulsion, and the International Police of Aliens," *Citizenship Studies* 6 (2002), 271.
[20] Ibid., 270.
[21] See also J. Torpey, *The Invention of the Passport* (Cambridge: Cambridge University Press, 2000), 19.
[22] J. Kristeva, *Strangers to Ourselves* (New York: Columbia University Press, 1991), 156. Cf. Torpey (2000), 24.

the territory of the French Republic. Some of the measures that were directed against them at that time may remind one of some of the contemporary national 'integration' policies in Europe:

> Many were imprisoned in town houses and requisitioned state buildings. It was proposed that 'hospitality certificates' be created, which would be given by municipalities to those foreigners having successfully passed the 'civics examination'; they would then wear an armband bearing the name of their country of origin and the word 'hospitality'.[23]

Not only France adopted restrictive measures but around the same time similar developments took place in other European countries and in the United States.[24] Here again we witness the inconsistency, already dealt with in detail above (chapters 2 and 3), between modern theory with its emphasis on universalism, and the actual practices which its ideas have given rise to, characterised by territorial particularism. And while this inconsistency is by definition magnified by the way in which the foreigner is treated, the meanings that are ascribed to territorial boundaries generally (thus not only with regard to *entering* foreign territory) reveal modernity's ambiguity in the clearest sense: as we have seen above, around the same time restrictions were imposed on freely leaving the country.

Nevertheless, liberal ideals continued to increase in importance, and during the nineteenth century freedom of movement had become the norm. Millions of people left their countries in order to start a new life elsewhere. Entry was generally an uncomplicated matter, due to an expanding economy in the Western countries, compatibility between source and destination countries, and the predominance of liberal thought in general.[25] The International Emigration Conference passed a resolution in 1889 that affirmed the right of the individual to come and go and dispose of his destinies as he pleased.[26] In 1891, the Institute of International Law rejected the idea that sovereign power entails an absolute right of exclusion and in 1892 it adopted the 'International Regulations on the Admission and Expulsion of Aliens', in which states were permitted to refuse entry solely in the public interest and for very serious reasons. It was stipulated that the protection of national labour in itself was not a sufficient reason for non-admission.[27] And although

---

[23] Kristeva (1991), 158.
[24] Plender (1988), 65.
[25] Nafziger (1983), 815; and Torpey (2000), 91–92.
[26] B. Thomas, *International Migration and Economic Development* (Paris: UNESCO, 1961), 9.
[27] Institute of International Law, "International Regulations on the Admission and Expulsion of Aliens," *Institut De Droit International Annuaire* 12 (1892). See on this also O'Connell (1970), 695; Nafziger (1983), 832; and T. Schindlmayer, "Sovereignty, legal regimes and international migration" *International Migration* 41 (2003), 113.

these documents did not contain binding norms, they do reflect perceptions on immigration that were common at the time of their adoption, but would presently be considered almost naive and certainly at odds with the way in which the law shapes the relation between state power and whoever is perceived as the 'foreigner'. Thus, expulsions in this era were seldom specifically directed at foreigners as such, but they were seen as a means of social regulation in the case of criminals. Their punishment consisted of removal from the territory of their countries of origin and they were transported to colonies or other areas.[28]

However, from the late nineteenth century onwards, states gradually started to impose border controls. Even though the attitude towards freedom of movement initially remained fairly liberal, states started to make distinctions between aliens and nationals. The changing connotations of nationalism, from freedom and equality for the people, to the particularistic language of national identity linked to territorial boundaries, and a common identity of the people, expressed themselves in a growing hostility towards foreigners. Ethnic, racial or national fault lines became the markers for political order and this period saw the introduction of racially, culturally and socially exclusive immigration laws.[29] With the onset of World War I, passports became obligatory in order to enter another country, and the 'foreigner' had to be identified by means of documentation.[30] Although these measures were initially seen as temporary, necessary in view of the war, the *laissez faire* era with regard to international migration had reached its definite end.[31]

We have seen that the perception of an unbreakable and necessary linkage between the state, people and identity reached its zenith in the period between the two world wars. Nationalism had changed citizenship's connotations of equality, freedom and self-government, and national identity was the first

---

[28] Walters, "Deportation, Expulsion, and the International Police of Aliens" (2002), 272.
[29] Such as laws preventing the immigration of 'paupers' or 'persons with low morals' and a number of specified nationalities. See D. Christie Tait, "International aspects of Migration," *Journal of the Royal Institute of International Affairs* 6 (1927); and H. Fields, "Closing Immigration Throughout the World," *American Journal of International Law* 26 (1932). Good examples of the latter are the US Chinese Exclusion Act of 1882 (Act of May 6th, f 1882, 22 Stat 58); and restrictions on Jewish migration to the United Kingdom and laws concerning "foreign Poles" working in Prussia. See W. Walters, "Mapping Schengenland: denaturalizing the border," *Environment and Planing D: Society and Space* 20 (2002), 571.
[30] See R. Aybay, "The Right to Leave and the Right to Return: the International Aspect of Freedom of Movement," *Comparative Law Yearbook* 1 (1977), 123; Plender (1988), 77; and Torpey (2000), 1.
[31] Torpey (2000), 112; and M.R. Marrus, The *Unwanted: European Refugees in the Twentieth Century* (Oxford: Oxford University Press, 1985), 62.

political priority while it had simultaneously become synonymous with citizenship. The international movement of people and the significance of territorial boundaries were greatly influenced by this shift in mentality. Most countries that had been welcoming towards immigrants before now imposed serious restrictions or even closed their borders completely.[32]

The idea that every nation should have its own state also influenced the right to remain. After the First World War and the break up of the last European empires, population transfers were seen as an acceptable way in which the ideal of the nation state could be achieved, especially in the new states that were formed after the disintegration of the Ottoman Empire.[33] And although Nazi Germany later took these practices to their extreme, they were by no means exclusive to Hitler's Germany, nor were they limited to the period between the two World Wars:

> While today it might be associated with ethnic cleansing, for statespersons at the middle of the century, population transfer was legitimated as an unpleasant but expedient and technical means of effecting national and international order. Hence population transfer did not end with the defeat of the Nazi regime. Under the Potsdam Protocol the Allies sanctioned a wave of transfers that would culminate in the removal of more than 14 million ethnic Germans from such countries as Poland, Hungary and Czechoslovakia.[34]

Precisely due to the way in which national identity, territory, and rights had become linked at the beginning of the twentieth century, an international refugee regime started to emerge around the same time. We will see below that international refugee law, on the one hand, and a system of sovereign states based on territoriality, on the other, are structurally connected to each other. The First World War with its break up of empires and subsequent revolution produced millions of refugees and a whole new category of people, the stateless.[35] While passports had become essential for international movement, for many refugees it was impossible to obtain the proper documents. The League of Nations recognised the difficult situation these people were in, and efforts were made in order to make movement easier for them. The Nansen Passport, named after the League's first High Commissioner for Refugees, initially

---

[32] See about the interwar situation: Christie Tait (1927) and Fields (1932).
[33] Lillich, *The Human Rights of Aliens in Contemporary International Law* (1984), 33.
[34] Walters, "Deportation, Expulsion, and the International Police of Aliens," (2002), 274. See on this also H. Arendt, *The Origins of Totalitarianism* (San Diego/New York/London: Harcourt Brace and Company, 1976), 276; Lillich, *The Human Rights of Aliens in Contemporary International Law* (1984), 62 and 76; and Marrus (1985), 327–328.
[35] The refugees from Russia were probably the most prominent amongst these. A vast majority were denationalised after departing and thus became stateless. See Torpey (2000), 124–125.

intended solely for Russian refugees, but later expanded to cover other groups, such as Armenians and minorities from the former Ottoman territories, was to provide a solution.

At first, these passports only facilitated movement: participating governments agreed to recognise those documents, but no state was obliged to receive refugees bearing such papers.[36] Later, in 1926, some of the participating governments to the original agreement extended the right of movement to encompass a right of return to the state that had issued the document. The League of Nations, in the 1933 Convention Relating to the International Status of Refugees, accorded Nansen Passport bearers some elements of what we might now have called 'supranational citizenship' by giving the High Commissioner for Refugees the authority to perform certain consular functions on behalf of those refugees in possession of such a document.[37] In addition, the Convention provided that a refugee had to be admitted by a Contracting State if he came directly from a state where he feared persecution.[38] The emergence of the Nansen passports can be seen as the birth of the international refugee regime: no longer was the protection of refugees a matter solely for the state that chose to afford them protection, but it became a concern for the international community at large.

International law's emerging concern with refugees after the First World War finds an interesting parallel with the way in which it dealt with the issue of national minorities during the same period, as was described in Chapter 3. Refugees, just as minorities, did not fit the population-territory-identity ideal of the sovereign state. In addition, both endangered the stability of a state system based on territoriality. Geopolitical considerations in the refugee regime were made apparent by the fact that the League of Nations only devoted attention to those refugees from regions that were considered most disruptive to the European order.[39]

The previous two chapters traced a changed perception of sovereignty in the period between the two World Wars, one that was "more jealous and absolute than anything known before."[40] We saw how that development caused citizenship to acquire new connotations, very far removed from those by which it had previously and originally been characterised. Citizenship

---

[36] R. Lui, "Governing Refugees 1919–1945," *Borderlands E-Journal* (1) 2002, at 36.
[37] Torpey (2000), 129.
[38] Lillich, *The Human Rights of Aliens in Contemporary International Law* (1984), 36.
[39] Lui (2002), at 38.
[40] K. Polanyi, *The Great Transformation: The Political and Economic Origins of Our Time* (Boston: Beacon Press, 1944), 202.

became instrumental in determining and establishing who belonged and who did not. In its most extreme uses, such as by the Nazis, this instrumental use of citizenship profoundly affected the right to remain.[41] The Nuremberg Laws of 1935, which deprived Jews of German citizenship, were the foundation for subsequent plans to expel all Jews from German territory.[42] The newly emerged sovereignty, with its accompanying system of controls on movement embedded in national membership, made sure that the victims of these measures could find refuge elsewhere only with difficulty. 'Paper walls' had been erected around all Western democracies, and at the Evian Conference, which was organised in 1938 in order to address the problem of Jewish refugees from Germany and Austria, it was made clear by Western governments that they had little intention of changing their perception of sovereignty as entailing an absolute right of exclusion. This had already been illustrated by the fact that only eight states had ratified the 1933 Convention on Refugees.[43]

After the Second World War, the number of displaced people in Europe finding themselves outside their countries of origin amounted to over 11 million. A refugee crisis of unprecedented magnitude presented itself, and a great part of the displaced persons over Europe were interned in camps. Already during the war, refugee relief operations were being planned. An international organisation, the United Nations Relief and Rehabilitation Administration (UNRRA), with the task of repatriating people, was established in 1943. In actual fact, the Allied Forces handled most 'resettlements'. In 1947 the UNRRA was succeeded by the International Refugee Organisation (IRO), intended to deal with the remaining one million displaced persons in Europe. The constitution of the IRO stated that if a displaced person had reasonable grounds to fear persecution on returning to his country of origin because of his race, religion, nationality or political opinion, he could refuse repatriation. And many of the remaining displaced persons did indeed refuse repatriation, especially those Eastern European refugees hostile to the Soviet regime and its expansionism. Thus, the IRO had to secure admission for these people somewhere. When it became clear that most Western European countries were reluctant to grant admissions on a large scale, the IRO searched for other solutions, encouraging non-European States to open their borders by

---

[41] Or the right to enter (return), as had already been shown by Soviet Russia, which, after the Revolution, denationalised a large part of the refugees who had left the country.

[42] See about pre-war Nazi plans for the mass departure of German Jews: Marrus (1985), 211–219.

[43] R.B. Lillich, *The Human Rights of Aliens in Contemporary International Law* (1984), 36.

linking the economic needs of these countries with the labour potential of the DP population.[44]

The IRO was succeeded by the UN High Commissioner's Office for Refugees in 1949. Although initially concerned only with Europeans, the United Nations High Commissioner for Refugees (UNHCR) gradually adopted a global mandate, less explicitly focussed on the events of the war in Europe. Whereas during the pre-war period, with the emergence of the Nansen Passports, refugees had been defined according to their membership of a particular national group, the UNHCR adopted the view that refugees had rights irrespective of their nationality.[45]

These developments were reflected in the 1951 Convention relating to the Status of Refugees and the modifications made to that Convention by the 1967 Protocol relating to the Status of Refugees. In spite of the fact that discretion on the entry and admission of aliens was reaffirmed as an essential attribute of the sovereign state, under the Convention national governments accepted certain restrictions to unlimited discretion in this field. The nature and extent of these restrictions will be dealt with in the section below. During the late forties, many refugees from Eastern Europe had started to come to the West, their departure prompted by harsh economic conditions combined with increasing political oppression. Before the Communist countries closed their borders completely to emigration, thousands of Eastern Europeans left their countries, seeking a safe haven or a better future in the West, which initially did not open its doors spontaneously, and neither did it welcome these people warmly:

> escapees who reached the American zone of Germany stood a reasonable chance of being jailed for illegal crossing of a frontier. By 1952, nearly 200.000 anti-Communist refugees were jammed into camps and centers in Berlin and West Germany, sometimes living in appalling conditions.[46]

However, as the Cold War hardened, Western countries started to maintain an open admissions policy for almost anyone coming from a Communist country, and refugee status was not reserved for the politically persecuted, but it was also offered to those individuals whose motivations to emigrate were largely economic.[47] On the one hand, this policy was clearly a tool in the

---

[44] Marrus (1985), 344–345. Three quarters of the approximately remaining one million DP's between 1947 and 1951 went to the United States, Australia, Israel, and Canada. Only 170.000 were received by Western European states.
[45] Torpey (2000), 144.
[46] Marrus (1985), 354.
[47] See A. Ghoshal and T.M. Crowley, "Refugees and immigrants: A Human Rights Dilemma," *Human Rights Quarterly* 5 (1983).

ideological struggle between the East and the West: refugee law was very useful for stigmatising the Communist regimes.[48] On the other hand, it was also a logical consequence of Western insistence upon the acknowledgement of the right to leave by the Communist countries. In any case, firm control over exit by the Soviets and their Eastern European allies prevented truly massive flows of people reaching the West.

At the same time, it should be noted that Cold War concerns could and did make entry (just as with regard to exit, as shown in the previous chapter) a more complicated issue for reasons of state and public security. In the case of the Federal Republic of Germany, foreigners crossing the border could receive severe penalties if they diverged from the route or destination prescribed in the visa.[49]

Because of shortages on the labour market, and in their efforts to rebuild post-war Europe, Western European countries encouraged the importation of foreign workers from the 1950s to the 1960s. These were mostly recruited from Mediterranean countries such as Italy, Yugoslavia, Turkey and Morocco. Around the same time, refugees started to come to Europe from the developing world. When applications for asylum kept increasing restrictive measures were taken in order to stem and control these flows of refugees. It should be noted that the Western European countries were more sympathetic to the plight of Eastern European refugees than to that of those coming from the third world. Another post-war development was immigration to European countries from their colonies or former colonies. Although the former colonial powers were initially fairly open to people from the overseas territories, these states changed their attitude fairly quickly and generally chose to close their borders to colonial-metropolitan migration, except to those who were perceived to have close ties to the European country in question.

From the 1970s onwards, due to economic concerns propelled by the 1973-1974 oil crisis, Northern European countries actively attempted to stem immigration flows and wished to repatriate many of the guest workers they had so enthusiastically recruited in the previous two decades. Nonetheless, it appeared that they were not always able to do so effectively. Asylum laws could be – and indeed were – made more restrictive, but repatriation programmes failed and

---

[48] In addition, the common perception might have been that communist poverty is attributable to the government, whereas poverty in capitalist countries is attributable to the individual. The US, for example, openly recognised the economic considerations of refugees from Communist countries, but refugees from non-Communist countries were sent back because they were economic refugees. See Editorial, "Political Legitimacy in the Law of Political Asylum," *Harvard Law Review* 99 (1985), 463.

[49] Torpey (2000), 148.

because family reunification had in most domestic jurisdictions become a legal right for resident immigrants, many new immigrants had to be admitted. The alarm caused by states' incapacity to reduce immigration pressures called for more restrictive measures, which in turn produced more illegal immigration.[50] The circle was complete when governments responded to this phenomenon with ever more strict legislation concerning the entry and sojourn of non-nationals.

Moreover, migration slowly but surely came to be regarded not only as an economic concern, but also as a security issue.[51] Political power in the twentieth century, especially with the advent of the welfare state after WWII, had come to be concerned with the wealth, health, welfare and prosperity of populations. As a result, immigration policy could, when the presence of aliens was perceived as an economic and social threat, become an instrument to defend and promote the welfare of a nationally defined population. This trend, originating in the ethnically and socially exclusive immigration laws at the turn of the nineteenth century, has become much stronger since the 1970s. Since the late 1980s, immigration has become a major political concern. The problems associated with immigration are presently worded in a rhetoric of 'threat, crisis, and 'invasion', which leaves one without doubt about the link with traditional notions of sovereignty and security. National identity once again plays a distinct role in public discourse. And even the legal, individual rights-based system of asylum is far from immune from political influences – refugees from countries which lack geopolitical importance generally do not enjoy priority status.[52] Even more importantly, the very *system* of refugee protection is deeply linked to the territorialisation of political organisation with its concurrent emphasis on identity, as we shall see below.

Generally speaking, since the early twentieth century onwards we have witnessed an ever more progressive assertion of sovereignty as inherently entailing the right to exclude foreigners. The idea of fundamental rights has made some inroads in this powerful and unhampered use of sovereignty, which is most clearly illustrated by the rights of long-term legal residents in liberal democracies, as we have seen in chapter 3. Nevertheless, in the course of the twentieth century, immigration control has become one of the ways to protect

---

[50] See Michael Samers who argues that the very phenomenon of illegal immigration is *produced* by migration and citizenship policy. M. Samers, "An Emerging Geopolitics of Illegal Immigration in the European Union," *European Journal of Migration and Law* 6 (2004).

[51] B. Melis, *Negotiating Europe's Immigration Frontiers* (Boston: Kluwer Law International, 2001), 11.

[52] Schindlmayer (2003), 119.

the essence of the nation, in whatever aspect one sees that essence expressed: population, borders, mythology or coercive power.[53]

Certainly, there are exceptions to this development, mainly at the regional level, the most notable being the European Union. But the very novel and revolutionary character of its notion of supranational citizenship, with the accompanying rights of freedom of movement throughout the countries of the Union, is perhaps all the more striking due to the fact that in general the development has been a reverse one. In addition, as was already observed in chapter 2, the European project has perhaps also emphasised the inside/outside distinction, notwithstanding the fact that the scales according to which who is labelled insider and who is an outsider have been shifting in important and unprecedented ways. With the abolition of internal borders in the EU, worries about the vulnerability of the external frontiers have equally arisen, and much action is being taken to strengthen these borders against unwanted immigration. Before I consider these issues and other questions specific to immigration law and policy in contemporary Europe in greater detail, it is necessary to sketch the international legal framework governing the right to enter and remain. Which, if any, legal constraints does it formulate against an unlimited sovereign right to exclude?

5.3 *The Right to Enter and Remain in International Law*

Only a brief glance at international law is sufficient to see that the right to leave and the right to enter a country are not symmetrically protected. Whereas the right to leave a country should be guaranteed for any person irrespective of his or her nationality, a general right to enter a country in international human rights instruments is reserved for nationals of the country in question. The corresponding duty of states to admit their nationals is well established in international law, and as such it is regarded as the logical correlative of the right of other states to expel non-nationals.[54] In classic international law, this duty raised obligations only between states, but presently the right to enter one's own state is incorporated in all major human rights instruments. The situation is similar with regard to a general right to remain: only nationals are inexpellable.[55] In the following paragraphs, I will focus on the international

---

[53] C. Dauvergne, "Sovereigty, Migration and the Rule of Law in Global Times," *The Modern Law Review*. 67 (2004), 592.
[54] Goodwin Gill, *International law and the movement of persons between states* (1978), 137. See also ECJ Case 41–74, *Van Duyn v. Home Office* [1974] ECR 1337.
[55] But see Doehring (1992), 110. In the ECtHR, the right to remain is guaranteed for nationals by Article 3 Protocol 4 ECHR.

legal framework concerning a qualified right to enter or remain in a state of which one is not a national.[56]

It is widely argued that there exists no right for aliens to enter the territory of a foreign state, except in particular cases, resulting from treaties, and that states similarly possess a general competence to require aliens to leave.[57] Yet, certain concerns have caused concepts such as domestic jurisdiction or *domain réservé* to undergo profound changes during the last century, and as we shall see below it is these very concerns – considerations regarding the fundamental rights of the individual and his or her dignity – that have brought about important limits to the sovereign right to exclude. The extent to which such considerations put limits on the right to exclude would perhaps not be so very wide if only taking into account customary international law or *ius cogens*. However, in chapter 3, I have pointed out that one misunderstands the discourse of fundamental rights if one deems an investigation into their origin indispensable in order to evaluate their impact on the sovereign claims of the modern state. Thus, be it treaty obligations or the case law of domestic courts that limit the alleged sovereign right to exclude, they are as much about restraining a particular assertion of sovereignty, as *ius cogens* or customary international law would be in the same case. This is especially so when we take into account the fact that the traditional perception of the sovereign power to exclude entails extensive executive discretion, with little or no room for the legislative or judiciary powers.

5.3.1 *General Limitations on the Sovereign Right to Exclude*

The main venues for legal migration into the Member States of Europe consist of immigration on humanitarian or human rights-related grounds; family reunification or formation; and primary labour migration. Concerning the two former categories, international law places important constraints on national sovereignty, which will be dealt with in the sections below (5.3.2 and 5.3.3). However, with regard to migration for employment or other general purposes, international law seems to limit the national state's discretionary powers in matters of immigration only marginally. As a general rule, the principle of non-discrimination puts constraints on the way in which the state uses

---

[56] As in section 4.2.2, concerning the legal framework of the right to leave, the ICCPR and the ECHR occupy a central place in the discussion below.
[57] Doehring (1992), 108; O'Connell (1970), 707; and G. Fourlanos, *Sovereignty and the ingress of aliens* (Stockholm: Almqvist & Wiksell International, 1986), 61.

its power to exclude.⁵⁸ The prohibition on racial discrimination can be seen as *ius cogens*,⁵⁹ but states would also act in contravention of the norm such as contained in Article 26 ICCPR if their decisions on requests for entry or applications for visa would be discriminatory on grounds such as race, sex, language, religion, opinion, national or social origin, property, birth or other status.⁶⁰ While the principle of non-discrimination thus seems to be the only international principle bearing upon a *general* right of the individual to enter, with regard to a right to remain, international law offers more protection by imposing certain restraints on the circumstances in which a state may expel an alien from its territory.⁶¹ It should be noted, however, that this extended protection is usually only offered to those individuals who were initially authorised to enter or stay in national territory. International law thus treats irregular residents on the same footing as those who never entered, therewith endorsing and even reaffirming a view of territorial sovereignty as a right to decide on matters of exclusion, at least initially.

---

⁵⁸ Note that the principle of non-discrimination plays an ambiguous role in international migration law as discrimination on the grounds of nationality is inherent therein. Additionally, it will often be difficult to prove discriminatory motives, precisely because of the existence of discretionary power. This problem is circumvented when the rights of nationals are involved as well: see the decision by the HRC in the *Mauritian Women's Case*, in which it decided that the Mauritian practice of affording alien wives automatic residence rights while denying such rights to alien husbands was discriminatory with respect to Mauritian women (*Amauruddyu-Cziffra et al. v. Mauritius*, 9 April 1981, Comm. No. 35/78, 1 Selected decisions H.R.C (New York: United Nations, 1985), at 67.

⁵⁹ See also the International Convention on the Elimination of All Racial Discrimination of 21 December 1961, entry into force 4 January 1969. Although the non-discrimination provision in the ECHR (Article 14) cannot be invoked independently from a claim concerning one of the rights set forth in the Convention, racial discrimination may of itself amount to degrading treatment, prohibited by Article 3 ECHR. See about the application of this provision to racially discriminatory immigration legislation: ECommHR, *East African Asians v. The United Kingdom*, 15 December 1973, E.H.H.R. 76. In *Timishev v. Russia* (13 December 2005, Reports 2005-XII) the Court found a violation of Article 14 in conjunction with the right to free movement *within* a state, as guaranteed by Article 2 of Protocol No. 4. Protocol 12 ECHR broadens the scope of article 14 ECHR by prohibiting discrimination in respect of the enjoyment of *any right set forth by law*.

⁶⁰ Goodwin Gill, *International law and the movement of persons between states* (1978), 81; and R. Cholewinski, Borders *and Discrimination in the European Union* (London and Brussels: ILPA and MPG, 2002), 51–52. But see HRC, *Vjatseslav Tsjarov v. Estonia*, 26 October 2007, Comm. No. 1223/2003, U.N.Doc. CCPR/C/91/D/1223/2003 in which the Committee sanctioned a blanket prohibition by Estonia of the issue of permanent residence permits to the former members of the armed forces of another state, without addressing the question whether such a prohibition was reasonable and justifiable in the individual case.

⁶¹ See Iran-U.S. Claims Tribunal, *Rankin v. Iran*, 3 November 1987, 17 Iran-U.S.C.T.R. 135 (1987), par. 22.

We have seen in chapter 3 that under international law foreigners are entitled to treatment in accordance with a minimum international standard. Such a standard applies equally to matters relating to their sojourn and the law of diplomatic protection thus decrees that they should not be subject to arbitrary expulsions.[62] The emergence of human rights has enhanced the international protection of the individual rights of aliens as such, and thus also with regard to matters relating to their sojourn. First of all, just as decisions pertaining to entrance should not amount to forbidden discrimination, neither should removal from national territory be effected on discriminatory grounds.[63] Secondly, a general principle of customary international law prohibits mass expulsions of aliens,[64] a prohibition which is closely related to the non-discrimination requirement and which is codified in Article 4 of the Fourth Protocol to the ECHR.[65] However, expulsions do not violate international law merely because numerous aliens are expelled; instead the prohibition concerns their expulsion as a group if that is not the result of decisions based on the merits of each individual case.[66] Thirdly, various provisions of international law stipulate that certain procedural guarantees need to be satisfied before a state may expel a foreigner in order to prevent arbitrary expulsions.[67] According to Article 13 ICCPR and Article 1 of Protocol 7 ECHR, an alien residing lawfully in a Contracting State's territory may be expelled from it only in pursuance of a decision reached in accordance with domestic law.[68] The HRC in applying Article 13 ICCPR does

---

[62] R. Higgins, "The Right in International Law of an Individual to Enter, Stay in and Leave a Country," *International Affairs* 49 (1973), 346; and Oda (1968), 482.

[63] HRC, *General Comment 15*, The position of aliens under the Covenant (Twenty-seventh session, 1986), U.N. Doc. HRI/GEN/1/Rev.6 at 140 (2003).

[64] J.-M. Henckaerts, *Mass Expulsion in Modern International Law and Practice* (The Hague: Martinus Nijhoff Publishers, 1995); and A. Cassese, *International Law* (Oxford: Oxford University Press, 2005), 121.

[65] And in Article 22 of the *International Convention on the Protection of the Rights of Migrant Workers and their Families* (Convention adopted by General Assembly Resolution 45/158 of 18 December 1990: Entry into force: 1 July 2003).

[66] EcommHR, *Becker v. Denmark*, 3 October 1976, Yearbook of the European Convention on Human Rights 19 (1976), 454.

[67] International laws that expressly give the individual a substantial, instead of a mere procedural guarantee against arbitrary expulsions are rare. See, for example, Article 19(8) of the 1961 European Social Charter, which decrees that migrant workers may only be expelled if they form a danger to national security, public interest or public morality.

[68] Other important provisions in this respect are Article 3 of the 1955 European Convention on Establishment and Article 22 of the International Convention on the Protection of the Rights of Migrant Workers and their Families. Article 3 of the European Convention on Establishment also enumerates permissible grounds for expulsion. Its provisions are only applicable to nationals of Contracting States who reside on the territory of another Contracting Party.

not deem it within its powers to evaluate whether national authorities have interpreted and applied the law correctly, unless it is established that they have not acted in good faith or that there was an abuse of power.[69] The Court in Strasbourg takes a less deferential approach by requiring that the national laws providing for deportation should contain minimum guarantees against arbitrary action by the authorities.[70] However, the importance of territorial sovereignty as entailing a right to exclude is simultaneously affirmed by the fact that the procedural guarantees are only applicable in the case of 'lawful residency', which lawfulness similarly refers to domestic law.[71] An inroad into this power is provided for by the HRC: when the legality of an alien's entry or stay is in dispute, any decision resulting in his expulsion or deportation should be taken in conformity with Article 13 ICCPR.[72]

Article 13 ICCPR and Article 1 of Protocol 7 ECHR accord lawful residents the right to advance reasons against the ordered expulsion and have their case reviewed by an authority that is capable of offering an effective remedy.[73] The reviewing authority may be the same as that which made the initial decision. Exceptions to these procedural guarantees are also provided for. In the ICCPR, compelling reasons of national security may justify the absence of an appeal and the entitlement to a review. In Protocol No. 7 ECHR, both public order and national security are grounds for derogating from these procedural rights. Nevertheless, according to the ECtHR, someone expelled on grounds of public order or national security does retain the right to invoke his procedural rights after expulsion. However, this can hardly be seen as an effective remedy.[74]

---

[69] HRC, *Maroufidou v. Sweden*, 5 September 1979, Comm. No. 58/1979, U.N. Doc. CCPR/C/OP/1 at 80 (1985).

[70] *Lupsa v. Romania*, 8 June 2006, Appl. No. 10337/04.

[71] See EcommHR, *Voulfovitch and Oulianova v. Sweden*, 13 January 1993, D&R 74, par. 3. See also ECtHR, *Sejdovic and Sulejmanovic v. Italy*, 14 March 2002 (Decision), Appl. No. 57575/00. Furthermore, aliens who arrive at ports or other points of entry are excluded from the protection of those provisions, just as 'overstayers' and those present on the territory awaiting a decision on a request for a residence permit. See the Explanatory Report to Protocol 7, par. 9; and HRC, *General Comment 15* (1986).

[72] HRC, *General Comment 15* (1986) at 9.

[73] HRC, *Hammel v. Madagaskar*, 3 April 1987, Comm. No. 155/198, U.N. Doc. CCPR/C/OP/2 at 11 (1990), par. 19.

[74] The ECtHR has in several cases, where other fundamental rights were at stake, stressed the importance of having remedies with suspensive effect when ruling on the obligations of states with regard to the right to an effective remedy in deportation or extradition proceedings. See ECtHR, *Bozano v. France*, 18 December 1986, A- 111, par. 48; *Conka v. Belgium*, 5 February 2002, Reports 2002-I, par. 79; and *Mamatkulov and Askarov v. Turkey*, 4 February 2005, Appl. Nos. 46827/99 and 46951/99, par. 124.

A national state, when invoking public order in order to avoid its obligations under Article 1 Protocol 7 needs to furnish proof that this is a necessary measure in the particular case.[75] However, if reasons of national security are advanced, these reasons are by themselves sufficient, and no further justification by the national state is required.[76] The HRC seems to limit its own powers of review in a similar manner when reasons of national security are advanced, therewith undermining the significance of the term 'compelling' in Article 13 ICCPR.[77] Thus, as no judicial check whatsoever is required on the invocation of national security by national states, one may well wonder what the guarantees contained in Article 13 ICCPR and Article 1 Protocol 7 in practice amount to.[78] In this respect it is worth noting that a proposal to include a similar provision in the European Convention system at an earlier date (namely in Protocol No. 4), in which it would also be for the national state alone to decide whether reasons of public security exist, was not adopted as the Committee of Experts felt that such a provision would not fit within the European system for the protection of human rights.[79] Moreover, in cases in which other fundamental rights are at stake, neither the Strasbourg organs, nor the HRC leave the assessment of whether a right balance is struck between national security concerns and individual rights solely to the national authorities.[80] On the contrary, the Court in Strasbourg has emphasised repeatedly that there are ways in which national security concerns can be accommodated and yet accord the individual with a substantial measure of procedural justice when fundamental rights are at stake.[81] It seems justified to conclude that procedural guarantees to protect against arbitrary expulsion as such – even if codified in the Convention system – do not amount to fundamental rights.

---

[75] See ECommHR, *Mezghiche v. France*, 9 April 1997, Appl. No. 33438/96.
[76] See the Explanatory Report to Protocol No. 7, par. 15.
[77] "It is not for the Committee to test a sovereign state's evaluation of an alien's security rating." *V.M.R.B. v Canada*, 26 July 1988, Comm. No. 236/1987, U.N. Doc. CCPR/C/80/D/1051/2002 (2004), at 8.4.; and *J.R.C. v Costa Rica*, 30 March 1989, Comm. No. 296/1988, U.N. Doc. Supp. No. 40 (A/44/40) at 293 (1989), at 8.4. See also S. Joseph, J. Schultz, and M. Castan, *The International Covenant on Civil and Political Rights: Cases, Materials and Commentary* (Oxford: Oxford University Press, 2004), 383.
[78] Martin (1989), 571.
[79] Explanatory Note to Protocol 4 ECHR, par. 34.
[80] See for the HRC: *Sohn v. Republic of Korea*, 3 August 1995, Comm. No. 518/1992, U.N. Doc. CCPR/C/54/D/518/1992 (1995), par. 10.4; *Mukong v. Cameroon*, 21 July 1994, Comm. No. 458/1991, U.N. Doc. CCPR/C/51/D/458/1991 (1994), par. 9.7.; and *Kim v. Republic of Korea*, 4 January 1999, Comm. No. 574/1994, U.N. doc. CCPR/C/64/D/574/1994 (1999), par. 12.4–12.5.
[81] *Al-Nashif v. Bulgaria*, 20 June 2002 (Judgment), Appl. No. 50963/99, par. 97; and *Liu and Liu v. Russia*, 6 December 2007, Appl. No. 42086/05, par. 59.

Such a conclusion is in accordance with the jurisprudence of the Strasbourg organs on the applicability of the fair trial provision of Article 6 ECHR on the decision to deport an alien or on the administrative proceedings relating to a prohibition of entry. Both the European Commission for Human Rights and the ECtHR have held that the right of an alien to reside in a particular country is matter of public law and the decision to deport him does not constitute a determination of his civil rights and obligations in the sense of Article 6.[82] For the Commission, it was the discretionary nature of the powers of the immigration authorities which was decisive in reaching this conclusion.[83] The Explanatory Report to Protocol No. 7 expressly states that its Article 1 does not affect this interpretation of Article 6.

Deference to national sovereignty in the context of procedural guarantees is in accordance with traditional perceptions of the power to exclude in which judicial review does not play a large role on account of the allegedly large extent of executive discretion.[84] Whether the HRC entertains similar views on the relevance of Article 14(1) ICCPR for exclusion cases is not entirely clear. The English version of Article 14 (1) ICCPR stipulates that a fair trial should be guaranteed to any person in the determination of his rights and obligations in a "suit at law", which refers to the nature of the right in question, instead of to the status of the parties concerned or the particular forum where the right is to be adjudicated.[85] However, the question whether a decision to deport an alien may amount to the determination of his rights and obligations in a suit

---

[82] ECtHR, *Maaouia v. France*, 5 October 2000, Reports 2000-X, par. 36–37; and the ECommHR: *Agee v. The United Kingdom*, 17 December 1976, D&R 7, 164, par. 28; *X v. The United Kingdom*, 18 May 1977, D&R 9, 224; and *Kareem v. Sweden*, 26 October 1996, D&R 87-A, 173. A confirmation of the approach taken in *Maaouia* can be found in the recent case of *Üner v. the Netherlands*, 18 October 2006, Appl. No. 46410/96, par. 56.

[83] EcommHR, *Uppal and others v. the United Kingdom*, 2 May 1979, D&R 17, 157; and *X, Y, and Z v. The United Kingdom*, 6 July 1982, D&R 27, par. 4.

[84] For an excellent discussion on how the so-called plenary powers doctrine (in the US) relates to territoriality and social contract theories see: S.H. Cleveland, "Powers Inherent in Sovereignty: Indians, Aliens, Territories, and the Nineteenth Century Origins of Plenary Power over Foreign Affairs," *Texas Law Review* 81 (2002). Interestingly, Cleveland does not limit her discussion of the origins of plenary powers to matters concerning immigration, but includes national power over Indians and the power to govern the inhabitants of newly acquired lands, all three areas implicating "persons who were non-citizens and who were racially, culturally, and religiously distinct from the nation's Anglo-Saxon, Christian elites" (Cleveland 2002, 11).

[85] HRC, *Y.L. v. Canada*, 8 April 1986, Comm. No. 112/1981, U.N. Doc. Supp. No. 40 (A/41/40) at 145 (1986), at. 9.1.; and HRC, *General Comment 13*, Article 14 (21st Session, 1984), U.N. Doc. HRI/GEN/1/Rev.6 at 135 (2003).

at law was never answered by the Committee, although it left open the possibility that it may do so in the case of *Madafferi*.[86]

Other important provisions in this regard are Article 13 ECHR and Article 2(3) ICCPR, granting the individual a right to an effective remedy before a national authority if he can present an arguable complaint that his rights as set forth in, respectively, the ECHR or the ICCPR are violated.[87] The precise relation between these provisions and Article 1 Protocol 7 ECHR or Article 13 ICCPR, both pairs of provisions involving procedural guarantees, is unclear. In this context, it is important to note that neither provision grants a right to review by a judicial authority. It is possible that, should it be concluded that Article 1 Protocol 7 or Article 13 ICCPR is violated, no additional assessment of a state's obligations under the more general procedural provisions would be considered necessary.[88] In any case, seeing that neither Article 1 Protocol 7, nor Article 13 ICCPR involve any guarantee relating to *substantive* grounds of expulsion, these grounds in themselves cannot become the subject of an effective remedy before a national authority by virtue of Article 13 ECHR or Article 2(3) ICCPR. The only way in which the grounds of exclusion can become relevant issues to consider in the framework of these provisions is when exclusion involves other rights or freedoms that are set forth in the ECHR or ICCPR.

5.3.2 *Refugee Law and the Prohibition of* Non-refoulement

When discussing international legal limits on the sovereign right to exclude, in the minds of many, refugee law provides the most obvious instances of just such limits. However, it is important to be aware of the fact that international refugee law does far more than that: it is an extensive body of international law, dealing with subjects ranging from the treatment of refugees on entry (including detention) to diverse rights of refugees who have permanently settled in their country of refuge, such as pertaining to housing, employment and education.

---

[86] HRC, *Madafferi v. Australia*, 26 July 2004, Comm. No. 1011/2000, U.N. Doc. CCPR/C/81/D/1011/2001 (2004), at 8.7. The issue was also raised in *V.M.R.B. v. Canada*; and *Nartey v. Canada*, 18 July 1997, Comm. No. 604/1994, U.N. doc. CCPR/C/60/D/604/1994 (1994), but these complaints were declared inadmissible.

[87] ECtHR, *Boyle and Rice v. United Kingdom*, 27 April 1988, A-131, par. 52–55; *Kudla v. Poland*, 26 October 2000, Reports 2000-XI, par. 157; *Christine Goodwin v. the United Kingdom*, 11 July 2002, Reports 2002-XI par. 112; and the HRC in *Kazantzis v Cyprus*, 19 September 2003, Comm. No. 972/2001, U.N. Doc. CCPR/C/78/D/972/2001 (2003), at 6.6.

[88] Much of the European Court's case law indicates that it considers Article 13 ECHR a *lex generalis* in respect of provisions that include separate procedural guarantees. See ECtHR, *Foti and Others v. Italy*, 10 December 1982, A-56, par. 78; and *Hentrich v. France*, 22 September

Here I will only investigate the way in which international refugee law restrains the sovereign right to decide on exclusion. Factually, this restraint is not premised on the right of asylum, which is nothing more than a right of a territorial state to grant asylum to an alien, and which, on the international plane, implicates solely interstate relations.[89] A provision such as Article 14 UDHR, declaring that everybody has the right to seek and enjoy asylum, although arguably more than merely an affirmation of the right to leave, was intended to provide a procedural right – the right to an asylum process.[90] Although many domestic legal systems have legislation containing a substantive right to asylum, national states have strongly resisted the codification of such a right in international law. An exception is provided by EU Council Directive 2004/83/EC on minimum standards for the qualification and status of third country nationals or stateless persons as refugees or as persons who otherwise need international protection and the content of the protection granted.[91] A person who according to the Directive qualifies for refugee status, should be afforded a residence permit that is valid for at least three years and which is renewable unless reasons of national security or public order so require.[92] Moreover, the EU Charter of fundamental rights appears to recognise an individual right to asylum.[93]

We will see that the way in which general human rights law constrains the national state with regard to its decisions on exclusion is in many instances more far-reaching than international refugee law's constraints on sovereignty. The relationship between the two areas of law is complex and at times confusing. Many of their differences are explained by the early twentieth century

---

1992, A-296-A, par. 65. However, a change in the Court's view on the subsidiary character of Article 13 ECHR may be apparent from its decision in *Kudla v. Poland*. The relationship between Article 1 Protocol 7 and Article 13 ECHR becomes especially interesting when the national state attempts to evade its obligations in the former provision on the grounds of national security as national security concerns should not lead to a state disregarding its obligations under Article 13, as transpired from the *Al-Nashif* judgment (par. 136-138).

[89] R.B. Lillich, "Civil Rights," in: *Human rights in international law: legal and policy issues*, ed. T. Meron (Oxford: Clarendon Press, 1984), 150; Plender (1988), 394; and Oda (1968), p. 490.

[90] Th. Gammeltoft-Hansen and H. Gammeltoft-Hansen, "The Right to Seek – Revisited. On the UN Human Rights Declaration Article 14 and Acces to Asylum Procedures in the EU," *European Journal of Migration and Law* 10 (2008). But see A. Grahl-Madsen, *Territorial Asylum* (Stockholm: Almqvsit and Wiksell International, 1980), 4-5.

[91] Council Directive 2004/83/EC of 29 April 2004 on minimum standards for the qualification and status of third country nationals or stateless persons as refugees or as persons who otherwise need international protection and the content of the protection granted, OJ L 304, 30 September 2004.

[92] Article 24(1).

[93] Article 18 of the Charter of Fundamental Rights of the European Union.

origins of modern refugee law and the fact that it has retained many classical international law characteristics, whereas human rights law is of a much more recent date, and explicitly attempts to break away from some of the notions underpinning classic international law. In this section, I shall first deal with the way in which international refugee law proper may limit national exclusionary powers. Subsequently, I will investigate how general human rights law has widened the scope of the cornerstone of international refugee law: the principle of *non-refoulement*.

Above I have already briefly traced the development of an international regime concerned with the legal protection of refugees. Refugee law was a response to the international legal dilemma caused by the denial of state protection for various groups in Europe during the early twentieth century.[94] In essence, the rationale for refugee law has remained the same today as it was then: refugees become an issue of international law because they cannot invoke the protection of their country of nationality,[95] despite the fact that, at present, the country of nationality is no longer the only entity capable of defending an individual's interests on the international plane.

This view of the underlying principles of refugee law is confirmed by the way in which the 1951 Convention Relating to the Status of Refugees as amended by the Protocol of 1967 (hereinafter the 1951 Convention) defines the refugee as someone who, owing to a well-founded fear of persecution, is outside his own country and is unable or unwilling to avail himself of the protection of that country.[96] Council Directive 2004/83/EC applies a similar definition of the refugee. There is ample legal scholarship concerning almost every single word constituting the core of the refugee definition.[97] It goes far beyond this study to discuss this scholarship in depth, but some brief remarks concerning the interrelated issues of fear of persecution and a lack of protection are called for in order to fully appreciate refugee law's constraints on national powers of exclusion.

---

[94] J. Hathaway, *Law of Refugee Status* (Toronto: Butterworths, 1991), 2.

[95] J. Hathaway, "Forced Migration Studies: Could We Agree Just to 'Date'?" *Journal of Refugee Studies* 20 (2007).

[96] Article 1F of the 1951 Convention excludes from refugee status persons who have committed crimes of great severity, such as war crimes, crimes against humanity or non-political acts of cruelty. Council Directive 2004/83/EC provides for exclusion on similar grounds in Article 12.

[97] D.J. Steinbock, "The refugee definition as law: issues of interpretation," in: *Refugee Rights and Realities: Evolving International Concepts and Regimes*, eds. F. Nicholson and P. Twomey (Cambridge: Cambridge University Press, 1999), 14; and V. Türk and F. Nicholson, "Refugee Protection in International Law: An Overall Perspective," in: *Refugee Protection in International Law*, eds. E. Feller, V. Türk and F. Nicholson (Cambridge: Cambridge University Press, 2003), 38.

In the first place, only EC law has explicitly defined the concept of persecution, but also in general international law its relationship with human rights law is fairly obvious: just as in Directive 2004/83/EC, persecution can be said to consist of severe human rights abuses. It is important to note that a well-founded fear of persecution is only relevant for the purposes of the Convention (and similarly for those of Directive 2004/83/EC), if persecution occurs or would occur on the enumerated grounds of race, religion, nationality, membership of a particular social group or political opinion. Especially the application and interpretation by national judiciaries of the ground 'membership of a particular social group' has been "pushing the boundaries of refugee law" as it is a plausible vehicle for claims to refugee status which do not fall under the other grounds set out in Article 1 of the Refugee Convention.[98]

In the second place, the lack of protection referred to in the refugee definition has been interpreted in various ways. Does it refer to the protection which the national state can offer within its territory, and thus impose an additional condition to be satisfied in order to conclude that a risk of persecution exits, namely "scrutiny of the state's ability and willingness to effectively respond to that risk"?[99] Or, should the lack of protection be understood as a lack of external protection, thus denoting the diplomatic protection that the refugee, once he is outside his country of origin, cannot avail himself of, for fear of a possibility of being returned to the country where the feared persecution could occur? The latter interpretation is certainly supported by a textual interpretation of Article 1 of the 1951 Convention and makes more sense from a general international law perspective.[100] Irrespective of the answers to these questions, both interpretations reveal the central place that the national state occupies in determining who is regarded as a refugee in international law. Precisely instances of persecution by non-state agents make clear that the question of persecution cannot be regarded separately from the issue of a lack of national protection. Some countries have consistently refused the application of the 1951 Convention to persons fleeing human rights violations committed by non-state actors, although that seems to be changing. EU Member States in

---

[98] T. Aleinikoff, "Protected characteristics and social perceptions: an analysis of the meaning of 'membership of a particular social group," in: *Refugee Protection in International Law*, eds. E. Feller, V. Türk and F. Nicholson (Cambridge: Cambridge University Press, 2003), 264. See also Council of Europe, Recommendation Rec (2004) 9 of the Committee of Ministers on the concept of membership of a social group in the context of the 1951 Convention relating to the status of refugees (adopted by the Committee of Ministers on 30 June 2004).

[99] Hathaway (1991), 135.

[100] See Türk and Nicholson (2003, 40) and the sources quoted there.

particular will no longer be able to maintain such a distinction between persecution by non-state actors and persecution by the state, seeing that Directive 2004/83/EC explicitly enumerates non-state actors as possible perpetrators of persecution.[101]

As already mentioned above, general international law does not contain a right to asylum, not even when an individual fulfils the 1951 Convention definition of a refugee. There are only three provisions in the 1951 Convention that have a direct bearing on the exclusionary powers of the national state in the case of refugees. Article 32 prohibits the expulsion of refugees who reside lawfully in national territory, save on grounds of national security or public order. Procedural guarantees comparable to those contained in Article 13 ICCPR are given if expulsion should be ordered on these grounds, in which case the refugee shall be allowed a reasonable period during which to seek legal admission into another country. Article 31 stipulates that states may not impose penalties on refugees on account of unauthorised entry or presence in their territories. The latter obligation is qualified by two conditions: the refugees should have come directly from territories where they feared persecution, and they should present themselves to the authorities without delay. But by far the most important provision in this respect is the first paragraph of Article 33 of the Refugee Convention, containing the norm of *non-refoulement*:

> No Contracting State shall expel or return ("refouler") a refugee in any manner whatsoever to the frontiers of territories where his life or freedom would be threatened on account of his race, religion, nationality, membership of a particular social group or political opinion.[102]

The second paragraph of Article 33 allows for two exceptions to the principle of *non-refoulement*: if an alien represents a danger to national security or, having been convicted of a particularly serious crime, constitutes a danger to the community of the state of refuge. Identical grounds for derogation are laid down in Article 21(2) of Council Directive 2004/83/EC. *Non-refoulement*

---

[101] Article 6 of Council Directive 2004/83/EC on minimum standards for the qualification and status of third country nationals or stateless persons as refugees or as persons who otherwise need international protection and the content of the protection granted. See on this and other implications of the Qualification Directive: H. Storey, "the EU Refugee Qualification Directive: a Brave New World?" *International Journal of Refugee Law* 20 (2008).

[102] According to Article 42 of the 1951 Convention, no reservations are permitted with regard to the non-refoulement provision. The prohibition of non-refoulement of refugees is codified in several other instruments, for example Article 3 of the 1967 Declaration on Territorial Asylum (United Nations General Assembly Resolution (A/RES/2132(XXII), 14 December 1967).

embodies the "humanitarian essence" of refugee law.[103] As we shall see below, its significance exceeds the area covered by the 1951 Convention. Before turning to the principle of *non-refoulement* in general human rights law, I will make some brief remarks concerning its role in the narrower context of the 1951 Convention. In the first place, it is important to understand the way in which *non-refoulement* relates to the lack of a right to asylum in international law. The only way to reconcile these two seemingly conflicting issues is by presuming that if a country is not prepared to grant asylum to a refugee, it must act in accordance with *non-refoulement*, as in the cases of temporary protection or removal to a safe third country.[104]

A second question is whether *refoulement* is only prohibited concerning those refugees who are already within the state's territory, or whether the principle also applies to non-admittance at the border. A consistent interpretation of the 1951 Convention combined with various Conclusions of the Executive Committee of the United Nations High Commissioner of Refugees (hereinafter ExCom) and other key instruments in the field of refugee protection support the view that non-refoulement also applies to rejection at the border.[105] However, an increasing number of states attempt to evade their obligations with regard to *non-refoulement* by physically separating control of the border from the territorial border, resorting to what Didier Bigo and Elspeth Guild have called *police à distance*, a term which connotes practices such as visa policies and airport carrier sanctions.[106] Indeed, the way in which the principle of *non-refoulement* increasingly gives way to "policies of non-entrée"[107] is painfully illustrated by incidents such as Australia's refusal to allow the MV Tampa to enter its territorial waters, the U.S. detention of Haitian asylum seekers on Guantanamo, and more recently,

---

[103] E. Lauterpacht and D. Bethlehem, "The scope and content of the principle of *non-refoulement*: Opinion," in: *Refugee Protection in International Law*, eds. E. Feller, V. Türk and F. Nicholson (Cambridge: Cambridge University Press, 2003), 107.

[104] Ibid., 113. On temporary protection measures see also Council of Europe, Committee of Ministers, Recommendation No. R (2000)9 on temporary protection, adopted on 3 May 2000.

[105] See R. Weinzierl, *The Demands of Human and EU Fundamental Rights for the Protection of the European Union's External Borders* (Berlin: German Institute of Human Rights, 2007); and V. Moreno Lax, " Must EU Borders have Doors for Refugees? On the Compatibility of Schengen Visas and Carriers' Sanctions with EU Member States' Obligations to Provide International Protection to Refugees," *European Journal of Migration and Law* 10 (2008). Cf. 1967 Declaration on Territorial Asylum; UNHCR ExCom Conclusion No. 6 (XXVIII) 1977 (Non-refoulement), par. (c); UNHCR ExCom Conclusion No. 15 (XXX) 1979 (Refugees Without an Asylum Country), at par. (b); and UNGA Resolution A/Res/55/74 of 12 February 2001.

[106] D. Bigo and E. Guild, "Le visa Schengen: expression d'une stratégie de 'police' à distance," *Cultures & Conflits* 49 (2003).

[107] J. Hathaway, "The emerging politics of non-entrée," *Refugees* 91 (1992).

the refoulement to Libya of more than 500 migrants intercepted by the Italian Navy in the Strait of Sicily in May 2009. Whether or not such policies are in violation of existing legal norms is not the interesting question *per se*.[108] What is much more fundamental is to find out how states make use of what they perceive as possible gaps in the law and expose the way in which these gaps are structurally related to territorialised sovereignty. The extraterritorialisation of European migration policies shall receive closer attention below, where we shall also be taking a closer look at Frontex, the agency that plays an important role in increasing the externalisation of migration control.[109]

In the third place, the prohibition on *refoulement* applies irrespective of the question whether or not a person is formally recognised as a refugee.[110] Seeing that the prohibition on *refoulement* is thus an autonomous concept in international law, that norm makes a significantly deeper inroad into the sovereign power to exclude than those norms that refer to domestic laws that regulate the legal status of individuals as were discussed above. That being said, there is also an important qualification to the limiting powers of *non-refoulement* in the 1951 Convention: if a refugee constitutes a danger to the community or security of the country in which he is present, *refoulement* is no longer prohibited.[111] Thus, however narrowly these grounds for derogation are to be interpreted, the core provision of the 1951 Convention preserves a crucial remnant of national sovereign power.[112]

It has been maintained that the norm of *non-refoulement* is a peremptory norm of international law.[113] Some authors have countered such an assumption with the argument that it is difficult to see how the *ius cogens* nature of

---

[108] See on this the Inter-American Commission of Human Rights, *the Haitian Centre for Human Rights et. al. v. United States*, 13 March 1997, Report no. 51/96, Case No. 10.675.

[109] See Section 5.4.2.

[110] See Article 21 Council Directive 2004/83/EC on minimum standards for the qualification and status of third country nationals or stateless persons as refugees or as persons who otherwise need international protection and the content of the protection granted; and Council of Europe, Committee of Ministers, Recommendation No. R (84)1 on the protection of persons satisfying the criteria in the Geneva Convention who are not formally recognised as refugees (adopted on 25 January 1984). See also UNHCR ExCom Conclusion No. 6 (XXVIII) 1977 (non-refoulement); and UNHCR ExCom Conclusion No. 79 (XLVII) 1996 (General conclusion on International Protection). Council Directive 2004/83/EC is explicit on this in the Preamble (at 14).

[111] G.S. Goodwin-Gill, *The Refugee in International Law* (Oxford: Oxford University Press, 1996), 139.

[112] See on this Lauterpacht and Bethlehem (2003), 133–140.

[113] J. Allain, "The *Jus Cogens* Nature of *Non-Refoulement*," *International Journal of Refugee Law* 13 (2001). See also UNHCR ExCom Conclusions No. 25 (XXXIII) 1982 and No. 79 (XLVII) 1996.

the norm as contained in the 1951 Convention can be reconciled with the fact that it simultaneously provides grounds for derogation.[114] Nevertheless, contemporary human rights law has added momentum to the norm of *non-refoulement* so as to make a good case for its peremptory or at least customary character.[115] Article 3 of the Convention against Torture and Other Cruel, Inhuman or Degrading Punishment (CAT) prohibits *refoulement* where there are substantial reasons for believing that a person would be subjected to torture.[116] Furthermore, the customary prohibition against torture in effect amounts to an obligation on national states not to expel a person to a country where substantial grounds have been shown for believing that he or she would face a real risk of being exposed to torture.[117] The HRC and the ECtHR have respectively construed Article 7 ICCPR and Article 3 ECHR as containing a principle of *non-refoulement* to a state where a real risk exists of torture or other cruel, inhuman or degrading treatment or punishment.[118] It is important to note that deducing a norm of *non-refoulement* from the prohibition contained in Article 3 ECHR and Article 7 ICCPR does not entail an extraterritorial application of human rights obligations. The real risk of a violation of an individual's rights is the result of a decision made in the territory of the Contracting State with regard to a person within that territory.[119]

---

[114] L. Hannikainen, *Peremptory Norms (Jus Cogens) in International Law: Historical Development, Criteria, Present Status* (Helsinki: Lakimiesliiton Kustannus, 1988), 261–263.

[115] Lauterpacht and Bethlehem (2003), 140–164.

[116] Convention against Torture and other Cruel, Inhuman or Degrading Punishment, Adopted by General Assembly Resolution 39/46 on 10 December 1984 (CAT). The majority of complaints under the CAT relate to Article 3. See among many CAT Committee decisions: *A. R. v. The Netherlands*, 14 December 2003 Comm. No. 203/2002, U.N. Doc. CAT/C/31/D/203/2002 (2003); *Tala v. Sweden*, 15 November 1996, Comm. No. 43/1996, U.N. Doc. CAT/C/17/D/43/1996 (1996); and *Kisoki v. Sweden*, 8 May 1996 Comm. No. 41/1996, U.N. Doc. CAT/C/16/D/41/1996 (1996). See also CAT Committee, *General Comment No. 1: Implementation of Article 3 of the Convention in the context of Article 22*, A/53/44 Annex IX (21 November 1997).

[117] Lauterpacht and Bethlehem (2003), 140–162.

[118] HRC, *General Comment 20*, Article 7 (Forty-fourth session, 1992), U.N. Doc. HRI/GEN/1/Rev.6 at 151 (2003), at 151; HRC, *C. v. Australia*, 13 November 2002 Communication No 900/1999, UN Doc CCPR/C/76/D/900/99 (2002); ECtHR, *Soering v. the United Kingdom*, 7 July 1989, A-161; *Cruz Varaz and Others v. Sweden*, 20 March 1991, A-201; and *Vilvarajah and Others v. The United Kingdom*, 30 October 1991, A-215.

[119] See ECtHR in *Bankovic and Others v. Belgium* (Decision), 12 December 2001, Reports 2001-XII, par. 68; and *Al-Adsani v. The United Kingdom*, 21 November 2001, Reports 2001-XI, par. 39. This is also the line of argument used by the HRC although the construction is slightly different: "The foreseeability of the consequence [of refoulement] would mean that there is a present violation by the State Party." *Kindler v. Canada*, Decision of 11 November 1993, Comm. No. 470/1991, U.N. Doc. CCPR/C/48/D/470/1991 (1993), at 6.2.

An important question is whether other rights than the right to be free from torture and other degrading treatment can be covered by the 'real risk' situation. According to the HRC, a real risk of a violation can occur with regard to any of the rights guaranteed under the Covenant,[120] although in practice only the right to life in Article 6 ICCPR has featured alongside Article 7 in *refoulement* cases.[121] The ECtHR case law is less clear on this point, and so far the Court has only found violations of the norms contained in Articles 2 (the right to life) and 3 as a result of removal.[122] It has explicitly allowed for the possibility of a violation of article 6 (fair trial) as a result of expulsion, although it has never established a violation of this provision as a result of deportation or expulsion.[123] However, with regard to other provisions, such as Article 5 or Article 9, it has for the most part been dismissive of the possibility that removal might engage the responsibility of the state under these provisions independently from Article 3.[124] It is difficult to see why a real risk of violations of other, derogable, human rights such as the freedom of religion or speech could not lead to a prohibition on expulsion or deportation in principle, in spite of obvious practical difficulties with regard to the assessment of the human rights situation in the country of return.[125] It can thus be concluded that international case law on *refoulement*, rather than being led by a consistent interpretation of the relevant human rights treaties, is largely inspired by the 1951 Convention, which prohibits

---

[120] HRC, *Kindler v. Canada*, at 13.2.

[121] HRC, *Judge v. Canada*, Decision of 17 July 2002, Comm. No. 829/98, U.N. Doc. CCPR/C/78/D/829/1998 (2003), (concerning a breach of Article 6 ICCPR as a result of extradition). In *G.T. v. Australia*, the applicant claimed a foreseeable breach of Article 14 ICCPR as a result of deportation. This claim was not examined on its merits. Decision of 4 November 1997, Comm. No. 706/1996, U.N. Doc. CCPR/C/61/D/706/1996 (4 November 1997).

[122] With regard to the application of Article 2, see: *Bader v. Sweden*, 8 November 2005, appl. No. 13284/04.

[123] See i.e. *Einhorn v. France*, 16 October 2001, Appl. No. 71555/01; and *Al Moyad v. Germany* (Decision), 20 February 2007, Appl. No. 35865/03, par. 101. See also EcommHR: *Aylor Davis v. France*, 20 January 1994, D&R 76A; *Alla Raidl v. Austria*, 4 September 1995, D&R 82-A.

[124] *Z. and T. v. United Kingdom*, 28 February 2006, Appl. No. 27034/05; *F. v. United Kingdom*, 22 June 2004, Appl. No. 17341/03; *Tomic v. United Kingdom*, 14 October 2003, Appl. No. 17837/03; and *Razaghi v. Sweden*, 11 March 2003, Appl. No. 64599/01. For an excellent and complete overview of the case law and an attempt to unravel the principles applied by the ECtHR see: M. den Heijer, "Whose Rights and Which Rights? The Continuing Story of *Non-Refoulement* under the European Convention on Human Rights," *European Journal of Migration and Law* 10 (2008).

[125] N. Blake, "Developments in the Case Law of the European Court of Human Rights," in: *Irregular Migration and Human Rights: Theoretical, European and International Perspectives*, eds. B. Bogusz et. al. (Leiden/Boston: Martinus Nijhoff Publishers, 2004), 437.

refoulement solely to territories where a refugee's life or freedom would be threatened.[126]

Nevertheless, if *non-refoulement* is applied as a component part of the general human rights obligations of the national state, it affords a far wider scope of protection than Article 33 of the 1951 Convention.[127] Whereas the latter instrument protects from *refoulement* solely persons whom it defines as refugees – which is additionally conditional on public order and security considerations, the prohibition on torture or other cruel and degrading treatment should be guaranteed to anyone without exception. Indeed, if the norm of *non-refoulement* flows from this prohibition, "the activities of the individual in question, no matter how undesirable or dangerous, cannot be a material consideration".[128]

In addition, the state-centred, territorial focus, apparent in traditional refugee law, by which different states are accorded responsibility for separate populations, is much diminished. Whereas we see that such an approach to human rights is still held by the CAT Committee (and necessarily so in view of the definition of torture in Article 1 CAT),[129] the ECtHR and HRC have both held

---

[126] The 'real risk' situation is to be distinguished from those cases in which immigration controls are *designed or imposed* to repress the exercise of fundamental rights by foreigners. The difference is that in the 'real risk' situation the *reasons* for exclusion and the existence of a real risk of human rights violations are unrelated: it is exclusion itself that may give rise to human rights violations. With regard to the situation in which a state uses immigration controls in order to repress the exercise of a fundamental right (such as the freedom of religion or of free speech), the Court in Strasbourg takes the stance that, "in so far as the measure relating to the continuation of the applicant's residence in a given State was imposed in connection with the exercise of the right to freedom of religion, such measure may disclose an interference with that right". See *Nolan en K. v. Russia*, 12 February 2009, App. No. 2512/04, par. 62 and the cases cited there (*Perry v. Latvia*, 8 November 2007, Appl No. 30273/03; *Al-Nashif v. Bulgaria*, 25 January 2001 (Decision), Appl. No. 50963/99; *Lotter v. Bulgaria* (Decision), 5 November 1997, Appl. No. 39015/97; and a decision by the EcommHR, *Omkarananda and the Divine Light Zentrum v. Switzerland*, 19 March 1981, Appl. No. 8118/77, D&R 25, 118).

[127] See also UNHCR ExCom Conclusion No. 103 (LVI) 2005 (Conclusion on the Provision on International Protection Including Through Complementary Forms of Protection); and UNHCR ExCom Conclusion No. 74 (XLV) 1994 (General Conclusion on International Protection), at par l-o.

[128] ECtHR, *N. v. Finland*, 26 July 2005, Appl. No. 38885/02, par. 159, 166. See also Council of Europe, Committee of Ministers, Recommendation (2005) 6 on the exclusion of refugee status (adopted on 23 March 2005) in which it is emphasised that exclusion from refugee status on grounds such as those provided for in Article 1F of the 1951 Convention does not equal removal.

[129] *G.R.B. v. Sweden*, 15 May 1998, No. 83/1997, U.N. Doc. CAT/C/20/D/83/1997 (1998), at 6.5.: "The Committee considers that the issue whether the State Party has an obligation to refrain

that treatment does not have to emanate from state agents in order to be contrary to the absolute protection offered by Article 3 ECHR and Article 7 ICCPR.[130]

Furthermore, it need not even amount to a breach of classical human rights obligations proper, nor needs the source of the risk of the proscribed treatment in the receiving country to engage either directly or indirectly the responsibility of the public authorities of that country, or taken alone to infringe the standards of Article 3.[131] In the words of the Court in Strasbourg: the absolute character of Article 3 ECHR requires flexibility.[132] As regards the European context, the landmark case in this respect is *D. v United Kingdom*, in which the ECtHR seized the absolute character of Article 3 "in order to subject *all the circumstances* surrounding the case to a rigorous scrutiny, especially the applicant's *personal situation* in the expelling state" (emphasis added).[133]

Lastly, in the application of the norm of *non-refoulement* by the ECtHR, the strict requirement of being 'singled out' in order to fall under its scope seems to be diminishing in importance.[134] The emerging EC case law on subsidiary protection takes a similar approach, albeit one that the ECJ has not so much based on Article 3 ECHR but on an autonomous interpretation of the grounds for subsidiary protection in EC law.[135]

If *refoulement* is forbidden by international law, states can still resort to removal to a third country, provided that such removal would not amount to

---

from expelling a person who might risk pain or suffering inflicted by a non-governmental entity, without the consent or acquiescence of the Government, falls outside the scope of Article 3 of the Convention." See also *V.X.N. and H.N. v. Sweden*, 15 May 2000, Comm. Nos. 130/1999 and 131/1999, U.N. Doc. CAT/C/24/D/130 & 131/1999 (2000), at 13.8; *S.V. v. Canada* 15 May 2001, Comm. No. 49/1996, U.N. Doc. A/56/44 at 102 (2001). at 9.5; and *M.P.S. v. Australia*, 30 April 2002, Comm. No. 138/1999, U.N. Doc. A/57/44 at 111 (2002), at 7.4.

[130] ECtHR, *H.L.R. v. France*, 29 April 1997, Reports 1997-III.
[131] ECtHR, *D. v. The United Kingdom*, 2 May 1997, Reports 1997-III, par. 49 (Deportation of an individual suffering from the final stages of AIDS to a country where he would not receive adequate medical treatment would amount to a breach of Article 3 ECHR). See also ECtHR, *T.I. v. The United Kingdom* (Decision), 7 March 2000, Reports 2000-III.
[132] *D. v. the United Kingdom*.
[133] Ibid., par. 49.
[134] *N.A. v United Kingdom*, 17 July 2008, appl. No. 25904/07; and *Salah Sheekh v. the Netherlands*, 11 January 2007, Appl. No. 1948/04.
[135] See Case C-465/07 *Elgafaji v. Staatssecretaris van Justitie* [2009] nyr on the interpretation of Article 15 (c) of Directive 2004/83/EC on minimum standards for the qualification and status of third country nationals or stateless persons as refugees or as persons who otherwise need international protection and the content of the protection granted.

indirect *refoulement*. In this context, the norm contained in Article 3 ECHR also opposes the automatic allocation of responsibility for safeguarding the rights of asylum seekers by the Dublin Convention: the receiving country is obliged to examine if the responsible country offers enough safeguards against refoulement.[136]

When national states allow an individual to stay on national territory on grounds related to the norm contained in Article 3 ECHR, they usually grant so-called subsidiary protection, the content of which is generally to be decided by each national state. Security of residence for persons enjoying subsidiary protection is recommended by the Council of Europe.[137] Council Directive 2004/83/EC requires states to issue a residence permit to persons qualifying for subsidiary protection, which should be valid for at least a year and renewable unless compelling reasons of national security or public order require otherwise, as long as the circumstances which have led to the affording of subsidiary protection continue to exist.[138] It should be noted that although Directive 2004/83/EC allows Member States to exclude persons from subsidiary protection (on grounds comparable to those leading to the exclusion of refugee status), they cannot act in contravention of their international obligations with regard to the principle of *non-refoulement*.[139]

Does *non-refoulement*, apart from thus significantly limiting states' sovereign powers with regard to substantive decision making, also put formal constraints on national decisions concerning issues of refoulement? Although most European states provide for a possibility to appeal in asylum procedures, the 1951 Convention leaves it to the state parties alone to shape the way in which decisions with regard to Article 33 are made.[140] Presently, the only international provisions that can be invoked in order to rely on rule of law guarantees with regard to decisions on admissibility or deportation are of a general character. As we have seen, Article 13 ECHR and Article 2(3) ICCPR give individuals the right to an effective remedy if one of their rights as guaranteed under the

---

[136] *T.I. v. The United Kingdom* (Decision). See L. Steendijk, "The Application of Human Rights Standards to Asylum Cases: The Dutch Example," *European Journal of Migration and Law* 3 (2001), 187.

[137] Council of Europe, Committee of Ministers, Recommendation No. R (2001)18 on subsidiary protection, adopted on 27 November 2001, par. 14.

[138] Article 24 (2) (residence permits) and Article 16 (Cessation).

[139] Article 21.

[140] Although it implies access to fair and effective procedures for determining protection needs. See UNHCR ExCom Conclusion No. 82 (XLVIII) 1997 (Safeguarding Asylum), under d(ii) and UNHCR ExCom Conclusion No. 103 (LVI) 2005, under (r).

respective instruments is violated.[141] Drawing on the case law of the ECtHR, the Committee of Ministers of the Council of Europe has adopted a recommendation on the application of Article 13 in conjunction with Article 3 with regard to the entry and removal of aliens.[142] An effective remedy should be guaranteed when somebody seeking admission or leave to stay is to be expelled to a country concerning which that person presents an arguable claim that he or she would be subject to torture or other inhuman treatment. A remedy is effective if it is carried out by a judicial authority, or, if it is an administrative authority, it should be impartial and independent, as well as have competence to decide on the substance of the appeal. Furthermore, the execution of the deportation order should be suspended until the decision is taken, also in the case where a claim has been dismissed as being manifestly unfounded.[143]

National states may find in the arguable claim requirement of Article 13 ECHR certain opportunities to evade their obligations with regard to persons seeking entry or leave to stay: if in their interpretation a claim is not arguable because the country of destination in the expulsion order is designated as a safe third country, the recommendation of the Committee of Ministers does not apply, unless the claim concerns substantial grounds which prove that the asylum seeker will be persecuted.[144] Perhaps EC legislation will contribute to strengthening rule of law elements internationally in asylum procedures seeing that Council Directive 2005/85/EC sets minimum standards on national procedures for granting and withdrawing refugee status.[145] Chapter V of the Directive requires Member States to ensure that applicants for asylum have the right to an effective remedy before a court or tribunal against a decision on their application.[146] However, these rights of appeal concern only requests for international protection under the Geneva Convention; requests for subsidiary protection fall outside their scope.[147]

---

[141] See also HRC, *General Comment 31*, Nature of the General Legal Obligation on States Parties to the Covenant, U.N. Doc. CCPR/C/21/Rev.1/Add.13 (2004).

[142] Recommendation No. R (98) 13, *on the right to an effective remedy by rejected asylum-seekers against decision on expulsion in the context of Article 3*, adopted by the Committee of Ministers of the Council of Europe on 18 September 1998.

[143] See ECtHR, *Jabari v. Turkey* (Decision), 28 October 1999, Appl. No. 40035/98.

[144] See the Explanatory Memorandum to Recommendation No. R (98) 13, par. 13.

[145] Council Directive 2005/85/EC of 1 December 2005 on minimum standards on procedures in Member States for granting and withdrawing refugee status, OJ L 326, 13 December 2005, 13–34.

[146] Also in the case where an application is not examined (Art. 36) or declared inadmissible (Art 25(2)) on the grounds of the safe third-country concept. See article 39 of Directive 2005/85/EC.

[147] Article 2(b) in conjunction with Article 39 Directive 2005/85/EC.

Above I have set out the legal framework concerning exceptions to the exclusionary powers of the sovereign state based on international refugee law or related human rights grounds. And while states are careful to sustain the pretension of formal compliance with these fields of international law, they simultaneously attempt to reduce the number of recorded asylum seekers.[148] Contemporary practice demonstrates that Western states are apt to minimise the scope of the limits on their exclusionary powers by the use of concepts such as safe third country, safe country of origin and manifestly unfounded claims. In addition, states endeavour to evade human rights obligations towards individuals who are not authorised to enter or stay on the national territory by making it very difficult for them to reach their national territories. The interception of asylum seekers on the high seas, the use of airport liaison officers, carrier sanctions and visa regulations serve to ensure that states can control movement without having to assume responsibility for the people who move. The way in which European States increasingly make use of novel concepts and techniques in order to (re)assert (national) exclusionary powers shall be dealt with later in this chapter.

5.3.3 *Family Life and Limits on Immigration Control*

I shall now turn to the way in which a right to remain or enter is construed against the background of family rights in international law, family reunification being one of the most significant sources of immigration into the European Union. The main emphasis will be on the way in which states' immigration policies are constrained by Article 8 ECHR, but European case law regarding the application of this provision in immigration decision-making will be placed in a larger perspective by referring to the ICCPR and decisions made by the HRC. More so than with regard to the application of Article 3 ECHR in immigration cases, the way in which the right to family life influences decision-making in immigration law involves significant extraterritorial aspects. The ECtHR has however refused to address the question of how this extraterritoriality relates to the term 'jurisdiction' in Article 1 ECHR. The Court has considered that, as soon as family life is at issue, no distinction can be drawn between applicants living *within* the respondent State and other applicants who are living in a third state.[149]

In the ECHR, Article 8 stipulates that everyone has the right to respect for his family and private life. Paragraph 2 of this article contains the familiar formula for derogable rights under the ECHR: interferences with family or

---

[148] Martin (1989), 574.
[149] See *Haydarie v. the Netherlands* (Decision), 20 October 2005, Appl. No. 8876/04.

private life should be "in accordance with the law" and "necessary in a democratic society in the interests of national security, public safety or the economic well-being of the country, for the prevention of disorder or crime, for the protection of health or morals, or for the protection of the rights and freedoms of others." In the ICCPR, the family is protected by two separate provisions. Article 17 deals with the family and private life of the individual and establishes a prohibition on interference. According to article 23(1), the family is to be protected by the law.[150] Although there seems to be a difference between the two provisions, generally decisions on violations have involved the two articles simultaneously.[151]

If, as a result of immigration decision-making, a breach of Article 8 ECHR is alleged, the Court in Strasbourg will first establish the existence of family life. The Court – and similarly the HRC in applying Article 23 ICCPR – regards this question as one of fact, depending on the existence of close personal ties.[152] A person who has no family life can nonetheless benefit from the protection of Article 8 ECHR on account of his private life, including links connected to educational or professional activities.[153] Especially in the case of second-generation immigrants, the right to private life has played a prominent role in deciding on the lawfulness of expulsion after criminal convictions.[154]

When the existence of family life is ascertained, the *removal* of a person from a state where close members of his family are resident may amount to an infringement of the right to respect for family life as guaranteed in Article 8(1)

---

[150] HRC, *General Comment 19*: Article 23 (Thirty-ninth session, 1990), U.N. Doc. HRI/GEN/1/Rev.6 at 149 (2003), at 149.

[151] Joseph, Schultz and Castan (2004), 591.

[152] Family life exists *ipso iure* between a child born of a marital union and his parents and this bond can only be broken by exceptional circumstances. See *Berrehab v. the Netherlands*, 21 June 1988, A-138, par. 21; *Hokkanen v. Finland*, 23 September 1994, A-299-A, 54; *Gül v. Switzerland*, 19 February 1996, Reports 1996-I, par. 32, and *Ciliz v. the Netherlands*, 11 July 2000, Reports 2000-VIII, par. 59 and 60. Regarding relations between couples, both marriages as well as *de facto* relationships can constitute family life, depending on a number of factors, such as "whether the couple live together, the length of their relationship and whether they have demonstrated their commitment to each other by having children together or by any other means." *Al-Nashif v. Bulgaria* (Judgment), par. 112. See also *Kroon and Others v. the Netherlands*, 27 October 1994, A-297-C, par. 30; and *X, Y and Z. v. the United Kingdom*, 22 April 1997, Reports 1997-II, par. 36. For the HRC see: *Balaguer Santacana v. Spain*, 15 July 1994 Comm. No. 417/90,U.N. Doc. CCPR/C/51/D/417/1990 (1994).

[153] *C. v Belgium*, 7 August 1996, Reports 1996-III, par. 25.

[154] See *Üner v. the Netherlands*, par. 59.

ECHR.[155] In this context, the Court in Strasbourg always reiterates the fact that "no right of an alien to enter or to reside in a particular country is as such guaranteed by the Convention," and that "as a matter of well-established international law and subject to its treaty obligations, a State has the right to control the entry of non-nationals into its territory." However, if such control leads to interference with the right protected under Article 8 ECHR, it needs to be in accordance with the requirements under the second paragraph of this provision. It will not be difficult for the state to argue that the contested measures fall under one of the legitimate aims of Article 8(2) ECHR, but it is the necessity of the deportation that will generally be the main point of contestation.

With regard to a *right to enter* for the purposes of family reunification or formation, the nature of the obligations by the state are somewhat different in character; while the main aim of Article 8 ECHR is to protect against arbitrary interference, the refusal of a request for entry may constitute a breach of a positive obligation inherent in an effective respect for family life.[156] However, in both cases, the Court has considered that the question to be decided is whether a fair balance has been struck between the interests of the individual and the community as a whole.[157]

The duty imposed by Article 8 ECHR cannot be considered as extending a general obligation on the part of a contracting state to respect the choice made by married couples of the country of their residence and to accept non-national spouses for settlement there, or otherwise authorise a family reunion in its territory.[158] The test applied by the Court is whether it can reasonably be expected from the persons concerned to establish family life in their own or their families' home countries. This test is to be more stringently applied when it concerns requests for family formation than in the case of family reunification.[159] Similarly, the HRC does not deduce from Articles 17 and 23 ICCPR a guarantee for establishing family life in a particular country, but the test to be applied is simply whether there can be effective family life, wherever that may be.

As always when assessing whether encroachments by the state on individual liberties constitute violations of fundamental rights, the Court engages in a

---

[155] *Al-Nashif v. Bulgaria* (judgment), par. 114.
[156] C. Forder, "Family Rights and Immigration Law: a European Perspective," in: *Migration, Integration and Citizenship: A Challenge for Europe's Future*, ed. H. Schneider (Maastricht: Forum, 2005). 72–73.
[157] *Konstantinov v. the Netherlands*, 25 April 2007, appl. No. 16351/03.
[158] *Abdulaziz, Cabales and Balkandali v. The United Kingdom*, 28 May 1985, A-94, par. 68; and, *Gül v. Switzerland*, par. 38.
[159] *Sen v. The Netherlands*, 21 December 2001, Appl. No. 31465/96, 96.

balancing act by which the interests of the applicant in maintaining family life are balanced with those of the sovereign state in controlling entry and residence. However, when a right to enter or remain is at stake, the HRC and the ECtHR seem to put rather more emphasis on national sovereign power than in cases where mere jurisdiction over nationals is involved. Indeed, the case law implies that the right to control entry and residence on national territory as inherent in territorial sovereignty is in itself a fundamental interest of the state, from which only special circumstances can result in a departure. The Court's acquiescence to territorial sovereignty's aim of allocating distinct populations to separate states by the use of a formal concept such as nationality[160] is perhaps most clearly expressed in those cases in which it has dealt with deportation of second-generation immigrants after conviction for serious criminal offences. For while it has regularly concluded that the state's actions which interfere with a person's existing residence may in such cases constitute a violation of Article 8,[161] it has in a significant number of cases condoned the expulsion of a person from a country which he could call his own in every sense except for the fact that he did not possess its nationality.[162] It can be argued that in these cases, territorial sovereignty stands in the way of a full application of the proportionality principle – no interference with fundamental rights is justified if there are other, less intrusive measures available – as national states do have adequate means at their disposal to deal with *national* criminals which do not consist of removal from national territory.[163] Indeed, already in 2001, while highlighting the fact that second-generation immigrants, for whom their parents' country is often unknown territory, cannot be

---

[160] Compare the discussion in Chapter 3 (section 3.4.2) on the *Nottebohm Case*.
[161] *Moustaquim v. Belgium*, 18 February 1991 A-193; *Nasri v. France*. 13 July 1995, A-320-B; and *Mehemi v. France*, 26 September 1997, Reports 1997-VI.
[162] See amongst others: *Kaya v. Germany*, 28 June 2007, Appl. No. 31753/02; *C. v. Belgium*; *Baghli v. France*, 13 November 1999, Reports 1999-VIII; *Bouchelkia v. France*, 29 January 1997, Reports 1997-I. See also the judgments in *El Boujaidi v. France*, 26 September 1997, Reports 1997-VI; *Boughanemi v. France*, 24 April 1996, Reports 1996-II; and *Boujlifa v. France*, 21 October 1997, Reports 1997-VI. Nevertheless, the HRC has proved to be much more deferential to national sovereignty than the Court in Strasbourg: if the decision to deport as a result of a criminal conviction takes into account the effect of the deportation on the deportee's family life and if there are no evident flaws in the domestic proceedings, deportation is permissible under the ICCPR. *Stewart v. Canada*, 1 November 1996, Comm. No. 538/93, U.N. Doc. CCPR/C/58/D/538/1993 (1996).
[163] M-B. Dembour, "Human Rights Law and National Sovereignty in Collusion: the Plight of Quasi-Nationals at Strasbourg," *Netherlands Quarterly of Human Rights* 21 (2003), 67. The seriousness of the crime heavily influences the legitimacy of the decision to deport. See for example *Chair and J.B. v. Germany*, 6 December 2007, Appl. No. 69735/01.

seen – humanly or sociologically – as foreigners, the Parliamentary Assembly of the Council of Europe called upon the Committee of Ministers to guarantee that migrants who were born or raised in the host country and their underage children cannot be expelled under any circumstances.[164]

On the other hand, the early decision by the European Court in *Berrehab* also shows that the reasons for deportation, if the latter constitute a serious interference with someone's family life, need to go beyond a simple enforcement of immigration legislation. In *Dalia*, the Court attached importance to the fact that the applicant's Algerian nationality was not a mere legal fact, but a reflection of certain social and emotional links.[165] And indeed, some judgments of a more recent date have at times – and in varying degrees – signalled a departure from the Court's deferential stance with regard to territorial sovereignty as well. In *Sen*, a case concerning family reunification, according to the Court the issue to be decided was not whether the Netherlands was the *only* country in which the applicants could establish family life, but rather the question pertained to what was the most *adequate* way for the family members to continue their family life together (*"le moyen le plus adéquat pour développer une vie familiale"*).[166] And in the case of *Sezen*, the removal of the applicant, even on the grounds of a serious crime, would constitute a violation of Article 8, partly because to ask of Mr Sezen's family members to follow him to his country of origin in order to continue family life would constitute a "radical upheaval" for them.[167]

Nevertheless, the importance which the Court ascribes to the exclusionary powers of the national state is evident by the way in which the Court deals with family life that is established while an applicant was unlawfully present within the territory. The Court regards the obligation flowing from Article 8

---

[164] Recommendation 1504 (2001) of the Parliamentary Assembly of the Council of Europe on the non-expulsion of long-term immigrants, text adopted by the Standing Committee, acting on behalf of the Assembly, on 14 March 2001. See about the criteria that the ECtHR uses to assess the lawfulness of the expulsion of second-generation immigrants or long-term legal residents after a criminal conviction: *Boultif v. Switzerland*, 2 August 2001, Reports 2001-IX; and for an elaboration: *Maslov v. Austria*, 23 June 2008, Appl. No. 1638/03; and *Grant v United Kingdom*, 8 January 2009, Appl. No. 10606/07.

[165] *Dalia v. France*, 19 February 1998, Reports 1998-I.

[166] *Sen v. the Netherlands*, par. 40. See also *Tuquabo-Tekle and others v. the Netherlands*, 1 December 2005, Appl. No. 60665/00.

[167] ECtHR, *Sezen v. The Netherlands*, 31 January 2006, Appl. No. 50252/99. See also *Mehemi v. France*, par. 36. But see: *Cherif and Others v. Italy*, 7 April 2009, Appl. No. 1860/07, in which case *suspicions* pertaining to terrorist activities by the applicants were crucial in the Court's finding that his expulsion was permitted. See the dissenting opinion by Judges Tulkens, Jočienė and Popović.

ECHR as positive in the case that an applicant enjoys family life without being entitled to legal residence,[168] and family life that is established during such unlawful presence will only be protected in "the most exceptional circumstances".[169] Although the HRC seems to attach less importance to the fact whether family life is established during lawful or unlawful residence, its adherence to the territorial sovereignty of the state is proven by its statement that only extraordinary circumstances may require a State to demonstrate factors justifying the removal of persons within its jurisdiction that go beyond a simple enforcement of its immigration policies.[170]

It should be observed that EU Member States' decisions regarding family reunification with regard to third-country nationals residing on their territories have to be in accordance with the EC Directive on family reunification.[171] At fist sight, the Directive seems to afford rather little scope for the assertion of territorial sovereignty with the sole aim of 'governing' populations as the entry of children and spouses of lawfully residing third-country nationals, who have a "reasonable prospect of obtaining permanent residence," can only be refused on the grounds of public order, internal security or public health. Nonetheless, Member States are afforded some discretion to make the right conditional upon (*inter alia*) integration requirements, while the concept of integration as such is not defined in the Directive, but refers to national laws.[172] Even if that fact cannot be interpreted "as authorising the Member States to employ that concept in a manner contrary to general principles of Community law, in particular to fundamental rights,"[173] it should be fully appreciated that the lack of even formal harmonisation in this field is due to Member States' reticence in abandoning *national* exclusionary powers. We have seen in chapter 3 that a

---

[168] ECtHR, *Ahmut v. Netherlands*, 28 November 1996, Reports 1996-VI, 63.
[169] ECtHR, *Mitchell v. The United Kingdom* (Decision), 24 November 1998 Appl. No. 40447/98. See also *Darren Omoregie v Norway*, 31 July 2008, Appl. No. 265/07, par. 57. See for such 'exceptional circumstances': *Rodrigues da Silva and Hoogkamer v. the Netherlands*, 31 January 2006, Appl. No. 50435/99. In this case it was the interest of the child – who was a *national* of the respondent state (!) – that made the scales tip in favour of the interest of the 'illegally' staying mother in not being expelled.
[170] HRC, *Sahid v. New Zealand*, 28 March 2003, Comm. No. 893/99, U.N. Doc. CCPR/C/77/D/893/1999 (2003), at 8.2. See for the HRC acknowledging such extraordinary circumstances: *Winata v. Australia*, 26 July 2001, Comm. No. 30/2000, U.N. Doc. CCPR/C/72/D/930/2000 (2001).
[171] Council Directive 2003/86/EC of 22 September 2003 on the right to family reunification, OJ L251, 3 October 2003.
[172] Article 7(c) of the Council Directive 2003/86/EC on the right to family reunification.
[173] ECJ Case C-540/03, *European Parliament v. Council of the European Union* [2006] ECR I-5769, par. 70.

similar mechanism is at work in Directive 2003/109/EC on the status of long-term legal residents, and as such, the rights that attach to the status of legally residing third-country nationals are far weaker than those that are enjoyed by Union citizens on the basis of Directive 2004/38.[174] In addition, not all third-country nationals are covered by EC law as former spouses after divorce, unmarried partners, and the economically less advantaged are not fully included.[175]

I will conclude this section with a few remarks on procedural guarantees, which, as transpired from the decision by the ECtHR in *Al-Nashif*, can form an inherent part of the safeguards contained in Article 8 ECHR, so as to ensure that the discretion that is left to the executive is exercised in accordance with the law.[176] In other words, if deportation or expulsion is ordered pursuant to a regime that does not provide the necessary safeguards against arbitrariness – thereby including some form of review of the decisions made by the executive – there will be a breach of Article 8. Even where national security is at stake, the concept of the rule of law requires that measures affecting the fundamental rights of individuals must be subject to some form of adversarial proceedings before an independent body.[177] The way in which the Court has interpreted the requirements of Article 8(2) ECHR in *Al-Nashif* come close to the fair trial guarantees of Article 6 ECHR, therewith weakening the effect of the exclusion of this latter provision on immigration decision-making whenever there are family rights involved in a decision to deport an individual.

Finally, if there is an arguable complaint that family rights are violated as a result of immigration decision-making, an effective domestic remedy should be available to the individual pursuant to Article 13 ECHR. Again, national security considerations cannot justify the absence of such a remedy, although they may legitimately give rise to certain limitations on the type of remedies available. Nonetheless, the reviewing authority "must be competent to reject the executive's assertion that there is a threat to national security where it finds it arbitrary or unreasonable".[178] The decision in *Al-Nashif* on procedural

---

[174] Council Directive 2003/109/EC of 25 November 2003 concerning the status of third-country nationals who are long-term residents, in its preamble (par. 3) refers to the Presidency Conclusions of the Tampere European Council of 15 and 16 October 1999 where the Council stated that European integration should aim at approximating the legal status of third-country nationals to that of Member States' nationals.
[175] S. Peers, *EU Law and Family Reunification: A Human Rights Critique*, ECLN Essay No. 4 (Essays for civil liberties and democracy in Europe, 2005), 4.
[176] *Al-Nashif v. Bulgaria* (judgment).
[177] Ibid., 122–128.
[178] Ibid., 137.

safeguards in the context of both Article 8 and Article 13 ECHR contrasts sharply with the requirements under Article 1 Protocol 7 ECHR as discussed above (5.3.1). Once again we thus find that the visibility of the interests of non-nationals appears to improve if there are a limited number of well-known and recognised fundamental rights involved in the decision to deport or expel these individuals.

5.4 Immigration into and within the EU: The Obduracy of the National Border?

Any account on freedom of movement without dealing at least in some detail with the special legal order of the EU would be incomplete. It is in the context of the EU that individual rights of free movement have developed most extensively, and they have arguably done so in a way that opens up a way of thinking about citizenship on a global scale.[179] The scope of this study is not such as to permit me to deal with the free movement rights of citizens of the Union as such, except for the way in which they impact on immigration policies vis-à-vis third-country nationals. Thus, the two sections below investigate the impact of European laws and policies concerning the immigration and sojourn of third-country nationals on national sovereignty and the notion of territoriality. In order to do that, I shall first discuss the free movement rights of third-country nationals *within* the 'area without internal frontiers' (5.4.1), after which I shall focus on the common immigration policy and the crossing of *external* borders (5.4.2).

It is helpful to address the EU in this chapter for three reasons. First, the Member States' pursuing of supranational policies in some areas, while displaying a reluctance to do so in others, shows that they make highly selective use of the concept of national sovereignty. This, in turn, reveals that they still perceive national sovereignty as decisive for unity, notwithstanding the fact that the way in which that unity is imagined may have changed in important and unprecedented ways as a result of the European project. Second, the common asylum and immigration policy shows unambiguously how states endeavour to find means by which they can circumvent the constraints put upon them by international law. The third reason, related to the former two, is that EU law and policies with regard to free movement provide an excellent example of the changing connotations of the *physical* border.

---

[179] See D. Kostakopoulou, "EU Citizenship: Writing the Future," *European Law Journal* 13 (2007).

5.4.1 *Freedom of Movement* within *an Area without Internal Borders*

While EU citizens benefit from extensive freedom of movement rights between the Member States, the Treaty provisions on freedom of movement are not applicable to third-country nationals who are long-term residents in a Member State.[180] The assertion of exclusionary powers *per se* is no longer deemed necessary, nor legitimate, with regard to EU citizens, but national states wish to keep their discretionary powers with regard to the entry and sojourn of third-country nationals in their own hands. According to the ECtHR, such preferential treatment of EU citizens as compared to third-country nationals does not constitute prohibited discrimination on the ground of nationality on account of the special legal order of the EU.[181] This is a clear illustration of the way in which Member States' perception of national sovereignty has changed in keeping with the European project, but is far from being abandoned.

Council Directive 2003/109/EC on the status of third country nationals who are long-term residents has somewhat rectified this situation, but substantive possibilities for national discretion remain.[182] Indeed, as we saw in chapter 3, through the introduction of national integration requirements, long-term resident status can ultimately be made contingent on each Member State's notion of its 'nationness'. And although the Directive accords long-term residents the right to reside in other Member States, the right to free movement can be limited by applying quotas for third-country nationals and allowing preferential treatment for Union citizens.[183] Furthermore, the right to reside in another Member State may be made conditional upon requirements that are not allowed in the context of the free movement of Union citizens, such as (again) integration requirements.[184] Notwithstanding these shortcomings, it should be appreciated that the Directive departs from the notion of "Union citizenship as the sole route to autonomous free movement

---

[180] Other fields of EC law are much more inclusive of third-country nationals, such as the rules on the free movement of capital or the transfer of undertakings, consumer law and transport policy, and rules regarding working conditions and social security schemes. S. Boelaert-Suominen, "Non-EU nationals and Council Directive 2003/109/EC on the status of Third Country Nationals who are long-term residents: Five paces forward and possibly three paces back," *Common Market Law Review* 42 (2005), 1014.

[181] ECtHR: *C. v. Belgium*, par. 34; and *Moustaquim v. Belgium*, par. 49.

[182] OJ 2004, L 16/44, 23 January 2004. See S. Carrera, "'Integration' as a Process of inclusion for Migrants? The Case of Long Term Residents in the EU," in: *Migration, Integration and Citizenship: A Challenge for Europe's Future*, ed. H. Schneider (Maastricht: Forum, 2005).

[183] Article 14.

[184] Article 15.

rights."[185] In addition, the Directive has in a general sense added momentum to international restrictions on national states' exclusionary powers by stipulating that Member States may expel a long-term resident solely where he/she constitutes an actual and sufficiently serious threat to public policy or public security, in which case he/she must have the possibility of judicial redress.[186]

Nonetheless, a vivid image of national sovereignty as control over access to territory was affirmed by the (temporary) reservations that many Member States made with regard to the free movement rights of the new EU citizens in Central and Eastern Europe.[187] Nationality, rights and the possibility for transnational movement remain firmly linked in the post-national entity of the EU as for non-EU citizens (or new EU citizens); national borders are still a factor to be reckoned with if they want to move from the territory of one Member State to another. This is not to say that the creation of a single market in which goods, persons and capital move freely has not made a real difference for them too, caused by the fact that the internal border is control-free. But instead of according them more freedom, the absence of internal border controls, combined with Member States' insistence on their exclusionary powers vis-à-vis third-country nationals, has led to a situation in which, quoting Malcolm Anderson and Didier Bigo, "controls are still there, but now over the whole of the territory, although perhaps not applied to everyone, but certainly to persons categorised as dangerous and especially as 'unwelcome migrants with dark skins'.'[188] The enlargement of the Schengen Area has certainly not reversed this situation. On the contrary, it may even have enhanced national sovereign control, as it has witnessed a "multiplication of alternative, functional borders [...] not only spatially scattered and diversified in terms of authorities but [...] also mainly subject to national discretion."[189]

---

[185] M. Bell, "Civic citizenship and Migrant Integration," *European Public Law* 13 (2007), 327.
[186] Article 12.
[187] The Accession treaties contain provisions that make this possible in order to "phase in" free movement rights for the new EU citizens. See for the 'newest' citizens (from Romania and Bulgaria) and the possibilities for the EU 25 to phase in their free movement rights: Annexes to the Act of Accession, Annex VI, List referred to in Article 23 of the Act of Accession: Transitional measures, Bulgaria OJ L 157/278 and Annex VII, List referred to in Article 23 of the Act of Accession: Transitional measures, Romania, OJ L 157/ 281.
[188] M. Anderson and D. Bigo, "What are EU frontiers for and what do they mean?" in: *In Search of Europe's Borders*, eds. K. Groenendijk, E. Guild and P. Minderhoud (The Hague: Kluwer Law International, 2002), 18.
[189] A. Faure Atger, *The Abolition of Internal Border Checks in an Enlarged Schengen Area: Freedom of movement or a scattered web of security checks?* (Brussels: CEPS Research Paper No. 8, March 2008).

Thus the European aim of creating a single market may have led to a willingness on the part of the Member States to part with elements of national sovereignty, but this willingness has a clear limit: when the right to exclude those whom Member States perceive as 'real' outsiders is threatened, national sovereignty becomes pivotal once again. Supranational policies to abolish internal borders are only acceptable to the Member States if the national state is able to maintain and control its linkage of population and territory, if not in a formal sense, then at least in reality. The controversial *Chen* judgment by the ECJ provides an excellent example of Member States' strategic use of the concept of national sovereignty in the European context.[190] Legislation pertaining to nationality has been held firmly within their sovereign prerogatives, while the issue of free movement rights for EU citizens is within the competence of the EC. As EU citizenship is dependent on citizenship of the Member States, national states retain the power to decide who can fully benefit from free movement rights, but the reverse side of the coin is that they have to respect, on an equal basis, other Member States' decisions in this area.[191] Their interest in preserving their prerogative over the recognition of citizenship status is indicative of their will to retain crucial elements of sovereign statehood.[192]

However, the *Chen* case showed that such an approach to EU citizenship may also result in a backlash in the individual Member State wishing to preserve its ultimate powers to exclude. The Chens were a Chinese couple living in Wales (where the father worked for a Chinese company) and were expecting their second child. As this contravened China's One-Child Policy the mother chose to give birth to her daughter, Catherine Chen, in Belfast, whereupon baby Chen automatically acquired Irish nationality (she had expressly chosen Ireland as mere birth in the UK does not automatically give rise to UK nationality). Her Chinese mother then returned to the UK with her (without having to cross any international border), where she held a temporary residence permit. The ECJ decided that as an EU citizen, baby Chen had the right to reside in any Member State, under the usual conditions laid down in various directives. As her right of residence would be illusionary without her mother to take care of her, her mother acquired a right of residence as well.[193]

---

[190] Case C-200/02, *Chen Kunqian Catherine Zhu and Man Lavette Chen v. Secretary of State for the Home Department* [2004] ECR I-9925.

[191] Naturalisation is an exclusive national competence.

[192] See A. Dashwood, "States in the European Union," *European Law Review* 23 (1998), 203; and E. Kveinen, "Citizenship on a Post-Westphalian Community: Beyond External Exclusion?" *Citizenship Studies* 6 (2002), 31.

[193] Compare *Rodrigues da Silva and Hoogkamer v. the Netherlands*, where the fact that the minor child was a national was not of itself a sufficient reason for the ECtHR to consider the exclusion of the mother to be a violation of Article 8 ECHR.

The argument which was used by the UK government in the proceedings is revealing: the mother's travelling to Belfast to give birth to her daughter and thus to acquire residence rights in the UK would constitute an abuse of EC law. It is difficult to imagine any other case in which a Member State would voluntarily ask the ECJ to usurp "the power of the Member States to decide on whom they can confer nationality and consequently also citizenship."[194] It is equally easy to understand why the UK did precisely that in the *Chen* case: suddenly Irish nationality law in a real sense affected its powers to exclude with possibly far-reaching consequences.

The decision in *Chen*, based upon the fundamental status of EU citizenship, is to be distinguished from cases in which the Court decided that the exercise of free movement rights by EU citizens necessitates effective respect for their family life.[195] However, it should be recognised that this construction has similarly led to a situation in which the concept of EU citizenship has made significant inroads in Member States' power to exclude third-country nationals from their territories. Thus, Directive 2004/38/EC on the right of citizens of the Union and their family members to move and reside freely within the territory of the Member States grants the right of all Union citizens to move and reside freely within the territory of the Member States also to their family members. Until recently the precise extent to which third-country nationals could derive a right of *first admittance* in the EU as a family member of a Union citizen remained unclear.[196] In *Akrich* the ECJ had repealed some of the principles established by its earlier case law by refusing the use of Community law in order to rectify the illegal status of a third-country national by the exercise of the free movement rights of his Union citizen wife.[197] However, in

---

[194] B. Kunoy, "A Union of National Citizens: the Origins of the Court's Lack of *Avant Gardisme* in the *Chen* Case," *Common Market Law Review* 43 (2006), 190.

[195] Case C-459/99, *Mouvement contre le racisme, l'antisémitisme, et la xénophobie ASBL (MRAX) v. Belgian State* [2002] ECR I-6591. See also Case C-60/00, *Carpenter v. Secretary of State for the Home Department* [2002] ECR I-6279 (the freedom to provide services (primary Community law) necessitated respect for family life).

[196] All the cases preceding *Metock* were decided under the previous directives which were repealed by Directive 2004/38/EC of the European Parliament and of the Council of 29 April 2004 on the right of citizens of the Union and their family members to move and reside freely within the territory of the Member States. See also Case C-503/03, *Commission v. Spain* [2006] ECR I-1097; and Case C-1/05, *Jia v. Migrationsverket* [2007] ECR I-1.; and Case C-291/05, *Minister voor Vreemdelingenzaken en Integratie v. Eind* [2007] ECR I-10719.

[197] Case C-109/01, *Secretary of State for the Home Department v. Akrich* [2003] ECR I-9607. See also E. Spaventa, "Case C-109/01, *Secretary of State for the Home Department v. H. Akrich*, judgment of the Full Court of 23 September 2003, [2003] ECR I-9607," *Common Market Law Review* 42 (2005).

Metock, the Court established unambiguously that Directive 2004/38 precludes national legislation which requires a third-country national who is a family member of a Union citizen residing in that member state but not possessing its nationality to have *previously* been *lawfully* resident in another Member state before arriving in the host Member State in order to benefit from the free movement provisions of that Directive. In this respect, the Court made clear that it is also irrelevant how the third-country national entered the host Member State.[198] The reason that the Court adduced in order to draw its conclusion in *Metock* shows how (just as it did in the *Chen* case), Member States' preservation of their sovereign powers in the field of exclusion may result in a backlash against them:

> Indeed, to allow the Member States exclusive competence to grant or refuse entry into and residence in their territory to nationals of non-member countries who are family members of Union citizens and have not already resided lawfully in another Member State would have the effect that the freedom of movement of Union citizens in a Member State whose nationality they do not possess would vary from one Member State to another, according to the provisions of national law concerning immigration, with some Member States permitting entry and residence of family members of a Union citizen and other Member States refusing them. That would not be compatible with the objective set out in Article 3(1)(c) EC of an internal market characterised by the abolition, as between Member States, of obstacles to the free movement of persons.[199]

Thus, the very fact that national immigration policies are not harmonised constitutes a reason finding in favour of a right of first-admittance of third-country nationals who are family members of a Union citizen in EC law.[200] In this light, the furious reactions that the *Metock* judgment received in several Member States are not surprising.[201]

We can conclude that the post-national constellation of the EU is ambiguous in its potential for inclusion/exclusion. Whereas for Union citizens, territorial borders have lost considerable relevance, with regard to third-country nationals Member States insist on their sovereign right to exclude. However, at the same time the case law of the ECJ shows that European integration follows

---

[198] Case C-127/08, *Metock and others v. Ministry for Justice, Equality and Law Reform* [2008] nyr.

[199] Ibid., par. 3.

[200] As such, the crossing of internal borders by third-country nationals cannot be seen in isolation from the delimitation of competences between the EC and the Member States with regard to external border crossings, to which we shall turn shortly (5.4.2).

[201] See D. Martin, "Comments on *Förster* (Case C-158/07 of 18 November 2008), *Metock* (Case C-127/08 of 25 July 2008) and *Huber* (Case C/524/06 of 16 December 2008)," *European Journal of Migration and Law* 11 (2009).

a logic which is independent of Member States' national sensitivities: judgments such as *Metock* and *Chen* exemplify the radical potential of post-national citizenship – and not only with regard to persons who possess the nationality of one of the Member States.[202] And yet – paradoxically as it may seem – in other areas again, internal (national) borders have not really diminished in importance. Rather, the location of their control has shifted, so that the regulation of transnational movement is increasingly located *inside* the country instead of at its *physical* border.[203] In this respect, Enrica Rigo effectively counters the "Fortress Europe" metaphor by pointing out that it is only partially true that controls have been relocated from national borders to the external frontiers of the Union. In reality, she argues, the "very concept of borders itself underwent deep transformation".[204] That is not to say that the external borders of the EU are not important when we investigate the way in which the Member States hang on to their exclusionary powers. On the contrary, as we will see below, the control of these borders may well have reinforced the territory-identity link by the use of novel techniques.

5.4.2 *The External Border: The Common Immigration and Asylum Policy*

Before the Treaty of Amsterdam, which made immigration and asylum policy a matter of EC competence, co-operation on these matters had for a long time been purely intergovernmental. This was largely due to Member States' reluctance to communitarize an area which was so clearly labelled, both by them and their national constituencies, as constituting the core of national sovereignty. Nonetheless, from the 1980s onwards, a certain degree of Europeanisation of migration policies – although not part of the integration process in a formal sense – had taken place in the form of various forms of transnational cooperation by individual Member States.[205]

---

[202] See also Case C-503/03, *Commission v. Spain*, where the Court decided that the automatic refusal of entry by one Member State on the ground of an SIS alert issued by another Member State violates EC law if the refusal concerns a spouse of an EU citizen.

[203] R. Bauböck, *Multilevel citizenship and territorial borders in the EU polity* (Vienna: Österreichische Akademie der Wissenschaften, 2003), 7; and D. Bigo and E. Guild, "Policing at a Distance: Schengen Visa Policies," in *Controlling Frontiers: Free Movement into and within Europe*, eds. D. Bigo and E. Guild (Aldershot: Ashgate, 2005), 238.

[204] E. Rigo, "Citizens and foreigners in the Enlarged Europe," in: *Spreading Democracy and the Rule of Law? The Impact of EU Enlargement on the Rule of Law: Democracy and Constitutionalism in Post-Communist Legal Orders*, eds. W. Sadurski et al. (Dordrecht: Springer, 2006), 98 and 101.

[205] J. Huysmans, "The European Union and the Securitization of migration," *Journal of Common Market Studies* 38 (2000), 755.

Some authors have linked the beginnings of European co-operation with states' awareness of increasing legal constraints domestically. Immigration control authorities found that they had more freedom of action if they operated at the European level, where decision-making was largely free of judicial checks and public scrutiny.[206] Even when co-operation was institutionalised in the third pillar in the Maastricht Treaty, the situation in which primacy lay with national executives remained largely the same: apart from the absence of domestic constitutional constraints, there was little scope for action by the Commission, the European Parliament or the ECJ.[207] This is one instance through which it may be shown that the European project provides Member States with an opportunity to reassert national sovereignty with regard to control over international movement by turning to the traditional administrative culture of immigration decision-making where the rule of law is severely curtailed.[208] Thus it has been argued by some that, while European integration may superficially be perceived as limiting the pursuit of some elements of sovereignty, in reality it strengthens the kind of "sovereign authority emerging as central in a globalising world."[209]

Hence, when Member States' concern over immigration had risen sufficiently high and dissatisfaction with the intergovernmental approach of the Third Pillar emerged, at Amsterdam the Treaty on the European Union was changed in such a manner that immigration and asylum were moved from the third pillar to the first. Increasing immigration pressure on the European Union countries made the Member States realise that purely intergovernmental strategies would no longer be sufficient to protect their national states. Moreover, although it seems to have been only a secondary motivation, the absence of internal border controls made a common stance on immigration from third countries seem logically required. The complex manner in which the common immigration and asylum policy is shaped, with rules from many

---

[206] See A. Geddes, "International Migration and State Sovereignty in an Integrating Europe," *International Migration* 39 (2001), 28; C. Boswell, "The external dimension of EU immigration and asylum policy," *International Affairs* 79 (2003), 623; and V. Guiraudon, "The constitution of a European immigration policy domain: a political sociology approach," *Journal of European Policy* 10 (2003).

[207] Boswell (2003), 623.

[208] V. Guiraudon and G. Lahav, "A Reappraisal of the State Sovereignty Debate, The Case of Migration Control," *Comparative Political Studies* 33 (2000), 178; Geddes (2001), 36; and A. Geddes, "Europe's border relationships and international migration relations," *Journal of Common Market Studies* 43 (2005), 788.

[209] E.S. Cohen, "Globalization and the Boundaries of the State: A Framework for Analyzing the Changing Practice of Sovereignty," *Governance* 14 (2001), 84. See also: M.A. Schain, "The State Strikes Back: Immigration Policy in the European Union," *The European Journal of International Law* 20 (2009).

overlapping sources, opt-in and opt-out provisions for certain Member States and forms of policy making which depart from the traditional EC legislative process such as the open method of co-ordination is a reflection of Member States' ambiguous feelings regarding the loss of their exclusive competences in this area. Another such example is contained in the special provision for preliminary rulings under Title IV that deviates from the normal procedure for preliminary rulings. According to Article 68 EC only national courts of last instance can refer questions for preliminary rulings to the European Court of Justice.[210]

Furthermore, some of the cooperation between Member States still takes place outside the formal structure of the EU, such as multilateral cooperation between several Member States in combating illegal immigration under the Prüm Convention.[211] The explicit intention of such cooperation is the eventual transferral of the rules which the participating states have agreed upon to the level of the EU. Even though such intergovernmental cooperation may be motivated by a genuine wish of some Member States to achieve closer integration, the inevitable result is that checks on the executive are largely absent: the European Parliament has no say in the proceedings and outcomes within these multilateral frameworks.

Instead of analysing the bulk of EU legislation that has been enacted under Title IV of the EC Treaty, this section focuses upon the way in which EU law and policies in this area have changed the connotations of the territorial border. I shall argue that most of these changes have been triggered by Member States' wishes to retain their sovereign power to exclude in response to the evolving human rights norms as discussed above (5.3). They have done so by shifting and extending the enactment of their sovereign powers.

I have already touched upon the shift 'upwards', denoting the transferring of migration decision-making to the Community level.[212] The measures and policies

---

[210] The Council did not adapt this provision after the transitionary period expired on 1 May 2004 as required by Article 67(2) EC. See Communication from the Commission to the European Parliament, the Council, the European Economic and Social Committee, the Committee of the Regions and the Court of Justice of the European Communities, Adaptation of the provisions of Title IV of the EC Treaty relating to the jurisdiction of the Court of Justice with a view to ensuring more effective judicial protection, COM 2006 (346) final, 28 June 2006.

[211] Convention on the stepping up of cross-border cooperation, particularly in combating terrorism, cross-border crime and illegal immigration, signed at Prüm on 27 May 2005 (Schengen III). The participating states are Belgium, France, Spain, Luxembourg, Austria, the Netherlands, Germany and Italy.

[212] Guiraudon and Lahav (2000), 176–177.

which have so far been taken as a result of this upward shifting show that strong emphasis is laid on the traditional control of territorial borders.[213] In spite of the comprehensive approach to be taken to migration which was proclaimed indispensable at Tampere, legislation and other instruments, such as on harmonising existing practices on expulsions,[214] the mutual recognition of expulsion decisions,[215] voluntary repatriation,[216] the organisation of joint flights for expulsion,[217] the return of illegally staying third-country nationals,[218] and controlling illegal immigration in a more general sense,[219] all point to Member States' strong commitment to a rigid territory-identity link. In this respect, it is significant that law and policy making under Title IV of the EC Treaty is strongly unbalanced in favour of measures that emphasise security and border control.[220]

Apart from an upward shift, Member States have externalised migration control through various EU policies, in what can be described as a shift 'outwards'. They have done so in different ways which all lead to a separation between the concept of the border and the perimeter of European territory.[221] The first of such policies is the Schengen system of visa regulation. The Schengen visa system governs the movement of potential migrants in their

---

[213] Id.
[214] Various Recommendations, see for example OJ C 5, 10 January 1996 and OJ C 274, 19 September 1996.
[215] Council Directive 2001/40/EC of 28 May 2001 on the mutual recognition of decisions on the expulsion of third country nationals, OJ L 149, 2 June 2001.
[216] Council Decision 97/340/JHA of 26 May 1997 on the exchange of information concerning assistance for the voluntary repatriation of third-country nationals, OJ L 147, 5 June 1997.
[217] Council Decision 2004/573/EC of 29 April 2004 on the organisation of joint flights for removals from the territory of two or more Member States, of third-country nationals who are subjects of individual removal orders, OJ L261, 6 August 2004, pp. 28–35.
[218] Directive 2008/115/EC of the European Parliament and the Council of 16 December 2008 on common standards and procedures in Member States for returning illegally staying third-country nationals, OJ L 348/98, 24 December 2008.
[219] Communication of 13 February 2008 from the Commission to the European Parliament, the Council, the European Economic and Social Committee and the Committee of the Regions: Preparing the next steps in border management in the European Union, COM(2008) 69 final; and European Pact on Immigration and Asylum, Adopted at the European Council in Brussels, 15 and 16 October 2008, Presidency Conclusions, 16 October 2008, 14368/08.
[220] G. Papagianni, *Institutional and Policy Dynamics of EU Migration Law* (Leiden/Boston: Martinus Nijhoff Publishers, 2006), 292. Legislation in the field of legal migration is subject to unanimity voting in the Council (Article 63(3)(a) and the Treaty of Lisbon reaffirm national competence in this area (in Article 63a(5) FEU).
[221] Rigo (2006), 107.

countries of origin instead of at the moment of their arrival at the actual border of the Member States. Particularly in combination with carrier sanctions,[222] through which private actors are made responsible for the typical sovereign act of control over borders, the European visa requirements lead to a construction in which control over movement is more easily exercised, because the extra-territorialisation of such control facilitates the evasion of human rights obligations.[223] The regulation of visas under Schengen is also indicative of the fact that States are not averse to ceding formal sovereignty if they can win back substantive powers of exclusion: participating states are under an *obligation* to refuse entry if the Schengen conditions are not met.[224] Furthermore, the stationing of immigration liaison officers in third countries, in order to prevent what is called irregular migration, is another illustration of the extraterritorialising of sovereignty, and thus implicitly of the way in which Member States conceive of the importance of access to territory for their human rights obligations.[225]

A particular instance of *police à distance* that has received considerable attention recently is the way in which several European Member States have worked together on the sea, intercepting migrants who have departed or intend to depart from the coast of North-West Africa. Efforts by Member States in this area are increasingly managed by Frontex, the agency that aims at the co-ordination of operational activities concerning external border control by Member States.[226] Several Member States have participated in these operations, such as Spain, Germany, France, Italy, Luxembourg and Portugal. Predominantly, these operations have been based upon bilateral agreements

---

[222] Based upon Art. 26 of the 1990 Supplementation Agreement of the Schengen Convention.
[223] See Moreno Lax (2008).
[224] J.D.M. Steenbergen, "Schengen and the movement of persons," in: *Schengen: Internalisation of Central Chapters of the Law on Aliens, Refugees, Privacy, Security and the Police*, ed. H. Meijers (Leiden: Stichting NJCM-Boekerij, 1992), 65.
[225] Council Regulation (EC) No. 377/2004 of 19 February 2004 on the creation of an immigration liaison officers network, OJ L 64, 2 March 2004, 1–4.
[226] Council Regulation (EC) No. 2007/2004 of 26 October 2004 establishing a European Agency for the Management of Operational Cooperation at the External Borders of the Member States of the European Union, OJ L 349/1, 25 November 2004, amended by Regulation (EC) No. 863/2007 of the European Parliament and the Council of 11 July 2007 establishing a mechanism for the creation of Rapid Border Intervention Teams, OJ L 199/30, 31 July 2007. Apart from the coordination of operational activities by Member States, Frontex's tasks consist of assisting Member States in the training of border guards, carrying out risk analyses and research, assisting Member States in circumstances requiring increased technical and operational assistance and providing Member States with support in organising joint return operations. See Article 2 of Council Regulation (EC) No. 2007/2004.

between Spain and third countries, such as Mauritania and Senegal.[227] Member States' co-operation within the framework of Frontex entails providing material assistance such as ships, helicopters or other aircraft and making personnel available.[228] The intercepted migrants are diverted back to the shores from which they intended to depart by the third-state law enforcement officials who are aboard the vessels of participating Member States. Frontex has also been involved by co-financing the material used in these operations, such as an aircraft based in Senegal for the detection of migrants onboard boats leaving Senegal, who are subsequently returned to Senegal by Spanish or Senegal vessels on the basis of a bilateral agreement between Senegal and Spain.[229] As a result of these policies, thousands of migrants were intercepted in the territorial waters of northwest African countries and have been diverted back to the coast of the territories that they attempted to leave.[230]

Other venues for extending the control and policing of transnational movement consist of shifting responsibility to third countries: "third countries are encouraged, or in the case of candidate countries, obliged, to apply EU standards of migration management, or to enter into agreements for readmitting irregular migrants."[231] Readmission agreements in particular, as a means to govern populations both inside and outside a state's territory, fit very well in a system based on territoriality.[232] We have seen above that the contemporary preoccupation with political territoriality, according to which each and every individual belongs to a certain, delimited piece of the earth, can be disrupted on the grounds of a limited number of human rights considerations. However,

---

[227] Although Frontex is also directly involved in the concluding of Working Agreements (which are not legally binding) currently being negotiated with *inter alia* Libya, Cape Verde, Senegal and Mauretania on the basis of Article 14 of Council Regulation (EC) No. 2007/2004 establishing a European Agency for the Management of Operational Cooperation at the External Borders of the Member States of the European Union,. See COWI, *External evaluation of the European Agency for the Management of Operational Cooperation at the External Borders of the Member States of the European Union, Final Report, January 2009* (Kongens Lyngby, COWI, 2009), 63.

[228] For instance, within the framework of Frontex, Luxembourg made available a helicopter to Mauritania. This is based in Nouakchott and undertakes air patrols along the Mauritanian coast. Amnesty International, *Mauritania: "Nobody wants to have anything to do with us": Arrests and collective expulsions of migrants denied entry into Europe.* AFR/38/001/2008 (Amnesty International Secretariat: London, 2008).

[229] COWI (2009), 62.

[230] Amnesty International (2008). See also Frontex Annual Report 2006, and documents that it makes available to the press on its website: www.frontex.europa.eu.

[231] Boswell (2003), 624. Much of this is currently done within the framework of the EU Neighbourhood Policy. See Gammeltoft-Hansen and Gammeltoft-Hansen (2008).

[232] Walters, "Deportation, Expulsion, and the International Police of Aliens," (2002).

concepts such as a safe third country and a safe country of origin, now commonly used by all Member States, attempt to reinstate a rigid system of territorial governance. These practices are comparable to the interception practices described above, in that they distribute responsibility for the fundamental rights of individuals along a strict territorial logic. In addition, both mechanisms will inevitably undermine the assessment of fundamental rights at stake in each and every individual case.[233]

Further proof of the desire to push borders outwards, thereby de-territorialising sovereignty, is provided by proposals made by Italy, Germany, and the UK, for so-called Transit Processing Centres. These countries seem to have been inspired by Australia's 'pacific solution', its asylum policy consisting of "patrolling a naval barrier created around Australia's territorial waters in order to prevent unauthorized vessels carrying asylum seekers from entering. Intercepted vessels are diverted to off-shore processing centres in counties to host [these] in return for financial incentives. […] if granted refugee status, the refugees are then resettled in third countries."[234] European ideas for Transit Processing Centres similarly envisaged the processing of claims that were made in one of the Member States outside the territory of the EU, thereby facilitating the contracting out of asylum services to third countries.[235] It is persuasively argued by several authors that significant legal obstacles would be encountered in realising these plans,[236] which perhaps explains why they have, to date, not been adopted by the Commission.

Member States, however, seem to think that these obstacles can be evaded if camps for illegal immigrants are set up in countries such as Algeria, Tunisia, Mauritania, Morocco, and Libya, not under the formal supervision of the EU, but of these respective countries.[237] Increasing co-operation

---

[233] See also P. Tuitt, "Racist Authorization, Interpretative Law and the Changing Character of the Refugee," in: *Nationalism, Racism and the Rule of Law*, ed. P. Fitzpatrick (Aldershot: Dartmouth Publishing Company, 1995); on interception practices and legal remedies: A. Fischer-Lescano and T. Löhr, *Menschen- und flüchtlingsrechtliche Anforderungen an Maßnahmen der Grenzkontrolle auf See* (Berlin: European Center for Constitutional and Human Rights, 2007); and Weinzierl (2007).

[234] O. Lynskey, "Complementing and completing the Common European Asylum System: a legal analysis of the emerging extraterritorial elements of EU refugee protection policy," *European Law Review* 31 (2006), 242.

[235] Ibid., 247; and I. Saint-Saens, "À distance," *Vacarme* 29 (2004).

[236] Lynskey (2006); and G. Noll, "Visions of the Exceptional: Legal and Theoretical Issues Raised by Transit Processing Centres and Protection Zones," *European Journal of Migration and Law* 5 (2003).

[237] D. Helmut, "The Desert Front: EU refugee camps in North Africa?" *Statewatch* (March 2005); and R. Andrijasevic, "How to balance rights and responsibilities on asylum at the EU's southern border of Italy and Libya," Compas Working Paper 27 (Centre on Migration, Policy and Society, University of Oxford: Oxford, 2006), 15–16.

between individual Member States and third countries shows a willingness on both sides to contain the alleged threat of migration on the non-European side of the Mediterranean.[238] Such co-operation has also been institutionalised within the framework of the EU. In Libya, the European Commission has four projects: centres to house illegal immigrants, information campaigns, the training of immigration officials and improvements to border controls.[239] It has furthermore recently adopted a package of measures to help Mauritania contain the flow of illegal immigrants to the Canary Islands. Resources for detention form part of the package, a € 2.45 million programme, which furthermore includes capacity building for detection and apprehension; the revision of existing legislation; and institutional support.[240] The background of such initiatives is a growing unwillingness on the part of the EU to deal with the effects of migration on its own soil, but to contain the problem in non-Member States, which are enticed to co-operate with political and financial advantages. Although occasionally worded in terms of humanitarian concern,[241] Member States use EU cooperation with third countries to export their views on territorial sovereignty, even though the situation in these third countries is hardly comparable to the situation in Europe. Similarly, plans for regional protection programmes, although arguably partly motivated by a genuine wish to provide more accessible and effective protection for refugees in their regions of origin, also fit within an image of a Europe which is reluctant to be engaged in refugee protection on account of its territorial responsibility.[242]

I have said above that a communitarian perspective on international movement reveals important insights with regard to national sovereignty

---

[238] Such as Italy financing the construction of detention camps in Libya. See European Commission, *Technical Mission to Libya on illegal immigration* 27 November-6 December 2004, Report. Brussels: 2005. Spain has agreed to pay for the construction of detention centres for illegal immigrants in Mauritania (Reuters, 17 March 2006).

[239] See European Commission Press Release, 10 July 2006, Brussels, IP 06/967. Libya "does not recognize the mandate of the UNHCR, has no asylum system, is not a signatory of the Geneva Convention and in which, as NGOs documented, irregular migrants and asylum seekers are at risk of arbitrary detentions, unfair trails, disappearance and torture while in detention." Andrijasevic (2006), 22. See also Human Rights Watch, *Libya: Stemming the Flow*, HRW Vol. 18, No. 5, September 2006.

[240] Id.

[241] With regard to plans for the establishment of reception camps in North Africa, the Austrian Minster of the Interior remarked: "Ce ne sont pas seulement des camps, ce sont des programmes pour créer de l'emploi, pour leur offrir un enseignement, pour les aider à commencer une vie par eux-mêmes." (Liberation, 13 January 2006).

[242] Communication from the Commission to the Council and the European Parliament, Regional Protection Programmes, COM (2005) 388 final, 6 April 2005. See Gammeltoft-Hansen and Gammeltoft-Hansen (2008), 457.

and territoriality. The way in which the Union and its Member States look upon and have regulated free movement *within* and *into* the territory of the European Union shows that national sovereignty plays a decisive role in shaping the legal and political framework dealing with free movement and immigration. Nevertheless, it is undeniable that the (imaginary) unity with which national sovereignty is concerned has changed as a result of the European project: the capacity to control the entry and stay by EU citizens has greatly diminished and the Court of Justice has shown in cases such as *Metock* and *Chen* that European citizenship has a distinctly 'post-national' potential. As such, it can doubtlessly inspire future conceptions of citizenship as a more "inclusive, multilayered and multicultural" concept, as Dora Kostakopoulou urges us to imagine.[243] Furthermore, the abolition of internal border controls has conceptually 'problematised' border controls as obstacles to individual freedom, and in certain respects the Schengen *acquis* has thus 'denaturalised' the border.[244]

Yet again we also find that in other areas Europeanisation has not altered the quintessential function of the territorial border, although its location and the manner of its enforcement on the individual are evolving.[245] Indeed, whereas before the concept of nationality was the essential tool with which national states monopolised the question of transnational movement, the EU and its Member States have brought about a considerably more sophisticated system of international government of populations. Concepts such as EU citizens, third-country nationals, safe country of origin and safe third country are the constituent elements of this novel structure. However, notwithstanding the novelty of the tools, maintaining the self-evident link between territorial exclusion and the individual who is defined as the other is the rationale behind that very structure. Similarly, the pushing of Europe's borders outwards through various policies fits within a traditional image of sovereignty, but instead of solely facilitating control over access to territory, these policies operate from a complementary logic. In order to protect national territory, they exploit the fact that access to fundamental rights is still largely contingent on presence within the *physical* borders of the nation state.

---

[243] Kostakopoulou (2007).
[244] W. Walters, "Mapping Schengenland: denaturalizing the border," *Environment and Planing D: Society and Space* 20 (2002),.
[245] See Rigo (2006).

5.5 Free Movement: Territoriality Shapes the Relation between State Power and Rights

This chapter has dealt with the exclusionary powers of the sovereign state by unravelling the assumptions that underlie the dominant perception of sovereignty as entailing an inherent right to exclude. We have seen that perceiving the power to control immigration as inextricably bound up with territorial sovereignty and thus falling within a field that is characterised by large executive discretion is a phenomenon that made its appearance relatively recently on the political stage. It was only in the late nineteenth century, at the time that the modern state's link between sovereignty, identity and rights had become exclusive and rigid that immigration began to be portrayed as a threat to sovereignty's claim to determine the inside from the outside and the unity of the state. As a result, it could become a domain that was largely excluded from normal processes of legal and political accountability. The tendency to depict immigration as a threat and a danger has gained momentum in the last three decades, during which it is being increasingly represented as a challenge to the modern state's national identity, its welfare provisions and its security.[246] At present, the individual has no right to enter or stay in national territory without state authorisation and unauthorised entry or sojourn is seen as a violation of the state's territorial sovereignty with allegedly grave consequences for its public order and domestic stability.[247] The preponderance of this view in Europe is amongst other things reflected in a growing body of national legislation that criminalises irregular entry or stay. At the very same time, as we have seen in the previous chapter, sovereignty has decreased in importance when it concerns matters relating to exit. In the concluding sections to this chapter I will seek to reconcile these seemingly opposing tendencies by pointing to the way in which modern law suffers from a serious blindness for the human interests that are affected whenever the state puts forward its territorial sovereignty as the basis for the exercise of power over individuals. The way in which modern law structures and categorises certain human interests as *rights*

---

[246] Huysmans (2000), 752. But see also A.W. Neal, "Securitization and risk at the EU Border: The Origins of Frontex," *Journal of Common Market Studies* 47 (2009).

[247] Anderson and Bigo (2002); D. Kostakopoulou, "Irregular Migration and Migration Theory: Making State Authorisation Less Relevant," in: *Irregular Migration and Human Rights: Theoretical, European and International Perspectives*, eds. B. Bogusz et al. (Leiden/Boston: Martinus Nijhoff Publishers, 2004); and Huysmans (2000).

whereas others are structurally ignored will be highlighted by pointing out how most limitations on the sovereign right to exclude operate from territoriality's logic (section 5.1.1). It is only by fully grasping territoriality's implications for modern constitutional discourse that we can subsequently account for what at first may seem a flagrant inconsistency in the contemporary global regulation of movement (section 5.1.2).

5.5.1 *Territoriality and Limitations on the State's Exclusionary Powers*

> Because of the way we label, define and categorise people who move, we obscure and make invisible their actual lived experience.[248]

In chapter 3 I have argued that, precisely because territoriality is very much taken for granted to the extent that our legal systems, domestically *and* internationally, are anchored in that very concept, modern constitutionalism is largely blind to the way in which territorial sovereignty implicates the interests of the individual. Whenever an issue is presented as engaging the territorial sovereignty of the modern state, modern constitutionalism seems to regress almost wholly to the discourse of classic international law, in which the sovereign state interest is central; territorial integrity paramount; and the interests of the individual remain inarticulable. As a consequence, the contemporary portrayal of immigration as impinging first and foremost on the 'integrity of national borders' overpowers the consideration of most – albeit not all – individual rights that may be at stake in its regulation. By failing to question the territorial assumptions that underlie both international and domestic legal systems, the law thus thwarts the communicability of the individual interests that are affected by the exercise of state power whenever this power is portrayed as being predominantly based upon territorial sovereignty.

At first sight, these claims seem to be in direct contradiction with the existence of international legal norms, such as pertaining to the protection of refugees and the application of the right to family life in the immigration context, which *do* make significant inroads into the sovereign power to exclude. Nevertheless – the exception of *non-refoulement* if based upon the prohibition of torture and degrading or inhuman treatment aside – the majority of these norms fit within a territorial image of the global political system. In these legal discourses, human interests are understood, categorised, and prioritised almost exclusively with reference to the existing structure of the territorial nation state and the system of which it forms part.

---

[248] A. Crosby, *The Boundaries of Belonging: Reflections on Migration Policies into the 21st Century*, Inter Pares Occasional Paper No. 7 (Toronto: Inter Pares, 2006), 3.

The international refugee regime in particular is far too intimately linked with the practices of excluding and including that the very concept of territoriality is about, to be able to challenge the perceived neutrality of that concept.[249] Perhaps, as a form of "geopolitical humanitarianism that has as its core business the preservation of the value of the nation-state form",[250] the refugee regime has even contributed to the reinforcement of the political-territorial ideal. The institution of asylum – which is in this respect comparable to the system of minority protection in the interwar period – was intended to safeguard the validity of an international order of states as a mechanism to govern human populations and to realise peace and stability.[251] This is not only apparent from the lack of the right to asylum for the individual in international law, but also from the central place that the state occupies in the definition of the notion of persecution in the refugee definition: the Geneva Convention does not protect against any kind of harm, but only when there is "a risk of a type of injury that would be inconsistent with the basic duty of protection owed by a state to its own population."[252] The protection afforded by the 1951 Geneva Refugee Convention thus applies only if an individual is the victim of clearly specified kinds of state violence; and the exclusion of victims of persecution by non-state agents from the scope of the Convention illustrates how international law in this area perceives the interests of individuals not so much in terms of their actual lived experiences, but instead with reference to the usual way in which (political and legal) responsibility over individuals is allocated: territorially.

The clear gaps that exist in international law when it concerns the protection of internally displaced persons provide a similar illustration of the stubborn and determinative influence of territorial borders on the question of which interests are able to be recognised *and* protected by the law:[253]

> (...) in international law a refugee is defined solely in state terms. The Geneva Convention and other international legal agreements limit refugee status to those

---

[249] See also P. Kumar and C. Grundy-Warr, "The Irregular Migrant as Homo Sacer: Migration and Detention in Australia, Malaysia, and Thailand," *International Migration* 42 (2004), 39.
[250] Lui (2002) at 6.
[251] Ibid.
[252] Hathaway (1991), 104. See also N. Nathwani, *Rethinking Refugee Law* (The Hague/London/New York: Martinus Nijhoff Publishers, 2003).
[253] See on these gaps: Report of the Representative of the Secretary-General, Mr Francis M. Deng, *Compilation and analysis of legal norms*, 5 December 1995, UN Doc. E/CN.4/1996/52/Add.2. See also Brookings-Bern Project on Internal Displacement, *Protecting Internally Displaced Persons: A Manual for Law and Policymakers* (UNHCR Refworld, October 2008). See also R. Cohen, "Response to Hathaway," *Journal of Refugee Studies* 20 (2007).

who have left their state of origin because of persecution or violence and who are unable to return for the same reason. In practice this means that an Ibo woman who is forced to leave her homeland in Nigeria can claim refugee status if she moves across the border into the Ibo part of Cameroon, but not if she moves in a culturally alien part of Nigeria.[254]

In this context, Robyn Lui writes that "categorisation and characterisation of population displacement are techniques of ordering" and she argues that the question of who is included and excluded from the category of 'refugee' is just as important as inclusion and exclusion from the nation-state community.[255] Indeed, the answer to both these questions is decided by the way in which rights, territory and political authority have become linked in a historically specific way. The 'techniques of ordering', to which Lui refers, reflect the territorial ideal in which this linkage is supposed to be perfectly embodied. And just as territoriality has determined the precise way in which rights are guaranteed in the domestic context (Chapter 3), in international refugee law it deeply affects the rights to be enjoyed by the individual as well.

Whereas the centrality of the state within traditional refugee law may be understandable when we take into account the period in which the international refugee regime emerged,[256] modern human rights law purportedly operates from a very different logic. Contemporary international human rights aim at the creation of a constitutional order over and across national boundaries, and in contrast to classic international law, human rights discourse is supposedly much less concerned with the principle of non-intervention or the notion of domestic jurisdiction. Below, I shall seek to answer the question as to whether this has reduced the logic of territoriality in international law's attempts to limit the sovereign right to exclude.

We have seen that the right to family life or private life may in certain cases constrain the sovereign state from exercising the full force of its exclusionary power. At first sight it seems that the way in which the ECtHR applies Article 8 ECHR (and similarly the HRC in applying Article 7 ICCPR) in exclusion cases amounts to the recognition of the fact that individual interests are involved in the assertion of a state's territorial sovereignty. For a right to enter

---

[254] Murphy, A.B. "The sovereign state system as a political-territorial ideal: historical and contemporary considerations," in: *State Sovereignty as a Social Construct*, eds. T.J. Biersteker and C. Weber (Cambridge: Cambridge University Press, 1996), 105.
[255] Lui (2002), at 66.
[256] Hathaway (1991), 30–31. Cf. B.S. Chimni, *International Refugee Law* (New Delhi/London: Sage Publications, 2000), 392. James Hathaway argues that it is still "the presence of refugees outside their own state [that] brings them within the *unconditional* protective competence of the international community (emphasis added). Hathaway (2007).

or remain is based upon the *interest of the individual* in being able to enjoy an effective family life. Nonetheless, when this proposition is closely scrutinised it becomes clear that family rights only constitute an effective barrier to the assertion of territorial sovereignty if a person's family members are legally residing within the state's territory. Accordingly, when the sovereign state's exclusionary powers are limited by an individual's family rights, there is a direct link with sovereignty's jurisdictional content, and as such, in applying Article 8 ECHR, the Court employs the traditional construction by which responsibility for the safeguarding of rights is assigned to states according to territoriality's logic.

Even so, it should nevertheless be valued that the recent case law of the ECtHR, which has taken the notion of *suitable* family life as a point of reference, suggests a growing reluctance to endorse territorial sovereignty's aim of allocating distinct populations to separate states by the mere use of a formal concept such as nationality. However, this does not signal an overall departure on the part of the ECtHR from the way in which international law looks upon the relationship between territorial sovereignty and the individual. This is evidenced by the fact that the invocation of the right to family life against the state has the most powerful potential if it concerns family life that was established *within* the territorial boundaries of the nation state by individuals who were at that time legally residing residents. The way in which the scales are tipped heavily in favour of territorial sovereignty and the state's power to guard the 'integrity of its border' can be deduced from the fact that family life that was formed during unlawful presence will only be protected in 'the most exceptional circumstances'.

The reification of territorial sovereignty and the distinction between sovereignty's territorial form and its jurisdictional content within a given body politic is also apparent from the way in which international law regards an individual whose presence on national territory is unauthorised, as someone who never entered. The Court in Strasbourg has followed this construction, thereby construing the family rights to which the undocumented migrant may appeal so as to relate to entry. And even as the Court has acknowledged that the distinction between positive and negative obligations is not always easy to draw in this field, it is important to establish unequivocally that such legal fictions do not reflect reality *at all*: in order to prevent entry or to remove irregular migrants from its territory, the national state is actively and positively performing. Movement controls *always* constitute an interference with individual liberty. By structuring rights discourse in such a way as to give priority to the fiction of territorial sovereignty over the actualities of the exercise of jurisdiction over individuals' lives, human rights law feeds "the contradiction between undocumented migrants' physical and social presence and their official negation as 'illegals'."²⁵⁷ Once more the human interests affected by state power remain invisible when the state bases its claims predominantly on sovereignty's territorial form.

Nevertheless, the application of the prohibition on torture and inhuman or degrading treatment in the immigration context shows that modern constitutionalism has at times recognised *and* protected the human interests that are affected by assertions of territorial sovereignty, even though until now it has done so only with regard to a limited amount of human interests that have been categorised as absolute rights. The revolutionary character of the norm of *non-refoulement*, resulting from the application of the prohibition on torture and inhuman and degrading treatment in the immigration context, lies in the fact that it has proven to be able to break away from a territorialised, state-centred, traditional conception of the interests that are involved in territorial sovereignty, and has instead framed these interests in terms of individuals' real lived experiences. In this respect it is also significant that for the application of Article 3 ECHR it is irrelevant whether the state bears responsibility, directly or indirectly, for the prohibited treatment, and as such, territoriality's logic by which different states are accorded responsibility for separate groups of individuals is largely absent here.

However, it should be noted that the individual interests that may be implicated in sovereignty's territorial form are narrowly interpreted, both by the ECtHR and the HRC. The real risk construction has so far only obstructed exclusion if there exists a real risk concerning "the life and limb" of the individual.²⁵⁸ Nonetheless, there is no logical reason why a consistent application of the way in which the norm of *non-refoulement* is constructed in Article 3 ECHR in cases where other fundamental rights are involved, could not lead to comparable limitations on the sovereign right to exclude. Maarten den Heijer has argued convincingly that in such cases, "the additional barrier to engage responsibility under the Convention lies predominantly in the fact that future treatment takes place in and under the direct responsibility of another country, i.e. a situation that is not normally – or automatically – covered by the reach of the Convention."²⁵⁹ Thus in the context of free movement, the Court still seems to divide responsibility for the safeguarding of most individual rights according to the traditional logic of territoriality.

---

²⁵⁷ N.P. De Genova, "Migrant "Illegality" and Deportability in Everyday Life," *Annual Review of Anthropology* 31 (2002), 427.
²⁵⁸ Heijer (2008), 314.
²⁵⁹ Ibid., 308. Compare *Bankovic and Others v. Belgium* (Decision), and the discussion in Chapter 3.

In addition, it is important to see that territoriality plays a more insidious role as well when it comes to *refoulement*. We have seen that especially in the context of the EU, a spatial extension of movement control has occurred far from Member States' physical borders.[260] States' increasing use of *police à distance* provides evidence of sovereign states' wish to control international movement without having to assume responsibility for the individual rights involved. The question as to how extraterritorial measures in the field of immigration may or may not engage the responsibility of states is without doubt an interesting and highly significant one. It is worth noting that national judiciaries have not been inclined to concede easily that they may do so.[261] The legal complexities of extraterritorial jurisdiction are compounded by the fact that these policies are increasingly carried out in the framework of the EU; Frontex's imprecise role in Member States' actions in the territorial waters of third states and the vagueness surrounding the legal bases upon which such schemes of international cooperation are based, prove a case in point.[262] But even without meticulously analysing these complexities, the very fact that states turn to *police à distance* policies reveals that they themselves feel that access to the perimeter of their territory is decisive for the extent of rights to be enjoyed, also with regard to their obligations flowing from the norm contained in Article 3 ECHR. Thus, even if territory and rights have to a certain extent become decoupled, states strategically make use of what they stubbornly wish to perceive as the territoriality of their responsibilities. And once again, irrespective of how a court of law may judge such an assumption, it certainly reflects contemporary reality where in most cases, even under the modern human rights regime, access to fundamental rights remains inexorably linked to presence within territorial boundaries of the national state because:

> For obvious reasons there are very few cases which could in fact challenge the policies constituting the non-arrival regime because the concerned individuals rarely get the chance to get in close contact with a lawyer who could bring their cases to court.[263]

---

[260] Samers (2004), 43.
[261] House of Lords, *Regina v. Immigration Officer at Prague Airport*, 9 December 2004, [2004] UKHL 55, at 21. But see UNHCR intervening in Regina v. Immigration Officer at Prague Airport (2005), *International Journal of Refugee Law* (2005).
[262] Thus introducing even more aspects to be considered with regard to Article 1 ECHR and the application of the Convention. See ECtHR, *Bosphorus etc. v. Turkey*, 30 June 2005, Appl. No. 45036/98, par. 136–137 and 156.
[263] M. Kjaerum, "Refugee Protection between State Interests and Human Rights: Where is Europe Heading?" *Human Rights Quarterly* 24 (2002), 525–526.

5.5.2 Territoriality and the Asymmetry of International Movement

European states' insistence on their sovereign prerogatives to control the entry and stay of foreign nationals has led to the contradictory situation that the function of Europe's eastern frontiers in controlling individual movement do not differ much from their role during the Cold War. This situation is especially paradoxical because the same countries that were vilified by the West because they infringed the right to leave during the Communist era were reprimanded for causing too many illegal entries in Western European countries shortly after the fall of the Berlin Wall. A country such a Romania introduced extensive regulations concerning exit controls in the years preceding its accession to the EU in 2007. For instance, Romanian citizens who had overstayed their visa in EU countries would, upon their return to Romania, be sanctioned by Romanian law varying from suspending the right of free circulation to the annulment of the right to have a passport.[264] In addition, anyone wishing to depart from Romanian territory had to prove that he or she would return within three months by showing transportation documents pertaining to a return trip.[265]

All of these requirements constitute clear interferences with the right to leave, the necessity and proportionality of which are very difficult to assess.[266] Romania is not the only country that exercised exit control in order to guard the 'integrity of Europe's external borders' – individual country agreements under the European Neigbourhood Policy also provide the basis for such measures, and as such they exemplify how the right to leave in the national (non-Western) context is affected by the exclusionary powers of European states.[267] Moreover, the right to leave is factually jeopardised by everyday practices of Western states: visa policies, the stationing of airport liaison officers in other countries and the vigilant patrolling of borders by the use of watch-towers, the military and the police all result in the inability of individuals to exercise their right to leave. Recently these policies have been complemented by

---

[264] S. Lazaroiu and M. Alexandru, *Controlling Exits to Gain Accession: Romanian Migration Policy in the Making* (Rome: CeSPI, 2005), 6. See also M. Baldwin-Edwards, "Navigating between Scylla and Charybdis: Migration Policies for a Romania within the European Union," *Southeast European and Black Sea Studies* 7 (2007), 10.

[265] Ibid., 6.

[266] HRC, *General Comment 27*, Freedom of movement (Art.12), (Sixty-seventh session, 1999), U.N. Doc. HRI/GEN/1/Rev.6 at 174 (2003), at 8.

[267] In August 2006, the Senegalese police force in Basse-Casamance interrogated 58 people who wanted to migrate 'illegally' to Spain (Source: JeuneAfrique.com, 3 august 2006, Senegal). The Senegalese authorities announced that they had arrested 15,000 candidates for 'illegal' emigration (Source: AFP, 22 May 2006). See also Amnesty International (2008).

measures that intercept migrants in the territorial waters of third states or on the high seas, and divert them back to the shores from which they intended to depart. Not only does such interception of migrants exemplify in the clearest terms possible that globalisation has caused heightened mobility for some, while resulting in immobility for others.[268] In addition, the official discourse dealing with these practices reflects a belief that such categorisation of movement has a clear and unequivocal basis in the law. In Frontex's documents, such as its annual or general report, or the information that it makes available to the press on its website, the notion of illegal *migration* seems to have pushed aside the notion of illegal *immigration*. As such, these documents give the impression that Frontex's mission is not merely to co-ordinate Member States' efforts in combating illegal immigration in order to protect the external border, but that the scope of its operations covers a far wider field of managing and controlling human movement in general.[269] However, if we examine the current practices of externalisation in a human rights law perspective and evaluate them in light of the very terminology of (il)legality, the most obvious difficulty on the legal plane lies in assessing the legality and proportionality of these measures in the light of international human rights law. Nevertheless, as soon as the sovereign right to exclude comes into play, the very contents of the fundamental rights at stake seem to alter drastically – the decision of the ECtHR in *Xhavara* proves a case in point, as the right to leave was not even considered a relevant constraint on sovereign power if that power was exercised in the context of immigration control.[270]

At first sight, a legal regime of international movement that does not squarely address these inconsistencies seems illogical. To understand it, it is necessary to appreciate the full implications of the fact that the contemporary system of movement controls is the result of political territoriality, a concept which has at the same time deeply structured the way in which international law categorises only certain human interests as rights. The result of territoriality's function in determining who belongs where – effectively allocating distinct populations to distinct states – is that rights, territory and state power have become linked to each other in a way that leaves certain interests inarticulable in the language of law simply because it cannot

---

[268] Z. Bauman, *Globalization: The Human Consequences* (New York: Columbia University Press, 1998).

[269] If seen in this way, we may also question the legal bases (Arts 62(2)a and 66 EC) for the establishment of Frontex, and widen the debate as regards legality by focussing on EC competence in this field.

[270] See ECtHR, *Xhavara and others v. Italy and Albania* (Decision), 11 January 2001, Appl. No. 39473/98 and the discussion of that case in the previous Chapter (4.4).

conceive of a corresponding *responsibility*. Thus, the right to leave is to be guaranteed for its bestowment is upon people for whom the state bears a clear and unambiguous responsibility: those individuals who are present within the state and whose presence within these territorial boundaries is not contested. In contrast, the claim of an individual to enter a state of which he or she is not a national cannot be fitted neatly in the normal paradigm that structures the relationship between rights, territory and power/responsibility, and consequently, to translate that particular claim into the language of rights is rendered very difficult. As such, the very phenomenon of international movement brings to the fore the limitations of a discourse of universal rights antecedently and independently of political power in our global political structure.

In addition to territoriality's structuring role in the global political system, effectively ascribing the responsibility for the protection of individual rights to a particular state, we have seen in chapter 3 that the perception of territory as a self-evident and innocent foundation for the body politic has resulted in little awareness of the individual interests that are involved in sovereignty's territorial form. In contrast, the exercise of jurisdiction by the state within this territorial frame has always been made subject to various processes of legal and political accountability. Raul Pangalangan captures this inconsistency when he argues that "norms of human dignity, whose enforcement was hitherto locked into state jurisdiction, have seen states yielding jurisdiction, but not territory which remains doctrinally entrenched."[271]

The fact that norms relating to human dignity have made a fundamental difference with regard to the right to leave, while leaving national discretion with regard to matters of exclusion largely intact, is the result of this conceptual distinction between sovereignty's form and content. Even though the right to leave also concerns sovereignty's territorial frame, the very visibility of the personal interests involved has resulted in the issue of leaving becoming a purely jurisdictional issue of the modern state where individual rights have an established role to play. At the same time, the implications of emigration for territorial sovereignty remain hidden and silent – and the logic of the territorial state system is often even deliberately overlooked by national states in their relations with various diasporas abroad.[272]

---

[271] R.C. Pangalangan, "Territorial Sovereignty: Command, Title and the Expanding Claims of the Commons," in: *Boundaries and Justice: Diverse Ethical Perspectives*, eds. D. Miller and S. Hashmi (Princeton/Oxford: Princeton University Press, 2001), 165.

[272] See on this A. Gamlen, "The emigration state and the modern geopolitical imagination," *Political Geography* 27 (2008).

With regard to the right to enter, it is precisely the other way around. Immigration is presented as engaging solely sovereignty's territorial frame, frequently even in a language that implicitly or explicitly alludes to the sanctity of territorial boundaries in the context of armed conflict.[273] The perception of a self-evident relation between territorial sovereignty and the exclusion of the foreigner means that we lose sight of the individual who is actually affected by exclusionary measures in the area of immigration. And as the discourse of territorial sovereignty – a discourse almost exclusively about the rights and duties of states amongst each other – dominates the state's stance on matters relating to immigration, modern constitutionalism is only in a very limited number of cases capable of challenging sovereign decisions of the state regarding the territorial exclusion of the other. This trend of limited accountability is much stronger at the European level, where measures relating to immigration are often concluded in secret and are difficult to access and control. The near blindness of modern human rights law towards the personal interests that are involved in sovereignty's right to exclude is further exacerbated by the fact that these are the interests of 'others' who are far away, or very different from 'us'.

Modern constitutionalism's distinction between sovereignty's form and content does not only surface when we look at the difference in legal recognition between the right to enter and the right to leave, but it is also apparent from the way in which the proliferation of human rights norms in the last sixty years has made significant inroads into the state's power to exclude legally residing foreigners. While the state is no longer able to dispose of aliens at will once their entry or sojourn has been authorised, these norms have not "markedly increased rights entitlements at the moment of border crossing," nor have they "significantly increased access to human rights for those without legal status, those illegals beyond the reach of law but at the centre of present rhetoric."[274] Human rights law's differentiation between the legal resident and the illegal immigrant lies precisely in the alleged violation of the latter of the territorial sovereignty of the state. In addition, with regard to legal residents who are present within the territory of the sovereign state, the jurisdictional aspect of sovereignty cannot remain hidden. Precisely on account of their authorised presence, their interests have become visible; they have clearly come within the ambit of the 'jurisdictional powers' of the state.

---

[273] See, for example, U.S Supreme Court in the *Chinese Exclusion Case* (*Chae Chan Ping v. United States* 130 U.S. (1889) 581.) The common use of the word 'invasion' when discussing immigration, in particular by those advocating an absolute right to exclude, provides a more recent example of the same attitude as was taken in this case.

[274] Dauvergne (2004).

Finally, when contrasting contemporary views on *internal* freedom of movement (i.e. within the territory of the national state) with those regarding international freedom of movement, the reification of territory as a natural foundation for political organisation is illustrated in yet another way. Freedom of movement within a country is regarded as one of the hallmarks of democracy and an indispensable condition for the free development of the individual.[275] Restrictions upon it, such as in South Africa under apartheid and the Soviet Union under communism, were generally and unequivocally condemned.[276] In the uneven perception of domestic and international movement, the interconnectedness of territoriality's implications becomes most palpable. Modern law's distinction between sovereignty's form and content plays an important role: it is clear that the regulation of internal movement merely concerns the exercise of jurisdiction over persons within a given body politic whose boundaries are not contested, whereas international movement impinges significantly on sovereignty's territorial form. Thus, internal movement is a matter for legal or political scrutiny as it concerns processes taking place within the nation state, and on account of territoriality "the categories through which we have attempted to pose questions about the political are precisely those that have been constructed in relation to the state."[277] In contrast, *international* movement presents an anomaly for a world where humanity is divided into "separate, closed and homogenous units at various stages of development."[278]

Ultimately then, the contemporary regulation of human movement exemplifies in the clearest sense the tension between the universal and the particular in a world divided into nation states. That might not be so very problematic if the nation state was indeed a closed container, its borders a perfect reflection of the way in which people wish to live their lives. They are not, and as we will see in the next chapter, state power has to be employed actively and continuously in order to reproduce the territorial state system. In contemporary liberal democracies, it is these very dimensions of state power – so closely bound up with violence, injustice and human suffering – that should be of the highest concern for any form of modern constitutionalism.

---

[275] HRC, *General Comment 27* (1999).

[276] R. Higgins, "The Right in International Law of an Individual to Enter, Stay in and Leave a Country," *International Affairs* 49 (1973), 343.

[277] A.P. Jarvis and A.J. Paolini, "Locating the State," in: *The State in Transition: Reimagining Political Space*, eds. J.A. Camilleri, A.P. Jarvis and A.J. Paolini (Boulder: Lynne Rienner Publishers, 1995), 5.

[278] J. Tully, *Strange multiplicity: Constitutionalism in an age of diversity* (Cambridge: Cambridge University Press, 1997).

Chapter 6

Reaffirming Sovereignty and Reproducing Territoriality: Deportation and Detention

> Spatial separation leading to enforced confinement was over the centuries almost a visceral, instinctual fashion of responding to all difference and particularly such difference that could not be, or was not wished to be, accommodated within the web of habitual social intercourse. The deepest meaning of spatial separation was the banning or suspension of communication, and so the forcible perpetuation of estrangement.[1]

6.1 Introduction

Deportation and detention are generally seen as no more and no less than the tools of 'fair' and effective immigration law enforcement. Thus, in official political discourse, they are portrayed as the appropriate and natural response by the sovereign state to those who have violated its territorial sovereignty. Indeed, deportation and detention have become so embedded within the contemporary administrative practice of liberal states that they receive far less attention in comparison with other forms of state violence and forced migration.[2] Criticism, be it political, academic or activist, revolves mainly around the conditions of their enforcement, but deportation and – albeit arguably to a somewhat lesser extent – detention, are seldom questioned as more than the unfortunate but predictable consequence of the fight against unwanted immigration. The way in which the removal of those that are not entitled to remain is portrayed as mere routine administrative state practice is highlighted by the way in which several countries have set up annual total numbers of persons to be deported or expelled, thus making statistics and not human beings the focus

---

[1] Z. Bauman, "Social Issues of Law and Order," *British Journal of Criminology* 40 (2000), 208.
[2] W. Walters, "Deportation, Expulsion, and the International Police of Aliens," *Citizenship Studies* 6 (2002), 256.

of law enforcement.³ The steep increase in the use of immigration detention, coupled with a tenacious belief in its effectiveness on the part of official authorities, reveal a similar logic according to which deprivations of liberty constitute a necessary part of a 'credible' and 'fair' immigration system. The way in which these increases are subsequently presented to the general public as an inevitable and proper response to deviant behaviour, i.e. behaviour that does not conform to the territorial ideal, is evidenced by statements such as those below, found on the webpage of the UK border agency where it elaborates upon the expansion of the "detention estate":

> Expanding the number of removal centres is a critical part of the UK Border Agency's plans to increase the rate of removal of failed asylum seekers and illegal immigrants, and to allow the fast removal of those who come to the United Kingdom and break the rules.⁴

The way in which a Dutch Minister responded to a question posed by an MP related to the growing use of immigration detention and the increasing periods that foreigners spend behind bars as a result of immigration decision making can be categorised along the same lines. Although the Minister confirmed the tendency of "ever-increasing and longer-lasting detentions" she did not squarely address the question whether she considered this trend to be a problematic one. Instead, she answered that this very development showed that previous governments have increasingly prioritised the fight against unauthorised presence on national territory, something that, she added, her government would continue to do.⁵

However, as so evocatively put by Nathalie Peutz, there must inevitably be something greater at stake in the practice of detention and removal, including "the (re)formulation of state sovereignty and of the law's exceptions and the (re)making of political subjectivities – both of 'citizens' and of those rendered 'deportable'."⁶ Her words accurately express the idea that deportation and detention constitute the litmus test for the way in which territoriality shapes the world and the life of its inhabitants. As both deportation and detention engage

---

³ France is one of these countries. See Council of Europe Commissioner for Human Rights, *Memorandum by Thomas Hammarberg, Commissioner for Human Rights of the Council of Europe further to his visit to the Zones d'Attente (Waiting Areas) at Roissy Airport and the Mesnil-Amelot Administrative Holding Centre*, CommDH (2008) 5 (Strasbourg, 20 November 2008), 6.
⁴ http://www.ukba.homeoffice.gov.uk/managingborders/immigrationremovalcentres/expansionofthedetention.
⁵ Questions by the MPs Van Velzen and De Wit to the Minister and the Answers, Aanhangsel Handelingen II 2007–2008, no. 843, 1801.
⁶ N. Peutz, "Embarking on an Anthropology of Removal," *Current Anthropology* 47(2006), 238.

the exposed core of state power ("there is no easy way to make those who do not want to depart actually leave; shackles and drugs are both on the menu"[7]), deportation and detention make it clear what sovereignty is all about; both with regard to its aspect of *monopolist violence* as well as with regard to its *claim to determine the inside and the outside*. Furthermore, deportation and detention when considered from a global perspective exemplify the idea of an international police of aliens: *territoriality* and *citizenship* as mechanisms of allocating responsibility over distinct populations.

These aspects of sovereignty and territoriality have been closely looked at in the previous chapters, together with the way in which they have shaped modern constitutional discourse. This chapter consists of a concise investigation into the logic of contemporary tools of immigration law enforcement which I shall relate to my findings from the previous chapters on state power in a global territorial system of sovereign states, so that we can thereafter turn to the way in which modern human rights law applies to cases of immigration detention (chapters 7 and 8).

Below, I shall first discuss the way in which the administrative practice of deportation relates to state power and territoriality by setting it in a wider field of political and administrative practice (section 6.2).[8] In doing so, I draw to a large extent on the work of William Walters who, by comparing modern deportation practice with historical forms of expulsion, offers a venue through which we can historicize and denaturalise deportation. After that, I shall address the relationship between immigration detention and state power (section 6.3). Michel Foucault's work on confinement and Hannah Arendt's reflections on Europe's post-war internment camps for displaced persons are briefly discussed in order to place the practice of immigration detention in a larger historical narrative of imprisonment. In the conclusions of this chapter, I shall seek to answer the question why in contemporary Europe the detention of unwanted foreigners increasingly prevails over other forms of administering the entry and removal of aliens.[9]

---

[7] C. Dauvergne, "Sovereignty, Migration and the Rule of Law in Global Times," *The Modern Law Review* 67 (2004), 592.
[8] See on the administrative character of deportation measures in most EU Member States: B. Nascimbene, *Expulsion and Detention of Aliens in the European Union Countries* (Milan: Giuffré Editore, 2001).
[9] See also G.N. Cornelisse, "Immigration Detention and the Territoriality of Universal Rights," in: *The Deportation Regime: Sovereignty, Space and the Freedom of Movement*, eds. N. De Genova and N. Peutz (Durham, NC: Duke University Press, forthcoming).

6.2 Deportation as Administrative Practice

By investigating several historical forms of expulsion (as a form of forced migration), William Walters intends to demonstrate that the linkage between deportation and contemporary immigration policy is not as self-evident or natural as it may seem at first sight. The first form of expulsion he addresses in his article "Deportation, Expulsion, and the International Police of Aliens" is exile or banishment.[10] In a lengthy period reaching from ancient Greece and early Rome until the late Middle Ages, exile was generally used as a form of punishment for serious crimes. The measure was directed against a person who was a member of the body politic, and Walters quotes the Italian jurist Beccaria (1738–1794) to illustrate the effect of banishment: It nullified all the ties between society and the delinquent citizen. Thus, with respect to the body politic banishment was a civil death, which should have purportedly produced the same effect as natural death.[11] The loss of citizenship put men at the mercy of sovereign power; and as such banishment illustrates the importance of citizenship while at the same time exposing the insignificance of 'bare life'[12] when confronted with sovereign power, despite declarations and theories in which rights are accorded to men prior to and independent of any political power. Hence, although banishment was frequently employed to lessen the punishment for serious crimes, its impact could be far more serious than imprisonment as the latter measure, although greatly restricting individual liberty, did not affect one's presence in the legal and political order as fundamentally as banishment did.

Subsequently, Walters considers expulsions that are associated with poor policy in early modern Europe. In England, for example, those who were likely to become a charge on the poor rate of a particular parish were subject to removal. Indeed, during the sixteenth and seventeenth centuries, the determination to restrict relief only to the local poor was a general feature of Western Europe, and paupers from other localities could be removed.[13] Thus, although the modern nation state had already started to take form, when it came to deportation the fault line between inside and outside was not yet determined by the concept of nationality but by the distinction of *local* versus foreigner. Nevertheless, it is important to take due notice of the fact that with regard to warfare and taxation, the fault line had started to shift slowly but decisively in

---

[10] Walters (2002).
[11] Ibid., 269.
[12] See G. Agamben, *Homo Sacer: Sovereign Power and Bare Life* (Stanford: Stanford University Press, 1998).
[13] Walters (2002), 270.

the direction of national versus foreigner. It is this very shift that is detectable in the third historic example of expulsion that Walters discusses: expulsion on the basis of group membership. Notwithstanding the fact that corporate expulsions in Medieval Europe were not targeted at other nationalities but rather at different religious groups, they were an important tool in the formation of national states, as political loyalties and religion were clearly intertwined in this period.[14]

Although the expulsion of religious groups became less commonplace when national states and the state system had consolidated in Western Europe, a new form of forced migration took over as a result of external colonisation and internal social regulation, the latter denoting the enormous growth of state power, penetrating ever more aspects of the lives of its citizens. One of the ways in which states dealt with those individuals that they perceived as undesirable in their social orders was to transport them to colonies overseas where they were subjected to forced labour. Thus, the poor and the criminal classes were not merely removed: the practice of transportation differed from classic exile as it sought to combine "forced removal with the game of colonization and economic exploitation."[15] Not only convicts were transported to the colonies: the legalisation of deportation in the English Vagrancy Act of 1597 shows that transportation as social regulation encompassed more than the pursuing of criminal law objectives.[16] An intriguing detail with regard to these policies, offering interesting parallels with the contemporary practice of readmission agreements, is the case of countries that did not have any significant colonies abroad, and for that reason sought to arrange the transportation of their 'undesirables' with other colonial powers.[17]

The final form of expulsion that Walters examines in his historical overview is the so-called population transfer. We have seen in chapter 3 that the way in which international law dealt with the case of minorities in Europe in the first half of the twentieth century resulted from, and simultaneously reinforced, the predominant perception of an inextricable link between identity, the nation, and the territorial state. International law was to afford minorities the protection they lacked because they did not fit in with the territory-identity ideal of the nation state. However, individual states found another, altogether less subtle way of dealing with the situation in which they found themselves confronted with minorities of another nation within their borders: the transferral of such minorities to their 'own' state. Examples of such "tidying

---

[14] Ibid., 270.
[15] Ibid., 272.
[16] Id.
[17] Id.

up of national frontiers"[18] have been described in Chapter 5, but for now it is important to appreciate how forced migration in the form of population transfer relates to *modern* state power. In this regard, Walters discerns a significant difference with group expulsions in the early modern period when the nation state had not yet grown to maturity:

> [...] with the early modern period expulsion was frequently used as a threat. It could be avoided if the subject agreed to accept baptism, conversion or foreswear the practice of usury. Expulsion as population transfer operates on a biopolitical territory where difference is marked indelibly.[19]

The changing connotations of expulsion which Walters tackles here correspond to the change from the medieval order based on individual differences and universal values to the modern state system where the principle of identity was pursued within states. The way in which the modern state came to assert a specific national identity – allegedly pre-political – and the impact of these collective processes of identity formation on theories on legitimate state power have been extensively addressed in chapter 2 and they explain the changing character of state-administered forced migration.

Walters' genealogy of deportation is significant in three respects. In the first place, through it, one comes to appreciate that deportation is not the particular response of the state to one singular situation. At various times in history, deportation has been a tool to facilitate state building; an instrument to regulate wealth; a means of social regulation; and a way in which to realise national ideology. Secondly, in the changing practices of deportation we may detect shifts in the in the significance and function of state power. Banishment in the early modern period was reserved for political enemies of the state and the transfer of religious residents was opportune for creating the modern sovereign state. With the risk of oversimplifying, one could say that such expulsions served to make sure that the emerging state could exercise effective power over a certain territory. The more modern modes of expulsion which became prevalent in the nineteenth and the first half of the twentieth century, such as the transportation of convicts and vagrants to colonies and population transfers based on ethnicity, exemplify that the state was no longer merely concerned with the territorial exclusiveness of power, but also with its substantial capacity to control its citizens' lives and identity. These tendencies were reflected in immigration policies: we have seen in Chapter 5 that during the same period laws were introduced that aimed at the prevention of the immigration of paupers or persons with 'low morals' and certain specific nationalities.

---

[18] A. Linklater, *The transformation of political community* (Cambridge: Polity Press; 1998), 160.
[19] Walters (2002), 247.

This link between forms of state power and modes of deportation leads us to the third important issue that Walters raises through his genealogy of deportation. He poses the question of what contemporary deportation practice may tell us about present forms of state power and images of political community. In order to answer his question, one needs to be aware of the fact that modern deportation practice is primarily the result of the territorial state system. Chapter 3 described how the institution of citizenship is rooted in and simultaneously produces a territorial system through which distinct populations are ascribed to distinct territorial entities. Thus, citizenship's role in a world made up of nation states is to allocate the responsibility for populations to states. Even conceptions of post-national citizenship depend on an initial authorisation for presence on national territory by the sovereign state and as such are consistent with Barry Hindess' idea of citizenship as international 'police'.[20] International law is deeply influenced by this construction of an international government of populations: it prohibits the expulsion of citizens and has legitimised the link between sovereignty and the deportation of foreign nationals, as we have seen in the previous chapter.

However, (and it is here that we find a first answer to the question of what the practice of deportation tells us about state power and political community) deportation is not merely the inevitable outcome of the notions of citizenship and territoriality. It is much more than that. Deportation itself is actively involved in producing and preserving the territorial order. A world made up of independent, sovereign nation states is the result of historical contingencies. It is neither a natural way of structuring the world, nor the inevitable outcome of a linear path of progress, and as such it does not and cannot reproduce itself naturally.[21] Therefore, Walters argues, the very practice of deportation is constitutive for the modern territorial order.[22] On the supranational level, EU return policy reveals a similar relation between territoriality, governance of populations and deportation: EU policies with regard to return that intensify cooperation with third countries find their "roots in the emergence of a dominant interpretative framework pertaining to the 'management of international migration'."[23]

---

[20] B. Hindess, "Citizenship in the international management of populations," *American Behavioral Scientist*. 43 (2000); and B. Hindess, "Divide and Rule: The International Character of Modern Citizenship," *European Journal of Social Theory* 1 (1998).
[21] Walters (2002), 288.
[22] Id.
[23] J.P. Cassarino, *The EU Return Policy, Premises and Implications*. Paper in the MIREM project: Migration de retour au Maghreb (Florence: EUI, 2006), 10.

The constitutive element of deportation in the modern territorial order brings us to a second element that is fundamental for an understanding of the way in which modern practices of deportation relate to state power. Deportation does not only function as a factual way in which to govern populations. In light of the ineffectiveness of many expulsion measures in several of the Member States,[24] its significance is perhaps more of a symbolic and indirect character. Matthew Gibney and Randall Hansen have argued that although deportation measures are often ineffectual, they are a necessity for governments which need to be seen to be in control of migration and borders. According to these authors, the established practice of deportation is necessary because it "assuages public opinion which would not view the states incapacity in this area with equanimity" and because it acts as a disincentive to other potential migrants.[25] William Walters uses the same arguments by placing deportation in the context of *governmentality*. Although I will not address conceptual distinctions between sovereign power and governmental power here, the latter supposedly a distinctly novel way of reflecting on and exercising state power, one aspect of governmentality deserves to be mentioned in the context of deportation. That is the concern of the state with the governmental mechanism of deportation itself:

> Governments are presently obsessed with the need to 'tighten up' their deportation and repatriation policies. One of the main reasons they give is the need to maintain the 'integrity' of their immigration and asylum systems. The problem identified is one where lax administration of deportation – the failure to execute deportation orders and actually to remove the subject – marks a particular state as a 'soft touch'. The fear is that asylum 'shoppers' will then flock towards that state to profit from its generous terms of admission. Strictly enforced migration policies send 'signals' to asylum seekers and 'illegal' migrants. What is being governed is not the population in a direct manner, as was with the population transfer or the socially undesirable, but the governmental system.[26]

Here again we can draw a parallel between national state practice and EU return policies, of which it has been said that they "reassert the managerial capacity of the state" and should lead to a "strengthening of the public credibility of states".[27]

Hence, the practice of deportation offers two images of state power. The first is an image of political power that is an intrinsic part of a global system of

---

[24] See Nascimbene (2001); and L. Schuster, "A Sledgehammer to Crack a Nut: Deportation, Detention and Dispersal in Europe," *Social Policy and Administration* 39 (2005), 612.
[25] M.J. Gibney and R. Hansen, *Deportation and the Liberal State*, (Geneva: UNHCR New Issues in Refugee Research Working Paper 77, 2003), 2.
[26] Walters (2002), 280.
[27] Cassarino (2006), 10.

sovereign territorial states. In this system deportation is central to the allocation of populations to states.[28] Governance of populations became territorial in the second half of the twentieth century, a development that is reflected in modern international law which has delegitimised historical forms of expulsion such as the expulsion of religious minorities, mass expulsions, and transportation of citizens, while at the same time naturalising the link between deportation and foreign nationals. Once again it is possible to discern international law's opposing tendencies: it couples concern with and limitations of the *content* of sovereignty with acquiescence to the state's exercise of power whenever it presents it as based on sovereignty's territorial *frame*. And although deportation clearly constitutes the exercise of jurisdiction over people, in the contemporary global structure, the basis for the exercise of this power is provided by territorial sovereignty. Only when taking into account the 'sacred' territorial foundation for the exercise of state power in migration law enforcement does it become possible to see why contemporary international law differentiates between transportation of the socially undesirable, religious minorities or citizens in general, on the one hand, and deportation of the foreigner on the other.

The second image of state power that is revealed by the practice of deportation is internal. Deportation is necessary to prove that a state takes control of its borders and it epitomises sovereignty as the power to distinguish between the inside and the outside. These two images of state power, the first structural and the second internal, are complementary and mutually reinforcing, as is illustrated by the continuity between the externalisation of border control such as visa requirements and readmission agreements and its internalisation resulting precisely from practices such as deportation and detention.[29] Similarly, the criminalisation of an illegal stay in national territory also shows how the internal and the structural features of state power complement each other: the international governance of populations has reached a peak when merely administrative sanctions no longer seem to suffice and the tendency to criminalise migrants internally gives a very powerful incentive to the inside/outside distinction. The widespread use of the word 'illegal' in conjunction with migration and migrants, also when discussing preventive and international approaches to migration – even though logically "a migrant can only be illegal once he finds himself within a state whose laws define his presence as

---

[28] Walters (2002), 267.
[29] E. Rigo, "Citizens and foreigners in the Enlarged Europe," in: Spreading Democracy and the Rule of Law? *The Impact of EU Enlargement on the Rule of Law: Democracy and Constitutionalism in Post-Communist Legal Orders*, eds. W. Sadurski et al. (Dordrecht: Springer, 2006), 11.

illegal"[30] – has the same effect of both emphasising each individual state's territorial sovereignty and calling attention to an international regime of the governance of the larger human population in which certain kinds of movement are taken for granted while other forms are undesirable and thus penalised.[31]

6.3 Immigration Detention, State Power, and Territoriality

The observations on state power and deportation that were made above hold equally true for the administrative practice of immigration detention: if its aim is to facilitate removal and to prevent illegal stay it fits within and simultaneously perpetuates a territorial image of the world. And even if the majority of those held in detention centres are eventually released,[32] just as deportation, detention is a necessity for states that want to be seen to be in 'control' of their borders. Furthermore, the symbolic function of immigration detention lies also in its deterrent effect to the outside world: detention centres are meant to signal that "'our' immigration policies are not a soft touch."[33]

However, immigration detention is special amongst the other venues through which states try to stem unwanted immigration such as deportation, readmission policies and the international governance of movement. In the first place, it is special because deprivation of liberty is the sharpest technique by which states attempt to preserve the global territorial order of sovereign states. We have seen in Chapter 2 that personal liberty and sovereignty are conceptually intertwined: the protection of the former is the reason for the existence of the latter. In societies based upon the rule of law there is no more serious interference with an individual's fundamental rights as depriving him or her of his or her liberty. The intimate relationship between personal liberty, sovereignty and violence warrants the utmost scrutiny when assessing the indiscriminate detention of thousands of people in light of traditional safeguards against sovereign power. But we shall see below that still more is at

---

[30] Elspeth Guild in House of Lords, The Hague Programme: a five year agenda for EU justice and Home Affairs, Report with Evidence: HL Paper 84 (London, 23 March 2005), 27.

[31] See also Cornelisse (forthcoming).

[32] ".... either because they cannot be removed because of conditions in the country of origin, or because travel documents for the person to be removed cannot be issued, or because they are allowed to appeal, or because they are granted leave to remain on compassionate grounds, or, finally, because their claim for asylum is allowed." Schuster (2005), 612–613. See also R. Andrijasevic, "How to balance rights and responsibilities on asylum at the EU's southern border of Italy and Libya," *Compas Working Paper 27*, Centre on Migration, Policy and Society, University of Oxford (2006), 18.

[33] Walters (2002), 286.

stake in the contemporary practice of immigration detention. It is this practice that, even more so than deportation, exemplifies in the clearest possible way the violent impact on the life of the individual of a world fully divided into territorial nation states. In order to see that clearly, we shall need to delve a little deeper into the role of detention in the history of the modern state.

In *Madness and Civilization*, Michel Foucault traced the origins of and the rationale behind the great confinement of the seventeenth century, which ascribed "the same homeland to the poor, to the unemployed, to prisoners and to the insane."[34] William Walters, by drawing a parallel between the logic of medieval poor laws and modern deportation practices, was able to highlight the constitutive role of deportation in governing populations. In much the same way, investigating the historical practice of confining the poor, the homeless, and the insane in the seventeenth and eighteenth centuries may tell us something about contemporary immigration detention.[35] It was precisely the poor laws of medieval Europe, the local logic of which seems at present to be reconstituted on a global, international scale through immigration policies, that in the seventeenth and eighteenth centuries were replaced by regulations which provided for the confinement of those who would have been previously expelled:

> It was, in any case, a new solution. For the first time, purely negative measures of exclusion were replaced by a measure of confinement; the unemployed person was no longer driven away or punished; he was taken in charge, at the expense of the nation but at the cost of his individual liberty.[36]

Indeed, whereas an edict of the parliament from 1606 ordered the beggars of Paris to be driven away from the city, fifty years later those people were hunted down and herded into the various buildings of the *Hôpital Général*.[37] This institution was a single organisation which united already exiting establishments which took care of the poor, but instead of merely consisting of an administrative reform, the establishment of the Hôpital Général in 1656 brought about a new "instance of order, of the monarchical and bourgeois

---

[34] M. Foucault, *Madness and Civilization: A history of insanity in the age of reason* (London: Tavistock Publications, 1967), 39.

[35] Note that 'vagabondage' still constitutes a legal ground for the deprivation of liberty according to Article 5 of the ECHR. The contemporary control of the fluidity of 'nomadic living' is also apparent from various forms of policing Gypsies and Travellers in Europe. See Z. James, "Policing Marginal Spaces: Controlling Gypsies and Travellers," *Criminology and Criminal Justice* 7 (2007).

[36] Foucault (1967), 48.

[37] Id.

order being organised in France during this period."[38] While the origin of the former measures of exclusion had been mostly local, the edicts that first established the *Hôpital Général* in Paris in 1656 and later prescribed the establishment of such institutions in every city of France in 1676, originated from the King. It was an early sign that one of the concerns of the emerging modern state was control over its citizens' lives and identity, because mere *local* territorial control – by means of the territorial exclusion of the undesirable from certain towns or provinces – would no longer function in a polity that aspired to *national* government.

The main aims of the 'great confinement' consisted of control and moral reform. Instead of being simply excluded, the poor and those without a fixed abode were now governed, albeit still by a logic which was driven by the "fear of pauperism, with its dangerous 'fluid, elusive sociality, impossible to control or utilise'."[39] In order to suppress such pauperism, the various *Hôpitals Généraux* provided for the "territorial sedentarization of populations"[40], but the difference with later measures aiming at a similar result such as public housing was the repressive nature of confinement. The near absoluteness of the power of the directors of the *Hôpitals Généraux* brings to mind contemporary conceptions of sovereign power over matters of immigration: it consisted of "jurisdiction without appeal" and it entailed "writs of execution against which nothing can prevail."[41]

The emergence of imprisonment as an instituted response to crime dates from the eighteenth century, and it is noteworthy that as a penal sanction for serious crimes it gradually started to replace transportation, banishment, corporal punishment and the death penalty.[42] Foucault has shown that the rise of the penitentiary is linked in important ways with ideas on liberal government.[43] Although I shall not investigate the history of this development in depth here, two of its aspects nonetheless deserve to be briefly mentioned. In the first place, practices of imprisonment had for centuries been linked with the worst abuses of royal power, of which the infamous *lettres de cachet* offer

---

[38] Ibid., 40.
[39] Walters (2002), 286.
[40] Ibid.
[41] Foucault (1967), 40.
[42] P. Spierenburg, "Four Centuries of Prison History: Punishment, Suffering, the Body, and Power," in: *Institutions of Confinement: Hospitals, Asylums, and Prisons in Western Europe and North America, 1500–1950*, eds. N. Finsch and R. Jütte (Cambridge: Cambridge University Press 1996), 24; and A.M. Durham III, "The Justice Model in Historical Context: Early Law, the Emergence of Science, and the Rise of Incarceration," *Journal of Criminal Justice* 16 (1988), 337.
[43] M. Foucault, *Discipline, toezicht en straf: de geboorte van gevangenis* (Groningen: Historische Uitgeverij, 1989).

the best example.⁴⁴ Yet, in modernity, prisons became a site where the very power to punish was made measurable and thus accountable, and as such imprisonment can be seen as an "enabling technology of what we would now call the rule of law."⁴⁵ Secondly, the imprisonment of criminals, just as the confinement of the poor, had important reforming functions. These two elements in particular meant that the "rise of the penitentiary […] is in a very real sense a story of rights and liberties as much as it is a story of prejudice and oppression."⁴⁶

Such a story of rights and liberties is conspicuously absent in Hannah Arendt's account of the internment camps which were set up for the stateless and refugees who fled totalitarian regimes during the thirties in Europe. Towards the end of the Second World War, millions of refugees and displaced people were kept in these camps, scattered all over Europe, and many of the former work and concentration camps in Germany were used as "assembly centres" for those people after the war had ended.⁴⁷ We have seen in Chapter 3 that the very existence of the internment camps made painfully clear that the Rights of Man were utterly dependent on citizenship. As national states were at loss about what to do with those foreigners who had lost the protection of their own states, these individuals were forced to live outside the jurisdiction of the law, interned in camps, which became "the only practical substitute for a non-existent homeland."⁴⁸

Arendt writes that it was not so much the loss of a home which led to this situation, but the impossibility of finding a new home, which was a problem not of "space but of political organisation."⁴⁹ In other words, the very construction of a world made up of territorial nation states with its unyielding and inextricable link between identity, territory and rights meant that the internment camp was "the only place which the world had to offer the stateless."⁵⁰ The stateless and the refugees were not interned on account of what they had done, but they were deprived of one their most basic rights because they did not fit within the territorial image of the world, and as such it seemed

---

⁴⁴ Ibid. and Foucault (1967), 38.
⁴⁵ J. Simon, "Refugees in a Carceral Age: The Rebirth of Immigration Prisons in the United States," *Public Culture* 10 (1998), 597. See also A.M. Durham III (1988).
⁴⁶ Simon (1998), 599.
⁴⁷ L.H. Malkki, "Refugees and Exiles: From 'Refugee Studies' to the National Order of Things," *Annual Review of Anthropology* 24 (1995), 499.
⁴⁸ H. Arendt, *The Origins of Totalitarianism* (San Diego/New York/London: Harcourt Brace and Company, 1976), 284 and 287.
⁴⁹ Ibid., 294.
⁵⁰ Ibid., 287.

easier to deprive these innocent people of their right to have rights than those who had committed a crime. It is clear that in Arendt's portrayal of the internment camps we do not encounter elements of reform or 'enabling technologies of the rule of law'. Rather, she presents us with an image of exceptionalism: sovereign power that is reduced to violence, a situation in which the rule of law has reached its limits. Evidently, the rationale for this exceptionalism was the assumed threat of the stateless and the refugees to the unity of the state and the overall order of the state system.

How, then, do contemporary immigration prisons feature in accounts of the modern state and the system it forms part of? Are they, like the confinement of the poor during the seventeenth and eighteenth century, essentially a means of territorial control and moral reform? Or do they additionally provide, just as the penitentiary did in the nineteenth century, an opportunity for legal accountability? Alternatively, can they be compared with the exceptionalism of the internment camp for the stateless that was set up in Europe during and after the Second World War?[51]

There are certainly similarities concerning the regulation of human mobility through immigration detention in contemporary Europe and the historic examples of internment that have been discussed above. The confinement of the poor as an answer to pauperism amounted to "territorial sedentarization" of the poor so that "fixed concentrations of populations" could be produced.[52] Similarly, the internment camp of post-war Europe was a "standardized, generalizable technology of power in the management of mass displacement."[53] Liisa Malkki writes that these refugee camps were a device of power as they provided for the spatial concentration and ordering of people.[54] The detention of the unwanted foreigner in contemporary Europe can be seen as a comparable "sedentarization campaign" to regulate and control "surplus humanity".[55] However, unlike confinement of the poor and imprisonment as a response to crime, immigration prisons do not function as a site for reform. Instead of aiming to produce proper citizens, their sole aim consists of territorial control of persons in order to hold onto the validity of the territorial ideal.

---

[51] It is worth noting that the Italian Prime Minister Berlusconi has compared the immigration detention centres in his country with yet another instance of imprisonment in the history of Europe: the concentration camp: "*È molto meglio esaminare nei luoghi di partenza se gli immigrati possano avere diritto di asilo. Non vorrei dirlo, ma questi campi di identificazione assomigliano molto a campi di concentramento*", Corriere della Sera, 20 May 2009.
[52] Walters (2002), 286.
[53] Malkki (1995), 498.
[54] Id.
[55] Walters (2002), 286.

Hence, it is certainly helpful to place immigration detention in a historical perspective of imprisonment in the modern state, for it exemplifies that, unlike deportation, immigration detention is not simply a technology to preserve the territorial state system and the concomitant allocation of citizens to states. In addition to being a means through which the national state, despite celebrations of universal human rights and assertions of post-national citizenship, violently guards the rigid link between territory, identity and rights, the immigration prison also provides an immediate place for those who do not fit within the global territorial ideal. Thus, the asylum seeker and the illegal immigrant "represent the nomadic excess that the state seeks to capture and normalize through panoptic confinement" in detention centres.[56] Hence, immigration detention is an explicit exception to the assumption that all the world's populations belong to a country, but at the same time, paradoxically, that very assumption is dependent on the existence of immigration detention.[57]

Furthermore, immigration detention is not only a way in which states violently guard the territoriality of the global state system and provide a solution for what is perceived as an anomaly in that system: people between national borders. In addition, by resorting to immigration detention, states seek to make ultimate use of territoriality's impact on modern constitutionalism: a discourse in which territorial demarcations drawn in the past determine which kinds of violence are prone to legal correction. Hannah Arendt argued that the internment camps were places of exceptionalism where people were placed outside the normal legal order. With regard to the immigration prison much the same arguments may be made: the indiscriminate detention of thousands of people, sometimes for periods which are not bound to a maximum by law, under special security administration, special laws and wide administrative powers in places which are difficult to access and control, certainly gives the impression of being a practice which is outside the usual legal framework of constitutional democracies. Bülent Diken and Carsten Laustsen recount the break-out from the Australian detention camp *Woomera*, where fifty people managed to escape. Most of them were subsequently captured, but "they are unlikely to be prosecuted or jailed – if they were, they would have visiting rights and a definite length of imprisonment, luxuries denied them as asylum seekers inside *Woomera*.[58] Precisely this situation would qualify for what

---

[56] B. Diken and C.B. Laustsen, "'Camping' as Contemporary Strategy – From Refugee Camps to Gated Communities," *Academy for Migration Studies in Denmark Working Paper Series* 32 (2003), 3.

[57] Walters (2002), 286.

[58] Diken and Laustsen (2003), 5. See also A. Bashford and C. Strange, "Asylum Seekers and National Histories of Detention," *Australian Journal of Politics and History* 48 (2002).

Arendt called one of the perplexities inherent in the concept of human rights: "it seems to easier to deprive a completely innocent person of legality than someone that has committed a crime."[59]

As such, we can perhaps regard the immigration prison as extraterritorial to the extent that it is outside the normal territorial legal and juridical order.[60] However, this extraterritoriality is at the same time governed by an unbending and relentless *territorial* logic: only those who are not authorised by the state to be present on national territory can be subjected to detention under these exceptional conditions. Legally permissive immigration detention is thus exemplary for the inability of modern constitutional discourse to make visible and protect the human interests that are affected whenever the national state bases the exercise of power on its territorial sovereignty. The insidiousness of detention in this context lies in the fact that the very measure of spatial confinement has – and here I paraphrase the words of Zygmunt Bauman – estrangement as its core function: reducing, thinning down and compressing the view of the other.[61]

Apart from bridging the territorial-extraterritorial dichotomy, the immigration prison operates within the zone of an indistinction between inside and outside in another, related sense as well. It has been argued that its two-folded logic of sedentarisation and exceptionalism leads to what Giorgio Agamben called "exclusionary inclusion".[62] Immigration detention differs from deportation because the former is not solely about exclusion. For although detention puts refugees and illegal immigrants outside the normal legal framework of the liberal state, their life inside the immigration detention centre is strictly determined and restricted by the law.[63] Thus, Diken and Laustsen draw attention to the fact that these individuals are thus in a very real sense included in the state's domain of sovereign power.[64] However, as I shall argue later, and contrary to Agamben's notion of 'exclusionary inclusion', the fact that immigration detainees are clearly included within the jurisdictional scope of the sovereign state may also provide the opportunity to subject the hitherto largely unrestrained exclusionary power of the sovereign state to legal contention.[65]

---

[59] Arendt (1976), 275.
[60] Walters (2002), 286.
[61] Bauman (2000), 208.
[62] Agamben (1998).
[63] Diken and Laustsen (2003), 2–3. See also Foucault (1989), 419–420.
[64] Diken and Laustsen (2003).
[65] It is indeed important to note that such a process would differ fundamentally from the situation which GiorgioAgamben has called 'exclusionary inclusion,' where "natural life is excluded from the public sphere of citizenship but included in the sovereign right to kill." R. Bailey, "Up Against the Wall: Bare Life and Resistance in Australian immigration Detention," *Law and Critique* 20 (2009), 117.

6.4 Maintaining the Territorial Order

I have argued in this chapter that it is important to recognise that immigration law enforcement is not merely the result of the contemporary system of territoriality. Practices such as deportation and detention actively contribute to reproducing the territorial order in which different populations are ascribed to distinct states. In this sense, immigration law enforcement is not only a "functional by-product of some presumed (and thus teleological) structural logic,"[66] but its operations are essential in maintaining and reproducing the global and national territorial *status quo*. The distinctiveness of immigration detention in particular lies in the fact that it attempts to provide a territorial solution for a problem which is perceived as a problem precisely because it cannot be reduced to the conventional territorial solution. Moreover, the appeal for national states in resorting to immigration detention lies in its additional value of providing an 'extraterritorial' way to deal with unwanted immigration. As a result, these states attempt to evade regular constitutional norms that apply to domestic deprivations of liberty. It is noteworthy that, during the nineties, infamous Guantanamo was used by the U.S. government to detain Haitian and Cuban asylum seekers, who could not rely on a constitutional right to liberty by invoking the habeas corpus jurisdiction of the federal courts.[67] Hence, by resorting to immigration detention, national states do not only aim to protect the territorial logic of fundamental rights protection, but in addition, they seek to make ultimate use of its structural limitations when it comes to the accountability of political power whenever its exercise is portrayed as being based on territorial sovereignty.

It is these structural limitations that Liza Schuster is essentially addressing when she asserts that the normalisation of detention as a way in which to deal with unwanted migration in contemporary Europe is disquieting, because it exemplifies that it has become acceptable to treat certain categories of people as less deserving of dignity and less deserving of their human rights.[68] She contends that, even disregarding the corrosive impact of such practices on society as a whole, the way in which they affect the group that is targeted is unacceptable.[69] However, whether immigration detention is a tale of mere exceptionalism or whether it has the potential to transform into a site for some

---

[66] N.P. De Genova, "Migrant "Illegality" and Deportability in Everyday Life," *Annual Review of Anthropology* 31 (2002), 424.
[67] *Cuban American Bar Association v. Christopher*, 43 F. 3d 1412, 1425 (11th Cir. 1995), 515 U.S. 1995) 1142.
[68] Schuster (2005), 618.
[69] See Gerald Neumann on the larger effects on society as a whole of what he calls 'anomalous zones'. G. L. Neumann, "Anomalous Zones," *Stanford Law Review* 48 (1996).

kind of legal investigation and accountability is a question that I have not yet answered. Some have argued that "there is little or no scope for a relationship of accountability when the refugee [and for that matter the illegal migrant] is cast outside the very parameters of responsibility and accountability."[70] This may be true with regard to deportation – an act through which the state "relinquishes all accountability" as "the deportee is divested of his legal rights as well of his access to the state apparatus of the deporting state."[71]

Yet, in the case of detention, the very fact that immigration detainees are in a very real sense included in the sovereign power of the state, may set in motion an altogether different process. Just as the imprisonment of criminals offered courts a venue through which to review the sovereign power to punish, I shall argue in the last part of this book (chapter 9) that, however minimal and embryonic the processes of legal investigation of practices of immigration detention may be, they hold the promise of bringing about legal claims that may possibly unsettle the notion of territorial sovereignty in modern constitutional discourse. In order to be able to address these issues comprehensively, we shall first need to examine closely the way in which contemporary human rights law features in cases of immigration detention.

---

[70] P. Kumar and C. Grundy-Warr, "The Irregular Migrant as Homo Sacer: Migration and Detention in Australia, Malaysia, and Thailand," *International Migration* 42 (2004), 40.

[71] Peutz (2006), 220. In so far as immigration law enforcement in such cases is placed beyond the pale of accountability mechanisms, Hans Lindahl interestingly argues that it becomes "a *de facto* response to *de facto* migration", an *alegal* act, which as such cannot be "attributed to members of the polity as its joint authors" and thus in that case "boundary-enforcement ceases to be an act of collective self-legislation." See H. Lindahl, "Border Crossings by Immigrants: Legality, Illegality, and Alegality," *Res Publica* 14 (2008), 134–135.

Chapter 7

International Human Rights Law on Immigration Detention

7.1 *Introduction*

This chapter and the next deal with the way in which the international human rights regime has placed limits on the state's power to resort to immigration detention. The focus in these chapters is on the international human rights norms and their application by international bodies, instead of on any particular national constitutional discourse because of international human rights' explicit aim of overcoming the 'particular universalism' that one finds in more traditional forms of constitutionalism. That is not to say that national courts do not have an important role to play in this area. On the contrary, especially in the area of human rights law, we have seen that the distinction between national and international law has become blurred and international norms in this field have a decisive impact on individual rights protection at the national level as domestic courts may apply a broad range of international norms pertaining to the protection of human dignity. However, for reasons concerning the length of this study, I do not examine the role of national courts in cases of immigration detention apart from occasional references as illustrations for a particular argument or position.

We have seen that the use of immigration detention by EU Member States can be divided into three categories: detention upon arrival; detention within the asylum system; and detention in the context of removal. In all these three – at times overlapping – instances detention is employed in order to protect and vindicate the presupposed sovereign right of the state to decide on matters concerning the entry and stay of foreign nationals. From the overview regarding state practice that was provided in chapter 1 it transpired that many of the usual constitutional guarantees are not applied by national states to cases involving deprivation of liberty under immigration legislation. Detention seems to be an attractive policy option for national governments that wish to combat irregular immigration and decrease the numbers of asylum applications, precisely because the perceived neutrality and naturalness of sovereignty's territorial form has made it easy to marginalise the human interests that are actually affected by it.

A good illustration of this position is provided by some of the arguments that sovereign states have put forward in cases with regard to complaints by individuals concerning their deprivation of liberty based upon immigration legislation. Australia, for example, has argued before the HRC that the purposes of mandatory immigration detention reflect the state's sovereign right under international law to regulate the admittance of aliens, and hence such detention cannot be unjust, inappropriate or improper.[1] If raised in a purely domestic context – dealing with, say, freedom of expression – in which the mere content of sovereignty and not also its territorial form was at stake, the inadequacy of such a line of legal reasoning would immediately be apparent. Nevertheless, when defending their policies of immigration detention it is all but exceptional to find comparable arguments brought forward by national governments and they provide the ultimate illustration of the assumption that territorialised sovereignty is immune to traditional modes of legal correction and forms an "unproblematic and legitimate site of legal violence".[2] Another, slightly more disguised, illustration of that assumption can be found in the contentions of the Belgium government in the Čonka case before the ECtHR, in which it argued that to employ a 'little ruse' in order to arrest irregular migrants and subsequently detain them could not be illegal as they had been served with orders to leave the territory, which expressly stated that they were liable to detention with a view to deportation if they failed to comply.[3]

In the remaining chapters of this book, I will investigate whether the application of international human rights to cases of immigration detention can destabilise such a perception of sovereignty's territorial form. Due to its unique manner of implementation and the right of the individual to appeal directly to the ECtHR, the case law of this Court is arguably the best place to conduct such an analysis with regard to the situation in Europe. However, before turning to the way in which the Strasbourg Court deals with the questions related to immigration detention (chapter 7), I shall first sketch a general outline of the international legal regime pertaining to immigration detention in this chapter. This will be done by providing a wide overview of the human rights instruments that are applicable to that practice, and by briefly focussing on relevant legal norms that have emerged in the context of EC law-making in the framework of Title IV TEC. It should be noted that not all instruments that are significant for the practice of immigration detention will be discussed in detail. The main focus of my analysis concerns the way in which the right to

---

[1] See i.e. *Bakhtiyari v. Australia*, 6 November 2003, Comm. No. 1069/2002, UN Doc. CCPR/C/79/D/1069/2002 (2003).

[2] A. Burke, "The Perverse Perseverance of Sovereignty," *Borderlands E-Journal* 1 (2002) on sovereignty in general.

[3] ECtHR, *Čonka v. Belgium*, 5 February 2002, Reports 2002-I, par. 37.

personal liberty is protected in international and European law. With regard to procedural guarantees it will be principally those that are included within the scope of this right which will receive attention.

I shall commence by providing an outline of the universal protection of the right to personal liberty as laid down in Article 9 ICCPR (section 7.2). Substantial guarantees as well as procedural requirements that have been formulated by the HRC and other international human rights bodies in applying this provision will be discussed with specific regard to their implications for the practice of immigration detention. After that, the focus will shift to international instruments which aim at the protection of asylum seekers and refugees as a separate category (section 7.3). Regional legal instruments pertaining to immigration detention will be investigated by taking a look at the soft law that has developed within the framework of the Council of Europe (section 7.4) and the binding instruments that form part of the emerging EC law on immigration and asylum (section 7.5). In the conclusions to this chapter, I shall present some preliminary observations regarding international human rights' potential for destabilising sovereignty's territorial frame.

7.2 *The Human Right to Personal Liberty: A Prohibition on Arbitrary Detention*

In the liberal democracies of the European Union, one of the most – if not the most – intruding forms of violence that the state can still legitimately resort to consists of depriving the individual of his or her personal liberty. However, it is important to realise that sovereignty is not only linked to state violence as such, but that liberty and sovereignty are equally intertwined: the protection of the former is the reason for the existence of the latter. A person's right to liberty is one of the oldest recognised rights, one that preceded thinking on the sovereign state:

> No free man shall be seized or imprisoned, or stripped of his rights or possessions, or outlawed or exiled, or deprived of his standing in any other way, nor will we proceed with force against him, or send others to do so, except by the lawful judgement of his equals or by the law of the land.[4]

---

[4] Article 39 of the Magna Carta of 1215. Thus, the English Habeas Corpus Acts of 1640 and 1679 codified and perfected an already existing procedure by which somebody deprived of his liberty could challenge detention by the King and Council. L. Marcoux, "Protection from arbitrary arrest and detention under international law," *Boston College International and Comparative Law Review* 2 (1982), 347. See also Article 7 of the 1789 French Declaration of the Rights of Men and the Citizen.

At present, the right to personal liberty is a fundamental principle of international human rights law that is recognised by all major human rights instruments.[5] However, as the right to liberty is not an absolute right, there are many instances in which international law recognises that deprivation of liberty is a legitimate form of state control.[6] The core of the right in question thus consists of a prohibition on *arbitrary* deprivations of liberty, and as such, international human rights law concerning the right to liberty revolves around the conditions that need to be fulfilled in order for a detention or an arrest not to be arbitrary.

The term liberty of person refers to freedom of bodily movement in the narrowest sense, which implies that interference with the right occurs only if a person is forced to remain at a certain narrowly confined space. All less serious restrictions on movement fall under the scope of the right to freedom of movement and are not covered by the protection offered by the right to liberty.[7] Noteworthy in this respect is Article 9 of the Universal Declaration of Human Rights, which combines the right to personal liberty with freedom of movement: this provision stipulates that no one shall be subjected to arbitrary arrest, detention or exile. However, when it comes to the scope of the right to personal liberty, only the individuals who are placed in closed centres, or are unable to leave any other narrowly confined location, such as an airport transit zone, fall under its protection.[8] When considering whether a

---

[5] Articles 3 and 9 UDHR; Article 9 ICCPR; Article 5 ECHR; Article 6 Charter of Fundamental Rights of the European Union; Article 7 American Convention on Human Rights; Article 6 African Charter on Human and Peoples' Rights; Article 20 Cairo Declaration on Human Rights in Islam; Article 20 Arab Charter on Human Rights. There are some instruments that deserve special mention: Article 5(a) of the Declaration on the Human Rights of Individuals who are not Nationals of the Country in which they Live, Adopted by General Assembly resolution 40/144 of 13 December 1985, and Article 16 of the International Convention on the Protection of the Rights of All Migrant Workers and Members of their Families. Most human rights instruments protect the right to personal liberty together with a person's right to security. Whereas the ECtHR has not accorded the right to security of person an independent status alongside the right to personal liberty, the right to security in Article 9 ICCPR aims to guarantee state protection against interference with personal integrity by private persons. See M. Nowak, *U.N. Covenant on Civil and Political Rights: CCPR Commentary* (Kehl am Rein: N.P. Engel, 1993, 163; and HRC, *Delgado Paez v. Columbia*, 12 July 1990, Comm. No. 195/1985, UN Doc. CCPR/C/39/D/195/1985 (1990).

[6] S. Joseph, J. Schultz, and M. Castan, *The International Covenant on Civil and Political Rights: Cases, Materials and Commentary* (Oxford: Oxford University Press, 2004), 304.

[7] See HRC, *Celepli v. Sweden*, 18 July 1994; Comm. No. 456/1991, U.N. Doc. CCPR/C/51/D/456/1991 (1994); and *Karker v. France*, 26 October 2000, Comm. No. 833/98, U.N. Doc. CCPR/C/70/D/833/1998 (2000).

[8] UN Commission on Human Rights, *Deliberation No. 5 of the Working Group on Arbitrary Detention*, Fifty-sixth session, Item 11(a) of the provisional agenda, Report of the Working Group on Arbitrary Detention, Annex II, E/CN.4/2000/4, 28 December 1999.

person is deprived of his or her liberty, the cumulative impact of the restrictions, as well as the degree and intensity of each one separately, should be assessed.[9]

Another restriction on the scope of the protection offered by the right to liberty is that it should be seen as applying only to the fact of deprivation of liberty itself and the specific procedural guarantees that form part of it.[10] In general, a person who is mistreated whilst in detention cannot claim a violation of the right to personal liberty or security. However, taking into account that the conditions of detention may in a limited amount of cases bear upon the question of its arbitrariness – which is arguably especially so in the context of immigration detention, I shall pay some attention to these conditions as well.

7.2.1 The Prohibition on Arbitrariness in Article 9 ICCPR

In order to flesh out the general prohibition on arbitrary detention in this section, I shall focus on Article 9 of the ICCPR, and the interpretation of this provision by the HRC and the Working Group on Arbitrary Detention, a UN body entrusted with the investigation of instances of alleged arbitrary deprivation of liberty and detention otherwise inconsistent with international legal instruments.[11] The first paragraph of Article 9 ICCPR reads as follows:

> 1. Everyone has the right to liberty and security of person. No one shall be subjected to arbitrary arrest or detention. No one shall be deprived of his liberty except on such grounds and in accordance with such procedures as are established by law.

Although the initial draft of Article 9 ICCPR contained a list of permissible grounds for detention, the final Article 9(1) ICCPR does not provide an exhaustive list of situations in which detention is permitted, but it simply forbids arbitrary detention as well as detention that is not in accordance with the law. This was not the original intention of the drafters, but it became obvious in the drafting process that to reach agreement on permissible grounds for the deprivation of liberty would be impossible. Moreover, an enumeration of about forty exceptions to the right to liberty (ever increasing reasons for restrictions were proposed by national states) was not considered to reflect the

---

[9] UNHCR, *Revised Guidelines on Applicable Criteria and Standards relating to the Detention of Asylum Seekers*, (IOM/22/99/Rev.1-FOM/22/99/Rev.1), February 1999, Guideline 1.
[10] Nowak (1993), 160.
[11] Established by Resolution 1991/42 of the Commission on Human Rights. The mandate of the Working Group was clarified and extended by the Commission in its resolution 1997/50 to cover the issue of administrative custody of asylum seekers and immigrants.

fundamental importance of that right.¹² Therefore two proposals that merely prohibited arbitrary and unlawful detention were accepted.

It is clear from the wording of Article 9 ICCPR and its drafting history that arbitrary cannot be equated with unlawful in the narrow sense of that latter term.¹³ The prohibition of *unlawful* detention is expressed in the third sentence of Article 9 ICCPR, which refers to the principle of legality, requiring that detention must be in accordance with a procedure laid down by domestic law. Accordingly, this principle is violated if someone is detained on grounds which are not clearly established by national law or if the act of deprivation of liberty disregards national law.¹⁴ Recently, the Working Group on Arbitrary Detention found Italy to be in breach of the requirement of legality with regard to first reception centres for asylum seekers, where, for a period varying between a few days and more than a month, asylum seekers had been de facto detained without a legal basis, as there was no procedure leading to this deprivation of liberty, nor any decision adopted.¹⁵

By adding a prohibition on *arbitrary* detention, the principle of legality is complemented with an autonomous international safeguard against those detentions that are authorised by unjust domestic laws. Such an additional safeguard was considered necessary by the majority of the members of the Commission on Human Rights if the right in question was to have any substance.¹⁶ Thus, with the introduction of the prohibition of arbitrariness, concepts of reasonableness and justice were introduced in the protection of the right to personal liberty. The definition in the *1964 Study of the Right of Everyone to be Free from Arbitrary Arrest, Detention and Exile* confirms that the protection of the right to liberty extends beyond protection against deprivation of liberty which is merely lacking a legal basis in domestic law or otherwise in violation of national legislation:

> Arrest or detention is arbitrary if it is: (a) on grounds or in accordance with procedures other than those established by law or (b) under the provisions of a law,

---

[12] Nowak (1993), 164.

[13] Ibid., 164–166; and Marcoux (1982), 359–364.

[14] Nowak (1993), 172. See also Principle 6 of *Deliberation no. 5 of the Working Group on Arbitrary Detention* (UN Commission on Human Rights, 28 December 1999).

[15] UN Human Rights Council, *Report of the Working Group on Arbitrary Detention, Addendum, Mission to Italy*, Tenth session, Agenda item 3, A/HRC/10/21/Add.5, 16 February 2009, par 70–72.

[16] Marcoux (1982), p. 363. See also R.B. Lillich, The Human Rights of Aliens in Contemporary International Law (Manchester: Manchester University Press, 1984), 138; and Y. Dinstein, "Right to life, physical integrity and liberty," in: *The International Bill of Rights*, ed. L. Henkin (New York: Columbia University Press, 1981), 130.

the purpose of which is incompatible with the right to liberty and security of person.[17]

The HRC uses a somewhat different approach to interpret the prohibition of arbitrary deprivations of liberty:

> Arbitrariness is not to be equated with 'against the law' but must be interpreted more broadly to include elements of inappropriateness, injustice, lack of predictability and due process of law.[18]

The prohibition on arbitrariness also disallows deprivations of liberty that are manifestly disproportional, and it entails that the specific manner in which the arrest is made and its implementation should not be discriminatory and must be proportional in view of all the circumstances.[19] The principle of proportionality constitutes only one aspect of the prohibition of arbitrariness, but it is a practical and useful criterion for the assessment whether the actual deprivation of liberty is compatible with the status of the right to liberty as a fundamental right. Human rights bodies such as the Working Group on Arbitrary Detention use it as a yardstick to evaluate state practice.[20] This latter body has repeatedly coupled the expression of its concern over ever increasing deprivations of liberty as a form of immigration control with a powerful reminder to governments that detention shall be a measure of last resort, permissible only for the shortest period of time, and that alternative non-custodial measures should always be considered before resorting to detention.[21] Furthermore, immigration detention is only

---

[17] See the "Draft Principles on Freedom from Arbitrary Arrest and Detention," UN Commission on Human Rights, *Study of the Right of Everyone to be Free from Arbitrary Arrest, Detention and Exile and the Draft Principles on Freedom from Arbitrary Arrest and Detention*, UN Doc. E/CN.4/826/Rev.1, at 7 (1964), 205.

[18] HRC, *Mukong v. Cameroon*, 21 July 1994, Comm. No. 458/1991, U.N. Doc. CCPR/C/51/D/458/1991 (1994), at. 9.8 and *Van Alphen v. the Netherlands*, 23 July 1990 Comm. No. 305/1988, U.N. Doc. CCPR/C/39/D/305/1988 (1990).

[19] Nowak (1993), 173.

[20] See for example UN Human Rights Council, *Report of the Working Group on Arbitrary Detention, Addendum, Mission to Italy*, 16 February 2009.

[21] UN Human Rights Council, Report of the Working Group of Arbitrary Detention, Tenth session, Agenda item 3, A/HRC/10/21, 16 February 2009, par. 65–67; and UN Human Rights Council, *Report of the Working Group on Arbitrary Detention*, Seventh session, Item 3 of the provisional agenda, A/HRC/7/4, 10 January 2008. See also UN Commission on Human Rights, *Report of the Working Group on Arbitrary Detention. Addendum: Report on the Visit of the Working Group on Arbitrary Detention to the United Kingdom on the issue of immigrants and asylum seekers*, Fifty-fifth session, Item 11(a) of the provisional agenda, E/CN.4/1999/63/Add.3, 28 December 1998, 12.

justified for as long as there is a reasonable prospect of removal, and it should not serve purposes other than those related to immigration law enforcement.[22]

A similar conclusion regarding the central importance of the principle of proportionality in immigration detention can be drawn from the approach that the HRC has taken to the Australian policy of mandatory detention of asylum seekers, already referred to above. The HRC does not deem the detention of asylum seekers or irregular immigrants as such arbitrary and in violation of Article 9 ICCPR:

> The fact of illegal entry may indicate a need for investigation and there may be other factors particular to the individual such as the likelihood of absconding and lack of co-operation, which may justify detention for a period. Without such factors detention may be considered arbitrary, even if entry was illegal.[23]

However, in most of the Australian cases that were brought before it, the HRC considered Australian detention policy to be in violation of Article 9 ICCPR as the government solely brought forward general justifications for the detention of asylum seekers, instead of stating any individual justification for the necessity of the detention.[24] Thus, immigration detention must be reasonable and necessary in view of factors which are particular to the individual in order to be in accordance with Article 9 ICCPR.[25] Accordingly, in *Jalloh v. The Netherlands*, the HRC did not consider it unreasonable to have detained the individual concerned for a limited time until the administrative procedure relating to his case was completed, taking into consideration that he had fled from the open facility at which he was accommodated from the time of his arrival for around eleven months.[26]

---

[22] Human Rights Council, *Opinions adopted by the Working Group on Arbitrary Detention, Opinion No. 45/2006 (United Kingdom)*, Seventh session, Item 3 of the provisional agenda, A/HRC/7/4/Add.1, 16 January 2008.

[23] HRC, *A. v. Australia*, 3 April 1997, Comm. no. 560/1993, UN Doc. CCPR/C/59/D/560/1993 (1993), par 9.4.

[24] See for example: *Baban v. Australia*, 18 September 2003, Comm. no. 1014/2001, UN Doc. CCPR/C/78/D1014/2001 (2003), par. 7.2; and *Bakhtiyari v. Australia*, par. 9.2. and 9.3.

[25] Recently affirmed in HRC, *Saed Shams et al. v. Australia*, 11 September 2007, Comm. Nos. 1255,1256,1259,1260,1266,1268,1270,1288/2004, UN Doc. CCPR/C/90/D/1255,1256,1259, 1260,1266,1268,1270&1288/2004 and *Danyal Shafiq v. Australia*, 13 November 2006, Communication No. 1324/2004, UN Doc. CCPR/C/88/D/1324/2004.

[26] *Jalloh v. The Netherlands*, 26 March 2002, Comm. No. 794/1998, U.N. Doc. CCPR/C/74/D/794/1998 (2002), par. 8.2. See also *Madafferi v. Australia*, 26 July 2004, Comm. No. 1011/2000, U.N. Doc. CCPR/C/81/D/1011/2001 (2004), in which case the HRC did not deem the initial decision to detain to be unlawful as it was based on an individual assessment that had shown that there was a risk of fleeing.

The importance of the criteria of necessity and proportionality becomes evident once more when the HRC assesses the duration of immigration detention, as it considers that "detention should not continue beyond the period for which the State can provide appropriate justification".[27] With regard to detention in order to secure removal, the HRC has clarified this requirement as entailing that once a reasonable prospect of expelling the individual concerned no longer exists, the detention should be terminated.[28] But more generally, when detention lasts for a longer period of time, considerations of proportionality start to play a more prominent role as well:

> [the Committee] observes that the authors were detained in immigration detention for three years and two months. Whatever justification there may have been for an initial detention, for instance for purposes of ascertaining identity and other issues, the State party has not, in the Committee's opinion, demonstrated that their detention was justified for such an extended period. It has not demonstrated that other, less intrusive, measures could not have achieved the same end of compliance with the State party's immigration policies by resorting to, for example, the imposition of reporting obligations, sureties or other conditions which would take into account the family's particular circumstances. As a result, the continuation of immigration detention for the authors, including two children, for the length of time described above, without any appropriate justification, was arbitrary and contrary to article 9, paragraph 1, of the Covenant.[29]

Concerning the duration of immigration detention, the Working Group on Arbitrary Detention further insists that a maximum period should be set by law and that the duration may never be unlimited or excessive.[30] As such, it considered the detention of a Somalian national by the British authorities to be arbitrary, seeing that it had lasted more than four years in a situation in which removals to Somalia could only take place if the deportees would sign a disclaimer indicating their voluntary return, something which the person concerned refused to do:

> With regard to duration, the Working Group notes that Mr. Abdi has been detained for four-and-a-half years as of today. The Working Group finds it difficult to think of circumstances under which this duration would not be excessive. [...] Where the chances of removal within a reasonable delay are remote, the Government's obligation to seek for alternatives to detention becomes all the more pressing. Looking forward, the possibility of Mr. Abdi's removal would

---

[27] *A. v. Australia*, par. 9.4.
[28] *Jalloh v. The Netherlands*, par. 8.2.
[29] HRC, *D and E v. Australia*, 11 July 2006, Comm. No. 1050/2002, UN Doc CCPR/C/87/D/1050/2002.
[30] *Deliberation No. 5 of the Working Group on Arbitrary Detention* (UN Commission on Human Rights, 28 December 1999).

appear to be currently as remote as it was ever before. His continued detention therefore has assumed an indefinite character.[31]

7.2.2 Article 9 ICCPR and Procedural Guarantees for Immigration Detainees

Paragraphs 2 to 5 of Article 9 ICCPR contain procedural safeguards for persons who are deprived of their liberty. These guarantees form an integral part of the right to personal liberty, and their violation will accordingly entail a breach of the right to personal liberty.[32] They read as follows:

> 2. Anyone who is arrested shall be informed, at the time of arrest, of the reasons for his arrest and shall be promptly informed of any charges against him.
> 3. Anyone arrested or detained on a criminal charge shall be brought promptly before a judge or other officer authorized by law to exercise judicial power and shall be entitled to trial within a reasonable time or to release. It shall not be the general rule that persons awaiting trial shall be detained in custody, but release may be subject to guarantees to appear for trial, at any other stage of the judicial proceedings, and, should occasion arise, for execution of the judgement.
> 4. Anyone who is deprived of his liberty by arrest or detention shall be entitled to take proceedings before a court, in order that that court may decide without delay on the lawfulness of his detention and order his release if the detention is not lawful.
> 5. Anyone who has been the victim of unlawful arrest or detention shall have an enforceable right to compensation.

Paragraph 2 of Article 9 ICCPR contains the right to be informed about the reasons for detention. In the *Body of Principles for the Protection of All Persons under any Form of Detention or Imprisonment* (hereinafter the *1988 Body of Principles*),[33] the obligation to provide information is further elaborated by the requirement that anyone detained should be provided with an explanation of his rights and how to avail himself of such rights.[34] Although Article 9 ICCPR does not state explicitly that the person concerned needs to be informed in a language that he understands, it would be difficult to maintain that someone is adequately informed if he does not understand what is being communicated

---

[31] Human Rights Council, *Opinions adopted by the Working Group on Arbitrary Detention, Opinion No. 45/2006 (United Kingdom)*.
[32] The Working Group on Arbitrary Detention takes due consideration of whether or not the alien is able to enjoy certain guarantees in order to determine whether a case of immigration detention can be considered arbitrary. See *Deliberation no. 5 of the Working Group on Arbitrary Detention* (UN Commission on Human Rights, 28 December 1999).
[33] UN General Assembly, *Body of Principles for the Protection of All persons under Any Form of Detention or Imprisonment*, UNGA Resolution 43/173, Annex, 43 UN GAOR Supp. (No. 49) at 298, UN Doc. A/43/49 (1988).
[34] Ibid., Principle 13.

to him.[35] Whether or not notification of the custodial measure is given in writing in a language understood by the asylum seeker or immigrant is one of the factors the Working Group on Arbitrary Detention considers when it assesses whether immigration detention is arbitrary.[36] According to the Working Group, the right to information in the case of immigration detainees should include the nature of and the grounds for the decision refusing permission to enter or reside in the territory.[37]

The right to information about the reasons for the deprivation of liberty serves, *inter alia*, to enable the detainee to make use of the right to challenge his detention in court, a fundamental procedural guarantee contained in Article 9 ICCPR. Hence, the Working Group on Arbitrary Detention requires the information provided to the immigration detainee to include a notification of the conditions under which he is able to apply for a remedy to a judicial authority.[38]

Article 9 ICCPR includes two habeas corpus provisions: its paragraph 3 is specifically meant for persons detained on criminal charges, who shall be brought promptly before a judge. With regard to persons detained on other grounds, such as immigration detainees, paragraph 4 of Article 9 ICCPR gives them the right to have the lawfulness of their detention reviewed in court, which shall decide without delay. Without delay means that the decision usually has to be made within several weeks, although this may depend on the type of deprivation of liberty and other individual circumstances.[39] The Working Group on Arbitrary Detention furthermore insists on a regular review of immigration detention within fixed time-limits, which must even stand in "emergency situations" such as in the case of large numbers of undocumented immigrants entering the territory of a State.[40]

---

[35] According to Principle 14 of the 1988 *Body of Principles*, anyone who does not speak or understand the language used by the authorities is entitled to receive the required information in a language he understands.

[36] *Deliberation no. 5 of the Working Group on Arbitrary Detention* (UN Commission on Human Rights, 28 December 1999), Principle 8.

[37] Ibid. Principle 1.

[38] Ibid. Principle 8.

[39] Nowak (1993), 179. According to the Working Group on Arbitrary Detention, immigration detainees must be brought *promptly* before a judicial or other authority, thereby according immigration detainees and persons detained on criminal grounds almost equal rights, were it not for the addition of the words 'other authority'. See *Deliberation no. 5. of the Working Group on Arbitrary Detention* (UN Commission on Human Rights, 28 December 1999 See also the 1988 *Body of Principles for the Protection of All Persons under Any Form of Detention or Imprisonment*, Principle 11).

[40] UN Human Rights Council, Report of the Working Group of Arbitrary Detention (16 February 2009), par. 67.

Article 9(4) ICCPR requires that recourse must eventually be had to a 'court'. This may be an administrative court, as long as certain requirements of impartiality and independence are satisfied. If the *initial* decision to detain is taken by a court in the sense of Article 9(4) ICCPR, this provision is usually complied with. The specific form of the judicial procedure in which the legality of the detention is challenged is irrelevant, as long as the court can order release if the detention is arbitrary or unlawful.[41]

> The Working Group considers that the right to challenge the legality of detention or to petition for a writ of habeas corpus or remedy of amparo is a personal right, which must in all circumstances be guaranteed by the jurisdiction of the ordinary courts.[42]

According to the HRC, the scope of the review of lawfulness by the domestic court is not limited to a mere review whether the detention is in compliance with domestic law, but it should include whether the detention is in accordance with the requirements of Article 9(1) ICCPR.[43] Thus, the court in question should evaluate the necessity, proportionality, and reasonableness of detention in the light of the individual circumstances, instead of merely assessing whether the law has been correctly applied.[44] Consequently, the HRC deems the procedure of habeas corpus in a state with immigration legislation containing mandatory detention provisions that have been declared constitutional by its highest court in violation of Article 9(4) ICCPR, as such a procedure would merely entail a verification of the applicability of the mandatory detention provisions to the detainee without due regard to the substantive grounds for the detention in each individual case.[45]

Paragraph 5 of Article 9 ICCPR gives anyone who has been deprived of their liberty in an unlawful manner the enforceable right to compensation. This right covers pecuniary as well as non-pecuniary damages.[46] Some additional guarantees particular to the situation of immigration detainees have been formulated by the Working Group on Arbitrary Detention. Asylum seekers or immigrants in custody must have the possibility of communicating with the outside world, and of contacting a lawyer, a consular representative, and

---

[41] HRC, *Danyal Shafiq v. Australia*. See also 1988 *Body of Principles for the Protection of All Persons under Any Form of Detention or Imprisonment*, Principle 32.
[42] UN Commission on Human Rights, *Report of the Working Group on Arbitrary Detention*, Sixtieth Session, Item 11(a) of the provisional agenda, E/CN.4/2004/3, 15 December 2003, 23.
[43] *Baban v. Australia*, par. 7.2.; and *Bakhtiyari v. Australia*, par. 9.4.
[44] See *Saed Shams v. Australia*, par. 7.3.
[45] *A. v. Australia*; *Baban v. Australia*, par. 7.2; *Bakhtiyari v. Australia*, par. 8.2 and 9.4; and *Danyal Shafiq v. Australia*.
[46] Nowak (1993), 182.

relatives.⁴⁷ The UNHCR and the Red Cross and other duly authorised NGOs must be allowed access to places of custody.⁴⁸ Furthermore, immigration detainees must be registered, and informed of the internal regulations.⁴⁹

7.2.3 Conditions of Immigration Detention: An Indication of Arbitrariness?

I have already mentioned that, as a rule, the conditions of detention do not fall under the scope of the right to personal liberty. Accordingly, the Working Group on Arbitrary Detention examines neither complaints about alleged torture during detention, nor complaints concerning inhuman conditions of detention.⁵⁰ Other general human rights norms such as Article 7 ICCPR, Article 3 ECHR and those contained in the 1984 Convention against Torture and other Cruel, Inhuman or Degrading Punishment (CAT) are applicable in these situations. In addition, international human rights law has accorded special attention to the treatment of detainees on account of the particular vulnerable position of persons who are deprived of their liberty, as exemplified by a provision such as Article 10 ICCPR. Also the *1988 Body of Principles* contains detailed provisions in this respect.⁵¹ These legal norms in themselves,

---

[47] *Deliberation no. 5 of the Working Group on Arbitrary Detention* (UN Commission on Human Rights, 28 December 1999), Principle 2. See also Article 36(1) under b and c of the Vienna Convention on Consular Relations and Article 6 of the European Convention on Consular Functions (1967) concerning the right of detained foreigners to have their consular representatives informed.

[48] *Deliberation no. 5 of the Working Group on Arbitrary Detention*, Principle 10.

[49] Ibid., Principles 4 and 5.

[50] UN High Commissioner for Human Rights, *Fact Sheet 26: The Working Group on Arbitrary Detention*, Human Rights Fact Sheet Series (Geneva: Office of the United Nations High Commissioner for Human Rights, last consulted online 5 June 2009).

[51] In the European context, the European Committee for the Prevention of Torture (CPT) is a key actor in this respect. The CPT examines, by means of visits to member states of the Council of Europe, the treatment of persons deprived of their liberty with a view to strengthening, if necessary, the protection of such persons from torture and from inhuman or degrading treatment or punishment (Article 1 of the 1987 European Convention for the Prevention of Torture and Inhuman or Degrading Treatment of Punishment). In recent years, it has paid special attention to the treatment of immigration detainees and it has repeatedly stressed that, if it is deemed necessary to deprive persons of their liberty under immigration legislation, it is by far preferable to accommodate them in centres specifically designed for that purpose, offering material conditions and a regime appropriate to the legal status of such persons, and staffed by suitably qualified personnel. CPT. *The CPT Standards: Substantive sections of the CPT's General Reports*. CPT/Inf/E (2002) 1 – Rev. 2006. Strasbourg, 2006, par. 25–29. See also CPT, *Report to the Finnish Government on the visit to Finland carried out by the European Committee for the Prevention of Torture and Inhuman or Degrading Treatment or Punishment (CPT) from 7 to 17 September 2003*, CPT/Inf (2004) 20, Strasbourg, 14 June 2004, 20.

however, do not limit the state's power to resort to immigration detention as such. This being said, it is conspicuous – and only all the more so as its mandate does not cover an examination of the conditions of detention – that the Working Group on Arbitrary Detention has in recent years insisted on calling attention to the harsh conditions of immigration detention in unambiguous and explicit terms:

> The Working Group has been able to observe during missions over the past few years the deplorable situation in the detention facilities in former conflict countries, countries otherwise in transition, or countries experiencing a large influx of foreigners either from a neighbour in crisis or because they are perceived to be a destination to realize the dream of a better life. Illegal immigrants, irrespective of their age, are detained for months, and held together with other detainees who are kept in custody pursuant to criminal law. They are often kept in custody without sufficient water, food, and bedding or any possibility of leaving the cells to go to the yard, to communicate with their relatives, lawyers, interpreters or consulates, or to challenge the legality of the deprivation of their liberty or deportation orders.[52]

Given the importance of the principle of proportionality in assessing the lawfulness of the deprivation of liberty, conditions of immigration detention may also play a role in balancing the interest of the state to resort to immigration detention, on the one hand, and the individual's interest in the enjoyment of his fundamental rights, on the other. Accordingly, it can be argued that in a limited number of situations, the conditions of detention may bear upon the question of its arbitrariness, and thus influence the question of the lawfulness of the deprivation of liberty itself, as was alluded to by the HRC in the case of *Madafferi v. Australia*:

> As to Mr. Madafferi's return to Maribyrnong Immigration Detention Centre on 25 June 2003, where he was detained until his committal to a psychiatric hospital on 18 September 2003, the Committee [...] observes the author's arguments, which remain uncontested by the State party, that this form of detention was contrary to the advice of various doctors and psychiatrists, consulted by the State party, who all advised that a further period of placement in an immigration detention centre would risk further deterioration of Mr. Madafferi's mental health. Against the backdrop of such advice and given the eventual involuntary admission of Mr. Madafferi to a psychiatric hospital, the Committee finds that the State party's decision to return Mr. Madafferi to Maribyrnong and the manner in which that transfer was affected was not based on a proper assessment of the circumstances of the case but was, as such, disproportionate.[53]

---

[52] UN Human Rights Council, *Report of the Working Group on Arbitrary Detention*, (10 January 2008), par. 49–50.
[53] *Madafferi v. Australia*, par. 9.3.

As the HRC accordingly found that the detention was in violation of article 10(1) ICCPR, a "provision [...] dealing specifically with the situation of persons deprived of their liberty and encompassing for such persons the elements set out generally in article 7 ICCPR", it did not deem it necessary to consider the claims arising under article 7 ICCPR separately.[54]

Support for the position that the conditions of detention may result in an unlawful deprivation of liberty can also be found in national case law. Dutch courts have considered unlawful deprivations of liberty lasting longer than six months on a so-called prison-boat (a facility specifically designed for immigration detention) or detention in police cells extending 120 hours, on account of the conditions of detention, which were deemed to result in a disproportional interference with the detainees' fundamental rights.[55]

7.3 Human Rights and the Detention of Refugees and Asylum Seekers

Refugees and asylum seekers will often constitute a large part of the population in immigration detention centres in Europe.[56] An increasing number of European states resort to the detention of asylum seekers whose claim to international protection has not yet been decided upon, if certain conditions are fulfilled, such as a lack of identification or travel documents.[57] According to the Working Group on Arbitrary Detention, a deprivation of liberty that results solely from the exercise of the right to seek and enjoy asylum as laid down in Article 14 UDHR constitutes an arbitrary deprivation of liberty, and is accordingly in violation of Article 9 ICCPR.[58] The Working Group estimates that thousands of people are subject each year to arbitrary detention, inter

---

[54] Ibid.
[55] Rechtbank's Gravenhage, 18 March 2005, AWB05/ 3107 and AWB 05/3109; and Rechtbank Haarlem, 20 March 2009, LJN: BH6982.
[56] See i.e. the United Kingdom, where the vast majority of those detained have applied for asylum at one stage or another. N. Hammond, "Chapter 26: United Kingdom," in: *Foreigners in European Prisons*, eds. A.M. van Kalmthout, F.B.A.M Hofstee-van der Meulen and F. Dünkel (Nijmegen: Wolf Legal Publishers, 2007); and A. Gil-Robles, Commissioner for Human Rights (Council of Europe), *Report on his Visit to the United Kingdom (4–12 November 2004) for the attention of the Committee of Ministers and the Parliamentary Assembly*, CommDH (2005) 6, Strasbourg, 8 June 2005.
[57] K. Hailbronnner, "Detention of Asylum Seekers," *European Journal of Migration and Law* 9 (2007), 160.
[58] UN High Commissioner for Human Rights, *Fact Sheet 26: The Working Group on Arbitrary Detention*.

alia, because of "the growing and pre-occupying practice of administrative detention, notably for those seeking asylum."[59] Similarly, the HRC has expressed concern over the detention of asylum seekers for reasons of administrative convenience, which it does not deem legitimate under the Covenant, and it has made clear that it considers the detention of asylum seekers in prisons to be unacceptable.[60] Undoubtedly the safeguards of Article 9 ICCPR are fully applicable to applicants for asylum, but as they are regarded as a particularly vulnerable group, additional guarantees concerning their detention have been formulated.[61] Below I shall provide a brief overview of some specific guarantees that apply to the detention of applicants for asylum and refugees, mainly formulated by the UNHCR.

Article 31 of the 1951 Convention Relating to the Status of Refugees is of key importance for the use of detention against refugees. The first paragraph of this provision prohibits criminal sanctions being used against refugees who come directly from a country of persecution, on account of their illegal entry or presence, provided they present themselves to the authorities without delay. It is not plausible that this provision would be violated when a refugee is detained on account of his illegal entry, if the deprivation of liberty is an administrative measure and is not categorised as a criminal sanction as such. But paragraph 2 of Article 31 extends protection in that case: states shall not apply to the freedom of movement of such refugees restrictions other than those which are necessary. Thus, this provision requires the detention to be proportional in view of the individual circumstances of each and every individual.[62]

The UNHCR has elaborated further on the principles of necessity and proportionality in its *Revised Guidelines on the Applicable Criteria and Standards Relating to the Detention of Asylum Seekers* (hereinafter the *1999 Guidelines*).[63]

---

[59] Ibid.
[60] Human Rights Committee, *Concluding Observations of the Human Rights Committee: United Kingdom of Great Britain and Northern Ireland*, Seventy-third session, 6 December 2001, CCPR/CO/73/UK;CCPR/CO/73/UKOT.
[61] Extra concern is warranted with regard to this group as the concerned individuals may have suffered persecution or other hardships, and detention in the supposed safe haven that they have fled to will thus be extra harsh. See also UN Commission on Human Rights, *Detention of Asylum Seekers*, Sub-Commission on Human Rights Resolution 2000/21, 27th meeting, 18 August 2000.
[62] See also A. Triche Naumik, "International Law and Detention of US Asylum Seekers: Contrasting *Matter of D-J-* with the United Nations Refugee Convention," *International Journal of Refugee Law* 19 (2007).
[63] UNHCR, *Revised Guidelines on Applicable Criteria and Standards relating to the Detention of Asylum Seekers*, IOM/22/99/Rev.1-FOM/22/99/Rev.1, February 1999.

The *1999 Guidelines* are not applicable to asylum seekers whose requests have been rejected on substantial grounds, but they do apply to those refugees whose claims are not investigated because of a principle such as a safe third country, or because, for other reasons, another country is responsible for handling the claim. According to the *1999 Guidelines*, the detention of asylum seekers must be avoided whenever possible, and alternative measures, such as reporting obligations, always need to be considered first.[64] The UNHCR has expressed scepticism about bail hearings as an alternative to detention as the focus would be on establishing the reliability of the surety and its relationship to the applicant as opposed to the reasons for detention.[65] In assessing whether the detention of asylum seekers is necessary, account should be taken of whether the detention is reasonable and whether it is proportional to the objectives to be achieved.[66] If detention is exceptionally resorted to, it is only permitted if it is prescribed by national law, which has to be in conformity with general norms and principles of international human rights.[67]

Apart from these more general requirements that flow, as we saw above, also from Article 9 ICCPR, the *1999 Guidelines* specify that the detention of refugees may only be used in order to verify identity; to determine the elements on which the claim for asylum is based; in cases where asylum seekers have destroyed their documents or used fraudulent documents; or to protect national security or public order.[68] Detention may certainly not be used to deter other asylum seekers; neither should it constitute a sanction for a failure to comply with administrative requirements or a breach of reception centre or other institutional restrictions.[69]

The inclusion in the *1999 Guidelines* of national security or public order as separate grounds for the detention of asylum seekers raises questions as regards the difference in the applicability of these grounds for detention to

---

[64] Guidelines 2, 3 and 4; and UNHCR Executive Committee, ExCom Conclusion No. 44 (XXXVII) 1986 (Detention of Refugees and Asylum Seekers). See also European Council on Refugees and Exiles, *Position Paper on the Detention of Asylum Seekers*, April 1996.

[65] UNHCR, *Detention of Asylum Seekers and Refugees: The Framework, the Problem and Recommended Practice*, 15th Meeting of the Executive Committee of the High Commissioner's Programme Standing Committee, Doc. No. EC/49/SC/CRP.13, 4 June 1999, Reprinted in *Refugee Survey Quarterly* 18 (1999), 168.

[66] UNHCR *1999 Guidelines*, Guideline 3.

[67] Ibid.

[68] Ibid. The same grounds are mentioned in UNHCR ExCom Conclusion No. 44 (XXXVII) 1986, under (b).

[69] UNHCR, *Revised Guidelines* (1999), Guideline 3. See also Amnesty International, *Cell Culture: The Detention and Imprisonment of Asylum Seekers in the United Kingdom*, London, 1996.

asylum seekers as compared to national citizens or regular immigrants.[70] In fact, if we take national executives' interpretation of national legislation as a point of reference, the public order and national security grounds carry in them a risk of becoming a licence to resort to the detention of asylum seekers on a very extensive scale.[71] More generally, it can be argued that the grounds of detention as specified in the *1999 Guidelines* are very wide and they can therefore be interpreted by states as providing the basis for detaining large numbers of asylum seekers.[72] Detention in order to determine the elements on which the claim for asylum is based may in particular conflict with the principle that there should be a presumption against detention. Similarly, the use of fraudulent documents as a ground for detention may raise serious objections in the case of refugees, a category that is often forced to have recourse to such documents in order to flee. However, it would clearly go against the text, object and purpose of the *1999 Guidelines* to interpret these grounds for detention in such a manner that the requirement of proportionality would no longer have any significance.

According to the *1999 Guidelines*, detention should only be imposed in a non-discriminatory manner. In addition, minors who are asylum seekers should not detained.[73] Detention of children in general should be a measure of last resort and is even subject to more severe restrictions than the detention of adults.[74] The *1999 Guidelines* also focus on the conditions of detention, which, they stipulate, should be humane with respect for the inherent dignity of every person.

---

[70] See the judgment by the House of Lords in *A v. Secretary of State for the Home Department*, UKHL [2004], in which the indefinite detention of the so-called Belmarsh detainees for reasons of national security was deemed unlawful as it was discriminatory. Parliament reacted by introducing new legislation allowing anyone of any nationality, thus including British, to be detained indefinitely.

[71] Especially when taking into account the way in which national governments interpret the term public order and codify it in national legislation with regard to immigration detention in general. See A. van Kalmthout, "Vreemdelingenbewaring," in *Detentie: Gevangen in Nederland*, eds. E.R. Muller and P.C. Vegter (Alphen aan den Rijn: Kluwer; 2005), 325–327 with regard to the situation in the Netherlands, where the public order criterion has lost much if its significance in daily practice. See also Article 59(2) of the Dutch Aliens Act 2000, a provision which employs the legal fiction that detention is required by public order if the necessary papers for removal are available or will soon be available.

[72] European Council on Refugees and Exiles, (April 1996), General Remark No. 9; and Jesuit Refugee Service, *Detention in Europe*, JRS-Europe Observation and Position Paper, 1 April 2004, 12.

[73] Guideline 6.

[74] See also Article 37 under (b) of the Convention on the Rights of the Child 1989/1990: No child shall be deprived of his or her liberty unlawfully or arbitrarily. The arrest, detention or

7.4 Regional Discourse: The Council of Europe and Immigration Detention

With regard to the human rights discourse relating to immigration detention in the framework of the Council of Europe, excluding the ECtHR, the most important document is Recommendation Rec (2003) 5 on measures of detention of asylum seekers adopted in 2003 by the Committee of Ministers.[75] It stipulates that measures of detention of asylum seekers should be in accordance with international standards and prescribed by a national law.[76] It is important to note that according to the Recommendation, alternative measures *always* have to be considered before resorting to detention.[77] If these are not feasible in the individual case, then detention is only permitted in the following situations: if the identity, including nationality, of the asylum seekers has to be verified (especially if they have destroyed their documents or used false ones); if detention is necessary to obtain elements on which their asylum claims are based; if a decision needs to be taken with regard to their right of entry to the territory; and lastly, if their detention is necessary with regard to national security or public order.[78]

These grounds are very wide, capable of leaving large discretion to national states. Accordingly, their inclusion in the Recommendation may raise similar concerns as were discussed above with regard to the grounds for detention included in the *1999 Guidelines*. Again, the principle of proportionality – detention should not be resorted to if alternative measures are feasible in the individual case – should curb a too extensive use of these grounds. In a similar vein as the HRC has done with regard to the detention of asylum seekers for administrative convenience, the Council of Europe Commissioner for Human Rights, Thomas Hammerberg, has expressed concern over the use of detention

---

imprisonment of a child shall be in conformity with the law and shall be used only as a measure of last resort and for the shortest appropriate period of time. Cf. the UN Committee on the Rights of the Child, *Concluding Observations adopted in respect of reports submitted by States parties to the Committee on the Rights of the Child: France*, 36th Session, UN Doc. CRC/C/15/Add. 240, 4 June 2004, par. 29–30. But see *D. and E. v Australia* where the HRC did not consider the detention of minors as a separate issue under Article 24 of the ICCPR.

[75] Council of Europe, Committee of Ministers, Recommendation Rec (2003) 5 of the Committee to member states on measures of detention of asylum seekers, Strasbourg, 16 April 2003.
[76] Ibid. General Provisions 4 and 5.
[77] Ibid. General Provision 6. Such as monitoring requirements, release on bail, stay in open reception centres and the provision of a guarantor. See Explanatory Memorandum to the Recommendation.
[78] See General Provision 3 of the Recommendation.

in so-called fast-track procedures, and urged governments to consider alternatives to detention.[79]

The Recommendation furthermore stipulates that the detention of asylum seekers should be reviewed regularly by a court.[80] Moreover, detained asylum seekers have the right to contact the UNHCR, a legal representative, NGOs, and family and friends.[81] The remaining provisions of the recommendation deal with guarantees for the mental, spiritual and physical well-being of the asylum seekers, and there are some special provisions with regard to minors, who, it is stipulated, should only be detained as a measure of last resort and for the shortest possible time.[82]

With regard to the detention of irregular immigrants who are subject to removal orders, the *Twenty Guidelines on Forced Return*, adopted by the Committee of Ministers, contain some relevant provisions.[83] In the first place, they require that a person may only be deprived of his liberty in accordance with a procedure prescribed by law with a view to ensuring that a removal order will be executed. In addition, it must be ascertained, after a careful examination of the necessity of the detention in each individual case, that compliance with the removal order cannot be ensured as effectively by resorting to non-custodial measures such as supervision systems, the requirement to report regularly to the authorities, bail or other guarantee systems.[84]

The latter requirement of an individualised examination of the necessity to detain in order to secure removal is deemed "part of a broader protection against arbitrariness."[85] It is further elaborated by stipulating that detention pending removal shall be for a time which is as short as possible and in any case justified only for as long as removal arrangements are in progress and executed with due diligence by the national authorities.[86] Furthermore, the person

---

[79] T. Hammerberg, *Memorandum by the Commissioner for Human Rights for the Council of Europe following his visit to the united Kingdom from 5–8 February and 31 March – 2 April 2008*, CommDH (2008) 23, Strasbourg 18 September 2008, 2.
[80] General Provision 5.
[81] General Provisions 16, 17 and 18.
[82] General Provisions 20–23.
[83] Committee of Minsters, *20 Guidelines on Forced Return*, CM (2005) 40 final, Strasbourg, 9 May 2005. These Guidelines are not applicable to detention upon arrival. See Ad hoc Committee of Experts on the Legal Aspects of Territorial Asylum, Refugees and Stateless Persons (CAHAR), *Comments on the 20 Guidelines on Forced Return*, 925 Meeting on 4 May 2005, CM (2005) 40 Addendum 40 final, Strasbourg, 20 May 2005, 2.
[84] *20 Guidelines on Forced Return*, Guideline 6(1).
[85] See CAHAR, *Comments on the 20 Guidelines on Forced Return*, 25.
[86] *20 Guidelines on Forced Return*, Guideline 7 and 8.

detained shall be informed promptly about the reasons for his detention in a language that he understands and he has the right to have access to a lawyer from the very outset of the detention.[87]

The administrative decision to detain is to be reviewed at regular intervals by the authorities and in the case of prolonged detention such reviews are to be subject to the supervision of a judicial authority.[88] Requirements regarding the immigration detainee's entitlement to resort to proceedings by which the lawfulness of the detention is decided upon by a court are similar to those flowing from Article 9 ICCPR, except for the explicit addition that legal aid should be provided for in accordance with national legislation.[89]

Similar guarantees have been formulated by the Commissioner for Human Rights and the European Committee for the Prevention of Torture (CPT), also with regard to detention upon arrival.[90] The CPT has repeatedly emphasised in several of its reports that in the case of immigration detention, the same procedural guarantees shall apply as with regard to other categories of deprivation of liberty.[91] Especially in waiting zones at airports this is often not the case, and the CPT cautions that this situation cannot be justified. It does not attach crucial weight to the typical argument made by states that the persons located in such places can leave at any time by taking any international flight of their choice: a stay in a transit, or international zone, can under certain circumstances amount to deprivation of liberty.[92]

The origin of the *20 Guidelines on Forced Return* lies in a Parliamentary Assembly Recommendation, urging the member states of the Council of Europe to guarantee, under regular supervision by the judge, the strict necessity and the proportionality of the use and continuation of detention for the enforcement of the deportation order, and to set the length of detention at a

---

[87] Ibid., Guideline 6(2).
[88] Ibid., Guideline 8.
[89] Ibid., Guideline 9.
[90] Commissioner for Human Rights, *Recommendation concerning the rights of aliens wishing to enter a Council of Europe member state and the enforcement of expulsion orders*, CommDH/Rec (2001) 1, Strasbourg, 19 September 2001, 3–4.
[91] See for example CPT *13th General Report on the CPT's activities covering the period 1 January 2002 to 31 July 2003*, CPT/Inf (2003) 35 (Strasbourg, 10 September 2003), 10; *Rapport au Gouvernement de la République française relatif a la visite effectuée en France par le Comité européen pour la prévention de la torture et des peines ou traitements inhumains ou dégradants du 17 au 21 juin 2002*. CPT/Inf (2003), Strasbourg, 16 December 2003, 40; and, more recently, *Rapport au Gouvernement de la Roumanie relatif à la visite effectuée en Roumanie par le Comité européen pour la prévention de la torture et des peines ou traitements inhumains ou dégradants du 8 au 19 juin 2006*, CPT/Inf (2008) 41 (Strasbourg, 11 December 2008).
[92] CPT Standards (2003), par. 25.

maximum of one month.⁹³ The recommendation by the Parliamentary Assembly also insists on member states favouring alternatives to detention that place less restrictions on freedom, such as compulsory residence orders or other forms of monitoring, such as the obligation to register.⁹⁴ Finally, it is important to note that the importance of the proportionality principle requiring an individual assessment of each case as well as the consideration of alternatives to detention has recently been underlined once again by the Commissioner for Human Rights in his report following his visit to the Netherlands.⁹⁵

7.5 Emerging EC Law on the Detention of Immigrants and Asylum Seekers

Although the focus of this chapter is on international human rights law, a few brief remarks on EC law are included, not only in order to obtain a fuller picture of the legal constraints which Member States may experience in resorting to immigration detention, but also because it provides an apt opportunity to observe how international legal norms operate in an allegedly post-national context.

In view of the discussion in the previous chapters on EU citizenship, it should not come as a surprise that the administrative detention of EU citizens pursuant to immigration law can only be highly exceptional practice, just to be resorted to if they constitute a genuine threat to public policy.⁹⁶ With regard to third-country nationals the situation is quite different, and in this context Daniel Wilsher argues that "so far as the Union legislature is concerned, we have seen some of the same attachment to detention as a means of policing the EU border that traditional states have maintained."⁹⁷ In the first place it should be underlined that – in accordance with general human rights law – the Charter of Fundamental Rights of the European

---

[93] Parliamentary Assembly, *Recommendation 1547 (2002) 1, Expulsion procedures in conformity with human rights and enforced with respect for safety and dignity*, Text adopted by the Parliamentary Assembly of the Council of Europe on 22 January 2002.

[94] Ibid.

[95] T. Hammerberg, *Report by the Commissioner for Human Rights for the Council of Europe following his visit to the Netherlands from 21–25 September 2008*, CommDH (2009) 2, Strasbourg, 11 March 2009, 15–17.

[96] ECJ Case C-215/03, *Salah Oulane v. Minister voor Vreemdelingenzaken en Integratie* [2005] ECR I-1215, par. 40–44.

[97] D. Wilsher, *The Liberty of Foreigners: A History, Law and Politics of Immigration Detention* (Nijmegen: Wolf Legal Publishers, 2009), 145.

Union permits limitations on the right to personal liberty only if these limitations are proportionate and necessary, and genuinely meet objectives of general interest that are recognised by the Union.[98] Member States, when implementing EC law, are furthermore bound to respect fundamental rights as guaranteed by the ECHR and as they result from the constitutional traditions common to the Member States, as general principles of Community law.

At present three instruments of EC law contain provisions on immigration detention. Article 7 of Council Directive 2003/9/EC on minimum standards for the reception of asylum seekers stipulates that, as a general rule, asylum seekers have the right to internal free movement within the territory of the host Member State.[99] Restrictions on free movement are provided for in paragraph 2, and in paragraph 3 Member States are given the power to detain applicants ("confine to a particular place") when this proves necessary, for example for legal reasons or reasons of public order in accordance with national law. As such, the provision on detention in the Reception Directive merely *authorises* the use of detention by national states, leaving the sovereign power to detain largely intact.[100] Still, the codification of a general norm of free movement within the state together with the requirement that the detention be a necessary measure can be used to challenge certain national practices, such as – again – detention for mere administrative expediency in the context of fast-track procedures.

If possible, Directive 2005/85/EC on minimum standards on procedures for granting and withdrawing refugee status provides even less safeguards for the individual, by merely requiring that Member States shall not hold a person in detention for the sole reason that he or she is an applicant for asylum.[101] As such, the Directive echoes a marginalised understanding of the norms that Member States are already bound to apply under general international law. By requiring that Member States shall ensure that there is a possibility of a speedy judicial review of the detention, it confirms a general and widely accepted principle of international human rights law.

Compared with the Directives on Reception Conditions and Procedures, the recently adopted Returns Directive contains more legal safeguards for the

---

[98] Articles 6 and 52(1) of the Charter.
[99] Council Directive 2003/9/EC of 27 January 2003 laying down minimum standards for the reception of asylum seekers, OJ L 31/18, 6 February 2003.
[100] Wilsher (2009), 159.
[101] Article 18 (1) of Council Directive 2005/85/EC of 1 December 2005 laying down minimum standards on procedures in Member States for granting and withdrawing refugee status, OJ L 326/13, 13 December 2005.

individual.[102] As such, in some respects, it provides a better reflection of international legal norms. Nevertheless, there are also aspects to the provisions on detention in the Directive that are problematic under international law, as we shall see below. According to Article 2(1), the Directive applies to third-country nationals staying illegally in the territory of a Member State. However, Member States may decide to exclude from the scope of the Directive third-country nationals who are refused entry at an external border, or those who have been intercepted or apprehended by the authorities in connection with the irregular crossing of an external border of that Member State. In Article 15, Member States are given the power to detain a third-country national who is subject to return procedures (also provided for by the Directive in Article 8) in order to prepare the return or carry out the removal process, but only if *other sufficient but less coercive measures* cannot be applied *effectively in a specific case*. As such, the Returns Directive clearly requires detention to be a proportionate measure. Also the Preamble (recital 16) explicitly declares that the use of detention for the purpose of removal should be limited and subject to the principle of proportionality with regard to the means and the objectives used. Detention should furthermore last for as short a period as possible and only be maintained as long as removal arrangements are in progress and executed with due diligence. If removal is no longer possible, detention ceases to be justified. Nevertheless, the clarity with which the principle of proportionality is thus introduced in the Directive is somewhat obscured by the way in which Article 15 enumerates two permissible but non-exhaustive grounds for detention: detention is allowed in particular when (a) there is a risk of absconding or (b) the third-country national avoids or hampers the preparation of the return or removal proceedings. Questions can be raised about the very fact of including these grounds for detention, as it seems that a consistent application of the principle of proportionality in itself aims to ensure that detention in the context of removal can *only* be resorted to if there is a risk of absconding. But while the first ground for detention can thus be seen as a mere affirmation of the importance of proportionality when it comes to the use of detention, the fact that the two enlisted grounds for detention are non-exhaustive is a cause for concern. In addition, with regard to the second ground for detention it should be noted that detention can never be used as a punitive measure or a means to pressurize the individual to co-operate in the removal proceedings.

---

[102] Directive 2008/115/EC of the European Parliament and the Council of 16 December 2008 on common standards and procedures in Member States for returning illegally staying third-country nationals.

The Directive also provides for a speedy judicial review of the lawfulness of the detention if it has been ordered by an administrative authority, which review is either to be provided by the authorities, or results from proceedings which are taken by the third-country national to challenge the lawfulness of the detention. If the detention is not lawful, the third-county national shall be released immediately. The Directive explicitly expands the *habeas corpus* requirement by requiring that the detention is reviewed regularly at reasonable intervals, either on application by the third country national or *ex officio*. While this review is to be carried out by the administrative authorities, in the case of prolonged detention periods, it should be subject to judicial review. Nevertheless, in Article 18 Member States are given the possibility to derogate from the requirement that judicial review takes place speedily in the case of an emergency situation, which is defined as a situation in which an exceptionally large number of third-country nationals to be returned places an unforeseen heavy burden on the Member State.

The most problematic aspect of the Directive may well be the maximum period that it sets to detention: 6 months with a possible extension of 12 months if the delay in removal results from a lack of co-operation by the third-country national or if it is due to delays in obtaining the necessary documents from third countries. In connection with the excessive time-limit of 18 months, the Working Group on Arbitrary Detention has publicly expressed its concern, together with some NGOs.[103] It is worth noting that there are not many Member States that permit detention to last longer than 18 months at present, and there is a real risk that the extremely lenient standard laid down by the Directive shall be used to lower standards significantly in this respect.[104] Moreover, the Working Group has called attention to the fact that it would also be permitted under the Directive to detain unaccompanied children, victims of human trafficking, and other vulnerable groups. Indeed, with regard to especially vulnerable persons the Directive only requires Member States to take account of their special situation as regards the conditions of detention whereas with regard to minors, it merely repeats the requirement that detention should only be resorted to as a last resort and for the shortest possible time, and it obliges Member States to provide leisure activities and access to education, depending on the length of their stay. With regard to conditions of detention generally, the Directive stipulates that immigration detainees shall

---

[103] UN Human Rights Council, *Report of the Working Group of Arbitrary Detention*, 16 February 2009, par. 66.

[104] See A. Baldaccini, "The Return and Removal of Irregular Migrants under EU Law: An Analysis of the Returns Directive," *European Journal of Migration and Law* 11 (2009), 14.

be held in specialised facilities. If this is not possible, they should be held separate from ordinary prisoners. It furthermore gives immigration detainees the right to information on their rights and obligations, and it obliges Member States to allow detainees to contact legal representatives, family members and consular representatives.

It seems justified to conclude that existing EC law does not add to the human rights norms that Member States are already bound to apply under general international law. With regard to the Returns Directive it has been argued that the provisions on detention in the final Directive have improved significantly if compared with the original draft in which mandatory detention provisions were included.[105] Even though this is undoubtedly true – mandatory detention provisions as such being in violation of Article 9 ICCPR – the Returns Directive and the way in which it was finally agreed upon can also be seen as archetypical of the shortcomings of EC law-making in the field of immigration policy: the very process of decision-making – even when Parliament is involved – is not sufficiently transparent, democratic accountability remains limited,[106] and harmonisation seems to be attainable only when the content of decision-making corresponds primarily to the *national* sovereign interest.

7.6 *The Right to Personal Liberty vs. Territorial Sovereignty*

This chapter has shown that international human rights norms place limits on the sovereign state's power to resort to immigration detention. The decision to detain immigrants and asylum seekers needs to satisfy certain substantial conditions, as well as some essential procedural requirements. Immigration detention is only allowed with an eye to specific purposes which are all narrowly related to the administration of immigration policies. These purposes consist of regulating entry and securing expulsion, and they have acquired an even stricter interpretation when it comes to a specific category of immigrants: refugees or asylum seekers. In any case, detention to deter or penalise immigrants is not allowed. Neither is it permitted to use immigration detention for purposes related to criminal law. Abuses of the law on immigration to

---

[105] Baldaccini (2009), 13.
[106] See on this Diego Acosta, who argues that the co-decision procedure did not guarantee enough transparency and accountability in the decision-making process owing to the institutionalisation of 'trilogues'. D. Acosta, "The Good, the Bad and the Ugly in EU Migration Law: Is the European Parliament Becoming Bad and Ugly? (The Adoption of Directive 2008/115: The Returns Directive)," *European Journal of Migration and Law* 11 (2009).

evade judicial safeguards and holding aliens in detention indefinitely have been explicitly addressed by the Working Group on Arbitrary Detention, and this body has repeatedly expressed concern about improper and discriminatory use of immigration laws by national states in order to circumvent the presumption of innocence and related judicial guarantees.[107]

Furthermore, detention should be a proportional measure with regard to the permissible purposes that it serves. According to the Working Group on Arbitrary Detention, one of the main causes of arbitrary deprivation of liberty is precisely the non-observance of the principle of proportionality in the relationship between the gravity of the measure taken and the situation concerned.[108] The requirement that detention needs to be proportional is to be found in almost all international instruments, either expressly articulated, or implied by the prohibition on arbitrary detention, or alternatively by formulating specific constraints on the use of immigration detention, such as, for example, the requirement that alternative measures need to have been considered before a state can resort to detention.

By categorising immigration detention as a legitimate form of state control, international human rights law reaffirms the sovereign right of the state to control the entry and sojourn of foreign nationals on its territory. However, the presumption that the regulation of the entry and sojourn of non-nationals is a matter falling within the sovereign prerogatives of the national state does not impede international law from recognising and safeguarding the rights of immigration detainees. Although immigration detention *per se* is not in violation of international legal norms, states may not resort to detention solely on the ground that a person does not have the right to enter or stay on national territory. International human rights law requires that there must be some substantive basis for detention in each individual case. In addition, international legal norms oblige national states to provide for a judicial procedure to review the lawfulness of immigration detention. In particular with regard to immigration detainees, the Working Group on Arbitrary Detention has placed considerable emphasis on states' duty to guarantee the effectiveness of the right provided by Article 9(4) ICCPR.[109] Moreover, according to the HRC, the scope of the review required by the this provision may not be limited to a

---

[107] UN Commission on Human Rights, *Report of the Working Group on Arbitrary Detention*, Sixtieth Session, Item 11(a) of the provisional agenda, E/CN.4/2004/3, 15 December 2003, 17, 18 and 20. These concerns became more prominent after 11 September 2001.

[108] Ibid., 18.

[109] UN Commission on Human Rights, *Report of the Working Group on Arbitrary Detention*, Sixty-second session, Item 11 (a) of the provisional agenda, E/CN.4/2006/7, 12 December 2006, 2.

mere review as to whether the detention is in compliance with domestic law, but it should include reviewing whether the detention is in accordance with the requirements of Article 9(1) ICCPR. As a result, the court in question should evaluate the case in the light of the individual circumstances, taking due account of the proportionality and necessity of the detention, instead of merely assessing whether national immigration legislation has been correctly applied.

By balancing the state's sovereign right to control the entry and residence of foreign nationals in its territory with the individual's right to personal liberty, international legal norms that apply to immigration detention fully acknowledge the individual interests that are involved in sovereignty's territorial frame. As such, they have the potential to undermine the perceived neutrality and self-evidence of sovereignty's territorial frame in modern law. Their consistent application to national practices of immigration detention, especially in view of the important procedural guarantees that they contain, could result in diminishing the immunity of territorial sovereignty against forces of legal correction. The way in which this particular process operates will be further dealt with in chapter 9.

Nevertheless, for now it is also important to point at some shortcomings in the international legal framework as was dealt with in this chapter. When it comes to the specific practice of immigration detention, the interests of asylum seekers are addressed far more often than those of irregular immigrants. This recurring emphasis on asylum seekers and refugees in international norms and documents that address the administrative detention of non-nationals, however understandable in view of their vulnerable position and particular need for protection, also runs a risk of resulting in an affirmation of the perception of territorial sovereignty as the site of legal and unproblematic violence when it comes to irregular migrants. A good example of this is to be found in the UNHCR Executive Committee's criticism regarding the failure on the part of states to make the necessary distinction between asylum seekers and illegal migrants, "therewith exposing the former to such control measures as automatic detention for indeterminate periods".[110] Although undoubtedly not the intention of the Executive Committee, remarks such as these, which subsequently fail to address the more fundamental sovereign assumptions that underlie the practice of immigration detention as a whole, may provide the impression that automatic detention for indeterminate periods of irregular migrants remains a sovereign prerogative.

---

[110] UNHCR, "Detention of Asylum Seekers and Refugees: The Framework, the Problem and Recommended Practice" (1999), 164–165.

In addition, many of the international documents that explicitly address the practice of immigration detention, such as those by the Council of Europe or the Working Group on Arbitrary Detention, articulate recommendations to states, or are in another way directed towards states. They do not accord rights to individuals and appealing to them or demanding their implementation by those who would supposedly benefit from them is not possible. Neither do they in themselves compel states to change existing policies.[111] An exception is Article 9 ICCPR, but the HRC in its rulings on individual cases under the Optional Protocol is sometimes simply ignored by states, of which Australia's stance affords a discouraging example.[112] Indeed, according to the UN Special Rapporteur on Migrant Workers, international human rights obligations of states are inadequately translated into practice at the national level. Measures aimed at stopping irregular immigration are all too often taken without due regard for international norms, standards and principles.[113] They undermine migrants' basic rights, including the right to be protected against arbitrary deprivation of liberty: detention is often resorted to without due regard to the individual history of the migrant; broad powers to detain are not checked by procedural guarantees; and detention is often very lengthy or even indefinite.[114]

---

[111] See for instance Australia's position as quoted in the *2003 Report of the Working Group on Arbitrary Detention*: "Immigration detention is an essential element underpinning the integrity of Australia's migration programme and the protection of Australia's borders. There is no recognition in the Working Group's report of the role Australia plays every year in the resettlement of thousands of refugees around the world. In conclusion, the Government considered that, yet again, a United Nations human rights body had produced a report misguidedly critical of Australia." (UN Commission on Human Rights, 15 December 2003, 15).

[112] In spite of several decisions in which the HRC found Australia's detention policy to be in violation of Article 9 ICCPR, the Australian Attorney-General believes that the Australian policies are consistent with its obligations under the Covenant. It holds on to the view that "The detention of unlawful non-citizens is necessary to uphold the integrity of Australia's migration system. It also ensures that such persons are available for processing of any protection claims, essential identity, security, character and health checks, and removal if found to have no right to remain in Australia. This approach is consistent with the fundamental principle of sovereignty in international law, which includes the right of a State to control the entry of non-citizens into its territory and to deport from its territory such aliens as it no longer finds acceptable." See the response of the Australian Government to the views of the Committee in *D. and E. v. Australia*, available at the website of the Attorney General at http://www.ag.gov.au.

[113] UN Commission on Human Rights, *Report of the Special Rapporteur, Ms. Gabriela Rodríguez Pizarro, submitted pursuant to Commission on Human Rights resolution 2002/62*, Fifty-ninth session, Item 14 (a) of the provisional agenda, E/CN.4/2003/85, 30 December 2002, 11.

[114] Ibid., 2 and 3.

In the European context, Member States' frequent and widespread lack of concern for the reasonableness, necessity and proportionality of immigration detention results in *de facto* violations of Article 9 ICCPR.[115] EC legislation has done very little to challenge these practices, and as such European law-making in this area reflects the conflicting tendencies that underlie the Europeanisation of national immigration policies, as elaborated upon in chapter 5. Furthermore, national judicial procedures such as at the highest administrative court in the Netherlands may well fall below the standards imposed by Article 9(4) ICCPR, as that court has limited the scope to review the lawfulness of detention in favour of the executive by repeatedly arguing that it is not for judges to assess what is essentially the proportionality of immigration detention.[116] The reservation by the United Kingdom to decide whether or not to comply with some of the *20 Guidelines on Forced Return* provides another clear example of national practice risking violations of binding international norms, because the requirements of some of the guidelines to which it made a reservation flow directly from Article 9 ICCPR.[117] An investigation into the way in which international human rights are actually implemented at the national constitutional level falls outside the scope of this book. Yet, in order to investigate the way in which international human rights law may more coercively restrain the state's power to resort to immigration detention, we shall now turn to the case law of the ECtHR.

---

[115] For example Hungary where the detention of asylum seekers depends on "accidental circumstances and arbitrary decisions of the authorities". T. Szabó et al., "Chapter 12: Hungary," in: *Foreigners in European Prisons*, eds. A.M. van Kalmthout, F.B.A.M. Hofstee-van der Meulen and F. Dünkel (Nijmegen: Wolf Legal Publishers, 2007), 444–445. Moreover, irregular migrants are detained on the sole ground that they have been found on Hungarian territory without a valid residence permit. Commissioner for Human Rights of the Council of Europe, *Follow-Up Report on Hungary (2002–2005), Assessment of the progress made in implementing the recommendations of the Council of Europe Commissioner for Human Rights*, CommDH (2006) 11, Strasbourg, 29 March 2006, 20.

[116] See Afdeling bestuursrechtspraak van de Raad van State, 6 September 2005, 200507112/1, JV 2005/452 and 16 August 2005, 200505443/1, JV 2005/396.

[117] The Permanent Representative of the United Kingdom indicated that, in accordance with Article 10.2c of the Rules of Procedure for the meetings of the Ministers' Deputies, he reserved the right of his Government to decide whether or not to comply with Guidelines 2, 4, 6, 7, 8, 11 and 16.

Chapter 8

The ECtHR: Detention as a 'Necessary Adjunct' to an 'Undeniable Sovereign Right'?

8.1 *Introduction*

We have seen in chapter 3 that the ECtHR and its enforcement mechanisms are by far the most effective and extensive of global and regional systems for the protection of international human rights. Some have argued that the ECtHR has become the Constitutional Court for Europe, promoting national Convention compliance which results in convergence in the "deep structure of national constitutional, legal and political systems."[1] As such, the key function of the Court lies in ensuring that national administrative and judicial procedures conform to "pan-European Convention standards ('constitutional justice') rather than affording "each deserving applicant with a personal remedy (individual justice')."[2] In addition, greater convergence between national systems in Europe with regard to the protection of fundamental rights is made possible by the fact that contracting parties to the Convention generally abide by the judgments of the Court, encouraged as they are by a number of pressures and interests, not the least important of which is that the Convention provides for important executive functions alongside its judicial functions.[3] The special position of the ECtHR in Europe makes it an exemplary site to conduct an analysis of the way in which national states are in a real sense restrained by international legal norms that aim at the protection of the human rights of immigration detainees. This is even more so as recent years have seen

---

[1] S. Greer, *The European Convention on Human Rights: Achievements, Problems and Prospects* (Cambridge: Cambridge University Press, 2006), 317.
[2] S. Greer, "Constitutionalizing Adjudication under the European Convention on Human Rights," *Oxford Journal of Legal Studies* 23 (2003), 405 and 406.
[3] Greer (2006), 317. The execution of the judgments of the ECtHR is supervised by the Committee of Ministers of the Council of Europe. Note that the 'Constitution' that the ECHR provides is only for a "partial polity" as it lacks legislative powers. See Greer (2006), 317.

Galina Cornelisse, Immigration Detention and Human Rights, pp. 277–312.
© 2010 Koninklijke Brill NV. Printed in the Netherlands.

a burgeoning in the amount of Strasbourg judgments in cases concerning immigration detention.

Whereas the previous chapter gave a wide overview of relevant international human rights law with regard to the right to personal liberty in immigration detention cases, the larger part of my investigation of the case law of the ECtHR below shall focus on the substantive conditions that need to be fulfilled in order for a state to have lawful recourse to immigration detention. I shall set the stage by addressing some general aspects of Article 5, the provision safeguarding the right to liberty in the Convention. When does the Court consider Article 5 to be applicable in the immigration context and how does that provision relate to national legislation are questions that shall be addressed in section 8.2. In section 8.3, the procedural guarantees which Article 5 provides are briefly discussed. Next, I will analyse how the Court interprets the prohibition on arbitrary deprivations of liberty in the immigration context, and we shall see that the Court's case law in this field lacks considerations of proportionality and necessity (section 8.4). Its approach to immigration detention is then compared with the method by which it generally interprets the Convention, as well as with the protection it offers to another category of individuals who may be deprived of their liberty under Article 5 ECHR (section 8.5). In the conclusions to this chapter (section 8.6), I shall argue that the Court's case law on immigration detention exemplifies the limits of the contemporary European system for the protection of human rights when it comes to those who are 'out of place' in the global territorial order.

8.2 *Immigration Detention and the Right to Personal Liberty in the ECHR*

In the ECHR, the right to personal liberty has been laid down in Article 5. The general rule set out by this provision is that everyone has the right to personal liberty, but it permits a limited number of exceptions to the general rule, under subparagraphs 1(a-f):

> Article 5(1) ECHR: Everyone has the right to liberty and security of person.
> No one shall be deprived of his liberty save in the following cases and in accordance with a procedure prescribed by law:
> (a) the lawful detention of a person after conviction by a competent court;
> (b) the lawful arrest or detention of a person for non-compliance with the lawful order of a court or in order to secure the fulfilment of an obligation prescribed by law;
> (c) the lawful arrest or detention of a person effected for the purpose of bringing him before the competent authority on reasonable suspicion of having committed an offence or when it is reasonably considered necessary to prevent his committing an offence or fleeing after having done so;

(d) the detention of a minor by lawful order for the purpose of educational supervision or his lawful detention for the purpose of bringing him before the competent legal authority;
(e) the lawful detention of persons for the prevention of the spreading of infectious diseases, of persons of unsound mind, alcoholics or drug addicts or vagrants;
(f) the lawful arrest or detention of a person to prevent his effecting an unauthorised entry into the country or of a person against whom action is being taken with a view to deportation or extradition.

The list of permissible cases of deprivation of liberty under Article 5(1) is exhaustive: if an actual case of detention or arrest cannot be classified as belonging to one of the categories mentioned in this provision, it is not permitted by the ECHR. The state's exercise of its power to deprive individuals of their liberty is further restricted by the notion that only a narrow interpretation of the exceptions to the right to liberty is consistent with the aim of Article 5, which, in conformity with general international law, consists of protecting the individual from *arbitrary* deprivations of liberty.[4] In this context it should also be highlighted that the concept of security in Article 5 has no independent meaning but the terms 'liberty' and 'security' in this provision must be read as a whole, with the notion of security explicitly denoting the protection against arbitrary interferences with the liberty of a person.[5]

Under subparagraph 1(f) of Article 5, states are allowed to control the liberty of aliens in the immigration context. We have seen in the previous chapter that also under general international human rights law, immigration detention can under certain circumstances be a legitimate measure, provided that it serves either the regulation of entry by foreign nationals, or their removal from national territory. Analogous to these general international norms, the European system for the protection of human rights also recognises the regulation of entry and removal as legitimate reasons for states to have recourse to immigration detention. Immigration detention based on any other reasons is prohibited by the ECHR, which is corroborated by Article 18 ECHR, which contains a prohibition on using the permitted restrictions by the Convention to the rights guaranteed by it for any purpose other than for which they have been described.

---

[4] See *Winterwerp v. the Netherlands*, 24 October 1979, A-33; *D.G. v. Ireland*, 16 May 2002, Reports 2002-III, par. 74; *Manzoni v. Italy*, 1 July 1997, Reports 1997-IV, par. 25; *Van der Leer v. the Netherlands*, 21 February 1990, A-170-A, 22; *Wassink v. the Netherlands*, 27 September 1990, A-185-A, par. 24; *Quinn v. France*, 22 March 1995, A-311, par. 42; *K.-F. v. Germany*, 27 November 1997, Reports 1997-VII, par. 70; and *Labita v. Italy*, 6 April 2000, Reports 2000-IV, par. 170.
[5] ECommHR, *Adler and Bivas v. the Federal Republic of Germany*, 16 July 1976, Yearbook of the European Convention on Human Rights 20 (1977), 102, par. 146.

8.2.1 *The Immigration Context: Deprivations or Restrictions upon Liberty?*

We have already seen in the previous chapter that detention as a result of immigration law enforcement may at times contain elements of ambiguity as it is not always unequivocally clear whether one can categorise a certain situation as a deprivation of liberty or as a mere restriction on freedom of movement. While the line between deprivations of liberty and restrictions on movement can be difficult to draw in purely 'domestic' situations as well,[6] in the area of immigration law and policy, which is a context defined by the very concept of human movement, these difficulties have generally played a more prominent role. Thus, sovereign states have repeatedly insisted before the ECtHR that holding aliens in the international zone of an airport does not involve a deprivation of liberty as these individuals are free to leave such an area in order to travel wherever they desire, as long as it is not into their sovereign territory.[7] Alternatively, they have argued that regular constitutional guarantees, therewith including those contained in the ECHR, do not apply in transit zones, as such areas purportedly benefit from an 'extraterritorial status'.[8]

In the case of *Amuur* the Court decided that to hold asylum seekers in the international zone of an airport upon arrival constitutes a restriction of liberty which under certain circumstances can turn into a deprivation of liberty.[9] According to the Court, a state cannot refute the existence of deprivation of liberty with the argument that the asylum seekers are not on its territory or that they are free to leave at any time. The possibility for asylum seekers to leave voluntarily the country where they wish to take refuge does not exclude the existence of a restriction of liberty, which can under certain circumstances turn into a deprivation of liberty.[10]

> Holding aliens in the international zone does indeed involve a restriction upon liberty, but one which is not in every respect comparable to that which obtains in centres for the detention of aliens pending deportation. Such confinement, accompanied by suitable safeguards for the persons concerned, is acceptable only in order to enable States to prevent unlawful immigration while complying with their international obligations, particularly under the 1951 Geneva Convention Relating to the Status of Refugees and the European Convention on Human Rights. States' legitimate concern to foil the increasingly frequent

---

[6] See *Guzzardi v. Italy*, 6 November 1980, A-39.
[7] See for example the argument raised by the Polish government in *Shamsa v. Poland*, 27 November 2003, Appl. Nos. 45355/99 and 45357/99, par. 38.
[8] Ibid., par. 45.
[9] *Amuur v. France*, 25 June 1996, Reports 1996-III.
[10] Ibid., par. 48.

attempts to circumvent immigration restrictions must not deprive asylum-seekers of the protection afforded by these conventions.[11]

Taking into account that the applicants were placed under strict and constant police surveillance and had no access to legal or social assistance, the Court concluded that their situation amounted to a deprivation of liberty which fell under the scope of Article 5 ECHR.[12] The Court's judgment in *Amuur* is of fundamental importance in that it takes due account of the individual interests that are involved in territorial sovereignty. Although the Court recognised the sovereign right of states to regulate the entry of foreigners, it acknowledged at the same time the actualities of individual movement in a global political system based on territoriality. As such, it effectively dismissed as artificial the argument that asylum seekers are free to go wherever they want as long as it is not on national sovereign territory – an argument that is at any rate questionable when made from a narrow, internal perspective, but which loses all validity when reminded of the global territorial order, where most people are anything but free to go wherever they please.

The Court decided the case of *Riad and Idiab* along similar lines. This case concerned two rejected asylum seekers who, according to the Belgian Government, had been "released from detention" after which they were taken to the transit zone of Brussels National Airport. There they spent eleven and fifteen days respectively, before they were deported. The Belgian government claimed that "the only restriction on the liberty of the applicants consisted in a prohibition to (re)enter Belgian territory."[13] Referring to *Amuur*, the Court held that:

> le maintien d'étrangers dans la zone internationale comporte une restriction à la liberté qui ne saurait être assimilée en tous points à celle subie dans des centres de rétention. Toutefois, un tel maintien n'est acceptable que s'il est assorti de garanties adéquates pour les personnes qui en font l'objet et ne se prolonge pas de manière excessive. Dans le cas contraire, la simple restriction à la liberté se transforme en privation de liberté.[14]

As such, according to the Court, the mere possibility of the applicants leaving the country voluntarily did not exclude a deprivation of liberty. Indeed, on account of the time the applicants had spent in the transit zone, taken together with the fact that they were sent there after having been detained in a regular

---

[11] Ibid. par. 43.
[12] Ibid., par. 45 and 49.
[13] *Riad and Idiab v. Belgium*, 24 January 2008, Appl. Nos. 29787/03 and 29810/03, par 66.
[14] Ibid., par. 68.

detention centre, the Court found that their situation amounted to a deprivation of liberty in the sense of Article 5. Similarly, in *Rashed*, the Court resolutely dismissed the claim by the Czech authorities that the pre-deportation detention of the applicant was 'voluntary' as he, being an 'economic migrant', should have been fully aware that his appeal against the rejection of his application for asylum was futile and he could thus have returned voluntarily to his country of origin at any moment.[15]

Nevertheless, in *Mahdid and Haddar* the Court took a somewhat different approach. In this case, concerning two asylum seekers whose applications had been dismissed by the Austrian government, the Court judged that the applicants' stay at Vienna airport fell outside the scope of Article 5 ECHR.[16] After the applicants' requests for asylum had been dismissed, they destroyed their travel documents so that they could not be removed. This – "a free choice for which the Contracting State cannot in any way be held responsible" – combined with the circumstances that the applicants remained without any special police surveillance; were unimpeded in establishing contact with lawyers and the public media; and had refused better accommodation in that part of the transit zone which was under constant surveillance, led the Court to conclude that their stay at Vienna Airport could not be categorised as a deprivation of liberty.[17] Although it can be argued that this case differed from *Amuur* in important aspects, the Court's quick characterisation of the situation as entirely due to the deliberate choice of applicants is questionable. For if one would assume that the Austrian government had been wrong in dismissing their requests for asylum (which was not a mere theoretical possibility, as it was still possible to appeal against that decision), the deliberate nature of the position of the applicants would have been much more problematic to defend.[18] If the applicants were indeed in need of international protection, the fact that they may have used their situation as a means to exert pressure on the government does not alter that conclusion, but rather becomes quite comprehensible.

8.2.2 'Lawful' Detention in 'Accordance with a Procedure Prescribed by Law'

As with all six permissible grounds of detention under Article 5(1), any deprivation of liberty under subparagraph f has to be 'lawful' and 'in accordance

---

[15] *Rashed v. Czech Republic*, 27 November 2008, Appl. No. 298/07, par. 58 and 68.
[16] *Mahdid and Haddar v. Austria* (inadmissible), 8 December 2005.
[17] Ibid.
[18] R. Lawson, "Annotatie bij Europees Hof voor de Rechten van de Mens 8 December 2005," *Jurisprudentie Vreemdelingenrecht* 7 (2006). See for a similar case in which the court's stance is more defensible: *Mogos v. Romania*, 13 October 2005, Appl. No. 20420/02.

with the law', and as such these requirements apply to so-called pre-admittance detention and pre-deportation detention alike. The Court has generally considered the two requirements together and as a result the distinction between them is often blurred in its judgments.[19] Primarily, they require that the deprivation of liberty conforms to procedural and substantive rules of national law.[20] Thus, the detention must always have a basis in national law. In addition, the domestic laws authorising detention have to be 'sufficiently accessible, precise and foreseeable' in their application to avoid the risk of arbitrary detention.[21] The 'quality of national law' in this senses gains in importance when it concerns the detention of asylum seekers or immigrants.[22]

In the particular context of immigration detention, the Court has repeatedly found violations of the 'legality' requirement – which is perhaps not very surprising in light of the arguments on immigration detention as a form of exceptionalism, which I have addressed in chapter 6. In the case of *Shamsa*, the Court found a breach of Article 5 because the Polish authorities had permitted the deprivation of liberty to last longer than ninety days, even if domestic legislation stipulated that the immigration detainee be released if removal had not been carried out within this period.[23] In another case, this time against Bulgaria, the applicant's detention had been based solely on the order that provided for his deportation. Although the Court conceded that such an order may imply "that he could be subjected to some sort of physical constraint for the purpose of being taken to the border" it did not allow for the possibility "that it additionally authorised his detention for a period which in fact lasted eight days but was apparently not subject to an upper limit."[24] Seeing that such detention was furthermore only possible under Bulgarian law if considered necessary by the authorities – a matter to which the order against the applicant gave no consideration whatsoever – his detention was deemed to be unlawful under Article 5. Similarly, in *Rusu* Austrian legislation only allowed detention if less coercive measures had been considered and not deemed sufficient. As the detention of the applicant was clearly not a measure of last

---

[19] See for example *Lukanov v. Bulgaria*, 20 March 1997, Reports 1997-II, par. 41.
[20] On the importance of this requirement generally: *Riera Blume and others v. Spain*, 14 October 1999, Reports 1999-VII, par. 31–35. Particularly in the context of immigration detention: *Amuur v. France*, par 50; and *Liu v. Russia*, 6 December 2007, par. Appl. No. 42086/05, par. 79.
[21] *Mohd v Greece*, 27 April 2006, Appl. No. 11919/03; *Mubilanzila Mayeka and Kaniki Mitunga v. Belgium*, 12 October 2006, Appl. No. 13178/03; *Sadaykov v. Bulgaria*. 22 May 2008, Appl. No. 75157/01, par. 49; *Shamsa v. Poland*, par. 49; and *Riad and Idiab v. Belgium*, par. 78.
[22] *Amuur v France*, par. 50; and *Rashed v. Czech Republic*, para. 73.
[23] *Shamsa v. Poland*, par. 52.
[24] *Sadaykov v. Bulgaria*, par. 25.

resort, it was in violation of domestic legislation, and as a result the Court decided that the deprivation of liberty was in violation of Article 5.[25] In *Mohd*, the deprivation of liberty was considered unlawful by the Court because no decision whatsoever had been taken with regard to the legal basis of a pre-deportation detention, although the authorities asserted that its legality was guaranteed by the mere fact that deportation procedures were initiated.[26] And in the aforementioned case of *Rashed*, Czech asylum legislation was so vague, especially concerning the periods during which asylum seekers could be detained and the place of detention, that it could not be seen as providing the kind of protection and the legal certainty necessary in order to prevent arbitrary deprivations of liberty.[27]

These cases make clear that compliance with domestic law becomes part of states' Convention-based obligations over which the Court in Strasbourg is competent to exercise jurisdiction.[28] However, when analysing the level of protection offered by the Convention in this respect, it must be taken into account that the scope of its jurisdiction in this sense is subject to certain limits. It is in the first place for the national authorities, notably the courts, to interpret and apply domestic law and who are allowed a certain margin of appreciation in this respect.[29] Thus the Court will generally limit its examination to whether the "interpretationof the legal provisions relied on by the domestic authorities was arbitrary or unreasonable."[30]

Even in the case that a deprivation of liberty is based upon and carried out in accordance with national laws that are sufficiently accessible and precise, a violation of Article 5 ECHR can still occur because the detention is not 'lawful':

> Where the 'lawfulness' of detention is in issue, including the question whether 'a procedure prescribed by law' has been followed, the Convention refers essentially to national law and lays down the obligation to conform to the substantive

---

[25] *Rusu v Austria*, 2 October 2008, Appl. No. 34802/02, par. 54–58.
[26] *Mohd v. Greece*, par. 23. In a more recent case decided against Greece, the Court decided once more that the domestic laws had not been correctly applied in a case concerning the detention of an asylum seeker. See *S.D. v. Greece*, 11 June 2009, Appl. No. 53541/07.
[27] *Rashed v. Czech Republic*, par. 73–76.
[28] And where a Member State of the EU is concerned, Community law must also be taken into consideration to the extent that it is self-executing. See ECommHR, *Caprino v. United Kingdom*, Decision of 3 March 1980, D&R 12, 14.
[29] See *Winterwerp v. the Netherlands*, par. 46; *Barthold v. Germany*, 25 March 1985, A-90, par. 48; *Bozano v. France*, 18 December 1986, A-111, par. 58; and *Kemmache v. France*, 24 November 1994, A-296-C, par. 42. See also K. Reid, *A Practitioner's Guide to the European Convention on Human Rights* (Sweet & Maxwell, 1998), 182.
[30] *Rusu v. Austria*, par. 55.

and procedural rules of national law. Compliance with national law is not, however, sufficient: Article 5 (1) requires in addition that any deprivation of liberty should be in keeping with the purpose of protecting the individual from arbitrariness It is a fundamental principle that no detention which is arbitrary can be compatible with Article 5(1) and the notion of 'arbitrariness' in Article 5(1) extends beyond lack of conformity with national law, so that a deprivation of liberty may be lawful in terms of domestic law but still arbitrary and thus contrary to the Convention.[31]

Thus, the terms 'in accordance with a procedure proscribed by law' and 'lawful' denote a far more fundamental requirement than mere conformity with positive law. They require that any measure depriving the individual of his liberty is compatible with the purpose of Article 5 ECHR: protecting the individual from arbitrariness.[32] Before turning to the way in which the Court fleshes out the prohibition on arbitrariness so as to arrive at the substantive conditions which immigration detention must satisfy in order to be legitimate under the ECHR, I shall first address some important procedural safeguards that Article 5 also provides.

8.3 *Procedural Safeguards against Arbitrary Detention*

The procedural safeguards that are contained in paragraphs 2 to 4 of Article 5 and the right to compensation in the last paragraph of that provision form an inherent part of the right to personal liberty. They read as follows:

> 2. Everyone who is arrested shall be informed promptly, in a language which he understands, of the reasons for his arrest and of any charge against him.
> 3. Everyone arrested or detained in accordance with the provisions of paragraph 1(c) of this article shall be brought promptly before a judge or other officer authorised by law to exercise judicial power and shall be entitled to trial within a reasonable time or to release pending trial. Release may be conditioned by guarantees to appear for trial.
> 4. Everyone who is deprived of his liberty by arrest or detention shall be entitled to take proceedings by which the lawfulness of his detention shall be decided speedily by a court and his release ordered if the detention is not lawful.

---

[31] *Saadi v. United Kingdom*, Grand Chamber judgment 29 January 2008, Appl. No. 13229/03, par. 67. See also *Brogan and others v. the United Kingdom*, 29 November 1989, A-145-B, par. 65; *Winterwerp v. the Netherlands*, par. 45; *Erkalo v. the Netherlands*, 2 September 1998, Reports 1998-VI, par. 52; and *Kawka v. Poland*, 9 January 2001, Appl. No. 25874/94, par. 48.

[32] See, for instance, *Winterwerp v. the Netherlands*, par. 39 and 45; *Bozano v. France*, par. 54; *Bouamar v. Belgium*, 29 February 1988, A-129, par. 47; *Benham v. the United Kingdom*, 10 June 1996, Reports 1996-III, par. 40; and *Chahal v. United Kingdom*, 15 November 1996, Reports 1996-V, par. 118.

5. Everyone who has been the victim of arrest or detention in contravention of the provisions of this article shall have an enforceable right to compensation.

8.3.1 The Right to be Informed of the Reasons for Detention

Paragraph 2 of article 5 contains the elementary safeguard that persons who are deprived of their liberty should know why they are being detained and it is applicable to all categories of deprivation of liberty.[33] Any person arrested should be told, in simple, non-technical language which he or she can understand, the essential legal and factual grounds for the detention.[34] The right to information is closely related to the right of *habeas corpus*, to be discussed below, as only someone who is promptly and adequately informed of the reasons for his or her detention can effectively use the right to challenge its lawfulness.[35] But apart from that, the right to be informed has an independent meaning as well, being the "embodiment of a kind of legitimate confidence in the relations between the individual and the public powers."[36]

Three requirements flow from the obligation laid down in article 5(2) ECHR: the information must be given promptly, it should be complete and correct as regards both the factual and legal grounds, and it ought to be communicated in an intelligible manner. Whether the content and promptness of the information conveyed to the immigration detainee are satisfactory in light of Article 5(2) is to be assessed in each case "according to its special features" and as such it is difficult to deduce general rules from the Court's case law.[37]

In any case, it seems that somebody deprived of his liberty should always be informed of the general reasons *at the moment* of arrest or detention. Only very special circumstances may justify a delay.[38] Detailed written reasons for the detention may be supplied somewhat later, as the Court confirmed in the case of *Čonka*.[39] However, if at the moment of arrest the applicant is only provided with general statements with regard to the grounds for detention, not too much time should lapse before he or she is informed of the specific reasons and correct legal grounds for detention. In *Saadi*, the Court found a violation of Article 5(2) as the applicant had been in immigration detention for some 76 hours before his lawyer was orally provided with the real reasons for

---

[33] *Rusu v. Austria*, par. 36. See also *Van der Leer v. the Netherlands*, par. 27–28.
[34] *Čonka v. Belgium*, 5 February 2002, Reports 2001-II, par. 50.
[35] *Rusu v. Austria*, par. 41. See also *X v. United Kingdom*, 5 November 1981, A-46, par. 66.
[36] See the dissenting opinion of Judge Evrigenis to *X v. United Kingdom*.
[37] *Čonka v. Belgium*, par. 50; and *Rusu v. Austria*, par. 36.
[38] P. van Dijk and G.J.H. van Hoof, *Theory and Practice of the European Convention on Human Rights* (The Hague: Kluwer, 1998), 369.
[39] *Čonka v. Belgium*, par. 47–52.

his detention.[40] The information needs to be complete, which in expulsion cases entails that somebody should not only be informed of the fact that he is detained in order to deport him, but also of the reasons underlying the decision to deport him (also because only in this way can he effectively make use of his right to challenge the lawfulness of his detention).[41] Finally, the reasons for the arrest or the detention need to be communicated in a language which the immigration detainee understands, and if an adequate translation is not provided, Article 5(2) is thereby violated. Thus, in *Rusu*, where it took ten days for the authorities to inform the applicant of the correct legal grounds for her detention in a language that she understood, the Court found a violation of Article 5(2).[42]

8.3.2 Habeas Corpus or the Right to Challenge the Lawfulness of Detention

The remedy of *habeas corpus* in Article 5(4) is a fundamental guarantee, judicial control being implied by "the rule of law and one of the fundamental principles of a democratic society."[43] The right to have the lawfulness of one's detention reviewed exists no matter how short the period of detention is.[44] Legitimate security concerns can never justify a complete lack of any judicial review of the detention.[45] Furthermore, the right to *habeas corpus* should not be "theoretical and effective, but practical and effective" which has led the Court to conclude that Article 5(4) had been violated in cases where the applicants had been deported before they could use the remedy contained in Article 5(4).[46]

In the Strasbourg case law a number of separate guarantees embodied in Article 5(4) have been distinguished. To begin with, the notion of a court in the sense of that provision does not necessarily imply the involvement of a traditional court, integrated in the normal judicial structures of a state. Instead the reviewing body needs to satisfy certain substantial requirements. In the first place, independence and impartiality are essential features of the concept of a 'court' in Article 5(4).[47] Consequently, an appeal to a higher

---

[40] *Saadi v. United Kingdom*, Chamber Judgment of 11 July 2006, Appl. No. 13229/03, par. 54–55, confirmed by *Saadi v. United Kingdom*, Grand Chamber Judgment of 29 January 2008, par. 83–85.
[41] *Chahal v. United Kingdom*, par. 13.
[42] *Rusu v. Austria*, par. 43.
[43] *Brogan and others v. the United Kingdom*, par. 58.
[44] *Al Nashif v. Bulgaria*, 20 June 2002, Appl. No. 50963/99, par. 92.
[45] Ibid., par. 95; and *Chahal v. United Kingdom*.
[46] *Čonka v. Belgium*, par, 45; *Sadaykov v. Bulgaria*, par. 35.
[47] *Neumeister v. Austria*, 27 June 1968, A-8, par. 24. See also *De Wilde, Ooms and Versyp v. Belgium*, 18 June 1971, A-12, par. 77; *Winterwerp v. the Netherlands*, par. 56; and *Weeks v. United Kingdom*, 2 March 1987, A-114, par. 61.

administrative authority to review the decision to detain would not satisfy the requirements of Article 5(4) ECHR.[48] Secondly, the court testing the lawfulness of the detention must provide fundamental guarantees of judicial procedure.[49] What kind of guarantees must be offered depends on the kind of deprivation of liberty in question.[50] In any case the proceedings must have a judicial character, and the individual affected by the deprivation of liberty must be able to participate properly in the proceedings.[51] Thirdly, the 'court' reviewing the lawfulness of the detention must have powers to order the detainee's release if it finds that the deprivation of liberty is unlawful. Accordingly, a reviewing body with merely consulting powers cannot be considered a court in the sense of article 5(4) ECHR.[52] Note that if the detention is ordered by a court that satisfies the above requirements, the supervision required by Article 5(4) ECHR is already incorporated in the initial decision to detain.[53]

The scope of the judicial review is the next aspect of article 5(4) ECHR to be considered. Article 5 ECHR should be read as a whole, which means that the meaning of the term lawfulness in the fourth paragraph of this provision is identical to that in the first paragraph.[54] Accordingly, even though the executive has a certain margin of appreciation with regard to the ordering of the detention, the review should in any case be "wide enough to bear on those conditions which are essential for the 'lawful' detention of a person according to Article 5(1) ECHR."[55] I shall address the substantive requirements that the first paragraph of Article 5 ECHR imposes on immigration detention below, but for now it is important to appreciate that Article 5(4) ECHR imposes an autonomous standard on the judicial procedure challenging the lawfulness of the detention. The question whether domestic law has been complied with thus contains only one element of the review required by Article 5(4) ECHR, which is in this respect comparable to Article 9 ICCPR.

Article 5(4) ECHR requires, furthermore, that the review takes place 'speedily'. The period to be measured commences when the appeal is lodged and it

---

[48] *Sadaykov v.Bulgaria*, par. 35.
[49] *De Wilde, Ooms en Versyp v. Belgium*, par. 76.
[50] *Weeks v. United Kingdom*, par. 61; *Wassink v. the Netherlands*, par. 30; and *Bouamar v. Belgium*, par. 57.
[51] *Weeks v. United Kingdom*, par. 66.
[52] Ibid., par. 64; *X v. the United Kingdom*, par. 61, and *Chahal v. United Kingdom*, par. 130.
[53] *De Wilde, Ooms and Versyp v. Belgium*, par. 76.
[54] *Dougoz v. Greece*, 6 March 2001, Reports 2001-II, par. 61; and *Ashingdane v. United Kingdom*, 28 May 1985, A-93, par. 52.
[55] *Chahal v. United Kingdom*, par. 127; *Kadem v. Malta*, 9 January 2003, Appl. No. 55263/00, par. 42. See also *Weeks v. United Kingdom*, par. 59.

ends on the day when the court decision is communicated to the applicant.[56] The Court has never pronounced a clear time-limit by which the review must have taken place as, once more, the question what is a 'speedy review' depends on the circumstances of the case.[57] In this context, the Court takes into consideration the complexity of the case; the behaviour of the applicant; the conduct of the authorities; and what is at stake for the applicant.[58] Yet, the term speedily in paragraph 4 of article 5 ECHR allows for less urgency than the notion of 'promptly'which is required for the review of deprivations of liberty under criminal law in Article 5(3).[59] In *Sanchez-Reisse*, periods of 31 and 46 days between requests for release and the judicial decisions on the lawfulness of the detention for the purpose of extradition were not deemed to be in compliance with the notion 'speedily'.[60] In *E. v. Norway*, concerning the detention of a mentally ill person, the Court found a period of eight weeks to be excessive.[61] In the particular context of immigration detention, the Court decided in *Kadem* that a period of more than three weeks is certainly in violation of Article 5(4).[62]

Related to the notion of a speedy review is the question whether article 5(4) entails a right to *periodical* judicial reviews. In cases of extended detention periods, a right of periodical judicial review at reasonable intervals is warranted because the reasons initially necessitating the detention may have ceased to exist.[63] Therefore, if an automatic periodical judicial review is not provided for, the immigration detainee should at least be entitled to institute proceedings to challenge the continuing lawfulness of his detention at reasonable intervals.

The final issue to be discussed briefly with regard to Article 5(4) concerns the question of legal assistance. In *Chahal*, the fact that the applicant was not

---

[56] *Singh v. Czech Republic*, 25 January 2005, Appl. No. 60538/00, par. 74.
[57] *Sanchez-Reisse v. Switzerland*, 21 October 1986, A-107, par. 55; and *E. v. Norway*, 29 August 1990, A-181-A, par. 64.
[58] R.A. Lawson and H.G. Schermers, *Leading Cases of the European Court of Human Rights* (Nijmegen: Ars Aequi Libri, 1999), 108. See also *Luberti v. Italy*, 23 February 1984, A-75. However, delays caused by an excessive workload or vacation periods can never be justified because the Contracting States are obliged to organise their legal systems in such a way as to enable their courts to comply with the Convention's requirements (*Bezicheri v. Italy*, 25 October 1989, A-164, par. 25).
[59] *E. v. Norway*, par. 64.
[60] *Sanchez-Reisse v. Switzerland*, par. 59–60.
[61] *E. v. Norway*, par. 64–66.
[62] *Kadem v. Malta*, par. 53. See also *Tekdemir v. the Netherlands* (Decision), 1 October 2002, Appl. Nos. 46860/99 and 49823/99.
[63] *Winterwerp v. the Netherlands*, par. 55; and *X v. United Kingdom*, par. 52.

entitled to legal representation before the panel that reviewed the lawfulness of his detention was one of the factors that led the Court to conclude that this reviewing body could not be considered a court in the sense of article 5(4) ECHR.[64] A right to legal aid can also be deduced from the requirement that the Convention rights need to be practical and effective: in Čonka the Court observed that a lack of legal assistance for immigration detainees would prevent them from making a meaningful appeal to a court.[65]

8.3.3 Compensation for Unlawful Deprivations of Liberty

The last paragraph of article 5 ECHR contains a unique provision in the Convention. It gives anybody the right to compensation if he has been deprived of his liberty in contravention of article 5 ECHR. This provision differs from article 50 ECHR in that it gives the individual whose rights under article 5 ECHR have been violated a right to compensation directly vis-à-vis the national authorities. In this respect it is not relevant whether it was the Court in Strasbourg or a national court that found a violation. In the absence of an enforceable right to compensation under national law for breaches of article 5 ECHR, paragraph 5 of that provision is violated, also if the detention was not unlawful according to national law.[66] However, Article 5(5) ECHR does not prohibit national states from making the award of compensation dependent upon the ability of the person concerned to show damage resulting from the breach. Indeed, in the Court's view there can be no question of 'compensation' where there is no pecuniary or non-pecuniary damage to be compensated.[67]

8.4 The Notion of Arbitrariness in the Strasbourg Case Law on Immigration Detention

As I have mentioned above, the term 'lawful', therewith including 'in accordance with a procedure prescribed by law' contained in Article 5(1) ECHR, requires that any measure depriving the individual of his liberty is compatible with the purpose of Article 5 ECHR, which consists of protecting the individual from arbitrariness. As we have seen in the previous chapter, in human

---

[64] Chahal v. United Kingdom, par. 130.
[65] Čonka v. Belgium, par. 44 and 55. In the case of Bouamar v. Belgium the Court deemed legal representation to be imperative in the habeas corpus proceedings of a minor.
[66] Brannigan and McBride v. United Kingdom, 26 May 1993, A-258-B, par. 37, and Brogan and others v. the United Kingdom, par. 67.
[67] Wassink v. the Netherlands, par. 38.

rights law the notion of arbitrariness can be understood to contain elements of 'injustice, inappropriateness, unpredictability and unreasonableness'. In this section, I shall flesh out the way in which the ECtHR applies the prohibition of arbitrary deprivations of liberty in the context of Article 5(1)(f). This will be done by first dealing with the way in which the Court assesses the legitimacy of the decision by the authorities to resort to detention, after which I shall address the application of arbitrariness to distinct aspects of the detention, such as the manner of its implementation, the place and conditions of detention, and its duration.

8.4.1 Chahal *and* Saadi: *Unnecessary and Disproportionate, but Lawful Detention*

We have seen above that the Convention recognises the prevention of unauthorised entry, on the one hand, and the enforcement of deportation proceedings, on the other, as the only two situations in which it is legitimate for states to deprive individuals of their liberty under immigration legislation. The issue to be dealt with here is the manner in which the Court interprets the exception under Article 5(1)(f) ECHR. In other words, under which conditions do the prevention of entry or the enforcement of removal justify the decision to resort to detention in the individual case?

The case of *Chahal* showed that the Court, at least when it concerns pre-deportation detention, barely perceives a difference between what the Convention recognises as legitimate aims of immigration detention, on the one hand, and the question under which circumstances the advancement of these aims by the state may justify the decision to deprive an individual of his liberty on the other:

> Article 5(1)(f) does not demand that the detention of a person against whom action is being taken with a view to deportation be reasonably considered necessary, for example to prevent his committing an offence or fleeing; in this respect Article 5(1)(f) provides a different level of protection from Article 5(1)(c). Indeed, all that is required under this provision is that 'action is being taken with a view to deportation'. It is therefore immaterial, for the purposes of Article 5(1)(f), whether the underlying decision to expel can be justified under national or Convention law.[68]

It is by elaborating the specific circumstances of each and every case, mitigating for or against detention in the context of deportation proceedings, that issues such as reasonability, proportionality and necessity come into play, of

---

[68] *Chahal v. United Kingdom*, par. 112; See also *Čonka v. Belgium*, par. 38; and *Riad and Idiab v. Belgium*, par. 70; and *Quinn v. France*, par. 48 (extradition).

which the decisions of the HRC discussed in the previous chapter provide a good example. However, according to the ECtHR, any person against whom deportation proceedings are taken can be detained without considering these otherwise important constitutional principles. The fact that an altogether different logic pertains to the right of liberty in the immigration context than which applies in other areas covered by the Convention is quite openly admitted by the Court, but in most of its judgments one is left in the dark as to what reasons underlie the difference. Thus, in the admissibility decision in *Batalov*, where the applicant argued that his detention in order to carry out his removal from Lithuania had been arbitrary as it was based on national security grounds which were unknown to him, the Court stated merely that:

> Article 5(1)(f) does not afford a detained alien the right to contest the 'proportionality' of the detention order, unlike other Convention issues, for example under Article 8 (2) of the Convention.[69]

In the case of *Čonka*, the applicants explicitly raised the argument that their arrest had not been necessary to secure their departure from Belgium. However, the Court quoted from earlier case law to state once more that an unnecessary or disproportionate pre-deportation detention is not an unlawful detention under the Convention.[70]

Its line of reasoning in *Chahal* and subsequent case law cannot be interpreted otherwise than to imply that even if the lawfulness of the deportation proceedings is in dispute, detention based upon those proceedings will not be unlawful in light of the ECHR. The only exception to the Court's deference to national authorities' decisions in this regard is provided by the situation in which there is no legal basis whatsoever for the deportation. In that case, the Court has found a violation of the requirement in Article 5(1)(f) that the deprivation of liberty needs to be carried out in accordance with a procedure prescribed by law.[71]

Until the case of *Saadi* was decided, the need to address the question of the necessity or the proportionality of pre-admittance detention had never arisen before the Court. It can be argued that the phrasing of the exception under the second limb of Article 5(1)(f) would compel the Court to take a different approach than that it has taken with regard to detention under the first limb, as it permits detention *to prevent* unauthorised entry. However, in a Grand Chamber judgment the Court pronounced unequivocally that the proportionality and necessity of the decision to resort to pre-admittance detention are as

---

[69] *Batalov v. Lithuania* (Decision), 15 November 2005, Appl. No. 30789/04.
[70] *Čonka v. Belgium*, par. 38. See also *Liu v. Russia*, 6 December 2007, par. 78.
[71] *Mohd v. Greece*, par. 20–24.

insignificant for the question of its lawfulness as they are with regard to the lawfulness of pre-deportation detention.

Saadi was a Kurdish refugee who had fled from Northern Iraq to the United Kingdom. After applying for asylum at Heathrow Airport, he was initially granted 'temporary admission' and he was only detained at Oakington Detention Centre (Oakington) on the third day after his arrival. The sole aim of detention at Oakington is to speed up immigration procedures by using a 'fast-track' procedure, and the decision whether an asylum claim is suitable for decision at Oakington is primarily based on the claimant's nationality. In addition, only those asylum seekers who are not considered likely to abscond are detained at Oakington with its 'relaxed regime'.[72] Saadi was released on the day that his asylum claim was rejected, after seven days of detention. He was once more granted temporary admission pending the appeal against the rejection of his application for asylum – which was allowed some two years later. At no point in the domestic procedures or in Strasbourg did the authorities argue that Saadi's detention had been necessary because there was a risk that he would abscond, which would in any case, according to the House of Lords, be a "flimsy reason".[73]

In the Chamber judgment, the Court accepted that Saadi's detention fell under the first limb of Article 5(1)(f), even though he had been granted temporary admission prior to his detention. His detention could "reasonably be considered to be aimed at preventing unlawful entry […] because, absent formal admission clearance, he had not 'lawfully' entered the country."[74] The Chamber also paid attention to the question whether it is permissible to detain an asylum seeker or immigrant in circumstances where there is no risk of his absconding or other misconduct. It argued that the level of protection for the right of liberty of would-be immigrants under the Convention is lower than for "individuals that are lawfully at large in a country" because the former "are not 'authorised' to be on the territory."[75]

> Accordingly, and this finding does no more than apply to the first limb of Article 5(1)(f) the ruling the Court has already made as regards the second limb of the provision, there is no requirement in Article 5(1)(f) that the detention of a person to prevent his effecting an unauthorised entry into the country be reasonably considered necessary, for example to prevent his committing an offence or fleeing.[76]

---

[72] Home Office, *Operational Enforcement Manual*, 21 December 2000, par. 38.3.
[73] House of Lords, *Regina v. Secretary of State for the Home Department Ex Parte Saadi (fc) and Others (Fc)*, 31 October 2002 [2002] UKHL 41, par. 21.
[74] *Saadi v. United Kingdom*, Chamber Judgment, par. 39–41.
[75] Ibid., par. 44.
[76] Id.

The Chamber did not deem it necessary to address the applicant's separate claim that Article 14 ECHR had been breached as a result of legislation that provided for a list of countries whose nationals could or could not be detained. Essentially, it seemed to allow for discrimination on the ground of nationality on account of the vast discretion it grants to the national state to decide on matters of immigration detention.

It was only a narrow majority of four judges (out of a total of seven) in the Chamber who found that Saadi's detention did not violate Article 5(1)(f) ECHR. The three dissenting judges considered his detention to be unlawful as the real reasons for this detention were "purely based on administrative or bureaucratic grounds aiming to follow the fast-track procedure with regard to the applicant."[77] Besides, one judge, in a concurring opinion, expressed the concern felt that a person should be deprived of his liberty for reasons essentially of administrative efficiency and the risks of arbitrariness which such detention may entail. He therefore emphasised that such a detention, if it were significantly in excess of the seven days that Saadi had spent in Oakington, would be difficult to reconcile with Article 5 ECHR.[78]

At Saadi's request, the case was referred to the Grand Chamber.[79] Essentially, in its judgment the Grand Chamber affirmed the view of the Chamber: a full test of the necessity and proportionality of the decision to detain asylum seekers is not required under the first limb of Article 5(1)(f).[80]

Before the Grand Chamber of the Court considered the 'lawfulness' of Saadi's detention, it addressed the question as to in which circumstances the deprivation of liberty of an individual can be characterised as being 'to prevent his effecting an unauthorised entry into the country' in the sense of the first limb of Article 5(1)(f).[81] In order to uncover the meaning of that phrase, the Court first stressed the often repeated "undeniable sovereign right of states to control aliens' entry into and residence in their territory." It deduced from that undeniable right of control a "necessary adjunct": the power to detain would-be immigrants who have applied for permission to enter.[82] Next, the

---

[77] *Saadi v. United Kingdom*, Chamber Judgment, joint dissenting opinion of Judges Casadevall, Traja and Sikuta.
[78] Concurring opinion of Judge Sir Nicolas Bratza.
[79] If a case decided by the Chamber in accordance with Article 29 ECHR raises a serious issue affecting the application or the interpretation of the Convention, or a serious issue of general importance, each of the parties may request that the case be referred to the *Grand Chamber*, consisting of 17 judges (Article 43 ECHR). It is a panel of five judges of the Grand Chamber who decides upon this request.
[80] *Saadi v. United Kingdom*, Grand Chamber Judgment, par. 72 and 73.
[81] Ibid., par. 61–66.
[82] Ibid., par. 64.

Court argued that as long as a state has not authorised the entry of these individuals, their detention could be classified as being 'to prevent unauthorised entry'.

The argument that detention under the first limb of Article 5(1)(f) is only justified if it can be shown that the person concerned will attempt to evade entry restrictions was rejected by the Court, as such a reading of Article 5(1)(f) was seen as placing too narrow an interpretation on that provision. It would moreover result in too large a restriction on the aforementioned 'undeniable right of control'.[83] In this part of the judgment, the Court seems to blur two issues that ought to be treated separately: On the one hand, the question as to whether the detention falls within the scope of Article 5(1)(f); and, on the other hand, the *ensuing* question as regards the compliance of the detention with that provision, thereby including particular justifications for that measure in the circumstances. As a result of this blurring, the requirement that pre-admittance detention be *necessary* for the prevention of irregular entry is implicitly and prematurely rejected by the Court in the part of the judgment where it should be merely assessing whether an actual deprivation of liberty falls within the ambit of the first limb of Article 5(1)f.[84] Almost inevitably, then, when subsequently addressing the notion of arbitrariness, the protection against which constitutes the core of Article 5, the Court merely refers to its case law on pre-deportation detention in order to reject a full test of the proportionality or necessity of pre-admittance detention.[85]

It can be concluded that regarding both pre-admittance detention and pre-deportation detention, the Court's interpretation of the exception to the right to personal liberty in Article 5(1)(f) ECHR can hardly be regarded as a narrow one. In this respect, the Court in Strasbourg offers immigration detainees a lower level of protection than the HRC. We have seen that according to the HRC, immigration detention needs to be reasonable *and* necessary in view of specific factors that concern the individual in order to be reconcilable with the right to liberty guaranteed by Article 9 ICCPR. Moreover, it is doubtful

---

[83] Ibid., par. 65.
[84] Compare par. 65 of the Grand Chamber Judgment. In other cases the Court has distinguished between these issues more clearly: "*la Cour estime que le placement et le maintien du requérant dans le centre d'accueil de l'aéroport international [...] visant à l'empêcher de pénétrer irrégulièrement dans le territoire tchèque, s'analyse en une privation de liberté au sens de l'article 5 § 1 f) de la Convention. Toutefois, le fait que la détention du requérant relève du paragraphe f) de l'article 5 ne signifie par pour autant que la détention soit régulière au sens de cette disposition.*" (*Rashed v. Czech Republic*, par. 70). See also *Merie v. the Netherlands* (Decision), 20 September 2007, Appl. No. 664/05.
[85] *Saadi v. United Kingdom*, Grand Chamber Judgment, par. 73.

whether the ECtHR has deduced the correct meaning from the international legal instruments that it refers to in its judgment in *Saadi*. When interpreting the first ground for detention under Article 5 (1)(f), it seems to argue that a full test of the necessity of pre-admittance detention would neither be required by Conclusion 44 of the Executive Committee of the UNHCR, nor by the 1999 UNHCR Guidelines for Detention of Asylum Seekers, nor by the Recommendation on Measures of Detention of Asylum Seekers by the Committee of Minsters of the Council of Europe.[86] However, as we have seen in the previous chapter, these instruments require, without exception, that detention is a necessary and proportionate measure in each individual case.[87]

8.4.2 *Immigration Detention and the ECtHR: Proportionality 'Lite'?*

Do considerations of reasonability, necessity and appropriateness, and the proportionality principle thus play no role at all in the Court's review of the lawfulness of immigration detention? They do – to a degree.

First and foremost, they may do so – on account of the 'legality requirement' – in the case that *national legislation* provides for the condition that detention must be necessary. In that case the Court has at times been willing to go quite far in its examination of the proportionality of the measure, as became apparent from its judgment in *Rusu*, a case which exemplifies the centrality of the passport in the 'monopolisation of the legitimate means of movement'. While travelling back from Spain to Romania (her country of origin), Rusu's passport was stolen in France. After reporting the theft, she continued her travel homewards via Italy and Austria. However, when she arrived at the Hungarian border, she was refused entry, and sent back to the Austrian border police. The Austrian authorities placed her in immigration detention because they believed there was a possibility that she would attempt to abscond and evade the deportation proceedings if released: a belief predominantly based on the fact that she had no passport and no fixed abode in Austria![88] On account of all sorts of bureaucratic complications, Rusu spent 25 days in immigration detention before being deported. As Austrian legislation required the detention to be a necessary measure, the Court observes that the authorities could only have resorted to detention if less severe measures had been considered and found insufficient to safeguard the public interest. According to the Court, such considerations clearly did not play a role with regard to the

---

[86] Ibid., par. 65.
[87] UNHCR Guideline 3; ExCom Conclusion 44; and General Provision 6 of Recommendation Rec (2003)5 (Strasbourg, 16 April 2003).
[88] *Rusu v. Austria*, par. 56.

decision to deprive Rusu of her liberty, and accordingly it found a violation of Article 5(1)(f).[89]

Furthermore, under Article (1)(f) the proportionality principle is also applicable to immigration detention to the extent that detention should not continue beyond a period of time that is reasonably required for the purpose pursued by it.[90] In *Saadi's* case, the seven-day period that he had spent in detention was not deemed to be unreasonable in view of its purpose, which was the speedy processing of his asylum claim.[91] When it concerns pre-deportation detention, the deprivation of liberty will be justified only as long as deportation proceedings are in progress.[92] If these proceedings are not carried out with due diligence the detention will cease to be lawful under Article 5 ECHR.[93]

When assessing the duration of the expulsion proceedings, the Court also takes the detainee's behaviour into account.[94] If his conduct was the cause for delays, the State cannot be held responsible for an exceedingly long duration.[95] Moreover, the interests at stake for the applicant also play a role. In *Chahal*, the applicant held that if he would be returned to his country of origin, he would be subjected to treatment that violated Article 3 ECHR. As his case accordingly involved considerations of an extremely serious and weighty nature, it was neither considered in his interest, nor in that of the general public, if decisions on his expulsion would be taken hastily.[96] Nevertheless, when assessing the duration of immigration detention, if the Court is satisfied that the national authorities have indeed acted diligently, it has at times approved of very long periods of detention, without fully balancing the competing principles at stake.[97]

The Court's case law presents three additional conditions that immigration detention must satisfy in order to be reconcilable with Article 5(1) – all of which bear some relation to the proportionality principle. Immigration

---

[89] Ibid., par. 58.
[90] *Saadi v. United Kingdom*, Grand Chamber Judgment, par. 72 and 74. See also *Gebremedhin v. France*, 26 April 2007, Appl. No. 25389/05.
[91] *Saadi v. United Kingdom*, Grand Chamber Judgment, par. 79.
[92] *Chahal v. United Kingdom*, par. 113.
[93] *Kolompar v. Belgium*, 24 September 1992, A-235-C, par. 36; and *Chahal v. United Kingdom*, par. 113. See also *Quinn v. France*, par. 48; and *Singh v. Czech Republic*, par. 61.
[94] D.J. Harris, M. O'Boyle and C. Warbrick, *Law of the European Convention on Human Rights* (London: Butterworths 1995), 127.
[95] *Kolompar v. Belgium*, par. 42.
[96] *Chahal v. United Kingdom*, par. 117.
[97] Thus, in *Chahal* the immigration detention had lasted for six years but was not considered unlawful. See also *Ntumba Kabonga v. France* (decision), 2 June 2005, Appl. No. 52467/99.

detention needs to be "closely connected" to the purpose of preventing unauthorised entry or deportation; it must be carried out in "good faith"; and the place and conditions should be appropriate, considering that "the measure is applicable not to those who have committed criminal offences".[98]

First, the requirement that there should be a *causal* relationship between a measure and its purpose is generally seen as the initial step in reviewing the proportionality of a measure, the so-called suitability principle.[99] However, the Court does not use the term causal, but instead it calls for a *close* relationship between immigration detention and its aims. In *Saadi* it was of the opinion that a sufficiently close connection existed between the purpose of detention at Oakington – facilitating a speedy and efficient decision regarding a claim for asylum – and the purpose of preventing unauthorised entry in Article 5(1)(f). This logic facilitates the construction of a 'chain' of permitted purposes, which renders the general rule – exceptions to the right to personal liberty must be narrowly interpreted – of little significance when it comes to the use of detention in immigration procedures. Indeed, if one considers the background of Saadi's case – detention in Oakington was indicated solely for asylum seekers who were not likely to abscond – it seems justified to conclude that the Court will accept a 'close' connection as long as the reasons for detention are genuinely related to immigration control. Nevertheless, such a general prohibition of *détournement de pouvoir* is already contained in Article 18 ECHR and as such it does not reflect the distinctive importance of Article 5 in the Convention.

Secondly, any deprivation of liberty will be in violation of the prohibition of arbitrariness if there has been 'an element of bad faith or deception on the part of the authorities'.[100] In the case of *Čonka* the Belgium police had sent a notice to a number of rejected asylum seekers, which invited them to attend a police station in order to complete the files concerning their applications for asylum. Once they arrived at the police station, they were served with an order to leave the territory, accompanied by a decision for their removal and their detention and they were taken to a closed transit centre. The Court condemned the use of a 'ruse' whereby the authorities tried, by misleading asylum seekers, to gain their trust in order to arrest and subsequently to deport them:

> The Court reiterates that the list of exceptions to the right to liberty secured in Article 5(1) is an exhaustive one and only a narrow interpretation of those exceptions is consistent with the aim of that provision In the Court's view, that requirement must also be reflected in the reliability of communications such as those sent

---

[98] *Saadi v. United Kingdom*, Grand Chamber judgment, para. 74. See also *Rashed v. Czech Republic*.
[99] J.H. Jans, "Proportionality Revisited," *Legal Issues of Economic Integration* 27 (2000), 239.
[100] *Saadi v. United Kingdom*, Grand Chamber Judgment, par. 69. See also *Liu v. Russia*, par. 82; *Gebremedhin v. France*, par. 7; and *Bozano v. France*, par. 59.

to the applicants, irrespective of whether the recipients are lawfully present in the country or not. It follows that, even as regards overstayers, a conscious decision by the authorities to facilitate or improve the effectiveness of a planned operation for the expulsion of aliens by misleading them about the purpose of a notice so as to make it easier to deprive them of their liberty is not compatible with Article 5.[101]

And although the Court accepted that the use of certain stratagems could be justified when it came to the arrest of criminals, it deemed such tactics to be unacceptable if they led to the apprehension of persons who were not guilty of criminal offences.[102] As such, in the ECtHR case law on immigration detention, the requirement of an appropriate relationship between the means employed and the end thereby served is not entirely absent. In *Saadi* the Court found that the authorities had acted in good faith, and in reaching this conclusion, it took into account that the reasons for which they had resorted to detention at Oakington were in the interest not merely of Saadi himself, but of those 'increasingly in the queue'.[103]

In the third place, the place and conditions of immigration detention need to be appropriate if such detention is to avoid being arbitrary. Thus, the Court's case law requires that there must be some relationship between the ground of permitted deprivation of liberty relied upon and the place and conditions of detention.[104] Here again, one can observe the – albeit limited – application of the proportionality principle, once more expressed in the restriction that immigration detention needs to reflect the fact that this measure concerns persons '*qui [...] n'avaient commis d'autre infractions que celles liées au séjour*'.[105] A violation of Article 5 has been found by the Court when asylum seekers were detained in the transit zone of an airport for an extended period without social or humanitarian assistance.[106] In the case of *Mayeka and Mitunga* an unaccompanied foreign minor had been detained in a closed centre intended for illegal immigrants in the same conditions as adults. As these conditions were not at all adapted to the position of extreme vulnerability in which the applicant found herself as a result of her position as an unaccompanied foreign minor, the Court found that the "Belgian legal system at the time and as it functioned in this instance did not sufficiently protect the applicant's right to liberty."[107]

---

[101] *Čonka v. Belgium*, par. 42.
[102] Ibid., par. 40–42.
[103] *Saadi v. United Kingdom*, Grand Chamber Judgment, par. 77.
[104] *Ashingdane v. United Kingdom*, par. 44; *Bouamar v. Belgium*; *Bizzotto v. Greece*, 15 November 1996, Reports 1996-V, par. 31; and *Aerts v. Belgium*, 30 July 1998, Reports 1998-V, par. 46.
[105] *Riad and Idiab v. Belgium*, par. 77.
[106] Id.
[107] *Mubilanzila Mayeka and Kaniki Mitunga v. Belgium*, par. 104.

In the same case the Court also found that the detention amounted to treatment prohibited by Article 3 ECHR, as the Belgian state did not fulfil its obligation to provide adequate care for the applicant in her position as an unaccompanied foreign minor. According to the Court, her detention in conditions as described above demonstrated a lack of humanity to such a degree that it amounted to inhuman treatment.[108]

Moreover, her detention was deemed to be in violation of the right to family life, enshrined in Article 8 ECHR, as the "effect of detention was to separate her from the member of her family in whose care she had been placed". The Court also scrutinised the measure of detention from the perspective of the right to private life, as protected by the same provision. The level of scrutiny when applying this provision differed significantly from the Court's application of Article 5(1)(f), seeing that the proportionality and necessity of the detention were explicitly addressed:

> in the absence of any risk of the second applicant's seeking to evade the supervision of the Belgian authorities, her detention in a closed centre for adults was unnecessary. Other measures could have been taken that would have been more conducive to the higher interest of the child guaranteed by Article 3 of the Convention on the Rights of the Child. These included her placement in a specialised centre or with foster parents.[109]

8.5 How to Reconcile the Human Right to Liberty with the Public Interest?

We have seen that the Court's interpretation of the right to personal liberty in the immigration context authorises the detention of asylum seekers and unauthorised migrants which is unnecessary and lacking in proportionality. Especially when seen in the context of constitutional adjudication, this position seems to be at odds with the very nature of human rights as such, the "special status" of which means that they cannot be "simply traded away for other social gains."[110] When called upon to resolve conflicts between human

---

[108] Ibid., par 50–59. Similarly, in *S.D. v. Greece* and *Dougoz v. Greece* the Court considered the applicants had experienced conditions that amounted to degrading treatment in the violation of Article 3.

[109] *Mubilanzila Mayeka and Kaniki Mitunga v. Belgium*, par. 83.

[110] "The language may be that of Nozickian "side-constraints" or Dworkinian "rights as trumps" or the Rawlsian "lexical priority of basic rights" but the moral instinct of the liberal is typically to give some special status (even if not an absolute priority) to the protection of basic liberties, which means that they cannot simply be traded away for other social gains." I. Loader and N. Walker, *Civilizing Security* (Cambridge, Cambridge University Press 2007), 55.

rights and competing public interests, judges have to reconcile the special status of such rights with the legitimate power of the state to set limits – under certain conditions – to their exercise. As we have seen in Chapter 2, this is usually done by reviewing the proportionality of the interference in question.

Generally, an interference with a human right on the ground of public interest is regarded as legitimate if the three sub-principles contained by the proportionality principle – the principles of suitability, necessity, and proportionality in the narrow sense – are satisfied.[111] The suitability principle requires that there is some causal relationship between the measure and the aim thereby pursued.[112] The need for necessity follows from the recognition that the special status of fundamental rights means that any invasion thereof should be kept to the minimum. Thus, if it is possible to resort to a less restrictive measure in order to safeguard the public interest, the measure in question is not proportionate.[113] Finally, the measure, even when considered suitable and necessary, should not impose an excessive burden on the individual concerned. Thus, the application of proportionality in the narrow sense entails an assessment of "whether there are sufficiently compelling reasons for the burdens and disadvantages suffered by individuals."[114] In the paragraphs below I shall first address the way in which the proportionality principle has featured in the Court's case law generally, after which I shall briefly address deprivations of liberty under Article 5(1)(e).

8.5.1 The Proportionality Principle as a General Principle in the ECHR

Proportionality as such is nowhere explicitly mentioned in the text of the ECHR.[115] The Court used the term proportionality for the first time in the *Belgian Linguistics Case* with regard to Article 14 ECHR, the provision prohibiting

---

[111] R. Alexy, "Balancing, Constitutional Rights and Rationality," *Ratio Juris* 16 (2003), 135.
[112] Jans (2000), 240.
[113] P. Craig, "Unreasonableness and Proportionality in UK Law," in *The Principle of Proportionality in the Laws of Europe*, ed. E. Ellis (Oxford: Hart Publishing, 1999), 97.
[114] N. Gibbs, "Getting Constitutional Theory in Proportion: A Matter of Interpretation?" *Oxford Journal of Legal Studies* 27 (2007), 185. Accordingly, proportionality in the narrow sense has also been called "the Law of Balancing": "The greater the degree of non-satisfaction of, or detriment to, one principle, the greater the importance of satisfying the other." Alexy (2003), 136.
[115] But note Article 15 ECHR in which the principle is all but mentioned. The Court has deduced from the term 'strictly necessary' in this provision the requirement of strict proportionality between the force used and the aims to be achieved thereby. See *McCann v. United Kingdom*, 27 September 1995, A-324, par. 48–149; *Andronicou and Constantinou v. Cyprus*, 9 October 1997, Reports 1997-VI, par. 171; and *Tanli v. Turkey*, 10 April 2001, Reports 2001-III, par. 140. See also *Brannigan and McBride v. United Kingdom*, par. 54.

discrimination. According to the Court, a difference in treatment does not always violate Article 14 ECHR, provided that a legitimate aim is pursued with the measure in question. However, it observed that if "the relationship of proportionality between the means employed and the aim sought" is not fully respected, the measure will be incompatible with Article 14 ECHR.[116]

The proportionality principle has featured most prominently in case law based on articles 8, 9, 10 and 11 of the Convention, provisions which contain a second paragraph in which limitations to the rights protected in the first paragraph are provided for, if they are necessary in a democratic society in order to achieve a legitimate purpose. In applying these provisions the Court often firstly ascertains whether the reasons given by the authorities for the restrictive measure are relevant and sufficient.[117] The term sufficient indicates that this examination entails more than a mere application of the suitability principle, as the Court has held that the reasons advanced by the authorities must specifically address the *necessity* of the measure.[118] In this respect, it is interesting to take at look at how the Court has interpreted the term 'necessary in a democratic society'. It has held that necessary in this context is not the same as indispensable, but neither does it have the flexibility of expressions such as admissible, useful, reasonable or desirable.[119] According to the Court, the notion of necessity furthermore implies a "pressing social need".[120] This interpretation is misleading insofar as it may pose a challenge to the legitimacy of

---

[116] Case "relating to certain aspects of the laws on the use of languages in education in Belgium", 23 June 1968, A-6, par. 32.

[117] See *Olsson v. Sweden*, 24 March 1988, A-130, par. 68; *Lehideux and Isorni v. France*, 23 September 1998, Reports 1998-VII, par. 51; *K. and T. v. Finland*, 27 April 2000, Appl. no. 25702/94, par. 135; *Barthold v. Germany*, par. 55; *Dudgeon v. the United Kingdom*, 22 October 1981, A-45, par. 54; *Handyside v. the United Kingdom*, 7 December 1976, A-24, par. 50; *Lingens v. Austria*, 8 July 1986, A-103, par. 40; *Sunday Times v. the United Kingdom*, 26 April 1979, A-30, par. 50; *Vogt v. Germany*, 26 September 1995, A-323, par. 52; and *Bergens Tidende and others v. Norway*, 2 May 2000, Reports 2000-IV, par. 48. See specifically for requirements of sufficiency and relevance the reasons given for interferences with the right to liberty in cases examined under Article 5(1) under c: *N.C. v. Italy*, 11 January 2001, Appl. No. 24952/94, par. 60; *Letellier v. France*, 26 June 1991, A-207, par. 52, *Tomasi v. France*, 27 August 1992, A-241-A, par. 91, *I.A. v. France*, 23 September 1998, Reports 1998-VII, par. 104; *Wemhoff v. Germany*, 27 June 1968, A-7, par. 12; *Kenmache v. France*, 27 November 1991, A-218, par. 52; *Van der Tang v. Spain*, 30 July 1995, A-321, par. 67; and *Muller v. France*, 17 March 1997, Reports 1997-II, par. 45.

[118] *Margareta and Roger Andersson v. Sweden*, 25 February 1992, A-226-A, par. 96.

[119] *Handyside v. United Kingdom*, par. 67.

[120] Ibid. §48. See also *Sunday Times v. United Kingdom*, 26 April 1979, par. 59; *Dudgeon v. the United Kingdom*, par. 51 and 60; and *Lehideux and Isorni v. France*, par. 51.

the purpose of the measure, which in itself is not relevant for assessing its proportionality.[121]

Apart from interpreting the words "necessary in a democratic society" so as to imply a pressing social need, the Court has also explicitly equated this requirement with the proportionality principle.[122] In this context, the Court may examine whether the legitimate interest can be pursued in another, less restrictive way. Thus, in a case involving a criminal conviction for publicly defending the crimes of collaboration, the Court considered that other means of intervention and rebuttal, particularly through civil remedies, would have been more suitable and proportionate, which made the measure unlawful under the Convention.[123] Along similar lines, it has held that if the measure does not have adequate and effective safeguards against abuse it cannot be said to be strictly proportionate to the aim pursued.[124] In other words, if the restrictions are "too lax and full of loopholes" they cannot be regarded as necessary to achieve a legitimate aim, and the authorities must look for measures which allow for less discretionary powers. Another approach is to be found in the case of *Handyside*, where the very elements of a democratic society – tolerance, pluralism and broad-mindedness – were presumed to imply that restrictions on freedom of expression had to be proportionate to the aim pursued.[125] In some other cases the Court has simply equated democratic necessity with proportionality: if the measure is not proportional, it is not considered necessary in a democratic society.[126]

Finally, with regard to 'proportionality in the narrow sense', the ECtHR case law has regularly addressed the question whether the measure places an

---

[121] See also F. Matscher, "Methods of Interpretation of the Convention," in *The European System for the Protection of Human Rights*, eds. R.St.J. Macdonald, F. Matscher and H. Petzold (The Hague: Martinus Nijhoff Publishers, 1993), 79.

[122] *Leander v. Sweden*, 26 March 1987, A-116, par. 58; *Gillow v. United Kingdom*, 24 November 1986, A-109, par. 55; *Olsson v. Sweden*, par. 67; *Schönenberger and Durmaz v. Switzerland*, 20 June 1988, A-137, par. 27; *Berrehab v. the Netherlands*, 21 June 1988, A-138, par. 28; *Beldjoudi v. France*, 26 March 1992, A-234-A, par. 74; and *Thoma v. Luxembourg*, 29 March 2001, Reports 2001-III, par. 48.

[123] *Lehideux and Isorni v. France*, par 57. See also *Campbell v. United Kingdom*, 25 March 1992, A-233, par. 48; and *Marckx v. Belgium*, 13 June 1979, A-31, par. 40.

[124] *Cremieux v. France*, 25 February 1993, A-256-B, par. 39; *Mihailhe v. France*, 25 February 1993, A-256-C, par. 38; and *Funke v. France*, 25 February 1993, A-256-A, par. 57.

[125] *Handyside v. United Kingdom*, par. 49.

[126] *Barthold v. Germany*, par. 59; *Margareta and Roger Andersson v. Sweden*, par. 97; *Berrehab v. the Netherlands*, par. 29. *Eriksson v. Sweden*, 22 June 1989, A-156, par. 69. See also J.J. Cremona, "The proportionality principle in the jurisprudence of the European Court of Human Rights," in *Recht zwischen Umbruch und Bewahrung: Festschrift fur Rudolf Bernhardt*, ed. U. Beyerlin (Berlin: Springer-Verlag, 1995), 330.

excessive burden on the individual concerned. For example, in cases concerning the right to property in Article 1 of Protocol 1 to the ECHR, the Court requires a proportional relationship between the means employed and the aim sought to be realised.[127] The fair balance which should be struck between the protection of the right of property and the requirements of general interest is considered to be upset if the person concerned has to bear an excessive and individual burden.[128] A somewhat similar approach by the Court can be observed in cases in which it has held that a measure was disproportionate because it impaired the "very essence of a right".[129]

The proportionality principle has also featured in judgments concerning provisions in the ECHR that do not explicitly allow for restrictions, such as Article 6 ECHR. Thus, when an individual's access to a court is limited, the Court will examine whether the limitation complained of pursued a legitimate aim and whether there was a reasonable relationship of proportionality between the measure and the aim sought to be achieved.[130]

At times the Court has also considered that, even though the authorities could have taken "less severe measures" to pursue a legitimate aim, they did not fail to strike a "fair balance" between the interest of the individual and the public interest.[131] In this regard it is important to keep in mind that the ECHR does not seek to establish a uniform framework for the protection of human rights, but that it aims to provide a minimum level of protection without erasing all the differences that may exist between national legal systems.[132] Thus, national states are allowed a certain "margin of appreciation" when they take action in the area of a Convention right.[133] The doctrine of the margin of appreciation has featured strongly in those cases where the principle of proportionality

---

[127] *Hakansson and Sturesson v. Sweden*, 21 February 1990, A-171, par. 51; *Immobiliare Saffi v. Italy*, 28 July 1999, Reports 1999-V, par. 59; *James and Others v. United Kingdom*, 21 February 1986, A-98, par. 50; *Vasilopoulou v. Greece*, 21 March 2002, Appl. No. 47541/99, par. 24; *Lithgow and others v. United Kingdom*, 8 July 1986, A-102, par. 120; *Beyeler v. Italy*, 5 January 2000, Reports 2000-I, par. 122; and *Ghidotti v. Italy*, 21 February 2002, Appl. No. 28272/95, par. 28 and 32.

[128] *Sporrong and Lönnroth v. Sweden*, 23 September 1982, A-52, par. 73.

[129] *F. v. Switzerland*, 18 December 1987, A-128, par. 40.

[130] *Ashingdane v. United Kingdom*, par. 57; *Z. and Others v. United Kingdom*, 10 May 2001, Reports 2001-V; and *Osman v. United Kingdom*, 28 October 1998, Reports 1998-VIII, par. 154.

[131] *Tre Traktorer Bolag v. Sweden*, 7 June 1989, A-159, par. 62.

[132] O. Jacot-Guillardmod, "Régles, méthodes et principes d'interprétation dans la jurisprudence de la Cour européenne des droits de l'homme," in *La Convention européenne des droits de l'homme: Commentaire article par article*, eds. L.E. Pettiti, E. Decaux and P.H. Imbert (Paris: Economica, 1995), 50.

[133] Harris, O'Boyle and Warbrick (1995), 12.

played a role, as national authorities are often in a better position than an international judge to weigh competing public and private interests.[134] In determining the scope of the national state's margin of appreciation in a particular case, factors of importance are the following: the rights involved; the aim that the domestic authorities pursue with the interference; as well as the question whether the case concerns general policies of the State.[135]

It is argued by some that the margin of appreciation obscures questions of appropriateness, and that it is due to the Court's uneven application of this concept that the principle of proportionality is implied less vigorously in some cases than in others.[136] Nonetheless, despite a general doctrinal uncertainty regarding the way the Court assesses restrictions on fundamental rights, it can be concluded that the proportionality principle serves as an essential tool in its assessment of whether a right balance has been struck between the protection of individual rights on the one hand, and the public interest on the other. As such, proportionality enjoys the status of a general principle embodied in the Convention.[137]

8.5.2 Detention of Persons who are Mentally Ill, Alcoholics and Vagrants

There are similarities between the grounds for detention in Article 5(1)(f), on the one hand, and Article 5(1)(e) on the other. Neither with regard to detention pending deportation, nor with regard to the detention of mentally ill people, alcoholics, drug addicts and vagrants does the text of the Convention spell out the aim of detention. Nonetheless, the detention of those persons mentioned in Article 5(1)(e) is not permitted merely on the ground of their condition as such, but instead there must be a specific aim underlying their deprivation of liberty. In the case of *Guzzardi* the Court shed some light on the reasons underlying the permissible detention of mentally ill persons, drug addicts, alcoholics and vagrants. The Convention permits the detention of these people, not only because they can be considered dangerous to public safety, but also because their own interests may necessitate their detention.[138]

---

[134] *Handyside v. United Kingdom*, par. 48.
[135] *Gillow v. United Kingdom*, par. 55. See also Dijk and Hoof (1998), 95.
[136] R.St.J. Macdonald, "The Margin of Appreciation," in *The European System for the Protection of Human Rights*, eds. R.St.J. Macdonald, F. Matscher and H. Petzold (The Hague: Martinus Nijhoff Publishers, 1993), 124. See also J. McBride, "Proportionality and the European Convention on Human Rights," in *The Principle of Proportionality in the Laws of Europe*, ed. E. Ellis (Oxford: Hart Publishing, 1999), 23; and A. McHarg, "Reconciling Human Rights and the Public Interest," *The Modern Law Review* 62 (1999).
[137] Dijk and Hoof (1998), 81.
[138] *Guzzardi v. Italy*, par. 98.

According to the Court an individual cannot be considered to be 'of unsound mind' for the purposes of Article 5(1)(e) and deprived of his liberty under that provision unless three conditions are met. First, the person concerned must be reliably shown to be of unsound mind. Second, the mental disorder must be of a kind or degree warranting compulsory confinement. And in the third place, the validity of continued confinement depends upon the persistence of such a disorder.[139] The last two conditions clearly imply that the Court regards the proportionality and necessity of the detention as indispensable requirements when assessing the lawfulness of such deprivations of liberty. The Court's requirement that an objective medical report must demonstrate to the competent national authority the existence of a genuine mental disturbance, whose nature or extent is such as to justify confinement, which cannot be prolonged unless the mental disturbance continues, is a more concrete statement of these conditions.[140]

Also in the case of *Varbanov* the Court explicitly referred, in general terms, to the required necessity of the deprivation of liberty in the sense that less restrictive measures would not suffice:

> The detention of an individual is such a serious measure that it is only justified where other, less severe measures, have been considered and found to be insufficient to safeguard the individual or public interest which might require that the person concerned be detained. The deprivation of liberty must be shown to have been necessary in the circumstances.[141]

The national authorities are granted a wide margin of appreciation with regard to the necessity of the detention of mentally ill persons, because it is primarily for them to evaluate the evidence brought forward.[142] Thus, normally the Court does not elaborate on what in its own view would constitute a kind or degree of mental illness to justify deprivation of liberty. In the case of *Winterwerp* it examined the Dutch legislation that authorised Winterwerp's confinement, and its conclusion that Article 5 had not been violated seems to have been motivated by the fact that this legislation allowed only for confinement which was proportional.[143]

In the case of *Witold Litwa*, the Court elaborated on the what is meant with the term 'alcoholics' in Article 5(1)(e). In light of the object and purpose of

---

[139] See *X v. United Kingdom*, par. 40; *Winterwerp v. the Netherlands*, par. 39; *Luberti v. Italy*, par. 27; *Johnson v. United Kingdom*, 24 October 1997, Reports 1997-VII, par. 60; *Varbanov v. Bulgaria*, 5 October 2000, Reports 2000-X, par. 45.
[140] *Herczegfalvy v. Austria*, 24 September 1992, A-244, par. 63.
[141] *Varbanov v. Bulgaria*, par. 46.
[142] See for example *Wassink v. the Netherlands*, par. 25.
[143] *Winterwerp v. the Netherlands*, par. 38.

this provision the Court considered that persons "who are not medically diagnosed as alcoholics, but whose conduct and behaviour under the influence of alcohol pose a threat to public order or themselves, can be taken into custody for the protection of the public or their own interests, such as their health or personal safety."[144] In the case at hand the Court found the detention to be unlawful under Article 5(1)(e), because it was considered unnecessary under the given circumstances.[145] The Court reiterated once again its generally formulated statement that the detention of an individual is such a serious measure that "it is only justified where other, less severe measures have been considered and found to be insufficient to the public or individual interest which might require that the person concerned should be detained."[146]

However, in an older precedent – a case dealing with the deprivation of liberty of vagrants – the Court seemed less observant of criteria such as proportionality and necessity. In *Ooms, Wilde and Versyp*, Belgian legislation defined vagrants as "persons who have no fixed abode, no means of subsistence and no regular trade or profession". If these three conditions were fulfilled, the authorities were allowed to order that the persons concerned be placed at the disposal of the Government in closed institutions. The Court considered that someone who would satisfy the definition of a vagrant in the relevant Belgian legislation would in principle fall within the scope of exception provided for in Article 5(1)(e). However, when subsequently assessing the legitimacy of the confinement of vagrants, the Court paid no heed to the proportionality principle or to considerations of necessity:

> Having thus the character of a 'vagrant', the applicants could, under Article 5 (1) (e) of the Convention, be made the subject of a detention provided that it was ordered by the competent authorities and in accordance with the procedure prescribed by Belgian law.[147]

It must be kept in mind that *Ooms, De Wilde and Versyp* was decided in 1971, when the Court had not dealt with many cases concerning deprivations of liberty. As we saw, in later cases it has consistently held that that the categories of persons mentioned in 5(1)(e) are to be narrowly interpreted and that the detention of such persons is allowed by the Convention, not only because they can be dangerous to public safety but also because their own interests may *necessitate* their detention.[148] It is possible, especially in light of more recent

---

[144] *Witold Litwa v. Poland*, Reports 2000-III, par 60–61.
[145] Ibid., par. 78.
[146] Id.
[147] *Ooms, Wilde and Versyp v. Belgium*, par. 69.
[148] *Guzzardi v. Italy*, par. 98.

case law concerning Article 5(1)(e), that it would pay more attention to the proportionality and necessity of the detention were it to decide such a case now.[149] At the same time, one cannot help drawing an uncomfortable parallel between the older precedent of *Ooms, Wilde and Versyp* and more recent cases concerning immigration detention, especially when keeping in mind the 'great confinement' as an instrument to achieve the sedentarisation of populations.

8.6 Immigration Detention as the Blind Spot of the ECtHR?

We have seen in this chapter that the level of scrutiny that is applied by the ECtHR when it assesses the lawfulness of immigration detention is not of the same intensity as it is when the lawfulness of several other categories of deprivation of liberty is examined. Nor are those principles applied which are considered intrinsic to the European system for the protection of human rights. With regard to all the three sub-principles contained in the proportionality principle, the Court's adjudication of migrants' claims to the right to liberty under Article 5(1)(f) is found wanting. The most serious issues arise with regard to the principles of suitability and necessity, its outright refusal to require that detention is a necessary measure if resorted to in immigration procedures being the most striking example. Reading the Grand Chamber judgment in *Saadi*, one feels an urge to remind the majority that *any* deprivation of liberty involves the state's monopoly on the use of violence, no matter how 'relaxed'(!) the regime at a particular detention centre may be.[150] That very fact, taken together with the existence of valid reasons to doubt the effectiveness of detention as a blanket tool of immigration control,[151] should mean – at least when

---

[149] In the two other complaints that were brought before the Court allegedly concerning unlawful deprivations of liberty on account on vagrancy, the issues of proportionality and necessity did not play a role. In *Bitiyeva*, the Court found that the detention was arbitrary as there was no legal basis for it in the domestic law and in *H.M v. Switzerland* it concluded that the situation was not covered by Article 5(1). See *Bitiyeva and X v. Russia*, 21 June 2007, Appl. No. 57953/00 and 37392/03; and *H.M. v. Switzerland*, 26 February 2002, Appl. No. 39187/98.

[150] With its concomitant dangers for abuse, which are well documented, as regards the situation in the UK, in: Birnberg Peirce & Partners, Medical Justice and the National Coalition of Anti-Deportation Campaigns, *Outsourcing Abuse: The Use and Abuse of State Sanctioned Force during the Detention and Removal of Asylum Seekers*, July 2008, at http://www.libertysecurity.org/IMG/pdf_outsourcing_abuse.pdf.

[151] London Detainee Support Group, *Detained Lives: The Real Cost of Immigration Detention* (January 2009) at www.detainedlives.org); and Amnesty International, *The Netherlands: The Detention of Irregular Migrants and Asylum Seekers* (EUR 35/02/2008), June 2008. But see K. Hailbronner, "Detention of Asylum Seekers," *European Journal of Migration and Law* 9 (2007), 161.

taking the idea of fundamental rights seriously – that in each individual case the suitability and the necessity of detention as a means to prevent unauthorised entry or to carry out deportation is ascertained. However, when it concerns the fundamental rights of those whose presence on national territory is not authorised, the Court seems to attach rather more weight to the logic of 'management' and 'control' concerning a whole category of persons, than to the individualised justice that should be the focus of human rights protection proper. Its susceptibility to the argument that Saadi's detention was in the interest of those asylum seekers "increasingly in queue" proves a case in point.[152]

Seven Grand Chamber judges wrote in a dissenting opinion to the judgment in *Saadi* that they 'fail[ed] to see what value or higher interest can justify the notion that [...] fundamental guarantees of individual liberty in a State governed by the rule of law cannot or should not apply to the detention of asylum seekers'.[153] Indeed, the ECtHR case law on immigration detention leaves one with a legion of pressing questions. Why is the lawfulness of the deportation order largely irrelevant to the question whether immigration detention is a lawful measure, whereas with regard to mentally ill persons, it is considered to be of crucial importance for the lawfulness of the confinement that the person concerned is really suffering from a mental illness? Why does the Court neither apply a 'necessity test' to immigration detention, nor insists that other, less severe measures have been considered and found insufficient, as it does with regard to interferences with the right to liberty in a purely domestic context? And how can legislation that provides for very wide discretionary powers, sometimes even allowing for discrimination based on nationality, be deemed to be in accordance with the Court's substantive interpretation of the expression 'in accordance with a procedure prescribed by law' in Article 5(1) ECHR? And, finally, how is Article 18 ECHR to be understood in the context of immigration detention, especially in view of the Court's position according to which the decision to detain someone who is not authorised to enter is justified, as long as it is a genuine part of the immigration procedures? With such an attitude, *détournement de pouvoir* is at best very difficult to prove; at worst it is encouraged.

Several factors contribute to the serious inconsistencies in the Court's case law. To begin with, it has been argued that the Court in general deals neither consistently, nor in a clearly reasoned way with individual rights protection versus the public interest, which is probably partly due to its general failure to

---

[152] The dissenting judges found this argument to be unacceptable. See *Saadi v. United Kingdom*, Grand Chamber Judgment, Joint Partly Dissenting Opinion of Judges Rozakis, Tulkens, Kovler, Hajiyev Spielman and Hirvelä.
[153] Ibid.

develop a coherent set of concepts to determine when and how rights prevail over the public interest.[154] In addition, the fact that recourse to immigration detention has increasingly become a general policy of European states is likely to result in those states being allowed a wider margin of appreciation.

Furthermore, it should be taken into account that there is no right to reside for foreigners to be found in the Convention. Nor does the ECtHR have direct control over the choices made by states as to priorities in the area of public policy. The dilemmas for the Court as to how far it may go in limiting the practices of states in this area are exacerbated by its international position, where it may at times need to be more deferential than national courts in order to retain its credibility. Thus, we should not discard the possibility that the Court grants national states a very wide margin of appreciation to decide on immigration detention because it is "silently conscious of the fact that the Strasbourg system of supervision needs to retain the fullest possible support and compliance of the contracting parties if it is to be at all effective."[155] Still, the political sensitivity of the area of immigration policy does not fully account for the Court's case law in this area. Indeed, as we have seen in Chapter 5, the Court's decisions with regard to Article 3 ECHR in the immigration context exemplify that it is not always so deferential to national sensitivities in a sensitive and highly politicised area.

The above-mentioned reasons considered separately do not adequately explain the inconsistency in the Strasbourg case law, but together they may well contribute to some of the difficulties that the Court has in defining adequate safeguards for immigration detainees. Nonetheless, I believe the very roots of the problem have to be sought elsewhere. It is precisely in the Court's portrayal of detention as a "necessary adjunct" to the sovereign state's "undeniable right of control" over its territory that we may find the deep cause for the substandard level of human rights protection for immigration detainees in Strasbourg. Its perception of territorialised sovereignty as a natural and innocent concept leads the Court to afford national states a very wide margin of appreciation when deciding to resort to deprivations of liberty in the immigration context. The Court's understanding of this specific aspect of sovereignty as entailing a nearly absolute right of states to control their territorial borders results in a clear failure to address the legitimacy of the coercive means that are used to assert this right.

Nevertheless, it is important to keep in mind that the Court's position is not one of inevitability, as is shown by some of the HRC decisions as were

---

[154] McHarg (1999) and Greer (2003).
[155] N. Mole, *Asylum and the European Convention on Human Rights* (Strasbourg: Council of Europe Publishing, 2007), 32.

discussed in the previous chapter. Indeed, even in the ECtHR case law on immigration detention, one finds an occasional awareness of the fact that the territorial frame of sovereignty cannot remain insulated against those processes of legal accountability that were accepted as being applicable to the content of sovereignty in a purely domestic context a long time ago.

In the first place, by insisting on the 'domestic legality' of the deprivation of liberty, the Court resolutely dismisses the possibility that immigration detainees can be held in a 'legal vacuum'. Likewise, its case law shows that the procedural guarantees provided by Article 5 are fully applicable to immigration detainees. Secondly, in *Amuur* and later similar cases dealing with the deprivation of liberty of aliens in transit zones of international airports, the Court has taken full account of the impact of the overall system of movement controls on the freedom of the individual in a global territorial structure of states.

In the third place, the proportionality principle and more general considerations with regard to the necessity, the reasonableness, and the appropriateness of the detention are not entirely absent from the ECtHR case law. They play a role when the Court examines the duration of the detention, which needs to be reasonable and proportionate. In addition, cases such as *Čonka, Riad and Idiab*, and *Mubilanzila Mayeka and Kaniki Mitunga* illustrate that the appropriateness and suitability of the specific manner in which the decision to detain is enforced or carried out have a bearing on its legitimacy as well.[156] In these cases, the Court has explicitly mentioned the fact that immigration detention affects persons whose only distinguishing characteristic is that they are not authorised to be on national territory, which accordingly meant that the authorities had to exercise due care in implementing the decision to detain them. Finally, if the right to privacy and family life is at stake, the judgment in *Mubilanzila Mayeka and Kaniki Mitunga* showed that the proportionality of the detention is fully measured against the interference – albeit not with the right to personal liberty but with the right protected by Article 8 of the Convention.

Apart from these exceptions, the ECtHR has embedded its case law on immigration firmly within a legal discourse that refuses to fully articulate and consider the interests of the individual. The Court's refusal in *Saadi* to examine the complaint under Article 14 ECHR is perhaps the most obvious manifestation of the 'territorial blind spots' that this discourse suffers, but the manner in which the rights of immigration detainees are generally protected in Strasbourg exemplifies the persistence of the political particularism that is

---

[156] See also the partly concurring and partly dissenting opinion of Mr Verlaers, Judge Ad Hoc in *Čonka v. Belgium*.

the result of territoriality in a discourse that explicitly aspires to surpass such particularism. The very institution whose founding document expresses a profound belief in human rights and fundamental freedoms as the foundation of justice and peace in the world, has thus "tamed and domesticated the promise of human rights"[157] by legitimating the silencing logic of territorial sovereignty. That very fact in itself could serve as a validation of the claim that human rights' contemporary institutionalisation in the global territorial order results in an inability to protect those individuals who are 'out of place'.

In this respect one cannot help noticing that the one case in which the Court meticulously analysed the proportionality of the decision to resort to immigration detention – albeit as a result of the requirement that the deprivation be in conformity with national law – concerned a person who was not at all 'out of place' in the global territorial ideal, but instead on her way back to the country where she 'belonged'. As such, the Court held that her situation "was fundamentally different from that of an illegal immigrant or asylum seeker."[158] Nevertheless, and although it may seem paradoxical, when it comes to the interests of the illegal immigrant and the asylum seeker, exposing territorial sovereignty to the full force of the original promise of human rights may be the only remedy to modern constitutionalism's obdurate and structural blind spots, a claim that will be carefully investigated in the conclusions to this book.

---

[157] N. Bohler-Muller, "Review Essay: On a Cosmopolis to Come," *Social & Legal Studies* 17 (2008), 566.
[158] *Rusu v. Austria*, par. 57.

Part III
Conclusions

Chapter 9

Destabilising Territorial Sovereignty through Human Rights Litigation in Immigration Detention Cases

> ... as long as we understand rights to imply a world building that is not incompatible with the project of building juridical institutions and safeguards, but also reaches beyond that project because it is wary of the sedimentations of power and discretion that accrete in such institutional contexts.[1]

9.1 Introduction

In this work I have sought to demonstrate that existing human rights adjudication proves inadequate to protect the individual and to safeguard his or her interests when the national state wishes to enforce its sovereign claims against those who have allegedly violated its territorial boundaries. The reason for human rights' failure to respond in accordance with its explicit aim of establishing a constitutional order over and across boundaries has to be sought in the doctrinal separation that has been made within the concept of sovereignty, that is, between its form and content. Indeed, whereas sovereignty's decisional content as the exercise of jurisdiction over people within a given territory has always been limited by various constitutional discourses, sovereignty's territorial form, although a relative latecomer on the political stage, has remained substantially insulated against the usual forces of political and legal correction. Such inoculation of territorial sovereignty could only occur as a result of the reification of territoriality in modern political and legal imagery. In this final chapter I shall first elaborate on my findings from the previous chapters in order to show that territorial sovereignty as an institution is founded upon and simultaneously maintains an important role in

---

[1] B. Honig, "Another Cosmopolitanism? Law and Politics in the New Europe," in *Another Cosmopolitanism: Hospitality, Sovereignty, and Democratic Iterations*, ed. R. Post (Oxford: Oxford University Press, 2006), 117, commenting on Hannah Arendt's unconditional "right to have rights".

Galina Cornelisse, Immigration Detention and Human Rights, pp. 315–344.
© 2010 Koninklijke Brill NV. Printed in the Netherlands.

shaping contemporary legal norms and actual practices; practices which, in turn, impact on these norms.[2] As such, we shall see that crucial normative assumptions are built into, but at the same time remain hidden by, the institution of territorial sovereignty, the implications of which on the life of the individual are best illustrated by the practice of immigration detention (section 9.3). In concluding this book, I shall argue that human rights litigation in immigration detention can make these normative assumptions open and explicit. The result is that they may be more effectively challenged in modern legal and political discourse, therewith facilitating novel ways of thinking about the relationship between political power, territory and individual rights (section 9.4).

9.2 Territorial Sovereignty as an Institution: The Shaping of Norms and Practices

> I once read the story of a group of people who climbed higher and higher in an unknown and very high tower. Their first generation got as far as the fifth storey, the second reached the seventh, the third the tenth. In the course of time their descendants attained the hundredth storey. With the passage of time they forgot that their ancestors had ever lived on lower floors and how they had arrived at the hundredth floor. They saw the world and themselves from the perspective of the hundredth floor, without knowing how people had arrived there. They even regarded the ideas they formed from the perspective of the hundredth floor as universal human ideas.[3]

In chapter 2, I briefly referred to the important argument made by John Agnew and Stuart Corbridge that the reification of territoriality as an organising principle for the global political system has been caused by the lack of attention to the historical relationship between two elements in the definition of the state in political theory: the exercise of state power through political institutions, on the one hand, and the clear spatial demarcation of the territory in which such power is exercised on the other.[4] The same shortcoming can be discerned in the field of law, exemplified by the way in which legal norms in their application simply take the territorial sovereignty of the state

---

[2] See for a somewhat similar definition of sovereignty as an institution in general terms: K. Claussen and T. Nichol, "Reconstructing Sovereignty: The Impact of Norms, Practices and Rhetoric," *Bologna Center Journal of International Affairs*, 12 (2009).
[3] N. Elias, *Time: an Essay* (Oxford UK, Cambridge USA: Blackwell, 1992), 135.
[4] J. Agnew and S. Corbridge, *Mastering space: Hegemony, territory and international political economy* (London: Routledge, 1995), 78 and 82.

for granted, without providing any reference to the normative assumptions that underlie that institution, even though, and this holds especially true for the constitutional ideas that have developed since the emergence of the modern state, these norms are only understandable against the normative assumptions underlying territoriality.[5]

In the field of constitutional law, the core function of which consists of making power accountable, this shortcoming is all the more serious because the state's claim to ultimate power within its territory (and its concomitant monopoly on the legitimate means of violence) is contingent on both the way in which the state determines its boundaries internally and the way in which its external sovereign claims feature in a global structure of mutually independent states. Below I shall first address the way in which, over time, social and political practices have lent the institution of territorial sovereignty its resilient and obdurate character. After that, I will elaborate on the way in which contemporary human rights law and modern migration laws have been decisively shaped by territorial sovereignty.

9.2.1 Nationalism as Social Practice and the Reification of Territorial Sovereignty

We have seen that the territorialisation of political organisation had largely become a reality by the time that the predominant mode of legitimising political authority consisted of an appeal to the sovereignty of the people. Indeed, the very process of territorialisation made possible the emergence of a notion as abstract as popular sovereignty: its very abstraction being one of the characteristics that distinguished popular sovereignty from earlier theories by which men had attempted to legitimise political authority. The result of the fact that ideas of popular sovereignty came to be executed in an emerging system of separate and independent political entities, demarcated by way of territorial borders, was that the enlightenment ideals on which the concept of the people was based quickly lost their universalistic implications.

Instead, under the influence of nationalism, they transformed into a particularistic conception of the *nation* constituted by the people whose bonds to

---

[5] Cf. Roberto Unger, who makes this argument with regard to the way in which modern legal analysis guards the treasured contrast between legal analysis and ideological conflict in general: "although the doctrinal ideas [contained in modern legal analysis] are neither justifiable nor even fully intelligible apart from the normative and empirical account of state and society that they take for granted, they are typically formulated, applied, and developed without clear reference to this account". See R.M. Unger, *The Critical Legal Studies Movement* (Cambridge, MA: Harvard University Press, 1983), 52.

each other were supposedly pre-political. The very survival of a political system in which loyalty was no longer required to the King, but to an anonymous and abstract multitude called the people, would probably not have been possible without an appeal that went deeper than the intangible notion of the *people* who were only united because they were subject to common government within a certain territory.[6] Within the state, nationalism was thus able to fill the gap that existed between the abstract and intangible notion of popular sovereignty and the actualities of a political system based on territoriality.

As regards the overall system of states, the emerging Westphalian logic firmly established the role of territorial borders in defining and limiting each state's jurisdiction. By establishing external sovereignty as a principle of international relations, the Peace of Westphalia thus ascribed to each territorial state the exclusive government of the population within its territory, and the ensuing external sovereign claims largely coincided with sovereignty's internal claim of distinguishing the inside from the outside. Again, such a global system of the governance of populations would not have been viable if states would not have had at their disposal an appeal to unity that supposedly went deeper than the mere fact of a shared presence in a certain territory. Thus, not only *within* the nation state had territory, identity and sovereignty become linked to each other in what from the end of the nineteenth century onwards was seen as a natural, necessary and inextricable linkage, but the same linkage provided the foundation for the system of sovereign states as a whole. Constitutional discourses, internationally as well as domestically, were profoundly influenced by the national-territorial ideal that was the embodiment of the triad of territory, authority and identity.

Roughly speaking, the establishment of the nation state and the Westphalian state system coincided with the establishment of constitutional government within the state, even though before that there had been theories concerning the limits to the power of the sovereign. The modern notion of individual rights distinguished itself from earlier notions of individual liberties in that, in theory, rights were accorded to the individual on account of his humanity, and no longer because of his specific place in the body politic or by reason of his personal relation to the sovereign ruler. However, the shift from the universal to the particular in the underlying ideals of the nation state, caused by the intricate relationship between territorialisation and nationalism, also affected the discourse of the Rights of Man. The Westphalian global structure, taken

---

[6] J. Habermas, "The European Nation-state – Its Achievements and Its Limits. On the Past and Future of Sovereignty and Citizenship," in *Mapping the Nation*, ed. G. Balakrishnan (London: Verso, 1996), 285.

together with the internal sovereign claims by the modern state, resulted in a construction in which citizenship, a particular form of membership in the territorially defined state, became a necessary condition for access to those rights that were supposed to be inalienable and pre-political. When, at the beginning of the twentieth century, citizenship's role had changed from a means by which to realise equality on a small scale to what has very aptly been called a 'gatekeeper of humanity', the link between rights, identity and territory seemed natural and inevitable. The result thereof was that, domestically, the legal venues for addressing state violence, if perpetrated against those individuals who did not share the identity of the national state, did not exist at all or were only very marginally developed.

The fact that an identity that found its roots in historically contingent territorial borders – notwithstanding the fact that it was presented as based on allegedly more profound ties – determined who could and who could not benefit from 'inalienable' and 'pre-political' rights, provides the ultimate example of how the process of territorialisation has deeply influenced questions relating to the legitimacy of the exercise of sovereign power and, ultimately, its accountability. However, the very appeal to more profound ties such as those based on blood and language or to the notion of a people united by a common destiny, merely buttressed the reification of territoriality, with the insidious result that only sovereignty's content – in the sense of jurisdictional claims made within a clearly defined territory – was open to challenge in domestic constitutional discourse.

Following a comparable logic, the process of territorialisation and the force of nationalism decisively shaped the way in which classic international law sought to limit state power as well. Here, the triumph of a particularistic reality over the universalistic ideals of the enlightenment era was expressed in the perception of international law as the law for and between sovereign states alone. In the few cases that the individual featured in this field of law, international law merely affirmed the rule that national sovereignty should embody a perfect link between identity and territory. Indeed, by providing a law of exception for those who "belied a different identity within,"[7] international law reinforced the perception according to which territorial belonging constituted a necessary criterion for access to the Rights of Man. In addition, the fact that only states were accorded international legal personality, combined with the fact that at the basis of international law lies the Westphalian notion that a

---

[7] N. Xenos, "Refugees: The Modern Political Condition," in *Challenging Boundaries. Global Flows, Territorial Identities*, eds. M.J. Shapiro and H.R. Alker (Minneapolis: University of Minneapolis Press; 1996), 233–246, on citizenship and nationalism.

state occupies a definite part of the earth within which it exercises jurisdiction over persons to the exclusion of other states, resulted in a system in which international law dealt mainly with the territorial form of sovereignty, with regard to which it took into account solely the interests of states in maintaining their so-called territorial integrity.

Accordingly, the separate nature of domestic constitutional discourses, on the one hand, and classic international law, on the other, and the distinct manner in which they made accountable and challenged the exercise of power by the sovereign state, reinforced the perception according to which sovereignty's content was conceptually distinct from sovereignty's territorial form, and according to which the latter aspect of sovereignty did not involve the interests of the individual. On a more practical level, the distinctiveness of external and internal constraints on state power resulted in the absence of enforceable rights for large groups of individuals who could not be fitted within the national-territorial ideal, as was exemplified by the unspeakable horrors committed against these people during the Second World War. The dreadful consequences of the very gap between international and national law led to the proclamation of yet another declaration insisting upon the equal and inalienable rights of all members of the human family. On December 10, 1948 the General Assembly of the United Nations adopted the Universal Declaration of Human Rights, a document that explicitly aims to secure that the Rights of Man have universal and effective recognition and observance.

9.2.2 *The Territorial Limitations of Modern Constitutionalism*

In the decades following the adoption of the Universal Declaration of Human Rights, the proliferation of binding and non-binding human rights law has been enormous, and it has been accompanied with an abundance of institutions, in the international arena as well as in the national context, both governmental and non-governmental in character, focussing on the promotion and protection of the human rights of the individual. And it is undeniable that the extensive body of human rights law that has developed since 1948 has succeeded in diminishing the gap between external and internal constraints on state power.

In the first place, by making the individual a subject of international law, international law is no longer the law for sovereign states alone: it offers venues for addressing the individual interests that are involved in the exercise of jurisdiction by the state within its own territory. Secondly, also *domestic* constitutional discourses have significantly altered under the influence of human rights norms: they have led to a weakening of the tie between identity and rights with regard to those individuals who are present within the territory of the nation state. Such a decoupling of rights and national identity with regard to sovereignty's content is most apparent in the case of individuals whose presence on national territory is authorised by the national state.

Nevertheless, even in the case of long-term legal residents, human rights have not utterly done away with the traditional linkage between the concept of identity and the notion of rights, a linkage that, ever since the Rights of Man were invented in the eighteenth century, has obstructed the attainment of true equality in dignity and rights for all human beings. Contemporary liberal democracies are no exception in this regard – also there national identity remains a factor of real significance for the individual's legal position within the body politic: those who do not share in its dominant identity can ultimately be made subject to the kind of sovereign discretion that, if applied to those who are formally recognised as members of the body politic, would be illegitimate.[8] And even though the very nature of such distinctions – based as they are on the sole fact that the person concerned 'belies a different identity within' – is not in accordance with the explicit aim of the human rights discourse (in addition to which they may, in their application, be difficult to reconcile with important constitutional principles), they have been affirmed in the Strasbourg case law. According to the ECtHR, the position of a nonnational, even if he or she holds a very strong residence status and has attained a high degree of integration, cannot be equated with that of a national when it comes to the sovereign power to deport or expel. The naturalisation of the link between deportation and foreign nationals is the immediate result of a discourse in which the responsibility for safeguarding the fundamental rights of the individual ultimately lies with the state to which that individual is allocated by way of an identity that is utterly contingent upon territorial boundaries.

In this context it should not be overlooked that the only formal instance of supposedly post-national citizenship – that of the EU – has retained a firm link between nationality and citizenship status. But perhaps even more fundamentally, celebrations of post-national citizenship that applaud the alleged decoupling of identity and rights tend to overlook the fact that the question of who has *access* to these rights is entirely determined by the way in which the territorial borders of the sovereign state have been drawn. For although human rights law may have achieved a certain decoupling of identity and rights *within* the territory of the constitutional democracy, outside its territory the two remain firmly linked on account of the global territorial system in which an

---

[8] *Article 3 Protocol 4 ECHR*: No one shall be expelled, by means either of an individual or of a collective measure, from the territory of the State of which he is a national.

individual's access to rights is almost entirely conditional on his or her presence on national territory. Just as traditional accounts of formal citizenship status, the discourse of post-national citizenship takes a predominantly internal perspective, which disregards both the global territorial structure of the state system and the ensuing importance of territory for the access to those rights that are supposed to be inalienable and pre-political. In other words, even today, the territorial borders of the national state retain their traditional role in determining the precise extent of the human rights to be enjoyed by the individual.

The failure of modern human rights discourse to remedy the impact of territoriality as an impediment to establishing truly universal guarantees for the equal dignity of each and every individual is amplified by its structural and paradigmatic inability to address the individual interests that are affected whenever the state bases its claims on sovereignty's territorial form. In other words, the fact that the *application* of human rights norms or the related question of who has *access* to these rights is dictated by the logic of territoriality are not the only obstacles that stand in the way of attaining human rights' original promise. Their underlying ideal is also persistently compromised because these norms are only very rarely applied to some important dimensions of power that the state needs to actively employ in order for the very system of territoriality to maintain its validity.

9.2.3 Constitutionalism's Limits Exemplified: The Legal Regulation of Human Movement

The contemporary legal regulation of migration exemplifies unequivocally how the reification of territorial sovereignty has shaped legal norms and the ensuing political practices, which practices, in turn, contribute to the solidification of territorial sovereignty in modern political and legal imagery. At present, human movement of all kinds is to a large extent governed by laws that find their origins in human rights norms, but the actual operations of these laws show that whenever an issue is portrayed as endangering the institution of territorial sovereignty, contemporary constitutionalism relapses to its 'pre-human rights' mode: it turns into a discourse in which sovereign state interest is central and territorial integrity paramount. In a system in which the law perceives sovereignty's content and its form as strictly separate, both subject to a different logic (the former open to full legal contention, the latter only very marginally subject to processes of accountability), the discursive force of presenting an issue as a threat to the state's territorial sovereignty comes most clearly to the fore when contrasting the opposing approaches that international norms have adopted with regard to various modes of human movement.

One example is the increasing acceptance of the constitutional dimensions of freedom of movement *within* the nation state – where its territoriality is not a factor to be reckoned with – which has occurred simultaneously with a hardening of views with respect to movement into its territory.[9]

Then there is also the fact that norms relating to human dignity have made significant inroads into the state's discretion to decide on *emigration* while leaving most decisions relating to the entry of foreign nationals securely embedded in the sovereign prerogative of the national state. At first sight it may seem illogical to seek to explain this difference by reference to modern law's distinction between sovereignty's form and content. Indeed, an historical perspective on sovereign states' responses to the phenomenon of international migration shows that states currently use the same justifications in order to restrict immigration *into* their territories as they have employed to curtail emigration *from* those territories in the past. In this context it is important to appreciate fully that, whenever the state decides on international movement, be it leaving or entering, sovereignty's content and its territorial form are actively engaged, both to an equal extent. Perhaps this is most obvious with regard to sovereign acts of immigration law enforcement: in order to detain and to deport, sovereignty's content must be actively employed. But border control in general, whether it is at the physical border or by means of *police à distance*, involves the exercise of jurisdiction over people.

Why, then, are legal norms dealing with the movement of individuals across international borders able to overlook and ignore most of the individual interests that are so unmistakably involved in immigration decision making? Why do they fail to make political power fully accountable whenever such power is exercised in order to protect national territories from unwanted immigration? The answer to this question has to be sought in the fact that national states portray immigration as engaging solely sovereignty's territorial form and the resonating force of the language that they employ to do so, a language clearly modelled upon the classic legal discourse reserved for interstate violence, which emphasised the sanctity of territorial boundaries and in which the individual had no role to play. In this context, the frequent use of the metaphor of war and aggression in political discourse on immigration is especially salient, which is, it should be underlined, a metaphor transgressing linguistic and

---

[9] See G.S. Goodwin Gill, "The Right to Leave, the Right to Return and the Question of a Right to Remain" in *The Problem of Refugees in the Light of Contemporary Law Issues*, ed. V. Gowlland-Debbas (The Hague: Martinus Nijhoff Publishers, 1996), 103, on the growing constitutional dimensions of freedom of movement within the nation state when compared to movement into its territory.

territorial boundaries in Europe.[10] The result of such a discursive approach to immigration is that the jurisdictional content of sovereignty remains hidden and that the personal interests that are affected by sovereign decisions in this field remain largely inarticulable, let alone that they can be conceived of as rights.

In contrast, in the contemporary state system, where the rights of the individual find the fullest expression if the responsibility for safeguarding these rights lies with the state to which this particular individual is allocated according to this system's territorial logic, the personal interests that are affected by a sovereign decision prohibiting emigration cannot be so easily overlooked. As a result, international norms constrain and make fully accountable the exercise of state power in the field of emigration, but only for as long as *emigration* control is not exercised in the context of *immigration* control.

Indeed, the fact that the steep increase globally in practices interfering with the right to leave serves the protection of the territorial borders of European nation states seems to be sufficient reason for these states to abandon their usual insistence upon adherence to human rights standards in their external relations. The result is that European states, in their attempts to stem immigration flows at their source, have become complicit in practices that involve the arbitrary and unaccountable exercise of sovereign power against individuals who certainly do not benefit from some kind of post-national citizenship status, but for whom the processes of globalisation have rather resulted in ever-decreasing opportunities to move freely in search of a more secure future. Thus, in May 2009, the Italian Minister of the Interior, Roberto Maroni, could publicly appreciate the fact that Libya is working "to keep illegal migrants from leaving."[11] Libya's actions to prevent departures are thus encouraged and even financed by Italy; yet there is strong evidence that the migrants who have been apprehended after earlier trying unsuccessfully to leave Libya are being mistreated and subjected to indefinite detention, often in inhuman and degrading conditions.[12]

---

[10] I. van der Valk, Difference, deviance, threat? *Mainstream and right-extremist political discourse on ethnic issues in the Netherlands and France (1990–1997)* (Amsterdam: Aksant, 2002). See also L. Jones, "Immigration and parliamentary discourse in Great Britain. An analysis of the debates related to the 1996 Asylum and Immigration Act," in *Racism at the Top*, eds. R. Wodak and T.A. van Dijk (Klagenfurt: Drava Verlag, 2002); and I. van der Valk, "Right-wing parliamentary discourse on immigration in France," *Discourse & Society*, 14 (2003).

[11] Human Rights Watch, News Release, 9 June2009, at http://www.hrw.org/en/news/2009/06/09/italylibya-gaddafi-visit-celebrates-dirty-deal.

[12] Id. See also Human Rights Watch: *European Union: Managing Migration means potential European complicity in Neighboring States' Abuse of Migrants and Refugees*, October 2006, at

The concealing of the human interests that are involved in immigration decision making is made easier by keeping the individuals concerned far away from us (a complementary logic underpinning policies of *police à distance*) or by portraying them as different from 'us' (an additional link between identity and rights is thus revealed). Similarly, the way in which populist discourse, becoming more and more mainstream in the Member States of Europe, describes immigration phenomena as 'floods', 'avalanches' and 'invasions' results in little awareness for the real persons who are actually affected by sovereign decision making in this area.[13]

The preponderance of powerful claims by the state that are derived from its territorial sovereignty on the legal regime of migration is exacerbated by the current trend in which immigration is increasingly portrayed as a security issue; the language of societal security being a political discourse that draws very directly from the vernacular of the "invading enemy", traditionally reserved for war and other threats to the territorial integrity of the modern state.[14] As such, 'securitisation' and its hidden assumptions offer ample opportunity to obscure the way in which the exercise of sovereign power implicates the freedom of the individual, not in the least also because its fundamental link with fear and danger reinforces "the indifference and the intentional blindness shown to the outside".[15]

Finally, it is worth taking a look at the various distinctions that the law draws with regard to the people who move – it distinguishes between illegal residents versus long-term legal residents; those whose family life was established while 'illegally' present within the territory versus those who have built

---

http://www.hrw.org/legacy/backgrounder/eca/eu1006/eu1006web.pdf. On the way in which Spanish authorities seem to be complicit, or at least knowledgeable, about unlawful and arbitrary state action conducted by Mauritanian officials against persons who have been suspected of attempting to migrate to the Canary Islands: Amnesty International, *Mauritania: Nobody wants to have anything to do with us, Collective expulsions of migrants denied entry into Europe*, AFR 38/001/2008, 1 July 2008.

[13] Some of the public media very explicitly avail themselves of parallels with war and aggression. On December 29, 2002 a British newspaper, the Sunday Express, wrote: "An army of 110,000 Iraqi refugees is heading for Britain to escape the looming war with Saddam Hussein. Ten thousand Kurds have already trekked to Turkish ports ready to cross into Greece – from where they can easily reach the UK." See for this and other examples: C. Gabrielatos and P. Baker, "Fleeing, Sneaking, Flooding: A Corpus Analysis of Discursive Constructions of Refugees and Asylum Seekers in the UK Press, 1996–2005," *Journal of English Linguistics* 36 (2008).

[14] See J. Huysmans, "The European Union and the Securitization of Migration," *Journal of Common Market Studies* 38 (2000), 757.

[15] H. van Houtum and R. Pijpers, "The European Union as a Gated Community: The Two-Faced Border and Immigration Regime of the EU," *Antipode* 39 (2007), 291, on the fear and politicisation of migration.

a family life whilst enjoying lawful residence; real refugees versus economic migrants, and so forth. The point is that these categorisations neither reflect the real experiences of people, nor have they been primarily thought of in order to safeguard the equal dignity of each and every individual. Instead, a historical perspective reveals that international law in this area has largely developed against the background of the territorial state system and the wish to retain a stable territorial order.

Accordingly, these legal norms are unintelligible without reference to the (conflicting) normative assumptions that underlie that very system, but these assumptions are conveniently not spoken about when the law is applied.[16] As a result, it seems to provide a neutral and impartial framework, itself effectively shielded from any serious challenge. Thus, the law's juxtaposing of the 'economic migrant' and the 'genuine refugee' serves to make sure that contemporary constitutional adjudication does not need to address the fact that denying 'economic migrants' the protection of international human rights law means in actual fact that rich democracies send these people back to face disease, extreme poverty and starvation.

9.3 Territorial Sovereignty as an Institution with Ontological Significance and Immigration Detention as the Litmus Test for the Modern Territorial Order

It has been said that the concept of ownership inherent in the traditional approach in international law to territorial boundaries reinforces and privileges a certain view of the state; and that it is unable to deal sufficiently with alternative perceptions of sovereignty.[17] Indeed, at this point, we can conclude that the present legal order is not prepared to accept a concept if it entails a clear and

---

[16] Of course, we should not forget that a whole range of other normative assumptions underlie modern immigration laws as well. Amongst the most prominent of those are assumptions about what constitutes a family and relations of dependence when it comes to family reunification.

[17] R. McCorquodale, "International Law, Boundaries and Imagination," in *Boundaries and Justice: Diverse Ethical Perspectives*, eds. D. Miller and S. Hashmi (Princeton/Oxford: Princeton University Press, 2001), 153. See also D. Kostakopoulou, "Irregular Migration and Migration Theory: Making State Authorisation Less Relevant," in *Irregular Migration and Human Rights: Theoretical, European and International Perspectives*, ed. B. Bogusz et al. (Leiden/Boston: Martinus Nijhoff Publishers, 2004), 44–50; and D. Kostakopoulou and R. Thomas, "Unweaving the Threads: Territoriality, National Ownership of Land and Asylum Policy," *European Journal of Migration and Law* 6 (2004).

visible challenge to the institution of territorial sovereignty.[18] I have sought to demonstrate that the way in which contemporary human rights law is applied to immigration detention provides the ultimate illustration of the claim that fundamental rights are to a large degree still "caught within the image of the sovereign, the territorial state and the traditional [...] institutions."[19]

Even a brief overview of state practice in this area warrants the conclusion that the normal constitutional safeguards do not apply to immigration detainees and that states refuse to treat them in accordance with international standards pertaining to the rights of the individual. As such, the very particularity of immigration detention lies in the cynical use that governments make of a system in which territory and rights remain firmly linked, despite the official rhetoric of universal rights and theoretical assertions of post-national citizenship. Immigrants who are deprived of their liberty at the borders of or within the European constitutional democracies are in many respects outside the pale of the law; even in the case that they are actually present within the territory of a national state, the absence of state authorisation for such presence means that the usual safeguards embodied in constitutional norms are not applied to them.

Even the European Court of Human Rights does not deem it within its powers to reverse this situation. In its case law on immigration detention, states' appeal to their territorial sovereignty in order to justify their decision to detain has immunised that decision against most forms of legal correction known to the Court. The way in which it endorses detentions that are very difficult to reconcile with the core of the right protected by Article 5 ECHR, as well as with important principles of constitutional adjudication in general, reveals that the Court in Strasbourg shares the dominant attitude in which immigration presents a 'threat' to the territorial border of the nation state that can only be 'controlled' and 'managed' with far-reaching measures.

Even more importantly, however, in deciding the cases of immigration detention that are brought before it, the Court does not once attempt to explain fully why it affords immigration detainees a lower level of human rights protection than those persons 'lawfully at large in the country'. A mere reference to the sovereign right to control borders as such seems inadequate, just as a simple reference to the sovereign right to control crime in a domestic context would be incomprehensible as an argument to do away with the usual constitutional protection for the individual in criminal proceedings – the

---

[18] McCorquodale (2001), 153, making this claim with regard to sovereignty in general.
[19] J. Huysmans, "Discussing Sovereignty and Transnational Politics," in *Sovereignty in transition*, ed. N. Walker (Oxford: Hart Publishing, 2003), 223, who makes a similar argument with regard to democracy.

rationale for the protection offered by human rights being precisely the dangers inherent in the exercise of sovereign power. The difference made by a mere invocation of territorial sovereignty becomes only understandable if we probe a little deeper into the normative assumptions that accompany the notion of territoriality.

As we have seen, these assumptions explain the operation of immigration laws in general. Yet, it is the practice of immigration detention in particular that serves as the litmus test for the way in which the institution of territorial sovereignty shapes contemporary norms and practices. This is so because, while most other exclusionary practices as resorted to by the modern state provide us only with a partial perspective on sovereignty's territorial form and its operations, immigration detention epitomises the whole range of the implications of the normative account that underlies the modern territorial order.

In the first place, we have seen that detention is a tool by which states violently reproduce the territoriality of the global state system. In this respect, detention is comparable to deportation, in that it shows how the structural features of the modern state system determine and shape the particular policies of individual nation states; policies which in turn contribute to the perpetuation of that system. When regarded from this perspective, the immigration prison can be categorised alongside a broader range of responses by the sovereign state to what it perceives as threats, not only to its unity within, but to the overall order of the system of which it forms part. The emergence of the refugee regime in the 1920s and the early system of minority protection constitute such responses, just like the population transfers that were resorted to in Europe's recent past in order to achieve the ideal of a stable order of nation states.

In the second place, immigration detention serves as a validation of sovereignty as the power to distinguish the inside from the outside. In this respect, immigration detention fits within a trend in which states make use of increasingly restrictive, at times even violent, tools of migration management in order to demonstrate that they are 'in control' of their borders. In the contemporary political climate, the fact that history shows that controlling flows across borders is far from being a "necessary criterion for legitimate statehood"[20] does nothing to alter states' perception to the contrary. Apart from the steep increases in detention, the most glaring examples of such assertions of sovereign power are constituted by the growing tendency to criminalise irregular stay by the EU member states. That these assertions are not merely

---

[20] R. Bauböck, *Multilevel citizenship and territorial borders in the EU polity* (Vienna: Österreichische Akademie der Wissenschaften, 2003), 8.

symbolical in character is, amongst other examples, proven by the legislative measures that have been adopted by a country such as Italy. A newly adopted public security decree does not only make 'illegal stay' a criminal offence, punishable with a fine of up to €10,000, but it also obliges civil servants, such as doctors and school principals, to report 'illegal immigrants' to the authorities. Moreover, without a valid residence permit, non-citizens cannot marry, nor register the birth of their children. Anyone who attempts to help unauthorised migrants, by offering or letting them accommodation, can be prosecuted for aiding and abetting illegal migration and risks a prison sentence.[21] Just as immigration detention, these measures bear witness to a dangerous tendency to marginalize people who do not conform to the territorial ideal by excluding them from the normal legal order, without paying attention to the question whether such responses to unwanted migration do not create infinitely more severe problems than they purportedly aim to solve.

Lastly, immigration detention is special amongst other tools of migration law enforcement because states do not only resort to immigration detention in order to keep the territorial ideal intact, but they employ the very tool of detention in order to reduce the visibility of disruptions to that ideal. The logic of the *Hôpitals Généraux*, driven by the fear of a "fluid, elusive sociality, impossible to control or utilise"[22] is presently reconstructed in the practice of immigration detention, which is a similar technology of power that provides for the "spatial concentration and ordering of people"[23]; the question of its fluidity and elusiveness now determined on the basis of their disruption not merely to the nation state, as was the rationale for the great confinement throughout Europe during the seventeenth century, but to the territorial system as a whole. The *spatiality* of detention is significant in another way as well, as it can be convincingly argued that spatially separating unwanted migrants from the population lawfully at large in the country reinforces modern constitutionalism's blindnesses and silences when it comes to the interests of these migrants, seeing that estrangement, 'reducing and thinning down the view of the other', is inherent in incarceration.[24]

It is the concept of *estrangement* that leads us to the ontological significance of the institution of territorial sovereignty: the deep cause of legally permissive immigration detention in contemporary societies. In order to understand the

---

[21] Legge 773b (affirmed by the President on 15 July 2009).
[22] W. Walters, "Deportation, Expulsion, and the International Police of Aliens," *Citizenship Studies* 6 (2002), 286.
[23] L.H. Malkki, "Refugees and Exiles: From 'Refugee Studies' to the National Order of Things," *Annual Review of Anthropology* 24 (1995), 498.
[24] Z. Bauman, "Social Issues of Law and Order," *British Journal of Criminology* 40 (2000), 208.

resilience of the legal norms that are associated with sovereignty's territorial form in the field of migration, we need to appreciate that the importance which states attach to the territorial ideal goes much deeper than the mere wish to maintain independent sovereign units, for exclusive territorial sovereignty is also feasible in a country that adheres to an open admissions policy (once again we can discern the artificiality of an ongoing construction in which immigration is perceived as per definition solely engaging sovereignty's territorial frame).

Accordingly, apart from exclusive and ultimate political authority within a certain demarcated territory, the territorial ideal primarily entails the homogenisation of these territorial units: the sovereignty that states seek to protect by invoking their territorial powers is about unity. In other words, although the discursive focus is on territorial boundaries, sovereign states' main concern is about their "conceptual and organizational borders" as those are the sites where membership conditions are stipulated.[25] At a time when the discourse of human rights has diminished the extent to which national states can distinguish between inside and outside *within* their territories with regard to the fundamental rights of persons under their jurisdiction, they rely on their territorial sovereignty in order to keep asserting what Catherine Dauvergne has called their 'nation's nationness'.[26]

Paradoxically, the importance that national states attach to the territorial ideal in this sense is exemplified by the Communitarisation of immigration policy by the EU Member States. The motives underlying that process and the way in which national states have strategic recourse to their sovereignty show that the process of integration in this field is driven by a deeply felt wish to maintain the traditional role of territorial boundaries in protecting the identity of the nation state, notwithstanding the fact that the location of border control has been shifting in important and unprecedented ways. Accordingly, although the tools with which the European Union and its Member States have refined the system of an international police of populations may be novel, their underlying rationale is provided by an understanding of sovereignty that regards control over identity crucial for the unity of the body politic. In this context, political geographers have drawn attention to contemporary practices of "bio-political classification of the origins of people in the world," such as EU legislation listing the third countries whose nationals must be in possession

---

[25] A. Geddes, "Europe's border relationships and international migration relations," *Journal of Common Market Studies* 43 (2005).

[26] C. Dauvergne, "Sovereignty, Migration and the Rule of Law in Global Times," *The Modern Law Review* 67 (2004), 595.

of visas when crossing the external borders and those whose nationals are exempt from that requirement.[27]

The legal framework that reflects the territorial ideal thus seeks to settle questions of identity – and as such migration laws do not merely provide a practical answer to these questions on an individual level (who belongs here and who does not?), but ultimately, these laws reflect assumptions on what it *means* to belong to the nation state.[28] Consequently, it is not some neutral adherence to the orderliness and tidiness of a world territorially divided amongst sovereign entities as such, but rather the elusive concept of identity that is at the root of states' appeal to sovereignty's territorial form when they assert the right to control their borders. That there is a gap between the discursive use of territoriality and the actual assumptions underlying it is best exemplified by sovereign states' willingness to disregard the implications of territoriality as soon as questions relating to *their* national identity and territory do not perfectly coincide.

Thus, ever since the Westphalian state system was established, states have regarded the treatment of coreligionists living in another state as a matter of their concern, just as they extend diplomatic protection to nationals who live in another state. Another example which shows how states, if their national identity is at stake, may deliberately act outside the narrow confines of the 'modern geopolitical imagination', is provided by the various mechanisms through which modern nation states relate to their diasporas abroad. The way in which 'the emigration state' has devised mechanisms of extraterritorial political and legal inclusion by extending expansive political and social rights to members of their diasporas has recently been mapped out by Alan Gamlen who, in the same study, has drawn attention to the various tools through which "states often encourage non-residents to identify with their imagined national communities."[29]

Of course, my claim that, ultimately, it is the concept of identity that lies at the root of the problem of legally permissive immigration detention in our societies should not surprise anyone. However, the crucial point is that the very notion of identity/otherness that determines modern law's perception of and responses to injustice and human suffering is the result of historical contingencies, which, if they were openly addressed, would not hold out as an

---

[27] According to Council Regulation (EC) No. 539/2001 of 15 March 2001, OJ L 81/1, 21 March 2003 (and as amended by later legislation). H. van Houtum and R. Pijpers (2007), 296.

[28] C. Dauvergne, "Confronting Chaos: Migration Law Responds to Images of Disorder," *Res Publica* 5 (1999), 38.

[29] A. Gamlen, "The Emigration State and the Modern Geopolitical Imagination," *Political Geography* 27 (2008), 843.

adequate justification for human inequality, that is to say, if we take the ideals underlying modern constitutionalism as a normative benchmark. As I shall argue below, human rights litigation in immigration detention may be the only site where the incongruity underlying constitutional adjudication on the basis of a legal system that is shaped by, and simultaneously reinforces, human inequality, can be openly addressed.

9.4 *Destabilising Territorial Sovereignty through Human Rights Law*

> Certain issues cannot be fitted within the categories, the description of certain violations cannot be harnessed through the procedures, certain claims remain unformulable, and other appear irrelevant, too subjective, extra-legal, or simply 'mad'. One should not, however, conclude that such difficult issues are necessarily improper for international law. After all international law is constantly in the making and the community is constantly in the process of (re)construction. Therefore, it is senseless to say that everything that is not clearly articulable or categorisable in international law is justly driven outside it, for it is the same to say that international law is a finished system and that we have arrived at the end of its progress. (…) there are always certain silences and incommunicabilities that may be investigated and reconsidered – arguably – to the benefit of the community and its ordering systems.[30]

9.4.1 *The Restrained but Radical Potential of Human Rights*

Modern law's failure in questioning the normative assumptions underlying the institution of territorial sovereignty means that, currently, for many the effective enjoyment of the universal right to equal dignity remains mere rhetoric. Even the majority of (international) constitutional norms that seemingly make inroads into the sovereign power to exclude fit within a territorial image of political order. Instead of challenging the deep cause that results in rights remaining firmly linked to territory and identity, most international rights bearing upon a right to enter or stay attempt to rectify the most glaring gaps in a system that harbours such a linkage, so that it may retain its validity.

By failing to address its inherent contradictions, these norms reinforce the perception of territoriality as a natural way of organising the global political system, which in turn buttresses modern constitutionalism blindnesses. This very mechanism itself could serve as a validation of the claim that human rights' contemporary institutionalisation in the global territorial order

---

[30] O. Korhonen, *International Law Situated: An Analysis of the Lawyer's Stance Towards Culture, History and Community* (The Hague: Kluwer Law International, 2000), 211–212.

inevitably results in their inability to protect those individuals who are 'out of place'. However, if we lose our belief in human rights, we simultaneously jettison "their potential to *transform* the predictable, normal and traditional" and we overlook the fact that they, "as an ideal unlinked from state power (*the polis*) can be used to challenge, resist and rebel against domination and the injustice of law from the point of view of the *cosmos*."[31]

Thus, although it may sound paradoxical, exposing territorial sovereignty to the full force of the original promise of human rights may be the only remedy to modern constitutionalism's 'territorial blindspots'. In this respect, it should not be overlooked that a radical role for human rights vis-à-vis modern territoriality is not utterly without recent precedent. The application of the prohibition on torture and inhuman or degrading treatment in the immigration context shows that modern constitutionalism has at times recognised *and* protected the human interests that are affected by assertions of territorial sovereignty, even though until now it has done so only with regard to those interests that have been categorised as absolute rights. The revolutionary character of the norm of *non-refoulement*, resulting from the application of the prohibition on torture and inhuman and degrading treatment in the immigration context, lies in the fact that it has proven to be able to break away from a territorialised, state-centred conception of the interests involved in territorial sovereignty, and has instead framed these interests in terms of individuals' real lived experiences. Moreover, it has refused to accept that the main responsibility for safeguarding the dignity of the individual lies with the state to which that individual is allocated on the basis of territoriality's logic.

However, there is a high threshold for an application of the norm of *non-refoulement* that breaks away from a territorialised conception of the relationship between interests, rights and responsibility: this will only occur in the case of 'very exceptional circumstances and compelling humanitarian reasons'.[32] In addition, the unleashing of at least some of the destabilising potential of human rights claims on the institution of territorial sovereignty through the application of the norm of *non-refoulement* has been accompanied with increasing attempts by states to resort to extraterritorial measures of immigration

---

[31] N. Bohler-Muller, "Review Essay: On a Cosmopolis to Come" *Social & Legal Studies* 17(2008), 568, discussing Costas Douzinas' ideas. See also C. Douzinas, *The End of Human Rights, Critical Legal Thought at the Turn of the Century* (Oxford, Hart Publishing, 2000) and C. Douzinas, *Human Rights and Empire, the Political Philosophy of Cosmopolitanism* (Oxford, Routledge, 2007).

[32] ECtHR, *D. v. United Kingdom*, 2 May 1997, Reports 1997-III, par. 54; and particularly ECtHR, *Bensaid v. United Kingdom*, 6 February 2001, Appl. No. 44599/98, par. 40, in which latter case the deportation of a patient suffering from schizophrenia did not breach Article 3 ECHR.

control.³³ Such practices show how sovereign states cling to territoriality as a dividing mechanism for responsibility: in their view presence on the territory is crucial for the enjoyment of rights and in many cases it will be impossible to vindicate claims to the contrary, not least because of practical obstacles.

Seeing that there can be no doubt about the fact that immigration detainees are fully included in the jurisdictional scope of state power (arguments pertaining to their supposedly 'extra-legal' status have been firmly rejected by modern constitutional discourse), I believe that the application of human rights claims to the practice of immigration detention could be more successful in destabilising some of the assumptions that accompany the paradigm of territorialised sovereignty. Just as the imprisonment of criminals offered courts an unprecedented way in which to review the sovereign power to punish in the eighteenth century, the very fact that immigration detainees are in a very real sense 'included in the state's domain of sovereign power' could very well provide the opportunity to subject the hitherto largely unrestrained exclusionary power of the sovereign state to full legal contention.

To be sure, courts must play a central role here, for unlike most issues bearing upon the territorial sovereignty of the state, which are largely excluded from normal processes of legal accountability, deprivations of liberty have always been intimately connected with constitutional ideas on judicial control.³⁴ In this respect, it is of key importance that essential procedural guarantees form an inherent part of the prohibition on arbitrary deprivations of liberty. Indeed, the procedural guarantees that accrue to someone on account of his detention are far better developed than those that he may appeal to in the case of his mere exclusion.³⁵ We have seen how the traditionally wide discretion in immigration law has resulted in the existence of only very marginal procedural guarantees with regard to a general right of the individual to enter or stay in a country that is not his own.³⁶ Exceptions are

---

[33] See i.e. G. Aubarell, R. Zapata-Barrero, and X. Aragall, *New Directions of National Immigration Policies: The Development of the External Dimension and its Relationship with the Euro-Mediterranean Process* (Euromesco Paper, February 2009), at http://www.euromesco.net/images/paper79eng.pdf.

[34] D. Wilsher, *The Liberty of Foreigners: A History, Law, and Politics of Immigration Detention* (Nijmegen: Wolf Legal Publishers, 2008).

[35] See P. Boeles, *Eerlijke immigratieprocedures in Europa: Standaarden voor effective procedurele rechtsbescherming in kwesties van toegang, verblijf en uitzetting* (Utrecht: Nederlands Centrum Buitenlanders, 1995), 189, who contends that the procedural guarantees in Article 5 (4) ECHR do not differ essentially from those laid down by Article 6 ECHR.

[36] In addition, practice at the national constitutional level shows that while in general the individual's procedural protection against administrative decision making has increased over time, with regard to immigration procedures the development is a reverse one. Ibid., 367.

contained in Articles 13 ICCPR and 1 of Protocol 7 to the ECHR, which provide for such guarantees with regard to the decision to expel, but these provisions are only applicable to those individuals who enjoy lawful residence. In addition, we have seen that they are subject to important public order and national security exceptions.[37]

Seeing that, in the European context, immigration procedures do not fall within the scope of Article 6 ECHR, the only other international norms pertaining to formal rule of law guarantees with regard to decisions dealing with entry or removal are those that can be invoked only when other fundamental rights are at stake. Thus, if an individual presents an arguable claim that as a result of immigration decision making, the norm contained in Article 3 ECHR is breached, or that his rights under Article 8 ECHR are violated (or, in theory, any other rights guaranteed by the ECHR), he has a right to an effective remedy under Article 13 ECHR.[38] However, even in this construction, states may simply refuse to afford procedural guarantees by arguing that a complaint is not arguable, such as in the case of the individual who comes from 'a safe country of origin'.

In contrast, the habeas corpus guaranteed by Article 5(4) ECHR is applicable to anyone who is deprived of his liberty under immigration legislation: whether someone is labelled as an 'illegal migrant' or a 'security risk', a 'bogus asylum seeker' or an 'economic migrant' is irrelevant when it comes to the procedural guarantees of the right to personal liberty. Moreover, the court to which the immigration detainee appeals should evaluate the case in the light of the prohibition on arbitrary deprivations of liberty, instead of merely assess whether national immigration legislation has been correctly applied. As a result, by resorting to the sharpest technique of exclusion, states risk greater accountability for their actions as well.

9.4.2 *Human Rights as Destabilisation Rights: Towards Territoriality 'Lite'?*

Thus, instead of presenting the immigration prison as the ultimate example of the immunisation of territorial sovereignty against modern constitutionalism, I will conclude this study by describing how it may possibly become a site

---

[37] The 1951 Refugee Convention is silent with regard to procedural guarantees applicable to decisions based on the norm contained in its Article 33, even though the Convention as whole implies access to fair and effective procedures for determining an individual's need for international protection. See UNHCR ExCom Conclusion No. 82 (XLVIII) 1997 (Safeguarding Asylum), under d(ii); and UNHCR ExCom Conclusion No. 103 (LVI) 2005 (Conclusion on the Provision on International Protection Including Through Complementary Forms of Protection), under (r).

[38] We have seen in chapter 5 that the ICCPR provides for similar guarantees.

where human rights transform into claims that unsettle territorial sovereignty as a "structural, paradigm-related and epistemic limitation" which stands in the way of the very communicability of individual interests.[39] In order to elaborate on this idea, I draw on the notion of destabilisation rights, a concept coined by Roberto Unger in a different setting, but which shall prove particularly useful for my purposes.[40] A recurrent theme in Unger's work is his concern with what he calls institutional fetishism: "the belief that abstract institutional conceptions [...] have a single natural and necessary institutional expression."[41] According to Unger, the pervasiveness of this belief should not prevent us from imagining alternative ways in which we can organise that society. Indeed, by ways of thinking that defy "the immunization of the basic institutions of society, defined in law, against effective criticism, challenge and revision," we may arrive at alternatives that are truer to our interests, ideals and hopes.[42]

Charles Sabel and William Simon have elaborated upon the idea of destabilisation rights in the area of public law litigation. They apply Unger's idea to a wide variety of policy fields such as pertaining to prisons, schools and housing, in order to show that the judicial recognition and enforcement of rights that "disentrench an institution that has systematically failed to meet its obligations and remained immune to traditional forces of political correction" may be effective in bringing about better compliance with legal obligations. I will not address their arguments with regard to the policy fields that they deal with in substance, as these are far too specific to be applicable to the institution of territorial sovereignty, but I shall refer to some of the "destabilization effects" which they describe in their analysis, in order to demonstrate how human rights applied to immigration detention may turn into destabilisation rights.

By not conforming to the usual judicial and legislative modes of exercise, the institution of territorial sovereignty satisfies the elements for what Sabel and Simon call the *prima facie* case for public law litigation: "failure to meet standards and political blockage."[43] With regard to the element of political

---

[39] O. Korhonen, *International Law Situated: An Analysis of the Lawyer's Stance Towards Culture, History and Community* (The Hague: Kluwer Law International, 2000), 210, about such limitations in international law generally.
[40] In Unger's theory, the central idea of destabilisation rights is 'to provide a claim upon governmental power obliging government to disrupt those forms of division and hierarchy that, contrary to the spirit of the constitution, manage to achieve stability only by distancing themselves from the transformative conflicts that might disturb them.' Unger (1983), 53.
[41] R.M. Unger, *What should legal analysis become?* (London, Verso, 1996).
[42] Ibid., 96.
[43] C.F. Sabel and W. Simon, "Destabilization Rights: How Public Law Litigation Succeeds," *Harvard Law Review* 117 (2004), 1062.

blockage, they distinguish between three different patterns, the first of which is directly applicable to the way in which sovereignty's territorial frame features in contemporary practices of immigration detention: it involves "majoritarian political control unresponsive to the interests of a vulnerable, stigmatized community."[44] In this study, I have focused mainly on the limits of constitutional processes and modern law in general when it concerns the accountability of the exercise of power based upon territorial sovereignty. Therefore, it is worth underlining here that in the case of immigration detention, the additional exclusion from processes of *political* control of those who Simon and Sabel call the stakeholders is the result of the very nature of territorial borders as constructs that define who can participate in a community's political decision making. As such, the laws governing the institution of territorial sovereignty – mostly ruling over those who have not consented to be governed – are a *prima facie* example of legislation that does not fit within standard democratic theory.[45]

However, as we have seen, a growing body of human rights law is concerned with the practice of immigration detention. In contrast to the application of the norm contained in Article 3 ECHR, which covers only a limited amount of human interests and can be invoked only in exceptional circumstances, the human right to personal liberty includes the interests of all that have been affected by the sovereign right to exclude, if the exercise of that right has resulted in a deprivation of liberty. We have seen that the destabilising potential of the right to liberty for the perceived neutrality of territorial sovereignty comes to the fore in some of the decisions on immigration detention by the UN Human Rights Committee. By insisting that the lawfulness of immigration detention requires an individualised test of its proportionality, this body invalidates sovereign claims to the effect that the particular mode of exercising the power to exclude cannot be contested. Furthermore, by balancing the interests of the individual against the state's interest in maintaining the 'integrity of its borders', it fully recognises the human interests that are involved in territorial sovereignty as *human rights*, the special status of which warrants that they cannot be 'simply' overridden by some abstract state interest.

A similar attitude can be encountered at the national level in judicial decisions that do not merely address the question of the lawfulness of immigration detention from a formal, legalistic perspective, but instead take full account of the effects of the restrictions on the individuals concerned.[46] Such an approach

---

[44] Ibid., 163.
[45] Dauvergne (1999), 27.
[46] Examples of such judgments are those that condemn the detention of children in immigration centres (see the Lithuanian Supreme Administrative Court Decision of 13 July 2005,

may receive an impetus through the recently adopted Returns Directive. We have seen that according to Article 15 of the Directive, the immigration detention of third-country nationals, who are or will be subject to a return decision or a removal order, is only justified if other sufficient but less coercive measures cannot be applied effectively in a specific case.[47] Moreover, it should not be overlooked that also the ECtHR has at times acknowledged the individual interests that are involved in sovereignty's territorial form. Even though its approach may be uneven and inconsistent in many respects, there are definite elements in its case law that can be exploited in order to increase the visibility of the interests of immigration detainees and their predicament.[48]

Taking human rights claims seriously in cases of immigration detention can have a series of destabilising effects on state practice in this area.[49] First, the fact that courts no longer treat territorial sovereignty as immune from most forces of legal correction, releases 'the mental grip of conventional structures on the capacity to consider alternatives'.[50] The regime of immigration detention, instead of appearing as a natural and justified response on the part of the sovereign state to those that have transgressed its boundaries, becomes simply one of the many responses of the state (and not even a very good one at that, in view of its ineffectiveness and financial burdens). Indeed, we have seen that most international norms which specifically address the practice of immigration detention prescribe that alternatives to detention have to be considered. Often, such alternatives are also provided by national laws, and countries' inconsistent, highly discretionary, and at times discriminatory recourse to

---

Lietuvos Vyriausiojo administracinio teismo nutartis No. N6–1514–05), or those that include the conditions of detention in their assessment of its lawfulness (see for a recent Dutch example: Rechtbank Haarlem, 20 March 2009, LJN: BH6928, *Jurisprudentie Vreemdelingenrecht* 197 (2009)). National constitutional law may play a significant role in this respect. See for example B. Kotschy, "Austria: Asylum Law in Conflict with the Constitution," *International Journal of Constitutional Law* 4 (2006).

[47] *Directive 2008/115/EC on common standards and procedures in Member States for returning illegally staying third-country nationals*, OJ L 326, 13 December 2008.

[48] As we saw in chapter 8, these cases concern situations in which young children are involved, or when the conditions of detention do not reflect the fact that these are persons who are not guilty of any crime.

[49] Charles Sabel and William Simon describe six "destabilization effects" resulting from the application of destabilisation rights in public law litigation. These are the veil effect; the web effect; the status quo effect; the deliberation effect; the publicity effect; and the stakeholder effect. My discussion of the application of destabilisation rights in cases of immigration detention is inspired by their description of the last five effects. See Sabel and Simon (2004).

[50] The *Status Quo Effect*. Ibid., 59.

such alternatives would no longer go unchallenged.[51] The use of alternatives to detention could result in a shift of balance in the particular logic of immigration law enforcement, not in the least because the symbolic force of using spatial incarceration as a standard response to unwanted migration would lose its significance.

Secondly, the abolition of the neutrality of territorial sovereignty may result in increased pressure on the state to support its position with regard to the exercise of its power to exclude with arguments that "persuade by the validity of their reasons".[52] Thus, in order to resort to immigration detention, states will have to support their positions with reasons that are grounded in the usual constitutional discourse pertaining to interferences with individual rights, instead of merely appealing to what is in essence a self-referential notion of territorial sovereignty. Even if courts would still condone the use of immigration detention by national states, the very fact that they are obliged to scrutinise the state's appeal to its territorial sovereignty in the same way as the invocation of any other public interest in constitutional adjudication would cause the normative controversies that underlie the institution of territorial sovereignty to become the subject of legal challenge. Such legal contention may be all the more forceful owing to the very act of extending equal human rights to immigration detainees in constitutional adjudication, thereby abandoning a mechanism that "generates an image of the other as unequal, anthropologically inferior, precisely because (s)he is juridically inferior."[53]

Thirdly, if the indiscriminate use of immigration detention by the state is repeatedly condemned, in particular if this occurs in higher national or international courts, that fact will inevitably result in greater public awareness of the plight of immigration detainees. In this way, the interests that are involved in territorial sovereignty become publicly visible and articulable, not only in a court of law, but also in the political arena, which in turn may result in powerful political pressures advocating a different approach.[54] Moreover, such condemnation provides official legitimation to the claims made by immigration detainees, which enhances the very visibility and communicability of the interests and rights of 'outsiders' in general. Instead of being merely a faceless mass consisting of those who do not belong, all those affected by the exercise

---

[51] See on these alternatives and countries' frequent inconsistent use of them: Amnesty International, *Irregular Migrants and Asylum Seekers: Alternatives to Immigration Detention*, AI Index POL33/001/2009 (Amnesty International: London, 2009).
[52] The *Deliberation Effect*. See Sabel and Simon (2004), 60.
[53] L. Ferrajoli, "Fundamental Rights," *International Journal for the Semiotics of Law* 14 (2001), 23.
[54] The *Publicity Effect*. Sabel and Simon (2004), 1077.

of the sovereign power to exclude thus become visible as persons towards whom the state is obliged to behave in accordance with certain fundamental norms.[55]

It is important to highlight that a full and consistent application of human rights norms to immigration detention would not only have a number of unsettling effects on the practice of immigration detention itself.[56] Indeed, the very fact that the state has become accountable for the exercise of its 'spatial powers' in the specific area of immigration detention, as well as the increased visibility and communicability of the interests of 'unwanted migrants' in the law, will inevitably have ramifications for other practices when similarly based on the self-referential notion of territorial sovereignty. Deportation will perhaps no longer seem to be such a self-evident and legitimate response on the part of the sovereign state towards those who have violated its territorial boundaries, as it does in contemporary societies. In a similar vein, externalisation policies may lose their image of necessity and legitimacy, and the constitutional pitfalls of such practices may be more easily addressed in a court of law.

The overall impact of the destabilisation of territorial sovereignty in modern legal discourse is of fundamental importance, for although the immigration prison may turn into a place of destabilisation, it would be naïve to overlook the real risk that such destabilisation carries as well. Just as states have exported important aspects of their immigration policy as a response to the enhanced protection of the individual's rights on account of the norm of *non-refoulement*, they may similarly react to increased protection for immigration detainees at home by offering incentives to non-European states to set up detention centres on their own soil in order to keep potential immigrants away from Europe's external borders, a development which is, as we have seen, not a mere theoretical possibility. The danger of the exportation of the immigration prison is compounded by the fact that the problem may then just become one of the many that are suffered by the faceless masses outside Europe's borders, reinforcing the very invisibility of the human interests involved. Seeing that the right to leave has become recognised as a fundamental right of the individual, the blanket detention of candidates for 'illegal emigration' is certainly not permitted by international human rights law.[57]

---

[55] The *Stakeholder Effect*. Id.
[56] Compare the processes that made incarceration result in the legal accountability of the sovereign power to punish, which came to cover far more than the actual decision to deprive convicted criminals of their liberty.
[57] See also G. Cornelisse, *European Vessels, African Territorial Waters and "Illegal Emigrants: Fundamental Rights and the Principle of Legality in a Global Police of Movement,"* Working Paper CHALLENGE 2008, available at: http://www.libertysecurity.org/article2365.html.

Perhaps if the institution of territorial sovereignty would have lost its 'halo of reasoned authority and necessity' from within, there would also be increased pressure on European States to take the norms pertaining to the right to leave seriously in their external relations.

9.5 Conclusions

We have seen that "territoriality is premised, foremost, on a control of ontology".[58] Inevitably, then, the destabilisation of territorial sovereignty as I have described above will result in a perception in which 'control over territory and borders […] no longer strikes at the heart of a society's self-determination.'[59] That is not to say that ideas of solidarity and identification as such can be done away with, for these remain important for every political community. Indeed, my objections against the institution of territorial sovereignty are not so much directed against the view often expressed by communitarian theorists that political arrangements should to a certain extent reflect the emotional commitments that people feel towards the community in which they live.[60] Rather, my critique focuses on the way in which contemporary legal and political practice refuses to acknowledge that the political institution of territoriality in our world is much more than a mere result of such affective commitments. By ignoring its role in the very act of constructing, reproducing and, ultimately, reifying these commitments, modern law and politics do not only give rise to and condone the unnecessary use of violence by the state, but they effectively obstruct the imagining of alternative conceptions of a political community that incorporates forms of human commitment that are more true to our ideals.

At this point it is well worth reiterating the fact that the very many images of *cosmopolitan* citizenship have their roots in a much older tradition than *national* citizenship, global citizenship having been present in "the margins of

---

[58] R. Prem Kumar and P. Grundy-Warr, "The irregular migrant as Homo Sacer: Migration and Detention in Australia, Malaysia, and Thailand," *International Migration* 42 (2004), 83, referring to Giorgio Agamben.

[59] D. Kostakopoulou, "Irregular Migration and Migration Theory: Making State Authorisation Less Relevant," in *Irregular Migration and Human Rights: Theoretical, European and International Perspectives*, eds. B. Bogusz et al. (Leiden/Boston: Martinus Nijhoff Publishers, 2004).

[60] I. Shapiro, *The Moral Foundations of Politics* (New Haven/London: Yale University Press, 2003), 179–180.

political thought for more than twenty-five hundred years."⁶¹ Under the influence of the diffuse processes that have been grouped together under the term globalisation, contemporary political and legal theory has added momentum to the ancient tradition of cosmopolitanism by addressing the feasibility of de-territorialised notions of sovereignty and political membership, for instance claiming that within the framework of cosmopolitan law:

> sovereignty can be stripped away from the idea of fixed borders and territory, and rethought of as, in principle, an attribute of basic cosmopolitan democratic law which can be drawn upon and enacted in diverse realms, from local association and cities to states and wider global networks.⁶²

With specific regard to the various ways in which we may rethink the individual's relationship to territory, Dora Kostakopoulou has proposed a system of "focal territoriality" in which territorial space is seen as a "dwelling place" where the inhabitants use and possess the territory, instead of owning it.⁶³ Along different lines, Seyla Benhabib advocates a world of "porous borders" where first-admittance rights are recognised, but the right of democracies to regulate the transmission of first admittance to full membership is retained.⁶⁴ Other theories defend a notion of "cosmopolitan economic membership" by reconciling a more conservative approach with regard to the role of national states "in protecting the individual vulnerabilities of their populations, and promoting the common interests that sustain their associational and political membership systems" with far-reaching proposals that will open national economies to foreign labour and remedy global inequalities through income transfers.⁶⁵ Another approach is Raffaele Marchetti's notion of a "world migratory regime," rejecting "the state-centric paradigm of national membership [...] in favour of a global political principle of residency."⁶⁶ Thus, Marchetti proposes that migration is no longer just regarded from the perspective of receiving states, which are currently dominant in deciding how to manage and control migration. Instead, she urges us to recognise a universal right to

---

⁶¹ H. Schattle, *The Practices of Global Citizenship* (Lanham: Rowman & Littlefield Publishers, 2008), 1–2.
⁶² D. Held, "Law of States, Law of Peoples: Three Models of Sovereignty," *Legal Theory* 8 (2002), 32.
⁶³ Kostakopoulou (2004).
⁶⁴ S. Benhabib, *The Rights of Others: Aliens, Residents and Citizens* (Cambridge: Cambridge University Press, 2004), 221.
⁶⁵ B. Jordan and F. Düvell, *Migration: The Boundaries of Equality and Justice* (Cambridge: Polity Press, 2003).
⁶⁶ R. Marchetti, "Toward a World Migratory Regime," *Indiana Journal of Legal Studies* 15 (2008), 479.

movement and to approach the right to residency in any state through principles of global distributive justice. Such a right would have to be embodied in a global institutional framework in which other claims are also recognised as fundamental rights.[67]

Novel forms of human commitment could also gain momentum by cultivating global political processes that would make it easier to address the violations of the human rights of those individuals whose political memberships have not proven to protect them from such violations. In this context, political theorists have suggested that "accountability [with regard to human rights] should link political decisions to universal agreements through global human rights institutions."[68] Along similar, but somewhat more radical lines, others have conceived of the 'human political community' as the addressee when human rights are violated, necessitating both a cosmopolitan constitutional order and a cosmopolitan dimension to democracy.[69] The newly imagined communities that could emerge from such rethinking of conventional processes of accountability do not necessarily imply a world state. Thus, Joshua Cohen and Charles Sabel suggest a form of global accountability which "depends on local debate, is informed by global comparisons, and works in a space of public reasons."[70] And even without belonging to a single state – indeed, precisely *on account of* the absence of conventional political authority and the struggle for control of it, such global administrative processes of accountability could bring about that "dispersed peoples might come to share a new identity as common members of an organized global populace".[71]

Within the scope of this book, it goes too far to explore the various concrete ways in which novel identities and new forms of affective attachment could be substantiated through the very process of destabilising territorial sovereignty in modern legal discourse. Therefore, whether such destabilisation could eventually bring about a global system where the right to free movement is universally recognised and protected as a human right is a question that I will not seek to answer here. Even if contemporary movement controls arguably give rise to the most glaring examples of entrenched social division and hierarchy globally, a belief in their abolishment or transformation will have to

---

[67] Ibid., 480.
[68] Which link should be sustained by deliberative procedures. E. Erman, "Rethinking Accountability in the Context of Human Rights," *Res Publica* 12 (2006).
[69] See J. Bohman, *Democracy across Borders: From Dêmos to Dêmoi* (Cambridge, MA: MIT Press, 2007), in particular 101–134.
[70] J. Cohen and C.F. Sabel, "Global Democracy," *NYU Journal of International Law and Politics* 37 (2005), 796.
[71] Id.

form part of a vision that encompasses much more than the way in which legal and political discourse perceives of human, cross-border movement and the relationship between political authority and territory. Thus, it would have to address the way in which economic, social and military relations of dependency contribute to structural global *and* national inequalities, and it would have to seek durable answers to existing and imminent conflicts over natural resources,[72] as well as to poverty and health inequalities.

In any case, it is important to underline that the immediate concern of this book is not so much with the practical arrangements of the world where the destabilisation of territorial sovereignty will eventually bring us. Rather than adding here to an already well-documented discussion of the possibilities and limitations of contemporary political organisation, I hope that I have been able to convey the urgency of the need to create a space in which we are really free to imagine alternative conceptions of the institutional expression of the values that underlie the human rights discourse. And just as the founders of the Rights of Man did not conceive of a political order that would do justice to the values of freedom and human equality by using the institutional blueprint of existing social organisation, we need to distance ourselves from contemporary forms of static social organisation in order to be able to imagine different ways of organising our world. By the very act of challenging the neutrality of territorial sovereignty, a stubborn and consistent application of human rights claims to deprivations of liberty in immigration procedures may well contribute to the opening up of such a space.

Accordingly, even if the destabilisation of sovereignty's territorial frame, as I have described above, has as the most immediate effect merely that the human interests which have thus far remained largely concealed acquire a platform where they can be addressed in substance, the very fact of their communicability will be a decisive step towards a more inclusive legal system, where accidental demarcations drawn in the past will no longer constitute legitimate reasons for turning a blind eye to the injustices of the present.

---

[72] In this context, one of the most pressing concerns at hand is the way in which climate changes will have the most devastating impact on the people who live in what are already the poorest regions of the world.

Bibliography

Abrunhosa Gonçalves, R. "Portugal." In *Foreigners in European Prisons*, edited by A.M. van Kalmthout, F.B.A.M. Hofstee-van der Meulen and F. Dünkel, 689-709. Nijmegen: Wolf Legal Publishers, 2007.

Aceves, W.J. "Relative Normativity: Challenging the Sovereignty Norm Through Human Rights Litigation." *Hastings International and Comparative Law Review* 25 (2002): 261-278.

Acosta, D. "The Good, the Bad and the Ugly in EU Migration Law: Is the European Parliament Becoming Bad and Ugly? (The Adoption of Directive 2008/15: The Returns Directive)." *European Journal of Migration and Law* 11 (2009): 19-39.

Ad hoc Committee of Experts on the Legal Aspects of Territorial Asylum, Refugees and Stateless Persons (CAHAR). *Comments on the 20 Guidelines on Forced Return*. 925 Meeting on 4 May 2005. CM (2005) 40 Addendum 40 final. Strasbourg, 20 May 2005, 2.

Agamben, G. *Homo Sacer: Sovereign Power and Bare Life*. Stanford: Stanford University Press, 1998.

Agnew, J. and S. Corbridge. *Mastering space: Hegemony, territory and international political economy*. London: Routledge, 1995.

Akritidou, M, A. Antonopoulou and A. Pitsela. "Greece." In *Foreigners in European Prisons*, edited by A.M. van Kalmthout, F.B.A.M. Hofstee-van der Meulen and F. Dünkel, 391-424. Nijmegen: Wolf Legal Publishers, 2007.

Aleinikoff, T. "Protected characteristics and social perceptions: an analysis of the meaning of membership of a particular social group." In *Refugee Protection in International Law*, edited by E. Feller, V. Türk and F. Nicholson, 264-311. Cambridge: Cambridge University Press, 2003.

Alexy, R. "Balancing, Constitutional Rights and Rationality." *Ratio Juris* 16 (2003): 131-140.

Allain, J. "The *Jus Cogens* Nature of *Non-Refoulement*." *International Journal of Refugee Law* 13 (2001): 533-558.

Allen, J.W. *A History of Political Thought in the Sixteenth Century*. London: Dawsons of Pall Mall, 1967.

Altiparmak, K. "*Bankovic*: An Obstacle to the Application of the European Convention on Human Rights in Iraq?" *Journal of Conflict and Security Law* 9 (2004): 213-251.

Amnesty International, *Cell Culture: The Detention and Imprisonment of Asylum Seekers in the United Kingdom*, London, 1996.

Amnesty International. *Europe and Central Asia: Summary of Amnesty International's Concerns in the Region (January-June 2004)*. AI Index EUR/01/005/2004. Amnesty International, 1 September 2004.

Amnesty International, EU Office. *The human cost of "Fortress Europe": Detention and expulsion of asylum-seekers and migrants in the EU: Open letter to Incoming UK Presidency on the occasion of World Refugee Day*. Amnesty International, 20 June 2005.

Amnesty International. *Greece: Out of the spotlight*. AI Index 25/016/20052005. Amnesty International, 5 October 2005.

Amnesty International. *The Netherlands: The Detention of Irregular Migrants and Asylum Seekers*. AI Index 35/02/2008. Amnesty International, June 2008.

Amnesty International. *Mauritania: Nobody wants to have anything to do with us, Collective expulsions of migrants denied entry into Europe*, AFR 38/001/2008, 1 July 2008.

Amnesty International. *Irregular Migrants and Asylum Seekers: Alternatives to Immigration Detention*, AI Index POL33/001/2009. Amnesty International: London, 2009.

ANAFE. *Visites dans la zone d'attente de l'aéroport de Paris-Orly: Observations et recommandations (juillet 2007-janvier 2008)*. Paris, September 2008.
Anderson, B. *Imagined Communities: Reflections on the Origin and Spread of Nationalism.* London: Verso, 1991.
Anderson, M. and D. Bigo. "What are EU frontiers for and what do they mean?" In *In Search of Europe's Borders*, edited by K. Groenendijk, E. Guild and P. Minderhoud, 7-26. The Hague: Kluwer Law International, 2002.
Andrijasevic, R. "How to balance rights and responsibilities on asylum at the EU's southern border of Italy and Libya." Compas Working Paper 27. Centre on Migration, Policy and Society. University of Oxford: Oxford, 2006.
Arendt, H. *The origins of totalitarianism.* San Diego/New York/London: Harcourt Brace and Company, 1976.
Asóciation Pro Derechos Humanos de Andalucía. *Centros de Retencíon e Internamiento en Espana.* October 2008.
Aubarell, G., R. Zapata-Barrero and X. Aragall. *New Directions of National Immigration Policies: The Development of the External Dimension and its Relationship with the Euro-Mediterranean Process.* Euromesco Paper, February 2009, at http://www.euromesco.net/images/paper79eng.pdf.
Aybay, R. "The Right to Leave and the Right to Return: the International Aspect of Freedom of Movement." *Comparative Law Yearbook* 1 (1977): 121-136.
Bailey, R. "Up Against the Wall: Bare Life and Resistance in Australian immigration Detention." *Law and Critique* 20 (2009):113-132.
Baganha, M.I.B. "From Close to Open Doors: Portuguese Emigration under the Corporative Regime." *e-Journal of Portuguese History* 1 (2003).
Baldaccini, A. "The Return and Removal of Irregular Migrants under EU Law: An Analysis of the Returns Directive." *European Journal of Migration and Law* 11 (2009): 1-17.
Baldwin-Edwards, M. "Navigating between Scylla and Charybdis: Migration Policies for a Romania within the European Union." *Southeast European and Black Sea Studies* 7 (2007): 5-35.
Balibar, E. "Propositions on Citizenship." *Ethics* 98 (1988): 723-730.
Balibar, E. "The Borders of Europe." In *Cosmopolitics: Thinking and Feeling beyond the Nation*, edited by P. Cheah and B. Robbins, 217-229. Minneapolis: University of Minnesota Press, 1998.
Balibar, E. "World Borders, Political Borders." *Proceedings of the Modern Language Association of America* 117 (2002): 71-78.
Balibar, E. *Masses, Classes and Ideas.* New York: Routledge, 1994.
Bartelson, J. *The Critique of the State.* Cambridge: Cambridge University Press, 2000.
Bashford, A. and C. Strange "Asylum Seekers and National Histories of Detention." *Australian Journal of Politics and History* 48 (2002): 509-527.
Bauböck, R. *Multilevel citizenship and territorial borders in the EU polity.* Vienna: Österreichische Akademie der Wissenschaften, 2003.
Baudoin, P., A. van de Burght and B. Hendriksen. *Vrijheidsontneming van vreemdelingen.* The Hague: Boom Juridische Uitgevers, 2002.
Baudoin, P.J.A.M. "De Vreemdelingenwet gewijzigd: rechterlijke toetsing terug naar af." *Migrantenrecht* 6 (2004): 225-226.
Bauman, Z. "Social Issues of Law and Order." *British Journal of Criminology* 40 (2000): 205-221.
Bauman, Z. *Globalization: The Human Consequences.* New York: Columbia University Press, 1998.
Bell, M. "Civic citizenship and Migrant Integration." *European Public Law* 13 (2007): 311-333.
Benhabib, S. *The Rights of Others: Aliens, Residents and Citizens.* Cambridge University Press, 2004.
Berger, P.L. *An invitation to sociology: a humanistic perspective.* Garden City, NY: Anchor Books, 1963.
Bibler Coutin, S. "Contesting criminality, Illegal immigration and the spatialization of legality." *Theoretical Criminology* 9 (2005): 5-33.

Bigo D. and E. Guild. "Le visa Schengen: expression d'une stratégie de 'police' à distance." *Cultures & Conflits* 49 (2003): 22–37.
Bigo, D. and E. Guild. "Policing at a Distance: Schengen Visa Policies." In *Controlling Frontiers: Free Movement Into and Within Europe*, edited by D. Bigo and E. Guild, 233–263. Aldershot: Ashgate, 2005.
Birnberg Peirce & Partners, Medical Justice and the National Coalition of Anti-Deportation Campaigns. *Outsourcing Abuse: The Use and Abuse of State Sanctioned Force during the Detention and Removal of Asylum Seekers*. July 2008. Available at http://www.libertysecurity.org/IMG/pdf_outsourcing_abuse.pdf.
Blackstone, William. *Commentaries on the Laws of England*. Volume I. London: Murray; 1865.
Blake, N. "Developments in the Case Law of the European Court of Human Rights." In *Irregular Migration and Human Rights: Theoretical, European and International Perspectives*, edited by B. Bogusz et al., 431–451. Leiden/Boston: Martinus Nijhoff Publishers, 2004.
Bobbio, N. *Democracy and Dictatorship*. Cambridge: Polity Press, 1989.
Boelaert-Suominen, S. "Non-EU nationals and Council Directive 2003/109/EC on the status of Third Country Nationals who are long-term residents: Five paces forward and possibly three paces back." *Common Market Law Review* 42 (2005): 1011–1052.
Boeles, P. *Eerlijke immigratieprocedures in Europa: Standaarden voor effective procedurele rechtsbescherming in kwesties van toegang, verblijf en uitzetting*. Utrecht: Nederlands Centrum Buitenlanders, 1995.
Bohler-Muller, N. "Review Essay: On a Cosmopolis to Come." *Social & Legal Studies* 17 (2008): 559–571.
Bohman, J. *Democracy across Borders: From Dêmos to Dêmoi*. Cambridge, MA: MIT Press, 2007.
Bolton. S. *Briefing Paper: The detention of children in Member States' migration control and determination processes*. European Parliament, Directorate-General Internal Policies, Citizens Rights and Constitutional Affairs, 2006.
Bosniak, L. "Human Rights, State Sovereignty and the Protection of Undocumented Migrants." In *Irregular Migration and Human Rights: Theoretical, European and International Perspectives*, edited by B. Bogusz, R. Cholewinski, A. Cygan and E. Szyszczak, 311–341. Leiden/Boston: Martinus Nijhoff Publishers, 2004.
Bosniak, L.S. "Human Rights, State Sovereignty and the Protection of Undocumented Migrants Under the International Migrant Workers Convention." *International Migration Review* 25 (1991): 737–770.
Bosniak, L. *The Citizen and the Alien, Contemporary Dilemma's of Contemporary Membership*. Princeton/Oxford: Princeton University Press, 2006.
Boswell, C. "The external dimension of EU immigration and asylum policy." *International Affairs* 79 (2003): 619–638.
Bosworth, M. "Border Control and the Limits of the Sovereign State." *Social and Legal Studies* 17 (2008): 199–215.
Boulbès, R. *Droit Francais de Nationalité: Les Textes, la Jurisprudence, les Regles Administrative*. Paris: Sirey, 1956.
Boutkevitch, V. *Working paper on the right to freedom of movement and related issues*. Prepared in implementation of Decision 1996/109 of the Sub-Commission on Prevention of Discrimination and Protection of Minorities, U.N. Doc. E/CN.4/Sub.2/1997/22 (29 July 1997).
Brand, R.A. "Sovereignty: The State, the Individual, and the International Legal System in the Twenty First Century." *Hastings International and Comparative Law Review* 25 (2002): 279–295.
Brenner, N. "Beyond State-Centrism? Space, Territoriality and Geographical Scale in Globalization Studies." *Theory and Society* 28 (1999): 39–78.
Brookings-Bern Project on Internal Displacement, *Protecting Internally Displaced Persons: A Manual for Law and Policymakers*. UNHCR Refworld, October 2008.
Brownlie, I. *Principles of Public International Law*. Oxford: Oxford University Press, 2003.
Brunkhorst, H. "Rights and the Sovereignty of the People in the Crisis of the Nation State." *Ratio Iuris* 13 (2000): 49–62.

Brunner, G. *Before Reforms: Human Rights in the Warsaw Pact States 1971-1988*. London: Hurst and Company, 1990.
Burke, A. "The Perverse Perseverance of Sovereignty." *Borderlands E-Journal* 1 (2002).
Burkens, M.C. *Algemene Leerstukken van Grondrechten naar Nederlands Constitutioneel Recht*. Zwolle: W.E.J. Tjeenk Willink, 1989.
Çalı, B. "Balancing Human Rights? Methodological Problems with Weights, Scales and Proportions." *Human Rights Quarterly* 29 (2007).
Caloz-Tschopp, M.C. "On the Detention of Aliens: the Impact on Democratic Rights." *Journal of Refugee Studies* 10(1997): 165-180.
Campbell, D. "Violent Performances: Identity, Sovereignty, Responsibility." In *The Return of Culture and Identity in International Relations Theory*, edited by Y. Lapid and F. Kratochwil, 163-179. Boulder: Lynne Rienner Publishers, 1996.
Caporaso, J.A. "Changes in the Westphalian Order: Territory, Public Authority and Sovereignty." *International Studies Review* 2, no. 2 (2000): 1-28.
Carr, E.H. *The Twenty Years Crisis: 1919-1939*. London: Macmillan, 1946.
Carrera, S. "'Integration' as a Process of inclusion for Migrants? The Case of Long Term Residents in the EU." In *Migration, Integration and Citizenship: A Challenge for Europe's Future*, edited by H. Schneider, 109-137. Maastricht: Forum, 2005.
Cassarino, J.P. *The EU return policy, Premises and Implications*. Paper in the MIREM project: Migration de retour au Maghreb. Florence: EUI, 2006.
Cassese, A. "International protection of the right to leave and return." In *Studi in Onore di Manlio Udina*, edited by A. Giuffre, 221-229. Milan: Multa Pacis AG, 1975.
Cassese, A. *International Law*. Oxford: Oxford University Press, 2005.
Chandler, D. "New Rights for Old? Cosmopolitan Citizenship and the Critique of State Sovereignty." *Political Studies* 51 (2003): 332-349.
Chimni, B.S. *International Refugee Law*. New Dehli/London: Sage Publications, 2000.
Cholewinski, R. *Borders and Discrimination in the European Union*. London and Brussels: ILPA and MPG, 2002.
Christie Tait, D. "International aspects of Migration." *Journal of the Royal Institute of International Affairs* 6 (1927): 25-46.
Claussen, K. and T. Nichol. "Reconstructing Sovereignty: The Impact of Norms, Practices and Rhetoric." *Bologna Center Journal of International Affairs* 12 (2009).
Cleveland, S.H. "Powers Inherent in Sovereignty: Indians, Aliens, Territories, and the Nineteenth Century Origins of Plenary Power over Foreign Affairs." *Texas Law Review* 81 (2002): 1-284.
Cohen, E.S. "Globalization and the Boundaries of the State: A Framework for Analyzing the Changing Practice of Sovereignty." *Governance* 14 (2001): 75-97.
Cohen, J. and C. Sabel, "Gobal Democracy," *International Law and Politics* 37 (2005): 763-797.
Cohen, R. "Response to Hathaway." *Journal of Refugee Studies* 20 (2007): 370-376.
Commission. Communication from the Commission to the Council and the European Parliament. *Regional Protection Programmes*. COM (2005) 388 final. 6 April 2005.
Commission. *Technical Mission to Libya on illegal immigration 27 November-6 December 2004*, Report. Brussels: 2005.
Conference on Security and Cooperation in Europe. "Charter of Paris for a New Europe and Supplementary Document to give effect to certain provisions of the Charter." 21 November 1990. Reprinted in *International Legal Materials* XXX (1991): 190-228.
Conference on Security and Cooperation in Europe. "Concluding Document of the Vienna Conference on Security and Co-operation in Europe held in 1989." Reprinted in *Human Rights Law Journal* 10 (1989): 270-296.
Conference on Security and Cooperation in Europe. "Document of the Copenhagen Meeting of the Conference of the Human Dimension of the Conference on Security and Co-operation in Europe." Reprinted in *Human Rights Law Journal* 11 (1990): 232-246.
Conference on Security and Cooperation in Europe. "Helsinki Accord, the Final Act of the Conference on Security and Co-operation in Europe in 1975." Reprinted in *International Legal Materials* 14 (1975): 1292.

Conversi, D. "Homogenisation, nationalism and war: Should we still read Ernest Gellner?" *Nations and Nationalism* 13, no. 3 (2007): 1-24.
Conversi, D. "Reassessing Current Theories of Nationalism: Nationalism as Boundary Maintenance and Creation." *Nationalism and Ethnic Politics* 1 (1995): 73-85.
Corbett, B. *This is Cuba: An Outlaw Culture Survives*. Cambridge, MA: Westview Press, 2002.
Cornelisse, G.N. "Immigration Detention and the Territoriality of Universal Rights." In *The Deportation Regime: Sovereignty, Space and the Freedom of Movement*, edited by N. De Genova and N. Peutz. Durham, NC: Duke University Press, forthcoming.
Cornelisse, G. *European Vessels, African Territorial Waters and "Illegal Emigrants: Fundamental Rights and the Principle of Legality in a Global Police of Movement."* Working Paper CHALLENGE 2008, available at: http://www.libertysecurity.org/article2365.html.
Cornelisse, G.N. "Human Rights for Immigration Detainees in Strasbourg: Limited Sovereignty or a Limited Discourse?" *European Journal of Migration and Law* 2(2004): 93-110.
Costa, P. "The Discourse of Citizenship in Europe, A Tentative Explanation." In *Privileges and rights of citizenship: law and the juridical construction of civil society*, edited by J. Kirshner and L. Mayali, 199-225. Berkeley: Robbins Collection Publications, 2002.
Council of Europe Commissioner for Human Rights, A. Gil-Robles. *Report on his visit to Spain from 10-19 March 2005*. CommDH (2005) 8. Strasbourg, 9 November 2005.
Council of Europe Commissioner for Human Rights, A. Gil-Robles. *Report on his visit to Malta from 20-21 October 2003*. CommDH (2004) 4. Strasbourg, 12 February 2004.
Council of Europe Commissioner for Human Rights, A. Gil-Robles. *Report on his visit to the Grand Duchy of Luxembourg from 2-3 February 2004*. CommDH (2004) 11. Strasbourg, 8 July 2004.
Council of Europe Commissioner for Human Rights, A. Gil-Robles. *Report on the effective respect for Human Rights in France following his visit from 5-21 September 2006*. CommDH (2006) 2. Strasbourg, 15 February 2006.
Council of Europe Commissioner for Human Rights. *Follow-Up Report on Hungary (2002-2005), Assessment of the progress made in implementing the recommendations of the Council of Europe Commissioner for Human Rights*. CommDH (2006) 11. Strasbourg, 29 March 2006.
Council of Europe Commissioner for Human Rights. *Follow-Up Report on Malta (2003-2005): Assessment of the progress made in implementing the recommendations of the Council of Europe Commissioner for Human Rights*. CommDH (2006) 14. Strasbourg, 29 March 2006.
Council of Europe Commissioner for Human Rights. *Follow-Up Report on Hungary (2002-2005), Assessment of the progress made in implementing the recommendations of the Council of Europe Commissioner for Human Rights*. CommDH (2006) 11. Strasbourg, 29 May 2006.
Council of Europe Commissioner for Human Rights. *Memorandum by Thomas Hammarberg, Commissioner for Human Rights of the Council of Europe further to his visit to the Zones d'Attente (Waiting Areas) at Roissy Airport and the Mesnil-Amelot Administrative Holding Centre*. CommDH (2008) 5. Strasbourg, 20 November 2008.
Council of Europe Commissioner for Human Rights. *Memorandum by Thomas Hammerberg following his visits to the United Kingdom from 5-8 February and 31 March-2 April 2008*. CommDH (2008) 23. Strasbourg, 18 September 2008.
Council of Europe Commissioner for Human Rights. *Memorandum by Thomas Hammarberg following his visit to France from 21-23 May 2008*. CommDH (2008) 34. Strasbourg, 20 November 2008.
Council of Europe Commissioner for Human Rights. *Recommendation concerning the rights of aliens wishing to enter a Council of Europe member state and the enforcement of expulsion orders*. CommDH/Rec (2001) 1. Strasbourg, 19 September 2001.
Council of Europe Commissioner for Human Rights. *Report by the Commissioner for Human Rights Mr Thomas Hammarberg on his visit to Austria from 21-25 May 2007*. CommDH (2007) 26. Strasbourg, 12 December 2007.
Council of Europe Commissioner for Human Rights. *Report by the Commissioner for Human Rights Mr Thomas Hammarberg on his visit to Germany from 9-11 and 15-20 October 2006*. CommDH (2007) 14. Strasbourg, 11 July 2007.

Council of Europe Commissioner for Human Rights. *Report by Thomas Hammarberg, Commissioner for Human Rights of the Council of Europe following his visit to Italy from 13–15 January 2009.* CommDH (2009) 16. Strasbourg, 16 April 2009.
Council of Europe Commissioner for Human Rights. *Report by Thomas Hammarberg on his visit to the Netherlands from 21-25 September 2008.* CommDH (2009) 2. Strasbourg, 11 March 2009.
Council of Europe Commissioner for Human Rights. *Report by Thomas Hammarberg following his visit to Greece from 8–10 December 2008.* CommDH (2009) 6. Strasbourg, 4 February 2009.
Council of Europe Commissioner for Human Rights. *Report on his Visit to the United Kingdom from 4-12 November 2004 for the attention of the Committee of Ministers and the Parliamentary Assembly.* CommDH (2005) 6. Strasbourg, 8 June 2005.
Council of Europe, Committee of Ministers. *Recommendation No R (2001)18 on subsidiary protection.* Adopted on 27 November 2001.
Council of Europe, Committee of Ministers. *Recommendation No. R (2000)9 on temporary protection.* Adopted on 3 May 2000.
Council of Europe, Committee of Ministers. *Recommendation No. R (84)1 on the protection of persons satisfying the criteria in the Geneva Convention who are not formally recognised as refugees.* Adopted on 25 January 1984.
Council of Europe, Committee of Ministers. *Recommendation No. R (98) 13 on the right to an effective remedy by rejected asylum-seekers against decision on expulsion in the context of Article 3.* Adopted on 18 September 1998.
Council of Europe, Committee of Ministers. *Recommendation Rec (2004) 9 on the concept of membership of a social group in the context of the 1951 Convention relating to the status of refugees.* Adopted on 30 June 2004.
Council of Europe, Committee of Ministers. *Recommendation Rec (2003) 5 of the Committee to member states on measures of detention of asylum seekers.* Strasbourg, 16 April 2003.
Council of Europe, Committee of Minsters. *20 Guidelines on Forced Return.* CM (2005) 40 final. Strasbourg, 9 May 2005.
Council of Europe, Parliamentary Assembly. *Recommendation 1547 (2002) 1, Expulsion procedures in conformity with human rights and enforced with respect for safety and dignity.* Text adopted by the Parliamentary Assembly of the Council of Europe on 22 January 2002.
COWI. *External evaluation of the European Agency for the Management of Operational Cooperation at the External Borders of the Member States of the European Unio, Final Report, January 2009.* Kongens Lyngby, COWI, 2009.
CPT. *13th General Report on the CPT's activities covering the period 1 January 2002 to 31 July 2003.* CPT/Inf (2003) 35. Strasbourg, 10 September 2003.
CPT. *Rapport au Gouvernement de la Belgique relatif a la visite effectuée en Belgique par le Comité Européen pour la prévention de la torture et des peines ou traitements inhumains ou dégradants du 18 au 27 avril 2005.* CPT/Inf (2006) 15. Strasbourg, 20 April 2006.
CPT. *Rapport au Gouvernement de la République française relatif a la visite effectuée en France par le Comité européen pour la prévention de la torture et des peines ou traitements inhumains ou dégradants du 17 au 21 juin 2002.* CPT/Inf (2003). Strasbourg, 16 December 2003.
CPT. *Rapport au Gouvernement de Roumanie relatif à la visite effectuée en Roumanie par le Comité européen pour la prévention de la torture et des peines ou traitements inhumains ou dégradants du 8 au 19 juin 2006.* CPT/inf (2008) 41. Strasbourg, 11 December 2008.
CPT. *Report on the visit to Finland carried out by the European Committee for the Prevention of Torture and Inhuman or Degrading Treatment or Punishment from 20 to 30 April 2008.* CPT/Inf (2009) 5. Strasbourg, 20 January 2009.
CPT. *Report on the visit to Greece carried out by the European Committee for the Prevention of Torture and Inhuman or Degrading Treatment or Punishment from 27 August to 9 September 2005.* CPT/Inf (2006) 41. Strasbourg, 20 December 2006.
CPT. *Report to the Austrian Government on the visit to Austria carried out by the European Committee for the Prevention of Torture and Inhuman or Degrading Treatment or Punishment, from 14 to 23 April 2004.* CPT/Inf (2005) 13. Strasbourg, 21 July 2005.

CPT. *Report to the authorities of the Kingdom of the Netherlands on the visits carried out to the Kingdom in Europe, Aruba, and the Netherlands Antilles in June 2007*. CPT/Inf (2008) 2. Strasbourg, 5 February 2008.
CPT. *Report to the Czech Government on the visit to the Czech Republic carried out by the European Committee for the Prevention of Torture and Inhuman or Degrading Treatment or Punishment from 21 to 30 April 2002*. CPT/Inf (2004) 4. Strasbourg, 12 March 2004.
CPT. *Report to the Finnish Government on the visit to Finland carried out by the European Committee for the Prevention of Torture and Inhuman or Degrading Treatment or Punishment (CPT) from 7 to 17 September 2003*. CPT/Inf (2004) 20. Strasbourg, 14 June 2004.
CPT. *Report to the German Government on the visit to Germany carried out by the European Committee for the Prevention of Torture and Inhuman or Degrading Treatment or Punishment from 3 to 15 December 2000*. CPT/Inf (2003) 20. Strasbourg, 12 March 2003.
CPT. *Report to the Government of Greece on the visit to Greece from 23 to 29 September 2008*. CPT/Inf (2009) 20. Strasbourg, 30 June 2009.
CPT. *Report to the Government of Ireland on the visit to Ireland carried out by the European Committee for the Prevention of Torture and Inhuman or Degrading Treatment or Punishment from 20 to 28 March 2002*. CPT/Inf (2003) 36. Strasbourg, 18 September 2003.
CPT. *Report to the Hungarian Government on the visit to Hungary carried out by the European Committee for the Prevention of Torture and Inhuman or Degrading Treatment or Punishment from 30 March to 8 April 2005*. CPT/Inf (2006) 20. Strasbourg, 29 June 2006.
CPT. *Report to the Polish Government on the visit to Poland carried out by the European Committee for the Prevention of Torture and Inhuman or Degrading Treatment or Punishment from 4 to 15 October 2004*. CPT/Inf (2006) 11. Strasbourg, 12 March 2006.
CPT. *The CPT Standards: Substantive sections of the CPT's General Reports*. CPT/Inf/E (2002) 1 –Rev. 2006. Strasbourg, 2006. Crosby, A. *The Boundaries of Belonging: Reflections on Migration Policies into the 21st Century*. Inter Pares Occasional Paper No. 7. Toronto: Inter Pares, 2006.
Craig, P. "Unreasonableness and Proportionality in UK Law." In *The Principle of Proportionality in the Laws of Europe*, edited by E. Ellis, 85–106. Oxford: Hart Publishing, 1999.
Cremona, J.J. "The proportionality principle in the jurisprudence of the European Court of Human Rights." In *Recht zwischen Umbruch und Bewahrung: Festschrift für Rudolf Bernhardt*, edited by U. Beyerlin, 323–330. Berlin: Springer-Verlag, 1995.
Cuesta, J.L. de la."Spain." In *Foreigners in European Prisons*, edited by A.M. van Kalmthout, F.B.A.M. Hofstee-van der Meulen and F. Dünkel, 751–780. Nijmegen: Wolf Legal Publishers, 2007.
Daes, E.I.A. *Freedom of the Individual under Law: an Analysis of Article 29 of the Universal Declaration of Human Rights*. New York: United Nations, 1990.
Dashwood, A. "States in the European Union." *European Law Review* 23 (1998): 201–216.
Dauvergne, C. "Confronting Chaos: Migration Law Responds to Images of Disorder." *Res Publica* 5 (1999): 23–45.
Dauvergne, C. "Sovereignty, Migration and the Rule of Law in Global Times." *The Modern Law Review*. 67 (2004): 588–615.
De Genova, N.P. "Migrant "Illegality" and Deportability in Everyday Life." *Annual Review of Anthropology* 31 (2002).
Décarpes, P. "France." In *Foreigners in European Prisons*, edited by A.M. van Kalmthout, F.B.A.M. Hofstee-van der Meulen and F. Dünkel, 317–340. Nijmegen: Wolf Legal Publishers, 2007.
Dell'Olio, F. *The Europeanization of citizenship: between the ideology of nationality, immigration and European identity*. Aldershot: Ashgate, 2005.
Dembour, M-B. "Human Rights Law and National Sovereignty in Collusion: the Plight of Quasi-Nationals at Strasbourg." *Netherlands Quarterly of Human Rights* 21 (2003): 63–98.
Deng, Francis M. Report of the Representative of the Secretary-General, *Compilation and analysis of legal norms*, 5 December 1995, UN Doc. E/CN.4/1996/52/Add.2.
Deudney, D. "Ground Identity: Nature, Place and Space in Nationalism." In *The Return of Culture and Identity in International Relations Theory*, edited by Y. Lapid and F. Kratochwil, 129–146. Boulder: Lynne Rienner Publishers, 1996.

Dieckhoff, A. and C. Jaffrelot, eds. *Revisiting Nationalism. Theories and Processes*. London: C. Hurst, 2005.
Dijk, P. van and G.J.H. van Hoof. *Theory and Practice of the European Convention on Human Rights*. The Hague: Kluwer, 1998.
Diken, B. and C.B. Laustsen. " 'Camping' as Contemporary Strategy – From Refugee Camps to Gated Communities." *Academy for Migration Studies in Denmark Working Paper Series* 32, 2003.
Dinstein, Y. "Right to life, physical integrity and liberty." In: *The International Bill of Rights*, edited by L. Henkin, 114–137. New York: Columbia University Press, 1981.
Dinstein, Y. *The International Law of Belligerent Occupation*. Cambridge: Cambridge University Press, 2009.
Doehring, K. "Aliens, Expulsion and Deportation." In *Encyclopedia of International Law*, edited by R. Bernhardt, 107–112. Amsterdam: Elsevier Science Publishers, 1992.
Donelly, J. "Human Rights in a New World Order: Implications for a New Europe." In *Human Rights in the New Europe*, edited by D.P. Forsythe, 3–32. Lincoln/London: Nebraska University Press, 1994.
Doty, R. "Sovereignty and the nation: constructing the boundaries of national identity." In *State Sovereignty as a Social Construct*, edited by T.J. Biersteker and C. Weber, 121–147. Cambridge: Cambridge University Press, 1996.
Douzinas, C. *Human Rights and Empire: The political philosophy of cosmopolitanism*. Milton Park: Routledge Cavendish, 2007.
Douzinas, C. *The End of Human Rights, Critical Legal Thought at the Turn of the Century*. Oxford, Hart Publishing, 2000.
Dowty, A. *Closed Borders, The Contemporary Assault on Freedom of Movement*. New Haven and London: Yale University Press, 1987.
Dünkel, F., A. Gensing and C. Morgenstern. "Germany." In *Foreigners in European Prisons*, edited by A.M. van Kalmthout, F.B.A.M. Hofstee-van der Meulen and F. Dünkel, 341–390. Nijmegen: Wolf Legal Publishers, 2007.
Düvell, F. *Illegal immigration: What to do about it*. Working Paper Working Group Migration-Mobility-Minorities-Membership. Florence: EUI/RSCAS, 2004.
Dummet, A and A. Nicol. *Subjects, Citizens, Aliens and Others: Nationality and Immigration Law*. London: Weidenfeld and Nicolson, 1990.
Durham III, A.M. "The Justice Model in Historical Context: Early Law, the Emergence of Science, and the rise of Incarceration." *Journal of Criminal Justice* 16 (1988): 331–346.
Easton, S and C. Piper. *Sentencing and Punishment: The Quest for Justice*. Oxford: Oxford University Press, 2008.
ECRE and ELENA. *Report on the Application of the Dublin II Regulation in Europe*. March 2006. Available at http://www.detention-in-europe.org/images/stories/ecre%20report%20 dublii.pdf.
Edwards, J. "Asylum Seekers and Human Rights." *Res Publica* 7 (2001): 159–182.
Elias, N. *Time: an Essay*. Oxford UK, Cambridge USA: Blackwell, 1992.
Ellinas, A. "Cyprus." In: *Foreigners in European Prisons*, edited by A.M. van Kalmthout, F.B.A.M. Hofstee-van der Meulen and F. Dünkel, 157–168. Nijmegen: Wolf Legal Publishers, 2007.
Engster, D. "Jean Bodin, scepticism and absolute sovereignty." *History of Political Thought* 14 (1996): 469–499.
Eriksen, E.O. "Why a Charter of Fundamental Rights in the EU?" *Ratio Juris* 16 (2003): 352–373.
Erman, E. "Rethinking Accountability in the Context of Human Rights." *Res Publica* 12 (2006): 249–275.
EU Network of Independent Experts on Fundamental Rights. *Report on the situation of fundamental rights in the EU and its Member States in 2005: conclusions and recommendations*. Ref.: CFR-CDF\Conclusions 2005, 2005.
European Commission Press Release. 10 July 2006. Brussels, IP 06/967.
European Commission. Communication from the Commission to the European Parliament, the Council, the European Economic and Social Committee, the Committee of the Regions and the Court of Justice of the European Communities. *Adaptation of the provisions of Title*

IV of the EC Treaty relating to the jurisdiction of the Court of Justice with a view to ensuring more effective judicial protection. COM 2006 (346) final. 28 June 2006.
European Commission. Communication from the Commission to the European Parliament, the Council, the European Economic and Social Committee and the Committee of the Regions. *Preparing the next steps in border management in the European Union.* COM (2008) 69 final.
European Council on Refugees and Exiles. *Position Paper on the Detention of Asylum Seekers.* April 1996.
European Council. *European Pact on Immigration and Asylum, Adopted at the European Council in Brussels, 15 and 16 October 2008, Presidency Conclusions.* 14368/08. 16 October 2008.
European Parliament, Committee on Civil Liberties Justice and Home Affairs. Rapporteur G. Catania. *Report by the LIBE delegation on its visit to the administrative detention centres in Malta.* PV 613713EN.doc. Brussels, 30 March 2006.
European Parliament, Committee on Civil Liberties, Justice and Home Affairs. Rapporteur A. Diaz de Mera Garcia-Consuegra. *Report by the LIBE delegation on its visit to the adminstrative detention centres in Paris.* PV 607993EN.doc. Brussels, 22 March 2006.
European United Left/Nordic Green Left. *Report by the GUE/NGL Delegation on the visit to the Canary Islands 10-11 April 2006.* GUE/NGL Website and Publications Unit, May 2006.
Faure Atger, A. *The Abolition of Internal Border Checks in an Enlarged Schengen Area: Freedom of movement or a scattered web of security checks?* Brussels: CEPS Research Paper No. 8, March 2008.
Feeley, M. and J. Simon. "Actuarial Justice. The Emerging New Criminal Law." In *The Futures of Criminology*, edited by D. Nelken, 173–201. London: Sage, 1994.
Feeley, M. and J. Simon. "The New Penology: Notes on the Emerging Strategy of Corrections and Its Implications." *Criminology* 30 (1992): 449–474.
Ferrajoli, L. "Beyond sovereignty and citizenship: a global constitutionalism." In *Constitutionalism, Democracy and Sovereignty*, edited by R. Bellamy, 151–160. Aldershot: Avebury, 1996.
Ferrajoli, L. "Fundamental Rights." *International Journal for the Semiotics of Law* 14 (2001): 1–33.
Fields, H. "Closing Immigration Throughout the World." *American Journal of International Law* 26 (1932): 671–699.
Finnis, J. *Aquinas: Moral, Political, and Legal Theory.* Oxford: Oxford University Press, 1998.
Fischer-Lescano, A. and T. Löhr, *Menschen- und flüchtlingsrechtliche Anforderungen an Maßnahmen der Grenzkontrolle auf See.* Berlin: European Center for Constitutional and Human Rights, 2007.
Fitzpatrick, J. "Sovereignty, Territoriality and the Rule of Law." *Hastings International and Comparative Law Review* 25 (2002): 303–340.
Fitzsimmons, M.P. "The National Assembly and the Invention of Citizenship." In *The French Revolution and the Meaning of Citizenship*, edited by R. Waldinger, P. Dawson and I. Woloch, 29–41. Westport/London: Greenwood Press, 1993.
Fontova, H.E. *Fidel: Hollywood's Favorite Tyrant.* Washington, DC: Regnery Publishing, 2005.
Forder, C. "Family Rights and Immigration Law: a European Perspective." In *Migration, Integration and Citizenship: A Challenge for Europe's Future*, edited by H. Schneider, 71–108. Maastricht: Forum, 2005.
Foucault, M. *Discipline, toezicht en straf: de geboorte van de gevangenis.* Groningen: Historische Uitgeverij, 1989.
Foucault, M. *Madness and Civilization: A history of insanity in the age of reason.* London: Tavistock Publications, 1967.
Fourlanos, G. *Sovereignty and the ingress of aliens.* Stockholm: Almqvist & Wiksell International, 1986.
Fox, G.H. "New approaches to International Human Rights: The Sovereign State Revisited." In *State sovereignty: change and persistence in international relations*, edited by S.H. Hashmi, 105–130. Pennsylvania: The Pennsylvania State University Press, 1997.
Frontex, Annual Report 2006.

Gabor, F.A. "Reflections on the Freedom of Movement in light of the dismantled 'Iron Curtain'." *Tulane Law Review* 65 (1991): 849–881.
Gabrielatos, C. and P. Baker. "Fleeing, Sneaking, Flooding: A Corpus Analysis of Discursive Constructions of Refugees and Asylum Seekers in the UK Press, 1996–2005." *Journal of English Linguistics* 36 (2008): 5–38.
Gaete, R. "Postmodernism and Human Rights: Some Insidious Questions." *Law and Critique* 2 (1991): 149–170.
Gamlen, A. "The emigration state and the modern geopolitical imagination." *Political Geography* 27 (2008): 840–856.
Gammeltoft-Hansen Th. and H. Gammeltoft-Hansen. "The Right to Seek – Revisited. On the UN Human Rights Declaration Article 14 and Acces to Asylum Procedures in the EU." *European Journal of Migration and Law* 10 (2008): 439–459.
Gatti, F. "Io, Clandestino a Lampedusa." *L'Espresso*, 7 October 2005.
Geddes, A. "Europe's border relationships and international migration relations." *Journal of Common Market Studies* 43 (2005): 787–806.
Geddes, A. "International Migration and State Sovereignty in an Integrating Europe." *International Migration* 39 (2001): 21–40.
Gellner, E. *Nations and Nationalism*. London: Basil Blackwell, 2006.
Ghoshal, A. and T.M. Crowley. "Refugees and immigrants: A Human Rights Dilemma." *Human Rights Quarterly* 5 (1983): 327–347.
Gibbs, N. "Getting Constitutional Theory in Proportion: A Matter of Interpretation?" *Oxford Journal of Legal Studies* 27 (2007): 175–191.
Gibney, M.J. and R. Hansen. *Deportation and the Liberal State*. Geneva: UNHCR New Issues in Refugee Research Working Paper 77, 2003
Giddens, A. *The nation state and violence*. Cambridge: Polity Press, 1985.
Gil-Robles, A. Commissioner for Human Rights (Council of Europe). *Report on his Visit to the United Kingdom (4–12 November 2004) for the attention of the Committee of Ministers and the Parliamentary Assembly*. CommDH (2005) 6. Strasbourg, 8 June 2005.
Goldsmith, J.L. and E.A. Posner, *The Limits of International Law*. Oxford: Oxford University Press, 2005.
Goodwin Gill G.S., *International law and the movement of persons between states*. Oxford: Oxford University Press, 1978.
Goodwin Gill, G.S., "The Right to Leave, the Right to Return and the Question of a Right to Remain." In *The Problem of Refugees in the Light of Contemporary Law Issues*, edited by V. Gowlland-Debbas. 93–108. The Hague: Martinus Nijhoff Publishers, 1996.
Goodwin-Gill G.S., *The Refugee in International Law*. Oxford: Oxford University Press, 1996.
Gordon, S. *Controlling the state: Constitutionalism from ancient Athens to today*. Cambridge, MA: Harvard University Press, 1999.
Grahl-Madsen, A. *Territorial Asylum*. Stockholm: Almqvsit and Wiksell International, 1980.
Greer, S. "'Balancing' and the European Court of Human Rights: A Contribution to the Habermas-Alexy Debate." *Cambridge Law Journal* 63 (2004): 412–434.
Greer, S. "Constitutionalizing Adjudication under the European Convention on Human Rights." *Oxford Journal of Legal Studies* 23 (2003): 405–433.
Greer, S. *The European Convention on Human Rights: Achievements, Problems and Prospects*. Cambridge: Cambridge University Press, 2006.
Guild, E. *Report for the European Parliament: Directorate General Internal Policies of the Union: A typology of different types of centres in Europe*. DG Internal Policies of the Union, Citizens Rights and Constitutional Affairs, 2006.
Guiraudon, V. and G. Lahav. "A Reappraisal of the State Sovereignty Debate, The Case of Migration Control." *Comparative Political Studies* 33 (2000): 163–195.
Guiraudon, V. "The constitution of a European immigration policy domain: a political sociology approach." *Journal of European Policy* 10 (2003): 263–282.
Gurowitz, A. "International law, politics and migrant rights." In *The politics of international law*, edited by C. Reus-Smit, 131–150. Cambridge: Cambridge University Press, 2004.

Habermas, J. "The European Nation-state - Its Achievements and Its Limits. On the Past and Future of Sovereignty and Citizenship." In *Mapping the Nation*, edited by G. Balakrishnan, 281-294. London: Verso, 1996.
Habermas, J. *Between Facts and Norms: Contributions to a Discourse Theory of Law and Democracy*. Cambridge, MA: MIT Press, 1996.
Hailbronnner, K. "Detention of Asylum Seekers." *European Journal of Migration and Law* 9 (2007): 159-172.
Halleskov, L. "The Long-Term Residents Directive: A Fulfilment of the Tampere Objective of Near-Equality?" *European Journal of Migration and Law* 7 (2005): 181-201.
Hammerberg, T. *Memorandum by the Commissioner for Human Rights for the Council of Europe following his visit to the united Kingdom from 5-8 February and 31 March-2 April 2008*. CommDH (2008) 23. Strasbourg 18 September 2008.
Hammerberg, T. *Report by the Commissioner for Human Rights for the Council of Europe following his visit to the Netherlands from 21-25 September 2008*. CommDH (2009) 2. Strasbourg, 11 March 2009.
Hammond, N. "United Kingdom." In *Foreigners in European Prisons*, edited by A.M. van Kalmthout, F.B.A.M. Hofstee-van der Meulen and F. Dünkel, 809-851. Nijmegen: Wolf Legal Publishers, 2007.
Hanagan, M. "Recasting citizenship: Introduction." *Theory and Society* 26 (1997): 397-402.
Hannikainen L., *Peremptory Norms (Jus Cogens) in International Law: Historical Development, Criteria, Present Status*. Helsinki: Lakimiesliiton Kustannus, 1988.
Hannum, H. *The right to leave and return in international law and practice*. Dordrecht: Martinus Nijhoff Publishers, 1987.
Happold, M. "Bankovic v Belgium and the territorial scope of the European Convention on Human Rights." *Human Rights Law Review* 1 (2003): 77-90.
Harding, C. and C.L. Lim. "The significance of Westphalia: an archaeology of the international legal order." In *Renegotiating Westphalia. Essays and commentary on the European and conceptual foundations of modern international law*, edited by C. Harding and C.L. Lim, 1-23. The Hague: Kluwer Law International, 1999.
Harris, D.J., M. O'Boyle and C. Warbrick. *Law of the European Convention on Human Rights*. London: Butterworths 1995.
Harvard Law Review Editorial. "Political Legitimacy in the Law of Political Asylum." *Harvard Law Review* 99 (1985): 450-471.
Harvey, C. and R.P. Barnidge. "Human rights, Free Movement and the Right to Leave in International Law." *International Journal of Refugee Law* 19 (2007): 1-21.
Hathaway, J. "Forced Migration Studies: Could We Agree Just to 'Date'?" *Journal of Refugee Studies* 20 (2007): 349-369.
Hathaway, J. "The emerging politics of non-entrée." *Refugees* 91 (1992): 40-41.
Hathaway, J. *Law of Refugee Status*. Toronto: Butterworths, 1991.
Heijer, M. den. "Whose rights and Which Rights? The Continuing Story of *Non-Refoulement* under the European Convention on Human Rights." *European Journal of Migration and Law* 10 (2008): 277-314.
Held, D. "Law of States, Law of Peoples: Three Models of Sovereignty." *Legal Theory* 8 (2002): 1-44.
Helmut D. "The Desert Front: EU refugee camps in North Africa?" *Statewatch* (March 2005).
Henckaerts, J.-M. *Mass Expulsion in Modern International Law and Practice*. The Hague: Martinus Nijhoff Publishers, 1995.
Henkin, L. "That 'S' Word: Sovereignty, and Globalization, and Human Rights, et Cetera." *Fordham Law Review* 68 (1999): 1-14.
Henrard, K. *Devising an Adequate System of Minority Protection: Individual Human Rights, Minority Rights and the Right to Self-Determination*. The Hague: Martinus Nijhoff Publishers, 2000.
Higgins, R. "La Liberte de Circulation des Personnes en Droit International." In *Liberte de Circulation des Personnes en Droit International*, edited by M. Flory and R. Higgins, 3-20. Paris: Economica, 1988.

Higgins, R. "The Right in International Law of an Individual to Enter, Stay in and Leave a Country." *International Affairs* 49 (1973): 341–357.
Hindess, B. "Citizenship in the international management of populations." *American Behavioral Scientist* 43 (2000): 1486–1497.
Hindess, B. "Divide and Rule: The International Character of Modern Citizenship." *European Journal of Social Theory* 1 (1998): 57–70.
Hinsley, F.H. *Sovereignty*. Cambridge: Cambridge University Press, 1986.
HM Chief Inspector of Prison, A. Owers. *Report on an unannounced inspection of Harmondsworth Immigration Removal Centre 17–21 July 2000*. London: Her Majesty's Inspectorate of Prisons, 2006.
HM Chief Inspector of Prisons, A. Owers. *Report on the unannounced inspections of five non-residential short-term holding facilities: Queen's Building and Terminals 1–4, Heathrow Airport 10–13 October 2005*. London: Her Majesty's Inspectorate of Prisons. 2006.
Hobbes, Thomas. Leviathan, edited by R. Tuck. Cambridge: Cambridge University Press, 1996.
Hoffman, J. *State, Power and Democracy*. Brighton: Wheatsheaf Books, 1988.
Hofmann, R. *Die Ausreisefreiheit nach Völkerrecht und staatlichem Recht*. Berlin: Springer, 1988.
Holsti, K.J. *International Politics. A framework for analysis*. New Jersey: Prentice Hall, 1995.
Home Office. Operational Enforcement Manual. 21 December 2000.
Hough, R.L. *The Nation-States, Concert or Chaos*. Lanham: University Press of America, 2003.
House of Lords, The Hague Programme: a five year agenda for EU justice and Home Affairs. Report with Evidence: HL Paper 84. London, 23 March 2005.
Houtum, H. van and R. Pijpers. "The European Union as a Gated Community: The Two-Faced Border and Immigration Regime of the EU." *Antipode* 39 (2007): 291–309.
Human Rights Watch. *European Union: Managing Migration means potential European complicity in Neighboring State's Abuse of Migrants and Refugees*. October 2006, at http://www.hrw.org/legacy/backgrounder/eca/eu1006/eu1006web.pdf.
Human Rights Watch. *Libya: Stemming the Flow*. HRW 18, September 2006.
Huysmans, J. "Discussing Sovereignty and Transnational Politics." In *Sovereignty in Transition*, edited by N. Walker, 209–227. Oxford: Hart Publishing, 2003.
Huysmans, J. "The European Union and the Securitization of migration." *Journal of Common Market Studies* 38 (2000): 751–777.
Ilareva, V. *Immigration Detention in International Law and Practice: In search of solutions to the challenges faced in Bulgaria*. 2008. Available at: http://www.statewatch.org/news/2008/jan/valeria-illareva-immigration-detention-bulgaria.pdf.
Inglés, J.D. *Draft Report of the Special Rapporteur: Study of discrimination in respect of the right of everyone to leave any country, including his own, and to return to his country*, Draft Report submitted by the Special Rapporteur, E/CN.4/Sub.2/L.234 (13 December 1961).
Inglés, J.D. *Study of Discrimination in Respect of the Right of Everyone to Leave any Country, Including His Own, and to Return to His Country*. Report Submitted by the Special Rapporteur on 23 November 1962, Commission on Human Rights, Sub-Commission on Prevention of Discrimination and Protection of Minorities, 15th Session, UN Doc E/CN.4/Sub.2/220/Rev.1 (1963).
Institute of International Law. "International Regulations on the Admission and Expulsion of Aliens." *Institut De Droit International Annuaire* 12 (1892): 218.
International Helsinki Federation for Human Rights. *Report 2006: Human Rights in the OCSE Region: Italy*. Vienna: IHF and IHF Research Foundation, 2006.
International Institute of Human Rights. "Strasbourg Declaration on the Right to Leave and Return (and Recommendation of the Meeting of Experts on The Right to Leave and Return to One's Country)." Adopted by the Meeting of Experts. Strasbourg: France, 26 November 1986. Reprinted in: *Human Rights Law Journal* 8 (1987): 478–480.
International Law Commission. *Draft articles on Responsibility of States for internationally wrongful acts*. Adopted by the ILC at its fifty-third session (2001) (extract from the Report of the International Law Commission on the work of its Fifty-third session, Official Records of the General Assembly, Fifty-sixth session, Supplement No. 10 (A/56/10), chp.IV.E.1) November 2001.

Isaac, J.C.A. "A new guarantee on earth: Hannah Arendt on human dignity and the politics of human rights." *Amercian Political Science Review* 90 (1996): 61-73.
Jacobson, D. and G.B. Ruffer. "Courts across Borders: The Implications of Judicial Agency for Human Rights and Democracy." *Human Rights Quarterly* 25 (2003): 74-92.
Jacobson, D. "The Global Political Culture." In *Identities, Borders, Orders. Rethinking International Relations Theory*, edited by M. Albert, D. Jacobson and Y. Lapid, 161-179. Minneapolis: University of Minnesota Press, 2001.
Jacot-Guillardmod, O. "Régles, méthodes et principes d'interprétation dans la jurisprudence de la Cour européenne des droits de l'homme." In *La Convention européenne des droits de l'homme: Commentaire article par article*, edited by. L.E. Pettiti, E. Decaux and P.H. Imbert. Paris: Economica, 1995.
Jagerskiold, S. "The Freedom of Movement." In *The International Bill of Rights: The Covenant on Civil and Political Rights*, edited by L. Henkin, 166-184. New York: Columbia University Press, 1981.
James, Z. "Policing Marginal Spaces: Controlling Gypsies and Travellers." *Criminology and Criminal Justice* 7 (2007): 367-389.
Jans, J.H. "Proportionality Revisited." *Legal Issues of Economic Integration* 27 (2000): 239-265.
Jarvis, A.P. and A.J. Paolini. "Locating the State." In *The State in Transition, Reimagining Political Space*, edited by J.A. Camilleri, A.P. Jarvis and A.J. Paolini, 3-20. London: Lynne Rienne Publishers, 1995.
Jean, P. "Le Contenu de la Liberte de Circulation." In *Liberte de Circulation des Personnes en Droit International*, edited by M. Flory and R. Higgins, 21-41. Paris: Economica, 1988.
Jesuit Refugee Service. *Civil Society Report on Administrative Detention of Asylum Seekers and Illegally Staying Third Country Nationals in the 10 New Member States of the European Union.* Malta, October 2007.
Jesuit Refugee Service. *Detention in Europe.* JRS-Europe Observation and Position Paper. 1 April 2004.
Johnson, A.K. "Sweden." In *Foreigners in European Prisons*, edited by A.M. van Kalmthout, F.B.A.M. Hofstee-van der Meulen and F. Dünkel, 781-808. Nijmegen: Wolf Legal Publishers, 2007.
Jones, L. "Immigration and parliamentary discourse in Great Britain. An analysis of the debates related to the 1996 Asylum and Immigration Act." In *Racism at the Top*, edited by R. Wodak and T.A. van Dijk, 283-310. Klagenfurt: Drava Verlag, 2002.
Joppke, C. "Why Liberal States accept Unwanted Immigration." *World Politics* 50 (1998): 266-293.
Jordan, B. and F. Düvell, *Migration: The Boundaries of Equality and Justice.* Cambridge: Polity Press, 2003.
Joseph, S., J. Schultz and M. Castan. *The International Covenant on Civil and Political Rights: Cases, Materials and Commentary.* Oxford: Oxford University Press, 2004.
Kaldor, M. *New and Old Wars. Organized Violence in a Global Era.* Cambridge: Polity Press, 1999.
Kalmthout, A. van. "Vreemdelingenbewaring." In *Detentie: Gevangen in Nederland*, edited by E.R. Muller and P.C. Vegter, 321-344. Alphen aan den Rijn: Kluwer, 2005.
Kalmthout, A.M. van, F.B.A.M. Hofstee-van der Meulen and F. Dünkel, *Foreigners in European Prisons.* Nijmegen: Wolf Legal Publishers, 2007.
Kalmthout, A. van and F. Hofstee-van der Meulen. "The Netherlands." In *Foreigners in European Prisons*, edited by A.M. van Kalmthout, F.B.A.M. Hofstee-van der Meulen and F. Dünkel, 621-660. Nijmegen: Wolf Legal Publishers, 2007.
Kant, I. *Perpetual Peace, A Philosophical Proposal*, translated by H. O'Brien. London: Sweet and Maxwell, 1927.
Kelly, M. *Immigration-related detention in Ireland. A research report for the Irish Refugee Council, Irish Penal Reform Trust and Immigration Council of Ireland.* Dublin: Irish Refugee Council/ Irish Penal Reform Trust/Immigrant Council of Ireland, 2005.
Kjaerum, M. "Refugee Protection Between State Interests and Human Rights: Where is Europe Heading?" *Human Rights Quarterly* 24 (2002): 513-536.

Korhonen, O. *International Law Situated: An Analysis of the Lawyer's Stance Towards Culture, History and Community*. The Hague: Kluwer Law International, 2000.
Kostakopoulou, D. and R. Thomas "Unweaving the Threads: Territoriality, National Ownership of Land and Asylum Policy." *European Journal of Migration and Law* 6 (2004): 5-26.
Kostakopoulou, D. "EU Citizenship: Writing the Future." *European Law Journal* 13 (2007): 623-646.
Kostakopoulou, D. "Irregular Migration and Migration Theory: Making State Authorisation Less Relevant." In *Irregular Migration and Human Rights: Theoretical, European and International Perspectives*, edited by B. Bogusz et al., 41-57. Leiden/Boston: Martinus Nijhoff Publishers, 2004.
Kotschy, B. "Austria: Asylum Law in Conflict with the Constitution." *International Journal of Constitutional Law* 4 (2006): 689-701.
Krasner, S.D. "Abiding Sovereignty." *International Political Science Review* 22 (2001): 229-251.
Kratochwil, F. "Citizenship: On the Border of Order." In *The Return of Culture and Identity in IR Theory*, edited by Y. Lapid and F. Kratochwil, 181-197. Boulder: Lynne Rienner Publishers, 1996.
Kristeva, J. *Strangers to Ourselves*. New York: Columbia University Press, 1991.
Kumar, P. and C. Grundy-Warr. "The Irregular Migrant as Homo Sacer: Migration and Detention in Australia, Malaysia, and Thailand." *International Migration* 42 (2004): 33-63.
Kunoy, B. "A Union of National Citizens: the Origins of the Court's Lack of *Avant Gardisme* in the *Chen* Case." *Common Market Law Review* 43 (2006): 179-190.
Kveinen, E. "Citizenship on a Post-Westphalian Community: Beyond External Exclusion?" *Citizenship Studies* 6 (2002): 21-35.
Lange, R. de. "Paradoxes of European Citizenship." In *Nationalism, Racism and the Rule of Law*, edited by P. Fitzpatrick, 97-115. Aldershot: Dartmouth Publishing Company, 1995.
Lapid, Y. "Identities, Borders, Orders: Nudging International Relations Theory in a New Direction." In *Identities, Borders, Orders: Rethinking IR Theory*, edited by M. Albert, D. Jacobson and Y. Lapid, 1-20. Minneapolis and London: University of Minnesota Press, 2001.
Lappi-Seppälä, T. "Finland." In *Foreigners in European Prisons*, edited by A.M. van Kalmthout, F.B.A.M. Hofstee-van der Meulen and F. Dünkel, 289-315. Nijmegen: Wolf Legal Publishers, 2007.
Lauterpacht and D. Bethlehem, E. "The scope and content of the principle of *non-refoulement*: Opinion." In: *Refugee Protection in International Law*, edited by E. Feller, V. Türk and F. Nicholson, 87-177. Cambridge: Cambridge University Press, 2003.
Lauterpacht, H. *International law and human rights*. Hamden: Archon Books, 1968.
Lawson, R.A. and H.G. Schermers. *Leading cases of the European Court of Human Rights*. Nijmegen: Ars Aequi Libri, 1999.
Lawson, R. "Annotatie bij Europees Hof voor de Rechten van de Mens 8 December 2005." *Jurisprudentie Vreemdelingenrecht* 7 (2006): 730-733.
Lazaroiu, S. and M. Alexandru. *Controlling Exits to Gain Accession: Romanian Migration Policy in the Making*. Rome: CeSPI. 2005.
Lee, M. "Women's imprisonment as a mechanism of migration control in Hong Kong." *British Journal of Criminology* 47 (2007): 847-860.
Lillich, R.B. "Civil Rights." In *Human rights in international law: legal and policy issues*, edited by T. Meron, 115-170. Oxford: Clarendon Press, 1984.
Lillich, R.B. *The Human Rights of Aliens in Contemporary International Law*. Manchester: Manchester University Press, 1984.
Lindahl, H. "Border Crossings by Immigrants: Legality, Illegality, and Alegality." *Res Publica* 14 (2008): 117-135.
Linklater, A. *The transformation of political community*. Cambridge: Polity Press, 1998.
Liu, G. *The Right to Leave and Return and Chinese Migration Law*. The Hague/Boston: Martinus Nijhoff, 2007.
Loader, I. and N. Walker, *Civilizing Security*. Cambridge: Cambridge University Press, 2007.
Locke, John. *Two Treatises of Government*. Edited by P. Laslett. Cambridge University Press: Cambridge, 1967.

London Detainee Support Group. *Detained Lives: The Real Cost of Immigration Detention.* January 2009. Available at: www.detainedlives.org.
London Detainee Support Group. *Indefinite detention in the UK: Length of detention snapshot statistics for 1 June 2009.* London, June 2009. Available at: www.ldsg.org.uk.
London Fell, A. *Origins of Legislative Sovereignty and the Legislative State.* Westport: Praeger Publishers, 1999.
Luban, D. *Legal Modernism.* Ann Arbor: University of Michigan Press, 1994.
Lucas, A.M. "Huddled Masses, Immigrants in detention," *Punishment and Society* 7 (2005), 323-329.
Lui, R. "Governing Refugees 1919-1945." *Borderlands E-Journal* (1) 2002.
Lush, C. "The territorial application of the European Convention on Human Rights: Recent case law." *International and Comparative Law Quarterly* 42 (1993): 897-906.
Lynskey, O. "Complementing and completing the Common European Asylum System: a legal analysis of the emerging extraterritorial elements of EU refugee protection policy." *European Law Review* 31 (2006): 230-250.
Macdonald, R.St.J. "The Margin of Appreciation." In *The European System for the Protection of Human Rights*, edited by R.St.J. Macdonald, F. Matscher and H. Petzold, 83-98. The Hague: Martinus Nijhoff Publishers, 1993.
Machiavelli, N. *The Discourses.* Edited by B. Crick. London: Penguin Books, 1987.
Madison, J., A. Hamilton and J. Jay. *The Federalist Papers*, edited by I. Kramnick. London: Penguin Books, 1987.
Malisauskaite-Simanaitiene, S. "Lithuania." In *Foreigners in European Prisons*, edited by A.M. van Kalmthout, F.B.A.M. Hofstee-van der Meulen and F. Dünkel, 539-571. Nijmegen: Wolf Legal Publishers, 2007.
Malkki, L.H. "Refugees and Exiles: From 'Refugee Studies' to the National Order of Things." *Annual Review of Anthropology* 24 (1995): 495-523.
Malloch, M.S. and E. Stanley. "The detention of asylum seekers in the UK: Representing risk, managing the dangerous." *Punishment and Society* 53 (2005): 53-71.
Mansbach, R.W. and F. Wilmer. "War, Violence and the Westphalian State System as a Moral Community." In *Identities, Borders, Orders: Rethinking International Relations Theory*, edited by M. Albert, D. Jacobson and Y. Lapid, 51-71. Minneapolis: University of Minnesota Press, 2000.
Mantouvalou, V. "Extending Judicial control in International Law: Human Rights Treaties and Extraterritoriality." *International Journal of Human Rights* 9 (2005): 147-163.
Marchetti, R. "Toward a World Migratory Regime," *Indiana Journal of Legal Studies* 15 (2008): 471-487.
Marcoux, L. "Protection from arbitrary arrest and detention under international law." *Boston College International and Comparative Law Review* 2 (1982): 359-364.
Marrus, M.R. *The Unwanted: European Refugees in the Twentieth Century.* Oxford: Oxford University Press, 1985.
Marshall, T.H. "Citizenship and Social Class." In *Citizenship and Social Class and other essays*, 1-85. Cambridge: Cambridge University Press, 1950.
Martin, D. "Comments on *Förster* (Case C-158/07 of 18 november 2008), *Metock* (Case C-127/08 of 25 July 2008) and *Huber* (Case C/524/06 of 16 december 2008)." *European Journal of Migration and Law* 11 (2009): 95-108.
Martin, D.A. "Effects of International Law on Migration Policy and Practice: The Uses Of Hypocrisy," *International Migration Review* 23 (1989): 547-578.
Matscher, F. "Methods of Interpretation of the Convention." In *The European System for the Protection of Human Rights*, edited by R.St J. Macdonald, F. Matscher and H. Petzold, 63-81. The Hague: Martinus Nijhoff Publishers, 1993.
McBride, J. "Proportionality and the European Convention on Human Rights." In *The Principle of Proportionality in the Laws of Europe*, edited by E. Ellis, 23-35. Oxford: Hart Publishing, 1999.
McCorquodale, R. "An Inclusive International Legal System." *Leiden Journal of International Law* 17 (2004): 477-504.

McCorquodale, R. "International Law, Boundaries and Imagination." In *Boundaries and Justice: Diverse Ethical Perspectives*, edited by D. Miller and S. Hashmi, 136–163. Princeton/Oxford: Princeton University Press, 2001.

McDougal, M.S., H.D. Lasswell and L. Chen, "The protection of aliens from discrimination and world public order: responsibility of states conjoined with human rights." *American Journal of International Law* 70 (1976): 432–469.

McGrath Dale, S. "The Flying Dutchman Dichotomy: The International Right to Leave v. The Sovereign Right to Exclude." *Dickinson Journal of International Law* 9 (1991): 359–385.

McHarg, A. "Reconciling Human Rights and the Public Interest: Conceptual Problems and Doctrinal Uncertainty in the Jurisprudence of the European Court of Human Rights." *Modern Law Review* 62 (1999): 671–696.

McIlwain, C.H. *Constitutionalism & The Changing World: Collected Papers*. Cambridge: Cambridge University Press, 1969. Médecins Sans Frontieres, *Violence and Immigration. Report on illegal sub-Saharan immigrants (ISSs) in Morocco*. 30 September 2005.

Melis, B. *Negotiating Europe's Immigration Frontiers*. Boston: Kluwer Law International, 2001.

Melzer, A. "Rousseau, Nationalism, and the Politics of Sympathetic Identification." In *Educating the Prince, Essays in Honor of Harvey Mansfield*, edited by M. Blitz and W. Kristol, 111–128. Lanham: Rowman & Littlefield Publishers, 2000.

Meron, Th. "Extraterritoriality of Human Rights Treaties." *American Journal of International Law* 89 (1995): 78–82.

Milanovic, M. "From Compromise to Principle: Clarifying the Concept of State Jurisdiction in Human Rights Treaties." *Human Rights Law Review* 8(2008): 411–448.

Miller, T.A. "Citizenship & Severity: Recent Immigration Reforms and the New Penology." *Georgetown Immigration Law Journal* 17 (2003): 611–666.

Miller, T.A. "Blurring the Boundaries Between Immigration and Crime Control After September 11th." *Boston College Third World Law Journal* 25 (2005): 81–124.

Mole, N. *Asylum and the European Convention on Human Rights*. Strasbourg: Council of Europe Publishing, 2007.

Moore, M. "Ireland." In *Foreigners in European Prisons*, edited by A.M. van Kalmthout, F.B.A.M. Hofstee-van der Meulen and F. Dünkel, 453–478. Nijmegen: Wolf Legal Publishers, 2007.

Moreno Lax, V. "Must EU Borders have Doors for Refugees? On the Compatibility of Schengen Visas and Carriers' Sanctions with EU Member States' Obligations to Provide International Protection to Refugees." *European Journal of Migration and Law* 10 (2008): 315–364.

Mubanga-Chipoya, C. *Analysis of the current trends and development regarding the right to leave any country, and some other rights or considerations arising therefrom*. UN doc. E/CN.4/Sub.2/1988/35 (1988).

Mubanga-Chipoya, C. *Draft Declaration on Freedom and Non-Discrimination in Respect of the Right of Everyone to Leave any Country, including his Own and to Return to his Country*. UN Doc. E/CN.4/Sub.2/1988/35/Add.1 (1988).

Murphy M. and S. Harty. "Post-Sovereign Citizenship." *Citizenship Studies* 7 (2003): 181–197.

Murphy, A.B. "The sovereign state system as a political-territorial ideal: historical and contemporary considerations." In *State Sovereignty as a Social Construct*, edited by T.J. Biersteker and C. Weber, 81–120. Cambridge: Cambridge University Press, 1996.

Nafziger, J.A. "The general admission of aliens under international law." *American Journal of International Law* 77 (1983): 804–847.

Nanda, V.P. "The Right to Movement and Travel Abroad: Some Observations on the U.N. Deliberations." *Denver Journal of International Law and Policy* 1 (1971): 109–122.

Nascimbene, B. *Expulsion and Detention of Aliens in the European Union Countries*. Milano: Giuffré Editore, 2001.

Nathwani, N. *Rethinking Refugee Law*. The Hague/London/New York: Martinus Nijhoff Publishers, 2003.

Neal, A.W. "Securitization and risk at the EU Border: The Origins of Frontex." *Journal of Common Market Studies* 47 (2009): 333–356.

Neumann, G.L. "Anomalous Zones." *Stanford Law Review* 48 (1996): 1197–1234.

Newman, D. "Boundaries, Borders and Barriers: Changing Geographic Perspectives on Territorial Lines." In *Rethinking International Relations Theory: Identities, Borders, Orders,*

edited by M. Albert, D. Jacobson and Y. Lapid, 137–151. Minneapolis: University of Minnesota Press, 2001.
Nijman, J.E. *The concept of international legal personality: An inquiry into the history and theory of international law*. The Hague: T.M.C. Asser Press, 2004.
Noll, G. "Visions of the Exceptional: Legal and Theoretical Issues Raised by Transit Processing Centres and Protection Zones." *European Journal of Migration and Law* 5 (2003): 303–341.
Nollkaemper, A. *Kern van het internationaal publiekrecht*. The Hague: Boom Juridische Uitgevers, 2004.
Nowak, M. *U.N. Covenant on Civil and Political Rights: CCPR Commentary*. Kehl am Rein: N.P. Engel, 1993.
O'Connell, D.P. *International Law*. London: Stevens and Sons, 1970.
Oda, S. "The Individual in International Law." In *Manual of Public International Law*, edited by M. Sørensen, 469–530. London: MacMillan & Co, 1968.
Ommeren F.J. van. "De rechtsstaat als toetsingskader." In *De rechtstaat als toetsingskader*, edited by F.J. van Ommeren and S.E. Zijlstra, 7–22.The Hague: Boom Juridische Uitgevers, 2003.
Oppenheim, L.F.L. *International Law*. Eight edition. Edited by H. Lauterpacht. London: Longmans, 1955.
Orford, A. "The destiny of international law." *Leiden Journal of International Law* 17 (2004): 441–476.
Orford, A. *Reading Humanitarian Intervention*. Cambridge: Cambridge University Press, 2003.
Ovey, C. and R.C.A. White, *European Convention on Human Rights*. Oxford: Oxford University Press, 2002.
Ozkirimli, U. *Theories of Nationalism: A Critical Overview*. Basingstoke: Macmillan, 2000.
Pacurar, A. "Smuggling, Detention and Expulsion of Irregular Migrants: A Study on International Legal Norms, Standards and Practices." *European Journal of Migration and Law* 5 (2003): 259–283.
Palmer, R.R. and J.A. Colton, *A History of the Modern World*. New York: Mc Graw-Hill, 1995.
Panglangan, R.C. "Territorial Sovereignty: Command, Title and the Expanding Claims of the Commons." In *Boundaries and Justice: Diverse Ethical Perspectives*, edited by D. Miller and S. Hashmi, 164–181. Princeton/Oxford: Princeton University Press, 2001.
Papagianni, G. *Institutional and Policy Dynamics of EU Migration Law*. Leiden/Boston: Martinus Nijhoff Publishers, 2006.
Partsch, K.J. "The Right to Leave and Return in the Countries of the Council of Europe." *Israel Yearbook on Human Rights* 5 (1975): 215–262.
Peers, S. *EU Law and Family Reunification: A Human Rights Critique*, ECLN Essay No. 4. Essays for civil liberties and democracy in Europe, 2005.
Petrovec, D. "Slovenia." In *Foreigners in European Prisons*, edited by A.M. van Kalmthout, F.B.A.M. Hofstee-van der Meulen and F. Dünkel, 729–750. Nijmegen: Wolf Legal Publishers, 2007.
Peutz, N. "'Criminal Alien' Deportees in Somaliland: An Ethnography of Removal." In *The Deportation Regime: Sovereignty, Space, and the Freedom of Movement*, edited by N. De Genova and N. Peutz. Durham, NC: Duke University Press, forthcoming 2009.
Peutz, N. "Embarking on an Anthropology of Removal." *Current Anthropology* 47(2006): 217–241.
Philpott, D. "Ideas and the evolution of sovereignty." In *State Sovereignty: Change and Persistance in International Relations*, edited by S.H. Hashmi, 28–33. Pennsylvania: Pennsylvania State University Press, 1997.
Pilgram, A. and V. Hofinger, "Austria." In: *Foreigners in European Prisons*, edited by A.M. van Kalmthout, F.B.A.M. Hofstee-van der Meulen and F. Dünkel, 91–125. Nijmegen: Wolf Legal Publishers, 2007.
Plamenatz, J. *Man and Society: Political and social theories from Machiavelli to Marx*. Volume I, *From the Middle Ages to Locke*. Longman Publishing Group: New York, 1992.
Plender, R. *International Immigration Law*. Dordrecht: Kluwer Academic Publishers, 1988.
Plender, R. *International Migration Law*. Leiden: Sijthof, 1972.
Poggi, G. *The State: Its nature, development & prospects*. Cambridge: Polity Press, 1990.
Polanyi, K. *The Great Transformation: The Political and Economic Origins of Our Time*. Boston: Beacon Press, 1944.

Pot, C.W. van der and A.M. Donner. *Handboek van het Nederlandse Staatsrecht*. Zwolle: Tjeenk Willink, 1995.
Preuß, U.K. "Two challenges to European citizenship." In *Constitutionalism in Transformation: European and Theoretical Perspectives*, edited by R. Bellamy and D. Castiglione, 122–140. Oxford: Blackwell, 1996.
Rahe P.A, ed. *Machiavelli's Liberal Republican Legacy*. Cambridge: Cambridge University Press, 2006.
Reid, K. *A Practitioner's Guide to the European Convention on Human Rights*. London: Sweet & Maxwell, 1998.
Reinke, F.W. "Treaty and non-Treaty Human Rights Agreements: A Case Study of Freedom of Movement in East Germany." *Columbia Journal of Transnational Law* 24 (1986): 647–675.
Reus-Smit, C. "Human rights and the social construction of sovereignty." *Review of International Studies* 27 (2001): 519–538.
Rifaat, A.M. *International Agression: A Study of the Legal Concept, its development and definiton in international law*. Stockholm: Almqist and Viksell International, 1979.
Rigo, E. "Citizens and foreigners in the Enlarged Europe." In *Spreading Democracy and the Rule of Law? The Impact of EU Enlargement on the Rule of Law: Democracy and Constitutionalism in Post-Communist Legal Orders*, edited by W. Sadurski et al., 97–119. Dordrecht: Springer, 2006.
Rodier, C. "'Emigration illégale': une notion á bannir." *Libération* 13 June 2006.
Rodier, C. "Not in my backyard, keeping refugees in camps outside Europe." *Vacarme* 24 (2003).
Rousseau, Jean-Jacques. *The Social Contract and other later political writings*, edited by V. Gourevitch. Cambridge: Cambridge University Press, 1997.
Rubenstein, K. "Globalization and Citizenship and Nationality." In *Jurisprudence for an interconnected globe*, edited by C. Dauvergne, 159–186. Aldershot: Ashgate, 2003.
Ruggie, J.G. "Territoriality and Beyond: Problematizing Modernity in International Relations." *International Organization* 47 (1993): 148–152.
Ruth, A. and M. Trilsch. "Bankovic v. Belgium (Admissibility), App. No. 52207/99." *American Journal of International Law* 97 (2003): 168–172.
Sabel, C.F. and W. Simon. "Destabilization rights: How Public Law Litigation Succeeds." *Harvard Law Review* 117 (2004): 1015–1101.
Sabine, G.H. *History of Political Theory*. London/Calcutta/Sydney: George G. Harrap & Co., 1941.
Saint-Saens, I. "À distance." *Vacarme* 29 (2004): 156–157.
Samers, M. "An Emerging Geopolitics of Illegal Immigration in the European Union." *European Journal of Migration and Law* 6 (2004): 27–45.
Sassen, S. "Beyond Sovereignty: De-Facto Transnationalism in Immigration Policy." *European Journal of Migration and Law* 1 (1999): 177–198.
Sassen, S. "The de facto Transnationalization of Immigration Policy." In *Challenge to the Nation-State: immigration in Western Europe and the United States*, edited by C. Joppke, 49–85. Oxford: Oxford University Press, 1998.
Sassen, S. "The Repositioning of Citizenship." In *People out of Place: Globalization, Human Rights and the Citizenship Gap*, edited by A. Brysk and G. Shafir, 191–208. London/New York: Routledge, 2004.
Schain, M.A. "The State Strikes Back: Immigration Policy in the European Union." *The European Journal of International Law* 20 (2009): 93–109.
Schapendonk, J. "Stuck Between the Desert and the Sea: The Immobility of Sub-Saharan African 'Transit Migrants' in Morocco." In *Rethinking Global Migration: Practices, Policies and Discourses in the European Neighbourhood*, edited by H. Rittersberger-Tiliç et al., 129–143. Ankara: KORA, METU & Zeplin Iletisim Hizm, 2008.
Schattle, H. *The Practices of Global Citizenship*. Lanham: Rowman & Littlefield Publishers, 2008.
Schermers, H.G. "Mensenrechten in de Slotacte van Helsinki." *Nederlands Juristenblad* 31 (1977): 801–803.

Schindlmayer, T. "Sovereignty, legal regimes and international migration." *International Migration* 41 (2003): 109–123.
Schmitt, C. *Constitutional Theory*, translated by J. Seitzer; edited by J. Seitzer and E. Kennedy. North Carolina: Duke University Press, 2008.
Schmitt, C. *Political Theology, Four Chapters on the Concept of Sovereignty*, translated by G. Schwab. Chicago: University of Chicago Press, 2005.
Schochet, G.J. "Introduction: constitutionalism, liberalism, and the study of politics." In *Constitutionalism*, edited by J.R. Pennock and J.W. Chapman, 1–11. New York: New York University Press, 1979.
Schuster, L. and M. Welch. "Detention of asylum seekers in the US, UK, France, Germany, and Italy: A critical view of the globalizing culture of control." *Criminal Justice* 5 (2005): 331–355.
Schuster, L. "A Sledgehammer to Crack a Nut: Deportation, Detention and Dispersal in Europe." *Social Policy and Administration* 39 (2005): 600–621.
Seth, S. "Nationalism in/and Modernity." In *The State in Transition: Reimagining Political Space*, edited by J.A. Camilleri, A.P. Jarvis and A.J. Paolini, 41–58. London: Lynne Rienner Publishers; 1995.
Shafir, G. "Citizenship and Human Rights in an Era of Globalisation." In *People out of Place: Globalization, Human Rights and the Citizenship Gap*, edited by A. Brysk and G. Shafir, 11–25. New York/London: Routledge, 2004.
Shapiro, I. *The Moral Foundations of Politics*. New Haven/London: Yale University Press, 2003), 179–180.
Shaw, M.N. *International Law*. Cambridge: Cambridge University Press, 1997.
Silove, D. and M. Fazel, "Detention of refugees." *British Medical Journal* 332 (2006): 251–252.
Simon, J. "Refugees in a carceral age: the rebirth of immigration prisons in the United States." *Public Culture* 10 (1998): 577–607.
Skinner, Q. *Machiavelli*. Oxford: Oxford University Press, 1981.
Škvain, P. "Czech Republic." In *Foreigners in European Prisons*, edited by A.M. van Kalmthout, F.B.A.M. Hofstee-van der Meulen and F. Dünkel, 169–206. Nijmegen: Wolf Legal Publishers, 2007.
Snacken, S. "Belgium." In *Foreigners in European Prisons*, edited by A.M. van Kalmthout, F.B.A.M. Hofstee-van der Meulen and F. Dünkel, 127–156. Nijmegen: Wolf Legal Publishers, 2007.
Sohn L.B. and T. Buergenthal. *The Movement of Persons across Borders*. Washington: American Society of International Law, 1992.
Soysal, Y. *Limits of Citizenship*. Chigaco: University of Chicago Press, 1994.
Spielmann, D. "Human Rights Case Law in the Strasbourg and Luxembourg Courts: Conflicts, Inconsistencies, and Complementarities." In *The EU and Human Rights*, edited by P. Alston, M. Butselo and J. Heenan, 757–780. Oxford: Oxford university Press, 1999.
Spierenburg, P. "Four Centuries of Prison History: Punishment, suffering, the Body, and Power." In *Institutions of Confinement: Hospitals, Asylums, and Prisons in Western Europe and North America, 1500-1950*, edited by N. Finsch and R. Jütte, 17–38. Cambridge: Cambridge University Press 1996.
Spiro, P.J. "Mandated Membership, Diluted Identity: Citizenship, Globalization and International Law." In *People out of Place: Globalization, Human Rights and the Citizenship Gap*, edited by A. Brysk and G. Shafir, 87–106. London/New York: Routledge, 2004.
Stacy, H. "Relational Sovereignty." *Stanford Law Review* 55 (2003): 2029–2060.
Stando-Kawecka, B. "Poland." In *Foreigners in European Prisons*, edited by A.M. van Kalmthout, F.B.A.M. Hofstee-van der Meulen and F. Dünkel, 661–687. Nijmegen: Wolf Legal Publishers, 2007.
Statewatch. "Update: MSF accused of 'disloyalty' over CPT Report." June 2004, available at: http://www.statewatch.org/news/2004/jun/23it-msf.htm.
Steenbergen, J.D.M. "Schengen and the movement of persons." In *Schengen: Internalisation of Central Chapters of the Law on Aliens, Refugees, Privacy, Security and the Police*, edited by H. Meijers, 57–73. Leiden: Stichting NJCM-Boekerij, 1992.

Steendijk, L. "The Application of Human Rights Standards to Asylum Cases: The Dutch Example." *European Journal of Migration and Law* 3 (2001): 185-198.
Steinbock, D.J. "The refugee definition as law: issues of interpretation." In *Refugee Rights and Realities: Evolving International Concepts and Regimes*, edited by F. Nicholson and P. Twomey, 13-39. Cambridge: Cambridge University Press, 1999.
Steiner, H.J. and P. Alston. *International Human Rights in Context: Law, Politics, Morals*. Oxford: Oxford University Press, 2000.
STEPS Consulting. *The conditions in centres for third-country nationals (detention camps, open centres as well as transit centres and transit zones) with a particular focus on provisions and facilities for persons with special needs in the 25 EU Member States*. European Parliament, Directorate-General Internal Policies, Citizens Rights and Constitutional Affairs, 2006.
Storey, H. "The EU Refugee Qualification Directive: a Brave New World?" *International Journal of Refugee Law* 20 (2008): 1-48.
Szabó, T. et al. "Hungary." In *Foreigners in European Prisons*, edited by A.M. van Kalmthout, F.B.A.M. Hofstee-van der Meulen and F. Dünkel, 425-449. Nijmegen: Wolf Legal Publishers, 2007.
Tamanaha, B.Z. *On the rule of law*. Cambridge: CamBridge University Press, 2004.
Thomas, B. *International Migration and Economic Development*. Paris: UNESCO, 1961.
Tilly, C. "The Emergence of Citizenship in France and Elsewhere." *International Review of Social History* 40, suppl. 3 (1995): 223-236.
Tilly, C. "Why worry about Citizenship?" In *Extending Citizenship, Reconfiguring States*, edited by M. Hanagan and C. Tilly, 247-271. Lanham: Rowman and Littlefield Publishers, 1999.
Tilly, C. *Coercion, Capital and European States: AD 990-1992*. Oxford: Basil Blackwell, 1992.
Torpey, J. *The Invention of the Passport*. Cambridge: Cambridge University Press, 2000.
Tóth, J. *Briefing Paper: A typology of Transit Zones*. European Parliament, Directorate-General Internal Policies, Citizens Rights and Constitutional Affairs, 2006.
Triche Naumik, A. "International Law and Detention of US Asylum Seekers: Contrasting *Matter of D-J-* with the United Nations Refugee Convention." *International Journal of Refugee Law* 19 (2007): 661-702.
Tuck, R. Introduction to *Leviathan*, by Thomas Hobbes, ix-xliv. Cambridge: Cambridge University Press, 1996.
Türk V. and F. Nicholson. "Refugee Protection in International Law: An Overall Perspective." In *Refugee Protection in International Law*, edited by E. Feller, V. Türk and F. Nicholson. Cambridge: Cambridge University Press, 2003.
Tuitt, P. "Racist Authorization, Interpretative Law and the Changing Character of the Refugee." In *Nationalism, Racism and the Rule of Law*, edited by P. Fitzpatrick, 45-59. Aldershot: Dartmouth Publishing Company, 1995.
Tully, J. *Strange multiplicity: Constitutionalism in an age of diversity*. Cambridge: Cambridge University Press, 1997.
Turack, D.C. "A Brief Review of the Provisions in Recent Agreements Concerning Freedom of Movement Issues in the Modern World." *Case Western Reserve Journal of International Law* 11 (1979): 95-115.
Turack, D.C. "Freedom of Transnational movement: The Helsinki Accord and Beyond." *Vanderbilt Journal of International Law* 11 (1978): 585-608.
UN Commission on Human Rights. *Report of the Working Group on Arbitrary Detention*. Sixty-second session. Item 11 (a) of the provisional agenda. E/CN.4/2006/7. 12 December 2006.
UN Commission on Human Rights. *Report of the Working Group on Arbitrary Detention*. Sixtieth Session. Item 11(a) of the provisional agenda. E/CN.4/2004/3. 15 December 2003.
UN Commission on Human Rights. *Report of the Working Group on Arbitrary Detention*. Sixtieth Session. Item 11(a) of the provisional agenda. E/CN.4/2004/3. 15 December 2003.
UN Commission on Human Rights. *Report of the Special Rapporteur, Ms. Gabriela Rodríguez Pizarro, submitted pursuant to Commission on Human Rights resolution 2002/62*. Fifty-ninth session. Item 14 (a) of the provisional agenda. E/CN.4/2003/85. 30 December 2002.
UN Commission on Human Rights. *Detention of Asylum Seekers*. Sub-Commission on Human Rights Resolution 2000/21. 27th meeting. 18 August 2000.

UN Commission on Human Rights. *Deliberation No. 5 of the Working Group on Arbitrary Detention*. Fifty-sixth session. Item 11(a) of the provisional agenda. Report of the Working Group on Arbitrary Detention, Annex II, E/CN.4/2000/4. 28 December 1999.
UN Commission on Human Rights. *Report of the Working Group on Arbitrary Detention. Addendum: Report on the Visit of the Working Group on Arbitrary Detention to the United Kingdom on the issue of immigrants and asylum seekers*. Fifty-fifth session. Item 11(a) of the provisional agenda. E/CN.4/1999/63/Add.3. 28 December 1998.
UN Commission on Human Rights. *Study of the Right of Everyone to be Free from Arbitrary Arrest, Detention and Exile and the Draft Principles on Freedom from Arbitrary Arrest and Detention*. UN Doc. E/CN.4/826/Rev.1, at 7 (1964).
UN Commission on Human Rights. *Report of the Third Session of the Commission on Human Rights at Lake Success*, 24 May to 18 June 1948, U.N. Doc. E/800 (28 June 1948).
UN Committee on the Rights of the Child. *Concluding Observations adopted in respect of reports submitted by States parties to the Committee on the Rights of the Child: France*. 36th Session. UN Doc. CRC/C/15/Add. 240, 4 June 2004.
UN General Assembly. *Body of Principles for the Protection of All persons under Any Form of Detention or Imprisonment*. UNGA Resolution 43/173, Annex, 43 UN GAOR Supp. (No. 49) at 298. UN Doc. A/43/49 (1988).
UN High Commissioner for Human Rights. *Fact Sheet 26: The Working Group on Arbitrary Detention*. Human Rights Fact Sheet Series. Geneva: Office of the United Nations High Commissioner for Human Rights, 5 June 2009.
UN Human Rights Committee. *General Comment 31*. Nature of the General Legal Obligation on States Parties to the Covenant. U.N. Doc. CCPR/C/21/Rev.1/Add.13 (2004).
UN Human Rights Committee. *General Comment 15, The position of aliens under the Covenant*. (Twenty-seventh session, 1986), Compilation of General Comments and General Recommendations Adopted by Human Rights Treaty Bodies, U.N. Doc. HRI/GEN/1/Rev.6 at 140 (2003).
UN Human Rights Committee. *General Comment 19: Article 23*. (Thirty-ninth session, 1990). U.N. Doc. HRI/GEN/1/Rev.6 at 149 (2003).
UN Human Rights Committee. *General Comment 27: Freedom of movement (Art.12)*. (Sixty-seventh session, 1999). Compilation of General Comments and General Recommendations Adopted by Human Rights Treaty Bodies, U.N. Doc. HRI/GEN/1/Rev.6 at 174 (2003).
UN Human Rights Committee. *Concluding Observations of the Human Rights Committee: United Kingdom of Great Britain and Northern Ireland*. Seventy-third session. CCPR/CO/73/UK;CCPR/CO/73/UKOT. 6 December 2001.
UN Human Rights Council. *Report of the Working Group on Arbitrary Detention. Addendum: Mission to Italy*. Tenth session. Agenda item 3. A/HRC/10/21/Add.5. 16 February 2009.
UN Human Rights Council. *Report of the Working Group of Arbitrary Detention*. Tenth session. Agenda item 3. A/HRC/10/21. 16 February 2009.
UN Human Rights Council. *Opinions adopted by the Working Group on Arbitrary Detention, Opinion No. 45/2006 (United Kingdom)*. Seventh session. Item 3 of the provisional agenda. A/HRC/7/4/Add.1. 16 January 2008.
UN Human Rights Council. *Report of the Working Group on Arbitrary Detention*. Seventh session. Item 3 of the provisional agenda. A/HRC/7/4. 10 January 2008.
UNGA Resolution A/Res/55/74 of 12 February 2001.
Unger, R.M. *False Necessity: Anti-Necessitarian Social Theory in the Service of Radical Democracy*. Cambridge: Cambridge University Press, 1987.
Unger, R.M. *The Critical Legal Studies Movement*. Cambridge, MA: Harvard University Press, 1983.
Unger, R.M. *What should legal analysis become?* London: Verso, 1996.
UNHCR. *Intervening in Regina v. Immigration Officer at Prague Airport (2005)*. International Journal of Refugee Law (2005): 427–453.
UNHCR Executive Committee. ExCom Conclusion No. 103 (LVI) 2005 (Conclusion on the Provision on International Protection Including Through Complementary Forms of Protection).

UNHCR. *Detention of Asylum Seekers and Refugees: The Framework, the Problem and Recommended Practice*. 15th Meeting of the Executive Committee of the High Commissioner's Programme Standing Committee. Doc. No. EC/49/SC/CRP.13. 4 June 1999. Reprinted in *Refugee Survey Quarterly* 18 (1999).
UNHCR. *Revised Guidelines on Applicable Criteria and Standards relating to the Detention of Asylum Seekers*. IOM/22/99/Rev.1-FOM/22/99/Rev.1. February 1999.
UNHCR Executive Committee. ExCom Conclusion No. 82 (XLVIII) 1997 (Safeguarding Asylum).
UNHCR Executive Committee. Excom Conclusion No. 79 (XLVII) 1996 (General conclusion on International Protection).
UNHCR Executive Committee. ExCom Conclusion No. 74 (XLV) 1994 (General).UNHCR Executive Committee. ExCom Conclusion No. 44 (XXXVII) 1986 (Detention of Refugees and Asylum Seekers).
UNHCR Executive Committee. ExCom Conclusions No. 25 (XXXIII) 1982 (General Conclusion on international Protection).
UNHCR Executive Committee. ExCom Conclusion No. 15 (XXX) 1979 (Refugees Without an Asylum Country).
UNHCR Executive Committee. ExCom Conclusion No. 6 (XXVIII) 1977 (Non-refoulement).
Uppsala Colloquium. "The Right to Leave and Return, A Declaration adopted by the Uppsala Colloquium, 21 June 1971." Reprinted in *Israel Yearbook on Human Rights* 4 (1974): 432–435.
Valk, I. van der. "Right-wing parliamentary discourse on immigration in France." *Discourse & Society* 14 (2003): 309–348.
Valk, I. van der. *Difference, deviance, threat? Mainstream and right-extremist political discourse on ethnic issues in the Netherlands and France (1990-1997)*. Amsterdam: Aksant, 2002.
Van Creveld, M. *Transformation of War*. New York/London: Free Press, 1991.
Vazquez, M.S. "Self-Determination and the Right to Leave." *Israel Yearbook on Human Rights* 12 (1982): 82–93.
Veit-Brause, I. "Rethinking the State of the Nation." In *The State in Transition: Reimagining Political Space*, edited by J.A. Camilleri, A.P. Jarvis and A.J. Paolini, 59–75. Boulder: Lynne Rienner Publishers, 1995.
VluchtelingenWerk. *Gesloten OC Procedure voor Asielzoekers, Onderzoek in Opdracht van UNHCR*. Vluchtelingenwerk Nederland, September 2007.
Walker, N. "Late sovereignty in the European Union." In *Sovereignty in transition*, edited by N. Walker, 3–32. Oxford: Hart Publishing, 2003.
Walker, R.B.J. *Inside/outside: International Relations as Political Theory*. Cambridge/New York: Cambridge University Press, 1993.
Walters, W. "Deportation, Expulsion, and the International Police of Aliens." *Citizenship Studies* 6 (2002): 256–292.
Walters, W. "Mapping Schengenland: denaturalizing the border." *Environment and Planing D: Society and Space* 20 (2002): 561–580.
Warbrick, C. "States and Recognition in International Law." In *International Law*, edited by M.E. Evans, 217–275. Oxford: Oxford University Press, 2003.
Weber, L. "Down that Wrong Road: Discretion on Decisions to Detain Asylum Seekers Arriving at UK Ports." *Howard Journal of Criminal Justice* 42 (2003): 248–262.
Weber, M. "Politics as Vocation." In *From Max Weber: Essays in sociology*, translated, edited and with an introduction by H.H. Gerth and C.W. Wright Mills, 77–128. New York: Oxford University Press, 1946.
Weiler, J. "Thou shall not oppress a stranger: On the judicial Protection of the Human Rigths of Non-EC Nationals – A Critique." *European Journal of International Law* 3 (1992): 65–91.
Weinzierl, R. *The Demands of Human and EU Fundamental Rights for the Protection of the European Union's External Borders*. Berlin: German Institute of Human Rights, 2007.
Welch, M. "The Role of the Immigration and Naturalization Service in the Prison Industrial Complex." *Social Justice* 27 (2000): 73–88.
Welch, M. *Detained: Immigration Law and the Expanding I.N.S. Jail Complex*. Philadelphia: Temple University Press, 2002.

Werner, W.G. and Wilde, J.H. de. "The Endurance of Sovereignty." *European Journal of International Relations* 7 (2001): 283-313.
Whelan, F.G. "Citizenship and the right to leave." *American Political Science Review* 75 (1981): 636-653.
Wilsher, D. *The Liberty of Foreigners: A history, Law and Politics of Immigration Detention.* Nijmegen: Wolf Legal Publishers, 2009.
Xenos, N. "Refugees: The Modern Political Condition." In *Challenging Boundaries. Global Flows, Territorial Identities*, edited by M.J. Shapiro and H.R. Alker, 233-246. Minneapolis: University of Minneapolis Press, 1996.
Yack, B. "Popular sovereignty and nationalism." *Political Theory* 29 (2001): 517-536.
Zeibote, L. "Latvia." In *Foreigners in European Prisons*, edited by A.M. van Kalmthout, F.B.A.M. Hofstee-van der Meulen and F. Dünkel, 515-535. Nijmegen: Wolf Legal Publishers, 2007.
Zoethout, C.M. "Wat is de rechtsstaat?" In *De rechtsstaat als toetsingskader*, edited by F.J. van Ommeren and Zijlstra, S.E. 55-77. The Hague: Boom Juridische Uitgevers, 2003.
Zolberg, A. "International Migrants and Refugees in Historical Perspective." *Refugees* 91 (1992): 37-39.

Table of Cases

International Court of Justice

Case concerning Military and Paramilitary Activities in and Against Nicaragua (Nicaragua v. U.S.A.), 27 June 1986, 1986 I.C.J 4.
Barcelona Traction Light and Power Co. Case (Belgium v. Spain), 5 February 1970 I.C.J. 3.
Nottebohm Case (Liechtenstein v. Guatemala), 6 April 1955, 1955 I.C.J. 4.

Permanent Court of International Justice

Panavezys-Saldutiskis Railway Case (Estonia v. Lithuania), Judgment of 28 February 1939, Ser A/B No 76.
Minority Schools in Albania, Advisory Opinion of 6 April 1936, Series A./B. No. 64.

Human Rights Committee

Vjatseslav Tsjarov v. Estonia, 26 October 2007, Comm. No. 1223/2003, U.N.Doc. CCPR/C/91/D/1223/2003.
Saed Shams et. al. v. Australia, 11 September 2007, Comm. Nos. 1255, 1256, 1259, 1260, 1266, 1268, 1270, 1288/2004, UN Doc. CCPR/C/90/D/1255,1256,1259, 1260,1266,1268,1270& 1288/2004.
El Dernawi v. Libyan Arab Jamahiriy, 20 July 2007, Comm. No. 1143/2002; U.N. Doc. CCPR/C/90/D/1143/2002.
Danyal Shafiq v. Australia, 13 November 2006, Communication No. 1324/2004, UN Doc. CCPR/C/88/D/1324/2004.
D and E v. Australia, 11 July 2006, Comm. No. 1050/2002, UN Doc CCPR/C/87/D/1050/2002.
Loubna El Ghar v. Libyan Arab Jamahiriya, 15 November 2004, Comm. No. 1107/2002, U.N. Doc. CCPR/C/82/D/1107/2002 (2004).
Madafferi v. Australia, 26 July 2004, Comm. No. 1011/2000, U.N. Doc. CCPR/C/81/D/1011/2001 (2004).
Kazantzis v Cyprus, 19 September 2003, Comm. No. 972/2001, U.N. Doc. CCPR/C/78/D/972/2001 (2003).
Sahid v. New Zealand, 28 March 2003, Comm. No. 893/99, U.N. Doc. CCPR/C/77/D/893/1999 (2003).
Bakhtiyari v. Australia, 6 November 2003, Comm. No. 1069/2002, UN Doc CCPR/C/79/D/1069/2002 (2003).
Baban v. Australia, 18 September 2003, Comm. no. 1014/2001, UN Doc. CCPR/C/78/D1014/2001 (2003).
C. v. Australia, 13 November 2002, Communication No 900/1999, UN Doc. CCPR/C/76/D/900/99 (2002).
Judge v. Canada, 17 July 2002, Comm. No. 829/98, U.N. Doc. CCPR/C/78/D/829/1998 (2003).
Jalloh v. The Netherlands, Comm. No. 794/1998, 26 March 2002, U.N. Doc. CCPR/C/74/D/794/1998 (2002).

Winata v. Australia, 26 July 2001, Comm. No. 30/2000, U.N. Doc. CCPR/C/72/D/930/2000 (2001).
Karker v. France, 26 October 2000, Comm. No. 833/98, U.N. Doc. CCPR/C/70/D/833/1998 (2000).
Kim v. Republic of Korea, 4 January 1999, Comm. No. 574/1994, U.N. doc. CCPR/C/64/D/574/1994 (1999).
G.T. v. Australia, 4 November 1997, Comm. No. 706/1996, U.N. Doc. CCPR/C/61/D/706/1996 (4 November 1997).
Nartey v. Canada, 18 July 1997, Comm. No. 604/1994, U.N. doc. CCPR/C/60/D/604/1994 (1994).
A. v. Australia, 30 April 1997, Comm. no. 560/1993, UN Doc. CCPR/C/59/D/560/1993 (1993).
Stewart v. Canada, 1 November 1996, Comm. No. 538/93, U.N. Doc. CCPR/C/58/D/538/1993 (1996).
Sohn v. Republic of Korea, 3 August 1995, Comm. No. 518/1992, U.N. Doc. CCPR/C/54/D/518/1992 (1995).
Balaguer Santacana v. Spain, 15 July 1994, Comm. No. 417/90, U.N. Doc. CCPR/C/51/D/417/1990 (1994).
Mukong v. Cameroon, 21 July 1994, Comm. No. 458/1991, U.N. Doc. CCPR/C/51/D/458/1991 (1994).
Celepli v. Sweden, 18 July 1994, Comm. No. 456/1991, U.N. Doc. CCPR/C/51/D/456/1991 (1994).
Kindler v. Canada, 11 November 1993, Comm. No. 470/1991, U.N. Doc. CCPR/C/48/D/470/1991 (1993).
Miguel González del Río v. Peru, 28 October 1992, Comm. No. 263/1987, U.N. Doc. CCPR/C/46/D/263/1987 (1992).
Van Alphen v. the Netherlands, 23 July 1990, Comm. No. 305/1988, U.N. Doc. CCPR/C/39/D/305/1988 (1990).
Delgado Paez v. Columbia, 12 July 1990, Comm. No. 195/1985, UN Doc. CCPR/C/39/D/195/1985 (1990).
Gueye et al. v. France, 3 April 1989, Comm. No. 196/1985, U.N. Doc. CCPR/C/35/D/196/1985 (1989).
J.R.C. v Costa Rica, 30 March 1989, Comm. No. 296/1988, U.N. Doc. Supp. No. 40 (A/44/40) at 293 (1989).
V.M.R.B. v Canada, 26 July 1988, Comm. No. 236/1987, U.N. Doc. CCPR/C/80/D/1051/2002 (2004).
Hammel v. Madagaskar, 3 April 1987, Comm. No. 155/198, U.N. Doc. CCPR/C/OP/2 at 11 (1990).
Y.L. v. Canada, 8 April 1986, Comm. No. 112/1981, U.N. Doc. Supp. No. 40 (A/41/40) at 145 (1986).
Lichtensztejn v. Uruguay, 31 March 1983, Comm. No. 77/1980, U.N. Doc. Supp. No. 40 (A/38/40) at 166 (1983).
Varela Nunez v. Uruguay, 22 July 1983, Comm. No. 108/1981, U.N. Doc. CCPR/C/OP/2 at 143 (1990).
Vidal Martins v. Uruguay, 23 March 1982, Comm. No. 57/1979, U.N. Doc. Supp. No. 40 (A/37/40) at 157 (1982).
Lopez Burgos v. Uruguay, 29 July 1981, Comm. No. 52/1979, U.N. Doc. Supp. No. 40 (A/36/40) at 176 (1981).
Pereira Montera v. Uruguay, 31 March 1981, Comm. No. 106/1981, CCPR/C/18/D/106/1981 (1983).
Celiberti de Casariego v. Uruguay, 29 July 1981, Comm. No. 56/1979, U.N. Doc. CCPR/C/OP/1 at 92 (1984).
Amauruddyu-Cziffra et al. v. Mauritius, 9 April 1981, Comm. No. 35/78, published at 1 Selected decisions H.R.C (New York: United Nations, 1985).
Maroufidou v. Sweden, 5 September 1979, Comm. No. 58/1979, U.N. Doc. CCPR/C/OP/1 at 80 (1985).

Convention Against Torture (CAT) Committee

A. R. v. *The Netherlands*, 14 December 2003, Comm. No. 203/2002, U.N. Doc. CAT/C/31/D/203/2002 (2003).

M.P.S. v. Australia, 30 April 2002, Comm. No. 138/1999, U.N. Doc. A/57/44 at 111 (2002).
S.V. v. *Canada*, 15 May 2001, Comm. No. 49/1996, U.N. Doc. A/56/44 at 102 (2001).
V.X.N. and H.N. v. *Sweden*, 15 May 2000, Comm. Nos. 130/1999 and 131/1999, U.N. Doc. CAT/C/24/D/130 & 131/1999 (2000).
G.R.B. v. *Sweden*, 15 May 1998, Comm. No. 83/1997, U.N. Doc. CAT/C/20/D/83/1997 (1998).
Tala v. Sweden, 15 November 1996, Comm. No. 43/1996, U.N. Doc. CAT/C/17/D/43/1996 (1996).
Kisoki v. Sweden, 8 May 1996, Comm. No. 41/1996, U.N. Doc. CAT/C/16/D/41/1996 (1996).

European Court of Justice

Case C-465-07, *Elgafaji v. Staatssecretaris van Justitie* [2009] nyr.
Case C-127/08, *Metock and others v. Ministry for Justice, Equality and Law Reform* [2008] nyr.
Case C-33/07, *Minsterul Ministerul Administrației și Internelor – Direcția Generală de Pașapoarte București v Gheorghe Jipa* [2008] nyr.
Case C-291/05, *Minister voor Vreemdelingenzaken en Integratie v. Eind* [2007] ECR I-10719
Case C-1/05, *Jia v. Migrationsverket* [2007] ECR I-1.
Case C-540/03, *European Parliament v. Council of the European Union* [2006] ECR I-5769
Case C-503/03, *Commission v. Spain* [2006] ECR I-1097.
Case C-209/03 *Bidar v. London Borough of Ealing*, 15 March 2005, ECR I-2119.
Case C-215/03, *Salah Oulane v. Minister voor Vreemdelingenzaken en Integratie* [2005] ECR I-1215.
Case C-60/00, *Carpenter v. Secretary of State for the Home Department* [2002], ECR I-6279
Case C-456/02, *Trojani v. Centre Public D'Aide Sociale de Bruxelles* [2004] ECR I-7573.
Case C-200/02, *Chen Kunqian Catherine Zhu and Man Lavette Chen v. Secretary of State for the Home Department* [2004] ECR I-9925.
Case C-109/01, *Secretary of State for the Home Department v. Akrich* [2003] ECR I-9607.
Case C-459/99, *Mouvement contre le racisme, l'antisémitisme, et la xénophobie ASBL (MRAX) v. Belgian State* [2002] ECR I 6591.
Case C-184/99, *Grzelczyk v. Centre public d'aide social d'Ottignies-Louvain-la-Neuve* [2001] ECR I-6193.
Case C-170/96, *Commission of the European Communities v Council of the European Union* [1988] ECR I-2763.
Opinion 2/94, *Accession by the Community to the European Convention for the Protection of Human rights and Fundamental Freedoms* [1996] ECR I-1759.
Case C-170/96, *Commission of the European Communities v Council of the European Union* [1988] ECR I-2763.
Case 41-74, *Van Duyn v. Home Office* [1974] ECR 1337.

European Court of Human Rights

S.D. v. Greece. Judgment of 11 June 2009, Appl. No. 53541/07.
Nolan en K. v. Russia. Judgment of 12 February 2009, Appl. No. 2512/04.
Grant v United Kingdom. Judgment of 8 January 2009, Appl. No. 10606/07.
Rashed v. Czech Republic, Judgment of 27 November 2008, Appl. No. 298/07.
Rusu v. Austria. Judgment of 2 October 2008, Appl. No. 34802/02.

Darren Omoregie v Norway. Judgment of 31 July 2008, Appl. No. 265/07.
N.A. v United Kingdom. Judgment of 17 July 2008, Appl. No. 25904/07.
Maslov v. Austria. Judgment of 23 June 2008, Appl. No. 1638/03.
Sadaykov v. Bulgaria. Judgment of 22 May 2008, Appl. No. 75157/01.
Saadi v. United Kingdom. Grand Chamber Judgment of 29 January 2008, Appl. No. 13229/03.
Riad and Idiab v. Belgium. Judgment of 24 January 2008, Appl. Nos. 29787/03 and 29810/03.
Liu and Liu v. Russia. Judgment of 6 December 2007, Appl. No. 42086/05.
Chair and J.B. v. Germany. Judgment of 6 December 2007, Appl. No. 69735/01.
Perry v. Latvia. Judgment of 8 November 2007, Appl. No. 30273/03.
Kaya v. Germany. Judgment of 28 June 2007, Appl. No. 31753/02.
Bitiyeva and X v. Russia. Judgment of 21 June 2007, Appl. No. 57953/00 and 37392/03.
Gebremedhin v. France. Judgment of 26 April 2007, Appl. No. 25389/05.
Konstantinov v. the Netherlands. Judgment of 25 April 2007, Appl. No. 16351/03.
Salah Sheekh v. the Netherlands. Judgment of 11 January 2007, Appl. No. 1948/04.
Bartik v. Russia. Judgment of 21 December 2006, Appl. No. 55565/00.
Földes and Földesné Hajlik v. Hungary. Judgment of 31 October 2006, Appl. No. 41463/02.
Üner v. the Netherlands. Judgment of 18 October 2006, Appl. No. 46410/96.
Mubilanzila Mayeka and Kaniki Mitunga v. Belgium. Judgment of 12 October 2006, Appl. No. 13178/03.
Saadi v. the United Kingdom. Judgment of 11 July 2006, Appl. No. 13229/03.
Lupsa v. Romania. Judgment of 8 June 2006, Appl. No. 10337/04.
Riener v. Bulgaria. Judgment of 23 May 2006, Appl. No. 46343/99.
Mohd v. Greece. Judgment of 27 April 2006, Appl. No. 11919/03.
Hussein v. Albania and others. Decision of 14 March 2006, Appl. No. 23276/04.
Sezen v. The Netherlands. Judgment of 31 January 2006, Appl. No. 50252/99.
Rodrigues da Silva and Hoogkamer v. the Netherlands. Judgment of 31 January 2006, Appl. No. 50435/99.
Timishev v. Russia. Judgment of 13 December 2005, Reports 2005-XII.
Mahdid and Haddar v. Austria. Decision of 8 December 2005, Appl. No. 74762/01, unpublished.
Tuquabo-Tekle and others v. the Netherlands. Judgment of 1 December 2005, Appl. No. 60665/00.
Batalov v. Lithuania. Decision of 15 November 2005, Appl. No. 30789/04.
Haydarie v. the Netherlands. Decision of 20 October 2005, Appl. No. 8876/04.
Mogos v. Romania. Judgment of 13 October 2005, Appl. No. 20420/02.
N. v. Finland. Judgment of 26 July 2005, Appl. No. 38885/02.
Bosphorus etc. v. Turkey. Judgment of 30 June 2005, Appl. No. 45036/98.
Ntumba Kabongo c. Belgique. Decision of 2 June 2005, Appl. No. 52467/99.
Singh v. The Czech Republic. Judgment of 25 January 2005, Appl. No. 60538/00.
Issa and others v. Turkey. Judgment of 16 November 2004, Appl. nr. 31821/96.
Ilascu and others v. Moldova and Russia. Judgment of 8 July 2004, Reports 2004-VII.
Shamsa v. Poland. Judgment of 27 November 2003, Appl. No. 45355/99 and 45357/99.
Napijalo v. Croatia. Judgment of 13 November 2003, Appl. No. 66485/01.
Slivenko v. Latvia. Judgment of 9 October 2003, Reports 2003-X.
Öcalan v. Turkey. Judgment of 12 March 2003, Appl. No. 46221/99.
Kadem v. Malta. Judgment of 9 January 2003, Appl. No. 55263/00.
Tekdemir v. the Netherlands. Decision of 1 October 2002, Appl. Nos. 46860/99 and 49823/99.
Christine Goodwin v. the United Kingdom. Judgment of 11 July 2002, Reports 2002-XI
Al Nashif v. Bulgaria. Judgment of 20 June 2002, Appl. No. 50963/99.
D.G. v. Ireland. Judgment of 16 may 2002, Reports 2002-III.
Gentilhomme and Others v. France. Judgment of 14 May 2002, Nos. 48205/99, 48207/99 and 48209/99.
Vasilopoulou v. Greece. Judgment of 21 March 2002, Appl. No. 47541/99.
Sejdovic and Sulejmanovic v. Italy. Decision of 14 March 2002, Appl. No. 57575/00.
H.M. v. Switzerland. Judgment of 26 February 2002, Appl. No. 39187/98.

Ghidotti v. Italy. Judgment of 21 February 2002, Appl. No. 28272/95.
Čonka v. Belgium. Judgment of 5 February 2002, Reports 2002-I.
Sen v. The Netherlands. Judgment of 21 December 2001, Appl. No. 31465/96.
Bankovic and Others v. Belgium. Decision of 12 December 2001, Reports 2001-XII.
Al-Adsani v. the United Kingdom. Judgment of 21 November 2001, Reports 2001-XI.
Boultif v. Switzerland. Judgment of 2 August 2001, Reports 2001-IX.
Rutten v. The Netherlands. Judgment of 24 July 2001, Appl. no. 32605/96.
Ilascu and Others v. Moldova and Russia. Decision of 4 June 2001, Appl. No. 48787/99.
Baumann v. France. Judgment of 22 May 2001, Reports 2001-V.
Cyprus v. Turkey. Judgment of 10 May 2001, Reports 2001-IV.
Z. and Others v. the United Kingdom. Judgment of 10 May 2001, Reports 2001-V.
Tanli v. Turkey. Judgment of 10 April 2001, Reports 2001-III.
Thoma v. Luxembourg. Judgment of 29 March 2001, Reports 2001-III.
Dougoz v. Greece. Judgment of 6 March 2001, Reports 2001-II.
Bensaid v. United Kingdom. Judgment of 6 February 2001, Appl. No. 44599/98.
Al-Nashif v. Bulgaria. Decision of 25 January 2001, Appl. No. 50963/99.
Xhavara and others v. Italy and Albania. Decision of 11 January 2001, Appl. No. 39473/98.
N.C. v. Italy. Judgment of 11 January 2001, Appl. No. 24952/94.
Kawka v. Poland. Judgment of 9 January 2001, Appl. No. 25874/94.
Öcalan v. Turkey, Decision of 14 December 2000, Appl. No. 46221/99.
Kudla v. Poland. Judgment of 26 October 2000, reports 2000-XI.
Maaouia v. France. Judgment of 5 October 2000, Reports 2000-X.
Varbanov v. Bulgaria. Judgment of 5 October 2000, 31365/96.
Ciliz v. the Netherlands. Judgment of 11 July 2000, Reports 2000-VIII.
Bergens Tidende and others v. Norway. Judgment of 2 may 2000, Reports 2000-IV.
K. and T. v. Finland. Judgment of 27 April 2000, Appl. no. 25702/94.
Labita v. Italy. Judgment of 6 April 2000, Reports 2000-IV.
Witold Litwa v. Poland. Judgment of 4 April 2000, Reports 2000-III.
Issa and others v. Turkey. Decision of 30 March 2000, Appl. nr. 31821/96.
T.I. v. the United Kingdom. Decision of 7 March 2000, Reports 2000-III.
Beyeler v. Italy. Judgment of 5 January 2000, Reports 2000-I.
Baghli v. France. Judgment of 13 November 1999, Reports 1999-VIII.
Jabari v. Turkey. Decision of 28 October 1999, Appl. No. 40035/98.
Riera Blume and others v. Spain. Judgment of 14 October 1999, Reports 1999-VII.
Immobiliare Saffi v. Italy. Judgment of 28 July 1999, Reports 1999-V.
Mitchell v. the United Kingdom. Decision of 24 November 1998, Appl. No. 40447/98.
Osman v. the United Kingdom. Judgment of 28 October 1998, Reports 1998-VIII.
I.A. v. France. Judgment of 23 September 1998, Reports 1998-VII.
Lehideux and Isorni v. France. Judgment of 23 September 1998, Reports 1998-VII.
Erkalo v. the Netherlands. Judgment of 2 September 1998, Reports 1998-VI.
Aerts v. Belgium. Judgment of 30 July 1998, *Reports* 1998-V.
Dalia v. France. Judgment of 19 February 1998, Reports 1998-I.
K.-F. v. Germany. Judgment of 27 November 1997, Reports 1997-VII.
Lotter v. Bulgaria. Decision of 5 November 1997, Appl. No. 39015/97.
Johnson v. the United Kingdom. Judgment of 24 October 1997, Reports 1997-VII.
Boujlifa v. France. Judgment of 21 October 1997, Reports 1997-VI.
Andronicou and Constantinou v. Cyprus. Judgment of 9 October 1997, Reports 1997-VI.
El Boujaidi v. France. Judgment of 26 September 1997, Reports 1997-VI.
Mehemi v. France. Judgment of 26 September 1997, Reports 1997-VI.
Manzoni v. Italy. Judgment of 1 July 1997, Reports 1997-IV.
D. v. the United Kingdom. Judgment of 2 May 1997, Reports 1997-III.
H.L.R. v. France. Judgment of 29 April 1997, Reports 1997-III.
X, Y and Z. v. the United Kingdom. Judgment of 22 April 1997, Reports 1997-II.
Muller v. France. Judgment of 17 March 1997, Reports 1997-II.
Lukanov v. Bulgaria. Judgment of 20 March 1997, Reports 1997-II.

Bouchelkia v. France. Judgment of 29 January 1997, Reports 1997-I.
Aksoy v. Turkey. Judgment of 18 December 1996, Reports 1996-VI.
Loizidou v. Turkey. Judgment of 18 December 1996, Reports 1996-VI.
Ahmut v. Netherlands. Judgment of 28 November 1996, Reports 1996-VI.
Chahal v. the United Kingdom. Judgment of 15 November 1996, Reports 1996-V.
Bizzotto v. Greece. Judgment of 15 November 1996, Reports 1996-V.
C. v Belgium. Judgment of 7 August 1996, Reports 1996-III.
Benham v. the United Kingdom. Judgment of 10 June 1996, Reports 1996-III.
Amuur v. France. Judgment of 25 June 1996, Reports 1996-III.
Boughanemi v. France. Judgment of 24 April 1996, Reports 1996-II.
Gül v. Switzerland. Judgment of 19 February 1996, Reports 1996-I.
S.W. v. the United Kingdom. Judgment of 22 November 1995, A-335-B.
McCann v. the United Kingdom. Judgment of 27 September 1995, A-324.
Vogt v. Germany. Judgment of 26 September 1995, A-323.
Van der Tang v. Spain. Judgment of 30 July 1995, A-321.
Nasri v. France. Judgment of 13 July 1995, A-320-B.
Piermont v. France. Judgment of 27 April 1995, A-314.
Loizidou v. Turkey. Judgment of 23 March 1995, A-310.
Quinn v. France. Judgment of 22 March 1995, A- 311.
Kemmache v. France. Judgment of 24 November 1994, A-296-C.
Kroon and Others v. the Netherlands. Judgment of 27 October 1994, A-297-C.
Hokkanen v. Finland. Judgment of 23 September 1994, A-299-A.
Chorherr v. Austria. Judgment of 25 August 1993, A-266-B.
Brannigan & McBride. Judgment of 26 May 1993, A-258-B.
Mihailhe v. France. Judgment of 25 February 1993, A-256-C.
Funke v. France. Judgment of 25 February 1993, A-256-A.
Cremieux v. France. Judgment of 25 February 1993, A-256-B.
Kolompar v. Belgium. Judgment of 24 September 1992, A-235-C.
Herczegfalvy v. Austria. Judgment of 24 September 1992, A-244.
Hentrich v. France. Judgment of 22 September 1992, A-296-A.
Tomasi v. France. Judgment of 27 August 1992, A-241-A.
Drozd and Janousek v. France and Spain. Judgment of 26 June 1992, A-240.
Campbell v. the United Kingdom. Judgment of 25 March 1992, A-233.
Beldjoudi v. France, Judgment of 26 March 1992, A-234-A.
B. v. France. Judgment of 25 March 1992, A-232-C.
Margareta and Roger Andersson v. Sweden. Judgment of 25 February 1992, A-226-A.
Kenmache v. France. Judgment of 27 November 1991, A-218.
Vilvarajah and Others v. the United Kingdom. Judgment of 30 October 1991, A-215.
Letellier v. France. Judgment of 26 June 1991, A-207.
Cruz Varas and Others v. Sweden. Judgment of 20 March 1991, A-201.
Moustaquim v. Belgium. Judgment of 18 February 1991, A-193.
Wassink v. the Netherlands. Judgment of 27 September 1990, A-185-A.
E. v. Norway. Judgment of 29 August 1990, A-181-A.
Kruslin v. France. Judgment of 24 April 1990, A-176 A.
Groppera Radio AG and others v. Switzerland. Judgment of 28 March 1990, A-173.
Hakansson and Sturesson v. Sweden. Judgment of 21 February 1990, A-171.
Van der Leer v. the Netherlands. Judgment of 21 February 1990, A-170-A.
Brogan and others v. the United Kingdom, Judgment of 29 November 1989, A-145-B.
Bezicheri v. Italy. Judgment of 25 October 1989, A-164.
Soering v. the United Kingdom. Judgment of 7 July 1989, A-161.
Eriksson v. Sweden. Judgment of 22 June 1989, A-156.
Tre Traktorer Bolag v. Sweden. Judgment of 7 June 1989, A-159.
Berrehab v. the Netherlands. Judgment of 21 June 1988, A-138.
Schönenberger and Durmaz v. Switzerland. Judgment of 20 June 1988, A-137.
Boyle and Rice v. the United Kingdom. Judgment of 27 April of 1988, A-131.
Olsson v. Sweden. Judgment of 24 March 1988, A-130.
Bouamar v. Belgium. Judgment of 29 February 1988, A-129.

F. v. Switzerland. Judgment of 18 December 1987, A-128.
Leander v. Sweden. Judgment of 26 March 1987, A-116.
Weeks v. the United Kingdom. Judgment of 2 March 1987, A-114.
Bozano v. France. Judgment of 18 December 1986, A-111.
Gillow v. the United Kingdom. Judgment of 24 November 1986, A-109.
Sanchez-Reisse v. Switzerland, 21 October 1986, A-107.
Lithgow and others v. the United Kingdom. Judgment of 8 July 1986, A-102.
Lingens v. Austria. Judgment of 8 July 1986, A-103.
James and Others v. the United Kingdom. Judgment of 21 February 1986, A-98.
Abdulaziz, Cabales and Balkandali v. the United Kingdom. Judgment of 28 May 1985, A-94.
Ashingdane v. the United Kingdom. Judgment of 28 May 1985, A- 93.
Barthold v. Germany. Judgment of 25 March 1985, A-90.
Luberti v. Italy, Judgment of 23 February 1984, A-75.
Foti and Others v. Italy. Judgment of 10 December 1982, A-56.
Sporrong and Lönnroth v. Sweden, Judgment of 23 September 1982, A-52.
X. v. the United Kingdom. Judgment of 5 November 1981, A-46.
Dudgeon v. the United Kingdom, Judgment of 22 October 1981, A-45.
Guzzardi v. Italy. Judgment of 6 November 1980, A-39.
Winterwerp v. the Netherlands. Judgment of 24 October 1979, A-33.
Marckx v. Belgium. Judgment of 13 June 1979, A-31.
Sunday Times v. the United Kingdom. Judgment of 26 April 1979, A-30.
Handyside v. the United Kingdom. Judgment of 7 December 1976, A-24.
Engel and others v. the Netherlands. Judgment of 8 June 1976, A-22.
Golder v. the United Kingdom. Judgment of 21 February 1975, A-18.
De Wilde, Ooms and Versyp v. Belgium. Judgment of 18 June 1971, A-12.
Wemhoff v. Germany. Judgment of 27 June 1968, A-7.
Neumeister v. Austria. Judgment of 27 June 1968, A-8.
Case "relating to certain aspects of the laws on the use of languages in education in Belgium." Judgment of 23 June 1968, A-6.
Lawless v. Ireland. Judgment of 1 July 1961, A-3.

European Commission of Human Rights

D. v. the United Kingdom. Decision of 2 May 1997, Reports 1997-III.
Mezghiche v. France. Decision of 9 April 1997, Appl. No. 33438/96.
Kareem v. Sweden. Decision of 26 October 1996, D&R 87-A, 173.
Alla Raidl v. Austria. Decision of 4 September 1995, D&R 82-A, 134.
Peltonen v. Finland. Decision of 20 February 1995, D&R 80-B, 38.
Illich Sanchez Ramirez v. France. Decision of 24 June 1994, D&R 86, 155.
Chrysostomides and others v. Turkey. Decision of 4 March 1993, Appl. Nos. 15299/89; 15300/89; 15318/89.
Aylor Davis v. France. Decision of 20 January 1994, D&R 76A, 164.
Voulfovitch and Oulianova v. Sweden. Decision of 13 January 1993, D&R 74, 209.
M v. Denmark. Decision of 14 October 1992, D&R 73, 193.
Stocké v. Germany. Report of 12 October 1989, A-199.
C. v. Germany. Decision of 2 December 1985, D&R 45, 198.
S.v. Sweden. Decision of 6 May 1985, D&R 42, 224.
W.v. Ireland. Decision of 28 February 1983, D&R 32, 211.
X, Y, and Z v. the United Kingdom. Decision of 6 July 1982, D&R 27, 205.
Omkarananda and the Divine Light Zentrum v. Switzerland. 19 March 1981, D&R 25, 118.
Caprino v. the United Kingdom. Decision of 3 March 1980, D&R 12, 14.
Uppal and others v. the United Kingdom. Decision of 2 May 1979, D&R 17, 157.
Caprino v. the United Kingdom. Decision of 3 March 1978, D&R 12, 14.
X. and Y. v. Switzerland. Decision of 14 July 1977, D&R 9, 57.
X v. the United Kingdom. Decision of 18 May 1977, D&R 9, 224.
X. v Germany. Decision of 16 May 1977, D&R 9, 190.

Agee v. the United Kingdom. Decision of 17 December 1976, D&R 7, 164.
Becker v. Denmark. Decision of 3 October 1976, Yearbook of the European Convention on Human Rights 19 (1976), 416.
Adler and Bivas v. Germany. Decision of 16 July 1976, Yearbook of the European Convention on Human Rights 20 (1977), 102.
Hess. v. the United Kingdom. Decision of 28 May 1975, D&R 2, 72.
Cyprus v. Turkey. Decision of 26 May 1975, D&R 2, 136.
East African Asians v. the United Kingdom. Report of 15 December 1973, 3 European Human Rights Reports 76.
X. v Germany. Decision of 14 December 1970, D&R 37, 69.
X. v Germany. Decision of 26 May 1970, Yearbook of the European Convention on Human Rights 13 (1970), 1028.
X. v. Germany. Decision of 5 February 1970, Yearbook of the European Convention on Human Rights 13 (1970), 688.
X. v. Germany. Decision of 25 September 1965, Yearbook of the European Convention on Human Rights 8, 158.

Inter-American Commission for Human Rights

Coard et al. V. The United States, decision of 29 September 1999, Report no. 109/99, Case No. 10.951.
The Haitian Centre for Human Rights et. Al. v. United States, decision of 13 March 1997, Report no. 51/96, Case No. 10.675.
Salas v. The United States, 14 October 1993, Case 10.573, Report No. 51/96.
Detainees in Guantanamo Bay, Cuba; Request for Precautionary Measures, March 13, 2002, at: http://www1.umn.edu/humanrts/cases/guantanamo-2003.html.

Iran-United States Claims Tribunal

Rankin v. Islamic Republic of Iran, 3 November 1987, 17 Iran-U.S.C.T.R. 135 (1987).

National Case Law

Lithuania

Lietuvos Vyriausiojo administracinio teismo nutartis Nr. N6-1514-05 [13 July 2005 Lithuanian Supreme Administrative Court Decision Nr. N6-1514-05]

Netherlands

Afdeling Bestuursrechtspraak Raad van State 22 January 2008, *Jurisprudentie Vreemdelingenrecht* 115 (2008).
Afdeling Bestuursrechtspraak Raad van State 11 January 2008, *Jurisprudentie Vreemdelingenrecht* 109 (2008);
Afdeling Bestuursrechtspraak Raad van State 31 October 2007, *Jurisprudentie Vreemdelingenrecht* 543 (2007).
Afdeling Bestuursrechtspraak Raad van State, 28 April 2005, *Jurisprudentie Vreemdelingenrecht* 308 (2005).
Afdeling Bestuursrechtspraak Raad van State, 6 September 2005, *Jurisprudentie Vreemdelingenrecht* 452 (2005).
Rechtbank Haarlem, 20 March 2009, *Jurisprudentie Vreemdelingenrecht* 197 (2009).
Rechtbank's Gravenhage, 18 March 2005, *Jurisprudentie Vreemdelingenrecht* 216 (2005).

United Kingdom

House of Lords, *Regina v. Secretary of State for the Home Department (Respondent) ex parte Khadir (FC) (Appellant)*, 16 June 2005, [2005] UKHL 39.
House of Lords in *A v. Secretary of State for the Home Department*, 16 December 2004, UKHL [2004] 56.
House of Lords, *Regina v. Immigration Officer at Prague Airport*, 9 December 2004, [2004] UKHL 55.
House of Lords. *Regina v. Secretary of State for the Home Department Ex Parte Saadi (fc) and Others (Fc)*, 31 October 2002 [2002] UKHL 41.

United States

Supreme Court, *Sale, Acting Commissioner, Immigration and Naturalization Service, Et. Al. v. Haitian Centers Council, INC., Et. Al.*, decided June 1991, 509 U.S. (1993) 15.
Supreme Court, *Haig v. Agee,* 453 U.S. (1981) 280.
Supreme Court, *Zemel v. Rusk*, 381 U.S. (1965) 1.
Supreme Court, *Aptheker v. Secretary of State*, 378 U.S. (1964) 500.
Supreme Court, *Kent v. Dulles*, 357 U.S. (1958) 116.
Supreme Court, *Nishimura Ekiu v. United States*, 142 U.S. (1892) 651.
Supreme Court, *Chae Chan Ping v. United States (Chinese Exclusion Case)*, 130 U.S. (1889) 581.
11th Circuit Court, *Cuban American Bar Association v. Christopher*, 43 F. 3d 1412, (11th Cir. 1995), 515 U.S. (1995) 1142.

Index

absolutism, 37, 40, 41, 47, 138
accelerated asylum procedures, 1, 13
 see also fast-track procedures
actuarial justice, 23–24
African Charter of Human and People's Rights, 147
Agamben, Giorgio, 244
Agnew, John, 61, 316
airport liaison officers, 195, 224
Akrich, 206
Algeria, 8, 199, 214
allegiance, 45–49, 53, 92, 94, 103, 137, 138, 141, 147, 165, perpetual, 47, 48, 138
Al-Nashif, 201
Althusius, Johannes, 38
American Convention of Human Rights, 147
Amuur, 280–282, 311
Arendt, Hannah, 81, 84, 96, 130, 137, 231, 241–244
armed conflict, 60, 90
 and legal discourse on immigration, 227
 see also war
Asylum Procedures Directive, 2, 11, 194, 269
asylum seekers, 194, 195, 243, 274, 335
 detention, 1, 2, 11–15, 24, 25, 27, 187, 236, 243, 245, 252, 254, 258, 261–264, 265, 266, 268, 269, 272, 274, 280, 281, 282, 283, 284, 293, 294, 296, 297, 298, 299, 300, 309, 312
asylum, 123, 173, 174, 209, 214, 219
 asylum procedures, 183, 193, 194
 right of asylum, 183, 186, 187, 219
Austria, 13, 19, 20, 171
 Federal Asylum Authority, 13

Bancovic, 115, 116, 118–121
banishment, 166, 232, 234, 240
bare life, 232
Batalov, 292
Bauböck, Rainer, 111
Bauman, Zygmunt, 244
Beccaria, 232
Belgian Linguistics Case, 301
Belgium, 17
Benhabib, Seyla, 342
Berlin Wall, 142, 146, 242

Berrehab, 199
Bigo, Didier, 187, 204
Bill of Rights, 70
Bodin, Jean, 37–40, 66, 72
Body of Principles for the Protection of All Persons under any Form of Detention or Imprisonment, 256, 259
border control, 2, 13, 168, 204, 211, 212, 215, 216, 237, 323, 330
Bosniak, Linda, 114
boundaries, 26, 34, 51–53, 55, 59, 78, 83, 138, 144
 international, 27
 national, 102, 104, 108, 127, 220
 social, 79
 territorial, 44–46, 57, 58, 60, 61, 83, 86, 89, 124, 125, 127, 128, 130, 161, 162, 164, 167–169, 221, 223, 226, 227, 316, 321, 323, 324, 327, 330, 340
boundaries of identity, 60, 62, 91
brain-drain, 144, 145, 154

Cameroon, 220
Canary Islands, 11, 215, 325
candidate countries, 213
carrier sanctions, 156, 187, 195, 212
Centro de Accoglienza, 12
Chahal, 289, 291, 292, 297
Charter of Fundamental Rights of the European Union, 183, 268
Charter of Paris for a New Europe, 147
Charter of the United Nations, 90, 98
 Chapter VII, 91
Chen, 205–208, 216
children
 detention of children, 3, 264, 266, 271, 299, 337
 rights of children, 3, 199, 200, 205, 255, 329
Chinese Exclusion Cases, 125, 227
Church, 36, 166
citizenship, 4, 52–55, 58, 64, 65, 70, 72–87, 92, 94, 97, 113, 114, 122–124, 127–129, 175, 231, 235, 241, 319, 322, 341
 citizenship and nationalism, 168–171
 cosmopolitan, 341
 deprivation of citizenship, 171, 232

European, 58, 59, 108–112, 129, 130, 203, 205, 206, 216, 268, 321
global institution of citizenship, 84
global, 164, 202, 342
post-national, 27, 103–108, 175, 208, 235, 243, 322, 324, 327
civil rights, 70, 106, 107, 112, 181
classic international law, 65, 86, 87, 89–97, 128, 135, 175, 184, 218, 220, 319, 323
coercion, 23, 34, 141
  legitimate means of coercion, 64, 85
  coercion and citizenship, 77
  see also force, the use of, and violence
Cohen, Joshua, 343
collectivism, 57, 141, 147
colonisation, 233
Commissioner for Human Rights for the Council of Europe, 16, 21, 265, 267, 268
Committee of Experts, 180
Committee of Ministers of the Council of Europe, 100, 194, 199, 265, 266
common asylum and immigration policy, 202
  development, 208–210
communitarian theory, 74, 341
Community law, 11, 109, 185, 192, 200, 201, 206, 207, 248, 249, 268, 269, 272
compensation
  in case of unlawful deprivation of liberty, 258, 290
conditions of detention, 2–4, 10–11, 19–22, 259–261, 264, 271–272, 299–300
Conference of the Interior Ministers of the Western Mediterranean, 159
confinement
  confinement of the poor, 239–242
  great confinement, 239–240, 241, 242
  see also detention
Čonka, 248, 286, 290, 292, 298, 311
constitution, 67–69, 72, 81, 115
  constitution of England, 68
  cosmopolitan constitution, 165
  French constitution, 68, 139, 166
constitutional government, 42, 44, 69, 72, 318
constitutional order
  cosmopolitan, 343
  domestic, 105
  human rights and a constitutional order, 102, 125, 220, 315
  international, 102
constitutionalism, 4, 27–28, 66–71, 127, 136, 218, 222, 227, 228, 243, 312, 320–322, 329, 323, 333, 335
  domestic, 27, 64
  international, 27
  traditional forms of constitutionalism, 67, 247

de-nationalisation of constitutionalism, 113
de-territorialisation of constitutionalism, 113
limits, 71–73
see also rule of law
Convention against Torture and Other Cruel, Inhuman or Degrading Punishment, 189, 259
Convention on the Elimination of Racial Discrimination, 147
Convention relating to the Status of Refugees 1951, 172, 184,185, 186, 194, 219, 262, 280
Corbridge, Stuart, 61, 316
cosmopolitanism, 56, 342
Council Directive 2003/109/EC concerning the status of third-country nationals who are long-term residents
  see Long-term resident directive
Council Directive 2003/86/EC on the right to family reunification
  see Family Reunification Directive
Council Directive 2003/9/EC on minimum standards for the reception of asylum seekers
see Reception Conditions Directive
Council Directive 2004/83/EC on minimum standards for the qualification and status of third-country nationals or stateless persons as refugees or as persons who otherwise need international protection and the content of the protection granted
  see Qualification Directive
Council Directive 2005/85/EC on minimum standards on procedures in Member States for granting and withdrawing refugee status
  see Asylum Procedures Directive
Council of Europe, 100, 101, 193, 249
  Council of Europe and immigration detention, 265–268, 275
Court of Justice, 112, 210, 216
courts
  national courts, 105, 107, 176, 210, 247, 258, 290, 310, 340
  see also judiciary
crime, 23, 242, 244, 327
  as distinct from war, 60–61, 89
crimes against humanity, 98
criminal justice, 22–26
CSCE Declaration of the Copenhagen Meeting, 148
customary international law, 99, 176, 178
Cyprus v. Turkey Case, 120
Cyprus, 5, 12
  Northern Cyprus, 120
Czech Republic, 8, 14, 17, 21, 284

D. v. United Kingdom, 192
Dalia, 199
De Genova, Nicholas, 136
De Jure Belli ac Pacis, 39
Declaration of the Rights of Man and the Citizen, 52, 54, 70, 75, 78, 80
decolonisation, 57, 144
democratic theory
  exclusion of migrants, 337
  cosmopolitan democratic theory, 343
deportation, 15, 23, 166, 179, 190, 193, 194, 197–199, 201, 229, 321, 328, 340
  pre-deportation detention, 15, 16, 17, 18, 157, 260, 267, 279, 280, 282, 283, 284, 291, 292, 293, 295, 296, 298, 305, 309
  link with modern territorial order, 230, 231, 235, 237, 243, 245, 328
  genealogy of deportation, 232–235
  symbolic function in the modern state, 236–237
  see also expulsion
deprivation of liberty
  see detention
destabilisation effects, 336, 338
destabilisation of territorial sovereignty, 28, 248, 249, 332, 333–345
destabilisation rights, 28, 336
detention
  of emigrants, 340
  of mentally ill persons, alcoholics, and vagrants, 305–308
  prohibition on arbitrary detention, 251–256, 290–300
  see also immigration detention, confinement
détournement de pouvoir, 298, 309
Diken, Bülent, 243–244
diplomatic protection, 86, 89, 92–97, 109, 178, 185, 331
direct rule, 76–77
Directive 2004/38/EC on the right of citizens of the Union and their family members to move and reside freely within the territory of the Member States, 201, 206, 207
Directive 2008/115/EC on common standards and procedures in Member States for returning illegally staying third-country nationals
  see Returns Directive
Discourses, The, 37
discrimination
  discrimination on the ground of nationality, 14, 73, 82, 109, 110, 177, 203, 294, 302, 309
  discrimination with regard to the right to leave, 150–151
  discriminatory use of the sovereign right to exclude, 176–178
  racial discrimination, 99, 177
  religious discrimination, 95
displaced persons, 79, 83, 97, 144, 171
  internally displaced persons, 219
  internment of displaced people, 231, 241
Divine Right, 36, 38, 41, 52
domain résérve, 92, 128, 161, 163, 176
Draft Declaration on the Right to Leave, 151
Du Contrat Social, 43
Dublin II Regulation, 1, 14, 21, 193

E. v. Norway, 289
EC law
  see Community law
economic migrants, 282, 326, 327, 335
effective control, 102
  state responsibility, 116–121
effective nationality, 94
effective remedy, 149, 159, 179, 182, 193, 194, 201, 335
emigration, 135–147, 324
  emigration as a crime, 142
  'illegal' emigration, 155, 159, 160, 340
  practice of Communist countries, 141, 142, 144, 158, 172, 173, 224
  right to leave, 147–154, 323
  sovereignty, 161, 226, 324
English Vagrancy Act 1597, 233
Enlightenment, 41, 43, 47, 48, 50, 52, 53, 56, 67, 69, 74, 80, 87, 88, 139, 140, 317, 319
equality, 43, 51, 53–55, 66, 67, 69, 70, 73–75, 96, 111, 168, 319
estrangement, 229, 244, 329
European Commission of Human Rights, 115, 116, 117, 118, 157, 181
European Commission, 209, 214, 215
European Committee for the Prevention of Torture and Inhuman and Degrading Treatment, 3, 19, 21, 22, 259, 267
European Court of Human Rights, 6, 24, 28, 100, 247–276, 327
  ECtHR as a constitutional court, 277
European integration, 207–210, 331
European Neighbourhood Policy, 224
European Parliament, 8, 11, 109, 110, 209, 210, 272
European Union, 58, 100, 108, 163, 175, 195, 209, 216, 249, 330
  migration, 202–216
Europeanisation
  of national immigration policies, 59, 208, 216, 276
Evian Conference, 171
exclusionary inclusion, 244

exclusionary power, 199, 200, 203, 204, 208, 217, 218, 220, 221, 224
  limits to the exclusionary power of the state, 184, 186, 195, 204
  legal contention of the exclusionary power of the state, 29, 244, 334
exile, 165, 166, 232, 233, 249, 250
expulsion, 135, 144, 135, 144, 179, 182, 62
  article 8 ECHR, 199–201
  expulsion and detention, 6, 12, 15, 17, 18, 20
  expulsion and human rights, 190
  expulsion as a criminal law sanction, 166, 196–198
  expulsion as a means of social regulation, 168
  expulsion in early international law, 164
  expulsion of refugees, 186
  historical forms of expulsion, 165, 166, 232–234, 237
  ineffectiveness of expulsion measures, 236
  mutual recognition of expulsion, 211
  prohibition on arbitrary expulsions, 178–180
  prohibition on mass expulsions, 178
  see also deportation
external borders, 59, 202, 208, 224, 331, 340
externalisation
  of immigration policies, 156, 188, 225, 237, 334, 341
extraterritoriality
  of immigration detention, 244, 245, 280
  of human rights obligations, 115–122, 189, 195, 212, 223
  extraterritorial political inclusion, 331

fair balance, 197, 304
fair trial
  applicability of Article 6 ECHR in immigration procedures, 181, 201, 335
family formation, 197
family life
  human right to respect for, 195–202, 218
  detention as an interference with the right to respect for family life, 300, 311
  family life established while unlawfully present in state territory, 200, 221, 325, 326
  family reunification, 143, 174, 176, 195, 197, 199, 200
  right to family life in EC law, 200, 206–207
Family Reunification Directive, 200
fast-track procedures, 13, 266, 269, 293, 294
  see also accelerated procedures
feudalism, 36, 53, 138
  fealty, 46
  see also serfdom

Finland, 12, 17, 21
force, use of, 26
  legitimate use of force, 34, 35
  monopoly on the use of force, 60
  use of force between states, 61, 65, 89–92, 102, 125
  see also coercion, violence
forced migration, 229, 232, 233, 234
  see also deportation, expulsion
foreign workers
  recruitment of, 173
Fortress Europe, 208
Foucault, Michel, 231, 239, 240
France, 3, 7, 19, 21, 36, 37, 53, 68, 139, 166–167, 212, 240
  Sécurité Public Regional, 21
  Gendarmerie, 21
free movement
  global system of free movement, 344
  historical perspective on free movement, 166
  within the EU, 110, 11, 202–207, 216
  within the nation state, 228, 323
  world migratory regime, 342
Frontex, 188, 212, 213, 223, 225

Geneva Conventions, 91
  see also war, laws of
Geneva Refugee Convention
  see Convention relating to the Status of Refugees 1951
geo-authoritarian culture, 124
German Democratic Republic, 142
Germany, 7, 14, 17, 19, 146, 169, 171, 172, 173, 212, 214, 241
Gibney, Matthew, 236
globalisation, 104, 225, 324, 342
God, 36, 38, 39, 55, 66
Gorbatchov, 146
governance
  governance of populations, 83, 113, 122, 235, 237, 238, 318
governmentality, 236
Grand Chamber (ECtHR), 24, 292, 294, 308, 309
Greece, 7, 13, 17, 19, 21–22
  Ancient Greece, 74, 232
Grenshospitium, 9
Grotius, Hugo, 39, 87, 101, 164
Guantanamo, 187, 245
Guild, Elspeth, 8, 187
Guzzardi, 305

habeas corpus, 245, 249, 257, 258, 271, 286–290, 335
  see also immigration detention, judicial review

Handyside, 303
Hansen, Randall, 236
Hegel, Georg, 56–57, 88
Helsinki Accord, 143
High Commissioner for Refugees
   Executive Committee, 187, 274, 296
   League of Nations, 169, 170
   United Nations, 172, 187, 259, 262, 263, 266
Hindess, Barry, 82, 84, 235
Hobbes, 39–44, 51, 66, 85
Home Office, 7, 230
Honecker, 146
Hôpital Général, 239–240, 329
hospitality
   right to, 164–165
Human Rights Committee, decisions on:
   Article 13 ICCPR, 178–181
   Article 7 ICCPR, 189–191, 220, 222
   immigration detention, 248, 249, 252, 253–255, 258, 260–262, 265, 273, 275, 292, 295, 310, 337
   right to family life, 195–198, 200
   right to leave, 148, 156,
   state responsibility for extraterritorial acts, 117, 118, 120
humanitarian intervention, 91–92
humanitarian law, 89–91, 115
humanity, 49, 51, 53, 54, 59, 78, 83, 120, 228, 242, 319
   humanity and rights, 70, 84, 318
   universal humanity, 51
Hungary, 16, 17, 20, 146, 196, 276

identity
   and international law, 94–97, 127–128, 319
   and rights, 97, 127, 130, 151, 169, 217, 241, 243, 319–321, 325, 332
   identity controls, 5, 8, 12, 16, 62, 263, 265, 330
   national or political identity, 34, 45, 49, 52, 53–59, 60, 62, 65, 74, 75, 83, 87, 93, 97, 103, 130, 141, 151, 168, 169, 174, 217, 233–234, 241, 318, 330–331, 343
Ilascu, 121
illegal emigration, 145, 156, 159–160, 224, 324, 340
illegal immigration
   see irregular immigration
illegal migration, 212, 225, 237, 274
immigration detention
   alternatives, 266, 268, 338, 339
   as a technique of sedentarisation, 242
   conditions, 3, 4, 9, 19–22, 251, 259–261, 271–272, 299–300, 324
   rights of refugees, 261, 265, 269, 274
   duration, 7, 10, 11, 17, 18, 255–256, 297, 311

   estrangement as core function, 244
   EU citizens, 268
   in accordance with domestic laws, 252, 282–284, 296, 311
   judicial review, 9, 14, 16, 18, 258–259, 267, 269, 271, 274, 276, 287–290, 337
   link with territoriality, 4, 26, 27, 28, 65, 230, 231, 238, 239, 243, 245, 248, 274, 327, 328, 329
   mandatory immigration detention, 24, 248, 272,
   procedural guarantees, 9, 10, 15, 19, 256–259, 267, 275, 285–290, 335
   proportionality, 16, 266, 267, 270, 271, 273, 276, 291–296, 309, 338
   state practice, 7–21, 247
   statistics, 7, 18
   symbolic function, 238, 328
   time limits, 10, 13, 17–18, 20, 257, 271
immigration law enforcement, 1, 23, 25, 26, 27, 28, 229, 231, 245, 254, 280, 323, 339
imprisonment
   as a response to crime, 23, 331, 239–242
   see also penitentiary
inalienable rights, 42, 69, 320
individual rights, 42, 67, 69–71, 98, 99, 102, 103, 106, 123, 223, 309, 318, 339
   as spheres of freedom, 70
   and citizenship, 79–82, 113
   and responsibility, 226
   and territory, 28, 122, 131, 163, 218, 222, 226, 247, 316
   and proportionality principle, 305
   individual rights of aliens, 178
individualism, 43, 55, 88
inequality, 4, 55, 332
inhuman and degrading treatment
   detention, 22, 259–260, 300
   non-refoulement, 189–194, 218, 222, 189
Institute of International Law, 167
institutional fetishism, 336
integration
   national requirements, 110, 167, 200, 203
   integration of migrants, 322
Inter-American Commission of Human Rights, 117
interception
   of migrants at sea, 156, 157, 195, 214, 225
intergovernmental cooperation
   in the field of migration, 208–210
internal borders, 203
   abolition of, 58, 175, 205
internal market, 207
International community, 92, 98, 102, 129, 170

International Court of Justice, 94
International Emigration Conference, 167
international human rights law, 7, 87, 89, 97–131, 147, 153, 225, 250, 259, 268, 273, 276, 279, 326, 340
international legal personality, 86, 88, 90, 93, 319
international minimum standard, 94
International Refugee Organisation, 171–172
International Regulations on the Admission and Expulsion of Aliens, 167
international relations, 47, 54, 60, 82, 90, 95, 318
  realism, 85
internment camp, 11, 97, 231, 241–243
irregular immigrants
  rights of irregular migrants, 107, 112, 221–222, 227, 312
Irregular immigration, 1, 4, 15, 18, 156, 174, 177, 221, 274–275
  criminalisation of irregular immigration, 23–24, 56, 217, 237–238, 328–329
Issa, 119–120
Italy, 12, 36, 156, 173, 212, 214, 252, 324, 329
Ius Cogens, 99, 176, 177, 188

Jacobson, David, 108
Jalloh v. the Netherlands, 254
Jefferson, Thomas, 48
judicial agency, 108
judicial review, 68–69, 71, 103, 108, 180–182, 194, 204
  of detention, 3, 9, 14, 16, 18–19, 257–258, 267, 269, 271, 273, 276, 287–290, 334
  speedy judicial review of detention, 289
judiciary, 24, 107, 108, 129, 145, 158, 176
  deference to executive, 127
  independent, 67–69, 126

Kadem, 289
Kaldor, Mary, 125
Kant, Immanuel, 164
Kellogg-Briand, 90
Kostakopoulou, Dora, 123, 216, 342
Kristeva, Julia, 54, 80

Lampedusa, 8, 11
Latvia, 12, 17, 20
Laustsen, Carsten, 243, 244
law of nations, 87, 88
League of Nations, 96, 169, 170
legal aid
  right to, 267, 290
  access to, 3, 9, 15, 18
legality
  of detention, 2, 11, 13, 16, 252, 283, 284, 296, 311
  of political power, 126
  of restrictions on the right to leave, 150, 153, 156, 225
legitimate political power, 35, 59
  see also sovereignty
lettres de cachet, 240
Leviathan, 51, 85
Leviathan, 39
liberal theory, 51, 54, 55, 80, 158
liberty, 41, 43, 48, 66, 68, 74, 76, 145, 221, 232
  individual liberty as a legal notion, 74
  republican notion of individual liberty, 74
Libya, 160, 188, 214, 215, 324
limited government, 66, 67, 69
Linklater, Andrew, 77, 78
Lithuania, 20, 292
Locke, John, 41–43, 48, 51, 68, 72
long-term resident, 58, 107, 110–111, 203–204
Long-term Residents Directive, 110–111, 201, 203
Luban, David, 124
Lui, Robyn, 200

Machiavelli, 36, 37
Madafferi, 260
Madness and Civilization, 239
Magna Carta, 68, 137, 138, 249
Mahdid and Haddar, 282
Malkki, Liisa, 242
Malta, 3, 8, 11, 12, 14, 17
mandatory detention, 24, 248, 254, 258, 272
mandatory residence requirements, 6
Mansbach, Richard, 128
Marchetti, Raffaele, 342
margin of appreciation, 284, 288, 304, 305, 306, 310
Maroni, Roberto, 324
Mauritania, 155, 156, 213, 215
Médicins sans Frontiers, 2
Melzer, Arthur, 55
membership
  membership of a particular social group in the refugee definition, 185–186
  national membership, 171, 172
  political membership, 319, 330, 343, 344
mercantilism, 138, 140, 166
Metock, 207, 208, 216
minorities, 46, 81
  expulsion, 165, 166, 237
  international law, 86, 89, 90, 92, 95–97, 128, 135, 170, 233

Index   385

Mohd, 284
monarchical power, 35, 40, 46
Montesquieu, 68
Moreno Lax, Violeta, 157
Morgenthau, 85
Morocco, 173, 214
Mubanga-Chipoya, Chama, 159
Mubilanzila Mayeka and Kaniki Mitunga, 299, 311

Nansen passports
  see passport
nation, 45, 49, 50, 52, 54, 55–58, 76, 78, 80, 81, 87, 88, 126, 136, 175, 233, 239, 317
national community, 55
national security
  Article 13 ECHR, 201
  Article 8 ECHR, 201
  detention of asylum seekers, 263, 264, 265
  expulsion, 179, 180, 186, 336
  immigration detention, 16, 17, 292
  refoulement, 186
  restrictions on the right to leave, 139, 142, 152
nationalism, 47, 57, 59, 75, 88
  citizenship, 75, 78, 79, 81
  impact on freedom of movement, 139–141, 147, 168
  link with liberal theory, 50–55
  social and political mobilisation, 79
  Westphalian state system, 50–55, 317–320
nationality, 14, 25, 45–49, 56, 58, 75, 78, 82, 83, 85, 88, 92, 94, 97, 98, 101, 103–113, 122–124, 130, 135, 148, 171, 172, 175, 184–186, 198, 199, 203–208, 216, 221, 232, 265, 293, 294, 309, 321
national-territorial ideal, 318, 320
  see also territorial ideal
natural law, 37, 39, 41, 42, 51, 69, 72, 74, 87, 88
natural rights, 39, 52, 66, 69, 79, 82, 87, 88, 139, 141
Netherlands, 3, 9, 20, 21, 24, 199, 268, 276
new penology, 23–25
non-refoulement
  at the border, 187
  in Directive 2004/83/EC, 193
  other human rights obligations, 190, 222
  prohibition in the 1951 Refugee Convention, 182, 186, 187, 188, 191, 193
  prohibition in the CAT Convention, 189
  prohibition of torture and inhuman or degrading treatment, 189, 191, 192, 218, 222, 333, 340
Nottebohm Case, 94, 198

Nuremberg laws, 171
Nuremberg tribunal, 90, 98, 124, 131

Oakington Detention Centre, 293, 294, 298, 299
Öcalan Case, 191, 121
Ooms, Wilde en Versyp, 307–308
open centres, 6, 12
open method of co-ordination, 210
Orford, Anne, 92
Ottoman territories, 170

Pacific Solution, 214
Palais de Justice, 21
paper walls, 171
Parliamentary Assembly of the Council of Europe, 199, 267, 268
particularism, 86, 103, 113, 135
  political, 55, 65, 75, 78, 79, 311, 312
  territorial, 51, 126, 167
  of citizenship, 75, 79, 83, 84
passport, 139, 140, 144, 145, 146, 148, 150, 168, 169, 296
  Nansen passports, 169–170, 172
Peace of Westphalia
  see Westphalia
penitentiary
  rise of the penitentiary, 240, 242
  link with legal accountability, 242
  see also imprisonment
Permanent Court of International Justice, 96
persecution, 170, 171, 184, 185, 186, 219
  according to Directive 2004/83/EC, 185, 186
  by non-state agents, 185, 186, 219
Peutz, Nathalie, 230
Piermont v. France, 109–110
Poland, 4, 13, 21, 169
police à distance, 187, 212, 223, 323, 325
police custody, 5, 19, 20
political participation, 73–74, 108
political rights, 70, 76, 82, 100, 107–109, 112, 113
poor laws and policies, 166, 239, 232
population transfer, 83, 169, 233, 234, 236, 328
Portugal, 12, 20, 141, 212
Prince, the, 37
prison, 241
  immigration detention carried out in prisons, 3, 5, 9, 19, 20, 262, 272
private life
  right to respect for, 195, 196, 220, 300
proportionality principle, 71, 151
  Article 5(1)(e) ECHR, 305–30

Article 5(1)(f) ECHR, 278, 291, 292, 294–300, 311, 312
Article 8 ECHR, 198
immigration detention, 16, 253–255, 258, 260, 262, 264, 265, 267, 268, 270, 273, 274, 276, 337
in ECtHR case law, 300–305
interferences with the right to leave, 152–156, 224, 225
protection
according to the 1951 Refugee Convention, 219
Protocol 4 ECHR, 148, 150, 153, 157, 321
Protocol 7 ECHR, 178–180, 182, 202, 335
Explanatory Report, 181
public order
Article 1 Protocol 7 ECHR, 179, 335
detention of refugees, 11, 263–265
immigration detention, 17, 269, 307
right to leave, 152–155, 157
Pufendorf, Samuel, 41, 51, 72

Qualification Directive, 183, 184, 185, 186, 193

Rashed, 282, 284
readmission agreements, 8, 213, 233, 237, 238
real risk, 189, 190, 222
reception centres, 3, 6, 12, 252
Reception Conditions Directive, 11, 269
Recommendation Rec(2003) 5 on measures of detention of asylum seekers, 265, 296
Reform Treaty, 110, 211
reformation, 36, 46
refoulement, 188, 223
indirect, 193
see also non-*refoulement*
refugee law, 169–170, 173, 182–185, 187, 191, 195, 220
refugees, 81, 144, 162, 166, 169–173, 174, 214, 241, 326
detention of refugees and asylum seekers, 15, 25, 97, 241–242, 244, 261–264, 272, 274
jewish refugees, 171
refugees from communist countries, 172–173
rights of refugees, 186–189
regional protection programmes, 215
religious freedom
Westphalian Treaties, 95
repatriation, 83, 171, 173, 236
voluntary, 211
republicanism, 37, 74
Res Publica Christiana, 36, 87
restrictions upon personal liberty, 6, 250, 268, 269, 280–282

return policy
EU, 211, 235, 236
Returns Directive, 2, 16–17, 22, 211, 269–272
Revised Guidelines on the Applicable Criteria and Standards Relating to the Detention of Asylum Seekers, 262–265, 296
revolution, 42, 146, 169
American Revolution, 44, 48
French Revolution, 44, 52, 53, 74, 75, 81, 139, 166
Riad and Idiad, 281, 311
right of exclusion, 163
see also exclusionary powers
Rights of Man, 52, 54, 70, 80–82, 84, 241, 319–321, 344
Rigo, Enrica, 208
Romania, 296
exit controls, 224
romanticism, 56
Rousseau, 43–45, 56, 85
Rubenstein, Kim, 113
Ruffer, Galya, 108
rule of law, 27, 66, 67, 103, 105–107, 118, 122, 126, 129, 131, 150, 193, 209, 238, 287, 335
and imprisonment, 241–242
denationalisation of the rule of law, 112–113, 131
in asylum procedures, 194
limits, 242, 309
link with territoriality, 102, 127, 129, 131, 137
national security, 201
see also constitutionalism
Russia, 140, 142
refugees from Russia, 170
Rusu, 283, 287, 296–297, 312

Saadi, 24–25, 286, 291–297, 308–309, 311
Sabel, Charles, 336, 337, 343
safe country of origin, 195, 214, 216, 335
safe third country, 187, 192, 194, 195, 214, 216, 263
Sahel, Mustafa, 159
Sanchez-Reisse, 289
Sarkozy, Nicholas, 159
Sassen, Saskia, 104, 107, 108, 123
Schengen, 204, 211, 212, 216
Schuster, Liza, 245
second-generation immigrants, 196, 198
secularisation, 37, 49
secular ideologies, 147
Security Council, 91
security of residence, 193
self-determination, 102, 146, 341
link with the right to leave, 137
Sen, 199

Senegal, 155, 213
separation of powers, 67–69, 126
serfdom, 138, 140, 142, 165
 see also feudalism
Sezen, 199
Shafir, Gershon, 130
Shamsa, 283
Simon, William, 336, 337
single market, 204, 205
Six Livres de la République, 38
Slovenia, 8, 17
social and economic rights, 70, 84, 106, 109, 112
social contract, 108
 novel forms, 108
 social contract theories, 41, 51, 69, 79
sovereignty
 and European integration, 58, 202–205, 208, 209, 212, 330
 and the use of force, 34, 35, 62, 231
 content, 33, 62, 65, 114, 124, 129, 131, 137, 160, 221, 226, 227, 215–216, 228, 237, 248, 311, 315, 319–322
 deterritorialised sovereignty, 213–214, 342
 external sovereign claims, 33, 47, 49, 54, 60–62, 82, 84, 85, 90, 95, 124, 128, 165, 318
 form, 29, 33, 61, 62, 63, 65, 86, 113–115, 119, 122, 124, 128, 129, 131, 137, 161, 162, 221, 222, 226, 227, 228, 237, 247, 249, 274, 311, 315, 320, 322, 323, 328, 330, 337–338
 frame, *see* form
 general theory, 37–39, 44, 45, 60, 62, 139, 164, 170–171, 238
 national sovereignty, 55–57, 81, 88, 89, 97, 99, 127, 128, 135, 136, 176, 181
 popular sovereignty, 34, 38, 41–44, 48, 50, 51, 53, 55, 59, 60, 64, 66, 67, 70, 74, 76, 79, 80, 81, 87, 107, 158, 317
 power to distinguish between inside and outside, 46, 60, 66, 103, 126, 128, 129, 237, 318, 328
 sovereignty and the exception, 72, 126, 165
 territorial sovereignty, 4, 27, 28, 29, 55, 63, 65, 86, 114, 123–125, 127, 136, 162, 177, 179, 188, 198–200, 215, 217, 218, 220, 226, 227, 229, 237, 238, 244–246, 248, 274, 281, 310, 312, 315, 316, 325, 327–330, 332–340
 ultimate political authority, 33, 35–41, 92–93, 102, 317
Soysal, Yasemin, 110, 123
spatial powers, 27, 63, 114, 123, 340
 and human rights, 124–126, 130
Special Rapporteur on Migrant Workers, 275

state formation, 46, 78, 166
state of nature, 39, 41–43, 48, 51, 85
stateless persons, 81, 83, 130, 169
 incarceration of, 25, 241–242
statelessness
 prevention of, 112
Stocké, 117, 119, 121
Strasbourg Declaration on the Right to Leave and Return, 148
Study of the Right of Everyone to be Free from Arbitrary Arrest, Detention and Exile, 252
Suarez, Francisco, 87
Sub-Commission on Prevention of Discrimination and Protection of Minorities, 150
subjecthood, 47
subsidiary protection, 192, 193, 194
supranational policies, 202, 205, 235
Supreme Court of the United States, 125, 145, 146, 158
Sweden, 20

Tampere, 211
taxation, 77, 232
territorial ideal, 57, 96, 219, 220, 230, 242, 243, 312, 329–330, 331
 see also national-territorial ideal
territorial integrity, 56, 90, 125, 128, 130, 218, 320, 322, 325
territorial state, 33, 46, 47, 49, 50, 52, 53, 57, 58, 60, 73, 81, 82, 84, 86, 89, 103, 111, 127, 128, 136, 160, 162, 183, 233, 237, 243, 318, 326
 territorial state system, 40, 83, 89, 226, 228, 236, 243, 326
territorialisation, 34, 35, 45, 46, 47, 49, 55, 59–61, 65, 90, 102, 113, 127, 129, 131, 318–320
 link with refugee protection, 174, 219–220
territoriality, 26, 29, 33, 35, 45, 52, 53, 54, 56, 61, 72, 78, 86, 123, 124, 131, 135, 226, 228, 330, 281, 315, 316, 317, 318, 319, 323, 328, 331, 332, 341
 and citizenship, 79, 83, 84, 130, 231
 and constitutionalism, 136, 137, 163, 218, 243, 312, 333
 and deportation, 235
 and immigration detention, 243, 245, 328,
 and rights, 28, 84, 103, 114, 120, 122, 123, 125, 126, 130, 220, 221, 222, 223, 225, 322, 333, 334
 focal territoriality, 342
 in EU, 163, 202, 213, 216, 235
 see also territorialisation
Thirty Years War, 60

Immigration and Asylum Law and Policy in Europe

1. E. Guild and P. Minderhoud (eds.): *Security of Residence and Expulsion*. 2000
ISBN 90-411-1458-0
2. E. Guild: *Immigration Law in the European Community*. 2001 ISBN 90-411-1593-5
3. B. Melis: *Negotiating Europe's Immigration Frontiers*. 2001 ISBN 90-411-1614-1
4. R. Byrne, G. Noll and J. Vedsted-Hansen (eds.): *New Asylum Countries? Migration Control and Refugee Protection in an Enlarged European Union*. 2002 ISBN 90-411-1753-9
5. K. Groenendijk, E. Guild and P. Minderhoud (eds.): *In Search of Europe's Borders*. 2003
ISBN 90-411-1977-9
6. J. Niessen and I. Chopin (eds.): *The Development of Legal Instruments to Combat Racism in a Diverse Europe*. 2004 ISBN 90-04-13686-X
7. B. Bogusz, R. Cholewinski, A. Cygan and E. Szyszczak (eds.): *Irregular Migration and Human Rights: Theoretical, European and International Perspectives*. 2004
ISBN 90-04-14011-5
8. H. Battjes: *European Asylum Law and International Law.* 2006 ISBN 90-04-15087-0
9. Elspeth Guild and Paul Minderhoud (eds.): *Immigration and Criminal Law in the European Union: The Legal Measures and Social Consequences of Criminal Law in Member States on Trafficking and Smuggling in Human Beings*. 2006 ISBN 90-14-15064-1
10. Georgia Papagianni: *Institutional and Policy Dynamics of EU Migration Law*. 2006
ISBN 90-04-15279-2
11. Elspeth Guild and Anneliese Baldaccini (eds.): *Terrorism and the Foreigner: A Decade of Tension around the Rule of Law in Europe*. 2006 ISBN 90-04-015187-7
12. Steve Peers and Nicola Rogers (eds.): *EU Immigration and Asylum Law: Text and Commentary*. 2006 ISBN 90-04-15374-8
13. Prakash Shah (ed.): *Law and Ethnic Plurality: Socio-Legal Perspectives*. 2007
ISBN 978-90-04-16245-7
14. Bruno Nascimbene, Massimo Condinanzi and Alessandra Lang: *Citizenship of the Union and Free Movement of Persons*. 2008 ISBN 978-90-04-16300-3
15. Evelien Brouwer: *Digital Borders and Real Rights: Effective Remedies for Third-Country Nationals in the Schengen Information System*. 2008 ISBN 978-90-04-16503-8
16. Nils Coleman: *European Readmission Policy:Third Country Interests and Refugee Rights*. 2008 ISBN 978-90-04-16554-0
17. Sergio Carrera: *In Search of the Perfect Citizen? The Intersection between Integration, Immigration and Nationality in the EU*. 2009 ISBN 978-90-04-17509-9
18. Jan Niessen and Thomas Huddleston (eds.): *Legal Frameworks for the Integration of Third-Country Nationals*. 2009 ISBN 978-90-04-17069-8
19. Galina Cornelisse: *Immigration Detention and Human Rights. Rethinking Territorial Sovereignty.* 2010 ISBN 978-90-04-17370-5

Martinus Nijhoff Publishers – Leiden · Boston

20. Ricky van Oers, Eva Ersbøll and Dora Kostakopoulou (eds.): *A Re-definition of Belonging? Language and Integration Tests in Europe.* 2010. ISBN 978-90-04-17506-8
21. Bernard Ryan and Valsamis Mitsilegas (eds.): *Extraterritorial Immigration Control. Legal Challenges.* 2010. ISBN 978-90-04-17233-3

Martinus Nijhoff Publishers – Leiden · Boston

Thomas, Robert, 123
Tilly, Charles, 60, 77
Tokyo tribunal, 90
Torpey, John, 122, 136
Transit Processing Centres, 214
transit zones, 1, 6, 7, 20, 280, 311
  see also waiting zones
transportation, 233, 234, 237, 240
travel documents, 150, 261, 282
Treaties of Westphalia
  see Westphalia
Treaty establishing the European Community, 1, 108, 109, 203
  Title IV EC Treaty, 210, 211, 270
Treaty of Amsterdam, 208
Treaty of Lisbon amending the Treaty on European Union and the Treaty establishing the European Community
  see Reform Treaty
Treaty of Versailles, 57
Treaty on European Union, 108, 209
third pillar, 209
Tunisia, 214
Twenty Guidelines on Forced Return, 266, 267, 276
Two Treatises of Government, 41

UN Sub-Commission on Prevention of Discrimination and Protection of Minorities, 150
undocumented migrants, 106, 108, 114, 221, 257
  see also irregular migrants
Unger, Roberto, 28, 336
United Kingdom, 13, 14, 230, 276, 293
United Nations Relief and Rehabilitation Administration, 171
United Nations' Commission on Human Rights, 99, 252
United States, 144, 145, 158, 167, 167
unity
  national 144
  political, 36, 38, 55, 62, 63, 65, 72, 126, 131, 202, 216, 217, 242, 328, 330
Universal Declaration of Human Rights, 122, 143, 250, 320
universalism, 49, 80, 86, 113, 118, 126, 127, 135, 167
  particular universalism, 247
USSR, 57

vagrants, 233-234
  incarceration of, 25, 279, 305-308

Varbanov, 306
Vattel, Emmerich de, 88, 93, 165
Vienna Convention of the Law of Treaties, 118, 157
violence, 4, 29, 33, 34, 35, 39, 46, 56, 57, 65, 77, 85, 86, 89, 90, 92, 97, 98, 125-128, 219, 220, 228, 229, 231, 238, 242, 243, 248, 249, 274, 308, 317, 319
  (i)legitimate, 34, 35, 59-62, 64
  interstate, 86, 97, 323
  see also coercion, and force, use of
visa policy, 187, 195, 211-212, 224, 237
Vitoria, Francisco de, 87
Volonté générale, 43-56

waiting zones, 9, 84, 267
  see also transit zones
Walters, William, 231-236, 239
war crimes, 98
war, 39, 42, 46, 52, 60, 77, 89, 90, 91, 125, 128, 137, 138, 323, 325
  civil, 36, 40, 51, 91, 144
  Cold War, 143, 145, 147, 172, 173, 224
  First World War, 57, 78, 79, 81, 90, 140, 141, 168, 169, 170
  laws of war, 90
  Napoleonic, 55, 76, 78, 166
  Second World War, 57, 82, 83, 97, 129, 137, 141, 144, 147, 158, 171, 241, 242, 320
  World Wars, 57, 97, 168, 169, 170
  see also armed conflict,
Warsaw Pact, 141
Weber, Max, 136
Westphalia
  Peace of, 26, 40, 47, 54, 60, 82, 85, 95, 318
  Westphalian state system, 50, 56, 59, 62, 73, 82, 83, 85, 89, 91, 92, 95, 128, 135, 166, 318, 331
Wilmer, Franke, 128
Winterwerp, 306
Witold Litwa, 306
Wolff, Christian, 87-88
Woomera, 243
Working Group on Arbitrary Detention, 18, 25-253, 255, 257-261, 271, 273, 275

Xhavara Case, 119, 156, 225

Yack, Bernard, 55
Yugoslavia, 120, 173

zones d' attente, *see* waiting zones
Zum Ewigen Frieden, 164